READINGS IN CURRICULUM

second edition

edited by

GLEN HASS

Professor of Education
Chairman, Graduate Curricula in
Curriculum Theory and Research
University of Florida

KIMBALL WILES

Late
Dean, College of Education
University of Florida

JOSEPH BONDI

Chairman, Department of Curriculum
and Instruction
College of Education
University of South Florida

ALLYN AND BACON, INC.   BOSTON

Contributors

ALEXANDER, WILLIAM, Professor of Education, University of Florida

ANDERSON, ROBERT H., Professor of Education, Graduate School of Education, Harvard University

ARNSTEIN, GEORGE, Consultant, Urban Study, American Council on Education, Washington, D.C.

AUSUBEL, DAVID P., Professor of Education, University of Illinois

AVILA, DONALD L., Associate Professor of Education, University of Florida

BELLACK, ARNO A., Professor of Education, Teachers College, Columbia University

BERGER, BENNETT M., Chairman, Department of Sociology, University of California at Davis

BERGESON, JOHN B., Assistant Professor of Teacher Education, Western Michigan University

BETHUNE, PAUL, Coordinator of Science, Nova High School, Broward County, Florida

BEVANS, LLOYD E., (Deceased) formerly Consultant in Elementary Education, California State Department of Education

BLOCKER, CLYDE E., Associate Professor of Education, University of Texas

BONDI, JOSEPH C., Chairman, Department of Curriculum and Instruction, College of Education, University of South Florida

BRADLEY, R.C., Faculty Member, North Texas State University

BRAMELD, THEODORE, Professor of Educational Philosophy, Boston University

BRUNER, JEROME S., Professor of Psychology and Director of Center for Cognitive Studies, Harvard University

BUSH, ROBERT N., Professor of Education, Stanford University

CANTRIL, HADLEY, Professor of Psychology, Princeton University

CHASE, EDWARD T., Writer on Public Affairs and Consultant to Private Industry and the U.S. Government

CLUTE, MORREL J., Associate Professor of Education, Wayne State University

COMBS, ARTHUR W., Professor of Education, University of Florida

CONANT, JAMES B., Former President of Harvard University and Chairman, NASSP Committee on the Study of the American Secondary School

COUNTS, GEORGE S., Professor of Education, Southern Illinois University

CUTTS, WARREN G., Specialist for Reading, U.S. Office of Education

DIEBOLD, JOHN, Head of Diebold Group, Inc., Management Cousultants, New York

DOAK, E. DALE, Assistant Dean, College of Education, University of Tennessee

DOXIADIS, CONSTANTINOS A., Architect, Author, City Planner, Head of Doxiadis Associates, Washington, D.C.

EDWARDS, ESTHER P., Associate Professor of Education, Tufts University

EMPEY, DONALD W., Director of Instructional Services of the Arcadia Unified School District, Arcadia, California

EURICH, ALVIN C., Fund for the Advancement of Education in the Ford Foundation

FANTINI, MARIO D., Program Officer, Ford Foundation

FLANAGAN, JOHN C., American Institute for Research and University of Pittsburgh

FORD, PAUL, Associate Professor of Education, Washington State University and Director of Small School Programs in the Northwest Regional Laboratory of the U.S. Office of Education

FOSHAY, ARTHUR W., Professor of Education, Teachers College, Columbia University

FOX, ROBERT S., Director of the University School, University of Michigan

FRANK, N.H., Professor of Physics, Massachusetts Institute of Technology

GILCHRIST, ROBERT S., Superintendent, University City (Missouri) Public Schools

GLASS, BENTLEY, Academic Vice-President and Distinguished Professor of Biology, State University of New York at Stonybrook

GLASS, CAROLYN A., Teacher at Lexington (Kentucky) Catholic High School

GORDEY, MICHEL, Chief Foreign Correspondent, *Look*

GORDON, IRA, Professor of Education, University of Florida

HABERMAN, MARTIN, Professor of Education, Rutgers University, New Brunswick

HARLACHER, ERVIN L., President, Brookdale Community College, Lincroft, New Jersey

HASS, GLEN, Professor of Education, University of Florida

HAVIGHURST, ROBERT, Professor of Urban Education, Fordham University

HEDGES, WILLIAM D., Curriculum Coordinator, Clayton, Missouri School District

HEFFERNAN, HELEN, Assistant Chief, Division of Instruction in Charge of Elementary Education, California State Department of Education

HERRICK, THERAL T., Director of Instruction and Guidance, Kalamazoo (Michigan) Public Schools

HUTCHINS, ROBERT M., Past President and Chancellor, University of Chicago and President of the Fund for the Republic

JENNINGS, FRANK G., Education Consultant to the New World Foundation and Editor-at-Large, *Saturday Review*

JOHNSON, IVAN, Head, Department of Art Education and Construction Design, Florida State University

JOHNSON, MAURITZ, JR., Professor of Secondary Education, Cornell University

KAUFMAN, BURT, Coordinator of Mathematics, Nova High School, Broward County, Florida

KLIEBARD, HERBERT M., Associate Professor of Education, University of Wisconsin

KUHLMAN, JOHN M., Professor of Economics, University of Missouri

LAMBERT, PHILIP, Associate Professor of Education, University of Wisconsin and Director of the Washington Elementary School, Madison, Wisconsin

LAW, NORMA R., Professor of Education, Wayne State University

LEE, DORRIS MAY, Professor of Education, Portland State College

LEE, THOMAS L., Deputy Superintendent of the Tucson (Arizona) Public Schools

LEVINE, DANIEL U., Associate Professor of Education, University of Missouri at Kansas City

LONSDALE, BERNARD, Consultant in Elementary Education, California State Department of Education

LOUNSBURY, JOHN H., Professor of Education, Georgia State College for Women

MacLEISH, ARCHIBALD, Pulitzer Prize Winner and Professor of Rhetoric, Harvard University

McCLUSKY, HOWARD Y., Professor of Education, University of Michigan

McGAUGH, JAMES L., Professor of Psychobiology and Acting Dean, School of Biological Sciences, University of California at Irvine

McLUHAN, MARSHALL, Director, Centre for Culture and Technology, University of Toronto

MASON, LOUIS D., Teacher, Business Education Department, Oshkosh (Winconsin) High School

MICHAELIS, JOHN U., Professor of Education, University of California

MIEL, ALICE, Professor of Education, Department of Curriculum and Teaching, Teachers College, Columbia University

MILLER, RICHARD I., Director of the Program on Education Change, University of Kentucky

MOORE, WILLIAM, JR, Associate Dean, General Curriculum, Forest Park Community College, St. Louis

MOSKIN, J. ROBERT, Senior Editor, *Look*

NALL, ALFRED W., Dean of Arts and Sciences, San Diego City College

NANCE, AFTON DILL, Consultant in Elementary Education, California State Department of Education

NEWSOM, CARROLL V., Senior Vice-President, Prentice-Hall, Inc.

OJEMANN, RALPH H., The Child Welfare Research Station, State University of Iowa

ORNSTEIN, ALLAN C., Teacher, Sands Junior High School, New York City

PIEL, GERARD, Publisher, *Scientific American*

POPPER, SAMUEL H., Professor of Educational Administration, University of Minnesota

POST, RICHARD L., Principal, Marcus Whitman Junior High School, Port Orchard, Washington

PURKEY, WILLIAM W., Associate Professor of Education, University of Florida

ROBINSON, DONALD W., Associate Editor, *Phi Delta Kappan*

ROGERS, CARL R., Professor of Psychology, University of Wisconsin

ROSENFELD, STANLEY S., Chairman of the Language Arts Department, Sands Junior High School, New York City

ROSENTHAL, SEYMOUR, Chief, Human Resources Coordinator, Model Cities Administration, U.S. Department of Housing and Urban Development

SHANE, HAROLD G., Professor, School of Education, Indiana University

SKINNER, B.F., Professor of Psychology, Harvard University

SMITH, B. OTHANEL, Professor of Education, University of Illinois, Urbana

SMITTER, FAITH, (Deceased) formerly, Director of Child Guidance, Santa Barbara County, California

SNIDER, BILL, Assistant Professor of Education and Consultant, University Computer Center, University of Iowa

THEUS, ROBERT, Assistant Professor, Kearney (Nebraska) State College

TILLMAN, RODNEY, Professor of Education and Dean, College of Education, George Washington University

VAN TIL, WILLIAM, Coffman Distinguished Professor of Education, Indiana State University

VARS, GORDON F., Professor of Education, Kent State University

VOCOLO, JOSEPH M., Director of Foreign Languages, Buffalo (New York) Board of Education

WAETJEN, WALTER B., Professor of Education, University of Maryland

WATSON, GOODWIN, Professor of Social Psychology and Education, Teachers College, Columbia University and Distinguished Professor, Newark State College

WEINSTEIN, GERALD, Professor of Education, University of Massachusetts

WHITE, WILLIAM D., Principal, Arvada West Senior High School (Colorado)

WHITE, WINSTON, Lecturer, Department of Social Relations, Harvard University

WILES, KIMBALL, (Deceased) formerly Dean, College of Education, University of Florida

WILHELMS, FRED T., Executive Secretary, Association for Supervision and Curriculum Development, Washington, D.C.

WILLIAMS, EMMETT L., Associate Professor of Education, University of Florida

Contents

Preface

Within the past half century, Americans have become more aware of the power of the school as the determiner of the future. As Nazi Germany and Soviet Russia have demonstrated the effectiveness of the school as an instrument of political policy, Americans, accustomed to regarding school as a place where the young have the opportunity to become literate, have begun to realize that education is a serious business for society, not just a freely extended privilege.

This new perception of the school curriculum has become the subject of much public and professional controversy. Various social groups and individuals have deep convictions about what and how the schools should teach. They use the mass media, professional journals, and local newspapers and assemblies to promulgate their beliefs. When authorities disagree—and they do—others become confused and disturbed.

This collection of readings is an attempt to help the reader see the scope of the curriculum decisions that must be made, identify some of the issues involved, understand the bases of curriculum building, and formulate for himself a clearer picture of what he wants the public school curriculum to be, at all levels, from nursery school to community college.

Some framework is necessary for presenting information that has significance for curriculum decisions. The editors have presented: first, the bases and criteria that give direction in deciding the role that the school should fulfill; second, other information that suggests the organization of educational experiences; and third, descriptions of programs and possible alternatives.

The material selected has come from many sources and authors. An attempt has been made to use persons who are recognized as authorities in their fields. Thus the statements on the bases of the curriculum are written largely by students of society, learning, and human development; while criteria and descriptions of programs and issues are written by individuals working in professional education.

Acknowledgment should be given to the many authors who have granted access to their writings. Their willingness to permit others to republish their ideas is an indication of their unselfish dedication to the continuous improvement of our way of life. It will be noted, too, that many selections were originally published in *Childhood Education, Educational Leadership, The Bulletin of the NASSP, NEA Journal, Teachers College Record, Phi*

Delta Kappan, Junior College Journal, The Saturday Review, The Clearing House, Journal of Secondary Education, Newsweek, Look, A.A.U.W. Journal, and the *Atlantic.* The assistance of the Center for the Study of Democratic Institutions, the NEA Research Division, the Association for Supervision and Curriculum Development, and the Edward A. Uhrig Foundation is also gratefully acknowledged.

It is the hope of the editors that the increased professional commitment of those who study this volume will amply repay the generosity of the associations and individuals that contributed so much to it.

Glen Hass and Kimball Wiles served as editors of the first edition of READINGS IN CURRICULUM and did the initial planning for the revised second edition. Following Dr. Wiles' death, Joseph Bondi worked with Glen Hass in completing the preparation of the second edition.

Part One

Bases and Criteria
for the Curriculum

1 Social Forces

To understand schools and school systems, one must relate them to the surrounding cultural, economic, historical, philosophical, and political circumstances. Since education is always an expression of a civilization and of a political and economic system, schools must harmonize with the lives and ideas of men in a particular time and place. Since the social environment today is in a state of change, descriptions of society in the nineteenth century or in the thirties or fifties no longer suffice. The situation must be regularly reexamined and an attempt made to understand its meaning and significance for the school program from kindergarten through the community college. This section is an attempt to analyze the social scene in America today and project what it will be during the rest of the century.

One way to gain an understanding of the close relationship of the social environment to the development of an appropriate educational program is to view the social setting from the standpoint of the individual. Some claim that in our society the role of each person is determined by his occupation. His friends are often drawn from those with whom he works and the whole tone of his life is related to this reference group. Moreover, a democratic society requires citizens who are prepared to deal with the current issues of government. Finally, each person faces problems of self-fulfillment and self-development. Thus from the individual learner's standpoint, the school program, if it is rationally developed, must provide for his vocational demands and requirements, the demands of citizenship, and the demands of self-fulfillment. In every society the nature of the demands on the individual is different. And because all industrial civilizations are undergoing rapid change, these areas of life and their requirements are also subject to constant modification within each society.

Aldous Huxley, author of *Brave New World,* in commenting on the ways in which human life is now rapidly changing into shapes as yet unknown,

3

said, "You must tell people they don't have much time. We must start thinking like mad. We must do something." What are some of the forces about which something must be done?

SCIENCE AND THE SCIENTIFIC REVOLUTION

Most historians agree that modern science is creating a revolution in living more violent than anything that has ever happened to mankind in the past. Because of the promise of the exploration of space in the near future the shape of things to come is but dimly seen. As machines relieve men of much manual and mental effort, they also cause uncertainty and change in the patterns and types of employment. Mathematics, physics, chemistry, and biological sciences are among the fastest growing fields. The number of technicians, engineers, and scientists in all fields is increasing rapidly. There are constantly increasing demands for teachers and for persons in the health professions and in many other fields requiring post-high school education. There are fewer opportunities for unskilled and skilled labor.

Schools are called upon to educate students for those occupations that are increasing in importance. They must also help people readjust to new living conditions and new ways of thinking. In addition to producing fundamental changes in technology and industry, science has provided a new way of thinking about problems. Probably 90 percent of the American population is unaware that human behavior has regularities that are as predictable as the phenomena of rockets, or arithmetic, or refrigerators.

George S. Counts ("Education and the Technological Revolution") traces the penetration of science and technology into our culture and shows how it will change the very character of the people nurtured by our civilization. He states that, due to the impact of science, the world is now confronted with "seven stark realities" that have brought about many things that "could not happen." "The task of bringing our old minds into accord with the facts of the new world is a gigantic and urgent educational undertaking."

Archibald MacLeish examines the sense of frustration and helplessness abroad in America today and defines its cause as science, which we have come to see as a kind of absolute beyond our reach. The human role in the shaping of civilization seems to be lost while a kind of automatism takes over. We need to believe in ourselves again and assume the mastery of our means.

Automation, a spectacular application of science and technology, is being used to operate entire factories, to predict the weather, to guide missiles and space ships, to make reservations on airlines, to check income tax returns. Automation has also been applied, with great success, to many aspects of agriculture. Without question many unskilled jobs are being eliminated. This change being wrought by the application of technology is confronting today's societies and schools with one of their severest challenges.

Computer systems will revolutionize business, communications, science and education in the years just ahead. John Diebold ("The New World Coming") warns that the new computer technology will produce enormous social change. Mr. Diebold, who generally is credited with coining the term "automation," sees both a threat and a promise in this new technology.

Whatever the net results, the impact of science on our society is pervasive and all-encompassing. It calls for reexamination of school programs.

THE KNOWLEDGE EXPLOSION

The rocketing growth of modern genetics has split it into countless specialties such as classical, population, molecular, and practical genetics. As a result of increased knowledge in this discipline, we are witnessing the efforts to explore the molecular structures of living cells and thus to control the growth and reproduction of such cells. Hopes are high that man will soon come to a complete understanding of life's basic chemical processes. The excitement and potential of the work now being done in genetics in the study of DNA, the chemical that is found in the nucleus of every living cell, is described in Bentley Glass' article, "What Man Can Be."

Robert M. Hutchins ("Is Democracy Possible?") forces us to face the questions that confront every citizen if he is to participate actively in the decisions which affect his life. He tells us of experts who state that there is no way in which the citizen can now take part in these decisions because of their enormous technical complexity. Hutchins believes that, through major improvements in education and in mass communication, the people could get the information necessary to make intelligent decisions about current problems.

CHANGING VALUES

Industrial culture today is characterized by different observers as materialistic, activistic, pragmatic, relativistic, extroverted, mystical, aesthetically sensitive, and idealistic. J. Robert Moskin ("Morality USA") asks whether bigness, the bomb, and the buck have destroyed our old morality. He finds that two Americans rarely agree on who is immoral or what is the moral thing to do. On the other hand, Edward T. Chase ("Money Isn't Everything") asserts that we have evolved beyond the consumption society to the society of self-realization. He believes that modern man is now experiencing, for the first time, the impact of a generation that is well educated and liberated from toil.

Many trends, directions, and opinions can be seen in the turmoil of changing values in our present world. The school may need to become an even more significant force to help us come to greater agreement regarding the values that will give us a sense of direction.

CHANGING ECONOMIC SYSTEM

The economic system exists to satisfy the wants of the society. In every society, but especially in industrial societies, the school has a role in sustaining and improving the economic system.

Gerard Piel ("Consumers of Abundance") perceives that technology is undermining the two mainstays of our economy: property and work. "In the place of work and property, illusions and old habits and compulsions now support the social edifice." Piel believes that fundamental changes in the social order are already underway and that public understanding must overtake this transformation.

How should the schools' goals and programs be reoriented to support the changing problems and circumstances of our economic lives?

CHANGING CITIZENSHIP ROLES

In the light of the many and varied changes noted thus far, it seems clear that the roles of citizenship in our society also must change. Awareness of the need for scientists and technicians will help bring about changes in school programs to provide retraining in these new specialties. Unfortunately, there is little comparable impetus from the society for more appropriate citizenship education and education for self-fulfillment.

"Do we as a people possess the wisdom, or even the interest and desire, to accept the challenges of our form of government?" asks C. V. Newsom ("Intellectual Demands on the Citizen"). As the functions of government expand, so do the responsibilities of citizens since, in a democracy, the citizens *are* the government. To meet these responsibilities, Newsom believes that the schools must provide better basic education, strongly oriented to the requirements of citizenship. Winston White ("Individual and Society: A New Perspective") claims that the individual today has unique opportunities to be an individual as a result of his new interdependence with others. Each person has a greater possibility of rejecting those roles and responsibilities for which he is not fitted and which do not interest him. If individuality is what we want, then specialization is the best arrangement, both for self-fulfillment and for society.

RISE OF DISADVANTAGED PEOPLES

Poverty in a rich country such as America is a complicated web of family, jobs, education, neighborhood, and national values. There seems to be no single cure because each of the elements reinforces the others. Can education make a difference? If education means that the individual learns, then, in the view of some observers, the slum school is often a failure factory.

Allan Ornstein and Stanley Rosenfeld ("Environmental and Other Factors Which Mitigate Against Disadvantaged Youngsters in School") state that the disadvantaged child is a victim from birth of an environment that is hostile. Our schools in many cases can do very little to save children who are lost before they ever walk through a school-house door.

The 1967 President's Riot Commission report pointed out very vividly the frustration of the disadvantaged in America. There seems to be an alarming loss of faith among blacks and whites, rich and poor, in the ability of their political system to find answers to America's problems. Michel Gordey, a French journalist who has visited and studied America, writes of an alarming change and an atmosphere of fear in the country ("A European Looks At America").

Nevertheless the 1960's and the 1970's are clearly the years of the rise of disadvantaged peoples, not only in this country, but all around the world. Former colonies have achieved independence, and hunger and disease everywhere are increasingly our own problems. Barriers of race, color, sex, and economic and social class are being broken. How will functional school programs take account of these changes in what and how students are taught?

CRISIS IN OUR CITIES

Since 1950 sixteen million rural refugees have fled to the cities, and they are still coming. They come because they have no other choice: they have faced starvation in the rural areas. The rural South no longer needs black people in large numbers after requiring Negro labor for 300 years. These poor, and others, have become a part of the city ghetto, which offers fear, unemployment, poor housing, and inadequate schooling.

The poor in the cities can wait no longer for white, affluent America to respond to their needs. Ghettos are exploding into open rebellion and suicidal anarchy. Daniel Levine ("Defaulting in the Schools and Rioting in the Streets") suggests that our schools have failed to break down the barriers separating Americans of differing social class and racial groups from each other.

A hope for cities comes from the Model Cities Program. Seymour Rosenthal and George Arnstein ("Where Schools Fit In the Model Cities Program") believe the Model Cities Program can be the vehicle for getting many new ideas going in our schools as a part of coordinated urban-planning ideas such as "lighted schools" to be open 24 hours a day, seven days a week.

What will life in our cities be like in the future? Doxiadis, a world-renowned architect and city planner, tells us we must project our thinking into the future in order to create a better present. He poses the question of whether cities of the future will serve man or tyrannize him.

OUR CHANGING SOCIAL GOALS

Our national ideals are based on our belief in the dignity and worth of the individual and his liberty. However, social forces that are transforming our society are making the implementation of individual liberty and dignity a very different matter from what it was when our nation was founded, or even 25, 15 or 10 years ago.

George Counts ("A Rational Faith in Education") reminds us that "our traditional faith in education as a liberator of mankind is justified only if education is carefully and effectively directed toward such a purpose." He considers several proposals for attaining this goal and describes the kind of curriculum he thinks is needed.

The social forces described in this section must be considered in curriculum planning. The next four sections of this book present other essential bases for thinking about curriculum planning at all levels of the school. In part II these bases can be applied to elementary, secondary, and community college programs.

EDUCATION AND THE TECHNOLOGICAL REVOLUTION

George S. Counts

Approximately a generation ago one of our greatest Supreme Court Justices, Oliver Wendell Holmes, observed that "what we need today is less inquiry into the abstruse and more thought about the obvious." While I would have no objection to more inquiry into the abstruse, I believe that Holmes was profoundly right.

The peoples of the world in the present epoch are leaving behind the material forms and agencies of a civilization which in its broad outlines endured for many centuries. This civilization was based on agriculture, animal breeding, handicraft, simple trade, and human energy—a civilization that in its many variants dates practically from the beginning of recorded history. The civilization which our fathers and mothers brought to the New World in the sixteenth and seventeenth centuries and molded into special patterns during the succeeding two or three hundred years was one of those variants.

A new civilization is rising in the West and spreading swiftly throughout the world—a civilization that is coming to be called industrial—a civilization so strange in its forms, so vast in its reaches, so complex in its patterns, and so mighty in its energies that thoughtful men and women fear that the control of its operations may prove to be beyond the powers of its creator. The fact must be emphasized, moreover, that in spite of the common reference to the "industrial revolution" as a limited series of changes in modes of production which took place in England in the eighteenth century and in other countries at later times, the revolution has actually been gathering momentum with every decade. Industrial *civilization* is probably still in its early infancy. What it will be like when fully matured we do not and cannot know. That it will assume, at least for a time, different forms in different societies, among peoples of diverse cultures, may be confidently expected. Moreover, although certain of its broad imperatives and potentialities are already clearly discernible, we may be sure that it will bring many surprises, challenges, hazards, and opportunities to mankind.

From *Teachers College Record*, LIX, No. 6 (March, 1958), 309-318. Used by permission of the author and publisher. This is the second in the series of lectures on "Education for a Society of Free Men in the Technological Era" delivered by Dr. Counts in Brazil in 1957.

The basic source of this new civilization is science. We must all concur in the judgment of Preserved Smith in his *A History of Modern Culture*. "Of all the elements of modern culture," he writes, "as of all the forces moulding modern life, science has been the greatest. It can be shown that all other changes in society are largely dependent on this. Thought, philosophy, religion, art, education, laws, morals, economic institutions, are to a great extent dependent upon the progress of science. Not only does science alter techniques in the production of wealth, but it alters man's view of the world in which he lives. The world-view is perhaps the decisive factor in moulding life and civilization." Undoubtedly the rise of science distinguishes our age from all the preceding ages of human history. And technology is the application of the methods and findings of science to the ways of life.

The penetration of science and technology into our culture involves education in two major tasks—the one relatively simple and the other profoundly complex. The first is the mastery and advance of scientific and technical knowledge, the training of engineers and scientists. Although at the moment this task arouses considerable excitement in my country because of the astonishing successes of the Soviet Union in this realm, it should not be our major concern. The real problem lies in the social, political, and moral sphere—in the sphere of values and understandings. We must strive in all haste to rear a generation capable of living with and directing toward humane ends all the resources of science and technology. The emphasis here will be placed on technology.

This question takes us again into an inquiry regarding the nature of culture. We must realize that a new cultural element changes the character of both the culture and the people involved. The introduction of such a powerful element as technology is therefore a most serious matter. It does not mean merely an addition to elements already present. A culture is much more than an aggregation of distinguishable elements. It is much more than the sum of its parts. It is essentially a system of functional relationships in which the diverse elements react upon one another and are bound together into a kind of organic unity. Consequently, a new element will affect eventually, according to its strength, the entire system of relationships. And this means that it will change the very character of the people nurtured by the given culture of civilization. A Connecticut clergyman, Horace Bushnell, saw this clearly in the middle of the last century. "This transition from mother and daughter power to water and steam power is a great one," he wrote, "greater by far than many have as yet begun to conceive—one that is to carry with it a complete revolution of domestic life and social manners."

Technology impresses its special character on a culture and on the bodies, minds, and hearts of those who use it. To think of technology solely in terms of its material products, of its discoveries and inventions, would be a grave mistake. In essence it is a process, a way of working, a method of attacking problems, a mode of viewing the world. As such, it has a number of characteristics. First, it is marked by emphasis on precision and ever greater precision, on orderly and defined relationships. Second, it is experimental in method, guided by bold imagination and careful observation, irreverent of the past, of great names, of authority as such in every form. Third, it is practical, concerned with the useful rather than the academic, with the application of knowledge to the ways of life rather than with the cultivation of knowledge for its own sake. Fourth, it is planful, insisting on the utility of design, on the rational ordering and coordination of materials and energies in the light of purpose. Fifth, it is dynamic, ever challenging the old, ever seeking new knowledge and new and more efficient ways of doing things, ever striving to push forward the boundaries of understanding and control. Its symbol is the laboratory. Clearly, in taking such a powerful and aggressive element to its bosom, any civilization is asking for trouble and crisis, excitement and adventure without limit.

The interaction of a culture and a new element, of course, works both ways. Every culture always impresses its special character on technology. Just as fire or the wheel has been put to the most diverse uses by different peoples, so technology can be directed toward the most diverse ends. It may be employed to destroy everything that is good in the world and to fasten some form of despotism on all peoples. Also, we have reason to hope, it may usher in the most glorious age of human history. At bottom the issue here is moral in character. Technology has raised anew and on a vaster scale than ever before the ancient question of the values by which men live.

The process of interaction between the old and the new of a culture may generate severe and even mortal strains in the society involved. Thus the swift transformation of the material foundations of life and the lag of institutional, ideological, and moral adjustment seem to be at the bottom of the terrifying crises, the wars and depressions, the revolutions and counterrevolutions of our time. Our world, in both its domestic and its international aspects, is out of joint. In 1937 the distinguished English archaeologist Stanley Casson published a book entitled *Progress and Catastrophe.* In this work the writer attempted, in the light of the entire human record, to answer the question as to whether the lot of man has been one of progress or of catastrophe. His answer, of course, was that man has experienced both. He concludes his review of the long human adventure with these words: "When his practical inventiveness ran ahead of his moral consciousness and social organization, then man has equally faced destruction. Perhaps today we are in this stage." The intervening two decades would seem to have strengthened rather than weakened his foreboding. Our "practical inventiveness" has been rushing ahead, while our "moral consciousness and social organization" have made little progress.

In the autumn of 1938, following the Munich Pact which was to "bring peace in our time," Anne O'Hare McCormick, one of our most distinguished commentators, observed in her column in *The New York Times* that "all of those things are happening in the world that could not happen." Mrs. McCormick, of course, knew that things don't happen that can't happen. Obviously what she meant was that many things were happening which could not have happened if our basic premises and assumptions about the world had been sound. She was also saying that our minds were dwelling in a world that had passed away, that we live in an age marked by changes involving the very foundations of civilization and the relations of nations, that we live in a revolutionary epoch which embraces the whole of mankind.

In this sense we have seen many things happen that could not happen. The First World War was such an event. All sensible people knew before August, 1914, that the statesmen of Europe would never allow their differences to reach the point of an internecine struggle that would place in dire peril the whole of Western civilization. And after the war began they knew that it could last only a few months because the economies of the several nations involved could not long bear the tremendous costs of the struggle. We in the United States, though we had our sympathies, resolved at the outset that we would never become directly involved. Yet we were drawn inexorably into the struggle and sent our young men into battle beyond the oceans, contrary to our entire isolationist tradition which had been built up during three centuries in North America.

We entered the war under the slogan of a "war to make the world safe for democracy." After it was over we were convinced that such had been its purpose and that democracy had triumphed. Had not the great autocracies of central and eastern Europe collapsed—first the house of the Romanovs, next the house of the Hapsburgs, and finally, the strongest of the three, the house of the Hohenzollerns? The road to the future was clear, and there could be only one road—the road to democracy and popular government. Anything else was unthinkable. Yet on the ruins of the ancient autocracies there arose new revolutionary systems which proved to be far more tyrannical than the old—the "popular despotisms" of Bolshevism and Fascism.

When the Bolsheviks, a tiny minority of revolutionaries, overthrew the promising Provisional Government in Russia by force and violence on November 7, 1917, we knew that they would survive only a few days or weeks because they were opposing the whole trend of the age—the trend toward popular rule. Moreover, in their proposal to abolish the institution of private property in land and the tools of production, they were obviously violating the laws of nature revealed by the classical economists of the nineteenth century. Indeed, an American Secretary of State in the late twenties declared Russia an "economic vacuum." That the Soviet Union under the dictatorship of the Bolshevik Party would develop into the towering industrial colossus of today was quite beyond the bounds of common sense.

The rise of Hitler also, not to mention Mussolini, was contrary to all the rules of logic. When he first appeared, shouting his barbarous doctrines of Nordic superiority, he seemed to all right-thinking people a comic figure on the stage of history. With his little black moustache he reminded one of Charlie Chaplin. With his arrest and subsequent imprisonment, following his "beer hall putsch" in Munich in 1924, all agreed that he was finished. While in prison he wrote *Mein Kampf*, in which he outlined his objectives and methods with utter clarity. Yet no one took him seriously because the German people were the most literate great nation in Europe—a people, moreover, who had contributed mightily to the development of European culture in the realms of art, music, literature, science, and philosophic thought. Yet he came to power and plunged the whole world into darkness.

The great economic depression which hit the United States and most of the rest of the world in 1929 likewise could not happen. The American economy had been moving from triumph to triumph, and every American family was to have a "chicken in every pot and a car in every garage." Yet, in spite of all the wise soothsayers, the depression came and lasted in some measure until the economy was rescued by the Second World War—by far the worst depression in the history of the Republic.

The Second World War, like the first, was also impossible. Again we resolved not to become involved. American soldiers, we were assured, would not be called upon to fight on foreign soil. Yet they died by tens of thousands in the most distant regions of the earth, on the land, in the air, and in the water, in the prison camps and on the death marches of Germany and Japan. Today we rightly fear the coming of a holocaust that would dwarf any previous death grapple of the nation.

The disaster at Pearl Harbor which precipitated the United States into the Second World War must also be listed. After the event several inquiries into the question of responsibility were launched. The fact is that the

American people generally were responsible. We lived under the spell of an illusion which we shared with practically all European nations. If it had been Germany in the Pacific, or any other Western state, we would not have been caught unaware. But it was the Japanese, a colored people, and therefore not to be taken too seriously. The following story went the rounds in those days: An American naval commander was asked what would happen if the Japanese fleet were to attack San Francisco early some morning before breakfast. The answer he made was that the American forces would get up, go out and sink the hostile vessels, and return in time for breakfast. Asked for an explanation of this happy disposal of the matter, he replied that the Japanese were mere imitators and incapable of creative and original thought. Their ships were badly constructed, their armaments were inferior, and their gunnery was bad.

The creation of the atomic bomb was another impossibility. Although this fateful advance in the destructiveness of weapons of warfare had been foreshadowed by the work of the physical scientists since the opening of the century, the suggestion that matter would be converted into energy made little sense to the ordinary citizen. And as the scientists who had fashioned the first atomic bomb awaited the outcome of the test on the deserts of New Mexico in July, 1945, they were by no means certain that the contraption would actually explode. But it did, and in so doing opened a new epoch in the history of the race.

The list could be greatly extended. It must suffice to say that the end is not in sight. During the next half century we shall doubtless see many more things that could not happen. As a distinguished student of the history of engineering and technology, R. J. Forbes of the University of Amsterdam, has recently written: "The heralding of the Atomic Age has rudely awakened us to the fact that, to paraphrase the words in which Newton summarized his life's achievements, we have picked up but a few pebbles on the shores of a great ocean that still remains to be explored." Perhaps the most revolutionary discoveries and inventions lie in the future, provided mankind has a future. To prepare a generation to expect and to live with the impossible should be one of the major objectives of a liberal education.

Already, as we have noted, the world has been profoundly transformed by the impact of science and technology on the heritage bequeathed to us by the nineteenth century. Out of this impact have emerged seven stark realities which are largely responsible for things happening that could not happen. These realities must be brought into our basic premises about the world if we are to deal rationally with problems and crises of the coming years. Indeed, any one of these realities would be sufficient by itself to mark the coming of a new age.

In the first place, the whole earth has been reduced to the dimensions of a little neighborhood. As a result of this development we may say that a major cycle in the life of man is closing in our time—a cycle which embraces hundreds of thousands, possibly a million years. It opened in that long-forgotten age, aeons before the dawn of recorded history, when man moved out from his place of origin, from some Garden of Eden, to occupy and sustain himself in practically all parts of the earth. In the process of migration, settlement, and adaptation, combined with the operation of factors of geographical barriers, great distances, and isolation, the several races and varieties of the human species, the many languages, religions, cultures, and political systems were formed.

For some time now, probably since the voyages of Columbus and Vasco da Gama, and particularly during the present epoch, this ancient tendency toward separation and differentiation has been reversed. In terms of means of communication and life conditions that bind men together into communities and societies, the whole earth is no larger than that tiny Garden in which man first ate of the fruit of the tree of knowledge of good and evil, and thus became man. And the divers members of the human family, with their long heritage of rivalry and conflict, of prejudice and hatred, are being pressed together in this tiny garden. As a consequence, the lot of each, including ourselves, is being joined in ever-growing measure with the lot of all. From this condition there is no retreat. We in the Americas in particular must realize that the great oceans, east and west, that protected us for centuries do so no longer.

In the second place, the colored peoples of the earth are rising everywhere, from Harlem to Tokyo and Timbuktu. So, a second great cycle, embracing approximately five hundred years, is passing into history. At the beginning of this period the light-skinned peoples of Europe were in imminent danger. Indeed, to the mythical visitor from Mars, it might have appeared at the time that they stood a good chance of being either enslaved or driven into the sea. The Tartars still occupied much of Russia; the Moors were still entrenched in Spain; and the Ottoman Turks were striking boldly and powerfully at the southeastern gates of Europe. Then, owing to a number of factors, one of which was certainly revolutionary inventions in the modes of warfare and another the advance of nautical science, the tables were turned. These Europeans took the offensive. They threw off the Tartar yoke, expelled the Moors, halted the advance of the Turks, discovered and conquered the New World, took possession of the islands of the eastern seas, swept over the Dark Continent, and penetrated the vast expanses of Asia. By the end of the nineteenth century they held nine-tenths of the land surface of the globe and dominated the remainder. As a result of their fabulous successes, they developed a sense of unqualified superiority, identified themselves with the advance of civilization, and assumed that they were destined by their own nature to rule the "lesser breeds" of man forever.

Again the tables are turning. The surviving colonial empires of the eighteenth and nineteenth centuries, the British, the French, and the Dutch, are in process of dissolution. And the colored peoples will not be satisfied until they have achieved equal status among the nations. Nor will they be satisfied until they have removed the last vestige of imputed inferiority which the power of the white man forced upon them.

In the third place, the center of gravity of industrial, military, and political power has already shifted from Western Europe, where it had rested during the modern period down to the end of the nineteenth century. It has shifted east and west, to Russia and the United States. Six of the eight so-called great powers which ruled the world fifty years ago have been reduced to the status of secondary powers by the wars of our period. The fiasco of the British and French attack on Egypt in the autumn of 1956 reveals to all eyes how the mighty have fallen. At present only two great powers remain. If they were alike in their traditions, institutions, and basic values, the situation would be critical, as any student of history would know. Thus, Charles A. Beard, the great historian, wrote to me on July 13, 1945, before the war was over in the east: "The sky is clear and ominous: only two mighty armed powers are on the horizon. What impends and with what portents? Day and night, I wonder and tremble for the future of my country and mankind." We have reached the point in history foreseen by Alexis de Tocqueville in 1835. Speaking of the Russians and the Americans, he wrote: "Their starting points are different, and their courses are not the same; yet each of them seems marked out by the will of Heaven to sway the destinies of half the globe."

That this situation will change in the decades ahead is clear. We may expect to see the renewal of the British Commonwealth, the integration of the West European states, and the rise of new great powers, perhaps in China, India, Brazil, and possibly in other regions of the earth.

In the fourth place, the whole world is threatened by a powerful and ruthless totalitarian movement—Soviet Communism. Stemming from the Russian Revolution of 1917, this movement constitutes a strange and dynamic synthesis of an old Russian revolutionary tradition, out of which Bolshevism came, and Marxian doctrines, Russian expansionism, and

Russian Messianism. With a sense of mission rarely equalled in history, the Soviet leaders see the eventual spread of Communism over the entire earth under their inspired guidance and through the extension of Soviet power. Their triumphs during and following the war in advancing their dominion in eastern Europe and Asia confirm these men in their doctrines. The death of Stalin and the rise of Khruschev to power should deceive no one on this point.

Today the members of the tiny oligarchy in the Kremlin, which holds sway over practically one-third of the human race, believe with the fanaticism of religious conviction that the forces of history are working swiftly and inexorably on their side. They are profoundly convinced that "all roads today lead to Communism." Through their own Communist Party of the Soviet Union and the network of Communist Parties embracing practically all countries, they are subjecting to implacable and pitiless attack the liberal and democratic forces of the world. With cold and careful calculation and guided by the ethics of battle, they are promoting strife and unrest everywhere beyond the borders of their own domain. And as they excoriate the decaying imperialisms of the past, they seek to fasten on mankind a new imperialism far surpassing in rigor and ruthlessness the colonial systems of the nineteenth century. In Hungary in October and November, 1956, they presented to the world a perfect exhibit of their methods, morals, and purposes.

In the fifth place, war threatens the very survival of civilization. Here is the supreme question confronting mankind in the second half of the twentieth century. While in the past the great destroyer has devoured and enslaved many tribes and peoples, today it places in jeopardy the entire human adventure. We know that total war, waged with the rapidly advancing military technology and with that spirit of ruthlessness which in our lifetime has greatly weakened the sense of mercy and humanity, threatens all the ways and values of civilized life. We know that it constitutes the most dangerous threat to the survival of civilization that mankind as a whole has ever encountered. We must remember that the earth today is a little neighborhood.

Unless this terrible scourge is driven from the earth, no civilization worthy of the name can be expected to endure. Otherwise, with the earth growing ever smaller and the engines of death ever more destructive, preparation for war may become the all-absorbing interest of mankind until the arrival of that fateful day when time shall be no more. A few short years ago we were contemplating the awful moment when, perhaps without warning, great cities would be consumed in the purple and orange holocaust of atomic explosion. Now we have the so-called hydrogen bomb, which, if let loose in the world, might exterminate the entire population of the earth and render it uninhabitable for centuries. As to what dreadful weapons may lie beyond the veil that mercifully shrouds the future, even distinguished scientists can only speculate. During the present respite, how long or short we know not, we have our chance of building a just and lasting peace.

In the sixth place, the advance of science and technology has put in the hands of men fabulous power for peaceful uses—power over material things, power over the life process, power over the human mind. In 1835, according to the German engineer and economist Leo Hausleiter, the total capacity of machines in the world was approximately 650,000 horsepower. By 1900 in the United States alone the figure stood at 70 million, and by 1935 at over 1 billion. Today it cannot be far from 2 billion. If one horsepower is reckoned as equal to the power of twelve men, this means that the American people have working for them over 20 billion mechanical slaves, almost ten times the total population of the earth. And Leland Olds, formerly chairman of the Federal Power Commission and a lifetime student of mechanical power, has recently predicted that power consumption in the United States "might increase six to eight times by 1970." When we consider that the age of atomic energy, electronics, and automation is upon us, we can see that not only the contours of the economy, but also the contours of labor and leisure, of our whole way of life are certain to be radically transformed. At this point we are reminded of the observation of Aristotle: "If every tool when summoned could work of its own accord, as the creations of Daedalus moved of themselves or the tripods of Hephaestus went of themselves about their sacred work; if the weavers' shuttles could weave of themselves; then the master workers would need no apprentices, and the landlords would need no slaves." Today, of course, in many respects we are far beyond the vision of the ancient philosopher.

Power over the life process is almost equally impressive. Unquestionably the advance and application of medical science constitute one of the glories of our civilization. Our fathers and mothers of the eighteenth and early nineteenth century had little more control over the life process than the people of antiquity. They multiplied without restraint, they lived on a monotonous and badly balanced diet, they were mowed down by disease, and they grew old in middle age. The average expectation of life in the most advanced communities and regions was between thirty and thirty-five years. Today most of the dread diseases of the past have been banished, control over births is widely practiced, and the life span has been raised to seventy years. With further developments in chemistry and the biological sciences, the time may not be far distant when man will be able to fashion himself into whatever image may strike his fancy. Given the present level of our ethics and our social organization we can view such a possibility only with deep misgivings.

The increase of power over the human mind constitutes, from the standpoint of free society, one of the most crucial problems of the age. Such a society rests not only on guarantees of individual security from the violence of mobs and the arbitrary acts of government, but also on general conditions of life that make possible the development of informed and independent judgment. The advance of technology has created new and powerful instruments of mind control; and the entire process of mind-forming has become more and more organized, or at least subject to organization. The individual has become increasingly dependent for information, political ideas, and social attitudes, upon organized education and the new media of mass communication, particularly the daily press, the comic, the movie, the radio, and television. That these new agencies have enormous power has been demonstrated in our time by both advertising agencies and totalitarian, states. If conducted with a high sense of public duty, personal integrity, and devotion to truth, they may serve mightily to promote enlightenment, understanding, and good will within the nation and throughout the earth. In a world as vast in its reaches, as complicated in its structure, and as dynamic in its movements as ours, they are indispensable to the successful functioning and perhaps the very survival of a democratic society. They are also equally indispensable to the totalitarian state.

We enter the atomic age with minds formed largely in pre-industrial times. And the fact must be emphasized repeatedly that the strange technological civilization which has burst upon mankind so suddenly and which is sweeping across the world so swiftly is still in its early stages. In certain of its phases it is far more advanced than in others. Our functional ideas, our moral conceptions, and our social organization lag seriously behind our modes of livelihood, forms of communication, use of mechanical energy, and scientific knowledge. This lag is doubtless responsible for many of the troubles and conflicts of our time. It is certainly the underlying source of the more powerful and disrupting tensions to be observed within our domestic society and among the nations of the world. Today a great gulf stands between many of the stubborn realities of our emerging industrial civilization and our customs, loyalties, understandings, and outlooks. It has been said that "distance has been annihilated, but the sense of distance remains." This could be said of so many things in the world today. The task of bringing our old minds into accord with the facts of the new world is a gigantic and urgent educational undertaking. Indeed, we shall not know peace and serenity until this is accomplished.

THE GREAT AMERICAN FRUSTRATION

Archibald MacLeish

That Americans have changed their nature since Andrew Jackson's day or Theodore Roosevelt's or even Harry Truman's is now taken as self-evident—at least among the Americans. No visiting European from Crèvecoeur to Somerset Maugham would have reported us to the world in the terms in which we now report ourselves, nor would Charles Dickens, who liked us least and used almost every other derogatory term to describe us, have used the word we repeat most frequently today. Arrogant, perhaps. Self-confident and bumptious, certainly. But frustrated? If there was one people on earth incapable of frustration it was the people who inhabited the United States . . . a hundred years ago.

But not now. Not to us. Not in the newspapers or the television programs or the lecture circuits or anywhere else our national mania for prodding and poking at our national psyche indulges itself. For a time last winter the word frustration was almost as frequently seen and heard in those quarters as the word America itself, and when Robert Kennedy was shot in Los Angeles, though the talk was all of the "sickness of American society," it was still the American sense of frustration and helplessness which spoke. We have not only accepted our frustration, we have embraced it. To the young it seems somehow to explain what is otherwise inexplicable in the numb uneasiness with which they approach their lives. To the old it provides an alternative to the exhausting labor of struggling to comprehend an increasingly incomprehensible epoch.

But what the great frustration actually means is not so obvious. Most of us, questioned about it, would reply Vietnam, meaning one of two quite different things: either that the stupidity of our involvement in the war in Vietnam has shaken our confidence in our ability to manage our own affairs, or that our astonishing failure to win the war once we had involved ourselves has undermined our belief in our greatness as a world power. But is either

From *Saturday Review*, LI, No. 28 (July 13, 1968), 13-16. Copyright 1968 Saturday Review, Inc. Used by permission of the author and publisher.

reply correct? Would we believe in our greatness as a world power today if we had used our incontestable superiority in weapons to blast what Governor Reagan refers to as "a water buffalo economy" off the earth? Or would we now regain our political self-confidence if we were to repudiate the President, whoever he was, who involved us in Vietnam in the first place? I doubt it. I think any such washing of the hands would end where, indeed, it has already ended; in the realization that no one, whether Eisenhower or Kennedy or Johnson, can usefully be blamed for the events which led to our involvement in Vietnam because no one of them was really in control of those events. And that realization, far from curing our sense of frustration, would only deepen it.

Or, more precisely, it would show us what this frustration which we confess so readily really is. It is not, as we like to think, Vietnam. Not the sense of individual helplessness which plagues the citizens of a large country when they become aware of the blindness and ineptitude of their rulers, the stupidity of those in power. Not the impotent rage which follows the failure of events to conform to expectations, the failure of history to keep to the plot as written—the refusal of the water buffalo economy to collapse before the electronic power. Not the first mistake which has left us in it, or anything else which has to do with Vietnam alone—which began in Vietnam and will end there. It is none of these things but something larger and more troubling: a numb, unformed, persistent sense, like the hinting pinch of a pain which is not yet brutal hurt but will be, that we, as Americans, we perhaps as members of our generation on this earth, have somehow lost control of the management of our human affairs, of the direction of our lives, of what our ancestors would have called our destiny.

It is a sense we have had in one form or another for a long time now, but not as an explicit, a formulated fear until we found ourselves deep in the present century with its faceless slaughters, its mindless violence, its fabulous triumphs over space and time and matter ending in terrors space and time and matter never held. Before that there were only hints and intimations, but they were felt, they were recorded where all the hints and intimations are recorded—in poems, fictions, works of art. From the beginning of what we used to call the industrial revolution—what we see today more clearly as a sort of technological coup d'état—men and women, particularly men and women of imaginative sensibility, have seen that something was happening to the human role in the shaping of civilization.

A curious automatism, human in origin but not human in action, seemed to be taking over. Cities were being built and rebuilt not with human purposes in mind but with technological means at hand. It was no longer the neighborhood which fixed the shape and limits of the town but the communications system, the power grid. Technology, our grandfathers said, "advanced" and it was literally true: it was technology which was beating the tambours, leading the march. Buildings crowded into the air not because their occupants had any particular desire to lift them there, but because the invention of electric elevators and new methods of steel and glass construction made these ziggurats possible and the possibility presented itself as economic compulsion.

Wildness and silence disappeared from the countryside, sweetness fell from the air, not because anyone wished them to vanish or fall but because throughways had to floor the meadows with cement to carry the automobiles which advancing technology produced first by the thousands and then by the thousand thousands. Tropical beaches turned into high-priced slums where thousand-room hotels elbowed each other for glimpses of once-famous surf not because those who loved the beaches wanted them there but because enormous jets could bring a million tourists every year—and therefore did.

The result, seen in a glimpse here, a perception there, was a gradual change in our attitude toward ourselves as men, toward the part we play as men in the direction of our lives. It was a confused change. We were proud—in England, and even more in America, raucously proud—of our technological achievements, but we were aware also, even from the beginning, that these achievements were not altogether ours or, more precisely, not altogether ours to direct, to control—that the *process* had somehow taken over leaving the purpose to shift for itself so that we, the ostensible managers of the process, were merely its beneficiaries.

Not, of course, that we complained of that, at least in the beginning. A hundred years ago, with the rare exception of a Dickens or a Zola, we were amenable enough—amenable as children at a Christmas party. Inventions showered on our heads: steam engines and electric lights and telegraph messages and all the rest. We were up to our knees, to our necks, in Progress. And technology had made it all possible. Science was the giver of every good and perfect gift. If there were aspects of the new world which were not perfect—child labor for example—progress would take care of them. If the ugliness and filth and smoke of industrial cities offended us, we put up with them for the sake of the gas lights and the central heating. We were rich and growing richer.

But nevertheless the uneasiness remained and became more and more evident in our books, our paintings, our music—even the new directions of our medical sciences. Who were *we* in this strange new world? What part did *we* play in it? Someone had written a new equation somewhere, pushed the doors of ignorance back a little, entered the darkened room of knowledge by one more step. Someone else had found a way to make use of that new knowledge, put it to work. Our lives had changed but without *our* changing them, without our intending them to change. Improvements had appeared and we had accepted them. We had bought Mr. Ford's machines by the hundreds of thousands. We had ordered radios by the millions and then installed TVs. And now we took to the air, flew from city to city, from continent to continent, from climate to climate, following summer up and down the earth like birds. We were new men in a new life in a new world ... but a world *we* had not made—had not, at least, intended to make.

And a new world, moreover, that we were increasingly unsure, as time went by, we would have wanted to make. We wanted its conveniences, yes. Its comforts, certainly. But the world as a world to live in? As a human world? It was already obvious by the beginning of this century that many of our artists and writers—those not so silent observers of the human world who sit in its windows and lurk in its doorways watching—were not precisely in love with the modern world, were, indeed, so little in love with it that they had turned against life itself, accepting absurdity and terror in its place and making of human hopelessness the only human hope. And there were other nearer, stranger witnesses. Before the century was two-thirds over numbers of our children—extraordinary numbers if you stop to think about it—were to reject, singly and secretly, or publicly in curious refugee encampments, the whole community of our modern lives, and most particularly those aspects of our lives which were most modern: their conveniences, their comforts ... their affluence.

It was inevitable under these circumstances that some sort of confrontation should occur between the old idea of man as the liver of his own life, the shaper of his own existence, and the new idea of world, the newly autonomous world—world autonomous in its economic laws, as the Marxists hoped, or autonomous in its scientific surge, its technological compulsions, as some in the West began to fear. And, of course, the confrontation did occur: first in rather fatuous academic ructions in which science and the humanities were made to quarrel with each other in the universities, and then, in 1945, at Hiroshima. What happened at Hiroshima was not only that a scientific breakthrough—"breakthrough" in the almost literal sense—had occurred and that a great part of the population of a city had been burned to death, but that the problem of the relation of the triumphs of modern science to the human purposes of man had been explicitly defined and the whole question of the role of humanity in the modern scientific age had been exposed in terms not even the most unthinking could evade.

Prior to Hiroshima it had still been possible—increasingly difficult but still possible—to believe that science was by nature a human tool obedient to human wishes and that the world science and its technology could create would therefore be a human world reflecting our human needs, our human purposes. After Hiroshima it was obvious that the loyalty of science was not to humanity but to truth—its own truth—and that the law of science was not the law of the good—what humanity thinks of as good, meaning moral, decent, humane—but the law of the possible. What it is *possible* for science to know science must know. What it is possible for technology to do technology will have done. If it is possible to split the atom, then the atom must be split. Regardless. Regardless of . . . anything.

There was a time, just after Hiroshima, when we tried—we in the United States, at least—to escape from that haunting problem by blaming the scientists as individuals: the scientists, in particular, who had made the bomb—the mysterious workers in the cellars at Stagg Field and the laboratories of the Manhattan Project. And the scientists themselves, curious as it now may seem, cooperated; many of them, many of the best, assuming, or attempting to assume, burdens of personal guilt or struggling, somehow, anyhow, to undo what had been done.

I remember—more vividly perhaps than anything else which happened to me in those years—a late winter evening after Hiroshima in a study at the Institute at Princeton—Einstein's study, I think—when Niels Bohr, who was as great a man as he was a physicist, walked up and down for hours beside the rattling radiators urging me to go to President Truman, whom I did not know, to remind him that there had been an understanding between Mr. Roosevelt and the scientists about the future neutralization of the bomb. I guessed that Bohr, even as he talked that evening, realized there was nothing Mr. Truman or anyone on earth could do to unknow what was known. And yet he walked up and down the freezing study talking. Things, of course, *were* "done"—attempted anyway. In the brief time when we alone possessed what was called "the secret," the American Government offered to share it with the world (the Baruch Plan) for peaceful exploitation. What we proposed, though we did not put it in these words, was that humanity as a whole should assert its control of science, or at least of this particular branch of science, nuclear physics, limiting its pursuit of possibility to possibilities which served mankind. But the Russians, with their faith in the dialectics of matter, demurred. They preferred to put their trust in *things*, and within a few short months their trust was justified: they had the bomb themselves.

The immediate effect in the United States was, of course, the soaring fear of Russia which fed the Cold War abroad and made the black plague of McCarthyism possible at home. But there was also a deeper and more enduring consequence. Our original American belief in our human capability, our human capacity to manage our affairs ourselves, "govern ourselves," faltered with our failure to control the greatest and most immediate of human dangers. We began to see science as a kind of absolute beyond our reach, beyond our understanding even, known, if it was known at all, through proxies who, like priests in other centuries, could not tell us what they knew.

In short, our belief in ourselves declined at the very moment when the Russian belief in the mechanics of the universe confirmed itself. No one talked any longer of a Baruch Plan, or even remembered that there had been one. The freedom of science to follow the laws of absolute possibility to whatever conclusions they might lead had been established, or so we thought, as the unchallengeable fixed assumption of our age, and the freedom of technology to invent whatever world it happened to invent was taken as the underlying law of modern life. It was not enough for a manufacturer of automobiles to announce on TV that he had a better idea—any better idea: pop-open gas-tank covers or headlights that hide by day. No one thought any longer of asking whether his new idea matched a human purpose.

What was happening in those years, as the bitterly satirical fictions of the period never tired of pointing out, was that we were ceasing to think of ourselves as men, as self-governing men, as proudly self-governing makers of a new nation, and were becoming instead a society of consumers: recipients—grateful recipients—of the blessings of a technological civilization. We no longer talked in the old way of The American Proposition, either at home or abroad—particularly abroad. We talked instead of The American Way of Life. It never crossed our minds apparently—or if it did we turned our minds away—that a population of consumers, though it may constitute an affluent society, can never compose a nation in the great, the human, sense.

But the satirical novels, revealing as they were, missed the essential fact that we were becoming a population of consumers, an affluent society, not because we preferred to think of ourselves in this somewhat less than noble role but because we were no longer able to think of ourselves in that other role—the role our grandfathers had conceived for us two hundred years ago. We were not, and knew we were not, Whitman's Pioneers O Pioneers.

It is here, rather than in the floundering failures and futile disappointments of Vietnam, that this famous frustration of ours is rooted. Vietnam alone, disastrous as that whole experience has been, could never have produced, in a confident and self-reliant people such as the Americans once were, a mood like the American mood of these past months. Not even the riots of last summer and this spring could have afflicted us as we are now afflicted if we had still believed that our principal business was the making of a nation, the government of ourselves. Indeed the riots are, if anything, the consequence of the *actual* causes of that doubt. It is not without significance that the targets of the mobs in the burning streets are supermarkets and television outlets rather than the courthouses and city halls which would have drawn the mobs of earlier times. Courthouses and city halls stand—or stood once—for The American Proposition. Supermarkets and television outlets are the symbols of The American Way of Life. Mobs strike for the Bastille in any rising and the Bastille in the United States today is whatever stands for the American Way of Life: the goods and services, the material wealth, which the majority claim as the mark of their Americanism and which the minority are denied.

It is because we are unwilling to recognize this fact and unable to face the crisis as a crisis in the long struggle for the creation of a true Republic—because, indeed, we are no longer primarily concerned with the creation of a true Republic—that the majority respond to these riots with nothing but a demand for more police and more repression, while the Congress sits impotent and paralyzed in Washington.

Which means, of course, however we put it, that we no longer believe in man. And it is that fact which raises, in its turn, the most disturbing of all the swarming questions which surround us: how did we come to this defeated helplessness? How were we persuaded of our impotence as men? What convinced us that the fundamental law of a scientific age must be the scientific law of possibility and that our human part must be a passive part, a subservient part, the part of the recipient, the beneficiary . . . the victim? Have the scientists taught us this? A few months ago one of the greatest of living scientists told an international gathering composed of other scientists: "We must not ask where science and technology are taking us, but rather how we can manage science and technology so that they can help us get where we want to go." It is not reported that Dr. René Dubos was shouted down by his audience, and yet what he was asserting was precisely what we as a people seem to have dismissed as unthinkable: that "we," which apparently means mankind, must abandon our modern practice of asking where science and technology are "taking *us*," and must ask instead how *we* can "manage" science and technology so that they will help us to achieve *our* purposes—our purposes, that is to say, as men.

Dr. Dubos, it appears, scientist though he is and great scientist, believes rather more in man than we do. Why, then, do we believe so little? Perhaps we can answer that question best by asking another: how was our original,

American belief in man achieved? Where did it come from? Thomas Jefferson, who had as much to do with the definition of our American belief as anyone, reflected on that subject toward his life's end. It was that famous trio at William and Mary, he decided, who "fixed" his "destinies." It was his education in his college, the teaching of Small and Wythe and the rest, which shaped his mind, gave it its direction. John Adams would have said the same and doubtless did: it was in Harvard College that he found those Greeks and Romans who taught him what a man could be and therefore *should*.

It is *our* education, then, which has shaped the very different estimate of man we live by? In part, I think; in considerable part. Education, particularly higher education, has altered its relation to the idea of man in fundamental ways since Adams's day and Jefferson's. From the time when Harvard President Charles Eliot introduced the elective system there—from the time, that is to say, of the renunciation by the university of an intention to produce a certain *kind* of man, a man shaped by certain models, certain texts—the university's concern with "man" as such has grown less and less and its concern with what it calls "subjects" has become greater and greater. The important thing has become the academic "offering" (revealing word): the range of subjects from which the student, with his eye on his career, may choose. And the ultimate consequence, only too evident in the time we live in, has been the vocationalization of the higher schools. The college no longer exists to produce men *qua* men, men prepared for life in a society of men, but men as specialized experts, men prepared for employment in an industry or a profession.

"Getting ahead in the world," says Professor Allen Tate of the University of Minnesota, "is now the purpose of education and the University must therefore provide education for our time, not for all time: it must discover and then give to society what society thinks it wants. . . ." Some of us, looking at the present state of American society—the decay of its cities, the bewilderment of its citizens—may wonder whether the university has really provided "education for our time," but no one, I think, will deny that Professor Tate's emphatic irony has its bite. The vocationalism which a technological society demands of the graduate schools has produced a secondary vocationalism which the graduate schools impose on the colleges, and the result is that undergraduate education—far more important to the preparation for citizenship than graduate education—is increasingly affected by the vocational taint.

What is happening, and in the greatest universities as well as in the less great, is that the entire educational process is becoming fixed—hung-up as the phrase goes now—on its vocational end result. The job out there in the profession or the industry dictates the "training" (their word, not mine) in the graduate schools, and the graduate schools dictate the preparation in the colleges, and the whole system congeals from the top down like a pond freezing. The danger is that, the society may congeal with it, for nothing is more certain in the history of our kind than the fact that frozen societies perish.

As specialized, professional training, higher education in the United States today is often magnificent. Young doctors are better and better as their specialties become more specialized: so much better that it is now a recommendation in almost any field to say of a young doctor that he is young. Student physicists in the great graduate schools are so notoriously productive at twenty-two that a professional physicist of thirty regards himself, or is regarded by his juniors, as middle-aged. But the educated *man*, the man capable not of providing specialized answers, but of asking the great and liberating questions by which humanity makes its way through time, is not more frequently encountered than he was two hundred years ago. On the contrary, he is rarely discovered in public life at all.

I am not arguing—though I deeply believe—that the future of the Republic and the hope for a recovery of its old vitality and confidence depend on the university. I am confining myself to Dr. Dubos's admonition that we must give up the childishness of our present attitude toward science and technology, our constant question where *they* are taking *us*, and begin instead to ask how *we* can manage *them* "so that they can help us get where we want to go." "Where we want to go" depends, of course, on ourselves and, more particularly, on our conception of ourselves. If our conception of ourselves as the university teaches it or fails to teach it is the conception of the applicant preparing for his job, the professional preparing for his profession, then the question will not be answered because it will not be asked. But if our conception of ourselves as the university teaches it is that of men preparing to be men, to achieve themselves as men, then the question will be asked *and* answered because it cannot be avoided. Where do we want to go? Where men can be most themselves. How should science and technology be managed? To help us to become what we can be.

There is no quarrel between the humanities and the sciences. There is only a need, common to them both, to put the idea of man back where it once stood, at the focus of our lives; to make the end of education the preparation of men to be men, and so to restore to mankind—and above all to this nation of mankind—a conception of humanity with which humanity can live.

The frustration—and it is a real and debasing frustration—in which we are mired today will not leave us until we believe in ourselves again, assume again the mastery of our lives, the management of our means.

THE NEW WORLD COMING

John Diebold

"It is an extraordinary era in which we live. It is altogether new. The world has seen nothing like it before. I will not pretend, no one can pretend, to discern the end; but everybody knows that the age is remarkable for scientific research into the heavens, the earth, what is beneath the earth; and perhaps more remarkable still is the application of this scientific research to the pursuit of life. The ancients saw nothing like it. The moderns have seen nothing like it until the present generation. . . . The progress of the age has almost outstripped human belief."

Those words were not spoken today—though I choose them to set today in perspective—but were used in 1847 by Daniel Webster when he opened a new stretch of railroad track in New Hampshire. A greater parallel exists between that era and our own than we normally realize. In that earlier era, science first began to be applied on a wide scale and out of that process came an entirely new society—an industrial society. Out of it, too, came problems, many of which still plague us. When we look back at that great technological upheaval, the real significance of those then-wondrous machines is the human and social change that accompanied their industrial use.

Just as yesterday's innovations proved to be moments in history—way stations leading to newer technology—so today the conception of the computer which we have learned to accept is becoming a thing of the past. Up-to-date systems are no longer glassed-in, carefully isolated accounting machines. Instead they perform an almost limitless variety of functions, and vary with individual requirements.

For example, the newest computer systems may appear as input/output units in individual desks; small television-like screens with keyboards and copying devices. When you ask a question you see the answer almost

From *Saturday Review*, XLIX, No. 30 (July 23, 1966), 17-18. Copyright© 1966 Saturday Review, Inc. Used by permission of the author and publisher.

simultaneously on the screen. If you want a copy of the answer, you can make it immediately. The heart of the system is a switching center rather like the telephone system. Computers, storage elements of many varieties, and many other devices used as part of the system are accessible as you need them, connected through the switching center to the terminal unit at your fingertips. Thousands of people may use such systems at the same time, and each need know no more about the operation of the system than the average person knows about the telephone. In the next decade the typical computer system is going to be of this kind.

Another radical change stemming from these new computer systems involves the relationship between man and machine. One no longer need carry data down to a computer center, or go through a laborious process of getting it into the machine and then waiting for results. Each technological development is moving us toward an easier, more productive relationship between man and machine. Already, for example, a computer can transpose a rough design into exact specifications. If an engineer makes a free-hand drawing of a bridge on such a system's television-like screen, the computer will convert the drawing into exact engineering specifications, will calculate and display materials and stress, and show the design in whole, in part, or in any perspective, in immediate response to the engineer's requirements.

Looking ahead, we see important changes in technology such as chemical memories; fluid and pneumatic systems that have instantaneous response; ability to store images, graphs, drawings and photographs, and to transmit them around the world. All these will be important elements of future computer systems. Graphic elements and the ability to communicate with TV screens are already becoming influential in progress being made in computer design. Yesterday these elements were undreamed of.

Work is being done on language translation by machine. Some document-translation is already on a regular production basis—in fact, people are now attempting to digest articles by machine. This work is still in its beginning stages and there are many problems to be overcome. But the history of this technology is that what seems impossible today becomes an accepted part of our lives tomorrow.

Development of voice recognition by computer, while rife with prob-lems, also is yielding results. Despite all the difficulties, voice-recognition equipment can be purchased today. No serious forecast about computer systems in the 1970s can omit voice recognition systems with several-thousand-word vocabularies. If this sounds unpromising, remember that only a few years ago people used to have two- and three-day meetings to discuss the problem of keeping records on magnetic tape. How naïve that seems to us now. Today, we already have machines that learn (they are called heuristic machines), that devise their own route to a goal or solution; machines that recognize patterns; and machines that can devise their own strategies—for example, winning at games with the men who design them.

Adding tremendous impetus to the technological explosion is the fact that, as computer capabilities are increasing, costs are decreasing. Between 1963 and 1972—a single decade—there will be a decrease of 85 per cent in the cost of completing a typical data-processing job. During this period, the cost of storage by magnetic tape will go down by 97 per cent; the cost of image storage by 96 per cent; and communication line costs, because of increased speeds of transmission, will decrease by 50 per cent. These changes in economics will mean that we will be able to do more with information technology than we now can even imagine.

Let me turn now to the problems of putting these machines to work.

Nowhere is the turn toward technology more obvious than in the *way* we manage. When we first started to apply computers to business operations in 1954, we went through a very difficult experimentation period and were faced with the most puzzling kinds of problems. We have largely emerged from that period, however, and today we are using computers in business for almost everything conceivable—and much that was not just a few years ago. Senior management has begun to realize that the application of this technology is too important to leave to technicians, and that dramatic things can be accomplished if people who know the objectives of a business will take the responsibility of putting these new capabilities to work. When this happens, you find remarkable achievements.

But along with this progress have come new questions and problems. There are, for instance, union negotiation questions. Throughout the country, a number of owners of newspapers have been willing to stake the very existence of their enterprises on the right to install a computer to prepare punch-tape to drive linecasting machines. Just over the horizon, it is clear that this entire process will be bypassed. Is it worth risking an enterprise on a process that is disappearing?

There are many similar questions. What kind of men, for example, should be trained as managers in the new technological environment? How do we create an atmosphere that is conducive to creative people—for more and more of our businesses must be staffed by highly educated and creative personnel? These are only a few of the problems we face.

Most important are the human aspects. They are related to every problem we have in this field: questions of fear and uneasiness when faced with technological changes; questions of education; questions of identification with an enterprise, with a profession.

But along with the question of how we manage are questions concerning what we manage—of new areas of business opportunity. Here, I will speak of four main new entrepreneurial opportunities. The first is the obvious one that has already taken form—the industry that supplies the systems and the equipment. It is already a multi-billion dollar industry, and this is only the beginning.

The second example, as yet nonexistent but about to bloom as an important basic industry, is the data utility field. This is analogous in some ways to the electrical utility industry: It is cheaper for many people to use a central utility than for each individual to have his own generator. The same economic reasoning applies to the data utility industry, where many people can use a machine simultaneously. The technology of realtime processing, time-sharing, and communication will allow this to happen. Small and medium-sized businesses—and for some purposes large businesses —will just plug in for data processing as we now do for electricity.

The third example is the one now being called the inquiry industry—in some ways, the publishing field of the future. This will allow the sale of proprietary data over a communications system in answer to a query placed by the customer. The possibilities are unlimited; practically any information can be provided. We have already started to see the purchase of publishing firms by electronic companies, and this is just the beginning. There will be major changes in ownership in this area in the near future as businesses begin to position themselves to offer such services.

The fourth example is an industry of computer-based educational systems. As technology allows a dynamic or "alive" relationship between a student and a machine system that answers questions as they are posed and discerns gaps in a student's basic grasp of a subject, the much-heralded but until now disappointing teaching machines (better, I think, called learning machines) will begin to mean something. Such systems are already at work in some industrial situations—IBM's Maintenance Training being a good example. Other precursors can be seen in mentally handicapped children's use of computer-driven typewriters to help them overcome some of their handicaps.

If there is one salient fact about information technology, it is that it is going to produce enormous social change. As the quality of life is changed, as the rate of learning, information, travel, and communications all change, we will see a major change in living patterns, in hopes and desires. In short, a complete new environment will exist.

WHAT MAN CAN BE

Bentley Glass

As man looks from his tiny planet out into the immensity of space with its whirling galaxies, he is, through science, master of all on earth and he dreams of flights across space and the settlement of other worlds. But he is also afraid. He is afraid of himself, for this is the age of human crisis, the age when human powers have become so vast that in an instant of anger or prejudice man can destroy himself and his entire planet. The problems of our age are in great measure the risks and the quandaries arising from our newfound scientific powers and our inability to find the honesty and courage, the insight and wisdom needed to deal with them safely.

As a geneticist concerned with human heredity, I believe one of the most remarkable achievements of scientific man in the twentieth century has been the development of our understanding of how the invisible genes in those tiny human sperms and eggs that form the only living connection between one generation and the next establish the nature and the potentialities of each individual.

In our 46 chromosomes we carry two sets of genes—one set from each parent—composed of deoxyribose nucleic acid (DNA) molecules. In all, there may be about 40,000 of these genes which endow us with the ability to synthesize the protein molecules that enable us to function. All our differences from other animals, indeed all our inherited differences from other human beings, reside in differences in the nature of our proteins and therefore of our genes.

The science of genetics, child of the twentieth century, is the science that relates to the study of these genes and what they do, as well as how they are transmitted in reproduction. All of the modern science of evolution revolves around a knowledge of how these genes mutate and what forces lead to the selection and perpetuation, over the generations, of those competing genes that endow their possessors with superior capacity to live to reproductive age and have offspring. With knowledge that has progressed from a few basic laws of the inheritance of genes known in 1900 to a complete picture today of the genetic code, man is now in

From *NEA Journal*, LVI, No. 6 (September, 1967), 11-14. Used by permission of the author and publisher.

almost full possession of the means to modify the hereditary nature of every plant and animal and microbe he wishes.

Indeed, there is nothing to prevent him from meddling with his own hereditary makeup. This staggering power over the nature of human evolution provokes a great crisis in human affairs—the crisis of values and goals, as I would like to call it. For the problem that faces us is not so much the problem of *how* to change man's nature as the problem of the kind of human being we wish to populate the earth. Should we breed for uniform superiority of physique, of health, of intellect? Or should we breed for the maintenance of human diversity? Is it possible that superiority in certain respects is incompatible with superiority in certain other ways? Should we produce castes for different callings? Should we regulate and impose social ends on the personal rights of reproduction? Let me urge everyone to reread Aldous Huxley's *Brave New World*. Do not think of it as fiction, for it isn't really that. Aldous Huxley was a prophet, and most, if not all, of the biological and psychological developments of human power he wrote about are already here, or are just around the corner.

By the end of the century, for example, biologists will, I suspect, have learned how to create some simple forms of living organisms, perhaps at the level of complexity of a virus. Such an accomplishment is not too far beyond the recently discovered steps toward synthesizing DNA or recombining two viruses, each with a mutation fatal to its growth, so as to recover a virus with no mutations and normal powers of growth and reproduction.

It should also be feasible by the year 2000 to bank human reproductive cells of both sexes in a frozen state as we now do with the sperms of sheep and cattle. In this way the reproductive cells of selected individuals might be utilized, even long after their death, to produce in the laboratory embryos that might be implanted in the womb of a foster mother, or even, after sufficient development of the technique, in bottle cultures. I do not expect that the latter "brave new world" technique will be realized by the turn of the century, however. On the other hand, I do expect that techniques will be developed for the cultivation in the laboratory of portions of human ovary and testis, permitting successful continuous production of mature ova and sperms. Recent success in producing mature mouse ova from cultured ovaries indicate that sufficient persistence by enough skilled biologists will make this goal attainable in a few years.

"Aren't the age-old ways of making babies good enough?" I am frequently asked. Several reasons may be given why it is important to explore new possibilities in human reproduction. Only by studying the development of the human embryo and fetus under continuous observation and under controlled conditions can medical science really learn what factors produce particular kinds of abnormalities and how these may be corrected or avoided.

Moreover, the practice of "prenatal adoption," that is, of implanting a healthy selected embryo in a foster mother's womb, appears to have fewer religious and legal objections than the present practice of artificial insemination of the woman, with or without the consent of her husband. The development of the implanted fetus within the mother and its normal delivery at full term will engender the maternal and paternal feelings of the "parents" far more fully than adoption of a child already several years old. Moreover, couples who are sterile may in this way have all the experiences of parenthood.

There are other reasons why such practices might be adopted—if not in the United States, then possibly elsewhere. From the standpoint of eugenics, parents should have their children while they are young. Banking of reproductive cells taken from individuals around 20 years of age may serve to prevent the accumulation of detrimental mutations which occurs with advancing age. From the standpoint of economics and population control, marriage is often long postponed and children are produced by parents in their thirties and forties. Healthy children may of course be produced by parents even at an advanced age, but the odds are not so good.

By banking the reproductive cells of young persons under conditions where mutation is reduced to the lowest level, and using implantation of an embryo produced by artificial fertilization, the older parents may have children as free of defect, on the average, as they would have been when the parents were young.

These practices would of course be ineffective without the practice of effective contraception. In spite of personal and religious objections, it seems clear that the use of present means, especially of steroid "pills" and intrauterine loops, will soon become worldwide. A promising recent advance appears to be that of inserting a dose of progesterone enclosed in a capsule under the skin of the female. Under these conditions, microdoses of the chemical will seep into the circulation and prevent conception even without modifying the usual female cycle. The capsule can be easily and painlessly put in place and may be removed at any time.

Modern methods of contraception, it seems clear, will be the quickest and surest means of securing control over the population increase, and are infinitely superior to the use of legal abortion, as is widespread in Japan today. We might even go so far as to predict that by the year 2000 many countries will have reached such a population density in relation to their

food supply that no further increase can be tolerated. A marriage certificate might then bear two coupons entitling the couple to produce two
children, no more.

We must now consider questions of eugenics, for complete and perfect
control by individuals and by society over reproduction opens up certain
eugenic possibilities like those of *Brave New World*. First, we must
recognize that under our present application of ethics to medical practice,
human society is already doing itself a considerable eugenic injury. When
an infant or child with a genetic defect is kept alive by medical means and
its defect is controlled or even eliminated, the child grows to adulthood.
The most common sequel is marriage and parenthood.

In the past, under a more cruel rule of nature, such persons never lived
to reproduce, and their defective genes were thus eliminated. The population thus maintained a balance between the defective genes being eliminated in each generation and the new ones being produced through
mutation. (Not all mutations produce defective genes, but over 99 per cent
of them do so, for the simple reason that the genes we now have are the
products of millions of years of selection of the best in guiding development suitably for our environment and in working harmoniously together.)
Medical practices thus tend to increase the frequency of defective genes in the
population. To a certain extent, doctors are only making more work for
themselves, for, since they have not removed the cause of the defect, the
gene, but have only corrected symptoms, the defective gene when transmitted does the same harm once again.

Geneticists are looking forward to the day when they can practice
genetic surgery, that is, really reach in and transform a defective gene and
make it functional again. This will not be easy. It will probably always
remain easier and simpler to discard defective reproductive cells and to
select others from banked or cultured material that is free of known
defect.

Now we come to the most serious aspect of the crisis of values and
goals. How can one select good strains of reproductive cells? If the same
materials are used to produce a great many embryos which are reared into
babies, they will be too much alike, like members of the same caste in
Brave New World. This difficulty might be avoided by never using a single
line of reproductive cells more than a few times.

There is another difficulty. Nearly all of us carry some defective genes.
The average is probably around eight. We lack visible signs of defect
because most defective genes are recessive—that is, must be inherited in a
double dose, coming from both father and mother, in order to produce an
evident defect. As long as we have one working gene per pair, enough of

the protein it controls is made to satisfy general needs. Close relatives, however, have a greatly heightened probability of carrying the same defective gene because they possess a common ancestor. We would therefore need strict rules to prevent offspring's being produced by persons who are derived from the same lines of banked or cultured reproductive cells, and careful records on the lineage of each person would have to be kept.

Another new development rapidly approaching realization is the provision of tests that will enable the laboratory specialist to determine whether or not a particular person carries even a single dose of a particular defective gene. For example, take the case of the recessive disorder phenylketonuria, which in an untreated affected baby produces a certain kind of idiocy. Both of the parents of a phenylketonuric child must possess a single dose of the defective gene, as otherwise the child could never have acquired two. By means of a test recently developed, we are able to detect carriers of that gene in the population, and advise them not to marry, or at least not to have children.

In the past decade, the ability to detect the carriers of recessive harmful genes has been extended to about a dozen conditions. It consequently seems very likely to me that before the year 2000 we will have genetic clinics in which by a battery of tests each prospective couple can learn whether or not both of them are carriers of the same defective genes. They could then be advised whether to avoid having children and to substitute prenatal adoption. A new type of medical man, the human geneticist, will take his place along with the other specialists in the near future.

In a population suffering severely from overcrowding and subject to rigorous limitation of births, eugenics might be related rather simply to the measure for population control. For example, if a couple that had used up their coupons for two babies wanted additional children, they might be required to meet certain genetic tests before receiving a special permit. Some additional children above two per couple would be needed in some families to maintain the population at a given level, since some women have no children or only one, for a variety of reasons. The simplest eugenic test, yet one that in the long run might be quite effective in improving the population, would be to examine the first two children to assure that neither one was physically or mentally below average.

Beyond the application of so simple a test, eugenic selection runs into frightening dilemmas. Who really possesses a "good" genotype? How do you judge, when the optimum genotype in one set of circumstances may well be inferior in another? If we knew how to define the goal of a "good race" objectively, we might breed human beings for it as we do animals;

but the lesson seems clear. In selecting for certain characteristics in their animal breeds, the breeders seem always to have sacrificed other very desirable traits. The human races are not animal breeds, but each has been tested out by selection in a natural environment. Probably each is somewhat superior in its own way.

The control of human behavior by artificial means will have become by the year 2000 a frightening possibility. Government—"big brother"—might use tranquilizers or hallucinogens like LSD to keep the population from becoming unruly or too independent. More and more subtle forms of conditioning will lead people to react in predictable ways desired by government or by commercial interests without people's quite knowing how they are hoodwinked. The added possibilities of controlled reproduction I have already described make these psychological methods of control over learning and behavior even more drastic. Here is our *Brave New World* in full, with bottled babies in different kinds of solutions that condition their mental growth to suit a certain caste.

One wonders, moreover, what the effect might be on society and on the family in particular of the complete liberation of the sexual life from its relationship to reproduction. Recently Robert S. Morison of Cornell University has pointed out the grave threat to the continuance of the family as the basic social unit. After a million years of human and prehuman evolution during which the family has been the basis of all protection, education, and nurture, can we safely give it up? What will be the psychological consequences of a population with no personal ties either to the older generation or to the younger generation? Can we look forward to the brotherhood of mankind when there are no more parents, brothers, or sons and daughters, but only people?

I have asked many questions that cannot at present be answered. I have predicted a future in which many cherished values of our society and many ethical standards may be questioned or superseded. It is not enough to have a few scientists raise such issues. Only prolonged and profound attention by many of the wisest men of our time, men of philosophy and religion, students of society and of government, and representatives of the common interests of men throughout the world, together with scientists, may achieve a wise and sober resolution of the crisis evoked in our world by scientific discoveries and their applications.

If we are going to develop a civilization broadly and soundly based on scientific foundations—and we can hardly escape that now—every citizen, every man in the street, must learn what science truly is and what risks and quandaries, as well as what magnificent gifts, the powers that grow out of scientific discovery engender. Surely, this is our primary task. Men who relinquish their birthright of scientific knowledge cannot expect to rule themselves. In order for the scientific society to be democratic and to remain democratic, the people themselves must understand the nature of the scientific forces and problems that dominate their lives. For those of us who are teachers, this is our task and our commitment.

IS DEMOCRACY POSSIBLE?

Robert M. Hutchins

The faith in which I was brought up was as simple and confident as the environment. Democracy was the answer to everything, including the ills of democracy. These ills would be cured by more democracy. The ideal toward which we were moving was the civilization of the dialogue, where everybody talked with everybody else about everything, where nobody tried to get his way by force or fraud, where everybody was content to abide by the decision of the majority as long as the dialogue could continue. Democracy meant self-government, and self-government meant primarily participation by the individual, at least through the selection of his representatives, in decisions affecting his life and happiness. Since decisions affecting the citizen's life and happiness were taken not merely by his government, but also by many other institutions, corporations, trade unions, and political parties, for example, the thing to do was to democratize them, as well as the government.

In this view the great crime is to try to prevent other people from speaking up, or to say that there are certain things you won't talk about, or certain people you won't talk to, either at home or abroad. In this view education and communication are of prime importance, because if you can't hear what the others are saying, or can't understand it, or if they can't hear or understand you, there can't be any dialogue, and democracy becomes meaningless.

The democratic faith is faith in man, faith in every man, faith that man, if he is well enough educated and well enough informed, can solve the problems raised by his own aggregation.

From *Saturday Review*, XLII, No. 8 (February 21, 1959), 15-17 and 58. Copyright © 1959 Saturday Review, Inc. Used by permission of the author and publisher.

One advantage of this faith is that it is practically shock-proof. Industrialization can sweep the world; nationalism and technology can threaten the extinction of the human race; and population can break out all over. Man can take off from this planet as his ancestors took off from the primordial ooze and try to make other planets from which to shoot. Education can be made trivial beyond belief. The media of communication can be turned into media of entertainment. The dialogue can almost stop because people have nothing to say, or, if they have something to say, no place to say it. And still it is possible to believe that if democracy and the dialogue can continue, if they can be expanded, if they can be improved, freedom, justice, equality, and peace will ultimately be achieved.

Some shocks I have received lately have bothered me a little. The first came when I was recommending my democratic panacea as a remedy for the ills of the labor unions to the people on the trade union project of the Fund for the Republic. They informed me that the idea of government by the people had little application to labor unions and that in any event democratic forms in unions were no safeguard against antisocial behavior on their part. In fact, they said, some of the unions in which democratic forms were most conspicuous were the most antisocial.

The second shock came when at the conclusion of my usual tirade against the wild irrationality of our foreign policy I explained to the people on the common defense project of the Fund for the Republic that we should subject that policy to democratic control. My colleagues pointed out to me that in addition to being impossible this was unconstitutional, and had always been regarded as such, and that whatever I might think of the policies followed by the President and the Secretary of State, and however much I might dislike being blown up or suffocated as a result of these policies, the Founding Fathers intended that I should be in precisely this position. In any event, they said, there was no way, particularly in view of the enormous technical problems of modern warfare and international relations, in which the citizens could actually participate in the decisions upon which their lives depended.

The third shock came when I was proposing my usual remedy to the people on the project on political parties, which deals with the political process in a free society. Participation was my watchword. Get out the vote. Or, as the Advertising Council has it, "Vote as You Please, but Please Vote." My associates indicated to me that getting people out to vote when they did not know what they were voting for was not helpful, and might be harmful, to the objects I had in view. Under modern conditions, they said, it might be that responsible political participation and decision by the citizens would prove to be impossible, anyway.

Somewhat shaken, I went to the conference on the Island of Rhodes on Representative Government and Public Liberties in the New States. The basic problem of the conference turned out to be whether government by the people is possible, or even desirable, in the modern world. The sense of relief with which members from the new states welcomed military dictatorships in their countries and with which the Frenchmen present welcomed de Gaulle was a measure of the current disenchantment with democracy. These men saw no way of adjusting democratic institutions to contemporary realities. What they hope for is a period of order in which the most acute problems, like Algeria in France and corruption in Siam, may be solved; after which they may, or may not, try government by the people again.

Eminent European philosophers and political scientists present reassured the members from the new states, three of whose governments turned into military dictatorships while the conference was in session, by telling them that democracy was an illusion in both old and new states, for different reasons. In the new states we could not expect government by the people because they lacked education, communication, organization, and law. In the old states it had been out of date since the Peloponnesian War, and even then it was not what we mean by democracy now. Pericles, a leader of the Left, struck thousands of voters from the rolls because they could not prove that both their parents were native-born Athenians. Greek democracy was based on a uniformity of ideas and practices appropriate to an extended family group. The kind of government by the people that may be said to have worked in Athens and in the New England town meeting could not possibly work in a large, heterogeneous, industrial, bureaucratic society. The most we could hope for was order, efficiency, and the maintenance of civil liberties, those rights historically carved out against governmental interference with private life. Alexander Pope, whose celebrated lines had always seemed to me as false as they were celebrated, was justified at last:

> For forms of government let fools contest
> Whate'er is best administered is best.

I came away from Rhodes with the foreboding that we might be at the beginning of something new in the last 100 years—a world-wide antidemocratic trend that had little or nothing to do with the intimidations or seductions of the Kremlin. (It was significant that in eight days of discussion no member from any new state said a word about Communism or Russia.) This antidemocratic trend would reverse the aspirations of all men of good will—at least since 1848—for government by the people. It would have alarming connotations for the United States in the realm of foreign policy. It should force us to re-examine the assumptions and slogans by which we have lived in the light of the actual operation of our institutions in the new industrialized, polarized, bureaucratic world.

If you ask how my democratic faith is doing,

> Whither is fled the visionary gleam,
> Where is it now, the glory and the dream?

I reply that it is still here. Perhaps the gleam is not quite as bright as it used to be, and somewhat more visionary, but it is still here. Yet, even at my age, I cannot long sustain a position to which my reason will not assent. The shocks I have received are recent; and I cannot claim that I have absorbed them or that I know how to repel others in the future. Perhaps what I can do is to communicate the sense of crisis that I feel and to ask others to join in thinking for a moment how that faith can be defended.

The faith rests on the propositions that man is a political animal; that participation in political decisions is necessary to his fulfillment and happiness; that all men can and must be sufficiently educated and informed to take part in making these decisions; that protection against arbitrary power, though indispensable, is insufficient to make either free individuals or a free society, and that such a society must make positive provisions for its development into a community learning together. For this is what political participation, government by consent, and the civilization of the dialogue all add up to.

If we are to become a community learning together, as I insist we can, the first thing we have to do is to make up our minds that we want to learn. We have lived on a note of triumphant philistinism. Here is a characteristically triumphant proclamation made by Carl D. Becker, perhaps the most celebrated American historian of his day, in 1931. He said, "Our supreme object is to measure and master the world, rather than to understand it. . . . Viewed scientifically, it appears as something to be accepted, something to be manipulated and mastered, something to adjust ourselves to with least possible stress. So long as we can make efficient use of things, we feel no irresistible need to understand them. No doubt it is for this reason chiefly that the modern mind can be so wonderfully at ease in a mysterious universe."

At ease, indeed! Anybody who feels at ease in the world today is a fool. And anybody who would say now that he was content to master and manipulate the environment without bothering to understand how it worked or what to do with it would show first that he did not know what science was, for science is nothing but organized understanding, and second that he had no grasp of the kind of problems we now confront. The great overwhelming problems of our country are how to make democracy a reality, how to survive in the nuclear age, and what to do with ourselves if we do survive. None of these problems is technological, though technology has helped to create all of them, and none of them will yield to the kind of measurement, manipulation, or mastery that Professor Becker had in mind. We may, in fact, reverse his statement of 1931 and come nearer the truth of 1959. Then it would go like this: no doubt it is because we have felt no irresistible need to understand the world that the modern mind can be so wonderfully ill at ease in a mysterious universe.

The next question is, how are we going to learn? History will have trouble with American education in the twentieth century. It will see a people who say they are dedicated to education and who are the richest in the world indifferent to education and unwilling to pay for it. It will see an educational system that delivers less education per dollar than any I can think of saying that all it needs is more money. The people and the educators are united only in this: they both want education without pain, either intellectual or financial. History will find it hard to explain how a nation that *is* one, a nation in which the political subdivisions have almost no relation to social or economic life and very little to political life, can entrust its future to these subdivisions by relegating education to them. History will smile sardonically at the spectacle of this great country getting interested, slightly and temporarily, in education only because of the technical achievements of Russia, and then being able to act as a nation only by assimilating education to the Cold War and calling an education bill a defense act.

We might as well make up our minds to it. If our hopes of democracy are to be realized, every citizen of this country is going to have to be educated to the limit of his capacity. And I don't mean trained, amused, exercised, accommodated, or adjusted. I mean that his intellectual power must be developed. A good way to start finding the money that is needed for education would be to kick out of it the subjects, the activities, and the people that make no contribution to the development of intellectual power. Such an operation would produce vast sums. I suggest that two things might be done with this money and with any more that may be needed: first, we should double teacher's salaries, not because all the teachers we have deserve twice as much as they are getting, but because we want to attract the ablest people into the profession; and second, we should establish a national system of scholarships that makes it possible for every citizen of this country to be educated to the limit of his mental capacity, regardless of the financial capacity of his parents.

If life is learning, and I think it is, and if our object is to become a community learning together, education ought to continue throughout life. Here is the great educational opportunity and obligation of the next generation. The education of adults is not only indispensable to the continuation, expansion, and improvement of the dialogue, but it is also an answer to the question of what we are going to do with ourselves if we survive. As automation advances, as new sources of energy are applied in industry, as the hours of labor decline, we have the chance to become truly human by using our new and disturbing leisure to develop our highest human powers to the utmost. Here we can build on the experience of such organizations as the Great Books Foundation, which has succored tens of thousands of refugees from television.

This brings me to the media of mass communications. If our hopes of democracy are to be realized, the media must supply full and accurate information on which the people can base their judgment on public affairs, and they must offer a forum for the discussion of those affairs. I doubt if there are six cities of any size in the United States in which the newspapers come anywhere near meeting these requirements. As for radio and television, with a few distinguished exceptions now and then, they make no attempt to meet them. A dozen years ago the Commission on the Freedom of the Press recommended the establishment of a continuing independent agency, privately financed, to appraise and report periodically on the performance of the media. Everything that has happened since, and especially the use of the most marvelous electronic methods of communication for the communication of the most insignificant material, makes the adoption of this recommendation more urgent every day.

If we were well-educated and well-informed could we make ourselves felt in the realm of political action? In the Republic as I have described it every act of assent on the part of the governed is a product of learning. Could we learn by doing in politics? Or would the archaic structure of our government and the vast bureaucratic machine that goes creaking on, following the right procedure instead of seeking the right result, prevent us from using our newly won education and information as active, deciding, responsible citizens?

Today the dialogue is impeded by obsolescent practices and institutions from the long ballot to the presidential primary, from the electoral college to the organization of cities, counties, and states. In too frequent elections, unknown persons by the hundreds running for insignificant offices and improper questions, like the dozens submitted at every California election, are presented to the electorate. This is not democracy, but a perversion of it. The political anatomy is full of vermiform appendices, many of them, like Arkansas, inflamed.

Some of these obsolescent practices stop the dialogue in its tracks, like the failure of the FCC and Congress to develop any concept of the public interest, convenience, and necessity. Some of them distort the dialogue by throwing false weights into it, as the electoral college gives a false weight to the large states and the laws on campaign expenditure give money an overwhelmingly false weight in elections. One thing is certain: If our hopes of democracy are to be realized, the next generation is in for a job of institutional remodeling the like of which has not been seen since the Founding Fathers.

Well, suppose we got this remodeling done. Could we then turn ourselves into active, responsible, participating citizens? Wouldn't the bureaucracy, though better, and administering better laws, still have us by the throat? The answer depends partly on our capacity for political invention, which in 1787 was quite large, and partly on what participation means. If we can be equipped for the dialogue and then invent the means by which the bureaucracy can hear it and be made responsive to it, we shall have come a long way from where we are now in relation, for example, to the State Department and the Atomic Energy Commission. Then political participation would mean not only what it too often means exclusively now, the ballot, but also participation in the dialogue about the ends and means of the political society. We would be a community learning together, and the bureaucracy would be learning, too.

The notion that the sole concern of a free society is the limitation of government authority and that that government is best which governs least is certainly archaic. Our object today is not to weaken government in competition with other centers of power, but rather to strengthen it as the agency charged with the responsibility for the common good. That government is best which governs best. Mr. Hoover could see no constitutional way of coping with depression, as Buchanan before him could see no constitutional way of coping with secession. We started out to show in 1932 that our institutions were sufficiently flexible to care for the welfare of all the people. The demonstration was never made. We have got instead the pressure-group state, which cares for the welfare of those who are well enough organized to put on the pressure.

The genealogy of this development is strange. When I was a boy, we knew what stood between us and freedom, justice, and equality: it was special privilege. Get rid of special privilege, we said, and the common good will be achieved. In our time pacification has been attained not by getting rid of special privilege, but by extending it, by extending it to those well enough organized to threaten the special privileges under attack.

Is the tariff hurting the farmers? Retain the tariff and subsidize the farmers. Are administered prices hurting labor? Let's have administered wages, too. Is industry demoralized by expense accounts and tax dodges? Let's have featherbedding in labor, too. Is something done by some group antisocial? Let's all of us—all of us who can put on the pressure—be antisocial, too. And if a Federal agency is established to regulate us, never fear, we have the pressure that will shortly make the agency the servant and mouthpiece of the interests it was intended to control. And as we laughingly count our gains at the expense of the public, we can reverently repeat the solemn incantation that helped to make them possible: that government is best which governs least.

The Constitution must protect the citizen against the government. The government must protect him against the pressure groups. The government must protect him against society and the rapacity of organizations in it by seeing to it that these organizations pursue purposes and programs consonant with the common good.

The stresses and strains in our society are obscured for us partly by our preoccupation with Russia, which plays a curious double role in our lives as the devil in our world and as the standard by which we measure our progress. If we weren't getting ahead of Russia, or falling behind her, how could we tell where we were?

Our real problems are also concealed from us by our current remarkable prosperity, which results in part from the production of arms that we do not expect to use and in part from our new way of getting rich, which is to buy things from one another that we do not want at prices we cannot pay on terms we cannot meet because of advertising we do not believe.

But beneath these superficial manifestations, fantasies of fear on the one hand and wealth on the other, are moving those great, fundamental, historic forces which will put our institutions and our democratic faith to the test. This is the basic fact of our life as a people.

I have never subscribed to the proposition once debated in the Oxford Union, that in the opinion of this House Columbus went too far. Nor can I bring myself to refer to man as he is now referred to in military technology, as a "biomechanical link." If Columbus had not gone so far, man might never have had the chance to become anything more than a biomechanical link. America is still the hope of mankind. It is still our responsibility, now more than ever, to see to it that government of the people, by the people and for the people does not perish from the earth.

MORALITY USA

J. Robert Moskin

Morality is the most intensely discussed subject in the United States. We argue about Elizabeth Taylor's love life, Billie Sol Estes's deals, Bull Connor's brutalities, Adam Clayton Powell's junkets, Nelson Rockefeller's divorce, Jimmy Hoffa's power. We debate stealing by youngsters in Darien, Conn., sterilization by doctors in Virginia, welfare restrictions by politicians in Newburgh, N. Y., the right to lie by officials in Washington, slant-well digging by Texans in Texas and gouging by slumlords in Chicago.

Rarely will two Americans agree on who is immoral or what is the moral thing to do. We are adrift without answers. We want to know:

Am I immoral if I don't want a Negro living next door?
Am I immoral if I pad my income-tax deductions?
Am I immoral if I let my daughter go on an all-night beach party?
Am I immoral if I object to giving "economic aid" to a lot of primitive, probably lazy, countries?

However you answer these questions, many Americans will disagree.

Each of us must make difficult moral decisions. We are witnessing the death of the old morality. In our world of masses of people, jet-age travel, nuclear power and fragmented families, conditions are changing so fast that the established moral guidelines have been yanked from our hands.

No single authority rules our conduct. No church lays down the moral law for all; no tribal customs and taboos define the limits of our immoralities. We are free to be prejudiced or promiscuous, to cheat or chisel. We are left floundering in a money-motivated, sex-obsessed, big-city-dominated society. We must figure out for ourselves how to apply the traditional moral principles of the problems of our times. Many find this burden too heavy.

Scientist J. Robert Oppenheimer expresses our dilemma: " 'Thou shalt not kill'—but a general says we can kill 400 million human beings."

Aware that pressures on our moral ideas worry many Americans, the editors of *Look* assigned me to talk with a broad selection of thinkers and

From *Look,* XXVII, No. 19 (September 24, 1963), 72-88. Copyright © 1963 by Cowles Communications, Inc. By the courtesy of the editors.

leaders who are concerned about where America is going. The heart of their message is a warning: We are heading into danger. We are in the midst of a moral crisis—because the great majority of Americans, who want to try to live moral lives, no longer can be certain what is right and what is wrong.

Most Americans hate to admit we are in a crisis. But its bitter fruits are all around us: the beatnik, the racist, the wild kid, the price-rigging executive, the pregnant high-school girl, the dope addict, the vandal, the bribed athlete, the uncared-for aged, the poor, the criminal. Television depicts shoot-'em-up violence as the American way, and the movies uphold stardom as a warrant for four husbands and a lover.

Out of today's moral confusion will come either a society of license and brutality or (if we are wise and lucky) a new moral code based on the realities of our new world. "There was never a time in the history of man," says University of Chicago sociologist Philip M. Hauser, "when man was as free to exercise his own intelligence and make his own decisions."

WHO HAS ENOUGH COURAGE?

Since we live in a society without a supreme moral authority, where can we get moral standards?

Not from the church, says Dean Samuel Miller of the Harvard Divinity School. "The church has become almost as monastic as the others in the Middle Ages. There seems to be no connection between what happens in the church and what happens in society, except that people living in a desperate age use it to tranquilize their disturbing experiences—like some kind of lullaby." Not from an elite serving as a moral example, says Dean Miller. "Morality depends on images of excellence. In the Middle Ages, this is what the saint was. We know what a rich man is, a scientist, an astronaut—but we don't have an image of moral excellence."

Left without minister or model, how can an individual act morally in a crowded, competitive society like ours? Historian Arnold Toynbee warns, "It is getting more difficult in our highly organized society for the individual conscience to break through."

Those who have the courage to set their own moral standards belong to a "personal elite," according to the renowned Protestant theologian Paul Tillich. "They have the courage to say 'No!' and this is a very great courage in certain societies. The individual has in himself essentially the responsibility to form his convictions and act accordingly. If conflict with society cannot be avoided, he has the responsibility to sacrifice himself."

The enormous material success of our industrial society has brewed this conflict between the organization and the individual conscience. It also gives us another serious moral problem: How can all Americans share our affluence? One economics expert figures 40 million U.S. citizens live below the poverty line. Says the Rev. William Sloane Coffin, Jr., the chaplain of Yale University, "In a competitive society, there have to be losers. We haven't faced up to what we are going to do about the losers. Here's where we are immoral."

We already need only a fraction of our rapidly growing labor force to produce the goods we consume. And with automation, some economists predict that in 10 years we will be able to produce all life's necessities without a single man on a production line. How can men live when there is no work? Some say we must create new kinds of work. President Kennedy says we must find 22 million jobs in the next decade. Others predict we must separate entirely the idea of work from the idea of income, so that nonworkers can still be consumers. This is fearsome to those who believe work is moral.

DO SCIENTISTS SPREAD IMMORALITY?

In great measure, the scientists are responsible for our moral crisis. Their discoveries—the computer, the Bomb, the oral contraceptive, the subconscious—have damaged man's traditional sense of responsibility. At the same time, they have bombarded us with difficult moral choices. Should we race the Russians to the moon, or spend the same talent and money fighting cancer and mental disease? To many scientific leaders, the space race compares less to Columbus's voyages than to the vainglorious building of the Pyramids. Atomic scientist Leo Szilard puts our choice bluntly: "This is a moral issue, and we are making the wrong choice. To race the Russians to the moon and let our old people live on almost nothing is immoral. The moon is not science—not bread. It is circus. The astronauts are the gladiators. It's lunacy, I say."

The most dangerous problem science has presented us is whether we shall use nuclear weapons. Says Dr. Oppenheimer, "The notion that we could have a great war and not use the stuff is even more dangerous. Virtuous nations are not virtuous when at war, although this is still a view held by some—despite Hiroshima."

Secretary of State Dean Rusk believes that the nuclear weapon has already had a moderating effect on morality in international relations: "It's had a sobering effect on national ambitions and appetites. It reminds people there are problems that make pygmies of us all." Perhaps the danger of annihilation would not seem so terrifying to many Americans if they had not lost the promise of heaven.

Our power and wealth have given us global responsibilities. How morally are we using our vast new power for leadership in the world? Secretary Rusk says, "Since World War II, United States power has been put behind the concept that men don't like to be pushed around." U Thant, Secretary General of the United Nations, sees a new moral attitude emerging: "The parochial concept of 'our town,' 'our country' is disappearing. I've been trained to be as objective as possible. If a Burmese boxer, maybe a middle-weight, fights a U. S. boxer, I will not feel any emotion. I've reached this stage. It has taken much training and meditation. This should be our aspiration. I feel very strongly about it. If we can think of one human species, it is only wisdom and vision." Toynbee adds, "Unless we develop a loyalty to the human race as a whole, we shan't survive."

Perhaps the most moral act in our national history has been the giving of postwar aid to other nations, from the Marshall Plan to the Peace Corps—without imposing our political views. Says Sen. Hubert H. Humphrey of Minnesota, "My people out home don't understand why there should be hunger in the world when there is a nation with surplus—want in the midst of plenty." And Toynbee poses our moral choice: "Should people have unreal wants when other people are starving? An Indian peasant doesn't need Madison Avenue to tell him what his wants are; his stomach does. Those who are relatively rich could feel more satisfied if their surplus money was going to meet the wants of people who have less, rather than for a tenth pair of shoes."

IS GOVERNMENT CLEAN?

In our country, three institutions have the power—and the responsibility— to influence our morality: government, business (with the labor unions) and the churches. Each has failed to provide moral leadership and has helped to precipitate our moral crisis.

Government makes moral decisions about nuclear weapons and the population explosion. It decides whether a businessman should take his wife along when he discusses business, and whether the astronauts should make a financial killing out of the space program. It was government that Negro leaders demanded should take a moral stand against segregation.

While it is widely agreed that politicians are less freewheeling today, we still have congressmen who are indicted for taking bribes and who tour the world at the taxpayers' expense, and city politicians and "county court-house gangs" who manipulate the law. Two former congressmen have appealed their convictions for trying to influence the Justice Department to drop a mail-fraud case. John Cogley, editor of a study of the American character, suggests that much immorality is covered up by the press. He says, "We never hear of sexual aberration or alchoholism among congress-men."

Conflict-of-interest problems gain attention when a Cabinet officer has to sell his stock holdings, but congressmen are not required to do so. A Secretary of the Air Force in the Eisenhower Administration was dropped for using Air Force stationery to solicit business for a firm in which he had been interested. But the late Sen. Robert Kerr of Oklahoma, for example, was well known for proposing gas and oil legislation while holding great gas and oil interests himself. Two New York state legislators who sponsored a middle-income housing law were revealed by the New York *Herald Tribune* to have connections with firms that earned $800,000 in legal and architec-tural fees from builders utilizing the law.

Politicians' most difficult moral dilemma is to draw a line between legitimate campaign funds and influence-seeking gifts. A senator may need a million dollars to get reelected. Almost every congressman is obligated to big contributors, many of whom expect something in return. An organiza-tion can only spend $3 million in a Presidential campaign, but Sen. Barry Goldwater of Arizona says, "It's a laugh. I know about what the Republicans spent. It's in excess of the law—not legally but in spirit. It's immoral."

Judges ultimately interpret the moral intentions of our laws. Prof. Robert G. McCloskey of Harvard, an expert on constitutional law, says, "In some ways, they are ill-fitted for their job. Judges are always lawyers, and the law is not the most broadening profession. . . . Lots of judges just don't read books. They are amazed when they pick up D. H. Lawrence. They haven't read anything since Tom Swift."

CAN WE MIX MORALS AND PROFITS?

The second institution with a moral responsibility in America is business. Business, on occasion, fails to provide moral leadership because profits and morality frequently clash.

Every businessman whose job it is to help his company make a profit faces moral choices. Even the most morally-minded businessman must decide questions of employment, wages, contracts, production quality, prices, competition, taxes. He is influenced by pressures from government and labor unions and by a growing awareness that what the public thinks of a company may affect its profits. The businessman who feels the strongest sense of responsibility to the public and his employees is precisely the one who suffers the most when he wrestles with his moral dilemmas.

The age-old moral problems of the small businessman are intensified by the vast impersonality of the big city. If you own a shop, should you pay off the fire, building and health inspectors, the union delegate and the police who come around with their hands out? Should you buy space in a publication that demands an ad before it will give you favorable publicity? Should you keep an able clerk who is swiping goods from the shop? Should you accept a kickback from a supplier? Whenever you answer yes, you may be acting immorally. But whenever you say no, you can hurt your business.

Most observers assert that the businessman has become more concerned about moral questions, but some operators still grab corporations, milk companies and bilk customers, manipulate markets, rig prices, conspire for excessive profits and bribe politicians and public commissioners. To these men, the Golden Rule is nonsense and the business world a jungle.

Business faces moral problems when it raises money for the public. Seventeen million people now own stock in U. S. corporations. Edwin D. Etherington, who became president of the American Stock Exchange as a reformer, describes the dilemma before a company selling stock to the public: Is the company obligated to get the highest price for its stock? If the public is eager enough to pay more than the stock is worth, should the company hold the price down? Etherington, who dreads government control, believes the only solution to this quandary is "full disclosure" of the facts and the "economic education" of the buying public.

Many businessmen worry about the moral line which competition should not cross. J. Irwin Miller, who is president of several corporations, a member of AT&T's board of directors and president of the National Council of Churches of Christ in America, asks what a businessman should do when a competitor offers one of his big customers a price cut. The businessman has to meet the competitor's price, but is he then morally required to offer the lower price to his other customers, so they can compete too? If he does not, he may be acting immorally, but if he does, he may go broke.

Supermarkets trading stamps raise moral questions about competition. A woman shopper may not be interested in collecting stamps to get a bridge table, but the stamps force her to pay more for food. Supermarket experts figure they must increase their volume of business by 16 percent to pay for the stamps. Deceptive packaging also hits the consumer. Under attack at present are companies that reduce the contents while keeping box sizes and prices the same. put false bottoms in bottles or conceal the amount of the contents in tiny, hidden type. Objections are also being raised against retailers who advertise products as "10 percent off," without indicating "off" what.

Some industries try to squelch competition by illegal agreements among competitors. Most notorious was the conspiracy in which 29 companies of the giant electrical industry were judged guilty in 1961 of price fixing, which resulted in excessive profits. They were fined a total of $1.7 million; seven executives went to jail, and 23 received suspended sentences. In addition, the companies have had to pay the Federal Government $8.6 million in damages, and they still face some 1,800 private damage suits.

In 1963, a grand jury indicted eight steel companies for conspiring to fix prices in the $75-million-a-year heavy-steel-casting industry, and recently, the Federal Trade Commission accused six major drug companies of rigging antibiotic prices.

In still another industry, prices are fixed and sales territories divided by "pilot-room agreements." By "coincidence" from time to time, top executives in this industry all find themselves and their private planes at the same airport waiting for fuel or repairs. While they wait, they sit in the pilots' ready room and talk business.

Says one hotel man, "Who can tell what is moral and immoral in competition? We do anything to get business. A competitor got a girl for a guy, and we lost the convention. I sit at home at night and realize they just outsmarted us." He draws the line for himself: "You drop out of competition when the dollars don't work out."

Senator Goldwater blames business immorality squarely on the Government and sets the date of The Fall at 1913, with the advent of the Federal income tax. He says, "Government is the biggest enemy of moral values. Why did we see the things we saw in General Electric and other companies—price fixing? What does high taxation do? The little businessman starts to connive—cutting corners in order to get along. Moral values decline as government grows."

Most authorities place the blame within business itself. In addition to the pressure to sell all we can produce, they blame the employee-manager who operates without real supervision from his stockholder-owners and behind platoons of "public relations" specialists who hush up his immoralities. The executive world is filled with distrust, says Yale's Prof. Chris Argyris, a specialist on business ethics; executive politicking costs one company he studied $186,000 every year. "At the moment," he says, "we have a world that has the cards stacked against the morally behaving man."

The self-interest of the professional manager can conflict with the best interest of his company. For example, it might cost the stockholders $20,000 to provide a car and chauffeur so their president can ride to work in style. If the president decides this is immoral, he would have to earn at least $50,000 more to be able to afford his own car and driver.

The classic case of conflict of interest occurred at the Chrysler Corporation in 1960 when its president was fired for profiting from companies that supplied Chrysler with parts and had to promise to pay Chrysler $450,000.

Many businessmen have discovered that higher standards of morality in business are not only necessary, but profitable. Etherington says, "The minute an individual steps out of line, he makes a problem. There is a practical reason, too, for being moral. We need to have everybody retain his own initiative about deciding what is moral—and doing it."

But the big-business organization often forces the individual to violate his conscience, to survive by conforming. Says Irwin Miller, "One of the dangers of bigness is the smothering of the individual." And Professor Argyris adds, "You are not asked how the sale was made. Morality is going down and will slide further unless we change the basic guts of the organizational world we have created."

Many businessmen agree. They are repeatedly torn between their responsibility to make a profit and their loyalty to their business associates. Says Preston R. Tisch, president of Loew's Hotels, "You have a tremendous responsibility to your stockholders, your company and your employees. You're affecting their lives." Another prominent businessman says his worst moral dilemma came when he had to decide whether to fire the aging executive who had originally brought him into the company. And a top executive, with a certain false bravado, says, "The nice guys I want to have lunch with are the guys I fire."

Other organizations, such as universities and labor unions, suffer from the same immorality. Governor Romney says of labor leaders, "Some are out to win, regardless of what it takes. To the extent the union leader is under the same temptation as the politician to make demagogic victory his prime consideration, there is a tendency to use union power for selfish and pressure reasons."

Speaking from his own business experience, National Council of Churches president Miller says the crucial moral question in business is: "What is fair, what is right? You take this problem to your preacher, and he takes to the hills. The church says do right—don't do wrong. This is no help. The problem is to choose between two evils."

The important fact is that the world in which businessmen must make their decisions has changed radically from the heyday of the "robber barons" and the sweatshop. The ethical standards of present-day business are certainly higher than those of 50 years ago. There are more restrictions on greed and more profit in seeking moral decisions—and as a result, businessmen's dilemmas are all the more acute and all the more puzzling.

HAVE THE CHURCHES FAILED?

The churches are the third American institution with a moral responsibility. They too have failed to supply moral leadership, and because their responsibility is the greatest, their failure is the worst. Harvard Divinity School's Dean Miller says, "The church simply does not have a cutting edge. It has taken the culture of our time and absorbed it. It's ghastly that the church is run not to serve the reality of human beings, but to conserve institutions."

Yale's Chaplain Coffin agrees: "We churchmen are gifted at changing wine into water—watering down religion. The problem of the church today is ineffectiveness. We've never had attendance so high and influence so low, and maybe the two are not unrelated."

Church leaders blame the churches' failure to be relevant to the tough moral issues of today on, a) their belief that moral leadership should be limited to private actions—drinking, dancing, smoking, etc.—and b) the intense competition among denominations. "What we have sold out to," says the Rev. John Morris, executive director of the Episcopal Society for Cultural and Racial Unity, is "financial strength and a successful career for the clergyman, the rising executive." Ralph McGill, the courageous publisher of the Atlanta *Constitution*, adds, "There's been a lot of intellectual dishonesty on the part of the churches. They have big building debts, and unhappily 85 percent of the big givers want to keep the status quo." Irwin Miller points out that there are more than 200 denominations of Christians, and warns, "If they won't lose their lives, how can they preach to you to lose your life?"

The tragedy of the churches' failure stands out vividly in America's suburbs. The churches' responsibility in suburbia, says Dr. Tillich, is "to undercut the false security in a well-to-do society." Self-satisfaction encourages many suburbanites to believe: "We are better than these masses in the city. We are what mankind should be." Pride, concludes Dean Samuel Miller, is "the cardinal *virtue* of our time."

In Deerfield, Ill., a Chicago suburb, which since World War II has tried to keep out Jews (unsuccessfully) and Negroes (successfully—so far), the Rev. John Usry, a young Congregationalist minister, says his suburban parishioners "feel no guilt about excluding, because those who are good succeed and come to Deerfield. In their own eyes, they are very moral. There are no wife beaters. But they live in isolation and are not in contact with problems of a metropolitan area. If we think we can go into the Loop and earn our money and come back here and barbecue and be happy, this is immoral."

A young minister wrestling with morality in the city slums is the Rev. Michael Allen, rector of St. Mark's-in-the-Bouwerie Protestant Episcopal Church in New York City. He says, "The Communists have a real vision, and they will work, bleed and die for that vision. They've stolen our thunder. That's what Christianity is supposed to do also. God is in the midst of teeming slums and horrendous social problems, but our society believes you can find salvation through caviar and champagne."

ARE OUR NEW IDEAS ABOUT SEX IMMORAL?

The two issues that trouble churchmen the most are sexual immorality and racial prejudice. There is widespread anxiety that our old sexual morality is going. "American society is no longer accepting the Christian morality of sexual life—that sex should not be outside marriage," says French scholar Raymond Aron. "Divorce is completely accepted; freedom of sexual intercourse between young men and young women is fully accepted. In sexuality, we are in revolt against Christianity."

Almost everyone is more candid about sex today. Prof. Lester A. Kirkendall of Oregon State University, a leading authority on family life, believes that one reason there is so much more youthful discussion of sex is that young people are trying to work out for themselves a new sexual code. Most of the people studying youthful behavior believe that sexual activity is also increasing. "If it is not increasing," comments Mrs. Helen Harris Perlman, professor of social work at the University of Chicago, "it would surprise me, considering the stimuli to sex and the rootlessness of the kids today." Professor Kirkendall says the proportion of women who have premarital relations is rising rapidly, but he adds, "our young people are not sex-obsessed. The culture is. We use it to sell products, as a come-on."

The greatest change in sexual morality is taking place among young women. Years ago, the authorities say, sexual prowess was something only boys talked about. Now, they cite cases of college girls keeping records, sharing experiences of a weekend, even borrowing birth-control devices in sororities.

Many parents, who would be shocked to admit it, are pushing their daughters into earlier sexual activity. Then they are appalled when a girl gets into "trouble." Says Professor Hauser, "It is a distorted society which gives 16-year-olds automobiles to drive, provides them with the opportunity to go out with the opposite sex, but does not teach them anything about sex or contraception."

Professor Kirkendall notes, "By the time they are in their teens, they are moving very close to a full physical relationship. The girl particularly is being pushed into marriage. This is one of the immoral things our culture does for girls. A girl feels extremely pressured to demonstrate she has the kind of attractiveness that is going to satisfy a boy."

Mrs. Katherine B. Oettinger, chief of the U.S. Children's Bureau, says, "We are too often lax about situations where experimentation goes on—the business of early dating, allowing youngsters so much freedom, sometimes promoting a boy friend at all cost. The youngsters who are unsophisticated have babies and are punished." The number of illegitimate births has tripled since 1940.

"In the United States, we have more high-school girls dropping out because of pregnancy, even girls who aren't yet in high school. They are 12 and 13 years old and come from all kinds of families," says Dr. Milton Senn, director of Yale's Child Study Center. Premarital pregnancy is now involved in 85 percent of all marriages in which both partners are high-school students. "This means," asserts Professor Kirkendall, "many more boys are being pulled into marriage through sex. Girls are becoming more aggressive in setting up dating relationships. They are devising more ways to take the initiative. Sometimes they press too hard. The boy may back off or may exploit her in turn. Girl wants boy. Boy wants sex. So they get together on that basis."

Harvard College's Dean John U. Monro, who has two daughters himself, warns there is a shock in store for young women: "They go along in 20th-century attitudes until the girl gets pregnant and 19th-century morality comes back into play." But he applauds the basis of the new relationship between young men and women. "This is moving so fast it would surprise you. They are much closer together. Girls are much more independent. Birth-control information and devices help a girl to be independent. This independence is great; comradeship is right. Women are people and should not think of themselves as dependents—second in line always."

Changing sexual mores have recently brought clashes between administrators and students at a number of colleges. Professor Kirkendall argues, "A college should not make a rule that chastity should be the rule. Because then you think if an act has or has not been performed indicates whether you have virtuous or nonvirtuous students. Rather than being concerned whether a sexual act has occurred, I would like to be concerned that we use all our powers and capacities with responsible concern for others. This is not permissiveness because relationships have rules. I'm more fearful about our inability to handle our aggressive and hostile impulses than our sexual impulses. You can use sex in a hostile way just as you use a bludgeon."

Our moral confusion over sex is not limited to the young. Kirkendall says, "As long as adults focus on youth, they don't have to look at themselves. It is essentially an adult problem. When a person uses sex in marriage to punish, control, manipulate, this becomes immorality too."

The absence of communication marriage experts find in many homes often results in using sex exploitively and in extramarital relations. The Rev. Gibson Winter, associate professor of ethics and society at the University of Chicago Divinity School, calls this "the pathos of the search for communication."

As a result of this adult problem, the 1960 census reported 1.8 million divorced women in the country, and there are estimated to be 13 million children who belong to broken homes. There are even extreme situations like the hundreds of suburban couples who, the San Francisco *Chronicle* revealed recently, were participating in "wife-swapping," that is, adultery with mutual consent. The newspaper reporters quoted one wife as saying, in her husband's presence, "It will save your marriage from going on the rocks if it's sexually stale and you're bored with going to bed with each other. It saved ours."

With one out of every four marriages today ending in divorce, the experts say we are practicing "serial monogamy." Father Walter Imbiorski, director of Chicago's Cana Conference, says, "We have to a great extent divorced sexuality from procreation and from love. In certain segments, sex is used as entertainment—without personal commitment, without being related to family and marriage."

CAN A CHRISTIAN SUPPORT SEGREGATION?

Of all the churches' failures, the most disastrous has been their inability to sell the idea that prejudice is immoral. Dr. Kenneth B. Clark, professor of psychology at New York's City College and a prominent Negro leader, says,

"I see institutions that are supposedly the custodians of our moral values and see that they are corrupt. The idea of a white church is so preposterous that it must reflect moral and intellectual bankruptcy."

"Of the major groups, the Baptists are the worst of all," said Ralph McGill. "They are largely rural and people from rural areas. They bring their prejudices with them." Recently, a Negro was still denied membership in Houston's First Baptist Church, whose paster is president of the Southern Baptist Convention. The Methodist Church has an all-Negro division called the Central Jurisdiction. Although the Mormon Church admits Negroes, they cannot become priests. And not until this year did the National Council of Churches finally set up an Emergency Commission on Religion and Race.

The record of the Catholic Church in the South has been cautious but better. "If you are a Catholic, you have to be color-blind," explains the Most Rev. Paul J. Hallinan, Roman Catholic Archbishop of Atlanta. "Christ's law is love thy neighbor as thyself. He didn't say your white neighbor." Because Atlanta has started to desegregate its public schools, the Archbishop has ordered the integration of Catholic schools and hospitals. "I am perfectly willing to take a moral stand," he says, "but I can't take the risk of closing some of these schools. Morality is made up of cases where we choose between a lesser and a greater evil."

The Negro, rising in revolt, is at last forcing the churches to face the immorality of his plight. As James Baldwin, the Negro writer, says, "White America has to face the question, why do you need the 'nigger' you invented?"

It is only relatively easier to fight discrimination in the "WASP" (white Anglo-Saxon Protestant) suburbs of the North. Says the Rev. Mr. Usry, "Even if a Negro had attained the status by which he could come to Deerfield, no realtor would sell him a house, no lending agency would lend him money to buy the house." In suburban America, the realtor and banker wield greater power over morality than the minister.

In Michigan, to which many Negroes have moved, Governor Romney says, "There is no justification under our system for anything other than equal civil rights and equal opportunity, regardless of race, color or creed." The Mormon Church to which Romney belongs has been criticized for its attitude toward Negroes, but he says, "There isn't anything we believe that the Caucasian world can attain in this world or the world beyond that they cannot attain too. It's equally clear that different people are at different places at any one time."

The late Rev. Martin Luther King, Jr., president of the Southern Christian Leadership Conference, asserted "The race question is at bottom a moral issue—a question of the dignity of man. It will ultimately have to have a moral solution. In five years from now, *legal* segregation will be broken down all over this country—education, public facilities. The job of real integration will take longer."

King says that a white American must ask himself: "Are Negroes being treated like you would like to be treated?"

The pain a Negro feels can be glimpsed in simple things white Americans take for granted

A highly educated, well-dressed woman enters a Southern airport with a suitcase in each hand. A man, with Southern courtesy, starts to hold open a door for her, sees she is a Negro and lets the door slam in her face.

A Negro, driving from Atlanta to Cleveland, has to drive straight through the night. He feels he can find no place to sleep until Ohio.

A Negro woman is given five days in jail in Gadsden, Ala., because the prosecutor insists on calling her "Mary" and she refuses to answer to her first name.

Ralph McGill said, "We've never seen the preposterousness of not sitting down on a bus with the same maid we entrust our children to."

Civil-rights leaders condemn business and union leaders. Says Martin Luther King, "There are those who seek to perpetuate human values that came into being in a slave-plantation society. These industries often move South because they want cheap labor." McGill said, "Ninety-seven percent of them in steel and textiles have a vested interest in retaining segregation and work at it." Throughout the country, many craft-union locals, especially in the skilled building trades, discriminate. Negroes have found it almost impossible to enter their apprentice-training programs and are restricted to nonskilled jobs. Business and unions pass the buck, each blaming the other.

The echoes of Birmingham, Ala., Oxford, Miss., Cambridge, Md., and Harlem are worldwide. The UN's U Thant says, "These developments have tarnished the American image. Governor Wallace should realize his activities are watched all over the world in terms of the United States of America, which has been regarded as a torch bearer of freedom and human dignity."

IS MONEY OUR GOD?

Even more baffling than how we shall overcome prejudice is how we can make money honestly. In our society, money is worshiped as the root of all happiness; it is more godlike than God. Says one young businessman, "Making $40,000 a year will be like getting an A on your report card."

How far will you go to win your A? Many an American will connive, lie and stomp over friends and competitors. Professor Winter condemns our values: "America is preoccupied with success in measurable terms. This is a self-defeating goal."

How far a man will go was demonstrated by Texas's Billie Sol Estes, who perpetuated a multimillion-dollar swindle on his neighbors and a dozen finance companies. It put him in the three-Cadillac, private-airplane class—which must rate an A-plus. Estes could have ballooned his schemes only by exploiting the greed for the quick buck of hundreds of farmers and businessmen. Harvard's Dean Monro says sardonically, "The ability to make money excuses everything else."

Money-as-God distorts lives much less notorious than Billie Sol's. A theological student in Connecticut, who had to resign because he could not pay his way, wryly told his roommate that his father had just bought a $12,000 boat. The president of a large company threatened with a stockholders' revolt said, "I won't give up this company. The president of a corporation lives better than a Louis of France. I have at my disposal a car and chauffeur, a yacht, an airplane, a hotel suite in New York and all the entertaining I want."

Our second moral dilemma over money results from the current idea that chiseling a big impersonal company is not really stealing at all. A dedicated churchgoer recently told proudly of returning a $5 bill to a drugstore clerk who had given him too much change. But when he completed a long-distance phone call from a pay booth and the operator returned his five quarters by mistake, he kept the money without a qualm. "The phone company's so darn big," he said, "they won't miss it."

This is so typical of our money morality that when a 10-year-old girl in Madison, N.J., found $6.30 in the return slot of a public telephone recently and gave it back to the operator, the New Jersey Bell Telephone Company made a big fuss over her, put her picture in the newspapers and treated her to lunch. The company was trying desperately to say that when a person faces a machine with a moral question, his answer should be the same as when he faces a human being.

It doesn't work that way. Scientist and writer C. P. Snow says, "We are more dishonest about money than our grandfathers were." In New Haven recently, an automobile-insurance broker advised his client after a collision to pretend his back had been injured. When his client protested, the broker said, "But everybody does it. The insurance company expects it. That's why the rates are so high." Insurance experts estimate that 75 percent of all claims are tainted with fraud, and damages in automobile accidents alone cost $7.4 billion last year.

The moral schizophrenia afflicts the Texas oilmen who stole, by slant-well digging, some $50 million worth of oil, chiefly from the lands of big oil companies. It encourages policemen to raid stores at night from Denver to Long Island. It inspired guests during the first 10 months at New York's spanking-new Americana Hotel to swipe (among other things) 38,000 demitasse spoons, 18,000 towels, 355 silver coffeepots, 1,500 silver finger bowls and 100 Bibles.

Personal morals often surrender to the worship of money. One New York hotel manager says he does not care if an unmarried couple sign the register as man and wife. But he is angered if a man takes a room as a single occupant and brings a woman in—that is cheating the hotel.

Supermarkets are especially vulnerable to "amateur" thieves, 80 percent of whom are women. One example: 500,000 supermarket shopping carts disappeared last year; at an average cost of $30 per cart, this comes to $15 million. One expert estimates that 15 percent of your food bill goes to cover what customers and employees take, salving their consciences with the thought that the big company can afford it. (The real question is: Can *you* afford it?)

One department-store chain, which does $100 million business a year, figures it loses, mainly from customer and employee thefts, more than $1 million annually. It is estimated that supermarket employees steal the equivalent of $300,000 every working day. Across the country, employee thefts of money and merchandise are estimated to total $2 billion a year. Such pilferage has destroyed many companies.

Much of this is in such innocent-seeming quantities that it hardly appears evil at all. Secretaries go home with pencils and carbon paper. Employees use the telephone for personal calls that add up to big money in a large company. (Says one executive, "If you asked a girl to put down a dime, she'd think you were crazy. She regards this as one of the benefits of working here.") Bartenders and waiters pocket cash or leave items off a customer's bill to get a bigger tip for themselves. Clerks damage goods intentionally so they can take them home. At the other end of the scale, a New York department-store executive has a crew from the store come up each spring and paint his Connecticut home—free.

Our third dilemma over money is the feeling that whatever is customary is ethical. In the television-quiz scandals a few years back, a college instructor, a lawyer and a minister were among those who took thousands of dollars by letting themselves be convinced that they were doing what came naturally in the TV world. The same moral question faces the traveler returning from abroad with false bills for the customs man. Or the doctor who uses experimental drugs on a patient without telling him—especially when the doctor owns stock in the drug company. Or the financial writer who buys a stock, plugs it and, when it climbs in value, swiftly sells it at a profit. Or the tax lawyer who tells his client to add some phony deductions because the revenue agent needs to find something to cross out.

Mortimer Caplin, director of the Internal Revenue Service, believes that no more than 3 percent of the people cheat on their income taxes. Of course, the great majority have no opportunity to. Caplin estimates that the IRS, which collected $100 billion in all taxes last year, would have collected an additional $5 billion if everyone were honest.

These are moral problems the individual faces in our big-money society. In business, we have changed from a society of the handshake to a society of the fine print. In charity, we have changed from personal help between families to massive fund drives. In medical care, we have changed from self-sacrificing family doctor to group practice and the profit motive.

Edward DeCourcy, the editor of the weekly *Argus-Champion* of Newport, N. H., and president of the International Conference of Weekly Newspaper Editors, says, "We who cover the small-town police station see the immorality of the driver who purposely breaks the law, while urging his kids to keep an eye out for a possible police cruiser in the rear. This is the guy who brags about cheating on his income tax, lies about his kid's age so he can get him into the show at half price, brags about getting his ticket fixed, and then wonders why his kid cheats on exams."

WHERE DO YOUR CHILDREN LEARN TO SIN?

Dean Samuel Miller asks, "How do we transmit any moral ethos from one generation to another in America? I see no sign of it being done in the home, where it can be done best, and what's being done in the church is extremely inadequate. There is something radically wrong with a society that does not know how to teach its children to behave in that society."

Professor Perlman of the University of Chicago concurs: "There are just too many freedoms kids have, and therefore too many temptations—cars, late hours, parents afraid to say, 'Be home,' parents pressing children to date earlier. The most important thing is the kids are not feeling inner-directed, not knowing who they are and where they are going."

Suicides among teen-agers are increasing, Dr. Senn of Yale's Child Study Center says: "What we are now seeing in our pediatric department are more suicide attempts of young adolescents with a peak of 15 years and as low as 12 and 13, both boys and girls." He concludes: "I believe our children are under particular stresses and strains because of the swiftness of change."

Dr. Lawrence Kohlberg, a University of Chicago psychologist who studies how children learn moral values, says, "Parents want their kids to be morally good, but they want their kids to be successful." According to Dr. Senn, "Parents say, 'You cheat where you can, and you teach your child to be adept at this because this is the way the world is.' "

Says Harvard sociologist David Riesman, "The confusion of parents themselves is communicated to children like a contagious disease." (Our society is even confused over whether it is right or wrong to spank a child.)

Parents pile on pressures to make good grades, to get into a good college, to choose careers and mates early. Last spring, Princeton University's admission office received a letter from an able freshman candidate, asking them to turn him down and not to tell his parents about his letter. The boy's parents had forced him to apply. Says Princeton admission director Alden Dunham, "Parental ambitions are often tied more to concepts of social prestige than education." The result of such pressures are seen in widespread college cheating, vandalism and promiscuity.

Sharing parents' burden to teach moral standards are our educational institutions. Dean Monro of Harvard is troubled about the moral values that colleges are teaching. Collegiate athletics, he feels strongly, are teaching youth to be cynical. "The greatest hypocrisy we have is professional athletics being conducted in the colleges under the guise of amateurism—the prospective doctor or teacher who is compelled to play football and whose college program is a joke. The morality is awful and getting worse with the television profits. Newspapers are for it because sports writers make a living off it. Colleges do it for money. That the institutions assigned a good part of the moral education of the young are this cynical—this is a moral cancer in our society."

But Dean Monro also feels that young people today are increasingly concerned about moral issues. He says, "What I've got here is concern, and this is true of a lot of colleges. It's important, it's growing, and it's intelligent."

Dean Miller tells of a friend of his whose son seemed irresponsible and only wanted to sing and play a guitar in coffee shops. Miller asked the boy to play for him, and discovered that his songs were about fallout (the rain on the prairies), lynching (the fruit of the tree). "In every one," says Miller, "there was a sense of moral judgment in what was happening. He was articulating the world, while the church was mumbling its old sacred formulas."

What the experts are saying about almost every aspect of American morality today is: In a rapidly changing world, we have lost our traditional moral guidelines. Philip Hauser sums it up: " When you begin to question

morality, it is a sign that the individual is becoming freed of the bondage
of tradition. You may think that this is tragic or deplorable, but there's
nothing you can do about it."

We are groping, painfully and often blindly, for new standards that will
enable us to live morally and decently. The experts feel strongly that we
cannot turn back to earlier, more rigid behavior patterns. Almost all the
thoughtful, worried people I talked with believe that, unlike people in so
many past ages, we have achieved some freedom of choice. We have choices
to make about power, money, sex, prejudice and our role in the world. We
must find a new moral code that will fit the needs of the society we live
in. We have a large measure of freedom to carve out lives we regard as
moral—if we will take the risks and pay the price.

MONEY ISN'T EVERYTHING

Edward T. Chase

A revolutionary shift from economic values to noneconomic values in our
decision-making has been quietly taking place since the war. Most
Americans still care mightily about money, to be sure, but a different
perspective is observable. To an unprecedented degree, things are being
decided on nonmonetary criteria, extending from the individual's choice of
a career to such matters as the public's support of preserving open land.

Since the economic theory proceeds on the premise that all except
frivolous motivations are at bottom pecuniary, it is only natural that
economists are mute on this point. Yet no discussion of the role of money
in American life can ignore this very important development. Furthermore,
the new appreciation of noneconomic values is the key to many of our
political differences; to misunderstandings between the older generations
and the new one; to the heightened tension between the businessman and
the intellectual, including the contempt for Madison Avenue; and to the

From *Atlantic*, CCIX, No. 4 (April, 1962), 131-134. Copyright ©1962, by the Atlantic
Monthly Company, Boston, Mass. Reprinted with permission of the author and publisher.

rise of the paperback, of the off-Broadway theater, of the art movie house.

An understanding of this revolution in values is of great consequence if we expect to comprehend not only the changing role of money in American life but also the strange new mixed economy that is replacing classical capitalism. Two underlying factors have created the possibilities of this revolution. The first factor is economic. A review of economic data on labor and productivity reveals striking changes within the past century. For example, within the lifetime of some of us, the average work week in the United States was 69 hours. Today it is about 35 hours, and union electricians in New York City have negotiated a new contract providing for a 25-hour week. The significance of these facts, which is not ordinarily discussed by professional economists, is that they are a prerequisite for the rising importance of noneconomic values.

No matter from what quarter you advance upon these statistics, they tell you the same thing: the imperative to toil for mere subsistence has suddenly lost steam. For the United States, at least, the battle has been largely won. In the jargon of professional economics, the shorter work week means a decline in the marginal urgency of goods.

A decline in the marginal urgency of goods, with its consequences of an abbreviated work week and labor force (our population of the non-productive—that is, the retired elderly and the young in training—is the largest in history) means at the very least that a young man today need not, as in past ages, be limited to a struggle for survival, nor even that he must feel compelled to embrace some conventional moneymaking career if he wishes to enjoy standard creature comforts. He has more choices of how to occupy himself than man has ever enjoyed before. So much is plain.

However, it does not follow that his choices will necessarily have a less economic character than heretofore. For this to be so, he must not only be free of excessive pressure to earn a buck; he must also be conditioned to make noneconomic choices (joining the Peace Corps, for example) by ideas, by his notions of what is worth doing. The second prerequisite for any general ascendancy of noneconomic values is mass education.

Social scientists refer to the educational changes in America in the last fifty years as one of the world's great social revolutions. In 1900 only one person in fifty stayed in school beyond the age of fifteen; now, thirty out of fifty finish high school. The percentage of the population aged eighteen to twenty-one enrolled in college nearly doubled between 1910 and 1920. The illiteracy rate in the population fell off about half between 1890 and 1910. The number of graduate students in U.S. colleges tripled between 1900 and 1920, tripled again in the 1930's, and more than doubled during each of the succeeding decades. We are now experiencing the combined impact of these two forces: the coming of age of a generation of the relatively well educated—the result of our unique mission of free public education for all; and our simultaneous liberation from toil through the triumph in economic productivity.

THE CULTURAL BOOM

The more obvious effects of this development are already dramatic. Take American post-war cultural and leisure-time pursuits, now for the first time within reach of a substantial majority of Americans. The cultural kick Americans have set off on since the war is astonishing, no matter how much you may like or dislike it. (It is *de rigueur* for intellectuals to dislike it, but since there is no corresponding diminution of high culture, they should not be so dismayed by mass culture.) The amount of money spent is all but incredible. A recent *Fortune* survey estimates that in 1961 Americans spent $5 billion on culture, 70 percent more than they did only ten years ago, while the population increased only 18.5 percent. This cultural explosion engages the public across all geographical and economic lines and involves every form of cultural activity.

Because of the didactic, information-spreading nature of literature (as opposed to an art form like the dance), the book boom is an especially significant aspect of the cultural explosion, since, by itself, the immense increase in reading is transforming the general level of sophistication. Consider these facts. In 1961 Americans spent twice as much for books as they did in 1955, some $1.2 billion, an extraordinary development no one predicted a decade ago. The American Library Association reports that book circulation nationally has increased 29 percent in the last five years, with the emphasis upon serious nonfiction. Sixty percent of the librarians surveyed attributed the reading boom to the "increased educational level" of the reader.

Significantly, many librarians reported that television, once considered the arch-villain, has been the prime spur to reading, with its promotion of new books and classics and its public-affairs programs. Book publishers, on the other hand, ungraciously claim that adults are increasingly abandoning television for reading, according to a *Wall Street Journal* survey, and ascribe the boom in book sales to the phenomenal rise in educational and cultural standards.

Attracted by the boom, more new book publishers are entering the field than ever before, with some twenty new firms having come into the paperback field alone since 1958. The sale of quality paperbacks totaled 13 million copies in 1960, eight times the number sold in 1952 and about a third more than in the preceding year. With college enrollments expected to rise more than 25 percent in the next three years, the incentives to publish are being intensified. Fat profits are predicted from textbooks and high-class paperbacks particularly. Thus, we are seeing magazine publishers like Time Inc., Macfadden Publications, Inc., and the McCall Corporation either already embarked on or about to embark on book publishing. At the same time, the distribution of books is being revolutionized, too. Supermarkets have become a recognized outlet.

The book and reading boom is matched by mass participation in the museums, which are making new records in attendance and winning greater financial support. In 1960 the number of art museums alone in the United States had grown to 630 (out of a grand total of 3900 of all types), and Americans spent just under $300 million to run them. A recent study by the New York *Times* carried revealing quotations from museum leaders about the sudden interest in the museum world. The operating administrator of the great Metropolitan Museum of Art in New York, James V. Noble, stated, "A cultural renaissance is occurring in this country, there is no question about it."

The fact that thirty years ago there were only twelve museums in the United States for each million of population, while today there are twenty-two for each million, strongly supports the renaissance thesis. Meantime, the sudden wave of building immense new cultural institutions, like Lincoln Center in New York, Los Angeles' $24-million Music Center, Saint Paul's new arts and science museum, and the Wayne State University cultural center in Detroit, is ensuring that new generations will not be culturally deprived.

The *Fortune* survey shows that in 1960 Americans spent $200 million to buy pictures or the materials to create them; $90 million for classical music recordings, including 25 million long-playing discs, or a 78 percent increase over the figure of just three years ago; $590 million for musical instruments; $26 million to operate symphony orchestras; $375 million for theater, opera, and concert seats.

Even more significant is the sudden advent of the off-Broadway serious and experimental theater, mushrooming in the post-war era from none to the present 32 houses; the similar flowering of art movie houses, from a handful in the 1940's to some 500 now, during a period when movie attendance over-all dropped from 60 million weekly to 40 million. Note, as well, the sudden growth of FM radio, the sprouting of foundations in support of education and culture, and that new campus figure, the resident writer and composer.

The threatened cancellation of the Metropolitan Opera's season was a most instructive episode. The acclaim accorded Labor Secretary Arthur Goldberg, for resolving the Met's labor problem emboldened him to urge direct government subsidy of the arts. This notion, hitherto alien to Americans, has come to have widespread popular as well as administration support. The interesting aspect of Goldberg's remarkable statement is his stress upon culture as so essential a part of democratic society as to justify large-scale federal aid. Referring to the performing arts, Goldberg said they are experiencing "a growth so rapid, so tumultuous, so eventful as to be universally described as an explosion. The specifics have no parallel in history. America today has some 5,000 community theaters—more theaters than radio and television stations. There are better than 500 opera-producing groups—seven times as many as fifteen years ago. Symphony orchestras now total 1,100—twice as many as only ten years ago. . . . An area of unequaled achievement may well be upon us."

Though disaffected intellectuals are appalled at the mass character of this culture, judging it to be a vulgarization, which much of it unquestionably is, nevertheless, this spate of cultural pursuits is primary evidence of the diminishing dominance of moneymaking as the tyrannical absorber of our time and energy.

THE NEW IDIOM OF SUCCESS

There is more subtle evidence of the change in our sense of values than the cultural boom. Much more pertinent, for example, is how the style-setting, opinion-making segment of the best-educated Americans is judging the ingredients of success. In the past, material success has traditionally been considered a sign of election of our dominant old Puritan Calvinist tradition. Today the sign of election is membership in the new elite, those who have intrinsically important work they enjoy, those for whom, in philosopher John Dewey's phrase, "earning one's living is at the same time living one's life." This is the newest idiom of success in America. In ever-increasing numbers, educated people are finding their primary concern and identification through their jobs, rather than through the incomes the jobs return.

All of us can cite supporting instances from personal experience: the man who takes a lower-paying job of four days so that on the fifth day he can pursue his personal research; the art connoisseur who takes a modestly paid job as assistant curator so as to be near paintings; the top graduates wooed en masse by commercial interests who instead choose obscure research fellowships, a stint as forest ranger, work in a settlement house, or the penury of being an assistant editor on a serious periodical.

The Peace Corps is a phenomenon that deserves very close scrutiny. The volume of 16,000 applications to date is extraordinary in itself. But the public support for the project is even more significant. So impressive has been the response, in fact, that plans are afoot in Washington for a domestic counterpart, an Urban Peace Corps, to strengthen some of the essential public services so desperately undernourished in our asphalt jungles.

This rise in noneconomic values reflects a rejection of the traditional system of rewards and bears the clear implication that monetary rewards have been too often unsustaining and even corrupting. Involved here is a revolt against the market system of free enterprise itself. For the market system, whose very successes have created the possibilities of an indulgence in noneconomic values, has been tyrannical in confining its rewards to those most fully absorbed with moneymaking. But today, as money weakens as an index of status and prestige, we are witnessing a revolt in which there are new heroes and new villains.

Robert Brustein writes perceptively of the "Madison Avenue villain" as the new symbolic figure, the type most widely and venomously rejected in the flood of self-critical American literature. One is reminded of Montesquieu's observation, at the onset of the Industrial Revolution whose fruits are now liberating us, that "It is the nature of commerce to make the superfluous useful." The heart of the contempt for the Madison Avenue type is his superfluousness. His life, as Brustein remarks, is selling something that he did not create and that people do not need. In short, Madison Avenue symbolizes the exact opposite of the new hero, the person who solves the peculiarly American problem of making meaningful use of time and finds self-fulfillment in his work. The successful man today is the one whom the intelligentsia define as the unalienated man. In the words of Sidney Hook, "the unalienated man is the creative man, any man engaged in significant or meaningful work voluntarily assumed as a means toward self-realization." If this is the new ideal which our affluence has made a practical possibility, then it is inevitable that the drive to make money becomes secondary.

The extraordinarily widespread deprecation heaped upon Madison Avenue from every quarter can be seen as an expression of the newly ascendant status of noneconomic values in various ways. For example, since the role of advertising is to guide the individual as a consumer, a contempt for advertising carries with it the rejection of consumption as a worthy end in itself, a rejection of the primacy of materialistic values. It is my belief that in fact we in the United States are evolving beyond what J. K. Galbraith calls the "consumption society"—one that has mastered the problems of production and are approaching a new order of society, the society of self-realization. This is a notch up the ladder from sheer consumption for its own sake or for the sake of maintaining full employment. In this higher society of self-realization whose outlines we are just perceiving, the effort to get meaningful work will be the paramount concern.

One of the dismaying developments of our time is the widespread incidence of juvenile delinquency. And a number of recent studies (*Growing Up Absurd* by Paul Goodman; *Delinquency and Opportunity* by Cloward and Ohlin; *Slums and Suburbs* by James B. Conant; *The Insecure Offenders* by T. R. Fyvel), by remarkable coincidence, all came out almost simultaneously with this finding: not lack of money but lack of jobs, of work with any meaning, is the bedeviling factor behind most of the delinquent behavior among adolescents. Affluence has not been enough, these studies show. The deprivation triggering delinquency has been a deprivation in noneconomic values, such as the sense of function and status, and the prestige that comes from having work of some significance. Hence, we see delinquency extend beyond the slum to the middle-class suburb, where money is not a problem.

Finally, we are increasingly encountering a shift to noneconomic values in our collective as well as our personal judgments. For example, there is a movement that has attracted wide public support across the nation to preserve open land. Rural and wilderness land is being acquired both by outright state purchase or by an ingenious leasing arrangement with private owners strictly for the sake of leaving land as it is, undeveloped and unexploited by commerce. Also, our planners are appealing, with increasing success, for the public to give precedence to noneconomic criteria in planning the major determinants of our environment, like urban renewal, highways, and airports.

Money isn't everything, and we are finding society acting on this radical premise in any number of ways. Harvard economist Alvin H. Hansen proposes in fact that Congress create a Council of Social Values comparable to the Council of Economic Advisers. The President, with the council's assistance, would report annually on our cultural gains and losses. He would be required to set forth goals for the coming year, review the progress or lack of progress in the year past, and propose necessary programs and policies. It is, says Hansen, "high time that we devote in our State of the Union message some attention to the cultural needs of an advanced society."

A wonderful paradox enters into this. The degree to which a society turns away from the immediacy of moneymaking to the cultivation of the resources of the mind and spirit substantially determines its ultimate economic growth. This is a new concept in economics that has been proved statistically only in the past several years. It was originally the brainchild principally of Arthur Burns of the National Bureau of Economic Research and of Chicago University's Milton Friedman. Now it enjoys the support of nearly all the younger economists.

It means that investment in physical capital, like factories and machinery, is less important to economic growth than investment in brains—in education, invention, research, professional skills, culture, technology. Dr. Walter Heller, the chairman of the President's Council of Economic Advisers, in his tour of the nation during past White House Regional Conferences emphasized at each conference that such investment in intangible human capital has accounted for over half of our economic growth in the twentieth century. The very subordination of moneymaking per se to concern about the quality of living in our emerging society of self-realization can beget wealth to an extent we have hardly contemplated.

Such a society, educated, self-aware, and free from overriding absorption with the pecuniary, is really the goal of democracy. Properly conceived, the end of democracy is the freedom and the capacity for self-fulfillment. This must be the commitment of all of us. In this light, the changing role of money in American life signifies a turning point in our history.

CONSUMERS OF ABUNDANCE

Gerard Piel

The advance of science has for many years been undermining the two pillars of our economy—property and work. Each at length has fallen from its place. Property is no longer the primary source of economic power, and ownership no longer establishes the significant, functioning connection between people and the things they consume. Work occupies fewer hours

From the Center for the Study of Democratic Institutions, Santa Barbara, California, June, 1961. Used by permission of the publisher.

and years in the lives of everyone; what work there is grows less like work every year, and the less the people work, the more their product grows. In the place of work and property, illusions and old habits and compulsions now support the social edifice. Public understanding must eventually overtake this transformation in the relationship of modern man to his physical environment. Fundamental changes in the social order—in man's relationship to man—are therefore in prospect and are already in process.

It is difficult and perhaps dangerous to forecast where these changes may lead. Full employment, for example, now seems to be not only an unattainable but an outmoded objective of economic policy. What takes the place of wages in a workless society? Does profit remain a useful standard of accounting in a propertyless society? But these questions are not only too big; they are premature. Before they can even be asked, the scientific revolution that occasions them must be more closely examined.

As the withering of these institutions from the life of society suggests, property and work are artifacts of civilization. In the kinship economies of pre-agricultural societies they have no place whatever or appear only in the faintest analogues. The wampum hoard that confers prestige in one culture becomes the potlatch of another. Hunting and food-gathering are not work, but adventure, assertion of manhood, magic, and craft.

Property and work make their appearance with the agricultural revolution. They are devices for gathering and impounding the surplus that four families at work upon the land can now produce to support a fifth family off the land. Property is the institution by which the church, the state, and their individual agents assert their control over the land as one of the two primary factors of production. Work is the institution by which they assert their control over the other primary factor of production—the energy of human muscle. The word "work" signifies toil and at the same time the product of toil; it is the measure ("according to his works") of the portion of the product that may be allocated to the unpropertied worker. The two institutions together furnished the rationale for the compulsions necessary to assure the removal of the surplus from the land. Thanks to these arrangements, even fairly primitive agricultural technologies were capable of supporting substantial urban civilizations, as in Mexico.

In the feudal societies identified with agricultural technology, land was the only economically significant property. It was typically inalienable, except by order of the suzerain; it was cherished and maintained from generation to generation, physically occupied by its possessors, who enjoyed all the rights of usufruct as well as the power to exploit. In medieval Europe the land so completely dominated economic life that the taking of interest was synonymous with usury, a crime as well as a sin. It took a religious revolution to establish the practice of selling things for more than they cost and to secure propriety for profit in the worldly virtue of thrift.

Profit, thrift, and the accumulation of capital brought an entirely new kind of property into ascendance in economic affairs. This was the machine. At first the machine had the same immemorial look of permanence as the land. It embodied a high ratio of brute material to design and was built for depreciation over at least one generation of ownership. Through such time periods, ownership of the machine carried the same stability of power and place as ownership of the mine or plantation.

It was not long, however, before the ratio of design to material in the machine began to rise and then reverse. As the machine became even less substantial, its lifetime grew shorter. Today the economically significant industrial property is not the machine, but the design, and not so much the design as the capacity to innovate design in process and product. This is scarcely property at all, but is rather a capacity inhering in an organization. To have that capacity encumbered by a gigantic plant can be hazardous. This is what the steel industry has found in the present technological free-for-all that has brought steel into competition with materials—glass, ceramics, reconstructed wood, plastics, and exotic new metals—that no self-respecting steelmaker ever heard of fifteen years ago. The most profitable manufacturing enterprises are those that show a shrinking ratio of plant to output and a rising ratio of instrumentation to plant. Not only the plant but the product and the very industry in which the company is engaged may be subject to obsolescence. The decisive factor of production is research and development.

As the nature of property, in the sense of the thing that is owned, has changed, so has the nature of the social institution of property. Property was subverted by another social institution, the corporation. With ownership represented by stock certificates, the proprietor ceased to occupy the premises. The right of property vested in the stockholder, as A. A. Berle, Jr. and Gardiner C. Means made clear more than a generation ago in *The Modern Corporation and Private Property,* was reduced to the right to vote for the directors of the corporation (if the stockholder bothers to return the proxy statement) and to a claim on earnings (if the directors declare them out in dividends on his class of stock). Even these vestiges of power are delegated today to a third party for the increasing percentage of the voting equities in American industrial enterprise that is held by insurance companies, pension funds, and mutual investment companies.

The puissance in research and development that determines the fortunes of a corporate enterprise is commonly valued at one dollar on the balance sheet. This accounting factor fiction hypothecates the talents of the men who make up the organization, and the common-stock certificate is a thrice-removed share in that hypothecation. Under the circumstances, it is hard to see how the stockholder could be vested with a larger claim. The instrumentalities of ownership have become as insubstantial as the decisive factor of production itself.

Against this statement of the terms on which the present owners of the American industrial system hold their property, it may be argued that the really giant new fortunes are being made in the old-fashioned kind of property; that is, land and the mineral riches underneath it. But even the discovery of mineral resources has moved into the realm of invention. It is *par excellence* a yield on instrumentation, implemented by an equally intangible talent for politics. As a result, most of the prospecting is carried on by large corporations, and ownership stands as removed as in other activities of the industrial system.

With the emergence of two to five corporations in control of assets and sales in all but a few realms of industrial activity, economic power has become highly concentrated in our society. But it is no longer attached to property. The power is vested in self-perpetuating managements. How they derive their legitimacy is a question that troubles a great many people, including those who exercise the power as well as those who are critical of the power-holders.

Edward S. Mason, of the Harvard economics faculty, has astutely asked what difference, if any, this transfer of power has made. It is true that the profit margin—the yield to ownership—remains the ruling discipline of corporate management. And it is also true that operation under this discipline chronically fails to realize the full potential of industrial technology. That failure is the measure of the present business recession: with the gross national product holding steady at an all-time high, fully one third of the steel plant and comparable percentages of capacity in other industries lie idle. As the self-appointed management contemplates the question of the legitimacy of its power, it must also face increasingly insistent questions about its stewardship of power.

The same transformation of the nature of property is to be seen again in the relationship of the owner to property as usufruct. There are more home-owners today in the United States than ever before in this century, more than 60 per cent of the occupiers of dwelling places compared with less than 50 per cent in 1900. But whereas 30 per cent of the homes were mortgaged to 40 per cent of their aggregate value in 1900, more than 60 per cent are mortgaged to more than half their aggregate value today. The builders and bankers of the new suburbs will tell you that the ownership of one out of six homes there turns over every year. Plainly, the so-called home-owner is buying not a home but a housing service, much as he buys transportation, not a car, from the auto industry. His equity in these two utilities rarely controls before he turns in the old house or car for the new model. By the same token, the total installment debt represents, from one year to the next, by far the major property interest in all of the other consumer durable goods in use in the country. The householder is correct in regarding these transactions as the purchase of a service rather than property. For the objects themselves are self-consuming, designed for depreciation to desuetude in 1,000 hours of service.

In sum, the typical American consumer owns no property in the classical meaning of the term. Out of current income he pays for services currently rendered. Through income set aside in social security taxes and in pension and insurance funds, he reserves a claim on services to be rendered in the future.

Mention of the social security now provided for the overwhelming number of United States citizens brings this discussion to the topic of work. Social security is one of the devices evolved in the recent history of our industrial economy to help solve the problem of "distribution." This, as is well known, is the last frontier of economics. Viewed from the vantage of the economy as a whole, it is the problem of finding people qualified to consume the increasing abundance of goods produced by a declining number of workers. From the point of view of the individual citizen, it is the problem of finding work in a shrinking labor market in order to qualify as a consumer of that abundance. Thus, as we shall see, the primary function of work in our economy today is to secure not the production but the distribution of goods. This is clearly a different situation from that which prevailed in the valleys of the Tigris and Euphrates 7,000 years ago, when the surplus had to be extracted from scarcity by coercion.

Modern industrial technology produces a vast material surplus of goods, many times greater than the need of the workers engaged in producing it. That surplus goes begging for consumers because technology has subverted the social institution of work. The subversion of work began, of course, with the displacement of the biologically generated energy of human muscle by the mechanically generated energy of steam engines. The reciprocal steam engine gave way after little more than half a century to the steam turbine, the generator of electrical energy in the huge quantities that are measured in kilowatts. Studies conducted many years ago, when muscles were yielding a day's work to steam, showed that one man can put out about 48 kilowatt-hours in useful work in a year. On that basis, the

750 billion kilowatt-hours of electricity generated in the United States puts the equivalent of eighty-five slaves at the disposal of each man, woman, and child in the population.

But this is an old story. The new story is the disemployment of the human nervous system. In industrial production the function of the human worker has been to set the tool, start up the machine, supervise its performance, correct its error, and keep its parts in working order. The machine has been doing all the work, including work that exceeds human physical capacity. But, for lack of a nervous system, it has had to depend upon human beings to regulate its operations.

The robot, or artificial nervous system, is the steam engine of the present phase of the industrial revolution. Unlike the steam engine, it does not announce its presence by huffing and puffing, and it has no easily recognized anatomical structure. But it does have a single underlying principle, which is as clear-cut and universal as the idea of converting heat into mechanical energy. This essential idea is known to engineers as feedback.

Feedback is the principle that underlies all self-regulating systems, including living organisms. The nearest and simplest example of feedback in action is the household thermostat: A mechanical sense organ absorbs a little of the heat generated by the household heating plant and thereby makes a measurement of its output. This small fraction of the output is fed back in the form of a signal to correct the input of fuel to the heating unit. By this feeding-back of output to input, the household heating plant is made to regulate itself.

Now the principle of converting heat to mechanical energy is embodied in about half a dozen economically important heat engines—including the steam turbine, the internal combustion engine, the gas turbine, and the rocket engine. The feedback control systems in our economy, on the other hand, appear in a host of species and varieties—electrical, electronic, pneumatic, hydraulic, mechanical—and in such diversity of design and appearance that they have only the essential feedback principle in common.

An accurate census of these robots has not been made. But the evidence is strong that they now outnumber the human workers employed in industry. Our entire energy economy—from the steam plant out across the high-tension lines to the rotating machinery of industry—is now subject to automatic control. The new technology of atomic energy is critically dependent upon automatic control; dozens of feedback circuits in the depths of a nuclear reactor control the dreadful flux of atomic particles in which no living things could survive. Our petroleum refineries and almost all of our chemical process plants are today so highly robotized that their entire operations are controlled by one or two human operators stationed at the central push-button control panel.

It is only a few steps from here to the fully automatic factory. In the petroleum industry, such a factory would make use of an instrument—such as the nuclear resonance spectrometer, which has only recently graduated from the laboratory—to analyze the output stream of a refinery. The spectrometer would feed back its reading to a mechanical computer, one of the "giant brain" variety. These machines are already equal to doing the work of the human operator at the control panel; they need merely to be equipped with instructions covering all possible contingencies in the operation of the plant. Comparing the spectrometer report on the output of the refinery with the instructions stored in its memory, the computer would check and correct the performance of the robot valves at all points on the process stream. In fact, the first full-scale refineries incorporating the principal elements of the self-regulating robot factory are now "on stream."

Obviously, the purpose in designing the automatic petroleum refinery is not to replace the one or two human operators who still remain on the payroll. This was the naïve idea of a Middle Eastern petroleum prince for whom an American oil company was building a refinery not long ago. Out of consideration for the underemployed *fellaheen* who were to squat in the sand outside the refinery fence, he asked whether jobs might not be created by disengaging the robots from the valves. The engineers took him seriously enough to re-examine the entire control system. They had to conclude that no team of human beings could be trained and coordinated to do its work.

So, also, the dial telephone, with the ramifications of direct long-distance and direct inward dialing, is designed not to save the wages of human female telephone operators, but to make the operation of the modern telephone system possible. The heart of that system is not the dial on the telephone but a computer in the central station known in the telephone company as the "line marker." Its self-regulating internal circuitry is so complex that its designers cannot tell at any given moment just which elements in it are performing the work at hand. The American Telephone and Telegraph Company estimates that, at the present rate of traffic, it would have to employ all of the women in the labor force, plus 20 per cent more, to do the work of its line markers. The task of coordinating the output of that many human nervous systems in a single telephone system is quite impracticable.

To engage the robot in functions of this kind takes some doing. The control system must be furnished with receptor organs, like the spectrometer or the dial on the telephone, to supply it with inputs from the world outside. And it must be linked with the world on its output side by means of effector organs, the hands that carry out its instructions. These may take the form of the electrical and pneumatic motors that drive the valves on a refinery or the relays that close connections in the telephone system.

Since the computer's function is to handle information, the easiest way to hook it up to the world outside it is by typewriter. Equipped with typewriters, it becomes a white-collar worker.

Thus far the impact of the automatic control revolution upon the industrial payroll has been felt most acutely by the production worker. Until about twenty-five years ago, the ranks of skilled and semi-skilled factory hands were the growing element in the labor force, absorbing the inward migration from farm to city. In the last ten years, however, as the index of manufacturing output has climbed from 75 to 110, the number of production workers has hovered around 12,000,000. It is evident that the number is now due to decline. In the electrical industry, for example, production employment shrank by 10 per cent in the six-year period from 1953 to 1959; during that same period production in this industry increased by 20 per cent. Even more striking records have been made by the larger units of the industry. In three years, from 1956 to 1959, the General Electric Company increased its output by 8 per cent and at the same time reduced its production payroll by 25 per cent. Its non-production workers now outnumber those on the factory payroll proper. Corresponding trends are to be observed in other industries. After the last retooling, the auto industry produced more units than ever before, and yet the auto cities of Michigan were rated as distress unemployment areas throughout the year of peak production. Projection of these trends into the future shows factory workers becoming as scarce as farmers toward the end of the century.

Vocal union organizations imbued with the Luddite spirit have made the public uncomfortably aware of these developments in recent years. Less is heard of what must be the already considerable impact of the white-collar computer. This movement has only just begun. Since typewriters furnish all the necessary linkage, it is clear that the liberation of the white-collar workers from their routine tasks is due to proceed at a much faster rate. Again it should be emphasized that the object is not labor-saving alone. With a computer to do the job, all the many records kept by a corporation become a deck of punched cards or a length of magnetic tape that serves as the single record for every function from inventory control to the computing of a salesman's bonus. Herbert A. Simon, of the Carnegie

Institute of Technology, has pointed out that the computer so programmed is not merely a clerk but stands ready to assume a large portion of the functions of middle and top management. As a decision-maker, the computer can subject much larger masses of data to more sophisticated analysis in much shorter periods of time. Not only does it know the theory of linear programming better than most of our highest-paid executives; it can also learn from experience to improve its performance in the managerial function.

From decade to decade, the American economy has adjusted to the subversion of the social institution of work with flexibility and something of the same inventiveness with which it has absorbed the consequences of the subversion of property. One man-hour of work today produces what it took three man-hours to produce sixty years ago. This means that we could be producing the same national product as in 1900 with one third of the 1900 labor force. That would leave 58,000,000 members of the present labor force unemployed. But, of course, the American people have elected to apply their rising productivity to the production of a much larger volume of goods, about six times as much as in 1900. A major part of this vast increase in output is represented by products not dreamed of in 1900. In other words, the workers disemployed by rising productivity in the old industries have been absorbed in new ones to produce an expanding variety of goods or in entirely new functions created by the flow of abundance.

They could be producing goods in even greater volume if not variety today, but they have chosen to take a substantial portion of the gain in leisure. With the work week shortened from around sixty hours to forty hours, the much larger 1960 labor force is putting in a total number of man-hours that is only 40 per cent larger than that worked by the 1900 labor force. If the sixty-hour work week still prevailed, only 40,000,000 workers would be needed to produce the 1961 national product and some 27,000,000 workers would be unemployed.

This invention—the spreading of the same amount of work over the larger labor force by giving everyone less work to do—constitutes only one of the measures so far evolved to handle the problem of distribution. Moreover, it should be distinguished from the desperate share-the-work measures taken in the Great Depression, because it does not involve sharing the wage.

On the contrary, the portion of the national income going to the labor factor—that is, compensation of employees as against profit, interest, rent, and so on—has risen slowly from 53 to 73 per cent since 1900. Some substantial portion of this shift must be attributed to the decline in the number of proprietors, large and small, especially in agriculture. That the shift also reflects a gain on the problem of distribution becomes clear, however, when it is considered in connection with the way the total income is shared among the income groups. Since 1929 the share of the national income going to the most fortunate fifth of the nation's families has shrunk from 55 to 45 per cent. Almost the entire 10 per cent subtracted from the income of the top fifth has gone to the three middle fifths, improving their relative position by about 25 per cent.

This redistribution of purchasing power is another important factor in reducing the amount of work people do in the course of their lives. It makes it possible for young people to postpone their entrance into the labor market through high-school and even college age, and it takes workers out of the labor market by voluntary retirement at the other end of their careers.

But the shortening of the work week and the working life still leaves untold the real story of how work has been spread in order to secure the spread of purchasing power. If work is defined with any sort of strictness to mean productive work—that is, the extraction of raw materials and the making of consumable goods from them (farming, mining, manufacturing, building, and transportation)—then less than half of the labor force, only 25,000,000 people, are really at work.

The distribution of the abundance they produce is secured in large part by employing people in the task of distribution. This is not to say that the distributors do not serve a valid economic function. But selling and distribution costs commonly mark up the manufacturing cost of durable goods by 250 per cent. The major portion of the profit on the sales price therefore comes from the distribution process. Since gimmickry is thus made to grow by what it feeds upon, the distribution system pays a premium on waste. Its principal economic justification is that it does provide "work" and so increases the number of consumers.

To the 12,000,000 employed in distribution should be added another 12,000,000 who qualify as consumers by virtue of their employment in financial, clerical, and service functions—necessary but again not productive work even as it is formally defined in our national bookkeeping. Another large group of consumers are qualified by their enrollment on government payrolls. Certain members of the community will stoutly deny that these people ever do a day's work. Not counting the armed forces, their number now exceeds 5,500,000. If the figure looks too big, it is because we usually forget local and state governments in these calculations. The figure comes back into scale when we recognize that $132,000,000,000, nearly 30 per cent of the gross national product, turned over in government budgets in 1959. Those expenditures not only set up 5,500,000 consumers for the goods made by those more productively employed; the money also made substantial direct purchases of goods and so generated millions of the jobs in the production sector.

Our roll-call ends with the approximately 2,000,000 household employees and the 2,000,000 or more who are employed in teaching or self-employed in the learned professions. Those whom we have here classified as nonproductive workers constituted only 30 per cent of the labor force of 1900; they make up 60 per cent of it today. Compared with the day's work that confronts most of mankind every morning, most American citizens are not engaged in work at all.

Thus, up to the present, the American society has managed to handle the subversion of the institution of work without undue stress upon the system of distribution that has carried over from the days of scarcity. Work, the illusion of work, and pleasant substitutes for work furnish an expanding population with the purchasing power to consume an even more rapidly expanding volume of production. For most of the past twenty years employment has been "full."

It now appears, however, that the advance of technology has begun to outstrip our capacity for social invention. Before the second World War, in the flux of technological change and the oscillations of the business cycle, the system chronically fell 5 or 10 per cent below full employment and fell as far as 25 per cent below in 1933. It is instructive to compare this experience with the present. During the past several years, despite a steady rise in gross national product, unemployment has been rising. Each wavelet in the now well-damped business cycle has left a larger number of workers high and dry on the beach. Unemployment now approaches 6,000,000, or nearly 10 per cent of the labor force. But this figure seriously understates the gap between the jobs available in the production and distribution of goods in the economy and the number of people who need employment in order to be able to purchase their share of those goods.

That gap has been filled for the past fifteen years by the war economy that has grown up alongside the consumer economy in our country. The rolls of the employed include today the 2,500,000 in the armed forces; they are certainly not employed in the production and distribution of goods. To their numbers should be added the 1,000,000 civilian employees of the Department of Defense, whose principal employment is that of housekeeping and procurement for those in uniform. Finally, we must add the 2,500,000 workers in industry engaged in filling the procurement orders of the military. The total of those unemployed or employed outside the civilian economy thus comes to 12,000,000, close to 20 per cent of the labor force, only 5 per cent below the unemployment peak of 1933—and this at a time when the gross national product has reached an all-time high. Wassily Leontief, of Harvard University, has recently adapted his "input-output" technique to permit detailed analysis of the prospective economic consequences of disarmament. Study of his tables indicate that even if the gross national product is maintained at peak levels through the transition period following an agreement to disarm, the civilian economy would very likely fall short of re-employing all of those who would be disemployed by the cut in military expenditure. The same study indicates that by 1965 technological disemployment will, in any case, eliminate about one fifth of the jobs in industry now generated by the procurement of arms (unless progress in the technology of armament continues to generate new starts on new weapons systems). In other industries, in the same period, technological progress promises to reduce employment by an average of close to 10 per cent.

The evidence that full employment is no longer an attainable objective seems to be growing. Of course, the arms budget can be arbitrarily increased, and the size of the armed forces along with it, to offset technological disemployment in the armament industries. But no one really wants to contemplate an indefinite continuation of the arms race. Alternatively, or concurrently, some of the slack can be taken up by a thirty-hour work week, a measure advocated by both presidential candidates as long ago as 1956. After that, the work week could be reduced to twenty-five, then twenty hours—and the inefficiencies inherent in such a short work week would help to create more jobs. At that point the nation will have come really close to being a workless society.

No reasonably predictable rate of growth in the productive sectors of the economy seems equal to overtaking the current rate of technological disemployment. Every step of progress in automatic control reduces the capital investment as well as the employment per unit of output. As the cost of investment goes down, the rate of technological progress must increase and with it disemployment. Even an expanding economy must employ progressively fewer workers in its productive sectors. At some point the terminus of full investment will be reached; even at the present level of opulence, the consumer economy shows signs of surfeit. There is, of course, a vast untapped market in the income groups at the bottom third of the economic pyramid. But how are their wants to be implemented with purchasing power when that bottom third already counts the disemployed among its members?

In the long run, larger questions must be asked and answered. If a fraction of the labor force is capable of supplying an abundance of everything the population needs and wants, then why should the rest of the population have to work for a living? Preposterous alternatives come forward: give-away programs on television suggest that television might be employed to give the abundance away instead of trying to sell it. If production cannot be maintained at a profit under such circumstances, then why should a profit be made? Some other standard of accounting might serve even better to reduce waste and inefficiency.

These questions are put in a deliberately extreme form. They suggest the kind of overturn in the values of our society which is already quaking the ground beneath our feet. The virtues of hard work and profit are rooted in scarcity. They have no relevance to the economics or the sociology of abundance.

Any hard work that a machine can do is better done by a machine; "hard" these days means mostly boring and repetitive, whether in the factory or in the office. But the instinct for workmanship, the need to feel needed, the will to achieve, are deeply felt in every human heart. They are not universally fulfilled by the kind of employment most people find. Full employment in the kind of employment that is commonly available, whether blue-collar or white-collar, has been plainly outmoded by technology. The liberation of people from tasks unworthy of human capacity should free that capacity for a host of activities now neglected in our civilization: teaching and learning, fundamental scientific investigation, the performing arts and the graphic arts, letters, the crafts, politics, and social service. Characteristically these activities involve the interaction of people with people rather than with things. They are admittedly not productive activities; nor are they profitable in the strict sense. But they are highly rewarding to the individuals involved and add greatly to the wealth of the nation. There is no question that our population numbers increasing millions of people qualified for such functions; our institutions of higher learning will have an enrollment of 6,000,000 before the decade is out. The nation's principal economic problem has become that of certifying its citizens as consumers of the abundance available to sustain them in tasks worthy of their time.

What disturbs the scarcity economist, of course, is that such certification is likely to be provided by the public payroll. It must be recognized, however, that these activities—along with urban rapid transit, the enhancement and conservation of natural resources, public works, the best kind of medicine, the operation of museums, and so on—have never been or can no longer be conducted at a profit. Most of these activities and institutions are now short-changed. With abundance to support the expanding portion of the population engaged in them, we may anticipate that they will assume a higher priority in our civilization.

In any event, so long as the institutions of work and property preside over our economic activities, it is clear that the distribution of material goods will be achieved as it has been in the past, by expansion of the "nonproductive" payroll in both the public and private sectors of the economy. The "peace corps" and the revival of the conservation corps proposed by the Kennedy administration are the latest steps in this direction. There is plenty of need, if not demand, for labor of this kind. A really adequate program of assistance to the underdeveloped countries might engage large numbers of disemployed factory workers in teaching their skills to people now entering on their industrial revolution. For some time to come, we can be sure, the real work that remains to be done in the world will stave off the specter of universal leisure.

As for profit, considerations other than profit are already being pressed upon the great corporations by society through governmental regulatory agencies. The self-perpetuating management is understandably wary of such invasion of its prerogatives. In the present ascendance of its reputation, however, it should be more concerned about its performance than its prerogatives. What is most to be asked of the corporate enterprise system is the vigorous promotion of technological progress. This, in fact, is the primary purpose served by profit in the industrial system today; as a kind of involuntary savings, extracted beforehand from the thriftless consumer, retained corporate earnings have furnished the principal capital for industrial expansion throughout the past fifty years. In the future, the "economic republic" of A. A. Berle envisions the insistent intrusion of the public interest in the councils of the private governments that operate our economy, especially when it comes to the deployment of investment funds.

Our society is probably closer to being propertyless than workless today. But the rate of technological progress is speeding up. It appears now to be moving faster than even the responsive and resilient American social order can evolve. Some of the changes may have to come in quantum jumps. For these we need economic and political leadership whose perception and judgment are not compromised in any fashion by commitments to the past.

INTELLECTUAL DEMANDS ON THE CITIZEN

Carroll V. Newsom

In spite of the braggadocio with which some of our "cultural missionaries" approach the underdeveloped nations, our society reveals primitive ideas as to the kinds of endeavor appropriate for women. A visitor from the outer world would be surprised to observe, as a correspondent of mine recently wrote, that "Many women college graduates seem to view social responsibility in terms of baking cookies for worthy causes or raising funds for organized drives."

My correspondent doubtless meant that many educated women define social responsibility too narrowly, in terms of "service to the community." They are content to carry out established policies instead of helping to determine new ones. They see their proper contribution as physical activity rather than intellectual effort. And they confine their citizenship sphere to the local community instead of reaching out to the nation and the world. Why is such a definition of the educated woman's obligation to society inadequate today?

On virtually every intellectual front there is controversy, requiring the judgment of all enlightened men and women. The United States, in common with the entire world, is living in an age of transition, the most important and the most painful in the chronicles of civilized man. All society is in ferment. Rapid advances in technology are creating social, political, and economic problems. The mandates of our time require reconciliation between conflicting cultures. Frames of reference are shifting and much of tradition is being cast aside.

Such turbulent changes must be reflected strongly in the dynamics of government. In fact, modern government must be in a continual process of adaptation.

But needed modifications of governmental program and organization do not occur spontaneously. In this nation especially, changes in government must represent the fulfillment of the desires of the citizens. No other way can be tolerated in a democratic political system. It remains true, as asserted by the Philadelphia Workingman's Committee of 1839, that "In a

From *A.A.U.W. Journal*, LV, No. 4 (May, 1962), 263-265. Used by permission of the author and publisher.

republic the people constitute the government, and by wielding its powers in accordance with the dictates either of their intelligence or their ignorance, [they] are the makers and rulers of their own good or evil destiny."

Do we as a people possess the wisdom, or even the interest and desire, to accept the challenges of our form of government? I am concerned that our willingness to accept responsibility for the political affairs of our nation has lagged intolerably behind the need for our involvement.

Our tradition that government, especially the Federal Government, should play a limited role in American life makes us reluctant to acknowledge what has happened in recent years. Within the past twenty-five years, we have seen the development of a tremendous governmental program of basic services to the indigent, the elderly, and the unfortunate. Public housing, first introduced as a stimulant to a depressed economy, has now been extended to include many kinds of activity, including urban development. As a result of the cold war, the Federal Government administers a huge military establishment, with fantastic ramifications upon our economy. There is a national space agency with a stupendous program for the exploration of outer space. Simultaneously elaborate governmental efforts to expand the uses of nuclear energy arc continued. Under the auspices of the Federal Government, there are extensive foreign aid projects, programs for the assistance of veterans, a nation-wide highway project, and programs that provide subsidies to farmers and to developers of certain natural resources.

WE ARE THE GOVERNMENT

Do we as American citizens really understand what has happened and what is happening in the realm of government? And do we have even some slight comprehension of the consequences to our social order, our economy, ourselves as individuals? After all, in essence, we of the United States *are* the government. We must recognize that as the functions of government expand, so do our responsibilities as citizens.

It is not enough that we concern ourselves with national issues. The problems of the rest of the world, of Ghana, of India, of Guatemala, of Ireland, of Iraq, have suddenly become our problems. This has been unavoidable. A policy of isolation for this country has become intolerable even for the rank conservative.

But what do we know about the problems of these other nations? Do we understand even the rudiments of the cultures of the countries now featured in the headlines of our newspapers? Many of our decisions are of great concern to people outside the United States. Undoubtedly some of our actions will determine the future of human relationships on this earth, an earth that has suddenly become so small that people must be able to live together. Where do we find the wisdom to provide proper judgment upon issues having international and intercultural significance?

To answer such a series of questions adds up to one simple fact: We are living in a day when the intellectual demands upon us as citizens transcend those of any period of our history. One must agree with the report of the President's Science Advisory Committee, issued on May 24, 1959, which stated in part that:

Until recent years the total intellectual capacities of our nation have never been fully challenged. But they are being challenged today. Our intellectual resources will be adequate to meet our needs only if all the brain power of our population is fully developed and utilized. Well-trained minds are among the most critical of our present national assets, among the scarcest and most valuable of our resources.

The complete acceptance of this challenge, it seems to me, requires much more than the rectification of minor inadequacies of school and college. It certainly means that we must demand a better basic education, strongly oriented to the requirements of citizenship. But, beyond this, it also means that we must move at once toward full utilization of the intellectual competencies of all our citizens, irrespective of race or creed or sex. And it means active acknowledgement that education for each person should become a continuing endeavor for all of life.

The very nature of the analyses demanded of our citizens in this age of gross turbulence requires the wisdom of intellectual maturity. School and college curricula can provide the individual only a foundation for his future studies and a guiding sense of perspective.

In the area of social sciences, for example, a student who specializes in sociology does not have time during his undergraduate career to understand fully the economic and political implications of his ideas. The student of economics, after his limited period of study in college, too frequently misunderstands the social and political consequences of his proposals. The fledgling expert on international affairs often fails to grasp the effect of his ideas upon domestic affairs. And few young possessors of the A.B. degree who advocate new public doctrine are able to comprehend its effects upon individuals.

The true intellectual effort that is demanded can be made only by the person who has risen above the mental stagnation and lethargy that plagues most adults, even college graduates. This country is desperately in need of educated people who are ready to maintain active, individualized programs of continuing study that will make it possible for them to participate in the shaping of public policy.

NEW DEPTH AND BREADTH

To be specific, each woman who would truly be a citizen of the modern world must maintain upon a ready basis the specialized tools of her mind. She must be prepared to make her own individualized contributions toward solving the problems that constantly challenge our civilization. She must attempt continuously to broaden the base of her understanding to provide adequate support for her judgments.

The adoption of this attitude would certainly give new meaning to the breadth and depth of her life. Acceptance of responsibility brings with it a greater sense of pride and confidence. And as an extra dividend, the lifelong student may find new values, including the kind of happiness that is frequently associated with true wisdom.

INDIVIDUAL AND SOCIETY: A NEW PERSPECTIVE

Winston White

Since the end of World War II, intellectuals have expressed a growing concern about the quality of American life, particularly about what they believe to be a loss of individualism and a surrender to conformity.

What good, they ask, are more cars and suburban homes, if Americans are losing their sense of purpose? What good are more television sets if what appears on the screen is trivial or degrading? What good is more income if spent on status-seeking and waste-making?

From *A.A.U.W. Journal,* LV, No. 4 (May, 1962), 269-274. Adapted from the author's *Beyond Conformity* (New York: The Free Press, 1961). Used by permission of the author and publisher.

The intellectuals are worried about the impact of a highly bureaucratized and industrialized society on the individual, who, they believe, has been cut off from relationships and experiences that once gave his life meaning and direction.

As the "togetherness" ethic of adjustment replaces the work ethic of achievement, individual responsibility declines, they say, and man becomes a passive approval-seeker. Mass production shapes consumer taste. Mass media seek the widest market through the lowest common denominator. Together they forge a mass culture whose vulgar banality undermines discernment and crushes diversity. Mass culture, by seducing talent and breeding passivity, robs the individual of his spontaneous creativity. Blind devotion to technology and science is leading us to a valueless disenchantment. This is the intellectuals' interpretation of what is happening.

I do not agree with this view, and I think an alternative explanation is badly needed. Of course everyone agrees that American society has undergone rapid changes in the last decade and a half. Many of us are deeply concerned about the meaning of these changes for the individual. But the intellectuals' pessimistic interpretation overlooks hopeful implications and real challenges. These changes, as I see them, create new opportunities for the individual to choose for himself. They are challenges because they make new demands on the individual, who is now confronted with choices for which his previous experience is not an adequate guide.

We might regard the kind of social change we have been going through as a process of *evolution:* Differentiation of structure and specialization of function. Under favorable conditions, this evolution means that each function can be fulfilled more effectively than before.

A pertinent illustration from American society is the structural differentiation between firm and family. In the case of the old-time family farm, both economic and familial functions were carried out by the same social unit. When the firm became differentiated from the family, "managerial" control of each became independent from that of the other. The family no longer had to be run like a business; the business no longer to concern itself with family problems.

Financing became independent. Decisions about spending money on plant or equipment no longer had to be weighed against decisions about spending money on household needs, education, and the like. Moreover recruitment of labor for the firm was no longer tied to available family members. The firm could hire those who might be better qualified than family members; sons gained more of a chance to fit their individual talents with occupational choice.

Similarly public education has meant that the teaching of children can be carried out independently of the financial and cultural resources of the family.

Today's family is more highly specialized and performs fewer functions. To compare the old-style family with the new-style family is like comparing the one-chamber heart with the right ventricle. This new-style family is able to perform its *essential* functions more effectively since it no longer has to be concerned with extraneous functions such as formal education and economic production.

With these changes, sex roles have become more differentiated and specialized. The father who was head of both family and firm (or farm) is not comparable with the father who goes off to business. In the former case, the father managed both family and firm, and woman's role was subordinated to his. Nor could he properly engage in the domestic activities the modern father does.

What was considered appropriate behavior for his wife was correspondingly limited. Although the nineteenth century farm woman may have performed a wider variety of tasks in the home than is the case today, they were all part and parcel of the same role definition. But today's mothers, particularly educated mothers, play a variety of roles differentiated from one another and more specialized. They are still mothers and wives, but they are also active in voluntary associations and many hold down jobs, often not from economic necessity but from personal need.

GREATER RANGE OF CHOICE

What is appropriate in one role need not be tied to what is appropriate in another. And since the individual has a greater range of roles from which to choose and the opportunity to play a variety of roles, he finds it easier to fit his own needs and talents into the slots that society provides.

This instance of family and firm illustrates my general interpretation of the way in which increasing social complexity affects individual choice. *The area of choice relinquished is of a lower order than that gained.* Let us take another example. When the small businessman goes to work for a large organization, he gives up deciding what products to make or services to perform. But he gains freedom to choose the occupational role suited to his particular productive capacities and interests and is freed from less congenial functions.

If the individual is to express his unique personality by developing his own particular productive capacities, as Fromm puts it, he has greater freedom to do so if he is not confronted with problems for which he has little talent and interest. If individuality is what we want and if we can assume that differences in heredity, "temperament," and experience equip individuals with different talents and interests, specialization is the best social arrangement.

The standardization of behavior often deplored as an aspect of "conformity" may also represent a surrender of *lower-order choices* that frees attention for more important matters. And with the reduction of behavior differences tied to class, income, and region come opportunities to be different in more individual ways.

Also *the number of choices gained is greater than the number relinquished.* Greater specialization opens a greater range of activities, both occupational and nonoccupational.

SOCIETY AND PERSONALITY

The increased complexity of society does not simply offer individuals a wider range of opportunities from which to choose. It may also develop their potentialities as human beings and their *capacity* to make choices.

Society is not something "out there" with which the "individual" is confronted. Personality is not an entity existing independently of society; its very nature and complexity are directly related to the complexity of society in three ways.

The first relationship flows from the fact that there are now more opportunities for individuals to express themselves, for unique talents to find outlets. Social complexity does not just *release* uniqueness in the individual; it helps to *create* it by developing the personality itself to higher levels of complexity and greater potentiality. Choices *and* the standards for making them become a structurally organized part of the personality.

The second relationship flows from the individual's greater freedom to pursue a range of activities independently of each other. As the person plays an increasing number of roles in a greater variety of situations, he has to discriminate among them, among the varying kinds of relationships he has with other people. This entails a higher level of organization in the personality. As the personality becomes more differentiated, the individual must *integrate* the larger number of roles he plays in order to maintain his identity.

As choices become available at higher levels, *upgrading* occurs, and this is the third aspect of the relationship between personality and society. Routinization of lower-level choices through social organization frees human effort for consideration of choices requiring more intense application and greater discrimination. Greater demands are made on individuals to achieve higher levels of performance, and this performance is of a qualitatively different type.

The most important shift is from working with things to *working with people*. This shift is due in part to the expansion of technology, which has reduced the extent to which human resources are applied to working with things and has made them available for action of a more completely human character. It is also a consequence of functional specialization, which requires increasing co-ordination of individual contributions.

BALANCE MUST BE MAINTAINED

In co-ordinating human effort, individual likes and dislikes, prejudices, and emotional needs must be taken into account. Greater demands for performance also intensify the problem of emotional needs. Therefore, as individual personalities play increasingly specialized roles in social interaction, a balance must be maintained between demands for performance and the need for emotional support. The individual must not only manage his own personality vis-à-vis others, he must also be sensitive to the fact that others have the same problem.

Indeed, one aspect of "conformity," preoccupation with what other people think and approve of, may be an effort to understand the nature of one's relationships with other people and, in so doing, discover the "self" in the looking glass of others' reactions. Much of what passes for anxiety about others persons' opinions may be an effort to understand and develop one's personality, an effort of increased importance in view of the demands being made on it to work with others in a complex society.

Of course, this effort may backfire and lead to crippling preoccupation with others' opinions. But it must be made; it cannot be abandoned because of its difficulty or dismissed as unnecessary and undesirable.

NEW STAGE OF GROWTH

The problems and challenges now emerging in interpersonal relations reflect a new and quite different stage of development in American society. As I see it, this new stage is *a shift from emphasis on the development of economic resources to the development of human resources,* particularly the capacities of personalities.

This does not mean that human resources have not been essential since the beginning of mankind. It does mean that new, higher-level uses of these resources are now both possible and necessary.

The resources of personality, as we have seen, have been emancipated in significantly new ways. Durable consumers' goods in the home, as well as automation in the factory and office, liberate human effort from tasks of a more physical nature. Upgrading the levels of performance requires greater skills on the job and in more complex interpersonal relationships.

IMPLICATIONS FOR WOMEN

The current preoccupation with education is the most salient symptom of this shift. Education, moreover, is not solely a matter of job-training, or "catching up with the Russians." It is also a matter of enlarging the individual's understanding of the complex world he lives in. And this understanding is a capacity of the personality.

It seems to me that this shift to human resources has important implications for the educated woman. What does it mean to her as a wife and mother, a jobholder, a citizen?

Let us first consider the new responsibilities she is assuming as a mother. As the needs of personality development become increasingly paramount, the family plays an increasingly important part. It provides the very foundation for the capacity to meet the demands on the personality to understand the complexity of human relations and personality problems. Given the attitudes that may underlie such decisions, it may not be too far-fetched to suggest that rearing larger families is one aspect of the rapidly emerging emphasis on developing human resources. A study of college women by Miriam Johnson revealed that those girls who wanted to have the largest number of children were already looking ahead to the time when their as yet unborn children would contribute to society as adults.

FAMILY PATTERNS CHANGING

Then, too, the greater demands on personality are reflected in changing patterns of family life, especially among the educated. The latitude given to children and their involvement in activities away from the home may be interpreted as encouraging them to become less dependent on their families and to learn how to confront new situations with a variety of other people. Greater permissiveness toward children when they are at home supplies the emotional support required by the greater demands for performance in contexts where the child is more "on his own."

In the occupational sphere, the demand for higher levels of performance, requiring advanced training, and the shift toward working with people challenge the special abilities of the educated woman. Talcott Parsons has suggested that woman, because of her role as mother and wife, tends to be oriented to personality concerns. Her experience in rearing children and providing an emotional retreat for her husband makes her, he says, particularly resonant to motivational problems and nuances. This distinction is roughly similar to the notion many psychologists hold to the effect that men tend to be interested in things and women in people.

Though there are, of course, male psychoanalysts and female engineers, women reveal capacities and interests in the direction noted to a greater extent than do men. And in those roles that are being newly developed and that require innovation in defining their nature, the difference between male and female capacities asserts itself with special force.

PRESSURES FORWARD FREEDOM

Closely allied to this interest in personality are women's interests, still relatively greater than men's, in education, religion, culture, and morality. These interests have enabled women to make distinctive contributions to the larger society. In her dissertation on *Social Change in the Feminine Role,* Janet Giele points out that American women have continually innovated *as women* in social roles related to women's particular concerns. As early as the 1820s and the 1830s, she notes, women were active in establishing basic equalities in education, property-owning, and suffrage for men. They moved on to an interest in the reform of individuals through church work and the early temperance movement. After the Civil War, there was a shift of interest from private to public morality, to a concern for the moral ends of social organization, associated with the Social Gospel and the Progressive Movement. Today's League of Women Voters is an example of this enduring concern. And with the advance of scientific knowledge of personality, the mental health movement has received impetus and support from educated women.

The patterns of life newly emerging on the American scene represent yet another stage in the development of man from prehistoric times. With the accumulation of past experience, changes have a way of occurring at a faster rate, so that now the impact of one is scarcely absorbed before another is upon us.

The impact of the current change has spread through the society virtually within a lifetime. Unlike previous changes, it cannot be absorbed *for* the individual by the family, the church, a class, or an economic or political interest. It is one that the individual must confront by making independent choices. He can no longer be guided by the same established patterns of behavior that characterized a simpler society. He no longer simply follows in his father's footsteps, or stays in his "class," or even in the community he grew up in.

As Dennis Wrong points out in his discussion of the family, this reduction in fixed guides to behavior undoubtedly creates uncertainty in courtship, in marriage, and in child-rearing, to which we might add occupational choice. But, as Wrong adds, it also creates an "inevitable expansion of the area of the personal freedom of the individual. . . . This is more difficult emotionally, and creates a confused situation socially and morally. But what else can freedom mean?"

ABILITY TO CHOOSE UPGRADED

This freedom *does* mean an upgrading of demands on personality of yet a different kind than those required by increasing specialization. It means an upgrading of the individual's *ability* to explore and to choose for himself. This requires sensitivity to personality problems, both of the self and of others. It requires the ability to take a complex view and abstract from concrete experience; it requires imagination.

If it is true that the individual now has *freedom from* older forms of ties and *freedom to* make a greater variety of choices, what is he to do with them? Because of the very fact that we are just entering this stage of development, we do not know the answer.

But as the economic stage required innovation in the face of uncertainty, so the present one requires another, perhaps more daring, certainly more personal, type of innovation. More important than knowing the answer now is being able to ask the question at all. In his new freedom from fixed patterns, in making choices that define his very identity, the individual is asking, *"Who am I?"* Does he find this quest for identity more difficult than primitive man found his struggle for survival, or Reformation man his concern for salvation? It is in the very nature of the choice, to be sure, that modern man faces it independently.

But he does *not* arrive at such independence without the resources that society and its culture make possible. He does not face an absurd, unordered world alone. Paradoxical as it may seem, his opportunities to be individual and his potentialities for taking these opportunities are the very consequence of his interdependence with others.

ENVIRONMENTAL AND OTHER FACTORS WHICH MITIGATE AGAINST DISADVANTAGED YOUNGSTERS IN SCHOOL

Allan C. Ornstein
and Stanley S. Rosenfeld

The exchange of knowledge and ideas, that subtle and elusive process we call education, is like any other exchange transaction in that it requires a purveyor and a customer. We were told from day to day about the new highs being reached by the Dow Jones averages and the steady climb of Standard and Poor's index. Yet, at the same time, the same financial pages were reporting more businesses filing under Chapter Eleven, and a walk in any local business area revealed closed shops and "going-out-of-business" sales with greater frequency. Thus, while General Motors had a record earning for the first quarter of 1966, and the general business picture was good, all was not as healthy as it appeared—and by the middle of the year (1966) it had become evident.

The situation in the field of education is highly analogous. College enrollment is at an all-time high, with the trend showing no signs of abating. State scholarships and incentive awards and federal grants vie with private money for the attention of prospective college students. Yet, the mass media are flooded with appeals from the President, state governors, mayors, sports figures, and other celebrated people, appeals to the potential dropout to remain in school. Somewhere, something is wrong.

The difficulty must lie with the product, the purveyor, or the intended consumer. Our concern in this paper shall be with the consumer—the student. What is the state of his health? Is there a GM here too, with record earnings, paying dividends to its investors? The records indicate that there most assuredly is. The better private schools, those of our public high schools which skim the cream of the school population through special entrance examinations, and the best students in the so-called "good" neighborhoods of our cities are turning out scholarship winners as never before. But it is the small businessman, the boy or girl from the ghettoes of our cities, who is the object of the appeals to stay in school. It is this disadvantaged youngster who is the personification of the conspicuous

From *Contemporary Education*, XXXIX, No. 4 (January, 1968), 156-160. Used by permission of the authors and publisher.

consumption which characterizes so much of American life. He represents the great waste or our natural resources, a waste we can no longer afford.

Why is the disadvantaged child being allowed to drift without direction into the ranks of the unemployed? There are some who would remind us of the old proverb, "You can lead a horse to water, but you cannot make him drink." They maintain that the boy or girl from the slum or racial ghetto is so alienated from the educational establishment that no amount of improvement in the school systems will improve his educational outlook; he does not want to learn. We are leading him to water, they say, but he will not drink no matter how we sweeten the water. What is closer to the truth is that we are indeed leading him to water, but he cannot drink. If a horse is tightly muzzled, it requires the greatest effort for him to open his mouth, great though his thirst may be.

Today (this is being written in August 1966) business is falling off at General Motors. Engineers suggest improvements in the product; efficiency experts suggest changes in personnel deployment or hiring procedures. But if the diffuculty were to lie outside the GM complex—with the consumer, greater problems would ensue. It would be unthinkable for GM callously to inhibit, almost to the point of complete crippling, the purchasing power of its consumers. This, however, is what society, and by extension, the education establishment, has done, and is doing, to the disadvantaged youngster. The child of the slum is so encumbered with handicaps, many of which are related to his inability to learn, that by the time he is ready to start kindergarten he is already one or two years behind his privileged brother. Here, then, is the crux of the matter. For the teacher, whether he be of the "child-centered" school or the "subject-centered" school is confronting a youngster who, through no fault of his own, is not ready to accept education. His lack of readiness may be attributed to problems which we may group into three broad and frequently overlapping categories: financial, physical, and emotional.

What kind of youngster are we discussing? Spindley's *The Deprived and the Privileged* lists 117 characteristics of the deprived child. Since this study was conducted in England in 1953, we in the United States may add at least one more—he is usually a member of a racial minority. This last characteristic has a profound effect on everything the youngster does. For if a white child has a fatalistic attitude and outlook on life, how much more so must Negro or Spanish-speaking children feel that there is no use!

One of the most frustrating situations that confronts a new teacher in a large urban school system—one in a low socioeconomic area—is the futility of a threat to call the parent to school. Often a child will laugh, inwardly or even to the teacher's face, because he knows that the teacher may call to his heart's content and no one will come. This youngster has been independent of his parents for many years and for many reasons. He may be dependent on an older sibling, but may just as likely be his own master. If he had a parent who would respond to a call from school, the call might not have been necessary. In such a situation, where parents are either absent or inaccessible, a child has too many other things on his mind to be burdened by assaults the school would like to make on his "ignorance."

Another consequence of the absent parent is the absent pupil. Where there is no father in the home, and where there is a working mother, a teacher will notice a great number of pupil absences, many of which are directly attributable to this situation. Either the child stays home because there is no one to see that he goes to school—a place that holds only failure for him, or the child, through neglect, suffers from real physical illness which keeps him at home.

A visit to the attendance office of any slum school at any level might be most enlightening. The attendance teacher—a modern euphemism for the truant officer—has brought a truant into school. They know each other quite well. The chances are the attendance teacher had no difficulty in finding the child; they have been playing hide-and-seek since the youngster started school. There is the formality of an interview with, perhaps, a warning of future legal action, and the child is returned to class. The attendance teacher then fills out the required forms and goes on to his next case. He knows that his interview will have the same effect that it had last time, and that it will have the next time.

Sometimes, the entry on the attendance form reads "illegally detained." This means simply that the parent is keeping the child at home for no apparent reason. This is a corollary to the absent parent—absent child situation. Here the "single" mother uses the child as a pawn in her battle with the welfare agencies. She withholds the child from the school as long as the welfare agencies withhold money from her. The youngster thus receives at an early age a feeling of contempt for the school. He cannot respect an institution that can be so easily duped; neither does he feel that such an institution can offer much of value. Therefore, he takes up truancy, apparently with his mother's blessing.

The disadvantaged child is sent to school at as early an age as possible. The parent seems eager to turn over to the school as quickly as possible the responsibility of caring for the youngster. What the child encounters at school, therefore, is hardly an improvement over what he had at home, or more precisely, in the streets around home. The classrooms are hopelessly overcrowded with the same children with whom he has been associating on the streets. Harried teachers are bound to shout and use other methods not subscribed to by the authors of textbooks on methods of teaching and classroom management. Thus the school not only offers no improvement over the home, but it applies restrictions to his movements that he does not find at home or in the streets. In her hurry to send the child to school, the mother has usually not bothered to prepare him for what awaits him at this strange place, and so he begins his education by disliking the school and all it stands for.

A child from a middle-class home has, from the time he was aware of such things, seen his parents reading. He is aware of and accustomed to reading materials around the house. He has probably accompanied his mother to the library. He has been read to and has been given books at an early age. The act of reading, therefore, is important to him; he has experienced it vicariously and he has seen his parents engaged in it. His curiosity is thus aroused. The disadvantaged child does not have this background. If he is among the fortunate ones, he may have seen a tabloid newspaper in the house. If he has older siblings, he may have seen comics, but the reading experiences which would stimulate his interest in learning to interpret the written word are virtually denied to him. Thus he is simply not ready to learn to read in the first or second grade.

There are of course other reasons why a disadvantaged pupil does not learn in school. There is the fifteen year old boy who entered his class at 9:00 each morning. By 9:10 he was sitting, head resting on his hands, fast asleep. The teacher, at first rather annoyed, investigated and allowed the practice to continue. It seems that by nine o'clock this boy had already been awake for five hours. He worked on a milk truck which started its rounds at 5:00 A.M. It seemed ludicrous to the boy to get a full night's sleep so that he could be awake and attentive in class, as the teacher had tried to persuade him. He was not earning ninety cents an hour in school learning that fog is like a cat. Who could refute this logic? He was helping to support a family which his father could not support alone. This was here and now. He could not buy himself or his brother a pair of shoes by reciting Carl Sandburg's poetry.

Another youngster sleeps in class because he spent the night roaming the streets. Of course he has a home to go to. But rather than listen to and watch his father argue with his mother again in a drunken rage—and stand the chance of a beating himself—he chose to spend the night "out." Can he, even with a night's sleep, be ready to face the unreal intricacies of percentage problems?

A girl comes to school late regularly. Inquiry reveals that she has difficulty getting up in the morning. She normally shares a bed with her mother, a common practice in impoverished homes. Perhaps, from time to time, one of her "uncles" comes to spend an evening with her mother, necessitating her waiting someplace outside the home until 'the "visit" is consummated. At the junior high school level a young adolescent cannot be put off with transparent stories of "uncle." This girl knew what was going on and appreciated full well the meaning of these visits. Can such a girl, realizing that her mother is engaged in prostitution, hope to pay any attention to what goes on in school? Will such a child seek fulfillment in her studies even after a maximum number of hours of sleep?

The preoccupation of sex may also be considered a manifestation of another problem that plagues the male adolescent in the Negro disadvantaged home. There seldom is an adult male in the home, and where there is a father, he is seldom the wage earner who contributes the major support of the family. Thus there is no model whom the young boy can seek to emulate. His family structure is matriarchal and, when he enters elementary school, he finds that that too is dominated by women, both teachers and administrators. Thus through promiscuous and precocious sexual activity he strives to establish his identity as a male.

Generally, the adult male with whom the child has most frequent contact is the policeman on the beat. He is the hated authority symbol, a natural enemy, called "the man," "fuzz" or "whitey." When the youngster enters junior high school, he may encounter his first male teacher. How the child reacts to this teacher can have a far reaching effect on his educational progress. If he rejects the teacher as another hated authority symbol, there is, naturally, no promise indicated.

The child is certainly influenced by his neighborhood environment. The child who is brought up on the street is going to be governed by the laws of the street. He is going to resort to violence as the only means of protecting himself from anything which he thinks makes him look foolish. He has seen this behavior at home where his parents and older siblings shout at him and thrash him when they are thwarted, and he has observed the older boys on his street do the same thing. Thus he believes this to be normal and acceptable behavior. In a school, where many provocations will arise early in his career, his normal pattern of behavior will be greeted with reprimands and limitations, adding to his confusion in his new, unfamiliar, and now unfriendly surroundings.

This feeling of strangeness and frustration is compounded by a decidedly poor self-image. The disadvantaged child feels, usually, dispirited and rejected. It is not a completely new thing for him, therefore, to be castigated and told he is doing something wrong. He simply retreats where, at least, he has the power to do something about what happens to him. At home and at school he as at the prey of adults who, he feels, don't want him in the first place. He can find neither comfort nor peace in the school situation, and so he rejects it.

His feelings of rejection and his unsatisfactory home experience also leave him ill-equipped to handle judgments of right and wrong. In Davis and Havighurst, *Father of the Man,* it is pointed out that an effective conscience depends upon parents loving their children (and the children knowing that they are loved) and parents making for their children socially appropriate prohibitions. In the experience of the disadvantaged child, the rightness or wrongness of an action depends, more often than not, on the mood or temper of the adult. Thus, no path has been defined for him, and what had always been acceptable on the street with his friends becomes anathema in school.

The disadvantaged child learns at an early age to take no stock in promises. His mother has lied to him, whether in promising him a reward for proper behavior and not delivering, or in telling him that he is going to visit grandma when he is actually going to the hospital, and he has learned his lesson well. Adults make promises which mean nothing; therefore, promises themselves mean nothing. I'll promise everything, he says, because nobody will expect me to deliver anything.

Promises also involve adults, and adults, as we have pointed out, represent authority. Adults whom he has known have lied to this child; why then should one with whom he has had no prior contact be obligated to tell him the truth? All authority then becomes suspect. He has long since learned that the police are enemies. The teacher is now a new kind of "cop" who keeps him in a different kind of jail, but a jail nevertheless. Many youngsters learn the new rules and "play the game," but many cannot, or simply will not.

"Playing the game" also means the disadvantaged child has learned the socio-psychological, educational clichés about himself. This is reflected in the child's answers and behavior which he thinks he is expected to say or do. Often the child is an astute appraiser and knowing manipulator of his environment; he must if he is to survive on the streets. He knows just when to stop before it becomes unsafe or before the teacher gets angry. When he is caught, he will often try to "con" or fake his way out, another game he has learned from the streets.

Sometimes, though the effort is sincere and the approach is sympathetic, the school, through no fault of its own, still fails the disadvantaged youngster. The constant questions, interviews, and advice from social workers, police, and now teachers, have helped to create an atmosphere of suspicion on the part of the child. Thus the well-intentioned teacher is greeted with what is to him unwarranted cynicism by a youngster in whom he has a sincere interest.

Despair and hopelessness also afflict the disadvantaged child. You cannot remain long in a slum area and not feel it in the air. Young men and old, "hanging out" on street corners or on stoops or near the local liquor store—of which there are many—find nothing but time on their hands. This is the picture which greets the child from the first time he leaves his home for school until he returns from school. Perhaps his father, if he knows his father, or an older brother is one of them. This is what he has to look forward to. In some instances this is the second generation subsisting on welfare checks. In other cases men have abdicated their bread winning responsibilities completely after years of frustration in finding and holding jobs which don't pay a living respectable wage. It is much easier for a woman to get a job as a domestic. So, the adolescent boy has no motivation to get an education. And you don't need a high-school diploma to scrub someone else's floors. This lack of intrinsic motivation is a wall which only the exceptional teacher can scale, and there are precious few good teachers, let alone exceptional teachers.

Thus, the disadvantaged child is the victim of an environment which is hostile from his birth. Since he is unwanted at home, he takes to the streets. He is forced by the law to enter a school which neither accepts nor understands his behavior. At school he is forced to fit a mold which does not fit him and which he does not need to prepare him for the life which he envisions for himself. He is surrounded on all sides by authorities which he does not accept, and he is then castigated and further rejected by the society which has imposed these authorities, for failing to appreciate what it has done for him.

A EUROPEAN LOOKS AT AMERICA

Michel Gordey

Only in America do people still talk, shout, speak their minds to a stranger as though he is one of them. You don't have to dig or beg.

On a recent visit to the States before the assassination of Sen. Robert F.

By the courtesy of the editors. From *Look Magazine,* XXXII, No. 16 (August 6, 1968), 25-27. Copyright 1968 by Cowles Communications, Inc.

Kennedy, I covered over 8,000 miles, crisscrossing the continent, coast to coast, from New York to the Middle West, then on to Arizona, Colorado, San Francisco, ending up in Washington, D.C. I talked with more than 200 Americans: young, old, rich, poor, black, white, men, women, for two months, about 15 hours a day.

They poured out their innermost thoughts on everything: jobs, neighbors, violence, crime, football, racial trouble, police, sex, high prices and peace. Usually, conversations started with my questions about the approaching election, the candidates—or with their comments about De Gaulle (because I am French). On the plane back to Paris, I summed up the topics. I found five "W's": worries, wealth, war, weapons, welfare.

"It's too much, really. Vietnam, the Negroes, the gold problem, those college kids. Sometimes, I feel like retiring on the top of a mountain in Vermont," said a 40-year-old executive, sitting next to me in a crowded air terminal in Chicago. On that Sunday morning, he was flying to a convention in Los Angeles, but would spend a few hours in Cleveland, to watch a football match: "I want to relax a bit," he said.

What happens to the U. S. has a direct bearing on my country, on the future of my children. My questioning was, indeed, a sort of investigation inside a friend's home. It did not take me long to realize that never before, in my lifetime, had Americans been in such a turmoil.

I was in New York City three times within nine months. I got the same advice from all of my friends: "Be careful at night. Don't walk the streets. Don't take the subway. Don't go to Harlem." During World War II, when I lived in New York, I used to face all the "dangers" with equanimity, as I do in Paris or Prague now. This time, I did not change my habits. Nothing happened, except some hostile glares in the Negro area, and several cabbies refusing to drive me there. But every day, the newspapers reported crimes, murders, rapes, burglaries, drug addicts. In my hotel room, when I switched on my TV set, I saw long or short sequences on the "risks" I had taken.

Yet something very important *had* changed. In Minneapolis, Detroit, Tucson, Denver and San Francisco. Also in Washington. On my nightly walks, I was alone—or almost—in the streets. Policemen looked at me suspiciously, swinging their nightsticks. I have made 22 visits to the States and *never* before sensed this strange atmosphere of anxiety and fear.

It was not like that five, ten or twenty years ago. Americans have now acquired the habit, at least in the big cities, of behaving after dark as though they live in a jungle. This, for a hospitable, open, basically trusting society whose homes are not protected by city walls, is something new and dangerous. "I never go to movies alone," said a pretty shopgirl in Detroit. "It's too scary."

Officials confirmed her opinion. The mayors of New York, of Minneapolis, of San Francisco, the police commissioner of Detroit, told me in various forms: "Crime is my No. 1 problem." Mr. John Lindsay said, however, that in New York, crime is not any worse than in other cities. Sitting in his office for half an hour, one realizes that it would take him five times more to simply enumerate his "other problems." Bravely, he smiled. My thoughts turned to Fiorello La Guardia, in that same building, laughing and joking with a much lighter heart. It was different 24 years ago. The city, the crowds, the mood and the air were easier to live with. All over America, it's the same.

In the big Midwestern cities—Minneapolis, Milwaukee, Detroit—I discovered what I think is the greatest threat. I had sensed it in Harlem. But after New York, I became even more acutely aware of a steady escalation of the racial crisis. One city's hell would have been heaven in the next one. As I went along, talking to black and white leaders or average people, I heard more and more people expressing fear, hatred, despair and distrust. Black Power militants spoke to a Frenchman with perhaps more frankness and less brutality than they would to an unknown white American. White liberals were less and less hopeful, though doing their best. Suburban residents were getting ready for a showdown in the summer. An extremist Negro leader told me in Detroit: "The white folks still think that we are summer people. I wonder why. We are used to the climate. We have lived here for a century. We can and will fight in any season. If they want to slaughter us, we'll first blow up the whole white Establishment."

The wife of a corporation lawyer in the same city, a resident of Grosse Pointe, the wealthy suburb where Mr. Henry Ford lives a few blocks from the lady's beautiful home, told me: "The blacks will kill and rape us right here in the next riot." She knew that her residence was 30 minutes away from the Negro ghetto. Her nightmare seemed unreal to me, but she was perfectly serious.

This mutual fear, this growing panic on both sides, is, of course, the ideal breeding ground for extremists. I talked to such people on several occasions. One of them, chairman of a right-wing organization, explained to me in Detroit that the Roman Catholic Church and the Negro organizations were infiltrated with Communists agents. He was going around making speeches and mailing leaflets about emergency precautions during the "next riot": get the easily acquired guns, store food and water supplies, establish shortwave radio communications with your neighbors, etc.

Also in Detroit, I was admitted to a private meeting of a shooting club where, for three hours, young and eager "sportsmen" explained to a quiet middle-class audience how to use and choose 20-odd short or long guns. It was like a prep school for the possible civil war threatening America. My fears were confirmed by an expert. "We are on the eve of a revolution which is going to split the country right down the middle. It is a class struggle, steadily building momentum, and we are not doing a damned thing about meeting this threat. There is an almost complete lack of communication between blacks and whites. Never in its history have there been as many guns in this city as now. And this has always been a rough city," said Detroit Police Commissioner Ray Girardin. He was talking on the record and looked more than gloomy.

About the guns, I went to see some other experts. At the National Rifle Association in Washington, I was told that a fair estimate of the number of guns in the country was 100 million, one for every second American (children included). Bearing arms, I was told, was an old tradition, guaranteed by the U.S. Constitution. I know enough about American history and national character to take such statements and statistics in my stride and keep cool.

What concerned me most was the amount of ignorance, the lack of interest among so many white Americans, about what was happening literally on the next block. I asked dozens of people in different cities: "Have you looked at the Negro ghetto? Have you been inside black homes? Have you taken some time to inquire personally about their life, their standards of living and education?" In most cases, I was met by a stony silence and puzzled glances.

Racism and blindness about one's neighbor's life exist in every country. In France, many of my compatriots take the same attitude toward the poor, unskilled Arab workers living in dreadful conditions on the fringes of Paris and other industrial centers. But at least the life of the country is not threatened by a potential civil war on the part of the Arabs. It was, on this last trip, that I fully realized the deep rift between black and white Americans. My friend, the late American Negro writer, Richard Wright, had written and spoken to me about it, back in the '50's. Now, I really understand what he meant.

But I had other surprises—pleasant ones. I had heard and read about the "generation gap" and wondered what it really meant. In Minneapolis, in Detroit, in San Francisco and in New York, I had long talks with young Americans, rebels, draft resisters, hippies, and just "normal" American boys and girls without special political or intellectual commitments. I was amazed, here again, by the change. In the '50's and early '60's, I had lectured on various American campuses and met the "practical generation." These were young people whose main interest was their future well-paid job, with a nice home, a flashy car and a good career in a big organization.

Many of them yawned at politics and did not care much about the world outside America.

This time, in 1968, I met in college dorms and at family tables a different breed of young Americans. They were either concerned by, or committed to, a cause: resistance to the Vietnam war, resistance to the draft, campaigns for racial equality, the fight against poverty. Some others were so critical of the society, so deeply opposed to the world and to the ideas of their parents, that they had withdrawn to a life of non-violence, a life of drugs and dreams, or of tribal customs, rejecting the values of the puritan, hardworking, moneymaking American tradition.

I witnessed bitter fights between fathers and sons, mothers and daughters. Everything was challenged: religion, sexual rules, political principles, importance of money. Sometimes, it was painful to listen to the arguments flying back and forth. Quite often, there was no more dialogue between parents and children. But both among those "rebels" and the young Americans who had not shed the established social values, I found an intellectual curiosity, with a most amazing amount of information and awareness about America and the world.

During the months I spent in America, a sort of slow landslide had started against the Vietnam war. Every day, every night, newspapers and television brought the war into American homes. Slowly, the well-established idea "America has never lost a war" was being eroded by free debate and fierce criticism, still the main strength of this nation. The young people were in the forefront, but many elders were in the same fight; and as I went from city to city, from home to home, I could see the meaning of that strange new slogan: "the credibility gap." The mass media and, above all, the impact of television, of the permanent debate on the small screen, and on the radio, had created a new political situation, both for the '68 elections and for the war. As a Frenchman, I know what government-controlled TV and radio can do to misguide public opinion. On this trip, I saw the definite proof of the vital role of free debate in shaping and changing the mood and even the meaning of patriotism in a great nation.

I had never doubted the basic desire of the American people for peace. Last year, I saw the whole population of a rather conservative small town—Glassboro, New Jersey—stand still for hours under the scorching sun, to cheer Johnson and Kosygin for a few minutes, because they were supposed to be making a step toward peace. This time, it was not a small town but, little by little, the new mood rolling over the whole country.

American waves of hope can sweep the continent as fast as the storms of disappointment. Because of the Vietnam war, I could feel in many talks undertones of bitterness or disappointment about the world's attitude toward the United States. Americans have always liked to be liked. In 1968, they feel lonely and misunderstood. Frequently, I ran into people who told me: "We ought to be ashamed of what we do in Vietnam and about the racial problem." Just as often, I heard indignant comments about the "betrayal," the "ingratitude" of the European allies, who, in this time of stress, criticize America or attack the dollar. I went home with the impression that it would not take long or much to have a growing number of Americans asking for a policy whereby Washington would care and spend more for the country's needs, for its own poor, ill-housed and unemployed, than for those in the outside world. Also, in almost every conversation, I could feel the first signs that America is learning to know the limits of its own power. This could change the whole world picture.

Finally, more than ever, America '68 is a land of contrasts. Ostentatious wealth and appalling poverty. Wide, brightly lit freeways with the latest model cars rolling at full speed through decrepit slum areas. Fantastic new technical progress in all fields that could benefit education, health, mankind; and old-fashioned, stale prejudices coming alive and getting sharper and meaner. Urban luxury and rural misery. Crowded cities and empty spaces where foreign nations could find enough room to live and flourish. The cultural explosion and, quite frequently, the bigotry—bigotry that quickly, easily, flares into violence and even assassinations.

One of the last images of my trip I shall remember for a long time. I was on a flight from California to the East Coast. Aboard were ten uniformed soldiers, returning from Vietnam, their chests bearing many battle ribbons. There were six Negroes, four whites. I looked at them and asked myself what kind of America they would now live in. How would their country receive and treat the black veterans? I had asked this question of many officials and average citizens. Nobody knew. Black militants had told me, quite frankly, that in the "coming battle of the races," they counted heavily on the Negro GI's returning from an integrated Army life to the iniquities of the ghettos. On that plane, they sat and chatted among themselves, sharing souvenirs and jokes. How long would it take to forget or continue that friendly dialogue? A crucial question for the whole nation.

On the day I was flying back to France, an American friend asked me to tell him in two sentences my impressions after 60 days in the States. I said: "Your greatest danger is the racial question. Your best hope is your young generation." He looked at me with surprise. "You did not mention Vietnam," he said. "No, I did not. As a European, as a Frenchman, I know that all wars always end, well or badly. In most cases, badly for both parties. But your 22 million black Americans will stay here forever. You better do something about them, or else your children's life will be tough," I said. He nodded.

DEFAULTING IN THE SCHOOLS AND RIOTING IN THE STREETS

Daniel U. Levine

The escalation in destructiveness of the civil disorders which began with rioting in New York and culminated in rebellious explosions in Newark and Detroit in the summer of 1967 has forced widespread realization that the nation's ideals and traditions may be destroyed unless rapid progress is made in solving the multiple social and economic problems of the inner core sections of our central cities.

Many perceptive observers have attempted to give the public informed guidance in considering why two great American cities faced what was virtually civil insurrection in the summer of 1967, and why officials in uncounted other cities were no longer able to maintain the fiction that, "It can't happen here." It has become frighteningly obvious that, "It *can* happen here," that "here" is nearly everywhere, and that the urban crisis which has developed in the United States can no longer be evaded or ignored.

Several of these observers, such as social scientist Daniel Moynihan, have pointed out that the rebellions in Newark and Detroit represented the economic protest of thousands who for various reasons are unemployed or underemployed and who, whether referred to as an "underclass" or a "lower class," realize that as conditions now exist they have no hope of fully participating in a modern economy. Others, such as author Piri Thomas,[1] have observed that overt violence generally can be traced to youngsters and young adults swept up in the excitement provided by the

---

From *The Clearing House*, XLII, No. 5 (January, 1968), 274-277. Used by permission of the author and publisher.

[1] Piri Thomas, "A Nightmare Night in 'Mi Barrio,' " *The New York Times Magazine*, August 13, 1967, pp. 16+.

chance to recklessly discharge accumulated anger and hostility which have been building over a long period of time.

These two observations are not mutually exclusive, nor do they exclude other factors which have been cited as igniting the spark that turns a smoldering fire into a raging eruption. There is evidence, for example, that organized effort by so-called black nationalist groups and by politically-radical elements played some part in fomenting the riots and in keeping them boiling after they started, and it is also widely recognized that small incidents involving the police can set off fireworks by bringing to the surface many years of intemperate and hostile relationships between law enforcement officials and the inhabitants of low-income ghettoes.

None of these explanations are fully satisfactory, however, because they miss the underlying cause which, unless adequately understood and dealt with, may eventuate in immeasurably more horrible confrontations in the future; the fact that in most large urban centers in the United States anywhere from one-fifth to two-fifths of the population consists of low-income people compressed into overcrowded and deteriorating communities where they feel—with good reason—that the mainstream of American life has passed them by.

As the United States has grown and as people have poured into the cities from rural areas, these neighborhoods have become so large that the social institutions which once reached into them with some effectiveness can no longer do so. Parents, as a result, are losing control of their children, who have become the victims of all the negative and soul-destroying influences that exist in the big city. That adults in the low-income core parts of the cities are losing an often desperate struggle to socialize their children in the middle-class goals of hard work and moderation is not very surprising, since the slums, as Joseph Lyford points out in an important book[2] about New York's West Side, exist precisely in order that the larger community may have a place to exile antisocial individuals unable to "make it" in polite society. Most people who live in the slums, however, bitterly resent the fact that their community is a malignant "dumping ground" for the rest of the nation.

Add to this the fact that many of the poor are non-whites whose residence in low-income ghettoes is an ever-present and inescapable reminder that forces beyond their control will seemingly forever limit their social as well as geographical mobility no matter how hard they might strive or how much they might achieve, and it is clear that one has sufficient incendiary materials to set off the most spectacular of explosions.

[2] Joseph Lyford, *The Airtight Cage* (New York: Harper and Row), 1965.

Behind all the specific causes which turn incipient brush fires into raging conflagrations, then, is the general bitterness and alienation created when large numbers of people live in circumstances which encourage them to see themselves as being deprived of and cut off from opportunities and rewards available to millions of persons in more fortunate communities.

The possibility that disastrous domestic conflict will recur is likely to exist as long as masses of the poor, particularly the non-white poor, live separated from their fellow man in socially stratified slums and racially segregated ghettoes. Recognizing also that very few teachers are able to conduct effective instructional programs in the fact of the alienation and the multiple social pathologies which permeate the inner-city classroom, it follows that the abolition of segregated educational patterns which help keep youngsters boxed in entirely low-income surroundings must be considered a priority goal for all educators. Granted that unemployment and intolerable housing conditions are more directly implicated as causes of violent social upheaval, it is also true that school experiences not only teach vocational skills needed to compete in an industrial society but also communicate attitudes and values which determine whether a student feels sufficiently a part of the larger society to function well in it or is alienated from it and unable to accept the demands it makes on him. The school may not be able to reach the present "lost generation" of hostile and embittered young adults and adolescents who are products of the segregated residential and educational patterns of the recent past, but it can provide desegregated educational experiences that combat the pervasive feeling of exclusion and isolation which is already beginning to cripple subsequent generations of younger students now growing to maturity in the inner core slums.

How well are we doing as a profession in helping to break down the barriers which separate Americans of differing social class and racial groups from each other? Judging by the fact that the overwhelming majority of low-income students are in predominantly low-income schools and the overwhelming majority of non-white students are in predominantly non-white schools, we have not been very successful in working to counteract the forces which lead to stratification and segregation in school district attendance patterns. Given the strength of these forces, it is patently unfair to expect the schools to fully overcome stratification and segregation created by other economic, political, and social institutions. Yet, the schools could do much more to destratify and desegregate attendance patterns than is now being done. Instead, we have allowed ourselves to be all but immobilized by what can be aptly characterized as the *"Yes, but"* Syndrome.

There are many manifestations of this syndrome at work with regard to the goals of placing youngsters in comprehensive-type schools which are not limited to a single social class or social group. One such example arises whenever educators pay verbal homage to this goal but show in their behavior that it is a low priority goal for them, a goal insufficiently important to warrant actually doing something to achieve: "*Yes,* it is desirable to have integrated education, and I am glad when Negro students enroll in previously all-white schools, *but* we are helpless to achieve more integration because to do so would require assigning some children to schools outside their immediate neighborhood." Thus it is assumed that traditional patterns of school district organization are somehow sacrosanct, and can brook neither reconsideration nor modification.

Similarly, the certainty that the schools cannot in the foreseeable future provide integrated educational experiences for every student—cannot, in other words, accomplish everything with respect to desegregation—becomes somehow transposed into the very different and illogical assertion that the schools cannot accomplish anything in the direction of desegregation, as when educators have argued: "*Yes,* segregation in education is undesirable and should not exist, *but* thousands of Negro students are piled up in the inner city far away from areas where whites are willing to attend school, and this prevents us from taking steps to reduce segregation."

When it comes to recent proposals for school district cooperation in allowing a limited number of non-white pupils from the city to attend suburban schools or to establish and maintain contacts among students and teachers of differing racial groups within the city districts or between city and suburban districts, once again verbal agreement about the importance of desegregation is all but universal, while willingness to act on this conviction has been evident in only a bare handful of suburban districts in the United States: "*Yes,* I sympathize with the problems the city schools are facing and feel that our predominantly-white student bodies would benefit greatly from contacts with non-white peers, *but* many of the parents in my district would oppose such programs and might even challenge them in the courts, so our hands are tied and there is nothing we can do to help our administrative colleagues in the cities."

Similarly, many suburban educators are aware of the existence of new curriculum materials, such as the basal readers published by the Ginn and Scott Foresman Companies, which show non-whites interacting in everyday surroundings with whites and which are every bit as good as previous versions that portrayed American society as if it consisted only of whites.

Yet, so few suburban school districts are taking advantage of the opportunity to replace materials which perpetuate racism by ignoring the fact that non-whites constitute a significant group in American society that one can almost hear educators in positions of authority attempting to excuse this inexcusable failure by pleading, *"Yes,* it is desirable to use multi-ethnic readers which make students aware that the United States is a pluralistic nation with diverse groups of people in it, *but* many of our clients are so imbued with racism that they would be alarmed and would register complaints at something so small as the appearance of non-whites in the school textbooks of their children."

It is impossible to deny that the educator in the grip of the *"Yes, but"* syndrome makes points which are valid if considered only in and of themselves. The inadequacy of this response, however, is clear the moment it is recognized that our nation as we now know it today may be doomed unless the schools, like every other key institution in our society, place paramount emphasis on the elimination of social and racial divisions which are moving us rapidly toward a state of continuous civil war. How responsible, in this context, is the superficially-defensible response of the educator whose position is epitomized by a line of reasoning which argues, *"Yes,* I realize that unless we turn out citizens who will practice brotherhood in their daily lives our country will be destroyed by hatred and violence, *but* our job in the schools is to concentrate on academic achievement and not try to solve social problems which we had no part in creating"?

How pick the most suitable terms to describe the crisis toward which we are drifting? Conflagration? Race and class warfare? Mass slaughter? Insurrection?

How pick the most suitable terms to describe the reaction-to-date of the educational profession in the face of this threat? Inaction? Apathy? Irresponsibility? Passivity?

It little matters which terms are chosen, since any of those in the second set can be paired with any from the first set to portray the general failure of nerve in a profession in which many once took great pride and showed great courage concerning their efforts to establish the foundations for a genuinely pluralist society. How sad that as a profession we have succumbed to the shortsighted *"Yes, but"* syndrome which is almost diametrically opposed to the school's historic mission as the crucible for pluralism in the United States.

WHERE SCHOOLS FIT IN THE MODEL CITIES PROGRAM

Seymour Rosenthal
and George Arnstein

The new Model Cities Program is not specifically designed to produce·
model cities; it does hope to have local leaders in towns and cities select a
substandard neighborhood, then devise an imaginative, far-reaching plan for
action to demonstrate that these neighborhoods can become visibly better
places to live. In this sense the selected neighborhood will become a model
for other parts of the city and for other cities as well.

FREE THINKING ENCOURAGED

The demonstration program began in 1967 when nearly 200 cities from
every region applied for planning grants. After May 1, the Washington staff
in the Department of Housing and Urban Development (HUD) reviewed
these proposals in the light of many criteria—local leadership, imagination
and initiative, and, above all, for evidence that the many different
components formed a cohesive unity and a commitment to overcome a
variety of substandard conditions which have torn apart the fabric of many
communities.

To repair and strengthen this fabric, the HUD guidelines sought to
encourage a "free zone of thinking"—a re-examination of current restrictions, attitudes and concepts toward institutions and people. The objective
is to encourage more experimentation and demonstration with the real
beneficiaries to be the residents of the selected Model City neighborhood.

If the parents and children of a given neighborhood are convinced that
education has nothing in it for them, there is little hope that a new,
well-designed school building will be truly successful. Similarly, there is
little to be said for a superb vocational guidance setup if there is no access
to jobs in the target area or in the city at large. A good job development
plan is probably doomed if there is no public transportation or an
ineffective system of communication. What ties together these and other
components of a good plan is the deliberate involvement of the citizens
and the active participation of all segments of the target area and its
population in the decision-making process.

From *Nations' Schools*, LXXX, No. 3 (September, 1967), 59-60 and 80. Used by
permission of the authors and publisher.

Schoolmen have long practiced community relations. They know it means more than an occasional newsletter or an unending series of PTA meetings. What is becoming obvious, however, is that community relations efforts have been most successful when aimed at the middle class. What has not been successful in many community relations programs is an active participation by the unorganized, the poor, the parents of the disadvantaged students from substandard homes.

Of the nearly 200 communities that have submitted proposals for planning grants, approximately 80 model cities will be selected as recipients. They will receive federal funds to translate their proposals into detailed plans that will then be supported by available federal funds from a variety of federal granting programs with different funding formulas. Also necessary are local public funds and participation by private organizations that take their civic responsibilities seriously.

To make these plans as good as possible, local agencies will have available, in addition to their own resources, consultants who can be employed through planning grants as well as technical assistance from various federal offices.

TRY OUT YOUR NEW IDEAS

For school administrators, the Model Cities program can be the vehicle that permits them to put into practice ideas and programs which, for a variety of reasons, have not been possible in the past. Example: The student who comes to school hungry has not been a good learner, for obvious reasons. Responsibility for this has been fragmented. The welfare department is supposed to look after his physical needs, the housing inspectors worry about the rat problem, the health department tries to contain or prevent epidemics, while the schools seek to educate. Even if the schools want to operate a breakfast program, a restrictive budget usually makes it difficult to stage a meaningful program.

The Model Cities program seeks to change this into an articulated, joint program by encouraging the local agencies to work together, to engage in a form of social systems analysis and design based on an interdisciplinary and interdepartmental commitment. Instead of by-passing the parents who hate the school, who denounce the landlords, and who blame the police, the Model Cities concept rests on two basic ingredients:

The complexity of modern society requires a pooling of knowledge and a sharing of resources.

An effective plan must be conceived with the active involvement of the citizens who are to be the beneficiaries. This will bring better understanding of the problem and diminish the accusations so often voiced against well-meaning social agencies.

The plan that emerges from this approach may differ sharply from what has gone before, but it should have a better chance of success. In many ways the interdisciplinary concept of Model Cities planning may be taken as an example of the systems approach. First, there is a statement of goals—specific, detailed outcomes to be sought through the plan. The goal, in the words of President Johnson, is: "To build not just housing units, but neighborhoods, not just to construct schools, but to create beauty and end the poisoning of our environment."

The specific local goals will vary from city to city but all of the plans will be based on HUD guidelines that spell out necessary components such as manpower development and education, health services and housing, transportation and welfare services. These and other components must be pulled together to reinforce each other rather than to survive as disparate pieces.

The comprehensive Model Cities approach seeks to avoid debacles like a crash program to build swimming pools without a budget for lifeguards, or to provide adult literacy classes with no plan to get the word to the target audience (except for stories in the daily press which illiterates can't read). Such efforts are ineffective. What the Model Cities program hopes to achieve is coordinated effort with a democratic framework headed by local leaders. The HUD staff knows that most local school boards and their superintendents value their autonomy and their non-political status. So does the Model Cities program, which is based on the assumption that local leadership and local efforts, supplemented by consultants as needed, can harmonize their interests to produce a comprehensive plan. The result is to be a whole greater than its parts, with the school playing a crucial role as an instructional center, as a physical focus for the neighborhood, and with education as the crucial ingredient enabling the target population to help itself.

HERE COME ALL-DAY SCHOOLS

Many of the applications included the concept of the "lighted school" to be open 24 hours a day, seven days a week. Through a combination of technical courses, regular academic offerings, and an enlarged array of community services, the "lighted school" is to be a literal and figurative beacon for all age groups.

Several communities included in their applications an understanding of the hereditary nature of poverty, calling for adult education as a means of breaking the cycle of poverty and increasing the familywide appreciation of education. A frequent proposal called for family nights at the school and other devices to involve parents and adults in educational activities.

In the Model Cities proposals are plans for the use of teacher aides and other nonprofessionals in many community services. There are calls for remediation, for upgrading of vocational education, and for industry-planned training programs. Particularly frequent are calls for educational parks, which are seen not so much as a solution to the classroom shortage but rather as a means of dealing with patterns of segregated housing and schooling and as a means of overcoming the disadvantages of the ghetto.

While educational forces have been accused of being resistant to change, a new resolution adopted by the NEA in July 1967 recognizes that many inner-city schools do not provide adequate education. The resolution calls for higher-than-average funds and compensatory education, then explicitly says that "education must transcend present patterns of urban school organization, programs and staff."

What remains unknown is the gap between paper and reality, between the words submitted by the authors of the proposals and the actual programs which will be launched with 80 per cent federal funds later this year. Here are some sample proposals:

City A has devised these approaches: It hopes to hold adult education classes in problem-solving technics, home management, consumer education skills, and job retraining based on modern equipment. *City A* hopes to use its high schools for the formulation of job market projections.

City A also has developed the concept of master teachers for the model neighborhood area. These teachers would spend one year studying the particular problems of the urban disadvantaged before they would qualify for this position. The master teachers would then head teams of professionals who would seek to reach every facet of the life of disadvantaged youths from Model Cities areas.

In recognition of the sometimes disruptive home atmosphere in the neighborhood the planners utilized the "cottage school." These schools would serve as overnight residences for preschool children from age 2 through 5. Similar to Head Start in theory, these schools would give the children the remedial education necessary to begin their formal education at the average national level.

City B wants an educational park for all grades, kindergarten through adult. This huge complex would be so situated as to cut across ethnic and economic barriers. The park concept would enable all ages to share common art and music facilities, libraries, gymnasiums and vocational workshops. This pooling of resources would provide funds for the best possible facilities, including the more efficient utilization of classrooms in this city of changing school populations.

City C has enlarged plans, all of which have been started in the first three years to enhance the opportunities of disadvantaged Negro youth. One project includes a series of recorded interviews with 60 Negroes prominent in a wide variety of occupations. The interviews are periodically broadcast over the radio and have been utilized by local guidance counselors as well. The second plan seeks to establish a personal relationship between the underprivileged pupil and an adult volunteer, who may be a teacher, a religious representative, or any interested local citizen. With one trip each month to nearby cultural, recreational and educational facilities, the project hopes to broaden the perspective of the student. City C also has established intercultural libraries to engender self-respect and self-confidence in minority groups of the area.

City D proposes "Great High Schools," a group of five comprehensive, strategically located high schools to serve the entire city. From 5,000 to 6,000 students are expected to attend each of these complexes which, by their very size, will be able to offer more than 100 vocational and technical programs. The Great High Schools will be located so as to bring together students from different sections of the community.

City D also wants nongraded sections for each class. Students will be able to progress at a rate commensurate with their abilities without the stigma of flunking a grade and without the delays which lead to boredom for other students.

City E proposes centers of innovation. Involving preschoolers through Grade 2, these centers would invite special teachers to develop new curriculums and teaching methods. The centers would function as a training base for teaching staff aides and community workers. Community involvement is an explicit goal.

City F visualizes an educational mall similar to the educational park plan. The educational mall seeks to maximize the facilities open to all neighborhood schools by pooling their resources. The mall will be situated between existing schools. It seeks to retain the intimate environment of the scattered schools while creating a large functional structure.

Given the newness of the Model Cities concept, it is not surprising that many of the applications show only a partial awareness of an overall approach to education.

There is a recurring weakness in the failure to include a truly comprehensive approach, reflecting in part the historic separation between city hall and the school administration building. The gap is not easy to bridge but the Model Cities staff hopes that the selected cities will use their planning grants to forge stronger bonds among the various specialists who have been concerned with health, nutrition, housing, education and social services, but who have not always used their special skills to help each other.

LIFE IN THE YEAR 2000

Constantinos A. Doxiadis

How will we ameliorate conditions of our life, of our educational system, of our human settlements? Dealing merely with the present is unrealistic because by the time we have analyzed the situation, defined our problems, and planned how to meet them, the present has become the past; by the time we are ready to act and create new conditions, the present is a distant past.

It is time that we learned to think about the present as a dynamically changing situation. If we wish to ameliorate the conditions of our life, we have to think far ahead in order to understand where we are going and to define whether we like our destination or not. If we do not like it, we must decide how we can take a different road at some time in the future, which, when we act, will be the present.

It is for these reasons that we must start thinking about life in the year 2000, life in the year 2050, life in the year 2100. If we can project our thinking into the future, if we can understand how life may be then, we will be able to help ourselves to create a better present, which will happen in the future.

How are we going to live in the year 2000? I have often been asked this question. Reasoning that I should make use of all the facilities offered by Greece's ancient civilization as well as the world's present one to get an answer, I decided to visit the Oracle of Delphi first and put the question to

From *N.E.A. Journal*, LVI, No 8 (November, 1967), 12-14. Used by permission of the author and publisher.

her. This I did some months ago and explained my worries about the contemporary great cities and the course they are following, my worries about the chances for them and the civilization we have created in them to survive. Patiently I waited outside the temple of Apollo for an answer.

The answer I received, scratched on a red tile, was quite typical of the Oracle: "Prospects of survival no death of city." Knowing how the Oracle enjoys playing with people's agony, I tried to puzzle out the prophecy and came up with two different interpretations. The first read, "Prospects of survival? No. Death of city"; the second, "Prospects of survival. No death of city."

Confused, I sat on the marble steps. Finally I decided I would combine modern technology with ancient imaginative capacity and explore the alternatives suggested by the interpretations.

In exploring the foreboding interpretation, I imagined myself taking the helicopter from Delphi (Why shouldn't I? Since helicopter noise does not allow me to be quiet even in Delphi anymore, I might as well make use of one) to the rocketport of Athens. Twenty minutes later, we land at the rocketport of New York City, 200 miles away from the heart of the metropolis. There, I board an airplane which, after a 30-minute delay waiting in line for the takeoff and an even longer one for landing, takes me to the nearest airport, 50 miles from downtown. There, I hail a taxi, which, guided by radar through the thick smog, gets me to my hotel after four more hours. In this way I discover one of the new laws of transportation: the longer the distance, the shorter the time needed to cover it.

Visiting the city is neither easy nor pleasurable. Some friends recommend that I use an oxygen mask; others suggest that I also use a guide. All insist that I should not stay out after sunset. Nobody is allowed to walk anymore, since the machines make walking both a luxury and very dangerous. Someone tells me about the special "walking hall" of our hotel, where a moving carpet gives the opportunity to those who want to move without using their weakened legs to do so, and where special mixtures of oxygen are provided for better breathing. The walking hall is specially recommended for those coming from nonconditioned areas.

I am informed that going out is rather meaningless anyway, since stores and other buildings have not outside windows, and flowers and trees survive only in the mountains. People do not like to meet foreigners; they suffer from all sorts of phobias, and have no time for new contacts, since work, commuting, and visits to their doctors and psychiatrists exhaust them completely.

No prospects of survival here!

Now let's explore in our imagination the more optimistic prophecy. From the temple of Apollo I walk back to my hotel, enjoying the peaceful surroundings, the yellow flowers, and the birds, including an occasional eagle which flies above and below me into the valley. I explain to someone that I have to take the speediest trip to New York and in 10 minutes a plastic bubble is in my room ready for my journey.

I hang my clothes in the bubble's special closet, close its door, lie in its armchair, fasten my belt, and push the buttons—Destination: New York, Waldorf-Astoria Hotel; Meal at 1300 hours G.T.; Passport, Greek 12/31/62; Do not disturb, please; I am not interested in the steward's stories.

My bubble is taken to the basement of the hotel and through an underground tube to the rocketport, loaded on a rocket, to be unloaded in New York, and guided to my hotel room there by another tube, while I work and rest. I know that I am traveling. I don't have any sense of motion.

After seven hours, I am told that I have arrived at the Waldorf. Emerging from my bubble, I leave the hotel for a walk on Park Avenue. Now that cars are all underground, the center section of the Avenue has become a sculpture garden. Here, shaded by trees and surrounded by flowers, a great collection of sculpture ranging from Rodin's to Henry Moore's is exhibited. The garden is flanked by marble pavements for those who wish to stroll along the avenue in the open air and by covered sidewalks for those who wish to window-shop.

Here in the midst of the best that mankind has created, I feel happy that industrial progress has allowed the planned order of New York City to be as enjoyable as the wilderness of the Greek mountains. Buildings and networks of transportation systems and other facilities have developed to the point that they serve man instead of tyrannizing him and imposing their demanding existence on him.

Leaving the world of imagination and poetic license, I turn to the modern methods of forecasting—to science and mathematics—in order to find which one of the two prophecies is the more realistic. There is no answer to this question since the two imaginary trips to New York in the year 2000 are equally possible. Which one we or our children will experience depends not on crystal-ball reading, but on decisions our generation will make.

If we continue to depend on what we like to call "present trends," there will be no hope of avoiding the road leading to disaster. If, for example, we accept as a fact the contaminated atmosphere of our cities, we will lay greater emphasis on the purification of the interiors of our buildings, and we will sell more and more devices to supply oxygen for breathing. This will mean that we will throw the contaminated air out into the public streets as people in the Middle Ages threw sewage. If this process continues, we will become more and more interested in private living space, and less and less in public space. We will become cave dwellers, and our society will disintegrate.

If, on the other hand, we decide that we want to continue only those present trends that serve man, we can start changing the course that we are following. There is no need to produce cars which can go over 100 miles per hour, thereby depriving us of the opportunity and pleasure of walking as free agents, meeting other people, and owning our world.

There is no need to turn man into a slave of the machine. We can get much better service from machines of all kinds if we understand the necessity of preserving human values. With this in mind, we can develop the most elaborate mechanism to serve us, starting with underground systems, which are the natural solution for the proper operation of our cities.

We need to develop the ability to change the course that we are following. In order to do this, we must understand the nature of the present course.

As Winston Churchill very aptly pointed out, we shape our cities and then they shape our way of life. This is an important fact to understand. And we must also understand that since we are shaping cities at random, our way of life is being formed at random.

I will use as an example the way we spend our time, since that is our most precious commodity. Man—in this case the average American citizen—spends 76 percent of his lifetime at home (males 69 percent and females 83 percent), and 24 percent away from it. He spends 36 percent sleeping, 20 percent working, and 10 percent eating, dressing, and bathing. He is left with 34 percent or one-third of his life which he should be able to devote to leisure, pleasure, or thought.

It is this one-third which constitutes the basic difference between man and animal. But males between 20 and 59 have only 20 percent of free time, of which some spend 90 minutes and others 3 hours in commuting. This means that such men are deprived of from one-third to two-thirds of their free time—the time that makes the great difference between a man and an animal, a free citizen and slave.

This waste of our most valuable commodity results from the fact that nobody plans our way of living and nobody facilitates it. Anybody is free to waste our energy by forcing us to wait longer at red lights, or by requiring us to cover longer distances, or by releasing contaminated air and exhaust fumes into our streets.

I think that it is important for us to remember that our houses and our factories, the corresponding ways of living or producing, follow our decisions but our cities do not. No businessman would allow me to sell him a factory plan without guaranteeing special economic performance, and he would not allow any machine to be included if it did not serve his goals. Not so in our cities; we all make decisions; we all produce; we throw all this into our cities and then we wonder why they are so bad; or maybe we get used to our urban environment and consider the great unreasonable heap of produce that we are building around us to be the city of man of which we can be proud.

It is time for us to understand that the way we are going to live in the year 2000 depends on the decisions we are going to make now. We cannot only predict; we have to decide.

A RATIONAL FAITH IN EDUCATION

George S. Counts

We in the United States have a long record of faith in both the *power* and *beneficence* of education. And we have commonly identified education with the work of the school. From early times we have associated education with the advance of civilization and the cause of human freedom. During colonial days, even as we struggled to survive in a strange land, we nurtured this faith. The founders of the Republic, under the influence of the revolutionary thought of the age in both Europe and America, believed that the strength of the new nation would depend on the spread of learning and enlightenment. "If the condition of man is to be progressively ameliorated, as we fondly hope and believe," wrote Thomas Jefferson, father of our democracy, "education is to be the chief instrument in effecting it." The great champions of popular liberty throughout our national history have generally insisted that the survival of free institutions requires an educated people. Horace Mann, father of the common school, a school open to all children regardless of class, religion,

From *Teachers College Record*, LIX, No. 5 (February, 1958), 249-257. Used by permission of the author and publisher.

or family circumstance, expressed the sentiments of succeeding generations when he said: "The Common School is the greatest discovery ever made by man." And the National Education Association chose as the slogan for its one-hundredth anniversary in 1957: "An educated people moves freedom forward." So, when confronted with difficult personal or social problems in the present critical epoch, we are inclined to turn to education as an unfailing solution.

Our historic faith has been translated into vigorous and sustained action. In 1837 Francis J. Grund, a Bohemian-born and Austrian-educated American writer, observed that "with the exception of Protestant Germany, there is no country in which so much has been done for the education of children, as in the United States of America." During the next century we developed a comprehensive system of public schools which has challenged and influenced the educational thought and practice of the Old World. In our justly celebrated "educational ladder" we repudiated the European aristocratic idea of separate schools for the "classes" and the "masses" and established the *principle* of a single educational system for all the people. Reaching from the kindergarten to the graduate and professional faculties of the university and designed to shatter the time-honored social barriers to advanced training, it is one of the finest and most distinctive expressions of our democracy. Although the measures adopted have by no means overcome differences in family income and cultural heritage or fully equalized educational opportunities at the higher levels, our secondary schools and colleges probably enroll as many young people from fourteen to twenty-two years of age as the corresponding institutions of all the rest of the world. Moreover, wherever the system of rigid social classes is rejected the "educational ladder" is welcomed.

The contribution to our democracy of this vast network of schools can scarcely be overemphasized. If they were to be closed for a generation, our entire economic and political fabric would disintegrate and we would be forced back to some relatively primitive and simple mode of life. That there are grave defects and shortcomings in both the conception and the administration of our schools must be granted. Yet with all their deficiencies they constitute one of the glories of our Republic.

Our faith in the beneficence of schools, however, has ofttimes been uncritical and superficial. As a people we have rarely, if ever, inquired deeply into the social, moral, and cultural foundations of education. We have failed to give sufficient thought to the diversity of educational conceptions and programs in history and in the contemporary world. We have equated education with enlightenment and enlightenment with education. We have assumed it to be a process that goes on more or less naturally and inevitably in the school and is good in any quantity for the ills besetting mankind and for the advancement of popular rule. We have assumed further that in essence it is a single thing, everywhere the same, governed by its own laws, feared by despotisms, and cherished by free peoples. We have tended to identify it with democracy and human progress, not sensing clearly and positively that there is an appropriate education for every society or civilization and that a form which is suited to one may destroy another. Long ago we could have read and pondered with profit the sage observation of Montesquieu that "the laws of education ought to be in relation to the principles of government." If we had, the National Education Association would not be proclaiming without qualification today that "an educated people moves freedom forward."

Our uncritical attitude may have had a certain justification in the nineteenth century when, with a single exception, autocratic states opposed the rounding of schools in order, as we used to say, "to keep their people in ignorance." The case of Prussia, which led the world in the development of an efficient system of elementary education for the masses, was conveniently disposed of as "the exception that proves the rule." We did not realize that the word "proves" in this old English adage actually meant "tests" and consequently implied that if the rule could not embrace the exception the rule itself would have to be abandoned. Certainly the renowned *Volksschule* strengthened rather than weakened the Hohenzollern dynasty. This was demonstrated in the Seven Weeks' War between Prussia and Austria in 1866. "The victory of the Prussians over the Austrians," wrote the German historian Oskar Peschel, "was a victory of the Prussian over the Austrian schoolmaster."

The rise of the contemporary totalitarian states, of the so-called "popular despotisms" of the twentieth century, has made imperative a critical re-examination of our historical conceptions. These states have equalled or surpassed the democracies in their devotion to and support of schools and other forms of organized education, most strikingly perhaps in the case of the Soviet Union. We should know now that literacy, earlier regarded as a reliable index of popular enlightenment, may be an instrument through which a controlled press may enslave a whole people. We should know also that the level of human culture cannot be measured by the number of schools and other agencies maintained by a society for the instruction of the young. Germany under the Nazis and Japan under the military caste were among the most literate and well-schooled lands on the face of the earth. Our traditional faith in education as a liberator of mankind is justified only if education is carefully and effectively directed toward such a purpose.

An unvarnished account of the role of organized education in history from the age of pre-literate man to the middle of the twentieth century fails utterly to support the traditional faith in the beneficence of schools and other agencies for the rearing of the young. The period between the great wars, as we have suggested, is particularly illuminating in this respect. The record should teach us that only an education designed to serve beneficent ends can ever be beneficent in any human conception of the term.

In *The Outline of History,* published in 1920, H. G. Wells, one of the prophets of our time, declared that "human history becomes more and more a race between education and catastrophe." During the 1920's this statement was probably quoted more widely and favorably than any other by educators in the United States. It was clearly in accord with our traditional faith. Early in 1939, in *The Fate of Man,* Wells observed that catastrophe "was well on its way," that education seemed "unable to get started," that indeed it had not even "readjusted itself to start." He concluded with the melancholy thought that "the race may, after all, prove a walk-over for disaster."

We know today that catastrophe triumphed and with terrifying swiftness. What went wrong? Did the nations of the world fail to build enough schools or train enough teachers? Or did education prove to be a feeble force in society? Actually the race was not between education in general and catastrophe, as Wells himself would have been the first to admit. The years between the wars witnessed an unprecedented expansion of organized education, of schools and colleges and other agencies for informing and molding the mind. In fact, never before had the problem of rearing the young and instructing the old received so much attention from the heads of government and the leaders of society. In the United States the number of students attending secondary schools increased from 2,500,000 in 1920 to 6,925,000 in 1940, while the enrollment in higher schools advanced from 750,000 to 1,800,000. During the same period Soviet Russia probably directed a larger *proportion* of the total national income to the support of education than any other country in history. The number of young and old attending schools and classes of all grades and types advanced from eight or nine millions to probably thirty-five millions. Following the Revolution and particularly after the launching of the First Five-Year Plan in 1928 the Soviet leaders conducted the most comprehensive campaign ever attempted to wipe out illiteracy. And the entire cultural apparatus, including the press, the radio, the theatre, the cinema, and even the circus, was directed toward the achievement of educational goals established by the Communist dictatorship. The Axis powers—Germany, Italy, and Japan—spent enormous sums on education and gave as close attention to shaping the minds of children and youth as to the reconstruction of the economy and the strengthening of the armed forces. In many other countries it was an era of educational expansion.

Comparatively little of this expansion was designed to prevent catastrophe. Indeed to a very large degree education between the wars was actually the handmaiden or midwife of catastrophe. This was obviously and avowedly true in the case of the totalitarian states. Children were taught in Italy that the time had come to restore the Roman Empire, that "it is better to live a day as a lion than a thousand years as a lamb"; in Germany that the Nordic race is immeasurably superior to all others, that the Third Reich is justified in extending its boundaries in all directions, that only in war does man fulfill his highest destiny; in Japan that the Japanese are the chosen people of God, that they should rightly covet the orange groves of California, that death in battle for the glory of the Son of Heaven is the most exalted purpose in life. In the Soviet Union the schools were employed to foster the class struggle, to misrepresent the social institutions of "capitalist" nations, and to propagate the doctrine that Russia was the spearhead of a world revolution which in time would spread to all countries and overthrow the existing order everywhere. And the schools in all of these totalitarian states sought to inculcate in the minds of the young blind and fanatical loyalty to the dictatorship. At the same time, no free society anywhere confronted the problem of education boldly and imaginatively. Throughout the world, education, either deliberately or unwittingly, helped to bring upon mankind the disasters that came close to destroying the best in our civilization. At the very least, it was not designed, either in conception or in practice, to oppose the swift advance of catastrophe.

We know today, if we have learned the lesson of the immediate past, that organized education may or may not serve the cause of peace, liberty, and justice on the earth. In fact, we know that it may serve any cause—tyranny as well as freedom, ignorance as well as enlightenment, falsehood as well as truth, war as well as peace, death as well as life. It may even lead men and women to think they are free even as it rivets upon them the chains of bondage. Education is indeed a force of great power, but whether it is good or bad depends, not on the laws of learning, but on the conception of life or civilization which it expresses.

The need today in every free society on the planet is for a great education—great in its conception and great in its operation. It is in such terms that the race, as Wells saw it more than a generation ago, is still on. We live today, to employ Arnold H. Toynbee's phrase, in a "time of troubles," perhaps the most fateful in the whole history of mankind. Since the early years of this century we have been living in a world increasingly strange and even terrifying. We have known an endless succession of crises at home and abroad. We have watched tragedy compounding tragedy in ever-mounting fury. We have seen our seemingly well-founded hopes ground under the heel of events. The solid verities and certainties of the nineteenth century seem to have vanished. Nothing appears to be secure and enduring. Social institutions, human relations, values systems, and conceptions of life and destiny are in flux. Thoughtful men and women everywhere are anxious and fearful about the future. After a retreat of centuries, despotism is on the march again.

In the 1930's we experienced a great economic disaster. At the very moment when our political and industrial leaders in the United States were confidently predicting an enduring and rising prosperity for an unlimited future under an economic system founded on the laws of nature, we were struck by an economic depression which rocked the foundations of the Republic and imperilled the entire free world. The marketing structure collapsed, banks, shops, and factories closed, farms turned backward to self-sufficiency, wheels of transport stopped turning, lifetime savings were wiped out, twelve to fifteen million workers lost their jobs, the total income was reduced by half, and rich and poor alike were gripped by fear. In response to the general distress revolutionary doctrines spread through the land and embryonic dictators on European models appeared in the United States. This traumatic experience tempered somewhat the traditional optimism of our people. Another disaster of such magnitude might bring additional victories to Communist totalitarianism.

Out of the dislocation of institutions, the conflict of classes, rivalries of the past, and the changing power structure of the world have come the great wars, revolutions, and counterrevolutions of our time. On this theme we need not dwell except to observe that a third world war waged with the new and ever more powerful engines of destruction might destroy advanced civilization everywhere and push mankind as a whole back toward barbarism, if it did not destroy the human race. And the epoch of revolution and counterrevolutions probably still has its course to run. It is assumed here that organized education must be conceived in the light of these troubled times and with a faith that it might illuminate the dark road which lies ahead for all mankind.

The twentieth century, as we have noted, has witnessed the growth of organized education and interest in organized education throughout the world. In the United States, as elsewhere, numerous teachers colleges and departments of education in our universities have been established, and an enormous amount of energy has been devoted to the improvement of education. Our literature, both lay and professional, is full of discussions of what is wrong with the school and of proposals to correct its weaknesses. The shelves of our libraries are laden with educational reports, surveys, and studies, including countless doctoral dissertations. New theories and experiments follow one another in an endless stream. This activity is by no means all lost motion; it has undoubtedly resulted in considerable improvement in the conduct of the school. Yet most of it deals with either the surface or the mechanics of the problem. Indeed, some of the most widely and hotly disputed proposals for reform during our generation are little more than nostrums which largely ignore the basic problem of all educational thought—the problem of the relation of education to the nature and fortunes of our civilization in its historical and world setting. Three such proposals have received much attention during the past fifty years.

The first and most fruitful of these proposals is the development of a science of education. Early in the present century the movement to convert education into a science aroused much enthusiasm and led to the launching of innumerable experimental and statistical studies. The learning process and child growth were subjected to tireless inquiry. Every aspect of the school program was brought under investigation. Vast attention was devoted to the perfection of the machinery of education, to the integration of parts, and to the elimination of friction, to the improvement of buildings and equipment, to the standardization of procedures, to the invention of pedagogical gadgets, to the construction of tests and rating scales for both pupils and teachers, and to the keeping of records of all actions and transactions. For a time philosophy was relegated to an inferior position and the prediction was confidently made in some quarters that all educational problems would be solved by the new science. Unfortunately the traditional program of the school was taken for granted and the emphasis laid on increased efficiency in the operation of that program. Education was regarded as an autonomous process which might be studied in isolation from society and civilization and perfected according to its own laws.

That this movement has contributed much of value to the advance of education cannot be disputed. The need today is for a more generous conception of a science of education—a science that is closely integrated with all the other sciences of society and human culture. We must realize that the answers to the most profound questions regarding the conduct of education, questions involving values and purposes, will have to be found outside the school and beyond the imperatives of scientific knowledge. A science can tell us how to produce a warrior or a pacifist, a slave or a free man, but it cannot tell us that we *should do* any one of these things.

Science can penetrate the secrets of the atom, but it cannot tell us whether we should make atomic bombs or convert atomic energy to peaceful purposes. Such questions lie in the realms of ethics and politics.

A second proposal seeks guidance in the interests and problems of children. The presumption here seems to be that the child achieves maturity through a process of spontaneous generation or inner unfoldment which the adult world through its educational agencies should merely guard and nourish. According to this view, the child, and not the teacher or the school, should play the decisive role in shaping both the processes and the ends of education. The interests and problems of boys and girls are assumed to constitute a more trustworthy guide than the experience and wisdom of their elders. It is argued, moreover, that any positive interference by members of the older generation is a form of imposition or indoctrination and is certain to lead to frustration and regimentation of the mind. Here, undoubtedly, is the most romantic interpretation of human nature since Rousseau.

In the proposal, however, there is an important insight. It recognizes the psychological truth that interest is a condition of effective and economical learning. The immediate concerns of the young, therefore, should always play a large role in education. Like the learning process and the "laws of the organism" generally, they provide the limits within which the teachers must operate. But those limits are known to be extremely wide and capricious. We must assume that children in their biological inheritance are essentially alike in all times and places, among all races and peoples, among all groups and classes. Yet their interests vary greatly from epoch to epoch and from society to society. Also they are extraordinarily fluid and subject to change. The interest that a child brings to school in the morning may be the result of the casual conversation of his parents at home, of a radio program devised to sell a hair tonic, of a moving picture produced with an eye on the box office, or of some incident observed in the street or on the highway. The responsibility of the school is not to follow the interests of the young, but rather to assist in arousing and building worthy, fruitful, and abiding interests.

It should be recognized also that this proposal contains a great moral affirmation. In conformity with the democratic ethic, it affirms that the child is a person and that his personality should always be treated with respect and regarded as precious. The historical record of the treatment of the young by their elders, including their teachers, is full of horrors. The liberation of boys and girls from the reign of adult tyranny and ignorance is one of the marks of a humane civilization. Yet respect for the personality of the child is expressed most fully in an educational program dedicated to the development of a mature personality deserving respect. "We see quite clearly," writes the great Polish anthropologist, Bronislaw Malinowski, "why the freedom of the child, in the sense of letting him do what he wishes and as he likes is unreal. In the interest of his own organism he has constantly to be trammeled in education from acts which are biologically dangerous, or which are culturally useless. His whims, his fits of idleness or disobedience must be gradually curtailed, formed and translated into culturally relevant choices. There is also no freedom in action except within the context of organized human groups."* We should never forget that societies rightly establish schools so that the child may become something which otherwise he would not become.

A third proposal which has been before us for about a quarter of a century finds the solution of the educational problem in the study of the so-called "one hundred great books" at the college level and preparation for their study in the lower schools. It must be admitted at once that from the standpoint of the teacher this is the most attractive proposal now current. It is the ideal answer of the pedagogue to the truly perplexing problems confronting education. In the first place, it would give him a virtual monopoly over a special body of knowledge, with no competitors. If he could only convince the other members of society of the worth of this esoteric knowledge, he would be in the enviable position of a long line of ancestors reaching back to the shaman and the medicine man of primitive society. In the second place, once having mastered the "great books" he could pursue his calling for the rest of his life without being disturbed by the issues of depression and prosperity, of war and peace, of tyranny and freedom, of the future of his country and mankind. He could withdraw from the world and dwell all his years in a scholastic paradise. He could be fairly sure, moreover, that only two or three books at most would be added in his lifetime, that their status would be uncertain for at least a century, and that anyway they could not equal in excellence those written by the "ancients" long ago.

The basic argument of the proposal seems to be that education is essentially a process of mental training, that the great literary classics are the finest product of the human mind, and therefore they are the best tools for the training of the mind. As a matter of fact, education is far more than mental training; it is first of all a process of inducting the young into the ways, privileges, and responsibilities of a given society. Also, these classics, precious as they are, cannot be said without qualification to be the

*Bronislaw Malinowski, *Freedom and Civilization* (New York, Roy Publishers, 1944), p. 145.

finest products of the human spirit: they scarcely rank above a great living civilization, a successful system of democratic government, a vast industrial enterprise, a splendid labor union, a famous scientific laboratory, or even a fine human being who possibly never read a single one of them. Likewise, that they are the best tools for the development of the mind is hardly supported either by the history of education or by psychological investigation. Experience suggests rather that this is the surest road that man has yet discovered to formalism, sterility, and stagnation in education. Although the proposal tends to correct the overweening concern of my countrymen for the immediate and the narrowly practical, directs attention to certain sublime achievements of the mind of man, emphasizes the processes of thought and reflection, and stresses universal and enduring elements in the human heritage, it is fundamentally a manifestation of academic nostalgia. It constitutes an attempt to retire, without sacrifice of glory, from the present troubled age.

From some things I have said the reader might infer that I have little faith in the beneficence of education. Such an inference would be a mistake. I share in large measure the historic faith of my people. The education of the younger generation is a sublime trust. With appropriate qualifications, I find myself in accord with the views expressed by the greatest Russian educator of the nineteenth century, K. D. Ushinsky. Even though working in an "impoverished and unpretentious school," he said, the teacher is a "living member of a great organism which is toiling for the perfection of mankind, which is striving for truth and justice." Even though his cause is modest at first sight, it is "one of the greatest causes of history—a cause on which kingdoms and generations rest." Such is the ideal to which we must all subscribe.

Education, however, as we have emphasized, can never be a purely autonomous process, independent of time and place, conducted according to its own laws. There have been as many educations in history as there have been human societies. It is as much an integral part of a culture or civilization as an economic or political system. The very way in which education is conceived, whether its purpose is to enslave or free the mind, is an expression of the society which it serves. Although all educational programs in the world today should embrace the conception of a common humanity, no such program as a whole should be regarded as an article of export either with or without the support of dollars or machine guns. Of necessity an education is a most intimate expression of a particular civilization.

We must seek the broad outlines of a great education therefore, not in the nature of the child, nor in the traditional practices of the school, nor yet in any single segment of our civilization. Such an education must embrace four great tasks in a free society. First of all, it must assure mastery on the part of the younger generation of the essential practical skills and knowledges of the social heritage. Second, it must promote with unflagging zeal an understanding of the world as it is and as it is becoming. Third, it must strive without apology to inculcate in the young loyalty to the great values of a society of free men. Fourth, it must stress the universal in the total human heritage, stimulate the creative faculties of man, and contribute to the advancement of all the humane arts and sciences. Such an education might serve to prevent catastrophe and facilitate the birth of an age of abundance, freedom, justice, beauty, and peace for all mankind.

QUESTIONS FOR DISCUSSION

SOCIAL FORCES

1. How are current social trends affecting schools with which you are familiar?
2. What are the implications of automation and computer technology for the school program? At the elementary level? Secondary level?
3. How can the school curriculum best cope with the "knowledge explosion?"
4. What democratic values should schools try to develop?
5. Do you share E. T. Chase's belief that we have evolved from a "consumption" to a "self-realization" society? If this change is occurring how should the schools reflect the change?
6. Does specialization contribute to individuality? If you agree with Winston White, how will you develop the school program?
7. What is the school's role in the "war on poverty" in America?
8. Do you believe that there is hope for effecting change in our cities?
9. Can education really be a liberator of mankind?
10. Try to summarize the implications of this section for the school curriculum as you view it now.

2 Human Development

The process of human development is generally accepted as one of the bases of the curriculum; most educators believe that the curriculum should be geared to it.

The study of child development is the most widely prevalent aspect of the undergraduate program of teacher education. The study of child and adolescent development is regarded as one of the basic sciences underlying education. Because of this, the study of human development as a part of teacher education is not now the particular property of any one theory of psychology or education.

The human development approach to the curriculum and to teaching includes a body of knowledge about human growth. It also includes a point of view with reference to learners; that they should be studied as individuals, so that the program of instruction can be shaped, in part, by their nature and needs.

The writers have been particularly influenced during the past twenty years by three books, which have attempted to apply knowledge about human development to the curriculum. These books still represent sources of great help to persons seeking to develop adequate understanding of this basis of curriculum planning.

The first of the three, *Child Development and the Curriculum*, by Arthur T. Jersild, first published in 1946, applied many insights about child growth to specific curriculum problems at both the elementary and secondary levels.

Developing a Curriculum for Modern Living first appeared in 1948 and applied the scholarly and extensive study of Florence Stratemeyer, Hamden Forkner, and Margaret McKim to the development of a reasoned theory of the curriculum, which would utilize our knowledge of students as they grow and mature in American society with its democratic orientation and

135

direction. This book presented the useful concept of the "persistent life situation" that learners face. Knowledge of child development and of the nature and values of a particular society were intermingled as the basis of the curriculum.

The third of the three books first appeared in 1953. It was *Human Development and Education* by Robert J. Havighurst. This book utilized physical maturation and cultural pressures and values as the basis of the "developmental task concept." A *developmental task* was defined as a task that arises during a certain period in the individual's life, due to physical maturation, the cultural pressure of society, and personal values and aspirations. Thus this book sought a workable synthesis of the maturational, cultural, social, and personal sources of the curriculum.

In the years that have elapsed since the publication of these three books, much additional information on human development has become available from research in biology, cultural anthropology, social and clinical psychology, social psychiatry, and sociology. The job of synthesizing this new research for application to curriculum development very largely remains to be done. This section attempts to present some of the conclusions of this new research, which should now be included in thinking about human development as a basis of the curriculum.

We are in a much better position today to view human development from the personal, cultural, social, and psychological viewpoints as well as from the biological. We clearly need to correct the earlier tendency to view learners according to patterns standardized for each age group. Although this was never the intention of the three books mentioned, other contemporary sources caused many teachers and parents to "normalize the child" and thus to stunt his individuality and growth.

Although each individual learner has similarities to all other learners, some of his characteristics are similar to those of some other learners only, and many of his most significant needs, interests, and problems are his alone and are characteristic of no other human being. These similarities and differences are now the subject of study by cultural anthropologists and sociologists, as well as by psychologists and biologists. All of these disciplines now provide much that is significant for the planning of the curriculum as it is related to likenesses and differences in human development.

The similarities among students are important in planning the curriculum because they are, to a large extent, instructed in groups. Understanding the likenesses among them aids in the formation of those aspects of the curriculum that may be considered suitable for many students at a particular age or grade level. For planning the curriculum and for teaching, an understanding of each learner's uniqueness is also a necessary guideline, since learning success often is determined largely by differences.

We now possess much greater understanding of the ways that culture, social forces, values, social groups, the family, social class, and peer groups interact with the individual's biological inheritance to affect his development. In addition, there is growing agreement among anthropologists, sociologists, and psychologists that these "external" factors in development must be combined with an understanding of the individual's "internal approach" to the various situational and constitutional factors that affect him. How the individual perceives his body, his home, his school, his family, his community, his daily experiences, and his future life constitute reality for him. Thus the three sources of all human development may be viewed as consisting of: 1) the genetic inheritance of each person, which he derives at the moment of conception from his father and mother; 2) all of the unique experiences he has had in interacting with his culture, beginning immediately after his birth; 3) his perceptions of his body and his social milieu, which determine their meaning for him.

Ira Gordon ("Developments In Human Behavior") describes seven basic concepts emerging in the behavioral sciences that are significant for human development and the curriculum. The concepts he discusses are "process," "the open energy system," "organization," "self," "growth," "individual variability," and "multiple causation."

David P. Ausubel ("Viewpoints From Related Disciplines: Human Growth and Development") presents a number of generalizations based on human growth concepts concerning the elementary and secondary curriculum. He shows that maximum breadth of the curriculum is desirable at all levels because of the wide scope of human abilities. He also analyzes readiness as a criterion for curricular placement, the child's voice in determining the curriculum, and the content and goals of instruction in relation to the organization and growth of intellect.

Jean Piaget is now influencing the curriculum through his ideas about the "stages of growth" in thinking abilities. His stages of "concrete operations" and "formal thinking" may have particular significance for the elementary and secondary school curricula. ("Jean Piaget: Notes on Learning" by Frank Jennings.)

Helen Heffernan and others ("The Organization of the Elementary School and the Development of a Healthy Personality") describe the six stages of growth toward a healthy, mature personality as they are developed by Erik Erikson. These stages are significant for developing the curriculum, according to Dr. Heffernan.

The most widely accepted assumption concerning human development today is probably the recognition of three periods of development: childhood, adolescence, and adulthood. These periods can be recognized psychologically, sociologically, and phsysiologically. The adolescent period has received the most attention during the past decade. The hypothesis that adolescence is a universal period of storm and strife is no longer tenable in the light of many anthropological studies. Bennett Berger, as a sociologist, states that adolescence is a violation of nature by the culture, and persuades us of the justice of the violation ("Teen-Agers Are An American Invention"). He identifies the functions of adolescence in an industrial society and relates them to the high school program.

In "Old Enough To ..." the question of whether eighteen-year olds are ready to assume adult responsibilities is discussed in light of the movement to lower the voting age to eighteen. "Best Years of Our Lives?" (*Newsweek*), tells us that almost a quarter of the U. S. population is made up of middle-agers between 40 and 60; yet there are still many erroneous beliefs about this age group.

Our knowledge of human development is now potentially of much greater help to the curriculum-maker than it has been in the past. Now we know that human development has many determinants and that there is danger in focusing too narrowly on the biological or sociological factors alone. The old argument of heredity versus environment no longer has any meaning, because they are so inextricably intermingled. The school program may contribute more significantly than ever before to the learner's physical, mental, emotional, and social growth, when these aspects of development and their interrelationships are viewed in the perspective of our new knowledge of human development.

DEVELOPMENTS IN HUMAN BEHAVIOR

Ira J. Gordon

It seems to me that we have reached a place in the behavioral sciences where it has become important to stop and take a look at the progress that

From *Educational Theory*, VIII, No. 4 (October, 1958), 259-268 and 274. Used by permission of the author and publisher. A modified form of this material appears as the first chapter of *Human Development: From Birth to Adolescence* (New York: Harper & Row, 1962).

has been made in the development of basic concepts, and to see what suggestions might grow out of this for educational practice and research.

This paper will attempt, therefore, to discuss some of the emerging concepts about human behavior that lie behind the descriptive data and that might be somewhat fundamental in any discussion of the directions for education.

I have selected, or rather ordered or organized, seven concepts for such a discussion. These all overlap to some degree; they are not nice discrete entities—at least they are not in my thinking. Why are there seven rather than another number? Perhaps it is because of the strong Hebraic concern with the magic of the number—seven days for a week, every seventh year a sabbatical one, and so forth—perhaps it's because I gave out of ideas at this point. Whatever the case, here they are:

1. The concept of "process."
2. The concept of "the open energy system."
3. The concept of "organization" and "order."
4. The concept of "self."
5. The concept of "growth."
6. The concept of "individual variability."
7. The concept of "multiple causation."

Each of these will be discussed in turn, including some definition, some discussion of its meaning, and some guesses as to its use in education.

PROCESS

We have been so used to thinking of "things" and "entities" that it is fairly difficult for us to think or feel in terms of ongoingness. We can visualize something in the process of changing continuously through time, but this is not what I mean. It seems to me that the individual is not something "in the process of" but the individual *is* a process or rather a series of interrelated processes.

I should like to explore this notion in terms of one particular facet that I feel is of tremendous importance in the field of human development. This particular notion is that of the inter-relatedness of structure and function. It used to be that we saw these as two discrete "entities" with the notion that structure determined function. We moved in biology, physiology, and other behavioral sciences to a recognition of the "inter-relatedness" of these two—a recognition that not only could structure determine function, but that function in turn could effect structure. It seems to me that we are now reaching the point of seeing structure and function simply as two different approaches to the same thing. It might be said almost that structure *is* the organization of function at a particular moment in space-time.

This is not only in terms of bodily processes where we might say that bone, muscle, etc., are structures, and the behaviors of the person are functions, but this way of seeing structure-function is also to be conceived of in terms of psychological and cultural processes.

For example, in the case of the differentiation of cells so that an animal or a worm differentiates out along a pole from head-to-tail, research has clearly shown that the development of structure is related to location in the field of the animal rather than to a "given" within the cell that is different than the "given" in a cell alongside it or ten cells down the line. As Gerard states: "Clearly there was nothing in the cell itself to determine which of these different paths (i.e. becoming a head or a tail cell) it would follow but only its position relative to the other cells"* so that "the head end gets the bumps and the bumps make the head end."**

Where does such a notion or principle of circularity lead us? First, let me say that this "principle of circularity" is based not only on biological research but also research in the field of perception† and in the field of self-regulating and servo-mechanisms in engineering.†† We can, if we wish to extend this, see that the physicist's definition of the atom is also in terms of process. Even though he uses the word "particles" as though they were actually entities, he *operates* with a recognition that they are not.

Let us now look at the meaning of this for us. First of all, by conceiving of the individual as an organization of processes all reciprocally related, it becomes easier to break down any mind-body dichotomy. It provides a background for understanding psychosomatic dynamics. It frees us, to some degree, from dealing with "givens" as though they were insurmountable barriers—for example, "native intelligence" becomes virtually meaningless as a "given." It makes more understandable several other concepts we will discuss, such as the extremely fascinating, implication-wise, generally accepted in lip service notion of individual variability.

It helps us to get away from some limits that are perhaps self-imposed as to the growth potential of the human being. For example, we are

---

*R. W. Gerard, *Unresting Cells* (New York: Harper & Brothers, 1949), pp. 359 - 360.
**Ibid., p. 357.
†F. Allport, *Theories of Perception and the Concept of Structure* (New York: John Wiley, 1955).
††N. Weiner, *The Human Use of Human Beings* (New York: Doubleday, 1954).

finding that, in relation to developmental norms in the United States, "the norms are in the process of changing . . . there is evidence that growth and rate of development in the present generation of North American infants has significantly advanced over the norms established on the Gesell, Cattell and Viennese infant development scales."*

In education, it may mean that seeing a child as constantly "becoming" gives a new impetus to seeing the teacher's role as being concerned with the processes of experiencing, particularly as they are perceived by the child, rather than being concerned with an end-product defined in terms of containment of so much knowledge, so much skill, thus-and-such an attitude, as though both the culture and the child were static or at best dynamic entities in constant contact with each other.

THE OPEN ENERGY SYSTEM

All living organisms can be defined as open energy systems or at least semi-closed systems. A system is an organized "something" that has a direction to it and some degree of internal unity. An organism as a system is partly continuous with its environment. In an open system such as an organism "there is a continuous input from the environment and a continuous output of products of the system's action."**

The system is greatly affected by the environment, and is not to be considered or understood apart from the situation in which it is. We cannot look at the system in isolation; we cannot understand the individual apart from the culture which has influenced and is continuing to influence him.

There are several characteristics of such a system: it maintains a "steady state," that is, it attempts to maintain its own integrity and balance of forces within the system. It does not reach "equilibrium"—this is death. It is constantly and continuously active, indeed this is its most outstanding characteristic.

In addition, the notion of ceaseless activity does not mean uncontrolled activity. The system has "built-in" regulators which we will look at in the next section. In this maintenance of a "steady state," the organism is not merely responding to the external environment but also to the "milieu interieur." Cannon's concept of "homeostasis" fits here.

Activity is ever present—even activity in the conceptual nervous system

*E. Jackson, "Child Development Patterns in the United States," In K. Soddy (Editor), *Mental Health and Infant Development* (New York: Basic Books, 1956), pp. 87–88.
**Allport, *op. cit.*, p. 471.

(CNS) is continuous. This CNS activity is self-sustained and does not rely on input of nervous energy from without. These circuits reverberate and are circular. To some degree, these circuits are sub-systems maintaining their own order and integrity. In terms of motivation, this has many implications, some of which we will look at at the end of the section on "self." These circular causal processes lead us to our third concept, which is perhaps the central concept or keystone of this paper, and that is the notion of "organization" or "order" or "control."

ORGANIZATION

We have said that a system by definition has an organization. We said of structure that it is momentary organization. An organism by definition is an organization.

An open energy system has a particular kind of organization or order. It is not like a building—the organization of the individual is organizing, ordering activity. A characteristic of such a system is direction—it can only go forward; it can't reverse itself as a closed system can. This order or organization, then, is a *directional* one—as seen in such activities as growth, learning, goal-setting, etc. It maintains its organization through activity, but it organizes this activity in a systematic way.

". . . living things do not just blindly explode their energy stores in response to environmental vicissitudes; they also direct them. The organism must maintain its complex integrity against the hostile forces of confusion, it must fend the 'slings and arrows of outrageous fortune' and so counter or adjust to the surrounding environmental whirl that it remains itself and yields as little as may be necessary. The more it changes the more it remains the same. True, over longer times, covering the evolution of the race or even the development of the individual, progressive change is a vital part of the life picture, and again along regular rather than random lines. But from moment to moment the individual acts to preserve itself in its current state. To environmental changes, or stimuli, living things respond adaptively, they make such changes in their behavior as most effectively preserve the status quo."*

How does the organism control its activity? What determines its direction of energy? At this stage, we are able only to theorize and hypothesize about these questions. But there are clues which come to us from biology, from cybernetics, from perceptual psychology.

*Gerard, *op. cit.*, pp. 211–212.

For example, from cybernetics we have the notion of "negative feedback" and the notion mentioned earlier of "built-in regulators." The basic homeostatic processes controlling the physical and chemical properties of the blood stream are examples of the operation of negative feedbacks.

This control is accomplished through the sending of information from tissues to the CNS, which then sends out impulses to bring the system back to a steady state. While control seems to reside in the CNS, any sub-system or tissue system can be the instigator of new activity. The CNS itself, since it is always active, can instigate organized activity.

The concept of "order" needs to be examined here. We have the idea that the universe is running down, that while we cannot reduce the amount of energy in the universe, the amount of useful energy is constantly being dissipated. The world, in effect, is becoming more disordered and disorganized. This concept of movement toward complete randomness is known as entropy. In seeming contradiction to this, the organism, when viewed as a system, is becoming more ordered, more organized, and is using its energy more efficiently. Organisms are characterized by their ability to wrench order from disorder or by negative entropy. We can look at this in the following fashion. The food we take in is free energy; we convert it into tissue; we store it as fat; we burn it up in behavior. We burn some of it up in the process of converting it into tissue and fat as well, so it is lost. But the remarkable thing is that we *can* convert and store it for future use. There is another kind of "energy" we take in—this is stimulus energy, or information. This can come either from outside the system or from within. In either case information serves to bring order out of chaos, to organize the system. Information is the reciprocal of entropy. Food energy provides the wherewithal; information provides the direction, the order, the organization.

All of this may seem very removed from education at the classroom level. Are there any meanings we can draw from this?

First, we are saying that the individual is always active, is in constant transaction with the environment, is always moving in the direction of increased complexity, and acts to order himself and his environment. We are imputing *direction* to him, and, in addition, we are saying the direction choice is within the system. As Freeman states:

"We are justified in taking this egocentric view, which says in effect that man conceives his world; for in the interests of preserving internal constancies, the exterofective system develops and maintains optimal external constancies. By means of overt reaction to specific external stimuli, the human organism stabilizes and betters its surroundings, eliminates potential dangers. . . . From our point of view, these self-constituted surroundings *are* the organism, and the behavioral processes by which they are maintained are homeostatic-regulatory. That is to say that a slander is just as much a threat to a man's good name—built up by a series of elaborate exterofective behaviors—as is a change in oxygen supply a threat to essential life processes. The organism will react to both displacements with behavior calculated to restore balance and equilibrium. The only difference in the two examples is that the 'good name' constancy is not nearly as stable and universal as is the oxygen requirement."*

It must be remembered, however, that the system includes the environment through the internalization of past experiences and the present field of forces.

Furthermore, this concept of organization presents another focus for us. This drive for order pervades the individual organism and the society. Order and predictability are security-giving. The gestalt concept of "closure" is an example of this. We perceive order, we *create* order where the field is such that there is a semblance of completeness. We attempt to see things as closed when they are not, because the closed system is more satisfying.

We are not only trying constantly to organize our world, we then get caught, so to speak, in our organization. It requires too much energy to change an organization. We maintain it even when, like the appendix, it may have outlived its usefulness. The organization becomes an end in itself. It becomes a dynamic. We tend to treat it not as our creation, but as a "given." We surrender to it some of our power. For example, social institutions, clubs, committees, etc., become self-perpetuating. Nobody questions their existence; or, if someone does, he's reminded that "we've done it this way for 87 years. . . ."

Our drive for order and organization, then, is what makes us, to some degree, human—it helps to explain our behavior as individuals because we strive to grow and perpetuate our organization. It helps explain individual resistance to change as well as cultural lags and the perceptions of social institutions as sacred and having an existence of their own apart from people.

In classroom operation, it means that pupils' needs for order need to be satisfied. I'm not talking about "discipline," but their need to see that the class or course has some system, some direction to it, whatever the particular organization may be. For example, introduction of newer teaching methods reflecting research in group processes or psychotherapy

*G. L. Freeman, *The Energetics of Human Behavior* (Ithaca, New York: Cornell University Press, 1948), pp. 146–7.

can be threatening to pupils when they perceive these approaches either as lacking any organization or as violating their already developed concepts of what a classroom situation "should be."

THE CONCEPT OF "SELF"

One way of seeing and labelling these organizing processes of the individual by which he attempts to structure his world is by using the concept of "the self." This permits us at one and the same time to talk about the consistency of an individual's organization and its ongoingness. Self here is defined as the processes by which an individual organizes the organism pole of the constantly fluid organism-environment field. The self-system might be defined as "what is" organized at a given moment.* As a part of one's self-system are those highly differentiated, integral, fairly persistent aspects which are one's concepts of himself. As Snygg and Combs say, "the self-concept includes those parts of the phenomenal field which the individual has differentiated as definite and fairly stable characteristics of himself."** This self-system fits the criteria for definition of an open-energy system—it attempts to maintain a "steady state"; it has direction to it; it has some degree of internal consistency; it is in continuous transaction with its environment. While its atomistic ingredients change—cells die and are replaced, behaviors, too, die and are replaced—the system goes on and has a recognizable identity. This recognizable identity, behavior-wise, is a function of the self-system and to a great degree of its self-concepts. By analogy, today's members of the First Division still wear the fourragère awarded to the Division by the French in World War I. I would guess that nobody in the present division was there at the time, but the identity of the Big Red One is continuous. Stretching a little bit, while we cannot predict the behavior of an individual soldier in the division, we might predict that the unit as a whole would maintain its organization, its traditions, etc., in battle. We might predict the future performance of the organization by knowing its present identity—its present self-system, and its concept of itself as visually displayed on the shoulders of its members.

The self-system, then, is at one and the same time a resultant of all the previous organism-environment transactions and it is one of the transactees. It is acting and being acted upon. We said the self has direction—it is going

*I. J. Gordon, *The Teacher as a Guidance Worker* (New York: Harper and Brothers, 1956), p. 168.
**Snygg and Combs, *Individual Behavior* (New York: Harper and Brothers, 1949), p. 112.

somewhere. This direction is not only in terms of time's arrow, but also in terms of purposes or goals. We can only understand the behavior of a person when we have some understanding of what he is striving *toward*.

The whole organism is goal-oriented. Understanding of self, then, means becoming aware of not where a person has been so much as becoming aware of *where he is going*. For education this has many implications. Education is concerned with present and future; the self-system is concerned with present and future. The past, of course, is embodied in the present and future. Both are goal-directed. The first task of the teacher is the clarification of goals—his own and his pupils'. This requires that he have a knowledge of the goals of man—the nature of the beast, so to speak—and then an understanding, as best he can, of the self-systems of his individual students. What are the goals of Man?

THE CONCEPT OF "GROWTH"

Growth may be seen as the ability and activity of the organism to preserve its steady state independent of its original conditions. For our purposes here growth may also be defined as the entire series of anatomic and physiologic changes, thus combining growth and maturation. Both increase in size and increase in complexity are growth processes. Growth itself is a "goal" of organisms. As a way of maintaining organization in a fluid environment, the organism reaches out into it, incorporates it both physically and psychologically, "feeds" on it (remembering our earlier statement about information being the reciprocal of entropy), and grows. While growth as increase in size stops, growth as increase in organization and complexity continues throughout the life cycle. At the risk of being teleological, the organism has growth as a goal or purpose. Growth is a means for maintaining organization and is also a directional process of organization.

Thus, a basic goal of man is continuous growth. This means a reaching out for experience, a curiosity, a need for coming to grips with his environment, a terrific urge to learn. As one of my undergraduates put it, a "ravishing appetite for knowledge." Cantril states: "the outstanding quality of man's motivation . . . appears to be a desire to bring forth and experience the value aspects latent in every concrete behavior."* He further says: "man is constantly making his environment more 'human' by extending his understanding of the significances of events or happen-

*Hadley Cantril, "The Qualities of Being Human." *American Quarterly*, VI, No. 1 (Spring, 1954), 8.

ings." * Man hunts for significance, for meaning in his world. He orders this world in terms of meaningfulness.

Man grows as he organizes. His goal is the development of a whole person, enhancement of the experiencing organism. As Sinott puts it, "the goal of the organizing process is a single, whole individual." **

Individual development can be seen, then, as the processes by which a person, from the moment of birth on, works toward self-actualization, fulfillment, completeness, or, to use the term we have been dealing with throughout, maximum organization and integration. This development can be studied, for example, from the observer's viewpoint by gathering data about those aspects of growth that are measurable or observable physically —height, weight, the appearance of secondary sex characteristics, etc. This development, however, needs to be seen in another way—in terms of how the person himself continuously organizes and re-organizes his world as he goes through progressive stages of development. It becomes necessary to not only observe that this child has reached his pre-adolescent growth spurt, but also to observe and infer from observations the *meaning* this has to the child—to discover as best we can what *he* is experiencing.

Let us now take a look at these last few concepts—organization, self, and growth, and explore some of their implications for education.

First, we have said that information is essential to the system. It takes information to maintain organization. There must be input. While some input is from the internal environment, much or most must come from outside the organism. The meaning of the input, the value of it, is determined by the system, not by the objective cue itself. It becomes information when it adds to the already developed pattern or structure. Nevertheless, growth cannot take place without information on which to feed. This means that the primary function of the school must be as a place where cues are readily available. Subject matter *is important.* It becomes information to the person when he sees it as assisting him in enhancing his self-system. He wants it—he needs it—and he seeks for it. There can be no such thing as process in the abstract—the concrete cues must be there for him to use. While it is true that he will fashion these to suit his particular organization, this does not relieve us of the responsibility for providing them. While his organization of them will differ from ours, we cannot escape our responsibility for providing a rich variety of resources.

This has many implications for administration and curriculum develop-

---

* *Ibid.*
** Edmund Sinnott, "The Biology of Purpose," *The American Journal of Orthopsychiatry,* XXII, No. 3 (July 1952), 466.

ment. Research is needed in the areas of thought and concept formation to aid us to plan the timing of experiences as well as the nature of the learning situations we wish to provide. Bruner's work* in this direction needs to be expanded so that we may understand how these strategies used in concept formation are acquired or developed as the child grows up. We have virtually no data on this crucial problem of how the child utilizes and organizes data to form concepts which become integrating forces in his self-system.

Allied with this is our notion that the individual is striving to learn, to grow, to have experiences, and to symbolize or interpret these experiences. The child or youth in school is active, thirsty (and not just for the many drinks of water he takes throughout the day), and inquisitive. We don't have to make him want to learn those things he perceives as meaningful. The older notion of motivation—that you could "motivate" another—makes little sense in this framework. Motivation is ever present, continuous, and internal. What the teacher can do is enable the child to see relationships between where he is going and the skills, attitudes, behaviors the school as an agent of society is attempting to convey. The teacher is an active agent in the process; he can serve as a guide and resource person. His task is not so much to arouse interests and curiosity, but to take those that are already there and extend the youngster's horizon, show him opportunities, offer data that he can then use as information. The task of the teacher is in no way diminished by recognizing that children basically want to learn. In some ways, the teacher's job becomes more complex, because he is dealing with a whole child constantly relating to his environment, whose needs for knowledge and experience may transcend the teacher's resources, or whose needs may differ from those of the teacher.

Third, knowledge of growth processes leads us to the recognition that one's presently developed self-system, including, of course, one's physical organism, sets limits on what will be perceived, experienced, turned into information, and therefore "learned." While we have said that structure-function may be seen as two approaches to process, it also must be recognized that external expectations must be related to the present system, and can only be utilized when the system has arrived at a particular point in space-time. For example, it is a cliché to say you can't teach a child to walk until he is ready. We are saying here you can't present any learning situation with hope of success to the individual until his total self-system is "ready." This means teachers need to know about the process

---

*J. S. Bruner, J. J. Goodnow and G. A. Austin, *A Study of Thinking* (New York: John Wiley and Sons, 1956).

of total development—physically and psychologically—since in behavior these two aspects are "all of a piece."

INDIVIDUAL VARIABILITY

Perhaps the concept most widely accepted in human development is that of individual differences. If there is one "law" about people, it is that no two are alike. We know this—yet so often we act as though we wish this were not so. Let me give you an example from my undergraduates again—a committee, in discussing the needs of children said, "the parent should realize that there are individual differences and that this is not necessarily bad."

We are constantly attempting to use both a nomothetic and an ideographic approach. We have this need for "order" ourselves, and it disturbs us when the concept of individual variability looks to us like chaos. If we could re-organize our thinking to see that the concept is lawful rather than chaotic, we might learn how to see it as the most promising idea for the future rather than one we'd like to do without.

In this search for order we've done another peculiar thing to the notion of individual differences. We say, "yes, they exist, but they exist in an ordered fashion—the normal curve." It would be so comforting if this were so—but unfortunately, it isn't. We have a nice normal curve on intelligence tests, but this is the result of the way we constructed the tests and is not necessarily the result of what exists in nature.

It seems to me at a time in education where we are talking so much about enhancing the individual, developing potentialities, and all our other pet phrases, that we must come to grips with the meanings of individual variability in our efforts to construct curricula, to develop sequences of experiences, to administer a program still designed—as for example, grade levels—much as the Procrustean bed. In practice, individual differences have often meant lopping off the feet or stretching the body to fit the predetermined size of the bed. We are faced with the task of re-designing the bed.

Perhaps the first place where a new design must emerge is in our philosophic approach. Do we see differences as a problem to be overcome, or as a challenge to create?

Research is needed here to increase our understanding of individual learning the the group setting. Certainly research is needed about what happens to the *total* development of the child who is at either of the ends of the "normal" curve and who is grouped accordingly. We need further to examine the kind of teacher education which is necessary to provide teachers with skills to enhance the individual development of individuals who must be met in a large group setting.

MULTIPLE CAUSATION

Historically, this concept has meant the recognition not only that behavior is caused but also that the causes are some sort of amalgamation of external and internal factors. For example, to explain why a boy might prefer to go to the library rather than go on the playground with his junior high school peers, we might hypothesize that this is due to: (a) he is a late maturer, and (b) he lacks skills in games, and (c) he has low energy output, and (d) his parents encourage him to read, and (e) his teacher has found some special books for him, etc. While this all may be so, the number of variables and the combination of variables are so many that one who wishes to explain behavior is faced with the virtually insurmountable task of gathering historical as well as contemporary data.

It is certainly important to recognize the many experiences that have been organized by the person into his self-system and his Weltanschauung—his view of the world. It reduces our task of understanding and predicting behavior if we attempt to gather and order our data in terms of his self-system. If we do this, it no longer is important to know that his baby sister was born when he was two. It is only important to know what place his sister holds in his present view of life.

What does this do to the concept of mulitple causation? It moves the multiplicity *within* the individual. While his present behavior is certainly a resultant of all he has experienced, we may now say that his present behavior is a function of his self-system, which is his unique organization of his past experiences including physiological processes as experiences.

Another way we can look at this is to recognize that man is integrating rather than integrated. This means that the self-system, while it attempts to maintain a steady state, is always to some degree in disequilibrium. Tensions may arise from any part of the system, or from the interplay among the various sub-systems. Multiple causation may then be perceived of as the behavior resulting from the disharmony existing among the sub-systems of the self-system. "Motives are not abstracts out in space that one dangles or creates to inspire learning; they are forever in operation in terms of tension distribution and development."* Any part of the system thus may be an instigator of behavior. The direction of the behavior is

*Gordon, *op. cit.*, p. 40.

determined by the *total* system.

Behavior is always a function of the total system operating in a situational field. To understand behavior we need to understand the self-system and the complex interactions of its sub-systems in the present situation.

This means that research needs to be done in helping teachers to find ways to analyze the situations in which they place children, and to infer from behavior the meanings these situations hold for children.

In summary we need to: (1) increase our knowledge of the conceptual and perceptual development of children, (2) develop skills which can be taught to teachers so that they may infer about the self-system of children with a high degree of accuracy, (3) build up our understandings of the role of situation in behavior, since we have repeatedly stated that this is a transactional process, (4) increase our knowledge of how and what individuals learn in group settings, (5) examine more fully the processes of concept formation and the various ways in which concepts are developed, (6) explore the role of "order" in the learning situation. How ambiguous can or should a situation be to be effective? What is the range of individual variation in the need for "order?" (7) raise our sights in terms of goals and free ourselves from setting what may be too low ceilings on the potentials for individual development, (8) clarify and increase our understandings of the process of changing goals and changing the self-system. Since organization seems to be an important force, and changes in organization are resisted, just how is change accomplished? How open to change is the self-system? Are there epochs (i.e. the adolescent period) where the system is more open to change? What kinds of environments produce change? And, for social scientists charged with responsibility, we cannot avoid exploring the question of what direction we set up as the one along which the developing child should move. We cannot avoid the choice-making process, but we may be able to make wiser choices as we increase our understandings of the development of human behavior in the cultural milieu.

BIBLIOGRAPHY

Allport, F., *Theories of Perception and the Concept of Structure* (New York: John Wiley, 1955).

Anderson and Anderson, "Social Development" in L. Carmichael (ed.) *Manual of Child Psychology*, 2nd edition (New York: John Wiley, 1954), ch. 19, pp. 1162-1215.

Bruner, J. S., Goodnow, J. J., and Austin, G. A., *A Study of Thinking* (New York: John Wiley & Sons, 1956).

Cantril, Hadley, "The Qualities of Being Human" *American Quarterly,* Vol. VI, No. 1 (Spring 1954).

Courtis, S. A., "Personalized Statistics in Education." Michigan Academy of Science, Arts and Letters, Univ. of Michigan, March 27, 1954.

Freeman, G. I., *The Energetics of Human Behavior* (Ithaca, New York: Cornell University Press, 1948).

Gerard, R. W., *Unresting Cells* (New York: Harper & Bros., 1949).

Goldstein, Kurt, "On Emotions: Considerations from the Organismic Point of View" *The Journal of Psychology*, 1951, 31: 37-49.

Gordon, I. J., *The Teacher as a Guidance Worker* (New York: Harper & Bros., 1956).

Hopkins, L. T., *The Emerging Self* (New York: Harper & Bros., 1954), pp. 4-13.

Ittelson, William H. and Hadley, Cantril, *Perception: A Transactional Approach*, Doubleday Papers in Psychology, 1954.

Jackson, E., "Child Development Patterns in the United States" in K. Soddy (ed.) *Mental Health and Infant Development* (New York: Basic Books, 1956).

Martin, William W., "Some Basic Implications of a Concept of Organism for Psychology" *Psychological Review,* Vol. 52, No. 6, November 1945, pp. 333-343.

Miller, James G., "Toward a General Theory for the Behavioral Sciences" *The American Psychologist*, Vol.10, No. 9 (1955), pp. 513-531.

Sinnott, Edmund W., "The Biology of Purpose" *The American Journal Of Orthopsychiatry,* Vol. XXII, No. 3, (July, 1952), pp. 457-468.

Snygg, Donald, "Scientific Method in Psychology" *The Journal of General Psychology*, 1955, 52: 189-196.

Snygg & Combs, *Individual Behavior* (New York: Harper & Bros., 1949).

Solley, C. and R. Sommer, "Perceptual Autism in Children" *J. General Psychol.,* 56(1) Jan. 1957, pp. 3-12.

Von Foerster, Heinz (Editor) *Cybernetics* (Josiah Macy, Jr. Foundation).

Weiner, N., *The Human Use of Human Beings* (New York: Doubleday, 1954).

VIEWPOINTS FROM RELATED
DISCIPLINES: HUMAN GROWTH AND DEVELOPMENT

David P. Ausubel

What light can the field of human growth and development throw on the issue "What shall the schools teach?" I only wish it were possible for me to list and discuss a dozen or more instances in which developmental principles have been validly utilized in providing definitive answers to questions dealing with the content and organization of the curriculum. Unfortunately, however, it must be admitted that at present our discipline can offer only a limited number of very crude generalizations and highly tentative suggestions bearing on this issue. In a very general sense, of course, it is undeniable that concern with child development has had a salutary effect on the educational enterprise. It alerted school administrators to the fact that certain minimal levels of intellectual maturity were necessary before various subjects could be taught with a reasonable degree of efficiency and hope of success; and it encouraged teachers in presenting their subject matter to make use of the existing interests of pupils, to consider their point of view, and to take into account prevailing limitations in command of language and grasp of concepts. On the other hand, premature and wholesale extension of developmental principles to educational theory and practice has caused incalculable harm. It will take at least a generation for teachers to unlearn some of the more fallacious and dangerous of these overgeneralized and unwarranted applications.

From *Teachers College Record,* LX, No. 5 (February, 1959), 245-254. Used by permission of the author and publisher.

Much of the aforementioned difficulty proceeds from failure to appreciate that human growth and development is a pure rather than an applied science. As a pure science it is concerned with the discovery of general laws about the nature and regulation of human development *as an end in itself.* Ultimately, of course, these laws have self-evident implications for the realization of practical goals in such fields as education, child rearing, and guidance. In a very general sense they indicate the effects of different interpersonal and social climates on personality development and the kinds of methods and subject-matter content that are most compatible with developmental capacity and mode of functioning at a given stage of growth. Thus, because it offers important insights about the changing intellectual and emotional capacities of children as developing human beings, child development may legitimately be considered one of the basic sciences underlying education and guidance and as part of the necessary professional preparation of teachers—in much the same sense that anatomy and bacteriology are basic sciences for medicine and surgery.

Actual application to practical problems of teaching and curriculum, however, is quite another matter. Before the educational implications of developmental findings can become explicitly useful in everyday school situations, much *additional* research at the engineering level of operations is necessary. Knowledge about nuclear fission, for example, does not tell us how to make an atomic bomb or an atomic-powered submarine, antibiotic reactions that take place in petri dishes do not necessarily take place in living systems, and methods of learning employed by animals in mazes do not necessarily correspond to methods of learning that children use in grappling with verbal materials in classrooms. Many of the better-known generalizations in child development—the principle of readiness, the cephalocaudal trend, the abstract to concrete trend in conceptualizing the environment, and others—fit these analogies perfectly. They are interesting and potentially useful ideas to curriculum specialists but will have little practical utility in designing a social studies or physical education curriculum unless they are rendered more specific in terms of the actual operations involved in teaching these subjects. This lack of fruitful particularization, although unfortunate and regrettable, does not in itself give rise to damaging consequences except insofar as many beginning teachers tend to nurture vague illusions about the current usefulness of these principles, and subsequently, after undergoing acute disillusionment, lose the confidence they may have felt in the value of a developmental approach to educational problems.

Much more detrimental in their effects on pupils and teachers have been the consequences of far-fetched and uncritical application to educational practice of developmental generalizations that either have not been adequately validated or only apply to a very restricted age segment of the total span of children's development. Two illustrations of the latter category of highly limited generalizations—the "internal ripening" theory of maturation and the principle of self-selection—will be given later in this discussion. A widely accepted but inadequately validated developmental principle frequently cited to justify general or over-all ability grouping of pupils is that a child's growth and achievement show a "going-togetherness." Actually, except for a spuriously high correlation during infancy, the relationship between physical status and motor ability on the one hand and intelligence and intellectual achievement on the other is negligible and declines consistently with increasing age. Even among the different subtests of intelligence and among the different areas of intellectual achievement, the weight of the evidence indicates that as a child grows older his component rates of growth in these various functions tend increasingly to diverge.

Keeping these qualifications about the relevance of child development for educational practice in mind, I propose briefly to consider from the standpoint of developmental psychology the following aspects of the issue under discussion: (1) readiness as a criterion for curricular placement; (2) developmental factors affecting breadth of the curriculum; (3) the child's voice in determining the curriculum; and (4) the content and goals of instruction in relation to the organization and growth of the intellect.

READINESS AND GRADE PLACEMENT

There is little disagreement about the fact that readiness always crucially influences the efficiency of the learning process and often determines whether a given intellectual skill or type of school material is learnable at all at a particular stage of development. Most educators implicitly accept also the proposition that an *optimal* age exists for every kind of learning. Postponement of learning experience beyond the age of optimal readiness wastes valuable and often unsuspected learning opportunities, thereby unnecessarily reducing the amount and complexity of subject-matter content that can be mastered in a designated period of schooling. It is also conceivable that beyond a certain critical age the learning of various intellectual skills becomes more difficult for an older than for a younger child. On the other hand, when a pupil is prematurely exposed to a learning task before he is ready for it, he not only fails to learn the task in question but even learns from the experience of failure to fear, dislike, and avoid it.

Up to this point, the principle of readiness—the idea that attained capacity limits and influences an individual's ability to profit from current experience or practice—is empirically demonstrable and conceptually unambiguous. Difficulty first arises when it is confused with the concept of *maturation* and when the latter concept in turn is equated with a process of "internal ripening." The concept of readiness simply refers to the adequacy of existing capacity in relation to the demands of a given learning task. No specification is made as to *how* this capacity is achieved—whether through prior practice of a specific nature (learning), through incidental experience, through genically regulated structural and functional changes occurring independently of environmental influences, or through various combinations of these factors. Maturation, on the other hand, has a different and much more restricted meaning. It encompasses those increments in capacity that take place in the demonstrable absence of specific practice experience—those that are attributable to genic influences and/or incidental experience. Maturation, therefore, is not the same as readiness but is merely one of the two principal factors (the other being learning) that contribute to or determine the organism's readiness to cope with new experience. Whether or not readiness exists, in other words, does not necessarily depend on maturation alone but in many instances is solely a function of prior learning experience and most typically depends on varying proportions of maturation and learning.

To equate the principles of readiness and maturation not only muddies the conceptual waters but also makes it difficult for the school to appreciate that insufficient readiness may reflect inadequate prior learning on the part of pupils because of inappropriate or inefficient instructional methods. Lack of maturation can thus become a convenient scapegoat whenever children manifest insufficient readiness to learn, and the school, which is thereby automatically absolved of all responsibility in the matter, consequently fails to subject its instructional practices to the degree of self-critical scrutiny necessary for continued educational progress. In short, while it is important to appreciate that the current readiness of pupils determines the school's current choice of instructional methods and materials, it is equally important to bear in mind that this readiness itself is partly determined by the appropriateness and efficiency of the previous instructional practices to which they have been subjected.

The conceptual confusion is further compounded when maturation is interpreted as a process of "internal ripening" essentially independent of *all* environmental influences, that is, of both specific practice and incidental experience. Readiness then becomes a matter of simple genic regulation unfolding in accordance with a predetermined and immutable timetable; and the school, by definition, becomes powerless to influence readiness either through its particular way of arranging specific learning experiences or through a more general program of providing incidental or nonspecific background experience preparatory to the introduction of more formal academic activities.

Actually, the embryological model of development implicit in the "internal ripening" thesis fits quite well when applied to human sensori-motor and neuromuscular sequences taking place during the prenatal period and early infancy. In the acquisition of simple behavioral functions (for example, locomotion, prehension) that characterize all members of the human species irrespective of cultural or other environmental differences, it is reasonable to suppose that for all practical purposes genic factors alone determine the direction of development. Environmental factors only enter the picture if they are extremely deviant, and then serve more to disrupt or arrest the ongoing course of development than to generate distinctive developmental progressions of their own. Thus, the only truly objectionable aspect of this point of view is its unwarranted extrapolation to those more complex and variable components of later cognitive and behavioral develop-ment where unique factors of individual experience and cultural environ-ment make important contributions to the direction, patterning, and sequential order of all developmental changes.

It is hardly surprising, therefore, in view of the tremendous influence on professional and lay opinion wielded by Gesell and his colleagues, that many people conceive of readiness in absolute and immutable terms, and thus fail to appreciate that except for such traits as walking and grasping, the mean ages of readiness can never be specified apart from relevant environmental conditions. Although the modal child in contemporary America may first be ready to read at the age of six and one-half, the age of reading readiness is always influenced by cultural, subcultural, and individual differences in background experience, and in any case varies with the method of instruction employed and the child's IQ. Middle-class children, for example, are ready to read at an earlier age than lower-class children because of the greater availability of books in the home and because they are read to and taken places more frequently.

The need for particularizing developmental generalizations before they can become useful in educational practice is nowhere more glaringly evident than in the field of readiness. At present we can only speculate what curricular sequences might conceivably be if they took into account precise and detailed (but currently unavailable) research findings on the emergence of readiness for different subject-matter areas, for different sub-areas and levels of difficulty within an area, and for different techniques of teaching the same material. Because of the unpredictable specificity of readiness as shown, for example, by the fact that four- and five-year-olds can profit from training in pitch but not in rhythm, valid answers to such questions cannot be derived from logical extrapolation but require meticulous empirical research in a school setting. The next step would involve the development of appropriate teaching methods and materials to take optimal advantage of existing degrees of readiness and to increase readiness wherever necessary and desirable. But since we generally do not have this type of research data available, except perhaps in the field of reading, we can only pay lip service to the principle of readiness in curriculum planning.

BREADTH OF CURRICULUM

One of the chief complaints of the critics of public education, both in the United States and in New Zealand, is that modern children fail to learn the fundamentals because of the broadening of the elementary school curriculum to include such subjects as social studies, art, science, music, and manual arts in addition to the traditional three R's. This, of course, would be a very serious charge if it were true, because the wisdom of expanding a child's intellectual horizons at the expense of making him a cripple in the basic intellectual skills is highly questionable to say the least. Fortunately, however, the benefits of an expanded curriculum have thus far not been accompanied by a corresponding deterioration in the standard of the three R's. Evidently the decreased amount of time spent on the latter subjects has been more than compensated for by the development of more efficient methods of teaching and by the incidental learning of the fundamentals in the course of studying these other subjects. Nevertheless, the issue of breadth versus depth still remains because there *is* obviously a point beyond which increased breadth could only be attained by sacrificing mastery of the fundamental skills; and even if we agreed to maintain or improve the present standard of the three R's, we would still have to choose between breadth and depth in relation to other components of the curriculum, particularly at the junior and senior high school levels. It is at these points of choice that developmental criteria can be profitably applied.

Generally speaking, maximal breadth of the curriculum consistent with adequate mastery of its constituent parts is developmentally desirable at all ages because of the tremendously wide scope of human abilities. The wider the range of intellectual stimulation to which pupils are exposed, the greater are the chances that all of the diverse potentialities both within a group of children and within a single child will be brought to fruition. By the same token, a broad curriculum makes it possible for more pupils to experience success in the performance of school activities and thus to develop the necessary self-confidence and motivation for continued academic striving and achievement. The very fact that elementary school children are able to make significant progress in science and social studies also indicates that myopic concentration on the three R's would waste much available readiness for these types of learnings and thus compel junior and senior high schools to devote much of their instructional time to materials that are easily learnable in the lower grades. In fact, one of the major failings of the secondary school curriculum today is that because it still has not adequately adjusted to the expansion of the elementary school syllabus, entering pupils are subjected to much stultifying repetition and fail to break the new ground for which they are obviously ready.

The relationship between breadth and depth must also take into account the progressive differentiation of intelligence, interests, and personality structure with increasing age. The elementary school child is a "generalist" because both his intellect and his personality are still relatively unstable and uncrystallized and lack impressive internal consistency. Thus, many different varieties of subject matter are equally compatible with his interest and ability patterns. Furthermore, unless he has experience with many different fields of knowledge and gives each a provisional try, he is in no position to judge which kinds of intellectual pursuits are most congruent with his major ability and value systems. Hence, quite apart from the future life adjustment values of a broad educational background, it is appropriate on developmental grounds for elementary and early high school curricula to stress breadth rather than depth.

Toward the latter portion of the high school period, however, precisely the opposite kind of situation begins to emerge. Interests have crystallized and abilities have undergone differentiation to the point where greater depth and specialization are possible and desirable. Many students at this stage of intellectual development are ready to sink their teeth into more serious and solid academic fare. but unfortunately suitable instructional programs geared at an advanced level of critical and independent thinking are rarely available. The changes that have taken place in secondary school curricula since the academy days have been primarily characterized by the belated and half-hearted addition of more up-to-date and topical information. Very little has been done in the way of providing the student with a meaningful, integrated, systematic view of the major ideas in a given field of knowledge.

THE CHILD'S VOICE IN CURRICULUM PLANNING

One extreme point of view associated with the child-centered approach to education is the notion that children are innately equipped in some mysterious fashion for knowing precisely what is best for them. This idea is obviously an outgrowth of predeterministic theories (for example, those of Rousseau and Gesell) that conceive of development as a series of internally regulated sequential steps that unfold in accordance with a prearranged design. According to these theorists, the environment facilitates development best by providing a maximally permissive field that does not interfere with the predetermined processes of spontaneous maturation. From these assumptions it is but a short step to the claim that the child himself must be in the most strategic position to *know* and *select* those components of the environment that correspond most closely with his current developmental needs and hence are most conducive to optimal growth. Empirical "proof" of this proposition is adduced from the fact that nutrition is adequately maintained and existing deficiency conditions are spontaneously corrected when infants are permitted to select their own diets. If the child can successfully choose his diet, he must certainly know what is best for him in all areas of growth and should therefore be permitted to select everything, including his curriculum.

In the first place, and refuting this theory, even if development were primarily a matter of internal ripening, there would still be no good reason for supposing that the child is therefore implicitly conversant with the current direction and facilitating conditions of development and hence axiomatically equipped to make the most appropriate choices. Because the individual is sensitive in early childhood to internal cues of physiological need we cannot conclude that he is similarly sensitive to cues reflective of psychological and other developmental needs; even in the area of nutrition, selection is a reliable criterion of need only during early infancy.

Second, unless one assigns a sacrosanct status to endogenous motivations, there is little warrant for believing either that they alone are truly reflective of the child's *genuine* developmental requirements or that environmentally derived needs are "imposed," authoritarian in spirit, and inevitably fated to thwart the actualization of his developmental potentialities. Actually, most needs originate from without and are internalized in the course of the child's interaction and identification with significant persons in his family and cultural environments.

Third, one can never assume that the child's *spontaneously* expressed interests and activities are completely reflective of *all* of his important needs and capacities. Just because capacities can potentially provide their own motivation does not mean that they always or necessarily do so. It is not the possession of capacities that is motivating, but the anticipation of future satisfactions once they have been successfully exercised. But because of such factors as inertia, lack of opportunity, lack of appreciation, and preoccupation with other activities, many capacities may never be exercised in the first place. Thus, children typically develop only *some* of their potential capacities, and their expressed interests cannot be considered coextensive with the potential range of interests they are capable of developing with appropriate stimulation.

In conclusion, therefore, the current interests and spontaneous desires of immature pupils can hardly be considered reliable guideposts and adequate substitutes for specialized knowledge and seasoned judgment in designing a curriculum. Recognition of the role of pupil needs in school learning does not mean that the scope of the syllabus should be restricted to the existing concerns and spontaneously expressed interests that happen to be present in a group of children growing up under particular conditions of intellectual and social class stimulation. In fact, one of the primary functions of education should be to stimulate the development of motivations that are currently nonexistent. It is true that academic achievement is greatest when pupils manifest felt needs to acquire knowledge as an end in itself. Such needs, however, are not endogenous but acquired—and largely through exposure to provocative, meaningful, developmental, appropriate instruction. Hence, while it is reasonable to consider the views of pupils and even, under certain circumstances, to solicit their participation in the planning of the curriculum, it makes little developmental or administrative sense to entrust them with responsibility for significant policy or operational decisions.

ORGANIZATION AND COGNITIVE DEVELOPMENT

The curriculum specialist is concerned with more than the appropriate grade placement of different subjects and subject-matter content in accordance with such criteria as readiness and relative significance for intellectual, vocational, or current adjustment purposes. More important than what pupils know at the end of the sixth, eighth, and twelfth grades is the extent of their knowledge at the ages of twenty-five, forty, and sixty as well as their ability and desire both to learn more and to apply their knowledge fruitfully in adult life. In light of these latter criteria, in comparing, for example, the quantity and quality of our national research output in the pure and applied sciences with those of European countries, the American educational system stands up relatively well even though our school children apparently absorb less academic material. We are dealing here with the ultimate intellectual objectives of schooling, namely, with the long-term acquisition of stable and usable bodies of knowledge and intellectual skills and with the development of ability to think creatively, systematically, independently, and with depth in particular fields of inquiry. Instruction obviously influences the outcome of these objectives—not so much in the substantive content of subject matter but in the organization, sequence, and manner of presenting learning experiences, their degree of meaningfulness, and the relative balance between conceptual and factual materials.

But obviously, before we could ever hope to structure effectively such instructional variables for the optimal realization of these designated objectives, we would have to know a great deal more about the organizational and developmental principles whereby human beings acquire and retain stable bodies of knowledge and develop the power of critical and productive thinking. This type of knowledge, however, will forever elude us unless we abandon the untenable assumption that there is no real distinction either between the logic of a proposition and how the mind apprehends it or between the logical structure of subject-matter organization and the actual series of cognitive processes through which an immature and developing individual incorporates facts and concepts into a stable body of knowledge. It is perfectly logical from the standpoint of a mature scholar, for example, to write a textbook in which topically homogeneous materials are segregated into discrete chapters and treated throughout at a uniform level of conceptualization. But how closely does this approach correspond with highly suggestive findings that one of the major cognitive processes involved in the learning of any new subject is progressive differentiation of an originally undifferentiated field? Once we learn more about cognitive development than the crude generalizations that developmental psychology can currently offer, it will be possible to employ organizational and sequential principles in the presentation of subject matter that actually parallel developmental changes in the growth and organization of the intellect. In the meantime let us examine briefly how such generalizations as the concrete-to-abstract trend, the importance of meaningfulness, and the principle of retroactive inhibition have been used and abused in educational practice.

Many features of the activity program are based on the premise that the elementary school child perceives the world in relatively specific and concrete terms and requires considerable firsthand experience with diverse concrete instances of a given set of relationships before he can abstract genuinely meaningful concepts. Thus, an attempt is made to teach factual information and intellectual skills in the real-life functional contexts in which they are customarily encountered rather than through the medium of verbal exposition supplemented by artificially contrived drills and exercises. This approach has real merit, if a fetish is not made of naturalism and incidental learning, if drills and exercises are provided in instances where opportunities for acquiring skills do not occur frequently and repetitively enough in more natural settings, and if deliberate or guided effort is not regarded as incompatible with incidental learning. Even more important, however, is the realization that in older children, once a sufficient number of basic concepts are consolidated, new concepts are primarily abstracted from verbal rather than from concrete experience. Hence in secondary school it may be desirable to reverse both the sequence and the relative balance between abstract concepts and supportive data. There is good reason for believing, therefore, that much of the time presently spent in cook-book laboratory exercises in the sciences could be much more advantageously employed in formulating precise definitions, making explicit verbal distinctions between concepts, generalizing from hypothetical situations, and in other ways.

Another underlying assumption of activity and project methods is that concepts and factual data are retained much longer when they are meaningful, genuinely understood, and taught as larger units of interrelated materials than when they are presented as fragmented bits of isolated information and committed to rote memory. This, of course, does not preclude the advisability of rote learning for certain kinds of learning (for example, multiplication tables) *after* a functional understanding of the underlying concepts has been acquired. Unfortunately, however, these principles have made relatively few inroads on the high school instructional program, where they are still applicable. The teaching of mathematics and science, for example, still relies heavily on rote learning of formulas and procedural steps, on recognition of traditional "type problems," and on mechanical manipulation of symbols. In the absence of clear and stable concepts which serve as anchoring points and organizing foci for the assimilation of new material, secondary school students are trapped in a morass of confusion and seldom retain rotely memorized materials much beyond final exam time.

This brings us finally to a consideration of the mechanisms of accretion and long-term retention of large bodies of ideational material. Why do high school and university students tend to forget so readily previous day-to-day learnings as they are exposed to new lessons? The traditional answer of educational psychology, based upon studies of short-term rote learning in animal and human subjects, has been that subsequent learning experiences which are similar to but not identical with previously learned materials exert a retroactively inhibitory effect on the retention of the latter. But wouldn't it be reasonable to suppose that all of the existing, cumulatively established ideational systems which an individual brings with him to any learning situation have more of an interfering effect on the retention of new learning material (proactive inhibition) than brief exposure to subsequently introduced materials of a similar nature (retroactive inhibition)? Because it is cognitively most economical and least burdensome for an individual to subsume as much new experience as possible under existing concepts that are inclusive and stable, the import of many specific illustrative items in later experience is assimilated by the generalized meaning of these more firmly established and highly conceptualized subsuming foci. When this happens the latter items lose their identity and are said to be "forgotten." Hence, if proactive rather than retroactive inhibition turned out to be the principal mechanism affecting the longevity with which school materials were retained, it would behoove us to identify those factors that counteract it and to employ such measures in our instructional procedures.

JEAN PIAGET:
NOTES ON LEARNING

Frank G. Jennings

The man behind the ideas of many of the plans and programs to improve the curricula in the schools is not an educator. Jean Piaget is the seventy-one-year-old French-speaking Swiss director of the Jean Jacques Rousseau Center for Genetic Epistemology, director of the International Bureau of Education, and professor of child psychology and of the history of scientific thought at the University of Geneva. Some psychologists are convinced that his work might become as influential as Freud's. Some educators are fearful that this may be true.

From *Saturday Review*, L, No. 20 (May 20, 1967), 81-83. Used by permission of the author and publisher. Copyright Saturday Review, Inc. 1967.

In March, Piaget came to this country to deliver three lectures on the nature and nurture of intelligence and on related matters in science, psychology, and education. He spoke at New York University and addressed the convention of the American Orthopsychiatric Association in Washington.

It has been said of Piaget that he is by vocation a sociologist, by avocation an epistemologist, and by method a logician. He tells his listeners and readers that he is not an educator, that he is a psychologist with an interdisciplinary bent, that he is an investigator using the tools of the related fields of biology, psychology, and logic to explore the genesis of intelligence in the human young. All his long life he has drawn upon these three fields to conduct research and to build his theories of the development of intelligence in children.

For Piaget, the crucial question in the study of the growing child is how he adjusts himself to the world in which he lives. And for Piaget there is nothing pejorative in the word *adjustment.* It involves backing and filling, winning and losing, understanding and gaining knowledge. As he expresses it:

Knowledge is not a copy of reality. To know an object, to know an event, is not simply to look at it and make a mental copy, or image, of it. To know an object is to act on it. To know is to modify, to transform the object, and to understand the process of this transformation, and as a consequence to understand the way the object is constructed. An operation is thus the essence of knowledge; it is an interiorized action which modifies the object of knowledge.

This is the voice of the epistemologist, but it speaks from the soul of the teacher. Piaget's techniques for observing, recording, and understanding the way a child thinks is quite literally to get inside of the child's mind and see the world through the child's eyes. One of his notable experiments, for example, was to join in a child's game as an equal. He would "learn how to make a good shot at marbles, how to make bad ones, and even how to cheat."

Rules and standards for three-year-olds, he found, are almost non-existent. Ask a three-year-old who won and you get the answer, "I won, you won, and we all won." The five-year-old sees and sometimes respects rules. For the seven-year-old they are sacred and immutable. When the Geneva boys were told that the game was played differently in Lucerne, they shouted, "But those kids over there never understood marbles, anyway."

Piaget found that ten-year-olds can get together and modify rules to meet new conditions, and with the onset of puberty, adjustments are freely made to meet unusual cases. In a ball game, the short-sighted child is allowed to stand nearer the pitcher, a cripple will be allowed a runner. Thus there is a logic of operations that is fitted to a logic of social relations. There is continuous observable growth in the way the child learns and adjusts his understanding to the requirements of the world around him.

Piaget sees four major stages of growth through childhood; the first is the *sensory-motor* stage, which lasts from birth to about two years. Here the child learns his muscles and senses and develops certain habits for dealing with external objects and events. Language begins to gain form. He can deal with and know that things exist even when they are beyond his sight or touch. He begins to "symbolize," to represent things by word or gesture.

The second stage is the *preoperational* or *representational* stage. It begins with the beginning of organized language and continues to about the age of six. This is the period of greatest language growth and through the use of words and other symbols the child can represent the outside world and his own inner world of feeling. It is a period when magical explanations make sense, when "God pushes the sun around" and stars must go to bed when he does. The child begins to gain a sense of symmetry, depends on trial and error adjustments, and manages things by a kind of intuitive regulation.

The third stage, between seven and eleven years, is one in which the child acquires the ability to carry out what Piaget calls *concrete operations.* He can move things around, make them fit properly. He acquires fine motor skills and can organize what he has and knows how to solve physical problems.

The fourth stage is one of *formal operations* and prepares the way for adult thinking. It usually begins between twelve and fifteen years and involves the development of "hypothetical reasoning based upon a logic of all possible combinations and to perform controlled experimentation."

In successive studies Piaget and his associates have explored the growth of intelligence, the development of moral awareness, the child's concept of physical reality, and the elaboration of appropriate logic to deal with complex nonrepresentational problems.

Although *The Language and Thought of the Child* was published in English in 1926, it was not until the early 1950s that Piaget's ideas made any significant impact in the United States. Professor Jerome S. Bruner of Harvard is probably responsible for the current public awareness, which can be traced to his important little book *The Process of Education* (1960), and his most recent book, *Toward a Theory of Instruction* (1966). Bruner describes Piaget as "unquestionably, the most impressive figure in the field of cognitive development." Piaget, he says "is often interpreted in the wrong way by those who think that his principal mission is psychological. It is not... What he has done is to write the implicit logical theory on which the child proceeds in dealing with intellectual tasks."

Some American psychologists and educators make precisely this "wrong" interpretation. They see Piaget as "cold-blooded," not interested in motivational problems, not responsive to curricular concerns. They criticize him for being intellectually seductive. They object to his children, who seem to have a fair view of the world, who appear to be distressingly happy with their existence. Put this down, perhaps, to a tough-minded myopia of those who must work in the slums, or to the necessary sentiment of those who give primacy to "feeling" and "socialization." It is not that Piaget overlooks the affective domain, but rather that he appears convinced that the world is manageable only to the degree that orderly intelligence can be brought to bear upon the inescapable transactions each human being must make with it and with his fellows.

One critic recently complained that Piaget's children "... react as if they trusted the world, as if the environment were waiting to welcome them." Indeed, they sometimes do, for they are engaged in explorations of the greater world and of the closer environment with patient, resourceful, interested, and perhaps even loving adults who seem to believe that sovereign reason has not yet been dethroned. The great strength of reason, Piaget seems to say, is in its very tentativeness before an uncertain and sometimes disorderly universe. Patience is required, and time to grow, time to take in the outside world to assimilate it, to understand it, and to use it generously.

THE ORGANIZATION OF THE ELEMENTARY SCHOOL AND THE DEVELOPMENT OF A HEALTHY PERSONALITY

Helen Heffernan, Lloyd E. Bevans, Mrs. Ruth Edmands,
Bernard J. Lonsdale, Mrs. Afton Dill Nance,
and Mrs. Faith Smitter

"For every child a healthy personality," the theme of the Mid-century White House Conference on Children and Youth, emphasized an important goal of education. One session of the 1951 California Conference of Elementary School Principals and District Superintendents of Schools was devoted to evaluating elementary school practices in relation to this goal. The practices evaluated were presented by the elementary education staff of the State Department of Education. The staff, basing its judgment on research and experience, chose for presentation the elementary school practices indicated by the following questions:

1. Does the practice of grade placement assure pupils opportunities to develop healthy personalities?

2. Does departmental teaching in the elementary school offer opportunities for pupils to develop healthy personalities?

3. Do current practices in reporting pupil progress to parents tend to give pupils good opportunities to develop healthy personalities?

4. Does the maintenance of grade standards assure opportunities for pupils to develop healthy personalities?

5. Does an articulated program of instruction provide superior opportunities for pupils to develop healthy personalities?

No brief was held for the selection of these questions in preference to others, but the staff believed that the questions cover areas that are of concern to every principal and teacher who sees in healthy personality development the major purpose of modern child-rearing.

From *California Journal of Elementary Education*, XX, No. 3 (February, 1952). Used by permission of the authors and publisher.

A HEALTHY PERSONALITY

Before approaching the problems set by the questions, common ground was sought for the meaning of the term "healthy personality." The concept of personality that was expressed during the White House Conference gave significant emphasis to the qualitative aspects of human relations and indicated that everyone who works in the service of children must take *children's feelings* into account. This way of looking at children leads inevitably to the conclusion that demeaning poverty, inadequate school and health services, and racial or ethnical discrimination not only are in and of themselves handicapping to children but also constitute a denial of the democratic ideal that every person is of precious and equal worth. As Allison Davis pointed out, these are serious considerations in a country which at this moment urgently needs all the skilled people it can get. More than 60 out of every 100 children in the United States live in families of low socioeconomic status. The ability represented in this large group of children is largely undiscovered and unused.

To be sure, emotional ill health may have many causes. Inadequate food and housing, racial discrimination, physiological malfunctioning, lack of guidance toward sound life values, and lack of love and affection of parents are all a part of the pattern which may disturb or obstruct well-balanced development in children. The problem in the elementary school is to determine ways to be sure that none of its practices constitute hazards to sound development.

The origin of the word "personality" is interesting. The word comes from the Greek *persona* or "mask," something which an actor puts on to conceal his true identity. Many advertisers seem to use the word in somewhat the same sense—the "man of distinction" becomes associated with a commodity available in bottles; an irresistible epidermis can be attained by liberal applications of a gooey substance in a tube or jar; social acceptability is somehow connected with the advertiser's toothpaste or deodorant.

But these were not the meanings of "personality" basic to the White House Conference. Rather, the philosopher, the psychologist, the physiologist, the sociologist, the psychiatrist pooled their ideas and came out with another meaning of personality. They said, "By personality we mean the thinking, feeling, acting human being, who conceives of himself as an individual separate from other individuals. The human being does not have a personality; he is a personality."

What then are the components of a healthy personality? These components, said Erikson, are the sense of trust, the sense of autonomy, the sense of initiative, the sense of accomplishment, the sense of identity, the sense of intimacy, the parental sense, and the sense of integrity.* These components will bear elaboration as bases for consideration of the organization of the elementary school.

The Sense of Trust

The first component of the healthy personality is the sense of trust. Trust can exist only in relation to something. The baby begins at an early age to develop the sense of trust as he learns that there are adults in this world who will relieve his hunger, provide for his physical comfort, and give him the affection he needs. Infants that are brought up in institutions in which the environments are unfavorable to their emotional stability show by listlessness, emaciation, pallor, immobility, unresponsiveness, poor appetite, poor digestion, and a wide variety of evidences of unhappiness that their experiences have not led them to develop a sense of trust. Fortunately most infants in our society find the comfort and affection that is essential to a developing sense of trust. Both nature and culture are conducive toward making mothers motherly at the very time the child's personality is in need of the nurture which develops this basic component of the healthy personality.

The Sense of Autonomy

Next in chronological order of development is the sense of independence or autonomy. The second and third years of life are roughly the beginning of the individual's struggle to establish himself as a human being with a mind and will of his own. The young child must experience over and over that he is a person who is permitted to make choices. Personal autonomy is an outstanding feature of the American way of life. Every red-blooded American resents being bossed, being pushed around; he maintains vigorously that everyone has a right to express himself, has a right to control his own affairs. The American people want each child to grow up to be the upstanding, look-you-in-the-eye kind of individual. That is the type of person Americans admire.

Although the beginnings of this sense of autonomy are important in the early years of life, independence is not established once and for all time

---

Fact Finding Report, A Digest . . . Children and Youth at the Mid-Century. Washington: Mid-century White House Conference on Children and Youth, 1950, pp. 1-56. See also Erik H. Erikson, *Childhood and Society.* New York: W.W. Norton and Co., Inc., 1950, pp. 219-31.

any more than is the sense of trust. The period during which these components of personality first emerge is crucial, but if we want youngsters to emerge into adulthood with healthy personalities, we must continue to nurture their sense of trust, respect their desire to assert themselves, help them learn to hold their desire for independence within bounds, and avoid treating them in ways to arouse any doubts in themselves or feelings of shame in connection with their accomplishments.

A Sense of Initiative

At four or five years of age, the young child wants to find out what kind of a person he can be. He watches the activities of adults about him; he recreates their activities in his play and yearns to share in their activities. It is important for the child's developing personality that much encouragement be given to the enterprise and imagination which characterize these years. The child is ready and avid to learn. This sense of initiative must be constantly fostered. If it is restricted, resentment and bitterness and a vindictive attitude toward the world may develop as a functioning part of the child's personality.

A Sense of Accomplishment

If during the early years of life a child has developed the sense of trust, the sense of autonomy, and the sense of initiative, we may expect when he is about six years of age to see the beginning of great development of the sense of accomplishment. While this sense is developing, a child wants to engage in real tasks that he can carry through to completion. After a period of time characterized by exuberant imagination, a child then wants to settle down to learning exactly how to do things and how to do them well. Much of this period of a child's life is spent in the elementary school. Under reasonably favorable circumstances, this is a period of calm, steady growth, especially if the problems of the previous stages have been well worked out. Although this is a rather unspectacular period in human growth, it is an important period, for during it there is laid the basis for responsible citizenship. And during this period children acquire knowledge and skills that make for good workmanship, the ability to co-operate and to play fair, and otherwise to follow the rules of the larger social game.

The chief danger a child may encounter during this period is the presence of conditions which may lead to a sense of inadequacy and inferiority. If in the home or school too much is expected of a child, or if a child is made to feel that achievement is beyond his ability, he may lapse into discouragement and lack of interest. It is important, therefore, that children have a feeling of successful accomplishment in connection with their school work. Studies of delinquent children frequently show that they hated school—hated it because they were marked as stupid, awkward, and not able to do so well as other children. Children who accept their inferiority passively are perhaps more damaged psychologically than those who react aggressively to frustrating experience.

Sense of Identity

At the onset of adolescence an individual begins to seek clarification of his concept of who he is and what his role in society is to be. During this period a youth is preoccupied with his appearance in the eyes of others—particularly his peers. If the course of personality development has been healthy up to this period, the young person will have acquired a reasonable feeling of self-esteem which will carry him through the tensions and strains that are biologically or culturally imposed on adolescents.

A Sense of Intimacy

Only if the young person has acquired a sense of identity can he achieve the next component of a healthy personality in his relation to others—a sense of intimacy. The surer the young person is of himself, the more successfully can he enter into relations of friendship, love, and inspiration.

The Parental Sense

In its broadest meaning, the parental sense involves the qualities of creativity and productivity. As the individual advances into adulthood, this sense develops normally if the preceding steps have been achieved with reasonable success.

The Sense of Integrity

The final component of a healthy personality is the sense of integrity. Throughout the child's development, his home and school have been helping him to accept the dominant ideals of the culture—honor, courage, purity, grace, fairness, self-discipline. These are the core of integration of the healthy personality. The acquisition of these values and ideals is the ultimate goal of American culture.

With this abbreviation of the background concepts that the White House

Conference used as a guide, present practices in elementary education may be examined to determine whether or not they contribute to healthy personality development.

THE EFFECT OF GRADE STANDARDS

Do grade standards contribute to the development of a healthy personality? Is the development of a healthy personality extended by a classification of pupils based on rigid grade standards? For those who accept the findings of research regarding individual differences, the answer is "No." Would healthy personality growth be furthered if the organization of the school provided a program of continuous learning and advancement in accordance with the growth patterns of individuals?

Research clearly indicates that the personality development of a child may be greatly affected by the maintenance of formal grade standards. Successful accomplishment gives the child confidence in himself, while retardation or assignment to slower groups tends to destroy the child's sense of personal worth and to cause him to have feelings of frustration. Rigid grade standards cannot be met by all members of any class. To the child with strong academic interest and ability, who succeeds almost effortlessly in school, the grade standard has no threatening consequences. To the child whose limitations are greater than average, the grade standard constantly threatens defeat and thereby prevents wholesome personality growth.

Grade standards originated as an administrative device and not as an answer to the question, What is best for the child? Can we justify the continuance of rigid grade standards as a basis for classifying pupils? Fixed grade standards are untenable in the light of what is now known about the best ways to meet the needs of children. A plan for continuous growth is widely recognized as more desirable than the experience of annual evaluation followed by promotion or nonpromotion. Learning is continuous and must progress according to individual rate and ability. Schools cannot, therefore, justify the continuance of annual promotion or retardation as sound practice.

An adult can never fully know how a child feels about school failure unless the adult has experienced such failure. Were you ever failed? Who knew that you failed? Did you lose status with your mother or your father, with big brother or sister? Children have feelings about failure even though some teachers say that children do not mind failure. How would you cover it up if you failed in your job? The hurt is deep, it must be hidden. To carry on, one must appear indifferent. Children are courageous. They are helpless in the face of adult decisions—decisions which so irrevocably affect their personality growth.

Can each of thirty-five children, all nine years old, make the third-grade standard on May 26? Can each of the thirty-five youth, fourteen years old, be expected to pass the *same test* in United States history for graduation from the eighth grade? Can thirty-five children, six years old, each read all the same pre-primers, primers, and first readers? Roma Gans in her book, *Reading is Fun*, says that "perhaps no subject has been taught with greater disregard for child development than has reading." The eyes of all six-year-old children do not focus well; the children may not speak in complete sentences; their family may speak Spanish at home; Dad may have gone to Korea and Mother may be working. Are children in each of these circumstances equally ready to read?

Statistics show that teachers fail over one-seventh of the children in their classes. Are teachers aware that under such circumstances it is the school that has failed? Grade standards for subject and skill mastery do not promote the development of healthy personalities. Yet there appears to be something compulsive about the desire of teachers and school authorities to make all children alike even though they know that each child differs from all other children.

A basic democratic principle is violated when the school fails to recognize the worth of the individual. The educational principle of individual differences is widely accepted. Equally widely accepted is the knowledge that learning is an individual, not a mass, accomplishment. More than twenty-five years ago psychologists publicized information about individual rates of development, abilities, interests, and needs. For many years William Heard Kilpatrick has directed our attention to the fact that a child learns what he lives. If the child is to learn democracy, teachers and principals must make the school environment such that he lives demo-cratically and successfully in accordance with his potentialities. Success motivates, failure frustrates children.

The child as a whole must be accepted. Intelligence, which is measurable to a degree, is but one of the factors which the child brings to the learning situation. To a high degree, ability to learn is conditioned by emotions, health, and past experiences as well as by native mental ability. Teachers must help children to grow, not attempt to force them not to drive them down standardized roads to learning through slavish attention to the same book. Children must be helped to know themselves, and to build their destinies in terms of their strengths. No one ever had his personality developed by constant emphasis on his weaknesses. Since individuals are different, fixed standards are not conducive to healthy growth. In a flexible program, differentiated materials and opportunities permit each child to explore and experiment, to figure, to discuss, to share and collect, and to find answers at a rate that is commensurate with his ability and interest.

When individuals have purpose they can master arithmetic combinations, learn to write a business letter, and read for information material adapted to their level of achievement. They will move steadily ahead, even though they may move slowly. When the child knows his needs, knows the next steps to be undertaken, and has had a part in planning how to attain his objectives, he is ready to learn. Interest motivates the child to put forth effort. Opportunities for continuous growth are challenging and stimulating to him. Attempts to force learning are not only unnecessary, but they are also futile unless the child is responding to inner drives of interest which encourage him to put forth effort.

Education to meet the needs of all children includes education to help parents understand their children and their children's problems. Parents must be helped to understand that there are some things that the school cannot do for children. Leaders in education to whom parents rightfully turn for information and guidance must help parents to understand individual differences and to accept their child and to love him as he is, even if he is a slow learner. Parents must know that the school cannot teach the child to read before he is ready and that no amount of effort to do so will produce the results desired. And parents must know that attempting to force a child toward mastery of a skill, before he is capable, produces frustration and delays learning. Schools must prevent frustrations, emphasize prevention, and do away with the need for remedying problems that they have created. Parents must realize that each child is unique; that his rate of learning, his ability, experiential background, health, and emotions strongly influence his learning. The individual's ability to learn differs from that of others as does his personal appearance or physical strength. Teachers must be honest and straightforward but kindly and understanding as they seek the help of parents. Parents and school people must become a team that believes in and supports each child.

Expediency should never be the basis for determining the treatment that a child shall be accorded. Democratic philosophy emphasizes the sanctity of individual personality. Change requires effort. When principles and teachers become dissatisfied with present practices in education they will willingly put forth the effort necessary to find improved ways of helping children. If inflexible grade standards do not meet individual differences or provide for continuous learning, schools must find better ways to do these things. The task of schools is to build, not destroy, personalities. Each child must be accepted as he is, where he is, and provided with opportunities for continuous growth. Democracy needs confident, healthy personalities. Schools must modify practices so that during each day each child has satisfying opportunities for growth toward the realization of his individual potentialities.

ARTICULATION OF UNITS OF THE SCHOOL SYSTEM

Does an articulated program of education contribute to the development of a healthy personality? Recently an elementary school teacher who is unusually adept in establishing friendly rapport with her pupils and who is teaching children in a large elementary school from which pupils enter a departmentalized junior high school was reviewing certain of her observations during the past three years. She said:

I have been teaching children in the sixth grade in this school for the past three years. The children who were with me during my first year in this position are now in the eighth grade of a highly departmentalized junior high school. Last year when they were in the seventh grade, and this year, too, they have invited me to their social gatherings which are usually held in a home of one of the group. Sometime before each evening is over they discuss their school activities. They tell one another and me, too, what they like about school. They also tell the things in elementary school that they miss, and one thing comes up over and over. It seems that in their junior high school the pupils not only have different teachers every hour on the hour but find themselves with different members of their group in the different classes. They miss most the opportunity to become acquainted with one another and with their teachers. They speak of one teacher as a home-room teacher but discern little difference between their home-room teacher and other teachers except that she appears to have more records to keep. They miss particularly a close association with one another. They enjoy and keep alive the social gatherings that were begun three years ago because they can meet with boys and girls they know well and with people who know them. They seek a sense of intimacy, friendship, love, and inspiration.

An eighth-grade teacher was talking about a boy who completed the eighth grade last June. She said:

I teach in a rural school. After students finish the eighth grade, they are picked up by a school bus provided by the high school district and ride many miles to the high school. I don't see them often after they start to high school because they leave early and get home late. Last week, however, one of the boys who finished the eighth grade last June came to talk with me. He was a good pupil in my class. I thought he was an unusually promising boy. While in the eighth grade, he had talked about taking courses in high school that would prepare him to work with the 'business part of getting fruit ready for the market,' to use his words. But now, after we had talked for awhile, he said he was thinking about quitting school and getting a job. When I asked him why he was thinking about quitting he said, 'My grades aren't very good. We have a lot more homework to do now than we had last year and I don't get mine done. Last year we didn't have much homework and I got along fine. Whenever we did have homework last year, I didn't get mine done at home. You know there are three of us kids at home and we still live in the trailer. When I try to do my homework I'm in everybody's way and I don't get it done. I've thought about it for a long time now and believe the thing for me to do is to earn some money. Maybe after I have earned some money to help at home I will be able to go to school again. Then, too, I'll have enough money to buy clothes and go places like the others do.' I felt depressed after he left and began to wonder what I could do to familiarize his high school teachers with the problems confronting him.

This statement by the eighth-grade teacher raises several questions. If feelings of discouragement persist in this once promising boy, can he have a healthy personality? Will such feelings give him the help he needs to develop a sense of accomplishment, a willingness to settle down to learning how to do things and do them well? Will they permit him to select desirable social goals and to feel reasonable security with his peers?

The two incidents mentioned are not isolated. They are typical of statements by teachers regarding young adolescents in many elementary schools.

A program of education contributes to the development of a healthy personality if each administrative unit is articulated in a total, continuous program. More specifically, schools which contribute to the development of a healthy personality are those in which the following statements describe school goals, planning, and procedures:

1.   Twelve years of education are regarded as minimum preparation for citizenship in today's complex society.
2.   School activities are guided by a unified philosophy of education which combines the guidance concept with intellectual education.
3.   The objectives or goals for each administrative unit are arrived at with joint representation and mutual understanding of all administrative units which constitute the school system.

4. The curriculum is planned jointly by elementary and secondary teachers, particularly for grades 6–7 and 9–10 in the 6–3–3 systems and for grades 8 and 9 in the 8–4 systems.

Educators today are accepting the idea of separate elementary and secondary schools only as convenient administrative units in a continuous, total program of public education. Educators today recognize that problems peculiar to elementary or secondary schools derive from the maturity levels of young people, not from any special institutional function or purpose. The elementary, junior high, and senior high schools joined end-to-end should provide an articulated program for the child from the time he enters school until he is prepared for adult citizenship in our modern society.

Healthy personality will be promoted as the elementary and secondary schools of a community put themselves through the process of developing and employing an educational philosophy that will make education a continuous, developmental experience for boys and girls.

TEEN-AGERS ARE AN AMERICAN INVENTION

Bennett M. Berger

Myth of Domination. There is a notion abroad in the land—one can hardly call it an idea—that ours is an adolescent-dominated society. The notion should not be taken seriously, and rarely is—least of all by those who voice it most frequently and audibly. It is, rather, typically expressed with that peculiar combination of coy bewilderment and mock helplessness which men affect when pleading their domination by women or by servants or by any group which actually has little power but which for one reason or another occupies a highly visible, perhaps strategic, and yet somewhat protected position in the society.

But the notion that we are a society dominated by adolescents is especially perverse because it is not only not true but is close to being the direct opposite of the truth. Indeed, it was not very long ago that the leaders of the world's major countries (Eisenhower, De Gaulle, Khrushchev,

From *The New York Times Magazine,* June 13, 1965. © 1965 by The New York Times Company. Reprinted by permission.

Mao, Macmillan, and Adenauer) were men who, were they not rich and powerful, would have qualified for the old folks' home. Far from being adolescent-dominated, modern societies tend to be gerontocracies.

The Teen-Age Problem. It is true, however, that most modern societies seem to have a problem with their adolescents, teen-agers—call them what you will. The very fact that we do not have a straightforward, unself-conscious, unmincing word in our language to describe the group is in itself evidence, as Edgar Friedenberg, the sociologist, has pointed out, of the problem that youth presents, and our apparent reluctance to face it squarely. I think that it is precisely because our kind of society has as yet found no honorable, serious, and productive place in it for young persons that we have no word to describe them with respect, and that our discussions of them have a tendency to be patronizing or cloying or clinical.

Postponement of Adulthood. Children everywhere, of course, pass through the sudden crisis of puberty, and the gradual maturation of their physical and sexual powers. But whereas in many societies the onset of puberty and the strength to do a man's or woman's work qualify a young person for membership in adult society (at a low status, perhaps, but at a low adult status), industrial societies like our own introduce into the culture a special *age grade* we call "adolescence"—a social category that *defines* that part of the population which fits it as not children, exactly, but not quite adults either. Adolescence is one of the ways in which culture violates nature by insisting that, for an increasing number of years, young persons postpone pressing their claims for the privileges and responsibilities of common citizenship, and by persuading young and old alike of the justice of that postponement.

Since the early nineteenth century in England, and probably the middle of the century in the United States, that postponement has been both institutionalized and prolonged, as more and more occupations required higher levels of skill. The most usual defense of postponed adulthood is the alleged "complexity" of our society, and hence the longer period of preparation needed for adequate functioning in it. But although there is little question that many modern occupations require extended training, the evidence is far from convincing (far, even, from being adequately gathered) that an American adolescent, for example, has more to learn about functioning *in general* than a young member of a "primitive" society, who may have to master the intricacies of a very complex kinship system or a system of highly elaborate religious ritual.

In any case, it is clear enough that adolescence is a relatively recent social invention which prolongs the exclusion of young persons from adult society until they are deemed "ready" to assume adult roles. There have always been people between the ages of twelve and twenty, but "teen--agers" are an American invention (not discovery)—invented within living memory.

Sources of Conflict. The well-publicized conflicts and tensions of the teenage "transitional stage" stem from the combination of an acceleration in the individual's physical and cultural growth with the continued refusal by society to grant to adolescents many of the rights and opportunities of adults; when sexual desires are more powerful than they will ever again be, sexual opportunities are fewest; obedience and submission are asked of adolescents at precisely the time when their strength, energy, and desire for autonomy are ascendent; responsible participation in the major social institutions is denied or discouraged at the moment when their interest in the world has been poignantly awakened. These tensions, generated partly by our age-grading system itself and exacerbated by a decline in parental control and a world in a state of permanent crisis, are a major source of general adolescent problems.

Means of Control. But given the severe tensions of adolescence, the surprising thing is that there isn't more trouble and turmoil among teen-agers than there actually is. I say this not to defend adolescents against the bad press they have had in recent years nor to minimize the magnitude of the "adolescent problem" but simply to point out that despite the general problems of adolescent psychology and by now legendary storminess of the teen-age years, the overwhelming majority of adolescents seem to make their way through to full adult status without getting involved in riots, orgies, or other serious delinquencies; without a dominating hedonism; and without generalized attitudes of rebellion toward parents and the world.

We don't have nearly as much adolescent rebelliousness as the tensions of adolescence suggest we might have because society has at its disposal a great armory of means to control the implicit threat of adolescent disorder posed by the anomalies of their status. I mean not the police and the courts or the more informal weapons wielded by parents, school principals, and other authorities; I mean the community youth center, the chaperoned dance, organized sports, extracurricular clubs, and the junior auxiliaries of business, religious, fraternal, and veterans' organizations—to say nothing of the comprehensive high school itself. Potential adolescent rebelliousness is controlled by a complex network of adult-sponsored youth organizations and by their promise of a bright future to those adolescents who can learn to live with and tolerate the temporary frustrations and deprivations of adolescence.

Of course, the effectiveness of these organizational weapons in coping with youth varies with the location of particular youths in the social structure. Where adult leadership is poor and community facilities limited (as frequently occurs in urban slums and certain new suburbs) or where sudden discontinuities in style of life create intergenerational tensions (as frequently occur in immigrant or highly mobile families), or where failure or anticipated failure in academic competition leaves the failed with the perception of a bleak future and with no approved, alternative sources of self-respect (as frequently occurs among Negro and lower-class boys in predominantly middle-class schools)—where these conditions exist we can expect to find high rates of adolescent disorder.

Most of the kids who get into trouble, in short, are those who are denied *both* the rights of adults *and* the compensations for this deprivation which the society tries to provide.

Adolescence and the Labor Market. Now, for a society to subject so substantial a part of its population to such severe pressures, and then to devote so much of its energies to avoiding explosions, seems like a particularly wasteful way for it to handle its youth. But we really don't know what else to do with them, for the "problem" of adolescence is inherent in something we are unwilling to change—the very structure of industrial societies.

The imposition of adolescence on young persons is not a simple accident of history nor the ethical result of revulsion with the facts of child labor, nor even an attempt by gerontocracies to postpone the succession of generations. It is by now quite common knowledge that, as societies industrialize, their need for the relatively unskilled labor of the young declines, and this tends to render a large part of youth economically superfluous.

Such societies have the problem of coping with economically useless persons while encouraging them to develop the skills which the economy needs. "Adolescence"—that is, the definition of young persons as not fully competent citizens—justifies the control that society exerts over them. It helps keep youth juvenile until society has readied an adult place for the young.

One of the functions of adolescence, then, is to keep young people off the labor market. But not only must they be kept off the labor market but off the streets and out of trouble as well; hence the whole range of adult-sponsored organizations designed to keep the young wholesomely occupied and distracted while they are readied for participation in the world of grownups.

The comprehensive high school, of course, is the most important means of controlling adolescents, and although the current campaign to reduce the number of "dropouts" is without doubt correct in warning those who are contemplating dropping out that their future occupational chances will be severely reduced, staying in high school is less important for the jobs it will qualify one for than for the reduced pressure it provides on a labor market unable to absorb the unskilled. I severely doubt that a high school diploma equips one to perform very many jobs that a person with a tenth- or eleventh-grade education could not perform.

Detachment from Family. Another thing that adolescence helps industrial societies to accomplish is the detachment of young persons from their families and locales, which helps fit them for social mobility. One of the features of traditional societies that industrialism destroys is the capacity of families, particularly fathers, to train their children for economic roles. As families are rendered inadequate to the task of training children for making a living as adults, this task falls increasingly to public agencies, which segregate the young for a large part of the day in places called schools.

Peer-Group Ties. But schools do more than simply take over the educational function from families; by bringing large numbers of young people together for a common purpose, the schools help shift the orientations and loyalties of teenagers from their families to their peer groups, and in a way this makes excellent sense for the future. Getting ahead in the adult world increasingly means the necessity for physical removal from the persons and place of one's youth, and strong family and kinship feelings as well as sentimental ties to "soil" and locale discourage social mobility.

On the other hand, strong peer-group ties (so long as they are not ties to specific persons) equip one for mobility by promoting experience and poise in "getting along" with friends and acquaintances who are one's age-mates. Blood may indeed be thicker than water, but for the sustenance of the kind of society we are making, it had better not be.

The price of social advancement is frequently separation from kin and community. The telephone company knows this, and can undertake a national advertising campaign for long-distance calls under the safe assumption that one's kin live at such distances that one can see them only infrequently. Where this is true, friends must be able to serve as a kind of substitute for unavailable relatives. But friends not obligated by blood must be found, and once found, kept, and are kept best by the sort of skill in casual cordiality developed in an adolescence crowded with one's age-mates.

Adolescence, then, by creating teen-agers and defining them as less than fully competent citizens, helps keep young unskilled persons off a labor market which has little need for them and the pseudo-society of adolescents, created by their segregation for a large part of the day in schools, helps detach them from the more traditional kinship influences which might impede their mobility. But perhaps the most important function credited to adolescence is the achievement of personal "identity."

Development of Identity. One of the most civilizing features of adolescence is what certain psychologists and psychoanalysts call the "psycho-social moratorium" it provides, that is, a period of years free from adult pressures, commitments, and responsibilities, in which young persons may engage in "the search for identity," that stormy process in which adolescents may play and experiment with social roles in an attempt to find out who and what they are.

In this view, adolescence terminates with the development of a firm and stable "identity" capable of adult choices and commitments, and this development, promoted by a long adolescence, is frequently praised as one of the triumphs of modern civilization because of the individuality it engenders. I find two serious difficulties with this view.

First, I see little evidence that the institutions designed to care for adolescents during the "psycho-social moratorium" are contributing much to "identity play" or experiments with social roles. Rather, it seems that the high schools and other youth organizations are more devoted to the rapid, assembly-line fabrication of junior grownups than they are to the cultivation of individuality. Moreover, the feared shortage of college openings creates great pressures among middle-class children for premature commitment, which tends to restrict rather than expand the horizons of personal identity.

Second, even if the conditions were optimal, there would still be a serious question about the value of a "firm identity." I see no good psychological reason for the stormy search for identity to end with adolescence (though I see how socially convenient this would be); nor do I see any good reason to believe that a "firm" and "stable" identity is under all circumstances preferable to a flexible and unstable one.

These days, a firm identity often seems to manifest itself as pigheadedness, and a stable one as stubborn rigidity. Moreover, in a rapidly changing society where social and geographic mobility puts enormous pressures on larger and larger numbers of people to anticipate the new demands that unfamiliar life situations may make on them tomorrow, a flexible, unstable identity seems like a very useful thing to command—however offensive such plasticity of personality may seem to those who have been intellectually bred on psychiatric euphemisms for "strength" of character.

Youth Culture. If the very concept of adolescence is an idea which has functioned historically to keep the young out of adult society, the complex phenomenon we have come to call "youth culture" has functioned to keep them distracted and happy while kept out. Whatever sense there is to the notion that adolescents dominate our culture rests on the fact that they constitute a major market, perhaps *the* major market, for several of the important industries of mass entertainment and popular culture. Young persons "consume" TV, movies, and popular music, for example, so far out of proportion to their numbers in the population that in this country "popular culture" is very nearly identical with "youth culture."

But there are several varieties of youth culture in America, varieties as wide as the different cultural contexts and opportunity systems offered by a pluralistic society. At its broadest and most innocuous, youth culture touches the fringes of what is called "teen-age culture": popular songs, rock and roll, disc jockeys, jukeboxes, portable phonographs, movie stars, dating, and romantic love; hot rods, motorcycles, drag racing, and sports cars; panty raids and water fights, drive-in hamburgers and clandestine drinking, football games, basketball games, dances and parties, and clubs and cliques, and lovers' lanes.

At its delinquent extreme, youth culture is black-leather jackets, gang rumbles and switchblades, malicious mischief, and joyriding in stolen cars. Politically, it is expressed in sit-ins, freedom rides, peace marches, and folk songs; it is jazz at Newport, vacations at Fort Lauderdale—and their attendant riots. And it is also bohemians and beatniks and beards and hipsters, and coffee-shop desperadoes plotting everything from literary magazines to assaults on the House Committee on Un-American Activities.

To the extent that the sound and images of popular culture invade the eye and ear at every turn, they create much of the surface texture of perceived everyday life in America, and hence reflect the influential role played by youth in the creation and the marketing of mass culture.

Now this is rather puzzling because there is no immediate self-evident reason why popular culture should be dominated by youth except, perhaps, the very existence of adolescence and consequences attributable to it. By defining young persons as "teen-agers," that is, as "not ready" for the serious matters of adulthood, adolescence invites their absorption in the

frivolous matters of "teenage culture," and the leisure and the unprecedented affluence of teen-agers predispose them to accept that invitation.

Idealism of Youth. It may well be that the very fact of their *exclusion*
from responsible participation in the major adult social institutions
increases the sensitivity of adolescents to the more purely *symbolic* aspects
of the culture. The proverbial "idealism" of youth is without question
partly a matter of this absorption with the symbolic, and the "irresponsibility" which adolescence imposes on them.

The dominant tendency among teenagers is to channel this idealism into
a sentimental preoccupation with romantic love, as this is expressed in the
music, lyrics, and rhythm of popular culture; less often, the idealism is
channeled into politics. For some it is the purity of the Beatles and the
pure erotic frenzy of their appearances; for others it is topical folk songs,
freedom rides, and sit-ins.

I do not mean morally to equate these two modes, but only to
emphasize their common source in the adolescent condition: alienation
from practical adult affairs and a compensatory absorption with the
symbolic, the ideal, the ideological. But regardless of whether their major
preoccupations are the Beatles and basketball or peace and civil rights,
adolescents tend to throw themselves into these preoccupations with great
purity and idealism.

At the same time, adolescence as we know it in this country ill prepares
young persons for the futures that actually await most of them. The
qualities of the young that our culture celebrates the most—the purity and
the idealism, the passion, candor, bluntness, spontaneity, and so on—are
precisely the qualities that the conditions of adult life make most difficult
to sustain.

This is probably why most of the culture heroes of youth (not the men
and women they say they want to be like, but the figures who actually
affect their style, demeanor, and orientation) are not the political or
economic or religious or other leaders of major institutional sectors of the
adult world but figures from the various worlds of show business, whose
milieux are closest in feeling and style to the adolescent world itself.

No Teen-Age Solution. The "adolescent problem" is at root a problem of
age grading, to which our society has found no systematic solution—except
to keep pushing up the chronological age at which people may still be
legitimately referred to as "kids." It is altogether likely that the problem of
adolescence, like the problem of slums and poverty and urban traffic, is a

problem we will simply have to learn to live with and work at piecemeal since we are unwilling to change the basic conditions which generate it.

OLD ENOUGH TO . . .

Are teen-agers mature enough to vote? President Johnson had no doubts about the young when he recommended that Congress lower the voting age to 18. "The young people of America in this decade," he declared glowingly, "are far more ready, far better qualified, far more able to discharge the highest duty of citizenship than any generation of the past."

But the film "Wild in the Streets" depicts the young electorate in wildly psychedelic colors. In the film the teenage power bloc puts LSD in the water supplies to befuddle Congress into lowering the voting age to 14. Recalcitrant elders are dispatched on permanent acid trips, and the U.S. is turned into a teeny-bopper Utopia featuring cozy communal living, perpetual rock and a potted benevolence toward other nations in place of reliance on armed forces and a diplomatic corps.

It could conceivably happen, of course, but the weight of recent physiological and psychological evidence suggests that the U.S. 18-year-old is not appreciably different from his 21-year-old brother or sister. The voting age of 21, after all, survives in the U.S. as the age of maturity more because of legal convenience and medieval custom (it was the age at which knighthood was conferred) than through biological necessity. Furthermore, other countries, notably Israel, Uruguay and Brazil, have a voting age of 18 without troubles caused by young voters. "Based on everything we know," says Dr. C. Keith Conners, director of the Child Development Laboratory at Massachusetts General Hospital, "an extra three years is not going to add to emotional stability or maturity."

Peak: Because of better diets and better medical care, U.S. 18-year-olds are bigger and heavier than earlier generations. According to the Surgeon General's office, today's U.S. Army recruits are 1.2 inches taller and 18 pounds heavier than those of World War I. Puberty now occurs around the

From *Newsweek*, LXXII, No. 5 (July 29, 1968), 53. Used by permission of the publisher.

age of 14. In the late nineteenth century boys reached puberty around 16. Today, at 18, according to the researches of the late Dr. Alfred Kinsey, the male has already reached his peak of sexual excitability and interest.

Recent studies at Vassar and Smith show that freshmen today are 2 inches taller and 10 pounds heavier than they were at the turn of the century. Also, the average age for the onset of menstruation is 12.9, almost two years younger than in 1900. The speeded-up maturity means young women enter adulthood earlier. The average age of marriage for U.S. women has declined from 21.2 years in 1920 to 20.5, and 40 per cent of all new brides are between 15 and 18 years of age.

Such physical maturity has been well documented. More surprisingly, there is new evidence that emotional and intellectual maturity parallel physical growth. At 18, according to Conners, emotional and intellectual growth have been largely completed. Says Conners: "There is no surge of ability beyond the age of early adolescence as far as the basic ability to handle abstractions is concerned." By the age of 12, he reports, the average child has already begun to learn the rudiments of abstract thinking, the ability to form hypotheses and make deductions. Six years later the techniques of thought have been mastered. "I would be inclined to say," concludes Conners, "that there is little reason to assume the average 18-year-old is not prepared with the basic rudiments for abstract thinking." According to Conners, intellectual growth after this point consists largely of gaining information and experience.

Furthermore, by 18 most people have survived the tribulations of adolescence, according to Conners, and have achieved the basic stability of personality that they will carry throughout life. However, Conners notes, some individuals mature as early as 16 while others may still be coping with their "identity crisis" at 25. Some putative "adults" remain emotional children forever.

Informed: Equally important, according to Dr. Edward J. Shoben, director of academic affairs for the American Council on Education, today's 18-year-olds are well-informed. They stay in school longer, more of them get high-school diplomas, and more of them go on to college. Furthermore, the media all keep the young informed about what is happening. In fact, Shoben believes, the scores that young people make on achievement tests show that they know more about the world than their parents did at the same age.

"I am thoroughly in favor of having 18-year-olds vote," Shoben concludes. "One of the major problems for youth is that they are biologically men and women and they have the same information as men and women have, but they are excluded from making decisions and acting as adults."

Dr. Thomas E. Shuffer, professor of pediatrics at Ohio State University, agrees with Shoben. "The more responsibility you give a teen-ager, the more he responds with sensible behavior," Shuffer asserts. The rule also works inversely, according to Shuffer, who cites the recent upheavals on U.S. campuses as a case in point. "A lot of irresponsibility," he concludes, "is the result of not being given responsibility in the first place."

Medical men, however, differ on how 18-year-olds will use the vote once they get it. Some psychiatrists believe that the searching and rebellion that characterize the emergence into adulthood will lead 18-year-olds to choose candidates on the left. But there are signs that many may gravitate to the right. The sun-kissed, vitaminized state of California, where half the population is under 21, is widely regarded as the pattern for the U.S. future. Youth sets the tone—and adults elect some of the most conservative U.S. political figures. Far left or far right, Big Brother could well turn out to be the little brother who just turned 18.

BEST YEARS OF OUR LIVES?

Somewhere between the miniskirt and medicare there is a gap in the social scientists' knowledge of human affairs. The Federal government has a Children's Bureau to study the problems of growing up; armies of psychologists monitor even the faintest tremors given off by teen-agers; social security worries about the elderly. But the vast continent of the middle-aged remains shrouded in mythology. Yet the age group between 40 and 60 makes up almost a quarter of the U.S. population, earns more than 50 per cent of U.S. personal income and wields considerable social power as well. "They are the decision makers," says Bernice L. Neugarten, professor of human development at the University of Chicago. "They set the tone of society."

Furthermore, middle age is spreading: medical progress has put off old age so that the middle years occupy a growing segment of the life span.

From *Newsweek*, LXXI, No. 8 (February 19, 1968), 88-89. Used by permission of the publisher.

"We just don't call people old as soon as we used to," says Mrs. Neugarten. "At 50 we are much younger than our parents were."

Mrs. Neugarten an attractive, 52-year-old psychologist—is one of the pioneers who have set out to explore the middle-age gap. Along with researchers at the University of California, the Langley Porter Neuro-psychiatric Institute in San Francisco, the Russell Sage Foundation and other institutions, she has made discoveries about middle-agers that have already filled in important gaps and swept away many erroneous beliefs. A sampling of some of the major findings:

Belief: Middle age begins at 40.

Finding: Neugarten's research shows that middle age comes much later to the educated, higher-status American than it does to blue-collar workers. In general, Neugarten explains, "the later a man finishes his education, the later he becomes a parent and therefore the later he reaches middle age." A construction worker, however, gauges his age by his physical strength and consequently might feel himself growing middle-aged at about 35. A brain man, on the other hand, may not feel middle-aged until well after 40.

Belief: Middle-aged people would prefer to be in their teens and twenties.

Finding: Interviewing and studying 100 middle- and upper-middle-class men and women, Neugarten found that most middle-aged people would not want their twenties back again. "Youth for most of us," says Neugarten, "has not been a particularly comfortable period in our lives. It is full of groping and turmoil." In contrast, "a middle-ager has been through it all before," says Neugarten, "and he knows how to get the most mileage out of his efforts." But most middle-aged men, according to Neugarten, do worry about their physical vigor. Men begin to "body-monitor." They watch their weight and physical appearance, are attuned to every muscle twinge as a sign of coronary disease. More important, they begin to develop certain "executive" strategies—such as leaving details to subordinates, or lessening their emotional involvement with customers—that protect them from strain and too much exertion.

Middle-aged women, in contrast, worry less than men about their own health. "Instead," says Neugarten, "a woman is more worried about her husband's health and begins to specialize in his care and feeding." The U.S. matron also begins to "rehearse for widowhood" by living through the experience of bereavement in her mind and thinking about community service and other activities to lessen the impact of widowhood.

Belief: Middle age is a time of less sexual activity and even impotence.

Finding: It's mostly in the mind. According to Dr. William Masters, co-author with Virginia Johnson of "Human Sexual Response," anxieties at the office and in the home—not a decline in physical ability—create most sexual problems in the middle years. These problems are similar to those in younger age groups: impotence, frigidity and premature ejaculation. "However," says Masters, "the younger age group is more tolerant of these problems and feels that given time all will be right with the world." For the middle-aged, this tolerance is often lost and a sense of hopelessness developed.

Belief: Menopause is a major emotional crisis for middle-aged women.

Finding: Ninety-six out of 100 women whom Neugarten interviewed in another study claimed that menopause was a relatively minor event. Many of the women who found menopause traumatic, according to Neugarten, had had earlier difficulty in adjusting to other psychosexual events, or were simply reflecting old wives' tales they had heard.

Belief: Middle-aged women suffer a great feeling of loss when their children grow up and leave home.

Finding: This "empty-nest theory" is overdrawn. Neugarten found that many of the women she studied were relieved to see children leave home so that they could find new activities.

Belief: Middle age is a time of emotional stagnation and lack of growth.

Finding: Middle age is a period in which significant emotional development can take place. "In fact," says social psychologist Marjorie Lowenthal, 53, of the Langley Porter Neuropsychiatric Institute in San Francisco, "we believe there is in middle age a time of crisis very much like the crisis in adolescence. The components, however, are very different." The middle-age crisis is triggered, according to Lowenthal, by the realization that there is not much time left. With the clock running out, the middle-ager must decide "whether to keep moving outward, or to turn inward in order to survive—a sort of death in life." Lowenthal says: "You can keep going or you can find yourself spending more and more time in front of the television, and on self-maintenance."

For some men, according to Orville G. Brim Jr., 44, president of the

Russell Sage Foundation, the crisis has a bitter edge. In middle age they realize they are not going to rise as high as they had hoped, and rather than face the humiliation of acknowledging failure they try to "repot" themselves by learning new occupations. Consequently, a professor, observes Brim in "Socialization and Society," may start writing novels, a businessman go into public service or a lawyer into business. Blue-collar workers face a similar crisis, when they realize they may never become their own bosses. To compensate they maintain the notion that their work is only temporary, or make a fling at starting a small business.

What happens when middle age fades into old age? "Men," says Neugarten, "tend to become more tolerant, they get more interested in children and less interested in being aggressive and logical. In a sense they become more feminine." Women, in contrast, get more aggressive and dominating. Often the male, resenting his increasing dependence on his wife, gets irritable, and the woman who uses his dependence against him more and more begins to nag. Some marriages improve, however—the woman enjoys her increasing independence and the man does not mind at all.

Research into middle age still leaves many questions open. Middle age may be a time of personality change, but how is it manifested in different social, economic, ethnic and sexual circumstances? To answer this kind of question, the National Institutes of Health has made an $800,000 grant to Lowenthal and her group at Langley Porter to finance a study of human development from adolescence through old age. And next fall at the University of California at Berkeley, John Clausen, 53, of the Institute of Human Development, will begin interviewing 100 citizens whose lives have been followed since they were in junior high school in 1931. Clausen will be looking for connections between childhood and adolescent experience and the quality of life in middle years.

Whatever discoveries these researchers make, they are not likely to contradict Neugarten's basic finding. While middle-aged men and women by no means regard themselves as being in command of all they survey, Neugarten asserts, they recognize that they constitute a powerful age group vis-à-vis other groups. And says Neugarten, "they are saying that middle age is the best time of life."

QUESTIONS FOR DISCUSSION

HUMAN DEVELOPMENT

1. What behavioral science disciplines must the teacher utilize in reaching an adequate understanding of the individual learners in his classroom? How does each discipline contribute?

2. What likenesses among the learners of a particular age may be made the basis for group instruction?

3. Do you agree with Gordon that we need: (1) to increase our knowledge of the conceptual and perceptual development of children; (2) to build up our understanding of the role of situation in behavior? How may such understandings affect curriculum and teaching?

4. Should the school curriculum wait for "internal ripening" when considering the readiness of learners?

5. Does knowledge of human development aid in resolving the issue of breadth versus depth in the curriculum content?

6. Do you share Ausubel's view of the role of the learner in curriculum planning?

7. What are the implications of Piaget's four major developmental stages for curriculum planning?

8. What are the curriculum implications of Ausubel's statement that older children learn primarily from verbal rather than concrete experience, after a sufficient number of basic concepts are consolidated? Does your experience support this conclusion? Relate this statement to Piaget's stages of growth of cognition.

9. How are today's adolescents different? How should this affect the secondary curriculum?

10. Do you agree that middle-agers are the decision makers and set the tone of society?

11. Should the adult education programs of the community colleges attempt to serve today's senior citizens?

3 The Nature of Learning

The third basis of the curriculum is the nature of learning. An understanding of how learning occurs in human beings is obviously a matter of central importance for planning the curriculum and for teaching.

Today there are three major families or groupings of learning theory. There are many subgroupings within these families, but for the curriculum worker or teacher who is seeking to clarify his thinking in this area, it is usually enough to be aware of the three families of theory and then to base further generalizations on this knowledge.

One learning-theory position stresses stimulus-response association. It includes all the reinforcement and conditioning theories of learning. The key word in these theories is "experience." Thinking, if it really exists at all, is a part of an S-R sequence that begins and ends outside the individual learner. Learning is a conditioning process by which a person acquires a new response. Motivation is the urge to act, which results from a stimulus. Behavior is directed by stimuli from the environment and is not related to purpose of any kind. A person selects one response instead of another because of the particular combination of prior conditioning and physiological drives operating at the moment of action. A person does not have to want to learn something in order to learn it. Anyone can learn anything of which he is capable if he will allow himself to be put through the pattern of activity necessary for conditioning to take place.

Dr. B. F. Skinner ("Freedom and the Control of Men") describes some of the advantages and possibilities of this approach to learning, as he sees them. He states that the "so-called 'democratic philosophy' of human behavior" is "increasingly in conflict with the application of the methods of science to human affairs." He believes that if there are not enough good men in the world, the first step is to create more. The question as he sees it is this: "Are we to be controlled by accident, by tyrants, or by ourselves in effective cultural design?"

193

The second of the three learning-theory families contains the "Gestalt-field," cognitive-field, and perceptual-field points of view. Dr. Arthur W. Combs ("Seeing Is Behaving") states the major principles of perceptual psychology. The contrast between these two positions—Skinner's and Combs'—is seen clearly in the first principle stated by Combs: "People do not behave according to the facts as others see them; they behave in terms of what seems to them to be so." In the perceptual-field learning theory, man is an actor who originates and thinks. In the conditioning S-R bond theory, man reacts in response to forces outside himself.

Carl R. Rogers ("Learning to Be Free") also represents the perceptual-field position. As he learns to be free, Rogers says, man realizes that he is not compelled to be the creation of others or of unknown forces within himself. As a behavioral scientist, Rogers agrees that the sequences of cause and effect operate quite as much in the psychological world as in the physical. But he believes that man's freedom is an inner thing quite apart from the outward choices of alternatives which he makes. Hadley Cantril ("Perception and Interpersonal Relations") describes an unusual research study in which he recently engaged. Through the use of the stereoscope, he determined what will happen to perception when two conflicting photographs are presented to the viewer at the same time. Perhaps this evidence will aid you in reaching a conclusion regarding the various learning theories.

Donald Avila and William Purkey ("Intrinsic Motivation—A Regrettable Distinction") contend that those who make a distinction between intrinsic and extrinsic motivation are doing so because they feel they have to make a choice between perceptual-field psychology and behavioristic S-R psychology. Calling this folly, Avila and Purkey suggest that a teacher can utilize principles of both psychologies in making the learning process more meaningful and useful.

Robert Theus ("Cognitive-Field Theory: A Positive Approach to Learning") explains Cognitive Learning Theory, which deals with the problem of how people gain an understanding of themselves, and how they use their cognitions in acting in relation to environment. He describes the proper role of the teacher as similar to that of a "head scientist" in a laboratory.

The third group consists of those views of learning that have grown out of the work and ideas of Sigmund Freud as well as his numerous present-day followers. Donald W. Robinson ("Psychoanalysis and Education") describes the impact of Freud on learning theory. The Freudian learning theories are utilized freely and compatibly by the exponents of the S-R associationism and cognitive-field learning positions. It would be a major step forward if a more abstract viewpoint might be found which could successfully incorporate the associationist and the cognitive-field viewpoints, as well as the Freudian.

A number of psychologists have attempted to synthesize contributions from these various theories of learning so that they can be more readily utilized by teachers and curriculum workers. Two articles that attempt this job of synthesis are included in this section: "Facts About Learning" by Walter B. Waetjen, and "What Do We Know About Learning?" by Goodwin Watson.

McGaugh examines learning and memory from a biological perspective, as complex processes. He believes that the time may be near when drugs may be used to correct learning deficiencies, and sees the enormous social implications of this possibility.

Concepts from many sources are in use in education today which have the subject of promising research. These areas of research include:

1. *Identification.* Children learn by and through identification with others, including their parents, peers, and teachers. Thus it is important that they have good models.

2. *Learning by Discovery.* Obtaining knowledge for oneself by the use of one's own mind frequently has advantages in terms of motivation, organization of what is learned, retention, and meaningfulness.

3. *Empathy.* Openness, trust, and security in human relationships free intelligence and enable boys and girls, and teachers as well, to learn more and to be more successful in activities in which they are jointly engaged.

4. *Culture Potential.* Anthropological studies have emphasized that different societies and cultures cultivate different qualities and capacities. Learning experiences that build on the cultural capacities of individuals and groups are particularly successful.

5. *Knowledge about Learners.* Research has shown that students learn more when teachers know them as individuals.

6. *Methods of Increasing Transfer.* When the teacher points out the possibility of transfer and develops and applies generalizations with the learners, transfer is more likely to occur.

7. *Zeal for Learning and Knowledge.* Students learn to like learning from teachers who love knowledge, from communities that provide resources for learning, and from a home environment which supports the search for knowledge by example and by the materials provided.

8.   *Sex Differences.* Too little attention is given to the differences in interests, needs, and problems of boys and girls in the school curriculum.

Perhaps concepts such as these and those provided by Waetjen and Watson in their articles may help lead to the desired synthesis of learning theory. What position on learning or synthesis of learning theories do you view as the most helpful basis for curriculum planning?

FREEDOM AND THE CONTROL OF MEN

B. F. Skinner

The second half of the twentieth century may be remembered for its solution of a curious problem. Although Western democracy created the conditions responsible for the rise of modern science, it is now evident that it may never fully profit from that achievement. The so-called "democratic philosophy" of human behavior to which it also gave rise is increasingly in conflict with the application of the methods of science to human affairs. Unless this conflict is somehow resolved, the ultimate goals of democracy may be long deferred.

Just as biographers and critics look for external influences to account for the traits and achievements of the men they study, so science ultimately explains behavior in terms of "causes" or conditions which lie beyond the individual himself. As more and more causal relations are demonstrated, a practical corollary becomes difficult to resist; it should be possible to *produce* behavior according to plan simply by arranging the proper conditions. Now, among the specifications which might reasonably be submitted to a behavioral technology are these: Let men be happy, informed, skillful, well behaved and productive.

This immediate practical implication of a science of behavior has a familiar ring, for it recalls the doctrine of human perfectibility of eighteenth- and nineteenth-century humanism. A science of man shares the

From *The American Scholar*, XXV, No. 1 (Winter, 1955-56), 47-65. Used by permission of the author.

optimism of that philosophy and supplies striking support for the working faith that men can build a better world and, through it, better men. The support comes just in time, for there has been little optimism of late among those who speak from the traditional point of view. Democracy has become "realistic," and it is only with some embarrassment that one admits today to perfectionistic or utopian thinking.

The earlier temper is worth considering, however. History records many foolish and unworkable schemes for human betterment, but almost all the great changes in our culture which we now regard as worthwhile can be traced to perfectionistic philosophies. Governmental, religious, educational, economic and social reforms follow a common pattern. Someone believes that a change in a cultural practice—for example, in the rules of evidence in a court of law, in the characterization of man's relation to God, in the way children are taught to read and write, in permitted rates of interest, or in minimal housing standards—will improve the condition of men by promoting justice, permitting men to seek salvation more effectively, increasing the literacy of a people, checking an inflationary trend, or improving public health and family relations, respectively. The underlying hypothesis is always the same: that a different physical or cultural environment will make a different and better man.

The scientific study of behavior not only justifies the general pattern of such proposals; it promises new and better hypotheses. The earliest cultural practices must have originated in sheer accidents. Those which strengthened the group survived with the group in a sort of natural selection. As soon as men began to propose and carry out changes in practice for the sake of possible consequences, the evolutionary process must have accelerated. The simple practice of making changes must have had survival value. A further acceleration is now to be expected. As laws of behavior are more precisely stated, the changes in the environment required to bring about a given effect may be more clearly specified. Conditions which have been neglected because their effects were slight or unlooked for may be shown to be relevant. New conditions may actually be created, as in the discovery and synthesis of drugs which affect behavior.

This is no time, then, to abandon notions of progress, improvement or, indeed, human perfectibility. The simple fact is that man is able, and now as never before, to lift himself by his own bootstraps. In achieving control of the world of which he is part, he may learn at least to control himself.

Timeworn objections to the planned improvement of cultural practices are already losing much of their force. Marcus Aurelius was probably right in advising his readers to be content with a haphazard amelioration of mankind. "Never hope to realize Plato's republic," he sighed, ". . . for who can change the opinions of men? And without a change of sentiments what can you make but reluctant slaves and hypocrites?" He was thinking, no doubt, of contemporary patterns of control based upon punishment or the threat of punishment which, as he correctly observed, breed only reluctant slaves of those who submit and hypocrites of those who discover modes of evasion. But we need not share his pessimism, for the opinions of men can be changed. The techniques of indoctrination which were being devised by the early Christian Church at the very time Marcus Aurelius was writing are relevant, as are some of the techniques of psychotherapy and of advertising and public relations. Other methods suggested by recent scientific analysis leave little doubt of the matter.

The study of human behavior also answers the cynical complaint that there is a plain "cussedness" in man which will always thwart efforts to improve him. We are often told that men do not want to be changed, even for the better. Try to help them, and they will outwit you and remain happily wretched. Dostoevsky claimed to see some plan in it. "Out of sheer ingratitude," he complained, or possibly boasted, "man will play you a dirty trick, just to prove that men are still men and not the keys of a piano. . . . And even if you could prove that a man is only a piano key, he would still do something out of sheer perversity—he would create destruction and chaos—just to gain his point. . . . And if all this could in turn be analyzed and prevented by predicting that it would occur, then man would deliberately go mad to prove his point." This is a conceivable neurotic reaction to inept control. A few men may have shown it, and many have enjoyed Dostoevsky's statement because they tend to show it. But that such perversity is a fundamental reaction of the human organism to controlling conditions is sheer nonsense.

So is the objection that we have no way of knowing what changes to make even though we have the necessary techniques. That is one of the great hoaxes of the century—a sort of booby trap left behind in the retreat before the advancing front of science. Scientists themselves have unsuspectingly agreed that there are two kinds of useful propositions about nature—facts and value judgments—and the science must confine itself to "what is," leaving "what ought to be" to others. But with what special sort of wisdom is the non-scientist endowed? Science is only effective knowing, no matter who engages in it. Verbal behavior proves upon analysis to be composed of many different types of utterances, from poetry and exhortation to logic and factual description, but these are not all equally useful in talking about cultural practices. We may classify useful propositions according to the degrees of confidence with which they may be asserted. Sentences about nature range from highly probable "facts" to sheer guesses. In general, future events are less likely to be correctly described than past. When a scientist talks about a projected experiment, for example, he must often resort to statements having only a moderate likelihood of being correct; he calls them hypotheses.

Designing a new cultural pattern is in many ways like designing an experiment. In drawing up a new constitution, outlining a new educational program, modifying a religious doctrine, or setting up a new fiscal policy, many statements must be quite tentative. We cannot be sure that the practice we specify will have the consequences we predict, or that the consequences will reward our efforts. This is in the nature of such proposals. They are not value judgments—they are guesses. To confuse and delay the improvement of cultural practices by quibbling about the word *improve* is itself not a useful practice. Let us agree, to start with, that health is better than illness, wisdom better than ignorance, love better than hate, and productive energy better than neurotic sloth.

Another familiar objection is the "political problem." Though we know what changes to make and how to make them, we still need to control certain relevant conditions, but these have long since fallen into the hands of selfish men who are not going to relinquish them for such purposes. Possibly we shall be permitted to develop areas which at the moment seem unimportant, but at the first signs of success the strong men will move in. This, it is said, has happened to Christianity, democracy and communism. There will always be men who are fundamentally selfish and evil, and in the long run innocent goodness cannot have its way. The only evidence here is historical, and it may be misleading. Because of the way in which physical science developed, history could until very recently have "proved" that the unleashing of the energy of the atom was quite unlikely, if not impossible. Similarly, because of the order in which processes in human behavior have become available for purposes of control, history may seem to prove that power will probably be appropriated for selfish purposes. The first techniques to be discovered fell almost always to strong, selfish men. History led Lord Acton to believe that power corrupts, but he had probably never encountered absolute power, certainly not in all its forms, and had no way of predicting its effect.

An optimistic historian could defend a different conclusion. The principle that if there are not enough men of good will in the world the first step is to create more seems to be gaining recognition. The Marshall Plan (as originally conceived), Point Four, the offer of atomic materials to power-starved countries—these may or may not be wholly new in the history of international relations, but they suggest an increasing awareness of the power of governmental good will. They are proposals to make certain changes in the environments of men for the sake of consequences which should be rewarding for all concerned. They do not exemplify a disinterested generosity, but an interest which is the interest of everyone. We have not yet seen Plato's philosopher-king, and may not want to, but the gap between real and utopian government is closing.

But we are not yet in the clear, for a new and unexpected obstacle has arisen. With a world of their own making almost within reach, men of good will have been seized with distaste for the achievement. They have uneasily rejected opportunities to apply the techniques and findings of science in the service of men, and as the import of effective cultural design has come to be understood, many of them have voiced an outright refusal to have any part in it. Science has been challenged before when it has encroached upon institutions already engaged in the control of human behavior; but what are we to make of benevolent men, with no special interests of their own to defend, who nevertheless turn against the very means of reaching long-dreamed-of goals?

What is being rejected, of course, is the scientific conception of man and his place in nature. So long as the findings and methods of science are applied to human affairs only in a sort of remedial patchwork, we may continue to hold any view of human nature we like. But as the use of science increases, we are forced to accept the theoretical structure with which science represents its facts. The difficulty is that this structure is clearly at odds with the traditional democratic conception of man. Every discovery of an event which has a part in shaping a man's behavior seems to leave so much the less to be credited to the man himself; and as such explanations become more and more comprehensive, the contribution which may be claimed by the individual himself appears to approach zero. Man's vaunted creative powers, his original accomplishments in art, science and morals, his capacity to choose and our right to hold him responsible for the consequences of his choice—none of these is conspicuous in this new self-portrait. Man, we once believed, was free to express himself in art, music and literature, to inquire into nature, to seek salvation in his own way. He could initiate action and make spontaneous and capricious changes of course. Under the most extreme duress some sort of choice remained to him. He could resist any effort to control him, though it might cost him his life. But science insists that action is initiated by forces impinging upon the individual, and that caprice is only another name for behavior for which we have not yet found a cause.

In attempting to reconcile these views it is important to note that the traditional democratic conception was not designed as a description in the scientific sense but as a philosophy to be used in setting up and maintaining a governmental process. It arose under historical circumstances and served political purposes apart from which it cannot be properly understood. In rallying men against tyranny it was necessary that the individual be strengthened, that he be taught that he had rights and could govern himself. To give the common man a new conception of his worth, his dignity, and his power to save himself, both here and hereafter, was often the only resource of the revolutionist. When democratic principles were put into practice, the same doctrines were used as a working formula. This is exemplified by the notion of personal responsibility in Anglo-American law. All governments make certain forms of punishment contingent upon certain kinds of acts. In democratic countries these contingencies are expressed by the notion of responsible choice. But the notion may have no meaning under governmental practices formulated in other ways and would certainly have no place in systems which did not use punishment.

The democratic philosophy of human nature is determined by certain political exigencies and techniques, not by the goals of democracy. But exigencies and techniques change; and a conception which is not supported for its accuracy as a likeness—is not, indeed, rooted in fact at all—may be expected to change too. No matter how effective we judge current democratic practices to be, how highly we value them or how long we expect them to survive, they are almost certainly not the *final* form of government. The philosophy of human nature which has been useful in implementing them is also almost certainly not the last word. The ultimate achievement of democracy may be long deferred unless we emphasize the real aims rather than the verbal devices of democratic thinking. A philosophy which has been appropriate to one set of political exigencies will defeat its purpose if, under other circumstances, it prevents us from applying to human affairs the science of man which probably nothing but democracy itself could have produced.

Perhaps the most crucial part of our democratic philosophy to be reconsidered is our attitude toward freedom—or its reciprocal, the control of human behavior. We do not oppose all forms of control because it is "human nature" to do so. The reaction is not characteristic of all men under all conditions of life. It is an attitude which has been carefully engineered, in large part by what we call the "literature" of democracy. With respect to some methods of control (for example, the threat of force), very little engineering is needed, for the techniques or their immediate consequences are objectionable. Society has suppressed these methods by branding them "wrong," "illegal" or "sinful." But to encourage these attitudes toward objectionable forms of control, it has been necessary to disguise the real nature of certain indispensable techniques, the commonest examples of which are education, moral discourse, and persuasion. The actual procedures appear harmless enough. They consist of supplying information, presenting opportunities for action, pointing out logical relationships, appealing to reason or "enlightened understanding," and so on. Through a masterful piece of misrepresentation, the illusion is fostered that these procedures do not involve the control of behavior; at most, they are simply ways of "getting someone to change his mind." But analysis not only reveals the presence of well-defined behavioral processes, it demonstrates a kind of control no less inexorable, though in some ways more acceptable, than the bully's threat of force.

Let us suppose that someone in whom we are interested is acting unwisely—he is careless in the way he deals with his friends, he drives too fast, or he holds his golf club the wrong way. We could probably help him by issuing a series of commands: don't nag, don't drive over sixty, don't hold your club that way. Much less objectionable would be "an appeal to reason." We could show him how people are affected by his treatment of them, how accident rates rise sharply at higher speeds, how a particular grip on the club alters the way the ball is struck and corrects a slice. In doing so we resort to verbal mediating devices which emphasize and support certain "contingencies of reinforcement"—that is, certain relations between behavior and its consequences—which strengthen the behavior we wish to set up. The same consequences would possibly set up the behavior without our help, and they eventually take control no matter which form of help we give. The appeal to reason has certain advantages over the authoritative command. A threat of punishment, no matter how subtle, generates emotional reactions and tendencies to escape or revolt. Perhaps the controllee merely "feels resentment" at being made to act in a given way, but even that is to be avoided. When we "appeal to reason," he "feels freer to do as he pleases." The fact is that we have exerted *less* control than in using a threat; since other conditions may contribute to the result, the effect may be delayed or, possibly in a given instance, lacking. But if we have worked a change in his behavior at all, it is because we have altered relevant environmental conditions, and the processes we have set in motion are just as real as inexorable, if not as comprehensive, as in the most authoritative coercion.

"Arranging an opportunity for action" is another example of disguised control. The power of the negative form has already been exposed in the analysis of censorship. Restriction of opportunity is recognized as far from harmless. As Ralph Barton Perry said in an article which appeared in the Spring, 1953, *Pacific Spectator*, "Whoever determines what alternatives shall be made known to man controls what the man shall choose *from.* He is deprived of freedom in proportion as he is denied access to *any* ideas, or is confined to any range of ideas short of the totality of relevant possibilities." But there is a positive side as well. When we present a relevant state of affairs, we increase the likelihood that a given form of behavior will be emitted. To the extent that the probability of action has changed, we have made a definite contribution. The teacher of history controls a student's behavior (or, if the reader prefers, "deprives him of freedom") just as much in *presenting* historical facts as in suppressing them. Other conditions will no doubt affect the student, but the contribution made to his behavior by the presentation of material is fixed and, within its range, irresistible.

The methods of education, moral discourse and persuasion are acceptable not because they recognize the freedom of the individual or his right to dissent, but because they make only *partial* contributions to the control of his behavior. The freedom they recognize is freedom from a more coercive form of control. The dissent which they tolerate is the possible effect of other determiners of action. Since these sanctioned methods are frequently ineffective, we have been able to convince ourselves that they do not represent control at all. When they show too much strength to permit disguise, we give them other names and suppress them as energetically as we suppress the use of force. Education grown too powerful is rejected as propaganda or "brain-washing," while really effective persuasion is decried as "undue influence," "demagoguery," "seduction," and so on.

If we are not to rely solely upon accident for the innovations which give rise to cultural evolution, we must accept the fact that some kind of control of human behavior is inevitable. We cannot use good sense in human affairs unless someone engages in the design and construction of environmental conditions which affect the behavior of men. Environmental changes have always been the condition for the improvement of cultural patterns, and we can hardly use the more effective methods of science without making changes on a grander scale. We are all controlled by the world in which we live, and part of that world has been and will be constructed by man. The question is this: Are we to be controlled by accident, by tyrants, or by ourselves in effective cultural design?

The danger of the misuse of power is possibly greater than ever. It is not allayed by disguising the facts. We cannot make wise decisions if we continue to pretend that human behavior is not controlled, or if we refuse to engage in control when valuable results might be forthcoming. Such measures weaken only ourselves, leaving the strength of science to others. The first step in a defense against tyranny is the fullest possible exposure of controlling techniques. A second step has already been taken success-fully in restricting the use of physical force. Slowly, and as yet imperfectly we have worked out an ethical and governmental design in which the strong man is not allowed to use the power deriving from his strength to control his fellow men. He is restrained by a superior force created for that purpose—the ethical pressure of the group, or more explicit religious and governmental measures. We tend to distrust superior forces, as we currently hesitate to relinquish sovereignty in order to set up an international police force. But it is only through such counter-control that we have achieved what we call peace—a condition in which men are not permitted to control each other through force. In other words, control itself must be controlled.

Science has turned up dangerous processes and materials before. To use the facts and techniques of a science of man to the fullest extent without making some monstrous mistake will be difficult and obviously perilous. It is no time for self-deception, emotional indulgence, or the assumption of attitudes which are no longer useful. Man is facing a difficult test. He must keep his head now, or he must start again—a long way back.

Those who reject the scientific conception of man must, to be logical, oppose the methods of science as well. The position is often supported by predicting a series of dire consequences which are to follow if science is not checked. A recent book by Joseph Wood Krutch, *The Measure of Man,* is in this vein. Mr. Krutch sees in the growing science of man the threat of an unexampled tyranny over men's minds. If science is permitted to have its way, he insists, "we may never be able really to think again." A controlled culture will, for example, lack some virtue inherent in disorder. We have emerged from chaos through a series of happy accidents, but in an engineered culture it will be "impossible for the unplanned to erupt again." But there is no virtue in the accidental character of an accident, and the diversity which arises from disorder can not only be duplicated by design but vastly extended. The experimental is superior to simple observation just because it multiplies "accident" in a systematic coverage of the possibi-lities. Technology offers many familiar examples. We no longer wait for immunity to disease to develop from a series of accidental exposures, nor do we wait for natural mutations in sheep and cotton to produce better fibers; but we continue to make use of such accidents which occur, and we certainly do not prevent them. Many of the things we value have emerged from the clash of ignorant armies on darkling plains, but it is not therefore wise to encourage ignorance and darkness.

It is not always disorder itself which we are told we shall miss but certain admirable qualities in men which flourish only in the presence of disorder. A man rises above an unpropitious childhood to a position of eminence, and since we cannot give a plausible account of the action of so complex an environment, we attribute the achievement to some admirable faculty in the man himself. But such "faculties" are suspiciously like the explanatory fictions against which the history of science warns us. We admire Lincoln for rising above a deficient school system, but it was not necessarily something *in him* which permitted him to become an educated man in spite of it. His educational environment was certainly unplanned, but it could nevertheless have made a full contribution to his mature behavior. He was a rare man, but the circumstances of his childhood were rare too. We do not give Franklin Delano Roosevelt the same credit for becoming an educated man with the help of Groton and Harvard, although the same behavioral processes may have been involved. The founding of Groton and Harvard somewhat reduced the possibility that fortuitous combinations of circumstances would erupt to produce other Lincolns. Yet the founders can hardly be condemned for attacking an admirable human quality.

Another predicted consequence of a science of man is an excessive uniformity. We are told that effective control—whether governmental, religious, educational, economic or social—will produce a race of men who differ from each other only through a relatively refractory genetic difference. That would probably be bad design, but we must admit that we are not now pursuing another course from choice. In a modern school, for example, there is usually a syllabus which specifies what every student is to learn by the end of each year. This would be flagrant regimentation if anyone expected every student to comply. But some will be poor in particular subjects, others will not study, others will not remember what they have been taught, and diversity is assured. Suppose, however, that we someday possess such effective educational techniques that every student will in fact be put in possession of all the behavior specified in a syllabus.

At the end of the year, all students will correctly answer all questions on the final examination and "must all have prizes." Should we reject such a system on the grounds that in making all students excellent it has made them all alike? Advocates of the theory of a special faculty might contend that an important advantage of the present system is that the good student learns *in spite* of a system which is so defective that it is currently producing bad students as well. But if really effective techniques are available, we cannot avoid the problem of design simply by preferring the status quo. At what point should education be deliberately inefficient?

Such predictions of the havoc to be wreaked by the application of science to human affairs are usually made with surprising confidence. They not only show a faith in the orderliness of human behavior; they presuppose an established body of knowledge with the help of which it can be positively asserted that the changes which scientists propose to make will have quite specific results—albeit not the results they foresee. But the predictions made by the critics of science must be held to be equally fallible and subject also to empirical test. We may be sure that many steps in the scientific design of cultural patterns will produce unforeseen consequences. But there is only one way to find out. And the test must be made, for if we cannot advance in the design of cultural patterns with absolute certainty, neither can we rest completely confident of the superiority of the status quo.

Apart from their possibly objectionable consequences, scientific methods seem to make no provision for certain admirable qualities and faculties which seem to have flourished in less explicitly planned cultures; hence they are called "degrading" or "lacking in dignity." (Mr. Krutch has called the author's *Walden Two* an "ignoble Utopia.") The conditioned reflex is the current shipping boy. Because conditioned reflexes may be demonstrated in animals, they are spoken of as though they were exclusively subhuman. It is implied, as we have seen, that no behavioral processes are involved in education and moral discourse or, at least, that the processes are exclusively human. But men do show conditioned relfexes (for example, when they are frightened by all instances of the control of human behavior because some instances engender fear), and animals do show processes similar to the human behavior involved in instruction and moral discourse. When Mr. Krutch asserts that " 'Conditioning' is achieved by methods which bypass or, as it were, short-circuit those very reasoning faculties which education proposes to cultivate and exercies," he is making a technical statement which needs a definition of terms and a great deal of supporting evidence.

If such methods are called "ignoble" simply because they leave no room for certain admirable attributes, then perhaps the practice of admiration needs to be examined. We might say that the child whose education has been skillfully planned has been deprived of the right to intellectual heroism. Nothing has been left to be admired in the way he acquires an education. Similarly, we can conceive of moral training which is so adequate to the demands of the culture that men will be good practically automatically, but to that extent they will be deprived of the right to moral heroism, since we seldom admire automatic goodness. Yet if we consider the end of morals rather than certain virtuous means, is not "automatic goodness" a desirable state of affairs? Is it not, for example, the avowed goal of religious education; T. H. Huxley answered the question unambiguously: "If some great power would agree to make me always think what is true and do what is right, on condition of being a sort of clock and wound up every morning before I got out of bed, I should close instantly with the offer." Yet Mr. Krutch quotes this as the scarcely credible point of view of a "protomodern" and seems himself to share T. S. Eliot's contempt for ". . . systems so perfect/That no one will need to be good."

"Having to be good" is an excellent example of an expendable honorific. It is inseparable from a particular form of ethical and moral control. We distinguish between the things we *have* to do to avoid punishment and those we *want* to do for rewarding consequences. In a culture which did not resort to punishment we should never "have" to do anything except with respect to the punishing contingencies which arise directly in the physical environment. And we are moving toward such a culture, because the neurotic, not to say psychotic, by-products of control through punishment have long since led compassionate men to seek alternative techniques. Recent research has explained some of the objectionable results of punishment and has revealed resources of at least equal power in "positive reinforcement." It is reasonable to look forward to a time when man will seldom "have" to do anything, although he may show interest, energy, imagination and productivity far beyond the level seen under the present system (except for rare eruptions of the unplanned).

What we have to do we do with *effort.* We call it "work." There is no other way to distinguish between exhausting labor and the possibly equally energetic but rewarding activity of play. It is presumably good cultural design to replace the former with the latter. But an adjustment in attitudes is needed. We are much more practiced in admiring the heroic labor of a Hercules than the activity of one who works without having to. In a truly effective educational system the student might not "have to work" at all, but that possibility is likely to be received by the contemporary teacher with an emotion little short of rage.

We cannot reconcile traditional and scientific views by agreeing upon *what* is to be admired or condemned. The question is whether anything is to be so treated. Praise and blame are cultural practices which have been adjuncts of the prevailing system of control in Western democracy. All peoples do not engage in them for the same purposes or to the same extent, nor, of course, are the same behaviors always classified in the same way as subject to praise or blame. In admiring intellectual and moral heroism and unrewarding labor, and in rejecting a world in which these would be uncommon, we are simply demonstrating our own cultural conditioning. By promoting certain tendencies to admire and censure, the group of which we are a part has arranged for the social reinforcement and punishment needed to assure a high level of intellectual and normal industry. Under other and possibly better controlling systems, the behavior which we now admire would occur, but not under those conditions which make it admirable, and we should have no reason to admire it because the culture would have arranged for its maintenance in other ways.

To those who are stimulated by the glamorous heroism of the battle-field, a peaceful world may not be a better world. Others may reject ·a world without sorrow, longing or a sense of guilt because the relevance of deeply moving works of art would be lost. To many who have devoted their lives to the struggle to be wise and good, a world without confusion and evil might be an empty thing. A nostalgic concern for the decline of moral heroism has been a dominating theme in the work of Aldous Huxley. In *Brave New World* he could see in the application of science to human affairs only a travesty on the notion of the Good (just as George Orwell, in *1984,* could foresee nothing but horror). In a recent issue of *Esquire,* Huxley has expressed the point this way: "We have had religious revolutions, we have had political, industrial, economic and nationalistic revolutions. All of them, as our descendants will discover, were but ripples in an ocean of conservatism—trivial by comparison with the psychological revolution toward which we are so rapidly moving. *That* will really be a revolution. When it is over, the human race will give no further trouble." (Footnote for the reader of the future: This was not meant as a happy ending. Up to 1956 men had been admired, if at all, either for causing trouble or alleviating it. Therefore—)

It will be a long time before the world can dispense with heroes and hence with the cultural practice of admiring heroism, but we move in that direction whenever we act to prevent war, famine, pestilence and disaster. It will be a long time before man will never need to submit to punishing environments or engage in exhausting labor, but we move in that direction whenever we make food, shelter, clothing and labor-saving devices more readily available. We may mourn the passing of heroes but not the conditions which make for heroism. We can spare the self-made saint or sage as we spare the laundress on the river's bank struggling against fearful odds to achieve cleanliness.

The two great dangers in modern democratic thinking are illustrated in a paper by former Secretary of State Dean Acheson. "For a long time now," writes Mr. Acheson, "We have gone along with some well-tested principles of conduct: That it was better to tell the truth than falsehoods; . . . that duties were older than and as fundamental as rights; as Justice Holmes put it, the mode by which the inevitable came to pass was effort; that to perpetrate a harm was wrong no matter how many joined in it . . . and so on. . . . Our institutions are founded on the assumption that most people follow these principles most of the time because they want to, and the institutions work pretty well when this assumption is true. More recently, however, bright people have been fooling with the machinery in the human head and they discovered quite a lot. . . . Hitler introduced new refinements (as the result of which) a whole people have been utterly confused and corrupted. Unhappily neither the possession of this knowledge nor the desire to use it was confined to Hitler. . . . Others dip from this same devil's cauldron."

The first dangerous notion in this passage is that most people follow democratic principles of conduct "because they want to." This does not account for democracy or any other form of government if we have not explained why people *want* to behave in given ways. Although it is tempting to assume that it is human nature to believe in democratic principles, we must not overlook the "cultural engineering" which produced and continues to maintain democratic practices. If we neglect the conditions which produce democratic *behavior*, it is useless to try to maintain a democratic *form* of government. And we cannot expect to export a democratic form of government successfully if we do not also provide for the cultural practices which will sustain it. Our forebearers did not discover the essential nature of man; they evolved a pattern of behavior which worked remarkably well under the circumstances. The "set of principles" expressed in that pattern is not the only true set or necessarily the best. Mr. Acheson has presumably listed the most unassailable items; some of them are probably beyond question, but others—concerning duty and effort—may need revision as the world changes.

The second—and greater—threat to the democracy which Mr. Acheson is defending is his assumption that knowledge is necessarily on the side of evil. All the admirable things he mentions are attributed to the innate goodness of man, all the detestable to "fooling with the machinery in the human head." This is reminiscent of the position, taken by other institutions engaged in the control of men, that certain forms of knowledge are in themselves evil. But how out of place in a democratic philosophy! Have we come this far only to conclude that well-intentioned people cannot study the behavior of men without becoming tyrants or that informed men cannot show good will? Let us for once have strength and good will on the same side.

Far from being a threat to the tradition of Western democracy, the growth of a science of man is a consistent and probably inevitable part of it. In turning to the external conditions which shape and maintain the behavior of men, while questioning the reality of inner qualities and faculties to which human achievements were once attributed, we turn from the ill-defined and remote to the observable and manipulable. Though it is a painful step, it has far-reaching consequences, for it not only sets higher standards of human welfare but shows us how to meet them. A change in a theory of human nature cannot change the facts. The achievements of man in science, art, literature, music and morals will survive any interpretation we place upon them. The uniqueness of the individual is unchallenged in the scientific view. Man, in short, will remain man. (There will be much to admire for those who are so inclined. *Possibly the noblest achievement to which man can aspire, even according to present standards, is to accept himself for what he is, as that is revealed to him by the methods which he devised and tested on a part of the world in which he had only a small personal stake.)*

If Western democracy does not lose sight of the aims of humanitarian action, it will welcome almost fabulous support of its own science of man and will strengthen itself and play an important role in building a better world for everyone. But if it cannot put its "democratic philosophy" into proper historical perspective—if, under the control of attitudes and emotions which it generated for other purposes, it now rejects the help of science—then it must be prepared for defeat. For if we continue to insist that science has nothing to offer but a new and more horrible form of tyranny, we may produce just such a result by allowing the strength of science to fall in the hands of despots. And if, with luck, it were to fall instead to men of good will in other political communities, it would be perhaps a more ignominious humiliating defeat; for we should then, through a miscarriage of democratic principles, be forced to leave to others the next step in man's long struggle to control nature and himself.

SEEING IS BEHAVING

Arthur W. Combs

How effective we are in dealing with the great human problem of any generation will depend in large measure upon the accuracy and scope of

Adapted from an address presented at the ASCD annual conference, Seattle, Washington, 1958. Used by permission of the author.

the ideas we hold about what people are like and why they behave as they do. This is particularly true for what we do as educators. People can only behave in terms of what seems to them to be so. Hence, the methods we use to solve our problems of curriculum will depend upon what we believe about the nature of the people we seek to teach. Whenever, therefore, science changes our ideas of what people are like, it must have far-reaching implications for our profession.

In recent years, the social sciences have been discovering some fascinating and exciting new ways of looking at human behavior, and these discoveries seem to me to have vast implications for the whole field of education. In this article I would like to state just two of these principles and point out some of the things it seems to me they mean for education.

BEHAVIOR IS A PERSONAL MATTER

The first principle is this: *People do not behave according to the facts as others see them; they behave in terms of what seems to them to be so.* The psychologist expresses this technically as: Behavior is a function of perception. What affects human behavior, we are beginning to understand, is not so much the forces exerted on people from without as the meanings existing for the individual within. It is feelings, beliefs, convictions, attitudes, and understandings of the person who is behaving that constitutes the directing forces of behavior. In election, for example, the people who vote for the Democrats believe that the Democrats will save the nation while the Republicans will certainly ruin it. The reverse is true of the people who vote the other way. Each side behaves in terms of what seems to him to be so. But what is *really* the fact of the matter we shall never know, for only one party gets elected! In order to understand the behavior of people we must understand how things seem to them.

Our failure to understand this simple and "obvious" fact about behavior is one of the most potent causes of misunderstanding and failure in dealing with human problems. A good example may be seen in the case of the child who feels that people do not like him. Feeling that he is unliked and unwanted, the child is likely to make himself obnoxious in his attempts to attract attention. Parents seeking to put a stop to this kind of annoying behavior may say, "For goodness sake, Jimmy, stop annoying Mr. Jones and go to your room!" Such behavior on the part of adults simply serves to prove what the child already believes—"People don't like me very well."

When we fail to understand how things seem to people with whom we are working, we may make serious errors in our efforts to deal with them.

The moment, however, we understand an individual's behavior as it seems to him, our own behavior can be much more accurate, realistic, precise, and effective. If a child *thinks* his teacher is unfair, it doesn't make much difference whether the teacher is really unfair or not. If a child thinks his teacher is unfair, he behaves as though she were. Whether she is really unfair or not is, as the lawyers say, "irrelevant and immaterial information as far as the child is concerned." In this sense, seeing is not only believing; seeing is behaving! To understand behavior we need to understand the personal meanings existing for the people who are behaving.

THE EFFECT OF THE CONCEPT OF SELF

The second important point we are currently discovering is this: *The most important ideas which affect people's behavior are those ideas they have about themselves.* This, the psychologist refers to as the *self concept.* The beliefs we hold about ourselves, we are learning, are among the most important determinants of behavior. People who see themselves as men behave like men; people who see themselves as women behave like women. Our self concepts even affect the things we see and hear. If you don't think so, try going window shopping with a member of the opposite sex.

The self concept, we are finding, is so tremendously important that it affects practically everything we do. We are even discovering that a child's success in school depends in very large measure upon the kind of self concepts he has about himself. Some years ago, Prescott Lecky observed that children often made about the same number of errors in spelling per page when they were writing free material, despite the difficulty of the material! One would normally expect more errors on harder material, but these children spelled as though they were responding to a built-in quota. It occurred to Lecky that they were behaving more in terms of their beliefs about spelling than in terms of their actual skills. Accordingly, he arranged to have a group of these children spend some time with a counselor who helped them to explore themselves and their feelings about their abilities to spell. As a consequence of these discussions an amazing· thing happened. Despite the fact that these children had no additional work in spelling whatever, their spelling improved tremendously, and several of the children took up spelling as a hobby!

We are finding a similar phenomenon in the field of reading. Nowadays we catch children's visual difficulties fairly early so that it is rare these days to find a child coming to the reading clinic with anything very wrong with his eyes. More often than not, when a child is unable to read, the difficulty seems to lie in the fact that he has developed an *idea about himself* as a person who cannot read. Having developed such an idea, he gets caught in a vicious circle that goes something like this: Believing he cannot read, the child avoids reading and thus avoids the very practice which might make it possible for him to learn. Furthermore, believing that he does not read very well, he reads poorly when asked to do so. His teacher, in turn, observing this weakness, says "My goodness, Johnny, you don't read very well!" which proves what he already thinks! Once having developed the idea that he cannot read, a child's experience confirms his belief and his teachers, who should know, corroborate it. Just to make sure that the lesson is well learned, moreover, we may also send home a failing grade on his report card so that his parents can tell him too!

We are beginning to discover that the self concept acts very much like a quota for an individual. What a person believes about himself establishes what he can and will do. Once a self concept is established, furthermore, it is a very difficult thing to change, even if we would like to change it in a positive direction. The young man coming to the university believing that he is not very bright, for example, who is told by the test administrator that he has done very well, responds: "Are you sure? There must be some mistake!"

We are even discovering that the question of adjustment or maladjustment is very largely a question of the self concepts people have about themselves. Well-adjusted people, we now observe, are those who see themselves as liked, wanted, acceptable, able—as people of dignity and integrity. People who see themselves so are no trouble to anybody. They get along fine in our society. They are essentially happy people who work efficiently and effectively, and rarely cause difficulty in school or out. The people who cause us difficulty in our society are, almost without exception, those who see themselves as unliked, unwanted, unacceptable, unable, undignified, unworthy, and the like. These are the frustrated people of our generation who frustrate us. They are the maladjusted, unhappy ones who fill our jails, our mental hospitals and institutions.

SOME IMPLICATIONS FOR EDUCATION

We have now stated two modern principles of behavior:

1. That people behave according to how things seem to them.

2. That the most important ideas any of us ever have are those ideas about ourselves.

These two very simple ideas have vast implications for education. In some ways they corroborate things we educators have been feeling all along. They also raise questions about some of the things we have been doing. And, finally, they seem to point to some new ways of solving old problems. In the remainder of this article I would like to point out two or three of the important implications these ideas seem to have for me.

TWO WAYS OF SEEING BEHAVIOR

If these ideas I have been talking about are valid, it seems to me to mean that we have two ways at which we can look at human behavior. One of these I have called the fencing-in approach, and it is familiar to anyone who has ever driven cows home from pasture. If we believe that behavior is a function of the forces exerted on people, then the methods we will use in working with them will have to do with attempting to control the forces acting upon people. One first goes down the lane from the barn in search of the cattle, opening the gates where he wants the cattle to go, and closing the gates where he doesn't want them to go. Then, when one has reached the pasture the idea is to get behind the herd, and irritate it in such a way that it will move toward the barn. Because we have previously opened the gates where we want them to go, and closed the gates where we don't want them to go, the cattle effectively reach the barn. This is a method of dealing with animals that works fine. However, it does not work so well with people. People, being smarter than cattle, are always finding gates we forgot to lock, or climbing over the fences and scampering off over the countryside. This fencing-in method of dealing with people may be found in operation everywhere in our society. It is to be found in our homes, in business, in our schools, in our churches, and even in diplomatic affairs where we attempt to fence in the other person and make him do what we would like to have him do. Such a method of dealing with people sometimes works, but it also has unfortunate effects upon people on whom it is applied.

People who are dealt with in this way tend to become dependent upon the people who are manipulating them. This dependency, however, is directly contrary to what we hope to accomplish in effective education. What is more, because this method of operation depends upon somebody setting up the proper fences, it leads directly to a *great man philosophy* of dealing with people. Somebody must know where people should go in order to know how we should set up the fences in order to get them there. Fundamentally, this is a dictatorial approach. It is a strange thing therefore that it is the most used method of dealing with people in our society, despite the fact that we pride ourselves on living in a democracy, and abhorring dictatorships.

There is another point of view which grows out of the way of seeing people that we have been talking about in this lecture. That is thus: If it is true that people's behavior is a function of their perceptions, perceptions lie inside of people, and cannot be dealt with directly. This means that in order to deal with people, if we follow this point of view, it is necessary for us to find ways of helping, assisting, facilitating, aiding people, rather than attempting to direct, force, or coerce them.

When the meanings that govern people's behavior are seen as lying inside them, our own behavior in working with them has to do with encouraging and facilitating people and their behavior. This has quite different effects than the fencing-in approach we have been talking about. People do not become dependent upon their leaders under these kinds of circumstances. Rather, they develop faith in their own dignity and integrity and accept the responsibilities for their own behavior. This, it seems to me, is a far more desirable approach in a democratic society. It is consistent with the basic democratic idea that when men are free they can find their own best ways. The problem here is not, then, to take people to some preconceived place but to create the kind of freedom that makes it possible for them to achieve their own best good.

We might each ask ourselves, "Which of these methods do I characteristically use in my work?" The answer probably comes almost at once: "I use the second of these methods." But let us stop a minute. Do you really? If you use this second method of dealing with people, you will not be heard saying such things as, "I cannot make him!" "If I could just get him to see!" "How am I going to get people to?" If these are the kinds of words you use in describing your relationships with other people, then, almost certainly, you are using the fencing-in technique we have been talking about, rather than the perceptual or facilitating approach.

EDUCATION MUST DEAL WITH MEANINGS

If it is true that people's behavior is a function of the meanings which exist for them, another thing we must learn to do as teachers is to become sensitive to people's meanings. This is not so difficult as one might suppose. People, after all, are always telling us about how things seem to them, if we could only learn to listen. Children, for example, are continuously telling us about how things are with them, or how things seem to them, through the things they do in their play, in art, in composition, discussion, in every activity, if we can but learn to develop a sensitivity to hear these things when they are said in our presence. If it is true that a person's behavior is a result of his perceptions, then what we need to do in learning to understand how things seem to people is to learn to read their behavior backwards. We need to ask ourselves now, "How would I have to feel to behave like that?" Or, "How would a person have to see the situation to behave in that way?"

TEACHERS DO NOT HAVE TO BE PSYCHIATRISTS

One of the most exciting implications of these new principles is this: if it is true that behavior is a function of perception then the causes of behavior lie fundamentally in the present and not in the past. Psychologists for several generations have told us that in order to understand an individual we need to know all that has happened to him in the past. As a result many teachers have often felt helpless to deal with a child because for one reason or other they were unable to acquire knowledge of all his past experiences. Many educators have never been entirely happy with this point of view. We have often felt, as Gordon Allport once expressed it, that "people are busy living their lives forward while psychologists busily trace them backwards!" We are now finding that many modern psychologists are providing support for our suspicion that this preoccupation with the past may not always be essential.

If it is true that behavior is a function of perception, then behavior is a result of how people are perceiving right now, *today, as of this moment!* This understanding opens a whole new world for education. This is not to say that behavior is not *also* the result of what has happened in the past. We can look at the causes of behavior in two ways. A person's behavior is *historically* the result of all the things that have happened to him in the past. It is *immediately* the result of how things seem to him at this moment. For example, a child that has been badly rejected in his youth may come to feel about himself that he is unliked, unwanted, unaccept-able, that the world is a pretty tough place, almost too much for what he has to offer. These feelings he has acquired, of course, because of the things that have happened to him. But his behavior today, now, as of this moment, is the result of how he is *feeling* today. This way of looking at behavior opens a whole new frontier for educational practice.

When we believed that behavior was entirely a function of the past, there was, of course, very little we could do. It had all been done. Such a belief leads to preoccupation with the child's history instead of what is going on at the moment. The historical view of causation also encourages the old army game of passing the buck. The college says, "What can you do with youngsters who come so badly prepared from high school?" The high school says, "What can you do for the child from a home like that?" The poor parent in our society is low man on the totem pole. He's stuck with it; he doesn't have anybody he can pass the blame to, except maybe to say, "Well, he gets it from the father's side of the family!"

If we believe that a child's behavior is solely the result of the forces working upon him, there is very little we can do to help, and we are always able to charge off our failures to other people. If, however, behavior is a function of perception, then there are tremendous things we can do in the present. We can help a person to see differently now, even if we cannot change his past. It means that you and I can help children in school without the necessity of having to change their environments. It means that there is something we can do for *every* child no matter what kind of background he comes from. Although we can rarely do much about the past, there are important things we can do about the present.

This new understanding also lifts a great weight from the teachers' shoulders. It means that we do not have to be social workers or psychiatrists, we can just be teachers! It means we do not have to pry, we do not have to know all about a child's background in order to be able to deal with him effectively. This is not to say that knowledge of his past and of his home situation might not be helpful. It does mean that we *do not have to have* it as an absolute essential. I don't know how you feel about this, but this sets me free to do a lot of things I was never able to do before. This simple idea has already caused revolutions in the field of social work, in psychotherapy and in the field of human relations generally. It seems equally promising in what it may offer to education.

For one thing, teachers do not have to feel defeated. If behavior is a function of perception, then no matter what goes on elsewhere in the child's life, it is still important what you do and I do as teachers. People get their perceptions from those who surround them, and that means us. It may be that there are some children with whom we have to deal who are so sick that we cannot make *all* the difference. We may not be able to change a child completely, but neither are we helpless. Fritz Redl once said in a speech, "You know, the difference between a good child and a naughty child is not very great. The difference, however, between a naughty child and a real tough delinquent is a very great distance. Wouldn't it be wonderful if we could just keep them naughty?" I find this sentiment very reassuring. I think that what Redl is trying to tell us is that none of us need feel defeated. That whatever we do is *always* important even though for a particular child it may not be enough to produce immediate results.

THE SELF CONCEPT AND CURRICULUM DESIGN

Finally, if the self concept is as important as modern psychology tells us, this fact has vast importance for curriculum construction and design. One of the great tragedies of our time is that we have literally hundreds of thousands of people in our society who are the prisoners of their own perceptions. Believing they can only do x well, they only do x much. The rest of us, seeing them do only x much say, "Well, that's an x-much person," and this just proves what these people have thought in the first place! Such people are the victims of their own self concepts. Everyone loses as a result of this great waste of human potential.

But people get their self concepts from the ways they have been treated by the persons who surround them during their growing up. From the minute the child is born we begin to teach him who he is and what he is. Whether we are helpful, or hindering, or of no account at all in the development of children's self concepts will depend upon ourselves. We *can* behave in ways that don't count, ways that have nothing to do with meanings, and they will quickly disregard us. Or, we *can* behave in ways that are important in helping them discover who they are and what they are—in positive fashion. We are, in a sense, the architects of children's self concepts.

Society needs adequate, well-adjusted, informed people as never before in history. What then shall we do to produce these kinds of people? I think the answer lies in the above definitions of the kinds of people we want. Earlier in this article we stated that whether or not an individual was likely to be well adjusted was largely a matter of his self concept. We observed that people who see themselves as liked, wanted, acceptable, able, dignified, worthy, etc., are the kinds who make effective, efficient citizens. People, on the other hand, who see themselves as unliked, unwanted, unacceptable, unable; these kinds of people are the ones who cause us trouble. If this is true, we do not have to be psychiatrists to help children grow.

To be effective in these terms, we need teachers who can understand and perceive how a child is thinking and feeling. We need teachers who can understand the impact of the ways they are behaving and the things they are doing on the perceptions of children. We need teachers skilled in helping children explore and discover themselves and their relationship to the world in which they live. In the final analysis, the question of curriculum construction boils down to this: How can a child feel liked, unless somebody likes him? How can a child feel wanted, unless somebody wants him? And how can a child feel able, unless somewhere he has some success? In our answers to these questions related to the kinds of self concepts we seek lie the basic criteria for curriculum change and improvement.

LEARNING TO BE FREE

Carl R. Rogers

I would like to describe for you a pattern of experience which I have observed, and in which I have participated. It is an experience which I have seen repeated with many variations, in many individuals, with many differing outward expressions, but with a seemingly common core. It is an experience on which I have placed various labels as I have tried to think about it—becoming a person, freedom to be, courage to be, learning to be free—yet the experience is something broader than, and deeper than, any of its labels. It is quite possible that the words I use in regard to it may miscommunicate. The speculations and ideas I present, based on this experience, may be erroneous, or partly erroneous. But the experience itself *exists.* It is a deeply compelling phenomenon for anyone who has observed it, or who has lived it.

THE EXPERIENCE OF LEARNING TO BE FREE

The experience to which I am referring is a central process or central aspect of psychotherapy. It is the experience of becoming a more

From a paper "Conformity and Diversity" given at the Conference on Man and Civilization, sponsored by the University of California School of Medicine, San Francisco, July 28, 1962. Used by permission of the author.

autonomous, more spontaneous, more confident person. It is the experience of freedom to be one's self.

In the relationship with an effective therapist—and I shall have more to say about the qualities of this relationship—the client moves gradually toward a new type of realization, a growing recognition that in some sense he chooses himself. This is not usually any sudden burst of insight—it is a groping, ambivalent, confused and uncertain movement into a new territory. The client begins to realize, "I am not compelled to be simply the creation of others, molded by their expectancies, shaped by their demands. I am not compelled to be a victim of unknown forces in myself. I am less and less a creature of influences in myself which operate beyond my ken in the realms of the unconscious. I am increasingly the architect of self. I am free to will and choose. I can, through accepting my individuality, my 'isness,' become more of my uniqueness, more of my potentiality."

CHARACTERISTIC FEATURES OF THIS EXPERIENCE

There are a number of characteristics of this experience. The client moves from fearing his inner feelings, and defending himself against them, to letting those feelings *be* and exist in him, as accepted elements of himself. From being out of touch with some aspects of his experience he moves toward a freer inner communication, a greater awareness of what is going on from moment to moment within. A client says, "The real truth of the matter is that I'm *not* the sweet forebearing guy that I try to make out that I am. I get irritated at things. I feel like snapping at people, and I feel like being selfish at times; and I don't know why I should pretend I'm *not* that way."

The client also moves from living by values introjected from others to values which are experienced in himself in the present. From existing only to satisfy the expectations of others, he moves toward being a person in his own right, with feelings, goals and ideas of his own. Thus a young woman says, "I've always tried to be what the others thought I should be, but now I'm wondering whether I shouldn't just see that I am what I am."

Another important element of this experience is that the client moves from being a person driven and compelled by internal and external forces beyond his control, toward being a person who makes responsible choices. One client tells how he has always felt his family was to blame for all of his difficulties and then adds, "But now that I understand all they've done, I guess it's up to me." A man who has been in a state hospital for years improves in therapy to a point where he is now facing a most perplexing situation regarding his leaving the hospital. Reflecting both his confusion and his newly born autonomy, he says, "I don't know *what* I'm gonna do, but *I'm* gonna do it."

Another characteristic of this experience is that the client moves from a distrust of the spontaneous and unconscious aspects of himself to a basic trust of his experiencing, and of his organism, as a sound instrument for encountering life. Clients find many ways of expressing this tentative movement into a greater confidence in the deeper aspects of themselves. One man says, "I have a feeling that what I have to do is to leave the vantage points that I have now—from which I look myself over. In a way being *less* conscious, more spontaneous. Take more the position of passenger than driver. See how things go when they're left alone. It's awful kind of scary." At another time he expresses the same feeling when talking about the secret thoughts in himself. "The butterflies are the thoughts closest to the surface. Underneath there's a deeper flow.... The deeper flow is like a great school of fish moving under the surface. I see the ones that break through the surface of the water, sitting with my fishing line in hand, trying to find a better tackle. Or better yet, trying to find a way of diving in. That's the scary thing. The image I get is that *I* want to be one of the fish myself." The therapist says, "You want to be down there flowing along, too " (10, p. 340). This desire to be one with the subterranean and primitive spontaneity within is a real part of the experience I am trying to describe.

Still another element of this experience is the ambivalent and fearful way in which the client moves toward this responsible freedom. It is not an easy thing to have the courage to be, and clients shrink from it at the same time as they move toward it. Thus a young woman who has taken a large step forward in realizing, "I can't depend on some one else to *give* me an education. I'll really have to get it myself," follows this up a moment later by saying, "I have a feeling of strength, and yet I have a feeling of realizing it's so sort of fearful, of fright."

I hope that what I have said so far conveys some sense of what I mean when I say that clients, in a satisfactory therapeutic relationship, undergo a self-initiated process of learning to be free. This learning is composed of movement from as well as movement toward. From being persons driven by inner forces they do not understand, fearful and distrustful of these deeper feelings and of themselves, living by values they have taken over from others, they move significantly. They move toward being persons who accept and enjoy their own feelings, who value and trust the deeper layers of their nature, who find strength in being their own uniqueness, who live by values they experience. This learning, this movement, enables them to live as more individuated, more creative, more responsive, and more responsible persons. Clients are, as I have tried to indicate, often sharply aware of such directions in themselves, as they move with fearfulness toward being freely themselves.

THE MODERN-VIEW MAN IS UNFREE

To some, it must seem strangely out of tune with the modern world to speak, as I have, of learning to be free. The growing opinion today is that man is essentially unfree. He is unfree in a cultural sense. He is all too obviously a pawn of government. He is molded by a mass propaganda into being a creature with certain opinions and beliefs, desired and pre-planned by the powers that be. He is the product of his class—lower, middle, or upper—and his values and his behavior are shaped by the class to which he belongs. So it seems increasingly clear from the study of social institutions and influences, that man is simply the creature of his culture and his circumstances, and most decidedly is not free.

At a still deeper level the behavioral sciences have added to this conception of man as unfree. Man is determined in part by his heredity—in his intelligence, his personality type, perhaps even his tendency toward mental aberration. He is above all the product of his conditioning—the inevitable result of the fortuitous events which have "shaped up" his behavior. Many of our most astute behavioral scientists are agreed that this process of conditioning, of "shaping up" the individual's behavior, is developing a technology which will enable us to control the individual to a degree which at the present moment would seem fantastic.

Along with the development of this technology has gone an underlying philosophy of rigid determinism in the psychological sciences which can perhaps best be illustrated by a brief exchange which I had with Prof. B. F. Skinner of Harvard at a recent conference. A paper given by Dr. Skinner led me to direct these remarks to him. "From what I understood Dr. Skinner to say, it is his understanding that though he might have thought *he chose* to come to this meeting, might have thought he had a purpose in giving this speech, such thoughts are really illusory. He actually made certain marks on paper and emitted certain sounds here simply because his genetic makeup and his past environment had operantly conditioned his behavior in such a way that it was rewarding to make these sounds, and that he as a person doesn't enter into this. In fact if I get his thinking correctly, from his strictly scientific point of view, he, as a person, doesn't exist." In his reply Dr. Skinner said that he would not go into the question of whether he had any choice in the matter (presumably because the whole issue is illusory) but stated, "I do accept your characterization of my own presence here " (2, pp. 75-6, 79). I do not need to labor the point that for Dr. Skinner the concept of "learning to be free" would be quite meaningless.

Thus, though there are opposing voices, the general thrust of the cultural trend throughout both the Western and Communist world is to say that man is not free, that there is no such thing as a free man. We are formed and moved by forces—cultural forces without, and unconscious forces within—which we do not comprehend and which are beyond our control. We will soon be formed more knowingly and more precisely by a scientific technology which will replace the crude way in which we have been molded by partially fortuitous natural events.

THE INADEQUACY OF THE "SCIENTIFIC" VIEW

I have contended, and continue to contend, that this is not the whole picture. The experience I have had with my clients causes me profoundly to disagree with the notion that the individual is no more than a link between a series of complex causes and their inevitable and predetermined effects. When I think of the explanation in which Skinner concurs as to his presence at the conference, I cannot make it apply to human events as I know them. When I try to tell myself, for example, that a Freedom Rider did not choose to expose himself to danger, did not voluntarily risk his life for a right which he valued, and had, as a person, no part in his behavior, my judgment rebels. When I try to tell myself that he behaved in this way, went into a dangerous situation, accepted a brutal beating, served a jail sentence, simply because his genetic constitution and his individual and cultural conditioning caused him to move in certain geographical directions, emit certain sounds when beaten, and further vocalizations when arrested, and that all of these behaviors were emitted because he had been conditioned to find them rewarding—this seems to be a most inadequate and degrading view of man. He becomes a meaningless phenomenon in a world which has no sense.

It is clear, however, that if I object to the concept of man as a meaningless molecule in an equation which he had no part in writing, then I must be willing to define what I mean when I speak of freedom when I say that I have observed in others, and have experienced in myself, the process of learning to be free. This may seem especially difficult since, as a behavioral scientist, I quite agree with Dr. Skinner in the view that the sequences of cause and effect appear to operate quite as much in the psychological as in the physical world.

WHAT IS THE MEANING OF FREEDOM?

So what is this freedom of which we speak? In what sense does a client—in what sense can any person—learn to be free? What possible definition of freedom can there be in a modern world?

In the first place, the freedom which I have been trying to describe is essentially an inner thing, something which exists in the living person, quite aside from any of the outward choice of alternatives which we so often think of as constituting freedom. I am speaking of the kind of freedom which Frankl vividly describes in his experience of the concentration camp, when everything—possessions, identity, choice—was taken from the prisoners. But even months and years in such an environment showed only "that everything can be taken from a man but one thing: the last of the human freedoms—to choose one's own attitude in any given set of circumstances, to choose one's own way" (7, p. 65). It is this inner, subjective, existential freedom which I have observed. It is the realization that "I can live myself, here and now, by my own choice." It is the quality of courage which enables a person to step into the uncertainty of the unknown as he chooses himself. It is the discovery of meaning from within oneself, meaning which comes from listening sensitively and openly to the complexities of what one is experiencing. It is the burden of being responsible for the self one chooses to be. It is the recognition by the person that he is an emerging process, not a static end product. The individual who is thus deeply and courageously thinking his own thoughts, becoming his own uniqueness, responsibly choosing himself, may be fortunate in having hundreds of objective outer alternatives from which to choose, or he may be unfortunate in having none, but his freedom exists regardless. So we are first of all speaking of something which exists within the individual, of something phenomenological rather than objective, but nonetheless to be prized.

A second point in defining this experience of freedom is that it exists not as a contradiction to the picture of the psychological universe as a sequence of cause and effect, but as a complement to such a universe. Freedom rightly understood is a fulfillment, by the person, of the ordered sequence of his life. As Martin Buber puts it, "The free man ... believes in destiny, and believes that it stands in need of him" (4, p. 59). He moves out voluntarily, freely, responsibly, to play his significant part in a world whose determined events move through him and through his spontaneous choice and will. Again to quote Buber, "He who forgets all that is caused and makes decision out of the depths, ... is a freeman, and destiny confronts him as the counterpart of his freedom. It is not his boundary but his fulfillment" (4, p. 53). This is the answer of the modern philosopher to the prevailing view that man is no more than the sum of his conditioning. Even more convincing than the intellectual answer is the experience of one client after another, as he moves in therapy toward an acceptance of the realities of the world outside and inside himself, and also moves toward becoming a responsible agent in this real world.

We are speaking, then, of a freedom which exists in the subjective person, a freedom which he courageously uses to live his potentialities. We are speaking of freedom in which the individual chooses to fulfill himself by playing a responsible and voluntary part in bringing about the destined events of his world. This experience of freedom is for my clients a most meaningful development, one which assists them in becoming human, in relating to others, in being a person.

THE FACILITATION OF INNER FREEDOM

Interestingly enough, we now have a considerable body of knowledge, both clinical and empirical, as to the conditions which, in psychotherapy, foster the process of learning to be free, of becoming one's self. Essentially, we have found, this experience comes about in a close, warm, understanding relationship in which there is freedom *from* such things as threat, and freedom to choose and be. Let me spell this out in somewhat more detail.

From the practical and research information currently available, it seems that a growth-facilitating or freedom-promoting relationship contains at least three significant qualities. I would like to describe these in the very briefest fashion, and in everyday language, as we have studied them in psychotherapy.

It has been found that personal change is facilitated when the psychotherapist is what he *is*, when in the relationship with his client he is genuine and without "front" or facade, openly being the feelings and attitudes which at that moment are flowing *in* him. We have coined the term congruence to try to describe this condition. By this we mean that the feelings the therapist is experiencing are available to him, available to his awareness, and he is able to live these feelings, be them, and able to communicate them if appropriate. No one fully achieves this condition, yet the more the therapist is able to listen acceptantly to what is going on within himself, and the more he is able to be the complexity of his feelings, without fear, the higher the degree of his congruence.

To give a commonplace example, each of us senses this quality in people in a variety of ways. One of the things which offends us about radio and TV commercials is that it is often perfectly evident from the tone of voice that the announcer is "putting on," playing a role, saying something he doesn't feel. This is an example of incongruence. On the other hand each of us know individuals whom we somehow trust because we sense that they are being what they are, that we are dealing with the person himself, not with a polite or professional front. It is this quality of congruence which we sense which research has found to be associated with successful therapy. The more genuine and congruent the therapist in the relationship, the more probability there is that change in personality in the client will occur.

Now the second condition: When the therapist is experiencing a warm, positive and acceptant attitude toward what is in the client, this facilitates change. It involves the therapist's genuine willingness for the client to be whatever feeling is going on in him at that moment—fear, confusion, pain, pride, anger, hatred, love, courage, or awe. It means that the therapist cares for the client, in a non-possessive way. It means that he prizes the client in a total rather than a conditional way. By this I mean that he does not simply accept the client when he is behaving in certain ways, and disapprove of him when he behaves in other ways. It means an outgoing positive feeling without reservations, without evaluations. The term we have come to use for this is unconditional positive regard. Again research studies show that the more this attitude is experienced by the therapist, the more likelihood there is that therapy will be successful.

The third condition we may call empathic understanding. When the therapist is sensing the feelings and personal meanings which the client is experiencing in each moment, when he can perceive these from "inside," as they seem to the client, and when he can successfully communicate something of that understanding to his client, then this third condition is fulfilled.

I suspect each of us has discovered that this kind of understanding is extremely rare. We neither receive it nor offer it with any great frequency. Instead we offer another type of understanding which is very different. "I understand what is wrong with you;" "I understand what makes you act that way;" or "I too have experienced your trouble and I reacted very differently;" these are the types of understanding which we usually offer and receive, an evaluative understanding from the outside. But when someone understands how it feels and seems to be *me*, without wanting to analyze me or judge me, then I can blossom and grow in that climate. And research bears out this common observation. When the therapist can grasp the moment-to-moment experiencing occurring in the inner world of the client as the client sees it and feels it, without losing the separateness of his own identity in this empathic process, then change is likely to occur.

Studies with a variety of clients show that when these three conditions occur in the therapist, and when they are to some degree perceived by the client, therapeutic movement ensues, the client finds himself painfully but definitely learning and growing, and both he and his therapist regard the outcome as successful. It seems from our studies that it is attitudes such as these rather than the therapist's technical knowledge and skill, which are primarily responsible for the therapeutic change (13, pp. 61-63).

THE DYNAMICS OF A DEVELOPING INNER FREEDOM

You may well ask, "But why does a person who is seeking help find himself changing in a relationship which contains these elements? Why does this initiate a process of learning to be free, of becoming what he is, of choice and inner development?" Let me try very briefly to answer such questions.

The reactions of the client who experiences for a time the kind of therapeutic relationship which I have described are a reciprocal of the therapist's attitudes. In the first place, as he finds someone else listening acceptantly to his feelings, he little by little becomes able to listen to himself. He begins to receive the communication from within himself—to realize that he *is* angry, to recognize when he is frightened, even to realize when he is feeling courageous. As he becomes more open to what is going on within him he becomes able to listen to feelings which have seemed to him so terrible, or so disorganizing, or so unique, or so personal, that he has never been able to recognize their existence in himself.

While he is learning to listen to himself he also becomes more acceptant of himself. As he expresses more and more of the hidden aspects of himself, he finds the therapist showing a consistent and unconditional positive regard for him and his feelings. Slowly he moves toward taking the same attitude toward himself, accepting himself as he is, respecting and caring for himself as a person, being responsible for himself as he is, and therefore ready to move forward in the process of being free.

And finally as he listens more accurately to the feelings within, and becomes less evaluative and more acceptant toward himself, he also moves toward being more real. He finds it possible to move out from behind the facades he has used, to drop his defensive behaviors, and more openly to be what he truly is. As these changes occur, as he becomes more self-aware, more self-acceptant, more self-expressive, less defensive and more open, he finds that he is at last free to change and grow and move in the direction natural to the human organism. He can make imperfect choices—and then correct them. He recognizes that he can choose to be hurtful or constructive, self-aggrandizing or committed to the welfare of the group, and when these choices can be freely made, he tends to move in the socially constructive direction.

This is a brief picture of what we have seen time and again in the experience of psychotherapy.

A HOPE FOR EDUCATION

It is such experiences in individual and group psychotherapy which lead us to believe that we have here an important dynamic for modern education. We may have here the essential core of a process by which we might facilitate the production, through our educational system, of persons who will be adaptive and creative, able to make responsible choice, open to the kaleidoscopic changes in their world, worthy citizens of a fantastically expanding universe. It seems at least a possibility that in our schools and colleges, in our professional schools and universities, individuals could learn to be free.

THE CURRENT TREND TOWARD HARD-HEADED CONFORMITY

I say this in full recognition of the fact that the current trend in education is away from freedom. There are tremendous pressures today—cultural and political—for conformity, docility, and rigidity. The demand is for technically trained students who can beat the Russians, and none of this nonsense about education which might improve our interpersonal relationships! The demand is for hard-headedness, for training of the intellect only, for scientific proficiency. We want inventiveness in developing better "hardware," but creativity in a larger sense tends to be suspect. Personal feelings, free choice, uniqueness—these have little or no place in the classroom. One may observe an elementary school classroom for hours without recording one instance of individual creativity or free choice, except when the teacher's back is turned. And at the college level we know that the major effect of a college education on the values of the student is to "shape up" the individual for more comfortable membership in the ranks of college alumni (9).

I am, therefore, quite aware that for the general public and for most educators the goal of learning to be free is not an aim they would select, nor toward which they are, operationally, moving. Yet if a civilized culture is to survive, and if the individuals in that culture are to be worth saving, it appears to me to be an essential goal of education. So I would like to explore something of what it means when we take seriously the learnings from psychotherapy and endeavor to apply them to the field of education in order to foster the development of persons who are inwardly free.

SOME EFFORTS TO PERMIT FREEDOM IN EDUCATION

The past has not been devoid of such experimentation, and there has accumulated a considerable body of practical experience, and a smaller body of empiric knowledge regarding education which has inward freedom as one of its primary goals. I will comment very briefly on four of the practical efforts along this line.

August Aichorn, many years ago, carried on a radical experiment in the re-education of delinquents (1). He permitted them freedom, within the institutional setting, to conduct themselves as they desired in the group in which he was the leader. After a period of chaos which I am sure few of us could bear, these youths gradually chose a social and disciplined and cooperative life as something they *preferred*. They learned, through experience in an accepting relationship, that they desired responsible freedom and self-imposed limits rather than the chaos of license and aggression.

Another radical experiment was that conducted by A. S. Neill in his school, Summerhill. Started forty years ago, this school has become a current focus of great interest because of Neill's recent book telling of the experiences of his pupils and himself in this school (11). This is a book which is well worth a thoughtful reading by every educator. Neill's sincerity and genuineness, his faith in the potential of each individual, his firm respect for each child and for himself, shines through its pages. As in the case of Aichorn, few of us would have the courage to trust the individual, and his natural desire to learn, as completely as does Neill. Yet he has given us a challenging laboratory example of what it means to provide a setting in which children can learn to be free. Even the cautious report of the Ministry of Education makes it clear that the students develop a zest for living, a spontaneous courtesy, as well as initiative, responsibility, and integrity. They conclude, "a piece of fascinating and valuable educational research is going on here which would do all educationists good to see" (11, p. 85).

The core of the progressive education movement, now so frequently derided, was another attempt to help individuals to learn to be free. That its fundamental philosophy frequently became debased into turning education into a sugar-coated pill should not obscure its true aims, nor its effective results when it was true to its own philosophical base.

Still another type of experiment along this line is evident in the work being done in student-centered teaching. Here much of the work has been done in university classes and in intensive workshops for professional persons. The aims of such an approach have been summarized in the following terms:

> the goal . . . is to assist students to become individuals:
> who are able to take self-initiated action and to be responsible for those actions;
> who are capable of intelligent choice and self-direction;
> who are critical learners, able to evaluate the contributions made by others;
> who have acquired knowledge relevant to the solution of problems;
> who, even more importantly, are able to adapt flexibly and intelligently to new problem situations;
> who have internalized an adaptive mode of approach to problems, utilizing all pertinent experience freely and creatively;
> who are able to cooperate effectively with others in these various activities;
> who work, not for approval of others, but in terms of their own socialized purposes (12, pp. 387-8).

SOME CONDITIONS WHICH FACILITATE "LEARNING TO BE FREE"

If we review all of these streams of effort, it seems possible to abstract from the various experiences, and from the pertinent research, those conditions which appear to be essential if we are to facilitate in students this quality of inward freedom. I should like to describe these conditions as I see them.

Confronting a problem.   In the first place, if this self-initiated learning is to occur, it seems essential that the individual be in contact with, be faced by, a real problem. Success in facilitating such learning often seems directly related to this factor. Professional persons who come together in a workshop, because of a concern with problems they are facing, are a good example. Almost invariably, when they are given the facilitating climate I will describe, they at first resist the notion of being responsible for their own learning, and then seize upon this as an opportunity, and use it far beyond their expectations. On the other hand, students in a required course expect to remain passive, and may find themselves extremely perplexed and frustrated at being given freedom. "Freedom to do what?" is their quite understandable question.

So it seems reasonably clear that for learning of the sort we are discussing it is necessary that the student, of whatever level, be confronted by issues which have meaning and relevance for him. In our culture we tend to try to insulate the student from any and all of the real problems of life, and this constitutes a difficulty. It appears that if we desire to have students learn to be free and responsible individuals, then we must be willing for them to confront life, to face problems. Whether we are speaking of the inability of the small child to make change, or the problem of his older brother in constructing a hi-fi set, or the problem of the college student and adult in formulating his views on international policy, or dealing effectively with his interpersonal relationships, some real confrontation by a problem seems a necessary condition for this type of learning.

A trust in the human organism. I come now to those conditions which are essentially dependent upon the teacher. It is clear from the experience of Aichorn, Neill, or the many individuals who have tried a student-centered approach to teaching, that one of the requisites for the teacher who would facilitate this type of learning is a profound trust in the human organism. If we distrust the human being, then we *must* cram him with information of our own choosing, lest he go his own mistaken way. But if we trust the capacity of the human individual for developing his own personality, then we can permit him the opportunity to choose his own way in his learning. Hence it is evident that the kind of learning I am discussing would be possible only for a teacher who holds a somewhat confident view of man.

Realness in the teacher. Another element of the teacher's functioning which stands out is his sincerity, his realness, his absence of a facade. He can be a real person in his relationship with his students. He can be enthusiastic. He can be bored. He can be interested in students. He can be angry. He can also be sensitive and sympathetic. Because he accepts his feelings as his own, he has no need to impose them on his students. He can dislike a student product without implying that it is objectively bad or that the student is bad. It is simply true that he, as a person, dislikes it. Thus he is a *person* to his students, not a faceless embodiment of a curricular requirement, nor a sterile tube through which knowledge is passed from one generation to the next.

Acceptance.   Another attitude which stands out in the work of those who have been successful in promoting this type of learning is a prizing of the student, a prizing of his feelings and his opinions. The teacher values the individual student as having worth, and this prizing extends to each and all the facets of this individual. Such a teacher can be fully acceptant of the fear and hesitation of the student as he approaches a new problem, as well as of the satisfaction he feels in achievement. If the teacher can accept the student's occasional apathy, his desire to explore by-roads of knowledge, as well as his disciplined efforts to achieve major goals, he will promote this type of learning. If he can accept personal feelings which both disturb and promote learning—rivalry with a sibling, hatred of authority, concern about personal adequacy—then he is certainly such a teacher. I trust I am making it clear that this means an acceptance of the whole student by the teacher—a prizing of him as an imperfect human being with many feelings, many potentialities. This prizing or acceptance is an operational expression of the teacher's essential confidence in the capacity of the human organism.

Empathy.   Still another element in the teacher's attitude is his ability to understand the student's reactions from the inside, an empathic awareness of the way the process of education and learning seems to the student. This is a kind of understanding almost never exhibited in the classroom; yet when the teacher *is* empathic, it adds an extremely potent aspect to the classroom climate. When a child says, in a discouraged voice, "I can't do this," that teacher is most helpful who naturally and spontaneously responds, "You're just hopeless that you can ever learn it, aren't you?" The usual denial of the child's feeling by the teacher who says "Oh but I'm *sure* you can do it" is not nearly so helpful.

Providing resources.   These then are the essential attitudes of the teacher who facilitates a learning to be free. There is one other function performed by such a teacher which is very important. It is the provision of resources. Instead of organizing lesson plans and lectures, such a teacher concentrates on providing all kinds of relevant raw material for use by the students, together with clearly indicated channels by which the student can avail himself of these resources. I am thinking not only of the usual academic resources—books, workspace, tools, maps, movies, recordings, and the like. I am also thinking of human resources—persons who might contribute to the knowledge of the student. Most important in this respect is the teacher himself as resource. He makes himself and his special knowledge and experience clearly available to the students, but he does not impose himself on them. He outlines the particular ways in which he feels he is most competent, and they can call on him for anything he is able to give, but this is an offer of himself as a resource, and the degree to which he is used is up to the students.

What the teacher does not do. The teacher thus concentrates on creating a facilitative climate, and upon providing resources. He may also help to put students in contact with meaningful problems. But he does not set lesson tasks. He does not assign readings. He does not lecture or expound (unless requested to). He does not evaluate and criticize unless the student wishes his judgment on a product. He does not give examinations. He does not set grades. Perhaps this will make it clear that such a teacher is not simply giving lip service to a different approach to learning. He is actually, operationally, giving his students the opportunity to learn to be responsibly free.

THE PROCESS OF LEARNING TO BE FREE

When the teacher establishes an attitudinal climate of the sort I have described, when he makes available resources which are relevant to problems which confront the student, then a typical process ensues.

Initial frustration. First, for students who have been taught by more conventional means, there is a period of tension, frustration, disappointment, disbelief. Students turn in such statements as "I felt completely frustrated by the class procedure." "I felt totally inadequate to take part in this kind of thing." "The class seems to be lacking in planning and direction." "I keep wishing the *course* would start."

One mature participant observer described the way one group struggled with the prospect of freedom after an initial session in which opportunities and resources were described.

Thereafter followed four hard, frustrating sessions. During this period, the class didn't seem to get anywhere. Students spoke at random, saying whatever came into their heads. It all seemed chaotic, aimless, a waste of time. A student would bring up some aspect of the subject; and the next student, completely disregarding the first, would take the group away in another direction; and third, completely disregarding the first two, would start fresh on something else altogether. At times there were faint efforts at a cohesive discussion, but for the most part the classroom proceedings seemed to lack continuity and direction. The instructor received every contribution with attention and regard. He did not find any student's contribution in order or out of order.

The class was not prepared for such a totally unstructured approach. They did not know how to proceed. In their perplexity and frustration, they demanded that the teacher play the role assigned to him by custom and tradition; that he set forth for good and bad (14, p. 301).

This is a good description of the bafflement and chaos which is an almost inevitable initial phase of learning to be free.

Individual initiative and work. Gradually students come to various realizations. It dawns on them that this is not a gimmick, but that they are really unfettered; that there is little point in impressing the professor, since the student will evaluate his own work; that they can learn what they please; that they can express, in class, the way they really feel; that issues can be discussed in class which are real to them, not simply the issues set forth in a text. When these elements are recognized, there is a vital and almost awe-inspiring release of energy. One student reads as she has never read before—two books a week in the subject, and hopes this "will never end." Others undertake projects of writing, experimentation, work in a clinic or laboratory, with a new zest. The report of one student is typical of many, and is worth quoting at some length.

I feel that I want to share my joy with you in relation to the paper that I gave you earlier today—it is what I call "my first real learning experience" . . .

I took a few minutes after I finished typing my paper to think what had made this learning experience so different from the many others which I have had. These are my reactions, sketched briefly:

Based on *real* need—not superficial topic. . .

Reading was done to satisfy my need, not merely to collect material to fit topic and sound good. . . .

I found that I had to scrap my original approach toward writing a paper when I realized that it did not have to sound good or conform to a prescribed pattern. I jotted down my usual idea of a good outline for a paper only to find that it was not geared to my need at all, and I turned to writing about things of significance to me and then made an outline over that I had written.

One of the most "shocking" parts of this experience, as I have related to you one day, was the fact that I did not have to do this and yet I wanted to be working on it all the time and rushed through assigned requirements in other courses to devote time to this.

I wrote an annotated bibliography for the first time in my life because I wanted to have information regarding this material I had read, for future reference. . . .

There was no feeling of drudgery about this paper—I found myself saying "I'm going over to the library to work on my paper for a while" instead of "Oh, I suppose I've got to plow through some more books tonight or I'll never get that paper done on time." The lack of external pressure made this experience one of the most enjoyable things I have ever done. Basically, through experience, it has changed my whole approach to teaching. . . (3).

It is clear that this student is discovering what it means to be autonomous, what it means to be creative, what it means to put forth disciplined effort to reach one's own goals, what it means to be a responsible free person, and most important, is appreciating the satisfactions which come from these experiences.

Personal closeness. Another element which is a common part of the process is that the group develops a respect and liking for each other as individuals, as they emerge in the group discussions. A teacher trying this approach writes, "In this second group, also, I found that the students had developed a personal closeness, so that at the end of the semester they talked of having annual reunions. They said that somehow or other they wanted to keep this experience alive and not lose one another."

Individual change. As the learning continues, personal changes take place in the direction of greater freedom and spontaneity. Here is another report by a participant observer.

In the course of this process, I saw hard, inflexible, dogmatic persons, in the brief period of several weeks, change in front of my eyes and become sympathetic, understanding and to a marked degree non-judgmental. I saw neurotic, compulsive persons ease up and become more accepting of themselves and others. In one instance, a student who particularly impressed me by his change, told me when I mentioned this: "It is true. I feel less rigid, more open to the world. And I like myself better for it. I don't believe I ever learned so much anywhere." I saw shy persons become less shy and aggressive persons more sensitive and moderate (14, p. 306).

A more personal statement of this kind of change is given by a student at the end of the course.

> Your way of being with us is a revelation to me. In your class I feel important, mature and capable of doing things on my own. I want to think for myself and this need cannot be accomplished through text books and lectures alone, but through living. I think you see me as a person with real feelings and needs, an individual. What I say and do are significant expressions from me, and you recognize this. You follow no plan, yet I'm learning. Since the term began I seem to feel more alive, more real to myself. I enjoy being alone as well as with other people. My relationships with children and other adults are becoming more emotional and involved. Eating an orange last week, I peeled the skin off each separate orange section and like it better with the transparent shell off. It was juicier and fresher tasting that way. I began to think, that's how I feel sometimes, without a transparent wall around me, really communicating my feelings. I feel that I'm growing, how much, I don't know. I'm thinking, considering, pondering and learning (3).

Throughout this description of the learning process in such a climate, I am sure you will have observed the many similarities to the process involved in psychotherapy. Outstanding is the way in which the student begins to rely on his own values as he experiences them, rather than upon the values imposed on him by others. It is also clear that the student is closer to his own feelings, trusts them more, trusts himself more. He is not so afraid of his own spontaneity, not so afraid of change. He is, in short, learning what it means to be free.

Effect upon the instructor. I believe the story of this kind of classroom experience is incomplete without some mention of the effect upon the instructor when he has been the agent for the release of such self-initiated learning. One such teacher says, "To say that I am overwhelmed by what happened only faintly reflects my feelings. I have taught for many years but I . . . never have found in the classroom so much of the whole person coming forth, so deeply involved, so deeply stirred. . . . I can only . . . say that I am grateful and I am also humbled by the experience" (14, p. 313).

Another reports as follows: "Rogers has said that relationships conducted on these assumptions mean 'turning present-day education upside down.' I have found this to be true as I have tried to implement this way of living with students. The experience I have had, plunged me into relationships which have been significant and challenging beyond compare for me. They have inspired me and stimulated me and left me, at times, shaken and awed with their consequences for both me and the students. They have led me to the fact of what I can only call ... the tragedy of education in our time—student after student who report this to be their first experience with total trust, with freedom to be and to move in ways most consistent for the enhancement and maintenance of a core of dignity which somehow has survived humiliation, distortion and corrosive cynicism." (3).

Research corroboration.   Empirical investigations of the sort of teaching I have described are neither large in number, nor noteworthy for their research sophistication (5, 6, 8). Yet they bear out the student report quoted above in indication that improvement in personal psychological maturity is significantly greater in student-centered classes than in conventional ones. There is also a greater amount of self-initiated extracurricular learning, and evidence of greater creativity and self-responsibility. As to the factual and curricular learning, this seems roughly equal to that achieved in conventional classes. Some studies report slightly more, others slightly less. The fairest summary seems to be that if we are solely concerned with the teaching of teacher-selected content material, this approach is probably no better and no worse than the ordinary class. If we are concerned with the development of the person, with initiative, originality and responsibility, such an approach produces greater changes.

SUMMARY

Let me retrace briefly the pathway I have followed in this talk. I have pointed out that though freedom is a concept not at all acceptable to our modern intellectual culture, it is something which is undeniably experienced by clients in individual and group therapy. These individuals, when permitted to live, even for a small fraction of their time, in the special psychological climate of the therapeutic relationship, achieve a spontaneous, existential, and creative inner freedom. I have tried to show that the freedom they achieve is definable in ways which complement rather than contradict the current scientific view of man's behavior.

When students are permitted to be in contact with real problems; when resources—both human and technical—are made psychologically available by the teacher; when the teacher is a real person in his relationships with students, and feels an acceptance of and an empathy toward his students; then an exciting kind of learning occurs. Students go through a frustrating but rewarding process in which gradually responsible initiative, creativity, and inner freedom are released. The kind of personal and intellectual change which comes about has many parallels with the changes which occur in psychotherapy. The nature of these changes has to some extent been investigated empirically.

In closing, I would like to point out that for the most part modern culture—in its two main streams, Western and Communist—does not, operationally, want persons to be free, and is extremely fearful and ambivalent of any process which leads to inner freedom. Nevertheless it is my personal conviction that individual rigidity and constricted learning are the surest roads to world catastrophe. It seems clear that if we prefer to develop flexible, adaptive, creative individuals, we have a beginning knowledge as to how this may be done. We know how to establish, in an educational situation, the conditions and the psychological climate which initiate a process of learning to be free.

REFERENCES

1.   Aichorn, A., *Wayward Youth* (New York: Viking Press, 1935).

2.   Amer. Acad. of Arts and Sciences, Conference on Evolutionary Theory and Human Progress: Conference C, "The Individual and the Design of Culture," Dec. 2–4, 1960. Mimeographed transcription.

3.   Appell, Morey, "Selected Student Reactions to Student-centered Courses." Mimeographed mss., 1959.

4.   Buber, M., *I and Thou,* translated by R. G. Smith (Edinburgh: T. & T. Clark, 1937).

5.   Faw, V. A., "Psychotherapeutic Method of Teaching Psychology," *Amer. Psychologist,* IV, 1949, 104–109.

6.   Faw, V. A., "Evaluation of Student-centered Teaching," unpub. mss., 1954.

7.   Frankl, V. E., *From Death-Camp to Existentialism,* translated by I. Lasch (Boston: Beacon Press, 1959).

8.   Jackson, J. H., "The Relationship Between Psychological Climate and the Quality of Learning Outcomes Among Lower-Status Pupils," unpub. Ph.D. thesis, University of Chicago, 1957.

9. Jacob, P. E., *Changing Values in College* (New Haven: Hazen Foundation, 1956).

10. Lewis, M. K., C. R. Rogers, and J. M. Shiien, "Time-limited, Client-centered Psychotherapy: Two Cases," in A. Burton (ed.), *Case Studies in Counseling and Psychotherapy* (Englewood Cliffs, N. J.: Prentice-Hall, 1959).

11. Neill, A. S., *Summerhill: A Radical Approach to Child-Rearing* (New York: Hart Publishing Co., 1960).

12. Rogers, C. R., *Client-Centered Therapy* (Boston: Houghton Mifflin, 1951).

13. Rogers, C. R., *On Becoming a Person* (Boston: Houghton Mifflin, 1961).

14. Tenenbaum, S., "Student-centered Teaching as Experienced by a Participant," chapter 15 in C. R. Rogers, *On Becoming a Person.*

PERCEPTION AND INTERPERSONAL RELATIONS

Hadley Cantril

It is with a very profound feeling of humility that I, as a psychologist, offer any comments for the consideration of psychiatrists on the subject of perception and interpersonal relations. For the more one studies perception, the more one sees that what we label "perception" is essentially a process which man utilizes to make his purposive behavior more effective and satisfying, and that this behavior always stems from and is rooted in a personal behavioral center. Thus perception involves numerous aspects of behavior which we rather artificially and necessarily differentiate in order to get a toe-hold for understanding, but which, in the on-going process of living, orchestrate together in a most interdependent way.

From a paper read at the APA Regional Meeting in Montreal, Nov. 8–11, 1956. Published in the *American Journal of Psychiatry,* CXIV (1957–58), 119–126. Used by permission of the author and publisher.

This means, then, that the nature of perception can only be understood
if somehow we manage to start off with what some of us call a "first
person point of view" as contrasted to the "third person point of view"
represented by the traditional psychological investigator. And so my very
genuine feeling of humility in accepting an invitation of psychiatrists
derives from the fact that the psychiatrist, perhaps more than any other
specialist concerned with the study of human beings, is primarily concerned
with the first person point of view, is skilled in the art of uncovering what
this may be for his patient, and knows from his own experience the wide
gap that exists between this first person experience and the abstractions we
have created as scientists in order to analyze, conceptualize, and communicate. A very nice expression of this last state of affairs was, incidentally,
recently made by Aldous Huxley in his book *The Genius and the Goddess:*

What a gulf between impression and expression! That's our ironic
fate—to have Shakespearian feelings and (unless by billion-to-one chance we
happen to be Shakespeare) to talk about them like automobile salesmen or
teen-agers or college professors. We practice alchemy in reverse—touch gold
and it turns to lead; touch the pure lyrics of experience, and they turn into
the verbal equivalents of tripe and hogwash.

BACKGROUND

Most of you are probably familiar to some extent with a point of view that
has developed rather recently in psychology and has been dubbed "transactional psychology." While I do not want to spend time here repeating
what has been published in a variety of sources, I might at least very
briefly note some of the major emphases of transactional psychology
before discussing certain aspects of some experimental results which may
be of particular interest to psychiatrists.

Here, then, are some of the emphases of transactional psychology which
may give us a take-off for discussion:

Our perception depends in large part on the assumptions we bring to
any particular occasion. It is, as Dewey and Bentley long ago pointed out,
not a "reaction to" stimuli in the environment but may be more accurately
described as a "transaction with" an environment.

This implies that the meanings and significances we assign to things, to
symbols, to people, and to events are the meanings and significances we
have built up through our past experience, and are not inherent or intrinsic
in the "stimulus" itself.

Since our experience is concerned with purposive behavior, our perceptions are learned in terms of our purposes and in terms of what is important and useful to us.

Since the situations we are in seldom repeat themselves exactly and since change seems to be the rule of nature and of life, our perception is largely a matter of weighing probabilities, of guessing, of making hunches concerning the probable significance or meaning of "what is out there" and of what our reaction should be toward it, in order to protect or preserve ourselves and our satisfactions, or to enhance our satisfactions. This process of weighing the innumerable cues involved in nearly any perception is, of course, a process that we are generally not aware of.

CREATING CONSTANCIES

Since things in the world outside us—the physical world and more especially the social world—are by no means static, are not entirely determined and predictable, experience for most of us often carries at least some mild overtone of "concern" which we can label "curiosity," "doubt" or "anxiety" depending on the circumstances involved.

One of my favorite illustrations of this point is an incident described by Carl Sandburg in his autobiography, *Always the Young Strangers.*

I have always enjoyed riding up front in a smoking car, in a seat back of the "deadheads," the railroaders going back to the home base. Their talk about each other runs free. . . . Once I saw a young fireman in overalls take a seat and slouch down easy and comfortable. After a while a brakeman in blue uniform came along and planted himself alongside the fireman. They didn't even look at each other. Then the brakeman, looking straight ahead, was saying, "Well, what do you know today?" and kept looking straight ahead till suddenly he turned and stared the fireman in the face, adding, "for sure." I thought it was a keen and intelligent question. "What do you know today—for sure?" I remember the answer. It came slow and honest. The fireman made it plain what he knew that day for sure: "Not a damn thing!". . .

Thus we seldom can count on complete 100 percent surety in terms of a perfect correspondence between our assumptions concerning the exact experience we may have if we actually do a certain thing and the experience we actually do have as a consequence of the action we undertake.

In an attempt to try to minimize our potential lack of surety concerning any single occasion and thereby maximize our sense of surety concerning the effectiveness of our action in achieving our intent, we build up "constancies" and begin to count on them. And above all, we have a great deal to learn about constancy as we extend this concept into the field of our interpersonal relations.

Parenthetically, one of the most important things we have to learn is that the "constancy" we create and that we describe. usually by means of some word, symbol, or abstract concept is man's creation, the validity of which can only be tested and the meaning of which can only be experienced in terms of some behavior which has consequences to us and signals to us what the concept refers to.

We create these constancies by attributing certain consistent and repeatable characteristics to what they refer to, so that we can guess with a fair degree of accuracy what various sensory cues impinge upon us. We do this so that we will not have to make fresh guesses at every turn.

These significances we build up about objects, people, symbols, and events, or about ideas, all orchestrate together to give us what we might call our own unique "reality world." This "reality world" as we experience it includes, of course, our own fears and hopes, frustrations and aspirations, our own anxiety and our own faith. For these psychological characteristics of life—as the psychiatrist knows better than anyone else—are just as real for us in determining our behaviors as are chairs, stones, or mountains of automobiles. It seems to me that anything that takes on significance for us in terms of our own personal behavioral center is "real" in the psychological sense.

ASSIGNING SIGNIFICANCES

Let me illustrate with reference to a few recent experiments the way in which the significance we attach to others "out there" seems to be affected by what we bring to the situation. Incidentally but important: I do want to underscore that the experiments mentioned here are only exploratory; are only, I believe, opening up interesting vistas ahead. I am in no sense attempting to indicate what their full theoretical implications may be. But I mention them to show how experiments designed to get at the first person point of view may suggest to the experienced psychiatrist ways of using experimental procedures in his diagnosis and possibly even in therapy. And I also mention them because of my deep conviction that psychology can be both humanistic and methodologically rigorous.

A whole series of most promising experiments now seems possible with the use of a modern adaptation of an old-fashioned piece of psychological equipment, the stereoscope. Dr. Edward Engel who devised the apparatus has already published a description of it and reported some of his first findings. As you know, the stereoscope in a psychological laboratory has been used to study binocular rivalry and fusion, but the material viewed almost always consisted of dots and lines or geometrical patterns. Engel was curious to see what would happen if meaningful figures were used instead of the traditional material.

The results are really most exciting. In Engel's experiments he prepares what he calls "stereograms" consisting of photographs 2 X 2 inches, one of which is seen with the left eye, the other with the right. The photographs he used first were those of members of the Princeton football team just as they appeared in the football program. Although there were slight differences in the size and position of the heads and in the characteristics of light and shadow, still there was sufficient superimposition to get binocular fusion. And what happens? A person looks into the stereoscope and sees one face. He describes this face. And it almost invariably turns out that he is describing neither the face of the man seen with the left eye nor the face of the man seen with the right eye. He is describing a new and different face, a face that he has created out of the features of the two he is looking at. Generally the face seen in this particular case is made up of the dominant features of the two individuals. And generally the face created by the observer in this situation is more attractive and appealing than either of those seen separately. When the observer is shown the trick of the experiment by asking him to close first one eye and then the other and to compare the face he originally saw with the other two, he himself characterizes the face he created as more handsome, more pleasant, a fellow he'd like better, etc.

I hasten to add, however, that we should by no means jump to the conclusion that an individual picks out the "best" or the "most attractive" features of figures presented to him in a situation of binocular fusion. For example, Professor Gordon Allport recently took one of Engel's stereoscopes with him to South Africa and initiated some experimental work there, using photographs of members of the different racial groups which make up that complex community.

While the experiments in South Africa have only just begun and no conclusion should be drawn, it is significant to note that in recent letters communicating the early results, Allport reported that when the stereograms consist of a European paired with an Indian, a colored person compared with an Indian, etc. the Zulus see an overwhelming preponderance of Indians. For the Zulu is the most strongly prejudiced against the Indian who represents a real threat to him. Allport also reports that when

Europeans in South Africa view the stereogram they tend to see more colored faces than white. It would seem, then, that a person sees what is "significant," with significance defined in terms of his relationship to what he is looking at.

One pair of slides we use in demonstrating this piece of equipment consists of two stereograms, each a photograph of a statue in the Louvre. One of the statues is that of a Madonna with Child, the other a lovely young female nude. While I am unable so far to predict what any given individual will "see," no doubt such a prediction might be made after some good psychiatric interviewing. But let me describe what happened in a typical viewing of these stereograms. The viewers happened to be two distinguished psychologists who were visiting me one morning, one from Harvard, the other from Yale. The first looked into the stereoscope and reported that he saw a Madonna with Child. A few seconds later he exclaimed, "But my God, she is undressing." What had happened so far was that somehow she had lost the baby she was holding and her robe had slipped down from her shoulders and stopped just above the breast line. Then in a few more seconds she lost her robe completely and became the young nude. For this particular professor, the nude never did get dressed again. Then my second friend took his turn. For a few seconds he could see nothing but the nude and then he exclaimed, "But now a robe is wrapping itself around her." And very soon he ended up with the Madonna with Child and so far as I know still remains with that vision. Some people will never see the nude; others will never see the Madonna if they keep the intensity of light the same on both stereograms.

In the situation described above, we do not have conditions for genuine fusion, but rather a condition which introduces conflict and choice in the possible meaning of the content represented. In order to learn whether or not there might be differences in choice that would be culturally determined, a cross-cultural comparison was made by Dr. James Bagby. He constructed pairs of stereograms that would create binocular rivalry: in one stereogram of each pair he had a picture of some individual, object, or symbol that would be of particular interest to Mexicans; in the other stereogram of each pair he had a picture that would be of particular significance to Americans. For example, one pair of slides consisted of a picture of a bull fighter matched with a stereogram picturing a baseball player. When these pairs were shown to a sample of Mexican school teachers, an overwhelming proportion of them "saw" the Mexican symbol; when the same slides were presented to a group of American school teachers, the overwhelming proportion "saw" the American symbol.

Incidentally, the Engel stereoscope is so constructed that one can get some idea of relative "strength" of each of the stereograms by adjusting the intensity of the lighting on each. Hence, if the lighting is equivalent on two stereograms in a rivalry situation, one can reduce the amount of lighting on the one that originally predominates, increase the amount of light on the one that was not "seen," and find the point where the first one disappears and the second one "comes in."

A modification of the stereoscope has just been completed by Mr. Alderstein in the Princeton laboratory. Our thought was that it might be extremely useful both in the clinical and social areas, if instead of having to use photographs of objects or people, a person could view the real thing—that is, the faces of real, live individuals or pairs of actual objects. So by means of prisms and mirrors, this device was constructed and I have only very rarely had the opportunity of experiencing the resulting phenomena. I must say it is strange and wonderful. For example, when I viewed Mr. Alderstein and Mrs. Pauline Smith, Curator of our Demonstration Center, I seemed to be looking at a very effeminate Mr. Alderstein who was wearing Mrs. Smith's glasses. Though weird, he was extremely "real." At one point while I was observing them Mrs. Smith began to talk, yet it was Alderstein's lips that were moving! Tingling with excitement and with a certain amount of anxiety, I drove home and asked my wife and daughter to come down to the laboratory so that I could take a look at them. I was, of course, fearful that I might see only one or the other. But fortunately, again I got an amazing fusion—a blending of my daughter's hair and chin and my wife's eyes and mouth—an harmonious composition that would do justice to any artist and which I created almost instantaneously and without any awareness of what was going on. These pieces of apparatus seem to me to have enormous potential usefulness for studying the way in which we create the world around us. I am hoping, for example, that before long someone in a position to do so may use this sort of equipment in a study of disturbed children. The child, having two eyes and two parents, might in some situations and in a very few seconds reveal a good bit about his inner life and his interpersonal family relations.

An interesting series of experiments on perception and interpersonal relations began systematically a few years ago after an observation I made one Sunday morning in our laboratory. An old friend of mine, who was a distinguished lawyer in New York and has since died, called me at home to say that he and his wife had been in town for the weekend and would I be willing to show them some of Ames' demonstrations about which he had heard. It is important for this story to emphasize the fact that the gentleman in question was really a most unusual man in terms of his ability, charm, and accomplishments, and his devotion to his family and friends.

Many of you are familiar, I am sure, with the "distorted room" designed by Adelbert Ames, Jr. which produces the same image on the retina as a regular square room if it is viewed monocularly from a certain point. Since the room is seen as square, persons or objects within the room or people looking through the windows become distorted. I had shown this room to hundreds of individuals and among other phenomena had demonstrated that when two people look through the back windows, the head of one individual appeared to be very large, the head of the other to be very small. When the individuals reversed the windows they were looking through, the size of their heads appeared to the observer to change. But on this Sunday morning when my friend's wife was observing him and me, she said, "Well, Louis, your head is the same size as ever, but Hadley, your head is very small." Then we changed the windows we were looking through and she said, Louis, you're still the same, but Hadley you've become awfully large." Needless to say this remark made a shiver go up my spine and I asked her how she saw the room. It turned out that for her the room had become somewhat distorted. In other words, she was using her husband—to whom she was particularly devoted—as her standard. She would not let him go. His nickname for her was "Honi" and we have dubbed this the "Honi phenomenon."

This observation was followed systematically in a series of experiments on married couples by Dr. Warren Wittreich. He found that if couples had been married less than a year there was a definite tendency not to let the new marital partner distort as quickly or as much as was allowed by people who had been married for a considerable time. But, again, I hasten to add that it is not a simple matter of how long one has been married that determines how willing one is to distort the size or shape of one's marital partner! The original observation was made on a couple who were already grandparents. Preliminary investigation also seems to show that parents of young children will not allow their children to distort as readily as will parents of older children.

We could continue at some length reporting experiments which seem to show that what we "perceive" is, as already emphasized, in large part our own creation and depends on the assumptions we bring to the particular occasion. We seem to give meaning and order to sensory impingements in terms of our own needs and purposes, and this process of selection is actively creative.

SOCIAL CONSTANCIES AND SELF-CONSTANCY

It is clear that when we look for constancies in other people either as individuals or as members of a group, a variety of complications is introduced. For when people are involved, as contrasted to inorganic objects or most other forms of life, we are dealing with purposes, with motives, with intentions which we have to take into account in our perceptual process—the purposes, motives and intentions of other people often difficult to understand. The purposes and intentions of these other people will, of course, change as conditions change; and they will change as behavior progresses from one goal to another. Other people's purposes will be affected by our purposes, just as our purposes will be affected by theirs.

It is by no means a quick and easy process, then, to endow the people with whom we participate in our interpersonal relations with constancies and repeatabilities that we can always rely on. And yet we must, of course, continue the attempt to do so, so that our own purposeful action will have a greater chance of bringing about the satisfying consequences we intended. So we try to pigeonhole people according to some role, status, or position. We create constancies concerning people and social situations. These provide us with certain consistent characteristics that will ease our interpretation and make our actions more effective so long as there is some correspondence between the attribution we make and the consequence we experience from it in our own action.

The "social constancies" we learn obviously involve the relationships between ourselves and others. So if any social constancy is to be operational, there must also be a sense of "self-constancy." The two are interdependent. Since the human being necessarily derives so much of his value satisfaction from association with other human beings, his conception of his "self," his own "self-constancy" and "self-significance" is determined to a large extent by the significance he has to other people and the way they behave toward him. This point is, of course, a familiar one to the psychiatrist and has been eloquently illustrated in literature as, for example, in Shaw's *Pygmalion.*

But it seems to me of paramount importance in any discussion of perception and interpersonal relations that we should not slip into the error of positing an abstract "self" or "ego" that can somehow be isolated, pointed to, analyzed, or experienced apart from any social content. It is only through the life setting and the process of participation with others that meaning and continuity are given to the "self." If the constancy of "self" is upset, it becomes difficult for us to assess changes in our interpersonal relations and accommodate to them. We lose the compass that keeps us going in a direction. "We" are lost.

This does not mean in any sense that for self-constancy to be maintained there can be no development or growth. On the contrary, self-development and growth are themselves aspects of social constancy. but this development must, as the psychiatrist knows better than anyone, flow from form if it is to be recognized, if there is to be continuity, and if there is to be a standard for comparison. Obviously, each of us surrounds himself with anchoring points of one kind or another which help to maintain this self-constancy in the process of ceaseless change around us. In this connection, I think, for example, of Konrad Lorenz' interpretation of why people like dogs. In his book *King Solomon's Ring,* he wrote that we should "not lie to ourselves that we need the dog as a protection for our house. We do need him, but not as a watch-dog. I, at least in dreary foreign towns, have certainly stood in need of my dog's company and I have derived, from the mere fact of his existence, a great sense of inward security, such as one finds in a childhood memory or in the prospect of the scenery of one's own home country, for me the Blue Danube, for you the White Cliffs of Dover. In the almost film-like flitting-by of modern life, a man needs something to tell him from time to time, that he is still himself, and nothing can give him this assurance in so comforting a manner as the 'four feet trotting behind.' "

This interdependent problem of social constancy and self-constancy has been submitted to some preliminary investigation. For example, when a person is wearing a pair of aniseikonic spectacles, which greatly distort the shape of the environment when familiar monocular cues are ruled out, he will generally see another person as distorted if that person is standing in an environment which has itself already become distorted. With a certain pair of these spectacles, for example, an individual will be seen as leaning forward with the upper and lower half of his body distorted in length. Dr. Wittreich set up such a situation at the Naval Training Center at Bainbridge, Maryland to see what might happen when the relationship of the person who was doing the viewing and the person being viewed was altered. His subjects were 24 white male Navy recruits. They first observed an authority figure dressed up as a first-class petty officer and, second, a non-authority figure dressed up in a white enlisted uniform with the marks of a recruit. Wittreich found that the authority figure did not distort nearly as much as the non-authority figure. In other words, the disciplinary training imposed in an organization that depends for effective functioning on the rigid acceptance of roles had produced a "constancy" which overpowered physiological changes in the optical system.

Another finding using the aniseikonic spectacles may be of interest to psychiatrists; namely, that a person tends to report much less distortion of his own image when he looks at himself in a full-length mirror while wearing aniseikonic spectacles than he reports when he is looking at a stranger. When one looks at one's self, the changes that appear seem to be minor and detailed—for example, slight distortions in the hands or feet; when one looks at a stranger, there is the more general bodily distortion plus the leaning one way or another, depending on the kind of spectacles used.

A subsequent study by Wittreich and one which I emphasize is only suggestive, was made comparing 21 subjects obtained from the patient roster of the neuro-psychiatric unit at the Bethesda Naval Hospital. When these disturbed individuals were wearing aniseikonic spectacles and saw their own image in the mirror, they tended to see the gross distortions that the "normal" population attributed to others; and, conversely, when the disturbed clinic looked at others, they tended to see the more detailed and minor distortions which the "normal" population had seen in themselves. All I should like to conclude about this particular experiment so far is that there seems to be some difference between the normal individual and the clinical patient in the functional importance assigned to his bodily image; the patient may conceivably be operating in terms of a relatively fixed and homogeneous image of himself which does not alter readily with the demands of the environment.

PERCEPTUAL CHANGE

Laboratory experimentation as well as research in the field of opinion and attitude change seems to demonstrate beyond a shadow of a doubt that the major condition for a change in our perception, our attitudes and opinions is a frustration experienced in carrying out our purposes effectively because we are acting on the basis of assumptions that prove "wrong." For example, Dr. Kilpatrick has demonstrated that apparently the only way in which we can learn to see our distorted room distorted is to become frustrated with the assumption that the room is "square" in the process of trying to carry out some action in the room. It is clear that an "intellectual," "rational," or "logical" understanding of a situation is by no means sufficient to alter perception. The psycho-therapist has taught us how successful reconditioning requires a therapy which simplifies goals so that their accomplishment can be assured through an individual's action as he experiences the successful consequences of his own behavior and thereby rebuilds his confidence in himself.

In this connection I recall a conversation I had in 1948 in Paris with an extremely intelligent woman who was at that time a staff member of the Soviet Embassy in Paris. We were at some social gathering and she began to ask me about American elections and the two-party system. She just couldn't understand it. She wasn't trying to be "smart" or supercilious. She was simply baffled. She couldn't "see" why we had to have two parties. For, obviously, one man was better than another and why wasn't he made President and kept as President as long as he proved to be the best man? It was a difficult argument for me to understand, just as my argument was impossible for her to understand. It was much more than a matter of opinion, stereotype, or prejudice on either side. We were simply living in different reality worlds, actually experiencing entirely different significances in happenings which might appear to an "objective," "outside" observer to be the same for both of us.

Parenthetically, while one of the outstanding characteristics of man is often said to be his amazing capacity to learn, it seems to me that an equally outstanding characteristic is man's amazing capacity to "unlearn," which is, I think, not the exact opposite. Because man is not entirely a creature of habit, he has the fortunate ability to slough off what is no longer of use to him.

THE REALITY OF ABSTRACTIONS
AND THE COMMONNESS OF PURPOSES

In order to ease our interpersonal relations and to increase the commonness of the significances we may attribute to the happenings around us, man has created abstractions in his attempt to bring order into disorder and to find more universal guides for living, no matter what the unique and individual purposes and circumstances of an individual may be. Such abstractions are represented by our scientific formulations, our ethical, political, legal, and religious systems. The abstractions can be recalled and repeated at will. They can be communicated. They are repeatable because they are static and have fixed characteristics.

The value of these abstractions for us in our interpersonal relations seems to be that when the tangibles of our personal reality world break down, we can turn to the intangible—to the abstractions we have learned that have been created by others and have presumably proved useful to them. We can begin to check our own particular situation, possibly a frustrating one, against the abstraction and thereby, perhaps experience for ourselves what the abstraction is referring to. Only then will the abstraction become real for us. For when it does become functional for us in our own individual lives, it is real as a determinant of our experience and behavior.

I will close this discussion of perception and interpersonal relations with a story which seems to sum a good deal of what I have been talking about. The story concerns three baseball umpires who were discussing the problems of their profession. The first umpire said, "Some's balls and some's strikes and I calls 'em as they is." The second umpire said, "Some's balls and some's strikes and I calls 'em as I sees 'em." While the third umpire said, "Some's balls and some's strikes but they ain't nothin' till I calls 'em."

BIBLIOGRAPHY

Cantril, Hadley, *The "Why" of Man's Experience* (New York: Macmillan, 1950).

Kilpatrick, F. P. (ed.), *Human Behavior from the Transactional Point of View* (Hanover, N. H.: Institute for Associated Research, 1952).

Kilpatrick, F. P., "Recent Transactional Perceptual Research, a Summary." Final report, Navy contract N6onr 27014 (Princeton University, May, 1955).

Cantril, Hadley, *ETC: A Review of General Semantics,* 12: No. 4 (1955), 278.

Engel, Edward, *American J. Psychology,* 69: No. 1 (1956) 87.

Bagby, James, *A Cross-Cultural Study of Perceptual Predominance in Binocular Rivalry,* 1956.

Wittreich, Warren, *J. Abnorm. Soc. Psychol.,* 47 (1952), 705.

Kilpartick, F. P., *J. Exp. Psychol.,* 47: No. 5 (1954), 362.

INTRINSIC AND EXTRINSIC MOTIVATION—
A REGRETTABLE DISTINCTION

Donald L. Avila and
William Watson Purkey

In educational circles a distinction is usually made between two kinds of motivation. First there is intrinsic motivation, which is an internal, autonomous, energy source, inherent in the organism. Second, there is extrinsic motivation, which is an external energy source, apparently perceived as being similar in structure and function to the intrinsic source, that the teacher is able to draw on through his training and skill.

Little is done about intrinsic motivation aside from defining it. It is something that the student brings to class and is either directed towards the goals of the teacher or is not. The teacher can do little or nothing to tap this source if it is not already predisposed to function in his favor. Therefore, the majority of the educators' time is spent with the second kind of motivation; with discussing and defining ways in which the teacher can *extrinsically* motivate his students.

This form of categorization is perpetrated by the educator because motivation is perceived as being free from the processes of control or manipulation. Since these terms have singularly negative connotations, the teacher feels a need to engage in processes when teaching that have little or no "control" in them. He fears being accused of controlling or manipulating his students, and therefore claims not to control or manipulate, but to extrinsically motivate his students. It is the contention of the writers that this is an unjustifiable fear, that the intrinsic-extrinsic distinction leads to a tremendous amount of waste and failure, and that those individuals who persist in making the distinction are engaging in self-delusion. There is a distinction to be made, but the intrinsic—extrinsic distinction obscures the true nature of motivation, and prevents the teacher from becoming highly skilled in the process that is truly the essence of all human interaction, that is, controlled manipulation.

Let us first examine the nature of motivation. There is only one kind of motivation, and that is the personal, internal motivation that each and

From *Psychology in the Schools,* III, No. 3 (July, 1966), 206—208. Used by permission of the authors and publisher.

every human being has at all times, in all places, and when engaged in any activity. As Combs (1962) has stated, ". . . people are always motivated; in fact, they are never unmotivated. They may not be motivated to do what we would prefer they do, but it can never be truly said that they are unmotivated." Again turning to Combs (1965) we find a succinct statement of the nature of this motivation, which is, ". . . an insatiable need for the maintenance and enhancement of the self; not the physical self—but the phenomenal self, of which the individual is aware, his self-concept." For the teacher, this is a given, a basic drive toward self-fulfillment. It may be inherent, or learned, but in either case, it is present by the time the child enters school; it is a built-in advantage, a force that comes from within the individual that, by school age, cannot be appreciably altered. No human being can ever motivate another, no matter what the situation or how strong the desire.

To conjure up an external force that is similar to basic internal motivation is to create figments of the imagination, to confuse issues, and to distract from the real value of the teacher. The teacher is the external force, and a strong force, yet not as a motivator, but as a manipulator of his charges. He does not motivate, but he controls an environment in which he manipulates himself and other classroom variables in such a way that what he is trying to teach appears to be self-enhancing to his students. He casts the situation and himself in such a way that the information and knowledge he is presenting is personally meaningful and enhancing to the student.

All human relationships are controlled and manipulated. None are without these two processes. Human relationships differ only in the degree to which and the manner in which manipulation and control are administered. Each day we give to and withhold from our children love and material goods. In our classrooms we reward and punish our students by sending them first one place and then another, by praising or blaming, by giving good grades and bad. Each day we greet our friends in an accepting or rejecting manner, bring them into or force them out of our confidence. All of these activities are examples of how we manipulate ourselves and control the objects in our environment in an attempt to get others to do what we want, in an attempt to make our personal interactions satisfying to both ourselves and those with whom we interact. It is on the basis of one degree or another of manipulation and control that all human relationships are established, conducted, and maintained.

Acceptance of this position does not mean that one must give up his basic humanistic philosophy. Even the most student-centered teacher or client-centered counselor is engaging in a process of controlled manipulation when he sets up conditions in such a way, and conducts himself in such a manner that he creates a warm, friendly, accepting atmosphere. One can only be free if he is in a system in which those persons in control allow him to behave freely. Freedom for growth is a basic humanistic principle, yet it is actually not a great deal different, nor less controlling than the rule of the benevolent dictator.

However, unwarranted fear, and failure to accept the reality of control and manipulation have often caused teachers to reject useful ideas and techniques and engage in labored discussions that result in no concrete classroom applications; and schools to encourage slovenly educational practices. The fate that has so often been accorded the ideas of the more behavioristically oriented social scientists offers a perfect example of what can result from this unwillingness to accept the inevitability of manipulation and the responsibility of control.

The behaviorist has sincerely devoted the lion's share of his time to studying the nature of human interaction generally, and the learning process specifically. He has been conscientious and scientific in his explorations, and although his efforts have fallen far short of being a hundred percent fruitful, he has generated many concepts and techniques that are immediately applicable to classroom use. Yet, many teachers have been unwilling to even listen to these principles, let alone attempt to apply them in practice. The typical teacher responds to behavioristic principles, with statements such as "Those tricks are only good for cats and dogs. They are too mechanical. I want to motivate my students, not raise pets!" Or, if accepting their applicability to human behavior, responding with "Conditioning may be all right for some things, but it just involves too much control for me. It takes too much of the humanness out of learning." The teacher is suggesting that control and manipulation are processes apart from human interaction, and that he can have nothing in common with the behaviorist because the behaviorist is so frankly attempting to control human behavior. The teacher, being a humanist, has no use for control. And, therein, as this paper attempts to point out, lies the fallacy B. R. Bugelski (1964) has recently published a textbook that could well serve as a tremendously practical handbook for the teacher, and help to make him more efficient at his teaching task if he were to make daily use of the principles it enumerates. Yet, few teachers will probably ever read this little book because behavioristic psychology and humanistic education have little in common in the eyes of the teacher educator as well as the practicing teacher. It is hoped that the present discussion has helped to clarify the wastefulness and futility of perceiving such a cleavage, such a difference in purpose between behavioristic and humanistic philosophies. Such perceptions can prevail simply through a failure to distinguish between motivation and manipulation, and a failure to accept the reality of what is truly involved in the process of human interaction.

Humanistic psychologies, such as phenomenology and self-theory, have defined for the teacher the nature of the organism's motivation, namely self-enhancement, and the conditions that are most likely to result in the greatest amount of learning: a warm, friendly, accepting atmosphere that gives each student an opportunity to invest himself into the learning situation. Behavioristic psychologies, such as operant conditioning, suggest many techniques whereby the teacher can control and manipulate the learner and the learning situation so that the learner will perceive both the material being taught and the learning situation as being self-enhancing. Thus, humanism, behaviorism, the student, and the teacher can and should act as a well organized, cooperative, team that is playing the game for the common purpose of making the learning process as meaningful, useful, and successful as possible.

REFERENCES

Bugelski, B. R., *The Psychology of Learning Applied to Teaching.* (New York: Bobbs-Merrill, 1964).

Combs, A. W. (Ed.), "Perceiving, Behaving, Becoming," *Yearbook of the Association for Supervision and Curriculum Development,* 1962.

Combs, A. W., "Some Basic Concepts in Perceptual Psychology," Paper read at Amer. Personnel Guid. Assn., Minneapolis, April, 1965.

COGNITIVE-FIELD THEORY
A POSITIVE APPROACH TO LEARNING

Robert Theus

Cognitive theory deals with the problem of how people gain an understanding of themselves and their environments and how, using their

From *The Clearing House,* XLII, No. 8 (April, 1968), 501–505. Used by permission of the author and publisher.

cognitions, they act in relation to their environments. Field theory centers on the idea that all psychological activity of a person occurs in a field; it is a part of a totality of coexisting factors which are mutually interdependent.

A cognitive-field theory of learning often is called merely field theory. However, since it describes how a person gains understanding of himself and his world in a situation where his self and his environment compose a totality of mutually interdependent, coexisting facts, cognitive-field is more truly descriptive of the learning process. Within cognitive-field theory, learning, briefly defined, is a relativistic process by which a learner develops new insights or changes old ones. In no sense is learning a mechanistic, atomistic process of connecting stimuli and responses within a biological organism.

Cognitive-field psychology explains development of insight as change in cognitive structure of a life space. To think of learning as development of insight and apply the thinking to school situations most advantageously, we need a psychological structure upon which to build our thinking. A person's insights collectively constitute the cognitive structure of his life space. Cognitive structure means the way a person perceives the psychological aspects of the personal, physical, and social world. Such a world includes a person and all of his facts, concepts, beliefs, and expectations. Consequently, the cognitive structure of life spaces figures in development of language, motions, actions, and social interrelations.

There are some features of cognitive-field psychology which make it distinctively different from any of the mechanistic psychologies. The foremost of these features is its unique approach to the study of perception and reality. Other important characteristics are interpretation of intelligent behavior as purposive, emphasis upon psychological functions rather than objects, a situational as opposed to a historical point of view, and stress upon the principle of contemporaneity.

In defining perception and reality in a relativistic manner, neither the organism nor the environment alone is one main factor. "Rather, a person and his environment are simultaneously interacting and participating in perception; they constitute a simultaneous natural interaction. Perception thus is expanded to its maximum and includes more than mere consciousness. Children in a schoolroom with teacher A conduct themselves quite differently from when they are with teacher B. Yet, they may at no time consciously formulate the two patterns of behavior. Perception, then, must be constructed to cover all the different ways one has of getting to know his environment."[1] "What one perceives—his reality—consists of what he makes of what seems to be himself and his environment. Depending on the habits—insights and understandings—he brings to a particular occasion, he seems to give meaning and order to things in terms of his own needs, abilities and purposes."[2]

Within cognitive-field psychology purpose is nearly a synonym for intelligence. A unique characteristic of human beings is their capacity to pursue long-sighted, as well as short-sighted, self-interests. A student's goal to become a teacher is a goal toward teaching as he now sees it. This goal may be a far cry from teaching as it is eventually experienced. The purposefulness of cognitive-field psychology is immanent, not transcendental, to the world of experience; it prevails in workaday life situations.

A third important feature of cognitive-field psychology is its emphasis upon psychological functions or events as contrasted with objects of movements. Psychological is understood to mean in accordance with the logic of a growing mind or intelligence. Thus, to be psychological in his pursuits a field psychologist must look at the world through the eyes of a learner. To describe a situation psychologically, one must describe the situation which confronts an individual. Such a situation is viewed as a pattern of person-environmental relationship which provides and limits opportunity. Once the person-environmental structure is established, the problem is to use constructs and methods adequate to deal with the underlying dynamics of behavior and to do this in a scientifically sound manner.

The learning situation in a cognitive field approach always consists of the whole field. At no time are aspects of a field viewed as isolated elements. In the study of a life space with its various constructs, the idea constantly is kept to the forefront that no two constructs or concepts are mutually exclusive, but that everything to some degree and in some sense is dependent upon everything else.

The fifth essential feature of cognitive-field theory psychology is the one most often misunderstood. Contemporaneity literally means all at one time. A psychological field or life space is a construct of such nature that it contains everything psychological which is taking place in relation to a specific person at a given time. The unit of time, microscopically viewed, is a moment; however, macroscopically considered, it may cover hours or

[1]Morris L. Bigge and Maurice P. Hunt, *Theories of Learning.* (New York: Appleton Century Crofts, Inc., 1956), pp. 340-346.

[2]Alfred Kuenzli, *The Phenomenological Problem* (New York: Harper Brothers, 1959) Chapter 8.

even weeks, months, or years. Whatever the amount of time, everything is going on at once—that is the meaning of the field. Psychologically, there is no part or future except as it enters into the present.

Field psychology is a purposive psychology; it assumes that intellectual processes are deeply affected by an individual's goals and that learning activity, including habit formation, is goal directed. Goal or purpose, therefore, is central to cognitive-field learning theory.

Cognitive-field theory involves the kind of generalizations about learning which may be applied to actual persons in school situations. It is associated with the knowing and understanding functions which give meaning to a situation. It is built around the purposes underlying behavior, the goals involved in behavior, and the persons' means and purposes of understanding themselves as they function in relation to their goal. Factors of a life space acquire meaning as a student formulates his goals and develops insights into ways of achieving them. Learning so construed is a change in the cognitive structure of, or insights in regard to, one's life space, which consists of a person and his environment.

Thus, with a working knowledge of the basic assumption underlying cognitive-field psychology, how do we apply it to a school situation? Advocates of cognitive-field psychology think that a teacher should teach, not baby-sit or dictate to students. A baby-sitter usually performs a custodial function but teaches children little, if anything. A dictator imposes the right answers. A teacher, in contrast with both, should perform his special teaching role in a process of student-teacher mutual inquiry.

The role of a teacher should be similar to that of a head scientist in a scientific laboratory; he should lead children in such manner that he helps them formulate and solve problems. To accomplish this, he should have a rich, extensive background of varied knowledge; he should be alert to the habitual attitudes and outlooks students are developing; and his ideal should be to promote an atmosphere which fosters maximum insightful growth. This means that he should be able to judge which attitudes or insights are conductive to continued growth and which are detrimental. He also should have sympathetic understanding of students as persons and should develop an accurate idea of what actually is going on in the minds (life spaces) of those whom he is teaching.

In a cognitive-field approach to the study of a school situation, a teacher and his students each is considered as a person in his life space. The goal of a teacher should be to have a common intersection of these life spaces. To gain an understanding of each child and his cognitive world, a teacher has to develop a sort of disciplined naivete. In order to adequately see Tom through, he must see through Tom. He must see Tom's person and environment as Tom sees it. When a teacher gains rapport with a child—when he gains his confidence—his influence can extend to the child's central regions and he is in a position to speak of the child's needs. What a child needs depends primarily upon how he sizes up himself and his material and social environment.

For a teacher to analyze a psychological situation, he must see the relationships between the various regions or parts of the child's life space. A group of pupils are all in the same physical environment in the classroom, but it is possible for each of them to be in a completely different psychological environment. A life space can include, and as a whole does, a large number of regions and the entire life space is surrounded by a foreign hull. The foreign hull is composed of potential perceptions that may, as learning progresses, be absorbed into the life space but at the present time are completely oblivious to the person. Knowing these facts helps a teacher to determine what is possible and what is not possible in the classroom, and what could happen and what probably will not happen in a learning situation.[3]

Let's now examine a real teaching situation using the above teacher learning concepts.

The chief strengths of any successful unit are those which enable each individual pupil to experience situations in such a way as to provide patterns which can be recalled by the individual as an aid in solving his future problems of life. Thus, the objectives of any unit must be the joint effort of the teacher and his pupils working and cooperating together. Such is the procedure followed in the formulation and presentation of the following twelfth grade American government class unit. Objectives were not planned in advance but developed as the unit developed.

American Government—Grade 12

Time—no special limit to the amount of time was given.

Students—a varied class of twelfth grade students with varied intellectual, economical, social, and other abilities and needs.

The central objective developed along with the unit acquainted students with local social and economic problems which they, as future citizens and taxpayers of the community, would soon become involved with. In fact,

[3]Bigge and Hunt, *op. cit.,* pp. 339-364.

many of these problems were already facing many students and their parents.

The secondary objectives of the unit varied almost with each individual student. An objective of several students was to improve their own living conditions. Others indicated that these problems were the ones experienced by their parents either directly or indirectly. To others these problems became sources of information and realization. But to all they created a desire first to learn and be informed, then to present the problem and finally a source for action.

Procedure

The introduction of the unit became unique in that it was student initiated and motivated. The idea of a local problems unit first came to the teacher's attention when he heard a group of students talking about a local election concerning legalized gambling. The interest of the students climaxed when several of them brought local and state papers giving the details of the local election. Others expressed their own personal opinions and those of their families and friends. The teacher then asked the class what other issues were important to them. The class next selected a secretary to write a list of problems suggested by the students on the chalkboard. From the list several would be chosen which would constitute the units to be studied. Several students suggested slums. Others mentioned the integration problem of their own school. One or two students mentioned a strike at a local factory. Drinking and vice were mentioned along with various health problems. Since many students were now driving, auto safety and auto accidents became a favorite student subject—especially since only the month before one of the students was killed in an auto accident. Some older students mentioned the draft, military service and the role of the church.

The teacher brought in such problems as the local teachers' union and housing. Of course, the problem concerning gambling was mentioned. After the list on the board was completed, a sheet of paper was passed out to the students and one was given to the teacher. The students and the teacher listed the five problems they would like to study and the five receiving the most votes were selected as parts for the unit. The students selected gambling, auto accidents, slums, housing, and strikes. They decided to deal with areas of the units one at a time beginning with the problems of slums.

Activities

Each of the main areas such as the slums was subdivided into five sections and a committee of five students was selected for each section. The students in each section were selected according to their ability to do the work of that section, the interest they had in that section, and the personal problem relationship they had to that section. For example, the slums section was divided into:

(a) What caused the slum conditions.
(b) What factors are used in recognizing slum conditions.
(c) What other conditions are associated with the slums.
(d) What relationships exist between the city and the slums.
(e) What can be done to remedy slum conditions.

In group (a) were found students interested in early history of the community. In group (b) were found some of the more capable students. In group (c) were a policeman's son and the daughter of a city crime reporter. In group (d) were found students who had the ability to reason and point out relationships. In the last group were found some of the slum students who had a chance to see what could be done to improve their own home environment.

The students decided to use the following activities which would be climaxed with a student publication and open house for their parents. The early study phase of the problem by the students consisted of reading several articles, pamphlets, and books—both local and otherwise—about slums and slum conditions. A second phase consisted of writing letters to city officials and other interested persons in similar slum conditions in other areas of the state. The third phase consisted of interviews with local persons interested in the slums such as the chief of police, the mayor, the director of the zoning board, the head of the city planning commission and several city social and health officials. The fourth phase consisted of actually visiting the slum areas and the homes of some of the students in these slums.

With the information gathered the student committees met and each recorded their facts. One student from each of the sections was chosen to help type and run off the pages. All the students then met together and assembled the booklets. While this was going on other students in the sections were drawing pictures, making blueprints and maps, or designing models. Others prepared for a panel discussion. A time was chosen by the students for an informal get-together with their parents at the school. A census of the number of parents attending was made so that the proper amount of booklets and refreshments were provided.

The meeting with the parents proved a huge success because within a short time the city had adopted a plan for slum clearance and improvement. A bond issue was proposed for the next election calling for low rent housing. Many parents of the poor economic group visited the school for the first time and a spirit for a general clearing up of the unsanitary conditions of the area insued. This unit drew our students closer together for the first time in which we had a real understanding of the economic classes within our community. This same sense of nearness and urgency existed in the other four parts of our local problems unit.

Evaluation

The evaluation of the unit existed three fold. First was the actual grading of the effort and presentation of the students. Next, the students graded themselves and compared this grade with the grade given them by the teacher. But, perhaps the most important evaluation of all was that of the city which for the next several years worked towards the elimination of all slum communities.

To conclude, the old notion that the brain was the only seat of learning has been discarded by present-day psychologists who now accept the more modern idea that the entire nervous system is the instrument of learning. Motivation of a practical nature has now become the key to learning.[4]

PSYCHOANALYSIS AND EDUCATION

Donald W. Robinson

THE IMPACT OF PSYCHOANALYSIS ON OUR CULTURE

The influence of psychoanalysis on education is as indefinable as it is undeniable, because it has been indirect. Sigmund Freud wrote in 1909

---

[4]Nelson L. Bossing, *Principles of Secondary Education.* (Englewood Cliffs, N.J.: Prentice Hall, Inc., 1962), p. 58.

From *Phi Delta Kappan,* XLIII, No. 7 (April, 1962), 292-299. Used by permission of the author and publisher.

that the purpose of education is "to enable the individual to take part in culture and to achieve this with the smallest loss of original energy." However, neither he nor the later analytic theorists have had very much to say about how learning takes place or about what should be taught or how it should be taught. They are primarily concerned with the emotions, while the teacher has traditionally been more concerned with the intellect. Relating the former concern to the latter is the task recently assumed by the psychologist.

Sigmund Freud is often mentioned, along with Charles Darwin and Albert Einstein, as one of the great creative thinkers of modern times. Like the others, he formulated a new way of looking at things that has profoundly altered the way we think about man and his relations to other men and to the universe.

His writings constitute a body of doctrine commonly called psycho-analysis, a doctrine based on the concepts of unconscious motivation, conflict, and symbolism. In this paper the word psychoanalysis will refer to this theory of human behavior set forth by Freud and his disciples.

The profound influence of the theories which Freud presented in books and essays from 1888 to 1938, and which he personally introduced to this country in a series of lectures in 1908, has been especially felt in the fields of psychology, sociology, anthropology, psychiatry, and psycho-somatic medicine.

Increasingly this influence is extending to the non-academic world. The growing stream of popular books, the evident Freudian approach by writers on child care and marriage counseling, the prevalence of Freudian allusions in popular literature and drama, and the appeal of analytic speculations about the cause of any human frailty or deviation, all confirm the fact that we cannot escape the influence of Sigmund Freud.

A leading psychologist who resists the Freudian influence nevertheless admits that, "It would be difficult to overestimate the impact of Freud's thoughts on the thinking of our times, especially among the classes which may be considered as supplying the intellectual leadership for the nation."

The impact on the schools has been no less important. It is readily apparent in the current school jargon. Teachers are threatened. Students have guilt feelings, aggressive tendencies, frustrations. Teachers stand as parent symbols, help students to recognize identification and projection and deal with anxiety and tension. These terms and the attitudes they represent are direct outgrowths of the concepts formulated by Freud.

The American Handbook of Psychiatry acknowledges the influence of psychoanalysis on education in these words, "In education, there has been a continuous trend toward the introduction of mental health principles in schools and a greater acceptance of the principles of individual, familial, and social dynamics. The importance of a wholesome school atmosphere, leading the pupil to a greater security and a feeling of belonging, or worth, and of dignity, as well as the importance of the teacher-child and the teacher-family relationships have been generally recognized. Progressive methods of education have been studied in relation to mental health aspects, and such extensive projects as 'human relation classes' have been highly successful. Psychiatric attention is being extended to every school level, including colleges and universities."

The card catalogue in the education library of a typical state college contains, under the heading *Psychoanalysis,* over 200 book titles. Goodwin Watson reports that psychology textbooks published in the 1920's averaged four pages devoted to unconscious factors in motivation, while books published in the 1950's averaged forty-six pages on the same topic. Texts published in the earlier period devoted an average of seven pages to mental hygiene, while the more recent books averaged fifty-seven. The trend is well established.

The reaction of teachers to this trend is naturally mixed. Younger teachers may accept the Freudian orientation more wholeheartedly because their exposure to it has begun earlier and they have not had to overcome a previously established viewpoint. Some teachers resist the whole psychological approach with a blunt insistence that "our job is to teach our subject; let the parents and the doctors take care of the emotional problems. The schools do too much psychologizing already." Others are responsive to the mental health approach, recognizing that establishing emotional health in the child will enhance his intellectual learning, but are unaware of the debt this approach owes to Freud and psychoanalysis.

The origins of this reluctance are easy to find.

Man will resist any new idea which seems to contradict notions long held and accepted as "true," especially such a notion as the complete freedom of man totally to control his actions by sheer willpower. Men have held so tightly to this illusion that it has seemed immoral to suggest, as Freud did, that a man's power to control his actions is limited by forces which he is normally incapable of controlling or even recognizing. We do not actually believe that a person can by sheer determination control his emotions, but we know that in our culture he is expected to do so.

A conscious determination to exercise control is necessary, but not always sufficient, for effective living. Anyone who has been the victim of blushing, stuttering, claustrophobia, forgetfulness, overeating, alcoholism, migraine headaches, insomnia, hypochondria, excessive worry, or any of a hundred other unconsciously-induced torments, will testify that willpower, even when adroitly applied, is often not enough.

The early years are so dominated by the constant urging by parents to "try," to "control," and to "master yourself" that the ego is unable easily to admit defeat by conceding that we are unable by sheer willpower to conquer the disability that plagues us. All people bear some degree of disability, whether it is a compulsive urge to talk or merely being ill at ease in certain situations. Fortunate are those who can adjust to their own idiosyncrasies, accept them, and prevent them from becoming disabling or disqualifying.

Resistance to the full acceptance of Freudian analytic ideas is normal and often assumes one of these rational forms: 1. *That psychoanalysis reduces the self-reliance of man by encouraging him to find explanations in circumstances beyond his control.* (The answer is that the Freudian approach is to *discover* what influences may be beyond the individual's *conscious* control and to offer a method for bringing these too within his control. An extension of consciousness can lead to higher levels of self-control, based on self-knowledge. Psychoanalysis seeks to replace the question "Does man possess free will?" with "How *much* free will does he possess?" and then seeks to enlarge the area in which he can exercise free will by revealing to him the source of some of his problems.)

2. *That the Freudian doctrine is unverifiable and unscientific.* (This is partly true, but the fact does not reduce the effectiveness of analysis. It might be difficult to demonstrate that Christianity or democracy are scientific, but that does not reduce their usefulness. And the power of the unconscious *is* clearly demonstrable, as in posthypnotic suggestion.)

3. *That Freudian literature is filled with bizarre, if not obscene, overemphasis on sex and sexual symbolism.* (The explanation is that the ever-recurring phallic and vaginal symbols are expressions of the powerful libidinal forces which eventually find fulfillment, if they are not thwarted, in heterosexual activity. Some persons find this symbolism repulsive because it violates the rigid code they were taught that one does not talk about sex except in hospitals and bars, because it is dirty. Is the dream symbolism suggested by Freud more bizarre than everyday occurrences such as blushing and stuttering *without* an explanation?)

Novelists long before Freud knew and exploited the power of the unconscious and the compelling importance of libidinal drives. Scientists too had underlined the instinctive urge to reproduce or the inherent urge for race survival. It is inconceivable that such a powerful urge should not influence the lives of individuals, even beyond their specific sexual acts. In this light Freud's emphasis on sex (which he defines in a far broader way than mere genital associations) is normal and desirable.

A different kind of resistance is engendered in persons who have had the misfortune to gain their first impressions of analysis from charlatans, quacks, or incompetents. Every complex social or psychological theory inevitably becomes altered as it becomes popularized. As the ripples of information circle out from the original source they become ever weaker and more easily distorted. This is equally true of Deweyism, Christianity, psychoanalysis, or any doctrine. The farther the gospel is spread the less it resembles the preachings of the master.

Most people probably adopt new ideas by bits and snatches. With respect to psychoanalysis some accept the concept of the unconscious while rejecting the notion of the sexual stages of development. Some accept the idea of dreams as concealed expressions of unconscious urges while scoffing at the Oedipus complex. As a result, the popular notion of psychoanalysis, as of every complex system, becomes a mishmash of distortions, dilutions, and eclecticisms.

The aversion that many teachers display toward Freudian doctrines results largely from this kind of peripheral misconception. Extremists who associated themselves with Freudian thought as well as with the fringe groups of ultra-progressives have given analysis an undeserved reputation for sanctioning the removal of all control and restraint from the child. Neither Freud nor any reputable analyst recommended the absence of controls.

It is not surprising that some of Freud's emancipatory discoveries, like some of Dewey's, became the vehicles for extremist movements of permissiveness. The early extremist works were published during the late Victorian era when a reaction against excessive authoritarianism was beginning and every possible scrap of evidence was marshaled in favor of the new spirit of freedom. Freud was aware of the unhappy effect of excessive repression and inhibition, as today he would be equally aware of the tragic consequences of insufficient control and direction of children. Both extremes are equally at variance with his theory and with the ideas of reputable analysis today.

THE INFLUENCE OF PSYCHOANALYSIS ON EDUCATION

A generation ago the obstreperous youngster was described as acting up. Today he is diagnosed as acting out. If the effect of the psychological emphasis had been no more than to create a new terminology it would not warrant our serious attention. Some partisans are certain that the psychological impact has rescued the schools from utter collapse, while others are equally convinced that the effect has been nearly disastrous.

The teachers of this country have welcomed the psychologists, though frequently unaware of their debt to psychoanalysis, and have eagerly attempted to incorporate their ideas into school practice. This is not surprising, since, with the extension of compulsory school attendance through high school, teachers have been unduly preoccupied with the problems of the emotionally disturbed students. Any new knowledge from psychology was welcomed if it promised hope of assistance in understanding and dealing with the mass of students who would once have been eliminated from school by virtue of their intellectual and emotional limitations, but who now must remain until graduation or until they reach age sixteen or seventeen.

The direct influence of psychoanalysis on school curriculum is apparent and significant. Teaching units on mental health and sex education have been introduced and psychological testing has mushroomed in importance, as have the guidance and counseling services. Important as these influences have been, we are not here concerned as much with them as with the over-all changes in educational philosophy and the resultant effect on teaching methods.

Psychoanalysis and Progressive Education

Psychoanalysis has been frequently equated with progressive education. It has been extravagantly praised and vehemently damned for introducing the permissiveness which has so conspicuously marked our child-rearing in the past generation. It deserves neither the praise nor the blame.

Three brief quotations should help to clarify the analytic position:

Dr. Peter Neubauer says, in an article in *The Atlantic* in July, 1961, "Freud pointed out that denial and conflict were as essential a part of the process of growth as gratification, and he never minimized the child's need for direction."

Anna Freud wrote, "The task of a pedagogy based upon analytic data is to find a *via media* between these extremes—that is to say, allow to each state in the child's life the right proportion of instinct gratification and instinct restriction."

Dr. Pearson, whose 1954 volume, *Psychoanalysis and the Education of the Child,* is probably the most comprehensive book on this subject, says, "Every individual must learn that he is affected by two fields of influence, the external world of sensory perception and the inner world of instincts. The influence of the latter far outshadows the former and in case of conflict takes precedence. Both too much frustration and too much gratification will hamper the development of the ego."

Excessive authority neglects to train the youngster for emancipation from dependence on the parent figures. Extreme permissiveness in the early years fails to provide the needed authority figures whom the child can use as models in developing his own personality.

If this sounds like a truism known by every experienced teacher, it is. And one of the reassuring aspects of psychoanalysis is that it *does* confirm the common-sense wisdom of the best of human experience. Psychoanalysis, like education, has for its major goal the freeing of individuals for rational living, unhampered by the bonds of ignorance or emotional thralldom.

Dr. Pearson dwells at length on the importance for teachers of the reality principle. He says, "Every opportunity to test reality is useful in helping the child solve his intrapsychic conflicts. During the latency period there should be ample opportunities for unsupervised and unrestricted play so that each child may have the chance to work out his specific conflicts in the make believe of play." Note that this is a very different thing than suggesting that the child should never be supervised, directed, or corrected. It is interesting to note, as Lilli Peller reminds us, that the child often takes his play just as seriously as the adult takes his work.

Pearson continues, "In reality human life consists more of hard and tedious work than of pleasurable experience, and if the individual wishes to lead a pleasurable life he must develop the capacity to accept and adjust to reality—to the realities of the physical world, the needs and desires of other people in this world, and the customs and mores of the world in which he lives. Only when the individual has this capacity will he be able to attempt to change any part of the environment—the physical work, the other members of his social group, or the prevailing customs and mores."

It is recognized that a child is far more likely to attain a satisfactory adjustment to reality if he is exposed to teachers who operate from reality, for the child incorporates not only what the teacher teaches but all aspects of the teacher's personality.

If the teacher has an extremely rigid personality, or is sadistic, or too inhibited, the child may incorporate some of this quality.

Pearson suggests that this may benefit the child if it happens to be the opposite of extreme parental traits, or harm him if it reinforces parental extremes.

Psychiatric Examinations for Teachers

It is self-evident today that emotional "maturity" is especially essential in a teacher. Pearson and many others urge that student teachers be required to undergo a period of direct psychoanalysis, and, where this is impossible, that applicants for teaching be screened by a rigid psychiatric examination.

It is tempting to speculate on the emotional stability of teachers. Dr. Shipley presents data from a 1948 study of admissions records at the Mayo Clinic showing that while 17 per cent of the physicians admitted to the clinic were found to have emotional illness, 19 per cent of the farmers, 30 per cent of the dentists, and 36 per cent of the lawyers and housewives, 55 per cent of the teachers admitted were suffering from emotional illnesses! The assumption that teaching harbors a higher percentage of neurotics than other occupations is a popular one. Although it cannot be thoroughly proved or disproved, it can be supported by logical inference, based both on the emotional wear and tear of the job itself and on the attraction of teaching for persons emotionally reluctant to compete in the hurly-burly adult world.

It is just possible that the influence of psychoanalysis on our culture has helped to determine the type of person who tends to become a teacher. If the extreme traditional school with its "this hurts me more than that does you" spirit attracted and then aggravated the "hard" or sadistic personality, the newer, more "progressive" school may appeal to the "soft" or philanthropic personality. Although the analytic approach requires neither "hard" nor "soft" but reality-based teachers, still an indulgent school, spawned in a permissive community, may tend to recruit overly sentimental teachers, who in turn will extend the permissive atmosphere still further.

At present no way exists to determine accurately how many teachers have unconsciously selected teaching as a solution for some deep-seated personal conflict, especially a conflict involving authority.

Analysts recognize this hazard among themselves and attempted some years ago a substantial study of the unconscious reasons why some analysts elected to concentrate in *child analysis.* Although the study was never formally completed, the evidence that was collected indicated three unconscious motives that prompted the choice of child analysis. It is evident that these motives *might* operate equally in the choice of teaching as a career. They are:

1. Fear of overaggressive impulses toward adults, consciously controlled by feelings of marked inferiority with adults and feeling more comfortable with children.

2. Unconscious desire to get even with hated siblings by being in a position where they can control children.

3. Conscious or unconscious hatred of parents, expressed as a determination, "when I grow up I'll show you how children should be treated."

No implication is intended that unconscious motivations are necessarily bad, but they *can* be unfortunate if they are too intense, and especially if they are not recognized and understood.

THREE PITFALLS FACED BY THE ANALYTICALLY ORIENTED TEACHER

Warnings should be advanced about three danger areas where the well-meaning teacher frequently errs in his efforts to promote mental and emotional health in his students. These three errors occur and are frequently cited by critics as failures of the psychological viewpoint.

The first of the three pitfalls is overemphasis on the developmental aspects of the child's personality at the expense of his intellectual development. Properly handled, teacher attention to the psychological problems of the child, with all of the interviews, tests, sociograms, play therapy, or whatever techniques are indicated, can be helpful in freeing the child from emotional blocks, and enhancing his ego so that he becomes a more effective learner as well as a happier person. If, however, so much time and attention is directed to the study of the psychological problems that too little is left for planning and directing the program of intellectual accomplishment, the child's education suffers. Perhaps there cannot be an overemphasis on emotional adjustment, but there can be an underemphasis on essential factual learning. Teachers are sometimes accused of over-psychologizing. This charge makes little sense as stated, for no teacher can know too much about the psychological problems of his students, but he *can* know too little or care too little about the learning that results from his instruction. If he goes overboard in his enthusiasm for psychology to the neglect of his subjects, he is justifying the charge that the schools are producing well-adjusted ignoramuses.

If the teacher's enthusiasm for helping the youngsters with obvious emotional problems leads to the neglect of the healthy average child, who also requires attention, he is derelict in his responsibility.

In addition to the general danger of overenthusiasm, a teacher who is familiar with analytic concepts is susceptible to *special* enthusiasms which can be harmful. One of these is the excessive interest and anxiety sometimes aroused in the teacher for the welfare of the problem student. For example, the teacher may know that the lonely child may be queer and that the distance between queerness and schizophrenia may be short, and so may go overboard in his anxious efforts to help the child to socialize. The teacher, in his fear that the child may overdo fantasy or day-dreaming, may prevent the child from working or playing alone, when the child very much needs the constructive values which he can only find alone. This concern about children's day-dreaming has sometimes led to an overemphasis on togetherness that makes children almost incapable of remaining alone.

So long as interest in psychology and personality development of the child demonstrably contributes to the improvement of his intellectual performance it will receive general support. When it becomes a movement to substitute the development of the personality for the development of the mind it contradicts a long-held and deeply cherished notion of the purposes of education. When the concept of the power of the unconscious is overstated it becomes in effect a kind of anti-intellectualism (or at least anti-academicism), which has been the target of recent attacks on the public schools.

The Teacher as a Behavior Model

A second and equally serious pitfall is neglecting to fulfill the child's need for a satisfying parent figure by being a "real person." The extreme progressive era encouraged the teacher to seek the background, to be inconspicuous and nondirective, so that the child might develop freedom, self-confidence and initiative. Again common sense tells us that the advice might be an excellent antidote for extreme teacher domination, but that the opposite extreme can be equally unfortunate. Children at every stage need the teacher partly as a model of behavior after which to pattern their own conduct. The teacher who remains inconspicuous provides no pattern. At the same time, on the strictly conscious level, students need teachers to tell them what they should learn and show them how to learn it—in short, to teach them.

Teachers who simply let children grow by self-expression are, it is true, avoiding the error of overdomination, but they are not teaching. It seems likely that a share of the apparent neurosis and insecurity today results from the fact that young people have had insufficient direction from adults. They have anxieties because they have not been given standards by which to measure their own conduct. A major function of the teacher is to lead. As a parent symbol he should afford the child the security which the child can derive from the knowledge that he is accepted as a loved child, even while he is corrected for his mistakes and is punished for his wrongdoing. The child seeks this security, both consciously and unconsciously, from the teacher's admonitions and examples. Without it he cannot learn as much.

Lilli Peller is referring to this function when she writes, "The teacher who puts herself on the child's level all the time, who encourages indulgence, who shows lavish admiration for any scribble—this teacher fails to inspire the child's wish to identify himself with her. Much as she tries to captivate the child's interest, she fails to get it. This does not imply that the so-called old-fashioned school has the most effective ways to promote learning and growth, it only indicates that conditions are more complicated than we thought." A school program must be geared to children's abilities and interests, but the child also expects the teacher to make demands and is disappointed when he receives no assistance from her in dealing with his instinctual pressures. Teachers themselves retain enough of the childish need for parent figures so that they frequently place the very concept of learning, or more often a specific new formulation of ideas, such as the Freudian concept, in a parent role. Their intellectual reaction to it is very much colored by their emotional reaction, which betrays a striking similarity to the manner of a child reacting to a parent, either prostrating himself completely to the new demands or rebelling violently against them. The role of the parent symbol is always present, and it is a role that the teacher cannot refuse to play.

Dealing With Resistance to Learning

The third weakness that sometimes comes into teaching with those who profess the mental health point of view is the failure to recognize the importance of resistance. Resistance to learning in the classroom is just as normal and inescapable as is resistance in the analyst's office. Man has a deep-seated human instinct to keep what is his own, especially his beliefs and feelings. Learning, if it is to be meaningful, must alter some cherished misconceptions of the learner, and these he will relinquish only slowly and reluctantly. Therefore when certain of the progressive teachers interpret students' resistance to learning as unacceptable or as evidence that the learning situation has been badly planned, they are missing a major analytic point. If the learning is significant some students *must* resist it and be unhappy about it. This does not make either the teacher or the lesson wrong. Teachers who feel that all learning must be gay and pleasant, almost to the point of being carefree and effortless, are denying the essence of learning. It would probably be an indefensible overstatement to assert that without discomfort and resistance no valuable learning can take place, but this statement is valid if we accept literally the popular dictum that the only learning that is truly worthwhile is that learning which results in changed behavior.

This proposition too can be tested by reference to adults. If we observe teachers or others discussing the relative merits of traditional versus progressive methods of teaching it will soon become apparent that for most of them something more is involved than a rational desire to share viewpoints and discover the best way to teach. What is more powerfully though unconsciously involved is a resistance to having their notions of teaching challenged. The concept of resistance is as significant in learning as the notion of the parent image, and should be thoroughly understood by the teacher.

It now becomes apparent that the three separate dangers inherent in the analytic approach all result in the same damage. The teacher who emphasizes the psychological approach at the sacrifice of subject matter, the teacher who neglects the role of the demanding parent figure, and the teacher who tries to eliminate or avoid pupil resistance, are all playing into the hands of "easy learning" to the long-range disadvantage of the child.

The reader should of course beware of interpreting the three warnings as being pleas for a return to authoritarian methods, or for more homework for students, or for more attention to academic requirements, or any other prescription. If they are pleas at all, they plead for keeping psychological and intellectual goals in balance, for having the teacher understand his psychological as well as his academic role, and for recognizing the inescapability of student resistance to learning.

In exonerating Freud and psychoanalysis of responsibility for the errors and excesses of well-meaning but misdirected disciples, we do not intend to excuse the teachers who perpetrate the damaging excesses.

Analytic theory in the hands of incompetent teachers is dangerous, but no more dangerous than psychological ignorance in the hands of incompetents. Where there has been incompetent teaching by analytically oriented teachers, let us blame the incompetence, not the philosophy.

SUMMARY

Despite the pitfalls, we must learn to make the best possible use of all the available tools and techniques that give promise of aiding in the herculean task of educating all the children of all the people. We must master the psychological contributions in order to improve the excellence of our intellectual accomplishments. And we need some other emphases in the school also. Excellence in imagination, in persuasion, and in artistic creativity are not to be scorned. The point is simply that excellence can seldom be attained by teachers who are unaware of their own emotional limitations and who stoutly resist self-knowledge by asserting that intellectual content is all that matters.

Psychoanalysis seeks for its followers the rational life, through the control and understanding of the emotions. Education too has as its goal the rational life, and seeks to promote a way of life directed by reason rather than by emotion. The cooperation of education and psychoanalysis in the attainment of their common goal seems natural and desirable.

Teachers cannot be trained as psychoanalysts. They cannot attempt the reconstruction of pupil personality. Nevertheless in dealing with emotionally deficient children the teacher is compelled to make some effort to minimize the effects of the child's personality disorders, as well as to prevent their aggravation, if she is to have any hope of teaching the student.

Consequently the teacher who is equipped with an understanding of the child's normal and abnormal behavior is more likely to succeed.

The master teacher who can recognize compulsions, fantasies, projection, identification, and other similarly emotionally dictated behavior can no more eliminate them than the master mariner can eliminate the adverse winds and tides. Neither would be called a master if he failed to recognize the adverse influences and guide his teaching or his navigation accordingly. It is important to have teachers who are analytically sophisticated as long as we have students who are immature and unstable. Otherwise, teachers in positions of authority over children who are unable to respond wholesomely will cause still more maladjustment. A few rare souls learn this without recourse to analysis, as they did before Freud began the systematic study of the unconscious. Unfortunately, still fewer of these rare souls find their way into public school teaching.

Analytic sophistication by teachers is obviously not the only need. Attention to mental health at every level is called for. Dr. Neubauer says, "Perhaps the greatest lag in the field of mental health is the relative lack of action to implement our conviction that emotional health and pathology are determined in early childhood. More than half of all hospital beds in the U. S. are occupied by mentally ill patients, yet there exist almost no institutional facilities for the emotionally disturbed preschool child. As long as we neglect the needs of the very young, we will continue to have a large population of adolescents and adults suffering from neurosis or the acuter forms of mental sickness."

Four-fifths of all counties in the U. S. still have no psychiatric service whatsoever. Studies of school children indicate that from 7 to 12 per cent—between two and four million—are in need of psychiatric treatment.

The mental health problem is immense. It is not the school's problem, but the school cannot escape responsibility for doing everything in its power to avoid aggravating it.

The various statements of the role of the teacher in handling this problem have this in common: they are all predicated on a continually increasing awareness and sophistication of psychoanalytic concepts. This is all that can be safely suggested, for psychoanalysis is not prescriptive.

Dr. Lawrence S. Kubie presents a convincing case for the importance of psychoanalysis to education in his introduction to *An Application of Psychoanalysis to Education,* by Richard M. Jones. Dr. Kubie reminds us of the necessity for making emotional maturation a part of the educational process by a continuous concern from kindergarten to university for making self-knowledge in depth part of the main stream of education. He does not urge that teachers play at being analysts, but only that education take place in an atmosphere in which emotional disturbances can be recognized and resolved instead of being repressed and aggravated. He goes on to say:

"The child's fifth freedom is the right to know what he feels; but this does not carry with it any right to act out his feelings blindly. This will require a new set of mores for our schools, one which will enable young people from early years to understand and feel and put into words all the hidden things which go on inside of them, thus ending the conspiracy of silence with which the development of the child is now distorted both at home and at school. If the conspiracy of silence is to be replaced by the fifth freedom, children must be encouraged and helped to attend to their forbidden thoughts, and to put them into words, i.e., to talk out loud about love and hate and jealousy and fear, about curiosity over the body, its products and its apertures; about what goes in and what comes out; about their dim and confused feelings about sex itself; about the strained and stressful relationships within families, which are transplanted into schools."

Dr. Kubie's plea, and it was Sigmund Freud's foremost plea, is for awareness. If teachers are aware of the deepest needs and feelings of their students, and if the students are encouraged to become aware of their own thoughts and feelings, far more effective learning will take place.

Traditionalists and progressivists stand together in abstract acceptance of the notion that the proper study of mankind is man. Increasingly they are sharing the awareness that Sigmund Freud contributed greatly to this study and that teachers have much to learn from him that will make them better teachers by making their students better learners.

FACTS ABOUT LEARNING

Walter B. Waetjen

I want to share with you some ideas which, for lack of a better term, I am calling "Myths and Facts About Learning." It is of interest to see where the myths come from and where I think the facts come from.

The myths which I will cite are essentially those that are either fairly common among our own profession or held by people who, though unqualified to say what education should be, are very vocal. The facts are what have come to us from research in how people learn.

AN ACTIVE PROCESS

The myth: The teacher's job is to teach what is to be learned, and the student's job is to learn it.

Notice that this means that a student, whether graduate or undergraduate or in secondary school, is to accept the data or information that the teacher supplies. He's to memorize it, and then he is to apply this information or data in predetermined ways. Even worse, he then takes an examination to prove that he has learned the data and information and that he knows how to apply them even though he has not been given the opportunity to do so. Notice that this places an extremely heavy burden of responsibility on the teacher. It makes the teacher the active person in the teaching-learning situation, and places the student in a passive role.

This myth also assumes that there is a one-to-one relationship between what is taught and what is learned and, as many of you know from the studies on perception, that is a fallacious assumption. There is a vast difference between what a teacher attempts to communicate and what students learn.

This myth also assumes that what is significant to the teacher is equally significant to the learner. And I could tell you of many ways in which this is not true just from little tales that my three children bring home from school!

From *Baltimore Bulletin of Education,* XXXVIII, No. 2 (December, 1960), 22–28. Used by permission of the author and publisher.

The fact: We cannot teach another person directly nor can we facilitate real learning in the sense of making it easier for the learner.

We cannot teach a person directly. We cannot communicate to others fully what our meanings are.

A teacher can make learning possible, not easier. He can make learning possible by providing a number of things—specifically, information; the setting, which I will describe to you somewhat later; materials and resources. But especially can a teacher make learning possible by being present in the whole human sense of that word: by listening, by emphasizing, by supporting, by encouraging. This is the primary role that the teacher has in facilitating learning. This, you see, would make the learner the active person, the prime mover in the teaching-learning situation.

If we believe in the facts from research that support the statement, *learning is an active process,* children will come to see school as a place where they go *to do something rather than have something done to them.*

BEGINS WITH THE STUDENT

The myth: Knowledge taken on authority is educative in itself.

When an authority says something, because he has said it, it is educative, if you learned the proper words. And there is the trap. It is entirely possible to learn the proper words. It is entirely possible that this vocabulary substitutes for vision and insight which, from my point of view, are learning. Let me give you an example.

One of my children who is in a secondary school said, not too long ago, "Well, as you move up the phylogenetic scale, man or animals become more complex." And I said, "That's exactly right. By gosh, that's a good notion. What does phylogenetic scale mean?" He answered, "I don't know. That's what we had in science today."

Will you notice, please, he has the vocabulary, he has the fluency to use the proper words. He did not know what they meant; he did not learn what this evolutionary scale meant. He was merely saying, "I learned a few words."

This tendency to accept knowledge and to assume that because an authority has passed it along it is then educative means that learners, pupils, students, people surrender self-direction. They surrender their own valuing of their experience and tend to say, "What you tell me is more important than what I have experienced."

In our curriculum we are so busy having children explain the experience of other people that children do not have the opportunity to explain their own experience, to tell about it, to analyze it, and to evaluate it.

Let me give you an example or two of how this is seen in classrooms. Have you ever had a student come to you and say, "What does the book say?" Notice again, "What do the authorities say?" Not so much "What does my experience tell me about what I have read?" but "What does the book say?"

Undergraduate students do this differently. They will say to· one another, "What did the prof say?" Because that's what's important. That's what gets you by the exam!

Again, the myth: Knowledge taken on authority is educative in and of itself. And, again, notice that this places the learner in a passive role. He is receiving, waiting for, rather than reaching out, and shaping or fashioning what his experience tells him.

The fact: The educational situation which most effectively promotes significant learning is one that has certain characteristics. First and foremost is the characteristic that the uniqueness of the learner is valued, cherished, and his uniqueness is brought into play in the learning situation. In other words, his own purposes, perceptions, and meanings are the ones that are used to give meaning to the educational or learning situation. Notice again that I am trying to say that *learning begins with the learner and not with the body of knowledge.* This is so basic a point that a teacher has no alternative but to begin with the student.

Another characteristic of the educational situation that promotes significant learning is the one in which the learner is free to explore ideas, materials, and resources that are available to him in the light of his potentialities, interests, and perceptions. I am not using the word interests as it is often used in education. Interests are basic, motivational structures and tell us how a person will use his energy, how he will behave or learn and, therefore, are necessary for us in devising grouping and in devising all kinds of curriculum experiences.

I've tried to say that these points are in rank order: If a person is accepted and valued and esteemed, he becomes an inquiring person and he actualizes himself. If, on the other hand, a person is taught to imitate, if he is taught to parrot back, if he's rejected or criticized, he becomes a static person in the learning process.

AN INTEGRATED PROCESS

The myth: Education can be obtained through a series of disconnected subjects.

There are very few exceptions to this today, because the push is in the opposite direction. The exceptions are these: There are some places trying ungraded or nongraded ways of grouping, and some places are trying more of an integrated kind of learning experience which flies under the banner of a core curriculum. It occurs to me that some of the very best education that's taking place is in special education classrooms because these are integrated.

The current pressure is toward more departmentalization, more specification of subjects that are to be taught by special teachers. I have just come from a city that has had departmentalization down through the fourth grade for over twenty years. They are now pushing to get it down through the second grade.

At the time that departmentalization for disconnected subjects came into being, we had a psychology of learning, stimulus response, connectionism, and conditioning that grew out of experiments with animals. It made good sense with animals. It does not make the same good sense with human beings, but it still persists.

When we have a highly departmentalized, disconnected kind of subject approach to learning, we have abdicated and left the most difficult job in learning to the students. The most difficult job is that of seeing relationships among different ideas, concepts, facts, in different disciplines. This is the hardest job in learning—the business of building the relationships, seeing the relationships—and this is the job that we leave to the students.

The fact: Learning is an integrated process and not the acquisition of discrete elements or unrelated facts.

Learning means that a person sees differently; that he feels and thinks differently; and, by all means, that he behaves differently. It means, too, that when a person has learned, it may be that his needs are not all satisfied. We tend, too often, to think learning implies that, when a person has learned, his needs are now satisfied. A good learning situation is one that ofttimes creates more needs than it satisfies. Rather than bringing closure, terminating learning, a good learning situation is ofttimes one that tends to open things up rather than to close them.

I've tried to say that even though in learning a person's understandings can be deepened, his needs may be highlighted and also more needs may be created than he had before.

The myth: There are many, many, people who believe that pupils must be coerced, forced, driven to learning something.

And may I say, with shame, that there are many people within our own profession who feel this. They believe that when we force a person to stick to something, we can rationalize to ourselves that this is good, that something unpleasant builds character. I am not quite sure what the logic in this is, but all the studies on learning indicate that while a student or a learner may complete such a task it does not necessarily follow that this is good for him. He may come out of the experience with other learnings that are distinctly contrary to what we would like him to formulate; for instance, feeling that teachers are coercive people and that school is a horrible place.

Also, if a person must be coerced into working on tasks, that person learns to conform, learns to surrender to authority. It means that he's robbed of self-respect (by that I mean respecting his own self-direction), and he's also robbed of his own self-direction.

It may be that this is one of the reasons why we have so many children in mentally retarded classrooms. They are not really mentally retarded; they have given up. It may also be that this is why we have so many children who are in remedial reading instruction programs. They are quite capable, but they have surrendered. They've given up in learning.

AFFECTED BY ANXIETY

The fact: The individual learns what he wants to learn.

The individual learns significantly only those things which are involved in the growth of *his self,* and I use the last words in a psychological sense, that we learn significantly only those things involved in the growth of our own personality organization. This is what makes sense to us.

Learning under threat is temporary, transient. These learnings disappear when threats are removed. Studies show that when people are threatened into learning something, they will learn it and be able to hand it back to an instructor. It has also been shown that when people learn in threatening situations, they jump to gross conclusions and are unable to perceive nuances of meaning, fine discriminations. And their recall is practically nil.

Anxiety can be a motivating force in learning; that is, anxiety which pushes the learner a little bit off balance makes the learner find out something in order to resolve his anxiety.

In a classroom, however, when anxiety gets in the way of learning, then the teacher who injects anxiety into the learning situation is defeating his own objectives.

Let me cite some research. High anxiety and intelligence are negatively correlated, which means the higher one's anxiety, the lower one's intelligence test score. This means that anxious children take their anxiety to the intelligence testing situation. This anxiety gets in the way of their performance, and they score low.

Since you are talking about grouping today, may I then inject a note of discouragement when it comes to grouping? If we group according to I.Q.'s, do we know the level of anxiety? Isn't it possible that a youngster who had an I.Q. of 95 may have high anxiety and in actuality have intelligence up around 125, or at least higher than 95? Recent research done on anxiety would knock ability grouping according to intelligence quotients into a "cocked hat."

It occurs to me also that the research on anxiety as a factor in learning points out that anxious children are dependent children. For example, let's say you gave instructions, somewhat like the following, to children in a classroom: "Now, for the next fifteen minutes, we will be doing this and such. This committee will meet over here, and so and so is going to be chairman. This committee will meet over here; and this one, here. You will do this and such. Once you have finished, we will do this and such." Very clearly and explicitly are the instructions given. Finally you say, "All right, now let's get to work." Then, you turn around, and someone is tugging at your sleeve or tapping you on the arm, asking, "Did you say that my group meets over here? Did you say that I was supposed to do this? Am I supposed to hand this in on this and such day or at this and such time?"

Notice, please, that when children do this, they are putting themselves into a dependent relationship with you. *Anxious children are dependent children.* They cannot act on their own cues, their own clues, their own experience. They have got to get it from you. I might add that there are some distinct relationships here to grouping. Can we group anxious children in the same manner, since they are more dependent than children who have lower levels of anxiety?

Another thing from the research on anxiety having to do with learning is that *anxious children tend to be blaming children.* In an experiment, the children in a classroom were given an arithmetic test. When the first youngster finished, the test was terminated! Some of the children had high anxiety, as previously measured; when these children were asked why they didn't complete the test, they never once questioned the teacher's judgment in terminating it after only one child had finished. They said something like this: "Well, my mother and father didn't help me with this last night." Or, "That kid next to me was bothering me during the exam, and I couldn't finish." Or else they said, "I am stupid. I just don't know how to do arithmetic." Notice the tendency to blame others, blame self.

The children with much lower levels of anxiety said, when they were interviewed, "Why did you stop the test so soon?" These children were much more reality oriented and discerning of what was going on around them. They also had this to say: "Well, if I had had more time, I could have finished it." This is not blame: this is a statement of fact. They could have. Again, the point is that anxiety has a tremendous impact on what one learns.

The myth: Learning is an intellectual process.

The approach that is taken by some people is that learning is entirely intellectual in nature. They assume, for instance, something like the following: Mental capacity as measured by a test equals the number of facts to be learned. This is the key; this is the formula; this is the statement. Whatever one's I.Q. is, or his mental age is, this determines the number of facts to be learned. This is all one need be concerned about with learning! They assume that no human factors play a part in the learning process other than the intellect. Many school systems grade and group on this same assumption or method. Many school systems shrink from frank acceptance of the fact that personality, as well as physiological factors, also influence learning.

A COMPLEX PROCESS

The fact: Learning is a very complex process that includes the intellect.

What this means is that when an individual acts in accordance with his own being—as he is, as a total person—he is more and more fully able to realize his potential. The result is an expression of self, and I am using this differently than self-expression. We ofttimes feel that self-expression means the aberrant acting out, irrational, inconsistent behavior of people. Expression of self to me means that a person's behavior is unified. It is consistent. It is inquisitive, inquiring. It is moving forward. A person is open and can benefit by his experience.

Two recent research studies bear on this very point, that learning is a complex process including the intellect. One study done by Spalding at Stanford University has to do with the effects of a person's conception of his mental ability upon his scholastic achievement or academic achievement. This researcher identified two groups of sixth-grade children. The children in one group were described as having a very high conception of their mental ability, and those in the other group were identified as having a low estimation of their mental ability. *The high self-concept group was found to be significantly superior in reasoning ability,* the point being that both boys and girls who had the self-concept of having high mental ability, whether they actually did or not, had significantly better reasoning ability. If this is so, there is a relationship between the intellect and one's conception of self.

One other finding was: *The facilitating effect of high self-concept occurred primarily for boys of low ability in the areas of work-study skills and* (please note!) *reading.* If I may state that differently, it's something like this: For boys, a high personal estimation of mental ability, even though that mental ability tested low, was found to have a beneficial effect on work-study skills and reading.

Please notice that if this is accurate, if it's valid, then it means that one of our primary jobs in school is to help build into the child a concept of self, a perception of self, such as, "I am a person who has ability, mental ability."

I have always been perplexed by this problem in grouping. When we group according to ability levels, we do so primarily on the assumption that this will aid us in helping the children to learn. I am wondering, however, if children in low groups do not perceive themselves as being low-groupers and behave accordingly. They react and they read as low-groupers. "I'm a low-grouper so I'm really not expected, nor permitted, to read at a middle-grouper level." Please note that I raise this as a question and not as a fact.

The summarizing paragraph in this study indicates that among the high-ability children, boys tended to be more realistic in their self-concepts about mental ability than girls. Boys are more objective about their mental ability; their perception of their mental ability and their actual mental ability are much closer together than those of girls. But among the low-ability children, girls tended to be more realistic in their self-concepts. This tendency of the girls to tolerate a lower self-concept about their mental ability may reflect cultural role expectations; the boys, on the other hand, may have to maintain higher self-concepts regarding their mental ability in response to the masculine role expectations of the culture. Again, please, I'm trying to make another point here by quoting this paragraph:

"Learning is intellectual in nature. It involves one's self-concept, but as this study in this paragraph just indicated, it also involves the cultural role expectations of boys and girls. Girls are permitted by the culture to have lower conceptions of their abilities than boys."

Jerry Bruner, who is now at Harvard, has completed a study on the factors that influence the learning of what he called "over-achieving" and "under-achieving" children. Over-achieving meant children who were achieving considerably above what was expected of them; under-achieving, children who were learning at levels considerably below those anticipated.

It was found that all children, boys and girls, who have high achieve-ment motivation, who have D. Q. (drive quotient), also are the ones who are achieving. They not only have the motivation to achieve, but are achieving at high levels. He found, however, that children who have high achievement motivation have, in back of their motivation, fear of failure. We have many children in our schools who have this high drive to achieve, and we value it. I'm raising the question with you: Should we help them to taper off a little so that they don't have the fear of failure goading them?

For instance, Bruner (and also McClelland at Harvard) found that children who have only moderately high achievement motivation have as the genesis for their moderately high motivation the anticipation of success. Notice how much more salutary, mentally, this is than it is to have high motivation where you fear to fail. My point is that moderately high achievement motivation has behind it the anticipation of success; very high achievement motivation has behind it the fear of failure.

In this same study, Bruner went further and found these characteristics in over-achieving boys (you can almost say "over-learning" boys). They are more anxious in general and extremely anxious in test situations. He found, too, that they are more disturbed than the under-achievers over whether or not others consider them intelligent. The under-achievers really didn't "give a hang" whether or not somebody thought they were unintelligent. They were able to convince themselves that they were intelligent; and if a teacher reflected to them that they were, that was entirely commensurate with their self-image.

The under-achievers were not distressed about whether or not people thought them unintelligent, but the over-achievers were concerned about this. Over-achievers had general concern about success and achievement as well as concern about intellectual failure. (Notice how the self-picture enters into this learning.) The under-achieving boys were unconcerned about these things. They seemed to have little anxiety about tests, little anxiety in general, and they were not distressed by the picture or the conception that others had of them.

Girls presented a different picture. Over-achieving girls have lower need to achieve than under-achieving girls, and their need to achieve was decidedly lower than that for under-achieving boys. In other words, girls in general have much lower need to demonstrate that they are achieving. It may be, you see, that there is less pressure on them to achieve than there is on boys. Over-achieving girls were found to be much less anxious than under-achieving girls, and over-achieving girls had considerably less concern over failure than under-achieving girls.

Studies, supporting the conclusion that learning is a complex process including many human dynamics, suggest that there are very different roads to learning for boys and girls. Especially because of their psychological organization, boys and girls approach learning, and learn, differently. Their perceptions differ.

These findings have implications for grouping which should lead us to ask: Are we really helping our children when we group them on a bi-sexual basis? Or is it, perhaps, in order sometimes to group pupils along sex lines?

The myth: Learning situations created by teachers determine the meanings which children experience.

The emphasis here is on the myth that there is absolute meaning in a situation or even in a course.

We tend to attach labels to different jars in the curriculum pantry. Rarely do we look inside the curriculum jar and say to ourselves, "What happens in the situation?" This has given us a quantitative orientation to education.

We say, "Three years of English are better than two years. Four years of science are better than three and, by all means, five years of mathematics are better than four." Notice, five are better than four, three are better than two, two are better than one. This is quantitative orientation. We do not say to ourselves, "What happens in the two years? What happens in the three years?"

I am quite sure that in some schools two years of mathematics are better than four years of mathematics in other schools. But as long as we take the position that there is something in a situation that has absolute meaning, then we are doomed to this quantitative approach.

MEANINGS FROM LEARNER

The fact: The meaning that is derived from any curriculum teaching-learning situation is determined, in large measure, if not totally, by the meaning brought to the situation by the learner.

The flow of meaning is from the learner to the situation and not from the situation to the learner. In this sense, human beings are the only creative animals. We, as individuals, create meanings; we do not receive them. *We create meanings by virtue of what we bring to a situation.*

Another point is that there are occasionally times when each of us, as an individual, finds himself in a situation where things just seem to fall into place.

I hope you have experienced this! You're in a learning situation where all of a sudden, in an instant, you see new relationships, new implications, new applications. You say to yourself, "Well, now I can see what he was saying two months ago. And I also see that this is related to this, and how this has an impact on my income tax, and so on and so forth." Things just seem to come together. You get this feeling: "Aha! That is just what I have been after!" This is learning.

There are a number of characteristics in this situation. First, the learner enters this learning situation with his needs highly illuminated, clear-cut. And when these needs are satisfied, things fall into place.

The second characteristic of such a situation is that the people who are present are warm and permissive—permissive in the sense of permitting intellectual freedom. They are also creative people.

The third characteristic of such a learning situation—this "Aha experience"—is that the immediate environment is rich and varied in its perceptual content.

WHAT DO WE KNOW ABOUT LEARNING?

Goodwin Watson

What do we really know today about learning? Although no scientific "truths" are established beyond the possibility of revision, knowledgeable psychologists generally agree on a number of propositions about learning which are important for education. The educator who bases his program on the propositions presented below is entitled, therefore, to feel that he is on solid psychological ground and not on shifting sands.

Behaviors which are rewarded (reinforced) are more likely to recur.

This most fundamental law of learning has been demonstrated in literally thousands of experiments. It seems to hold for every sort of animal from earthworms to highly intelligent adults. The behavior most likely to emerge in any situation is that which the subject found successful or satisfying previously in a similar situation. No other variable affects learning so powerfully. The best-planned learning provides for a steady, cumulative sequence of successful behaviors.

From *NEA Journal*, LII, No. 3 (March, 1963), 20–22. Used by permission of the author and publisher.

Reward (reinforcement), to be most effective in learning, must follow almost immediately after the desired behavior and be clearly connected with that behavior in the mind of the learner.

The simple word, "Right," coming directly after a given response, will have more influence on learning than any big reward which comes much later or which is dimly connected with many responses so that it can't really reinforce any of them. Much of the effectiveness of programmed self-instruction lies in the fact that information about success is fed back immediately for each learner response. A total mark on a test the day after it is administered has little or no reinforcement value for the specific answers.

Sheer repetition without indications of improvement or any kind of reinforcement (reward) is a poor way to attempt to learn.

Practice is not enough. The learner cannot improve by repeated efforts unless he is informed whether or not each effort has been successful.

Threat and punishment have variable and uncertain effects upon learning: They may make the punished response more likely or less likely to recur; they may set up avoidance tendencies which prevent further learning.

Punishment is not, psychologically, the reverse of reward. It disturbs the relationship of the learner to the situation and the teacher. It does not assist the learner in finding and fixing the correct response.

Readiness for any new learning is a complex product of interaction among such factors as (a) sufficient physiological and psychological maturity, (b) sense of the importance of the new learning for the learner in his world, (c) mastery of prerequisites providing a fair chance of success, and (d) freedom from discouragement (expectation of failure) or threat (sense of danger).

Conversely, the learner will not be ready to try new responses which are beyond his powers or are seen as valueless or too dangerous.

Opportunity for fresh, novel, stimulating experience is a kind of reward which is quite effective in conditioning and learning.

Experiments indicate that lower animals (rats, dogs, monkeys) will learn as effectively when they receive rewards of new experience or satisfied curiosity as they will when the rewards gratify physical desires. Similarly, stimulating new insights have been found to be effective as rewards for the learning efforts of human beings.

The sense of satisfaction which results from achievement is the type of reward (reinforcement) which has the greatest transfer value to other life situations.

Any extrinsic reward—candy, or stars on a chart, or commendation —depends on its dispenser. There is no need to strive if the reward-giver is out of the picture. Also, cheating can sometimes win the extrinsic reward. The internal reward system is always present for the learner, and he sees little gain in fooling himself.

Learners progress in an area of learning only as far as they need to in order to achieve their purposes. Often they do only well enough to "get by"; with increased motivation, they improve.

Studies of reading speed show that practice alone will not bring improvement; a person may have read books for years at his customary rate, but with new demands and opportunities he may be able to double that rate.

The most effective effort is put forth by children when they attempt tasks which are not too easy and not too hard—where success seems quite possible but not certain. It is not reasonable to expect a teacher to set an appropriate level of challenge for each pupil in a class; pupils can, however, be helped to set their own goals to bring maximum satisfaction and learning.

Children are more likely to throw themselves wholeheartedly into any learning project if they themselves have participated in the selection and planning of the project.

Genuine participation (not pretended sharing) increases motivation, adaptability, and speed of learning.

Excessive direction by the teacher is likely to result in apathetic conformity, defiance, scapegoating, or escape from the whole affair.

Autocratic leadership has been found to increase dependence of members on the leader and to generate resentment (conscious or unconscious) which finds expression in attacks on weaker figures or even in sabotage of the work.

Overstrict discipline is associated with more conformity, anxiety, shyness, and acquiescence in children; greater permissiveness is associated with more initiative and creativity.

In comparisons of children whose parents were most permissive in home discipline with those whose parents were most strict (both groups of parents loving and concerned), the youngsters from permissive homes showed more enterprise, self-confidence, curiosity, and originality.

Many pupils experience so much criticism, failure, and discouragement in school that their self-confidence, level of aspiration, and sense of worth are damaged.

The pupil who sees himself at his worst in school is likely to place little value on study and to seek his role of importance outside the classroom. He may carry through life a sense of being not good for much. He is likely also to feel resentment at schools, teachers, and books.

When children or adults experience too much frustration, their behavior ceases to be integrated, purposeful, and rational. The threshold of what is "too much" varies; it is lowered by previous failures.

Pupils who have had little success and almost continuous failure at school tasks are in no condition to think, to learn, or even to pay attention. They may turn their anger outward against respectable society or inward against themselves.

Pupils think whenever they encounter an obstacle, difficulty, puzzle, or intellectual challenge which interests them. The process of thinking involves designing and testing plausible solutions for the problem as understood by the thinker.

It is useless to command people to think; they must feel concerned to get somewhere and eager to remove an obstruction on the way.

The best way to help pupils form a general concept is to present the concept in numerous and varied specific situations—contrasting experiences with and without the desired concept—and then to encourage precise formulations of the general idea and its application in situations different from those in which the concept was learned.

For example, the concept of democracy might be illustrated not only in national government but also in familiar situations of home, school, church, jobs, clubs, and local affairs. It is best understood when it is contrasted with other power structures such as autocracy, oligarchy, or *laissez faire.*

The experience of learning by sudden insight into a previously confused or puzzling situation arises when (a) there has been a sufficient background and preparation, (b) attention is given to the relationships operative in the whole situation, (c) the perceptual structure "frees" the key elements to be shifted into new patterns, (d) the task is meaningful and within the range of ability of the subject.

The term "cognitive reorganization" is sometimes applied to this experience. Suddenly the scene changes into one that seems familiar and can be coped with.

Learning from reading is facilitated more by time spent recalling what has been read than by re-reading.

In one experiment (typical of many), students who spent 80 percent of their learning periods trying to remember what they had read surpassed those who spent only 60 percent of the time on recollection. The students who spent all the time reading and re-reading the assignment made the poorest record.

Forgetting proceeds, rapidly at first—then more and more slowly. Recall shortly after learning reduces the amount forgotten.

Within twenty-four hours after learning something, a large part is forgotten unless efforts are made to prevent forgetting. A thing can be relearned more quickly than it was learned originally, however, and if it is reviewed several times at gradually increasing intervals, it can be retained for some time.

People remember new information which confirms their previous attitudes better than they remember new information which runs counter to their previous attitudes.

Studies consistently show that individuals who feel strongly on a controversial issue, and who are asked to read presentations of both sides, remember the facts and arguments which support their feelings better than they recall those on the opposite side.

What is learned is most likely to be available for use if it is learned in a situation much like that in which it is to be used and immediately preceding the time when it is needed. Learning in childhood, then forgetting, and later relearning when need arises is not an efficient procedure.

The best time to learn is when the learning can be useful. Motivation is then strongest and forgetting less of a problem. Much that is now taught children might be more effective if taught to responsible adults.

If there is a discrepancy between the real objectives and the tests used to measure achievement, the latter become the main influence upon choice of subject matter and method. Curriculum and teaching geared to standardized tests and programmed learning are likely to concentrate only on learnings which can be easily checked and scored.

The more rapid mental growth comes during infancy and early childhood; the average child achieves about half of his total mental growth by age five.

In the first two years a normal child transforms the "big, buzzing, blooming confusion" of his first conscious experience to organized perception of familiar faces, spoken words, surroundings, toys, bed, clothing, and foods. He differentiates himself from others, high from low, many from few, approval from disapproval. He lays a foundation for lifelong tendencies toward trust or mistrust, self-acceptance or shame, initiative or passivity; and these vitally condition further growth.

Not until adolescence do most children develop the sense of time which is required for historical perspective. The so-called facts of history—1492, 1776, and all that—can be learned by children, but without any real grasp of what life was like in another period or in a different country. Most instruction in ancient, medieval, and even modern history is no more real to children than are fairy tales.

Ability to learn increases with age up to adult years. The apparent decline is largely the result of lack of motivation. We can coerce children into school activities; adult education is mostly voluntary. Men and women *can*, if they wish, master new languages, new ideas, and new ways of acting or problem-solving even at sixty and seventy years of age.

SOME CHANGING CONCEPTS ABOUT LEARNING AND MEMORY

James L. McGaugh

Those who study man generally agree that it is our mental capacity that sets us apart from the other animals. Countless centuries ago, we domesticated plants and animals and began other technological achievements which surpass those of all other species. We also developed elaborate forms of communication, including language, which enabled us to transmit acquired knowledge to our offspring. All of these achievements are based, of course, upon our ability to learn: to record experiences and to utilize records of the past in dealing with the present. In adapting to our environment, we have relied upon learning ability to a greater extent than have any other animals. Learning ability is central to the biological and social evolution of man.

In most areas of human enterprise, technological achievements long preceded scientific understanding. Animal husbandry, agriculture, and even medicine antedated recorded history. In each of these areas, however, scientific discoveries of recent decades, in disciplines such as genetics, microbiology, and biochemistry, have so profoundly influenced technological developments and practices that the techniques of the farmer and the physician today bear little resemblance to those used even a few years ago. In areas essential for our survival, we have come to expect our technology to be continuously modified by scientific knowledge.

Although education is clearly essential for survival, the practices of

---

From *NEA Journal*, LVII, No. 4 (April, 1968), 8–9, 51–52 and 54. Used by permission of the author and publisher.

education have been less significantly influenced by basic research findings than have those of agriculture and medicine. Understanding of the nature and biological bases of learning and memory has not, as yet, significantly affected the educational technology. Most of the significant innovations have been concerned either with the *content* of education or with procedures for automating traditional teaching methods; few innovations and varied practices have grown out of basic research concerning the nature of learning and memory.

There are several possible reasons for this state of affairs. First, we simply may not yet know enough about the processes of learning and memory. Second, inadequate traditional views of the nature of learning and memory may have been misleading. Third, we may not have made sufficient effort to examine the implications of recent findings for educational practices. Whatever the reasons for the present situation, it seems clear that if we are to develop effective educational systems, teachers, like farmers and physicians, will need to develop and use more practices which are based on scientific understanding. Society cannot afford the luxury of ignoring this important problem.

The problem is complicated by the fact that at one time educators made a valiant attempt to understand and use principles of learning theory, but the theory they worked with was neither very good nor very helpful. From the time of Thorndike to the present, the dominant theories have emphasized the learning of stimulus-response connections and have stressed the value of rewards.

It has been difficult to reconcile these emphases with the obvious fact that much, if not most, learning consists of acquiring information or knowledge as a consequence of some sensory impact (watching, listening, reading). Learning may occur *prior to* responding and *prior to* rewards. While overt responding undoubtedly influences learning, it does not do so simply by strengthening stimulus-response connections. Responding provides a repetition or rehearsal of acquired information and, in addition, provides an opportunity for correcting errors if what was remembered was incorrect. But the response cannot occur unless some learning has already occurred.

Understandng of the nature and bases of learning and memory has increased steadily if not dramatically over the past several decades. Unfortunately, we have not yet reached the stage where such information is as relevant for the teacher as the findings of genetics, biochemistry, and microbiology are for the farmer and physician. Nonetheless, the theories and implications emerging from recent findings should not be ignored. In this brief essay, I will discuss a few of them, emphasizing three points—the increasing tendency to view learning and memory from a biological perspective, the considerable emphasis being placed on learning and memory as complex processes involved in the storage and utilization of information, and a cautious but increasing interest in considering the educational implications of these emerging facts and theories.

LEARNING AND MEMORY FROM A BIOLOGICAL PERSPECTIVE

Theories of learning have, to a considerable extent, ignored biological factors. The psychologist, John B. Watson, once proposed to take any one of a dozen well-formed, healthy infants and train them to become "... any type of specialist ... doctor, lawyer, artist, merchant, chief ... even beggar man and thief, regardless of his talents, penchants, tendencies, abilities, vocations. . . ." Beggar man and thief aside, this is, of course, the American Dream—an educational bill of rights that every one of us would like to accept as true.

In evaluating Watson's proposal, much depends upon the meaning of the words *healthy* and *well-formed*. Unfortunately, as far as ability is concerned, all men are not created equal. Because of inborn errors of metabolism, many infants will, regardless of training, never have the ability to become doctors and lawyers. They will be fortunate to learn to speak, feed themselves, and to tie their shoes.

"Normal" variations in intelligence also appear to be at least in part biologically based. Studies of the IQ's of twins have shown that in sets of identical twins the correlation of IQ scores is typically greater than +.80, while that for fraternal twins is usually approximately +.50. The similarity in IQ between pairs of fraternal twins is no greater than that of ordinary brothers and sisters. Numerous studies of this type show that, in general, similarity in IQ varies directly with the genetic similarity. Undoubtedly, heredity influences IQ scores.

Unfortunately, IQ tests were not developed to provide a measure of a psychological process or set of processes. They were developed simply on an empirical basis to provide a score which can be used to predict academic success. As such, IQ tests are used to predict—not to diagnose. They are, of course, not simply tests of learning and memory. They do, however, include subtests which provide measures of learning and memory.

Experimental studies using laboratory rats have shown that it is possible to develop, by selective breeding, strains of rats that are bright and strains that are dull on specific learning tests. Further, numerous different strains of mice specially developed for tumor incidence have been found to differ in learning ability on various tasks. In mice and men, learning ability is genetically influenced.

Learning ability is not, however, completely determined by genetic factors. David Krech and his colleagues at the University of California at Berkeley have found that environmental stimulation influences the learning ability of rats.

Rats reared in an enriched laboratory environment are better learners than rats reared in less stimulating surroundings. Again, however, biological factors appear to play a role; the rats who were better learners differed from the other rats in several morphological and biochemical measures.

We do not yet know in detail how genes and environmental stimulation act to produce normal variations in intelligence and learning ability. The learning tests used with rats and mice provide rather crude measures of learning ability—much in the same way that IQ tests provide crude measures of children's mental capacities. In spite of this crudeness, the tests are able to provide indirect measures of processes which are biologically based.

LEARNING AND MEMORY AS COMPLEX PROCESSES

The processes underlying learning and memory are undoubtedly extremely complicated. Consider what is involved in learning a telephone number. First, the information has to be attended to and received; second, the information must be registered or stored in some way; third, the information must be retained for a period of time; and fourth, it must be retrieved when needed. Learning ability depends upon the efficiency of each of these processes. Since deficiencies in one or more of the systems could cause poor learning, we need to know the nature of the brain processes underlying these systems.

Studies of memory in humans with memory defects have provided some leads. Dr. Brenda Milner at Montreal Neurological Institute has conducted studies of memory in patients with brain lesions in the temporal lobes of both hemispheres of the brain. In some ways, the memory processes of such patients are fairly efficient. Immediate or short-term memory may be normal, and there may be no impairment of the patient's ability to remember events which occurred some time prior to the brain damage. IQ scores are usually unaffected. However, although the patients may appear to be quite normal, they are not. They have completely (or almost completely) lost the ability to acquire and retain new information. The case of one such patient, who received brain damage 10 years ago, illustrates the nature of the defect:

"Ten months after [the occurrence of the brain damage] the family moved to a new house ... situated a few blocks away ... on the same street. ... A year later the man had not yet learned the new address, nor could he be trusted to find his way home alone because he would go to the old house. ... Moreover, he is unable to learn where objects constantly in use are kept. ... He will do the same jigsaw puzzles day after day without showing any practice effects and reads the same magazines over and over again without ever finding the contents familiar."

Research in my laboratory and in numerous other laboratories has shown that it is possible to produce amnesia in animals experimentally, by administering treatments including electroshock stimulation and various drugs, after animals are trained on a task. Amnesia results only if the treatments are given within a few minutes or hours after the training. The magnitude of the amnesia decreases as the interval between training and treatment is increased.

Findings such as these suggest that information can be retrieved from at least two memory systems: a short-term system and one for long-term storage. Both brain damage and the treatments such as drugs and electroshock stimulation appear to block storage processes in the long-term memory system.

It seems possible that at least some "normal occurring" deficiencies in learning and memory might be due to impaired functions of the two memory systems. Studies of memory disorders in geriatric patients and retarded children provide some support for this view. For example, W. K. Caird at the University of British Columbia reported results suggesting that, at least in some cases, the memory disorder in elderly patients may be due to a loss of efficiency in the long-term memory storage system.

Millard C. Madsen at UCLA has found that, in comparison with children with high IQ's (an average of approximately 120), children with low IQ's (an average of approximately 60) appear to have poorer short-term memory. Further, the lower-IQ children required longer intervals between training trials for optimal learning. This suggests that mental retardation may be due in part to deficiencies of short-term and long-term memory storage systems. In one study Madsen found that children with low IQ's could learn almost as efficiently as children with high IQ's when a relatively long interval lapsed between repetitions of the material.

Additional evidence that memory storage involves several systems has come from our studies of drug effects on memory storage. We have found in our laboratory that it is possible to enhance learning of laboratory animals by administering certain stimulant drugs shortly after training. These findings indicate that the drugs facilitate learning by enhancing long-term memory storage processes. The effects, like those obtained with memory impairing treatments, are time-dependent. Facilitation is obtained only if the drugs are administered within an hour or two following the training.

A large number of drugs are now known to enhance memory. Many appear to facilitate long-term memory storage in the manner just described. Others appear to act on short-term memory and retrieval systems. Unfortunately, not much is known about the specific ways in which the drugs influence neural functioning to produce memory effects, and we do not yet know whether comparable effects can be obtained with humans.

IMPLICATIONS

Although much has been learned in recent years about the nature and biological bases of learning and memory, we have probably not yet reached the point where such knowledge is of immediate significance for educational technology. All indications are that this point is rapidly being approached, however. Even at the present state of knowledge there are some important implications.

First, it is probably time to discard intelligence tests as we know them now—and time to develop tests designed to assess specific processes of learning and memory. Such tests could be used to diagnose individual differences in learning efficiency and might even prove useful (as IQ tests have not) in helping to develop teaching practices designed to deal with individual differences in learning and memory.

Second, it may be time to anticipate the possibility that, in the future, drugs might be used to correct learning and memory deficiencies in the same way that corrective lenses are now used to correct visual defects. Drug treatment of memory defects could become as common as drug treatment of allergies and emotional disorders. It may be that some day, by these means, educators will be able to fulfill John B. Watson's dream. Perhaps it will be the right of every child to have the opportunity to become a doctor, lawyer, merchant, or chief. The social and economic implications of this possibility are enormous. Perhaps we should begin to give them some thought.

QUESTIONS FOR DISCUSSION

THE NATURE OF LEARNING

1. The three learning theories presented in this section are said to view man as a reactive being (S-R association); as a reactive being in depth (Freudian theory); or as an active being in a constant state of becoming (cognitive-perceptual field theories). Which position is most acceptable to you? Which one is most extensively supported by research? Which is most compatible with a democratic society?

2. What are your reactions and conclusions in regard to man's freedom after reading the articles by Skinner and Rogers? How can scientific sequences of cause and effect in the psychological world be made compatible with man's freedom to choose? What implications do you see for the school curriculum in this discussion?

3. Is a synthesis of these three learning theories desirable? To what extent do you feel that this goal is achieved by Waetjen, Watson, or Avila and Purkey? What step toward this synthesis can you suggest?

4. The introduction to this section on learning lists eight concepts that may aid in a synthesis of learning theory. Would you add other concepts to this list? Try to decide which of the theories was the likely source of each of these concepts. What is the source of your additions to the list?

5. Which of the learning theories or what synthesis should be made the basis of classroom teaching and curriculum planning?

6. Should the same learning theory be the basis of curriculum and teaching at the elementary, junior high, senior high, and community college levels?

7. What is meant by "learning by discovery"? How does a teacher plan for this kind of learning?

8. How might the study of an individual learner affect curriculum planning?

9. Are there different kinds of learning? Is it possible that the different theories explain the different kinds? What implications would this have for curriculum planning?

4 The Nature of Knowledge

Man interacts with his environment and forms an interpretation of the world about him and his own nature. The accumulated products of these interactions, man's experience, is called knowledge.

Scholars have organized portions of knowledge into disciplines. A discipline consists of a set of generalizations that explain the relationships among a body of facts. Moreover, workers in the discipline develop a method of inquiry useful in discovering new facts. Each discipline is man-made and is subject to revision if a different organization of the facts proves more functional.

Some think of knowledge as an organized body of facts and believe that all the facts that man has discovered, learned, or invented have been collected, catalogued, and organized into the only logical structure. Further, they believe that the school's function is to accept the organization of facts that has been made in the past and devise ways of helping each pupil acquire as much of it as he can. According to this viewpoint, curriculum workers and teachers are confronted with the task of examining each subject or discipline and deciding upon a sequence in which the facts should be learned and the pace and procedures by which pupils should be brought into contact with them.

Certain problems have arisen for those who follow this logic. The facts available to man have accumulated at an extremely rapid rate and will multiply even faster in the years ahead. It is impossible, and will become increasingly so, to have any one pupil learn all of the facts available, even in a given discipline. Moreover, the new knowledge makes some present "facts" obsolete. What is to be done? Which shall be taught? How shall it be taught to enable the pupil to use his knowledge to greatest advantage and also to accommodate additional knowledge (Arthur W. Foshay, "Knowledge and the Structure of the Disciplines" and Jerome S. Bruner, "Structures in Learning")?

Others view knowledge as a much more flexible, fluid product of man's experience. They are not sure that the organization of facts that the scholars have created is the most functional for all purposes. They believe that the definition and the structure of a discipline are inventions of man and may be revised in light of new knowledge, and that new disciplines can be formed as needed.

They believe that each man attempts to understand himself and the environment about him. In the process, he invents interpretations of his environment and of his own actions. These interpretations are unique to him, and constitute the knowledge that is real and of value to him. Through his attempts to understand himself and his environment, he is brought into contact with facts that others have discovered and organized. The facts and the organization may or may not have meaning for him. He decides. He determines how the newly contacted data will be incorporated into his system of knowledge. His structure of knowledge—his actual structure and not the one he may verbalize—is personally invented and constructed.

Curriculum workers and teachers who hold this second conception of the nature of knowledge approach curriculum construction and teaching in a different manner. They are not sure that the traditional disciplines should be the guides for organizing the curriculum. They want to start with the concerns and needs of the pupil and permit him to use facts from any discipline that will help him.

Still other persons concerned with curriculum development and teaching fall between these positions. Arno A. Bellack ("Conceptions of Knowledge: Their Significance for the Curriculum") suggests that curriculum planners shift from an orientation based on individual disciplines to broader groupings of knowledge such as science, mathematics, social science, and the humanities. He pleads for scholars and curriculum workers to join in a search for new teaching structures that avoid undue fragmentation of knowledge.

A growing concern for disadvantaged learners has led to the suggestion that the affective dimensions of learning be emphasized in relation to knowledge content in organizing the curriculum (Mario Fantini and Gerald Weinstein, "Reducing the Behavior Gap"). Students can't be asked to give up "inner" content for "outer" content that bears little connection to them.

Some scholars have questioned the meaning and usefulness of such terms as "structure of the disciplines" (Herbert Kliebard, "Structure of the Disciplines as an Educational Slogan"). Still others have called for training teachers in logic so they can help students to understand how to arrive at conclusions (B. Othanel Smith, "Logic, Thinking And Teaching"). The question of how knowledge will be organized and taught is one that is not resolved.

McLuhan ("The Medium Is The Message") asserts that the medium is the thing to study. If you don't know the total environment of the knowledge or content, you don't know the message. Everybody pays too much attention to knowledge according to McLuhan; he says that we should pay more attention to the form, structure, and framework of knowledge.

McClusky believes that society increasingly will require that systems of formal instruction be reoriented to life-long educational needs and that this will necessitate emphasis on the structure of subject matter, the "why" of method, and the concept of the "spiral" curriculum ("The Demand for Continual Learning in Modern Society").

Each curriculum worker and teacher holds beliefs about the nature and organization of knowledge that influence his decisions. He may not be conscious of his point of view, but his unstated assumptions are the basis of his actions.

The clarification of such assumptions about the nature of knowledge is necessary if the curriculum worker is to make intelligent decisions about such questions as: (1) What information is most important to include in the curriculum? (2) What bases are to be used in deciding which information has the most value? (3) What organization of the knowledge that is selected should be made available to students? (4) How should students be brought into contact with the knowledge? (5) What do we want students to do with the knowledge they study? (6) How do we help students form a functional organization of knowledge?

KNOWLEDGE AND THE STRUCTURE
OF THE DISCIPLINES

Arthur W. Foshay

I wish to examine with you here the idea that the structures of the disciplines on which our school subjects are based may be taken as highly suggestive of the way the subjects should be conceived, taught, and learned. This is, of course, the hypothesis strongly implied by Bruner's book, to which reference has repeatedly been made during this conference.

The idea has roots that go deep into our intellectual history. For it to be meaningful to us as educators, however, we must understand the terms *subject* and *discipline* in the same way. In this paper, therefore, I shall deal first with the concept "discipline," then with the concept "school subject." If my way of dealing with these concepts is successful, it will then be meaningful to consider how the structures of the disciplines may be used for school purposes. In order to do this, I shall use as illustrations the structures of three diverse disciplines: chemistry, history, and poetry. If the proposition is meaningful that the structure of the disciplines suggests the way the disciplines may themselves be learned, then these illustrations should be suggestive of curriculum experimentation.

In the popular sense, a discipline is a branch of knowledge involving research. More helpfully, we may think of a discipline as a way of learning, or a way of knowing. Those people who pursue the way of doing research appropriate to a given branch of knowledge are members of a common discipline. We say, in common-sense terms, that historians are members of the discipline called history, chemists are members of the discipline of chemistry, poets are members of the discipline of poetry. There are branches of knowledge widely recognized as disciplines: the sciences, the social sciences, the various humanities. The scholars in these various fields have in common their attempt to create new knowledge, but their ways of working, or of knowing, differ. Let us accept for purposes of this discussion the characterization of a discipline as "a way of knowing," if for no other reason than that such a definition helps us to make a desirable distinction between the term *discipline* and the term *school subject*.

From *The Nature of Knowledge: Implications for the Education of Teachers,* William Jenkins, ed. (Milwaukee: University of Wisconsin–Milwaukee, 1962), pp. 28-40. Used by permission of the author and publisher.

If a discipline is a way of knowing its particular body of knowledge in its appropriate way, then a school subject can be thought of as a pattern of learning activities, worked out by an educationist (a teacher, if you please) which has as its purpose the introduction of students into the discipline. For example, we have a school subject called history that has as its purpose acquainting students with the discipline called history; we have a school subject called chemistry that has a similar purpose with respect to the discipline of chemistry, and so on. The fact that we call the school subject by the same name as its underlying discipline has tended to obscure the necessary distinction between the subject and its underlying discipline. A school subject, as organized and taught, represents an educationist's attempt to translate an underlying discipline into a pattern of activities that will make it available for a student's learning.

According to this view, a school subject could be evaluated according to the success of the translation. It would be meaningful to ask whether a given course in history successfully introduces students to the relevant portion of the discipline of history; it would be equally meaningful to ask whether a course in poetry successfully introduces students into the "discipline" of poetry. (I recognize that calling poetry a discipline introduces certain problems, for the poet does not think of himself as doing research, although the critic of poetry may well do so. Of this, more later.) For our purposes here, it is sufficient only that we accept the idea that a distinction can be made between a school subject and the discipline to which it is relevant.

In order that there be a discipline, it is necessary among other things that people be in agreement on the field of phenomena in question—the domain of the discipline. Biologists, for example, have to be in agreement about the phenomena they are to deal with. One of our problems in the field of education is that no such agreement appears to exist; that is, we are not in agreement on what phenomena fall within the field of education, and what phenomena fall without. Nor are we in agreement on what is more central and what is less central to the field of education —though efforts are being made to develop such an agreement.

Second, the members of a discipline agree upon a set of rules which are to apply to the scholar's attempt to create knowledge within the field of his inquiry. The success with which he applies these rules determines the quality of the output of his efforts. The scholar in any discipline must claim to be dealing with truth, though his truth may have a small "t." The success of his truth-claiming may be judged by other members of his discipline according to the criteria that the rules of evidence in the discipline suggest. Thus, a common criticism of Toynbee among the historians is that he is a better theologian than he is an historian—that is, that the rules he has used are more properly the rules of theology than they are the rules of the discipline of history.

It is of great importance that we recognize that these rules differ from one discipline to another. One cannot apply the rules of chemistry to the field of history; to do so would result in a kind of chemo-history, a scholarly monstrosity. One cannot apply the rules of physics to the field of poetry. I once heard a physicist comment on his view of poetry. Inevitably, he said that it was simply "noise." Of course it was, if one tried to look at it the way a physicist looks at the phonemena of his field. A good many of the difficulties we have in education arise from this same problem. If one looks at education as an economist, one sees only the arrangement of resources. What occurs to one is that these resources can be redeployed. An economist could look at education in this fashion forever, and never see a curriculum problem. The difficulty with the application of the wrong set of rules to a field like education (itself only half-formed as a discipline) is that it yields half-truths, such as "sufficient unto the improvement of the schools is the reorganization thereof." The difference between a well-rounded man and a narrow specialist could be found at this point: the "well-rounded" man would be aware of the nature and limitations of the rules he was applying as he tried to make sense out of things; the specialist might well blunder into the belief that the set of rules he knows are sufficient for all kinds of phenomena. For our purposes here, it is important only that we recognize that there are sets of rules associated with each of the major fields of inquiry, that the sets differ profoundly from one another, and that if one applies the wrong set of rules to a domain, one may get only half-truth, or perhaps mere nonsense for one's efforts. The mischievous element here arises from the fact that well-organized sets of rules do in fact yield truth when applied to the proper phonomena; it is hard to understand that one's discipline cannot deal with all fields of human knowledge. It makes no sense (that is, it makes nonsense) to apply the rules of the sciences to a field like theology, for example.

In many of the disciplines, the history of the discipline itself is of importance. It is important, for example, for the chemist to know the history of his own field, not only because this will help him to avoid repeating old mistakes, but also because it will help him to understand how some lines of inquiry are being pursued now at the expense of others. The more deeply one understands the history of one's own field, the more nearly one can be in control of the effectiveness of one's own efforts. Staying with chemistry for a moment longer, for example, it is helpful to the chemist to understand that very deep in the tradition of his field is magic and alchemy. Hence, some of the public attitude towards chemists. The high school student's image of the scientist that Margaret Mead described some time ago—of a withdrawn, "brainy" person in a white coat—comes directly out of this past. In the field of education, there is, of course, a long and potent tradition at work, much of it pejorative.

Of the three elements of a discipline—the domain, the rules, and the history, the first two contain whatever is vital about the discipline—vital in the sense that they provide for growth, change, and the production of new knowledge. The effect of history or tradition on a discipline is to define in some degree its domain and its rules.

One more thing may be said about disciplines, and we may then pass on to a consideration of certain disciplines we teach in school. We should recognize that the disciplines we teach in school have a certain arbitrary quality. This arbitrariness arises in part from their histories, and in part from the nature of the agreements on domain and rules that characterize them. The discipline of chemistry exists independent of the particular chemist at work in his laboratory and independent of the teacher who teaches chemistry in a high school. I repeat: it exists in this fashion by virtue of its own past, and by virtue of the working agreements that have been developed among chemists. The same kind of thing may be said for the other well-organized branches of knowledge. Each of them has an integrity of its own which is in large measure "given." While disciplines undergo constant modification, they are modified only in terms of agreements by members of the disciplines—that is, by the practicing scholars. This is a matter of considerable importance to educationists. As educationists, it is not our function to modify basic disciplines. If we wish to participate in modification, we must drop our role as educationists and claim authority as scholars in the discipline to be modified. Our function as educationists, I repeat, is to translate scholarly knowledge and scholarly ways of working into viable school subjects. This presents us with a good many problems. Quite apart from the problems associated with making viable school subjects out of scholarly knowledge and ways of working, we have the problem of deciding which authorities to listen to, in order that we may have a properly authoritative knowledge of the discipline itself. What are we to do when "doctors disagree?" I do not mean to enter into this question here; I mean only to emphasize the importance of our not confusing ourselves with the doctors.

On this matter of arbitrariness, one other observation is relevant. Not only are the disciplines undergoing constant modification by their members, but there is also a constant branching off of new disciplines, and a constant combination of disciplines. Some of the most interesting knowledge now being created arises from hyphenated disciplines like astrophysics and bio-chemistry among the sciences, and from fields like social psychology and cultural anthropology among the behavioral sciences. Teams of researchers have evolved multi-disciplinary approaches to complicated practical problems, so that many of us as laymen are aware of the multi-disciplinary approach. As an educationist, however, I must take a conservative view of these matters. Once more, it is important for me as an educationist to remember that the combination of disciplines is a highly complex and sophisticated matter, properly left in the hands of the members of the disciplines. If I am to maintain my role as an educationist, and to continue my attempts to contribute toward the development of the discipline of education, then my task is to discover and to apply an educationist's view of these matters. It is not within my province to create new multi-disciplines in the schools. To do so violates my major responsibility—that of translation.

A number of conclusions follow as a consequence of the view of disciplines described here. If a discipline is a way of knowing, then the productive capacity of a discipline lies in the successful application of this way of knowing. If a school subject is a teacher's attempt to translate a discipline into learning activities, then the success of a school subject depends on the degree to which the students learn how knowledge is made or discovered in each of the branches of knowledge being studied. Since each of the fields of knowledge exists in the terms of agreements on the domain and the ways of knowing appropriate to it, it follows that the integrity of the disciplines must be preserved in every instance as we attempt to make translations of them into school subjects. Since a discipline is a mode of inquiry, the translation should also be a mode of inquiry. There is a new view of the student imbedded in this set of ideas: the view of a student as one who is learning a way of inquiry, a way of knowing.

Our pedagogical history does not agree either with this view of school subject matter or this view of the student. When we try to consider school subjects as modes of inquiry, it is important that we recognize we are at war with our own tradition. Nor does the pedagogical tradition tolerate students as inquirers, happily. The pedagogical tradition calls for transmittal of the "given." It is a tradition of the transmittal of certainty, not of doubt. But doubt is precisely the quality of the scholar. The scholar, taken as an intellectual, is one "who makes the given problematic." Our pedagogical tradition does not deal with problematic material. If we obey our tradition, we take what is problematic and make it into sets of certainties, which we then call upon the students to "master." In too many instances, our sets of certainties have become dissassociated from the fields of knowledge out of which they originally grew. In some cases, the contrast between the school subject and its underlying field of knowledge is ludicrous. Thus, for example, we have taught dates and events in the name of history; we have taught prosody in the name of poetry; we have taught computation in the name of mathematics; we have taught grammar in the name of composition. Every one of these school subjects has been sterile precisely in the degree that it does not open up modes of inquiry to the student. Because our traditional approaches to mathematics and the sciences have become so detached from those disciplines as understood by the scholars, these fields are undergoing radical reform now—reform precisely in the direction of making the school subjects of mathematics and the sciences into fields of inquiry.

The implication that the integrity of the disciplines must be observed will lead many educationists to become concerned about the possibility that this kind of curriculum reform will make the schools less related to life, rather than more related to it. It would be too bad if, given the vitality and the promise of the reforms in the sciences and mathematics, we should wind up in a few years with a new sterility in the schools. It does not seem necessary that this happen. If it is not to happen, however, it is up to the educationists to prevent it.

In preventing it, we must recognize two realities where we have recognized only one in the past. In the past, we saw as a reality that the problems of life do not come in "disciplined" packages. For example, a good many of the public problems we must deal with—housing, crime, transportation, and the like—go beyond the boundaries of any one discipline and must be studied on a multi-disciplinary basis. The most notable of the curriculum reforms intended to deal with this reality was the core curriculum, a problem-centered approach to learning, in which the mode of inquiry was to be dictated by the nature of the problem itself. We don't want to leave our students ill-prepared for the practical problems of life, but there is another reality which we have tended to overlook. This second reality is that each of the disciplines, as they are organized, contains within its domain and methodology the best thought about reality in its own field. For example, one who knows how a chemist thinks can see more deeply into what is "chemical" about an industrial problem than one who does not know how a chemist thinks. A problem, industrial or other, has no "discipline" of its own. The disciplines are as they are, as I have pointed out at some length. The ideal problem-solver would be a man who was well enough educated in a number of disciplines to be able to look at a problem in a disciplined fashion, following the rules of one discipline after another. So equipped, hopefully, he could see into a problem with greater depth than he could otherwise. When educators have looked at multi-disciplinary problems, as in the core curriculum, the look has too often been superficial. In the absence of a neatly "disciplined problem," we have applied no discipline at all.

What, you say, of the discipline of practical judgment, of the method of intelligence, of problem solving taken simply as orderly thinking? It is necessary, once more, to remember that each way of knowing has its own rules. The method of intelligence does not really help one to become an effective biologist, for it does not take into account some real problems (such as the multiplicity of unknown variables operating in a given biological experiment) that the biologist has to live with. Similarly, the method of intelligence does not give the literary critic the means to deal at the required level of sophistication with the phenomena he tries to comprehend and explain. The method of intelligence, or the method of problem solving, has to be taken as a meta-method—a way of describing what thoughtful people have in common, not what they do in particular. It does not provide an adequate set of rules for the operation of scholars within particular fields. Before the meta-method can be used operationally, one must have the particular methods in mind. A multi-disciplinary approach involves knowledge of the many disciplines to be applied. It cannot operate in a sophisticated manner—and it may operate in a dangerously superficial manner—in the absence of knowledge of the appropriate disciplines.

One of the most useful demands we could be making of students would be that they deliberately look at a complicated problem the way a scientist would look at it, the way a humanist would look at it, the way a behavioral scientist would look at it. If a grand synthesis can be made by a student who has learned to look at a practical problem in these disciplined ways, he can claim the status of a well-educated man, and our attempt to teach him what is involved in multi-disciplinary thinking will have been successful.

We have to have it both ways, however. It won't do to become subject-centered at the expense of maintaining contact with life, nor at the expense of the application of the criterion of social utility to the school subjects we teach. Since we must also maintain the integrity of the ways of knowing that we intend to teach, lest we relapse into an all-too-familiar superficiality, we have a problem. It does not seem to me to be beyond solution; what is required is that we recognize that the problem exists and that both ways have to be honored, each in its own terms.

If the idea of subject matter as inquiry is to be pursued successfully, it is necessary that we attend to the nature of the disciplines that we intend to translate into school subjects. If this is to be done, and the necessary educational experimentation designed intelligently, we educationists have to become familiar with the scholar's approach to each of the disciplines in turn. In order to illustrate what it involved in this problem, I shall give brief descriptions of three disparate fields: chemistry, history, and poetry. I claim no authority in giving these descriptions; it may be that scholars in these fields will disagree with my descriptions of them, or find my descriptions superficial or in error. So be it; I have to take that kind of chance, and I think we all do, if the educational problem of translating these fields into subject matter is to be undertaken successfully. It seems to me that we educationists will, for the next few years, have to occupy ourselves with problems of this nature. We will have to re-educate ourselves concerning the nature of the major fields we teach, taken as modes of inquiry. I say, re-educate ourselves, because most of us were not educated in a way that leads us to think of these fields as modes of inquiry. We were educated in accordance with the pedagogical tradition that implied that knowledge is a given, and taught that the love of learning consists primarily of passive listening. If we are to depart from this tradition, we have to pay attention to the nature of the fields of knowledge.

I described my discipline as existing by virtue of its domain, its rules, and its history. I shall describe here one of the sciences, chemistry; a field that is part science and part art, history; and an art, poetry. It seems to me that the three-fold analysis that I have suggested as applying to all disciplines applies helpfully to these three diverse fields.

CHEMISTRY

The domain of the field of chemistry can be described in simple terms: chemists are concerned with the nature of matter. While this seems all-inclusive, it is not. There are other sciences that are not concerned primarily with matter. For example, the geographer is concerned primarily with areas, not primarily with matter; the biologist is concerned with living things, not primarily with the matter that makes them up. If there is any ambiguity about the domain of chemistry, it arises from the fact that it has become difficult to distinguish between matter and energy, and thus the physicists and chemists have been drawn closer together than once was thought necessary. However, there is still a relatively clear-cut distinction between matter and energy—clear-cut enough so that chemists and physicists can go their separate ways, each with full respect for the other's research. To be a chemist, therefore, is to be concerned with the nature of what we call "matter."

The rules that apply to the field of chemistry are, of course, elaborate and sophisticated. However, for purposes of this discussion, we may categorize them into those rules having to do with observation, those having to do with the analysis of what is observed, and those having to do with prediction. That is, if a student is to learn how a chemist thinks, he has to learn how a chemist observes, how he analyzes, and what enters into making a prediction within the field of chemistry. Moreover, there are rules that apply to the kind of truth that the chemist produces: the truth relating to the success of the chemist's hypothesis, the production of a chemical theory, and finally the development of a law in chemistry.

The history of chemistry, as I mentioned earlier, includes alchemy and magic. It also includes Lavoisier's experiment; it includes the history of some fruitless theories, and more recently it includes such dramatic experiments as the recent chemical synthesis of chlorophyl.

If one were going to make a school subject called chemistry out of elements of this kind, presumably the central activities for the student would take place in the laboratory, where he would try to learn to observe, to analyze, to predict; where he would also try to learn to formulate hypotheses, to take steps (at least) toward the development of theory and law. He would not, if he were trying to learn how a chemist thinks, spend most of his time listening to the results of experiments, which he was to master. His teacher would be less concerned with the amount of information the student had amassed and more concerned with the appropriateness of the intellectual processes relevant to the field of chemistry that he had learned to apply.

HISTORY

The domain of the field of history is, simply, the past, in a chronology. But since the past is gone, and may neither be revoked nor invoked, the historian deals with the records that happen to remain from the past. In principle, the domain of history is the past in a chronology. In practice, it is the records that remain from the past.

The rules that the historian follows may be described only in a preliminary fashion. While it is easy for the historians to agree on their domain, there is much less agreement among them on how they conduct their inquiry, since history is part science and part art. The degree to which it is one or the other varies with historians; Macauley was more artist than scientist, while Schlesinger is more scientist than artist. That is, Schlesinger and other modern historians do not feel free to go very far from the immediate evidence they are dealing with; Macauley felt free to invent likely incidents and write them in without qualifying remarks.

Some agreements on the rules, nevertheless, exist in the field of history. For one thing, there is agreement on what the historian seeks to produce. As an historian, he seeks to produce an historical period—to define it, and to assert that certain consistencies in it are explanatory and relevant to that portion of the past he chooses to deal with. Periodization, therefore, is the name of the historian's output. In producing historical periods (for example, in asserting that a certain time is better thought of as the Age of Franklin than as the Age of the American and the French Revolutions) the historian is called upon to state clearly the point of view he has chosen to adopt, openly to invite criticism of the consistency with which he has applied his point of view and the thoroughness with which he has applied to the point of view all of the relevant records. There are many kinds of historians, all honorable: social historians, economic, cultural, political, military, and intellectual. Each of these represents a worthy point of view—a principle according to which some events and their records within a period are taken to be relevant and others irrelevant. Modern historians do not try to deal with cause and consequence in the past, though the sequentiality of events—their chronology—is inevitably of great interest to them. In dealing with the past, any good historian is deeply aware of the ambiguity and uncertainty of the record he faces. There is always the possibility that an event took place of which there is no record, but which, if he knew of it, would wholly alter his view of what has happened. When the historian has consulted the record thoroughly, explained his point of view honestly and openly, and decided on the thesis he wishes to pursue, he finally writes literature. The aesthetic element in history is a prominent one; good history must be well written.

The history of history is of very considerable interest to the historian, naturally. It is of interest to laymen, too, though often overlooked. The historian has at various times been viewed as judge ("the judgment of history"), as archivist, as journalist, as scientist, as a member of one or another school of history. There is a good deal of fad and fashion among historians. A great study by one historian is highly influential on the approach used by subsequent historians until the next great study comes along. (I do not mean by saying this to denigrate this field; the historians are not easily influenced to change from one approach to another; the influential study must be what they will call "great.")

According to this analysis, history is what the historian writes. History does not exist outside of the books written by historians—it does not exist of itself.

Students who are going to learn how an historian thinks must, for one thing, learn to live with the ambiguity that the historian faces and with the subjectivity of history as written. It makes less and less sense, given this view of the field, to have a single textbook in any course in history. The documentary approach to the teaching of history, by contrast, makes more and more sense. The essential problem for the student when he reads history would be to learn to confront the historian's problem. He has to understand that he never reads about what happened, but rather reads someone's interpretation of the records that happen to remain from the past—and this separation of the past from its records is central to a proper understanding of the field. Otherwise, the student is at the mercy of the historian he reads. History, taken as the past, cannot of itself reveal anything. What we read is not the past revealed, but the past as interpreted by the historian.

POETRY

The domain of poetry is language itself, in an art form. The central quality of poetry is connotation, or evocativeness. The poet presses language beyond its limits, the art form—that is, the form of poetry he chooses to employ—is his means toward poetic meaning. Poetic forms exist on a kind of continuum from lyric to narrative, and the proper understanding of a poem involves an understanding of the art form and its likely purposes. That's why one doesn't read "Evangeline" the same way one reads "The Ode on a Grecian Urn." Poets don't talk to one another very much about their poems, for "a poem must not mean, but be." But they often think of themselves as craftsmen dealing with a difficult medium—language.

The rules of poetry are, of course, difficult to state, since there is little agreement about them. However, there are canons of criticism, according to which at least gross distinctions can be made between good and poor poetry. There are, that is to say, rules that make it possible to say with considerable authority that Blake's "Little Lamb Who Made Thee?" is a better poem than Edgar Guest's "It Takes a Heap O' Livin' to Make a Home."

If the output of chemistry is theory and eventually laws, and if the output of history is periodization, then one may say that the output of poetry as an art is *humanitas*—a deepened realization of the nature of man.

The general question to ask about any poem is, what does the poet mean to say about the nature of man? This is as true for one form as another and as true for one poet as for another. One can deepen one's own sensibility, which is to say one's self-understanding, by something as overwhelming as Milton's Satan or something as amusing as Josephine Miles' real estate salesman. The deepening, and the sensibility, of course, differ from the one to the other. It remains meaningful to ask of any poem, nevertheless, what does it contribute to my understanding of *humanitas,* the human condition?

The history of poetry is, of course, ancient. It includes the poet as a singer and troubadour, the poet as a soothsayer (that is, a truth sayer), and the poet as a free man, disaffiliated from his immediate society and its tensions. The history of poetry differs from the history of chemistry and of history in that it is less sequential than these other fields; all of these traditional views of the poet, once having been introduced, tend to remain with us. We still think of the poet as singer, as recounter of tales, as soothsayer, and as free man.

This account of the field of poetry does not fit what we have ordinarily taught in school. For example, it does not imply that the central fact of poetry is its meter or rhyme scheme, though the sound and pulse of a line may well be a major part of the poet's problem. It is the way the art form is subdued by the poet that constitutes his problem, and therefore the problem of the reader of a poem. Probably the teaching of poetry in the elementary and high schools has been the greatest of our failures, in that what we have taught has been in most instances almost wholly divorced from the poet's approach to poetry, and thus from the meaning of a poem. It is partly because of this disconnection that poetry has come to be slightly valued in the schools and in the larger culture. If the bad teaching of poetry in the American schools is not a sufficient explanation of the low estate of poetry in American culture, it is at least a partial explanation. If we were going to teach poetry in a way that would help a student to understand the poet's problem, we would, for example, give him a poetic problem, to be solved by the writing of poetry, and ask him to contrast his attempt with the attempt of practicing poets to deal with similar problems. We would ask of him that he examine closely the meaning of each of the words and each of the lines in a poem. We would not overlook the qualifiers poets use, nor would we become sentimental about the poet's imagery, for the poet's image is likely to have an exactness that is not possible in prose. I repeat: our approach to the teaching of poetry in the schools is so far removed from the art itself that almost any application of the poet's approach to poetry that we would attempt would be an improvement.

The same sort of thing can be said about our teaching of the arts generally. After children leave the elementary school, we make only the most superficial and inadequate provision for the teaching of the arts to them. At the very time in their lives when the arts might have their greatest impact, we deny them. One of the most helpful things we could do now in the public schools would be to develop experiments in the teaching of the dance, drama, the graphic and plastic arts, music, poetry, and the other literary forms. Our preoccupation with the criterion of social utility has left us at the mercy of the loudest (which is to say the most Philistine) voices in our culture, and the arts have suffered almost to the point of banishment.

I have described the disciplines of chemistry, history, and poetry, with some difference. Such descriptions would better be undertaken by members of the disciplines themselves. I repeat, however, that it seems necessary for educationists to attempt now to gain knowledge of this kind from those who have it, if curriculum experiments are to be undertaken which have as their intent making school subjects relevant to the modes of inquiry of the disciplines. The promise of such experiments seems very great indeed.

We hear much these days of the necessity that students learn to be creative. There can be no doubt that the development of creativity among students is necessary. Creativity, however, cannot take place in a vacuum. Being creative is much more than an act of will; creativity involves the use of materials and means. The promise of the approach to subject matter as inquiry lies precisely in its proffering both the materials and the means of intellectual life—which is to say, creativity—to students in school, an exciting prospect indeed. For this reason too, therefore, experimentation with the structure of the disciplines, translated into school subjects, is worth our most serious and prolonged attention.

STRUCTURES IN LEARNING

Jerome S. Bruner

Every subject has a structure, a rightness, a beauty. It is this structure that provides the underlying simplicity of things, and it is by learning its nature that we come to appreciate the intrinsic meaning of a subject.

Let me illustrate by reference to geography. Children in the fifth grade of a suburban school were about to study the geography of the Central states as part of a social studies unit. Previous units on the South-eastern states, taught by rote, had proved a bore. Could geography be taught as a rational discipline? Determined to find out, the teachers devised a unit in which students would have to figure out not only where things are located, but why they are there. This involves a sense of the structure of geography.

The children were given a map of the Central states in which only rivers, large bodies of water, agricultural products, and natural resources were shown. They were not allowed to consult their books. Their task was to find Chicago, "the largest city in the North Central states."

The argument got under way immediately. One child came up with the idea that Chicago must be on the junction of the three large lakes. No matter that at this point he did not know the names of the lakes—Huron, Superior, and Michigan—his theory was well reasoned. A big city produced a lot of products, and the easiest and most logical way to ship these products is by water.

But a second child rose immediately to the opposition. A big city needed lots of food, and he placed Chicago where there are corn and hogs—right in the middle of Iowa.

A third child saw the issue more broadly—recognizing virtues in both previous arguments. He pointed out that large quantities of food can be grown in river valleys. Whether he had learned this from a previous social studies unit or from raising carrot seeds, we shall never know. If you had a river, he reasoned, you had not only food but transportation. He pointed to a spot on the map not far from St. Louis. "There is where Chicago *ought* to be." Would that graduate students would always do so well!

Not all the answers were so closely reasoned, though even the wild ones

From the *NEA Journal,* "Special Feature on Learning," LII, No. 3 (March, 1963), 26-27. Used by permission of the author and publisher.

had about them a sense of the necessity involved in a city's location.

One argued, for example, that all American cities have skyscrapers, which require steel, so he placed Chicago in the middle of the Mesabi Range. At least he was thinking on his own, with a sense of the constraints imposed on the location of cities.

After forty-five minutes, the children were told they could pull down the "real" wall map (the one with names) and see where Chicago really is. After the map was down, each of the contending parties pointed out how close they had come to being right. Chicago had not been located. But the location of cities was no longer a matter of unthinking chance for this group of children.

What had the children learned? A way of thinking about geography, a way of dealing with its raw data. They had learned that there is some relationship between the requirements of living and man's habitat. If that is all they got out of their geography lesson, that is plenty. Did they remember which is Lake Huron? Lake Superior? Lake Michigan? Do you?

Teachers have asked me about "the new curricula" as though they were some special magic potion. They are nothing of the sort. The new curricula, like our little exercise in geography, are based on the fact that knowledge has an internal connectedness, a meaningfulness, and that for facts to be appreciated and understood and remembered, they must be fitted into that internal meaningful context.

The set of prime numbers is not some arbitrary nonsense. What can be said about quantities that cannot be arranged into multiple columns and rows? Discussing that will get you on to the structure of primes and factorability.

It often takes the deepest minds to discern the simplest structure in knowledge. For this reason if for no other, the great scholar and the great scientist and the greatly compassionate man are needed in the building of new curricula.

There is one other point. Our geographical example made much of discovery. What difference does discovery make in the learning of the young? First, let it be clear what the act of discovery entails. It is only rarely on the frontier of knowledge that new facts are "discovered" in the sense of being encountered, as Newton suggested, as "islands of truth in an uncharted sea of ignorance." Discovery, whether by a schoolboy going it on his own or by a scientist, is most often a matter of rearranging or transforming evidence in such a way that one is now enabled to go beyond the evidence to new insights. Discovery involves the finding of the right structure, the meaningfulness.

Consider now what benefits the child might derive from the experience of learning through his own discoveries. These benefits can be discussed in terms of increased intellectual potency, intrinsic rewards, useful learning techniques, and better memory processes.

For the child to develop *intellectual potency,* he must be encouraged to search out and find regularities and relationships in his environment. To do this, he needs to be armed with the expectancy that there is something for him to find and, once aroused by this expectancy, he must devise his own ways of searching and finding.

Emphasis on discovery in learning has the effect upon the learner of leading him to be a constructionist—to organize what he encounters in such a manner that he not only discovers regularity and relatedness, but also avoids the kind of information drift that fails to keep account of how the information will be used.

In speaking of *intrinsic motives* for learning (as opposed to extrinsic motives), it must be recognized that much of the problem in leading a child to effective cognitive activity is to free him from the immediate control of environmental punishments and rewards.

For example, studies show that children who seem to be early over-achievers in school are likely to be seekers after the "right way to do it" and that their capacity for transforming their learning into useful thought structures tends to be less than that of children merely achieving at levels predicted by intelligence tests.

The hypothesis drawn from these studies is that if a child is able to approach learning as a task of discovering something rather than "learning about it" he will tend to find a more personally meaningful reward in his own competency and self-achievement in the subject than he will find in the approval of others.

There are many ways of coming to the *techniques of injury,* or the heuristics of discovery. One of them is by careful study of the formalization of these techniques in logic, statistics, mathematics, and the like. If a child is going to pursue inquiry as an eventual way of life, particularly in the sciences, formal study is essential. Yet, whoever has taught kindergarten and the early primary grades (periods of intense inquiry) knows that an understanding of the formal aspect of inquiry is not sufficient or always possible.

Children appear to have a series of attitudes and activities they associate with inquiry. Rather than a formal approach to the relevance of variables in their search, they depend on their sense of what things among an ensemble of things "smell right" as being of the proper order of magnitude or scope of severity.

It is evident then that if children are to learn the working techniques of discovery, they must be afforded the opportunities of problem solving. The more they practice problem solving, the more likely they are to generalize what they learn into a style of inquiry that serves for any kind of task they may encounter. It is doubtful that anyone ever improves in the art and technique of inquiry by any other means than engaging in inquiry, or problem solving.

The first premise in a theory concerning the *improvement of memory processes* is that the principal problem of human memory is not storage, but retrieval. The premise may be inferred from the fact that recognition (i.e., recall with the aid of maximum prompts) is extraordinarily good in human beings—particularly in comparison to spontaneous recall when information must be recalled without external aids or prompts. The key to retrieval is organization.

There are myriad findings to indicate that any organization of information that reduces the collective complexity of material by imbedding it into a mental structure the child has constructed will make that material more accessible for retrieval. In sum, the child's very attitudes and activities that characterize "figuring out" or "discovering" things for himself also seem to have the effect of making material easier to remember.

If man's intellectual excellence is the most important among his perfections (as Maimonides, the great Hispanic-Judaic philosopher once said), then it is also the case that the most uniquely personal of all that man knows is that which he discovers for himself. What difference does it make when we encourage discovery in the young? It creates, as Maimonides would put it, a special and unique relation between knowledge possessed and the possessor.

CONCEPTIONS OF KNOWLEDGE: THEIR SIGNIFICANCE FOR THE CURRICULUM

Arno A. Bellack

In current debates about what should be taught in the schools, the "conventional wisdom" long honored in pedagogical circles about the

From *The Nature of Knowledge: Implications for the Education of Teachers,* William Jenkins, ed. (Milwaukee: University of Wisconsin-Milwaukee, 1962), pp. 42–52. Used by permission of the author and publisher.

nature of knowledge and the role of knowledge in the curriculum is being called into question. The enemy of conventional wisdom, Professor Galbraith (the originator of that felicitous term) tells us, is the march of events. The fatal blow comes when conventional ideas fail to deal with new conditions and problems to which obsolescence has made them clearly inapplicable. The march of events in the world at large that is placing new demands on the schools, and in the world of scholarship that is making available new knowledge in great quantities is forcing us to re-examine our ideas about the nature of knowledge and its place in the instructional program.

It is well to remind ourselves that the current debates about knowledge and the curriculum are not over the question of whether knowledge is relevant to the school's task. Although there are different views as to what knowledge should be taught and how it is to be taught, most educators would agree that knowledge is the stock in trade of the school. Few would deny that the fields of organized inquiry are significant aspects of our culture that the school is uniquely equipped to introduce to students. No other agency or institution in our society has the personnel or other resources to perform this function effectively. Unless students become acquainted with these important facets of the culture in school it is doubtful that they will learn about them elsewhere, at least not so well.

It is important to stress this at the outset, for today one frequently hears the view expressed that educationists responsible for planning the curriculum of the elementary and secondary schools have only recently, and belatedly, come to recognize that knowledge is a significant factor in teaching and in preparation for teaching. A brief glance at the historical development of the school curriculum should help to set the record straight on this score. Throughout our history, most elementary and secondary programs have been organized around the time-honored school subjects, even during the heyday of progressivism in the decades prior to World War II. The progressives too had a place for knowledge in their scheme of things: the curriculum was to be organized around personal and social problems, and the academic disciplines were to serve as resources in dealing with these problems. It was this central idea that attracted the sympathies of many educators who questioned the ability of traditional school to provide an effective way of preparing students to face the increasingly complex problems of modern living.

If then the fields of knowledge are no strangers to curriculum theory and practice, what is significantly different in contemporary efforts to redefine the role of knowledge in the curriculum? The activities and proposals of the projects in physics, chemistry, biology, mathematics, economics, geography, and English reveal certain common viewpoints and approaches.

1.   Their aim is to introduce students to the universe of discourse, or more grandly, the ways of life, represented by the fields of scholarship. Students are to engage in activities patterned after those of the practicing physicist, chemist, or economist. Whereas formerly factual and descriptive content of the various fields was stressed, now the emphasis is on the basic concepts and conceptual relationships that scholars in the various fields use as intellectual tools to analyze and order their data.

2.   Although most of the projects have developed programs for specific groups of students, particularly the college-bound, the view is widely held that similar approaches should be followed with all students. On this view, the disciplines are significant not only for the specialist, but for the average man as well. The aim is excellence in intellectual affairs not only for the academically talented, but for all students at levels commensurate with their ability.

3.   Furthermore, these projects attach great importance to the participation of university scholars in continuing revision of the curriculum. Through such collaboration, schools are to keep their programs up to date with recent developments in university research.

The situation developing in the elementary and secondary schools thus begins to reflect, at least to some degree, the state of affairs in the universities with respect to the development and organization of knowledge, which Professor John Randall has described in this way:

As reflected in the microcosm of the modern university, the world of knowledge has today become radically plural. It is a world of many different knowledges, pursued in varied wasy to diverse ends. These many inquiries are normally carried on with little thought for their relation to each other. The student of John Donne's poetry, the student of the structure of the atom—each gives little enough attention to what the others are doing, and none at all to any total picture of anything. Each has his own goals, his own methods, his own language for talking about what he is doing and what he has discovered. Each seems happiest when left to his own devices, glad indeed if he can keep others from treading on his toes. Each is convinced that what he himself is doing is worthwhile. But none has too much respect for the others, though he is willing enough to tolerate them. They have all too little understanding of each other's pursuits—what they are trying to do, how they are doing it, and what they really mean when they talk about it.[1]

The projects sponsored by the various curriculum commissions reflect this thoroughgoing diversity. Proposals for the teaching of biology, chemistry, and physics have, to the present time, been developed with little or no relationship to each other. The project in economics was unrelated to the other social sciences, although the Task Force recognized that these fields could also marshall cogent arguments for a place in the school program. In the field of English, three domains have been staked out: language, literature, and composition. Only in mathematics has there been a disposition to view the field as a whole, but this too is a reflection of developments within the field of mathematics at the highest levels of scholarship.

I emphasize this pluralism in the academic world not to deplore it, but to call attention to the problem that it presents for those who are concerned with the organization of the total curriculum. For there is not only the question of the structures of the individual disciplines, but also the question of the structure of the curriculum as a whole within which the fields of knowledge find their place. The problem can be very simply stated, if not easily solved: What general scheme of the curriculum can be developed so that autonomy of the parts does not result in anarchy in the program as a whole? This is one of two questions I propose to discuss briefly this morning.

The second question grows out of the proposal that students be introduced to the ways of thinking associated with the various disciplines in such fashion that they in fact become physicists, chemists, or economists. Professor Bruner puts it this way:

What a scientist does at his desk or in his laboratory, what a literary critic does in reading a poem, are of the same order as what anybody else does when is is engaged in like activities—if he is to achieve understanding. The difference is in degree, not in kind. The schoolboy learning physics is a physicist.[2]

I take it this does not mean that the goal of general education is to train all students as specialists in mathematics, geography, history, or

[1] John H. Randall, Jr., "The World to be Unified," in Lewis Leary, ed., *The Unity of Knowledge* (Garden City: Doubleday & Company, 1955), p. 63.

[2] Jerome Bruner, *The Process of Education* (Cambridge: Harvard University Press, 1960), p. 14.

whatever other subjects they might study. Rather, the goal is to make available to students the intellectual and aesthetic resources of their culture in such a way that they become guides for intelligent action and help students create meaning and order out of the tangled world in which they find themselves. Professor Bestor, who scarcely qualifies as an advocate of education for life adjustment, has made this same point:

The modern scientist or the modern scholar knows the delight of intellectual endeavor for its own sake, and he rightly resents the undervaluing of this motive. But when all is said and done he knows that the principal value to society of a man's cultivating the power of abstract thought is that he is thereby enabled to deal more effectively with the insistent problems of modern life. . . . The basic argument for the intellectual disciplines in the education is not that they lift a man's spirits above the world, but that they equip his mind to enter the world and perform its tasks.[3]

How is this widely accepted objective to be realized? Is the ability to relate what is learned in school to the world of human affairs to come as an inevitable by-product of the study of the disciplines, or must teachers give explicit attention to helping students see the relevance of such study for their own lives as individuals, citizens, and workers? This is the second issue I propose to discuss briefly.

KNOWLEDGE AND THE DESIGN OF THE CURRICULUM

When we look beyond the structures of the disciplines and ask about the structure of the curriculum within which the various fields of study take their places, we face a problem of the greatest complexity. What knowledge from the vast array of intellectual resources shall the schools teach? The accumulated and ever-growing knowledge in all fields has reached such proportions that comprehensive grasp of the total range of knowledge is out of the question for any one individual. The question raised by Spencer a hundred years ago, "What knowledge is of the most worth?" is even more relevant today than it was in his time. Indeed, it is an ever-renewed problem, one that apparently every generation has to solve over again for itself. Given the limited time and capacity of the school, what shall the schools teach to secure results that can be generalized beyond the immediate situation in which the learning takes place?

[3] Arthur Bestor, *Educational Wastelands* (Urbana: University of Illinois Press, 1953), p. 15.

The progressives, taking their cue from Dewey, found their answer to this question in the "scientific method" (or the "method of intelligence" as it was frequently labeled) that was assumed to characterize all types of rational, intelligent activity in academic pursuits and in practical affairs as well. The problem-solving method came to be viewed as the basic ingredient in programs of general education.

But by no means is there agreement among scientists that there is a single all-encompassing set of procedures, even in the natural sciences, as assumed by those who talk about *the* scientific method. There seems to be little warrant for assuming that there is one over-arching method sufficiently flexible and inclusive to deal with problems in the various scientific fields, to say nothing of the arts, crafts, and applied areas. Indeed, as we have already noted, the intellectual world today is characterized by a plurality of methods and conceptual schemes developed by the disciplines to deal with problems within their individual spheres. Analysis of the various disciplines reveals a wide range of organization and intellectual methods associated with them. Instead of a unity of method or a single universe of discourse, we are confronted with a vast confederation of separate areas of study. Modes of thinking and analysis differ from field to field, and even from problem to problem within the same field.

The heterogeneous character of the resources that are a part of the culture is a fact of major significance for the curriculum builder. We would do well frankly to recognize this and make a place in our programs for the variety of organizations and logical orders that characterize the fields of knowledge on which we draw in building the curriculum. But *what* knowledge deserves a place in the curriculum? Let us consider two contrasting approaches to the curriculum that involve two conceptions of knowledge, both of which are significant for our purposes here.

But first we must take notice of the viewpoint recently expressed by a prominent Harvard historian, Oscar Handlin. Professor Handlin contends that the expansion of knowledge and the range of backgrounds and abilities of students now required to attend school make it futile to attempt to plan a program of common knowledge for all. Writing in the September, 1961, issue of *The Atlantic*, he argues that any effort "to define a body of knowledge that every educated man ought to have is futile and needless. By what criteria can we tell the boys and girls who enter high school next year to take French or Latin rather than German and Russian, Medieval rather than Oriental history, physics rather than chemistry? . . . The high school cannot endow its students with everything they ought to know. It can only equip them to get what they need as they come to recognize the need for it." And how is the school to go about doing this? "It ought to impart to its students the ability to communicate and to be communicated with, and it ought to introduce them to the quantitative techniques on which modern science and technology rest. If it succeeds in these tasks, it will give its graduates the equipment for future learning." Language and mathematics are thus to be required of all, with the rest of the curriculum tailor-made for each student on the basis of interests and ability.[4]

This viewpoint seems to me to be a counsel of despair that need not delay us long in our search for an answer to the question: What shall we teach? Without denying the importance of language and mathematics. other fields have equally legitimate claims to a place in the program of studies for all students.

The first approach I would like to have us examine briefly takes seriously the responsibility of the school to introduce students to the fundamental intellectual resources of their culture. These resources, communicated in meaningful fashion to succeeding generations, provide indispensable working capital in the management of human affairs and serve as the foundation from which continued progress is made. The supporters of this viewpoint are individuals and groups representing widely divergent backgrounds and philosophical outlooks. Nevertheless, there is remarkable unanimity among them when it comes to identifying the disciplines or broad groupings of disciplines that represent the basic cultural interests of our society. A few illustrations will make clear the nature of this approach.

Dr. Conant suggests that the curriculum in its general phases should include three major areas of study: (1) the humanities (art and literature); (2) the study of man (the social sciences, with history and philosophy the connecting links between these fields and the humanities; and (3) the natural sciences and mathematics.[5]

Professor Broudy contends that all students need knowledge that helps them understand their relationships to the physical environment, the social environment and the environment of their own psychic self. His curriculum is therefore organized around three major areas: (1) the natural sciences (including mathematics); (2) the social sciences; and (3) living with the self or self-science (which includes literature, fine arts, and philosophy).[6]

The Council for Basic Education proposes a curriculum organized around five groupings with the constituent fields taught as separate

[4] Oscar Handlin, "Live Students and Dead Education," *The Atlantic,* September, 1961, pp. 32–33.

[5] James B. Conant, *Education in a Divided World* (Cambridge: Harvard University Press, 1948), chapters 5, 6, 7.

[6] Harry H. Broudy, *Building a Philosophy of Education* (New York: Prentice-Hall, Inc., 1954), chapter 7.

subjects: (1) citizenship, history, geography; (2) composition and literature; (3) languages; (4) mathematics and science; (5) art, music, speech and philosophy. [7]

Sidney Hook outlines a program of studies that includes: (1) sciences and mathematics; (2) social sciences; (3) philosophy and logic; (4) language and literature; (5) art and music. [8]

Other illustrations might be cited; but these four, representing very different philosophical and educational orientations, are sufficient to show that there is substantial agreement regarding the disciplines and broad areas to be included in the program for all students: the natural sciences, mathematics, social sciences, and humanities. The primary differences among them have to do with the extent to which these areas of knowledge should be taught as separate fields or as broad areas of study.

The second approach views the world of ideas to which students are to be introduced from a different perspective, one concerned primarily with "the principal modes of intellectual activity." In making suggestions for the reform of general education in British secondary schools, Professor Peterson of Oxford University urges that educators cease thinking of general education in terms of "general knowledge":

It is not a sign that a man lacks general education if he does not know the date of The Treaty of Utrecht, the latitude of Singapore, the formula for nitro-glycerine or the author of the *Four Quartets*. It does denote a lack of general education if he cares nothing for any of the arts, confuses a moral judgment with an aesthetic judgment, interprets the actions of Asian political leaders in terms of nineteenth century English parliamentarianism or believes that the existence of God has been scientifically disproved. [9]

He urges therefore that the British secondary schools devise programs of general education not in terms of wide general knowledge, but in terms of general development in the main modes of intellectual activity, of which he identifies four: the logical, the empirical, the moral, the aesthetic. These different modes of thought are associated with different uses of language. For example, the empirical mode has to do with statements about the world based on our experience of it. The moral and the aesthetic are concerned with statements of preferences, evaluations, and judgments of

[7] James D. Koerner, ed., *The Case for Basic Education* (Boston: Little, Brown and Company, 1959).

[8] Sidney Hook, *Education for the Modern Man* (New York: The Dial Press, 1946), chapter 5.

[9] Oxford University Department of Education, *Arts and Science Sides in the Sixth Form* (Abingdon-Berkshire: The Abbey Press, 1960).

the good and the evil, the beautiful and the ugly, the desirable and the undesirable. Any one discipline gives opportunity for the development of more than one mode of thought and each mode can be developed through more than one of the disciplines. For example, literature can contribute to the development of both moral and aesthetic judgment. Mathematics and philosophy both contribute to the development of the logical mode.

If students are to gain understanding of the nature of knowledge, the different modes of mental activity must be made explicit to them:

They must have time and guidance in which to see that what is a proof in the Mathematics they pursue on Tuesday is not the same kind of thing as a proof in History, which follows on Wednesday; that the truth of George Eliot or Joseph Conrad is not the same thing as the truths of Mendel or Max Plank; and yet that there are similarities as well as differences.

Peterson accordingly suggests that in addition to giving attention to these varying modes of thought in the subject fields, the secondary program include a special course in which these ways of thinking are the object of study. One important aspect of such teaching has to do with ways in which these modes of thought are verified. Verification is particularly significant in that it is the guide to meaning of the various types of thought. For example, empirical statements are verified by tests conducted in terms of experience, whereas moral statements are verified by reference to criteria or principles of judgment.

The two complementary ways of viewing knowledge incorporated in these two curriculum approaches provide a fruitful basis for curriculum planning. In the first, emphasis is on the conceptual schemes and methods of inquiry associated with the disciplines and grouping of disciplines. In the second, attention is focused on modes of thought that transcend the boundaries of the individual fields. They thus represent two mutually reinforcing conceptions of knowledge that deserve consideration in curriculum building.

Professor Toulmin has coined two terms that might be helpful in clarifying what is meant here. He distinguishes between participant's language and onlooker's language.[10] Participant's language is the language used by members of a professional group or discipline as they carry on their work within these fields. Hence we talk today about the language of science, the language of psychology, the language of mathematics and even

---

[10] S. Toulmin, *Philosophy of Science* (London: Hutchinson University Library, 1953), p. 13.

the language of education. Ralph Barton Perry once observed that you can tell the specialty of a man by the words he uses carefully and with precision. Participant's language has to do with the language systems that are the distinguishing characteristics of the various disciplined areas of study such as history, science, literature, mathematics, and the like.

Now if we want to examine or talk about the language we use in any one of these fields, we must use another level of discourse. We must, in Toulmin's terms, use onlooker's language. For example, Peterson is quoted above as saying that students need help in understanding that a proof in mathematics is not the same as a proof in science or that the "truth" of a scientist is not the same as the "truth" of the poet or novelist. To make these comparisons and contrasts we need a language system that enables us to look at these various areas of study from the outside, as it were. The modes of thought identified by Peterson furnish us with language tools that are useful for this purpose. Hence their importance in teaching.

These two complementary conceptions of knowledge deserve consideration in curriculum building. Such planning would include:

1. A program of general education built around the structures and strategies of the four major areas of knowledge: the natural sciences, mathematics, the social sciences, and the humanities.

2. Explicit attention in the teaching of these fields to the various modes of thought and different uses of language incorporated in them.

In view of the significance of knowledge in our lives today, it seems reasonable to suggest that knowledge itself should become an object of study in the schools. At what points in their educational career students are able to carry on such study with understanding is an empirical question, certainly not answerable in the abstract. High schools might experiment with courses similar to the one suggested by Mr. Peterson for British schools. Already there are available in Britain excellent teaching materials prepared specifically for the kind of teaching here envisaged.[11]

One point implicit in the above proposal deserves special emphasis. I think it important that the context for curriculum planning be shifted from the individual disciplines, as is now the vogue, to the broad groupings of knowledge suggested above. I am not calling for indiscriminate scrambling of superficial knowledge. Indeed, at this point we would do well to

[11] See, for example, the following: E. R. Emmet, *The Use of Reason* (London: Longmans, Green and Company, Ltd., 1960); John Wilson, *Language and the Pursuit of Truth* (London: Cambridge University Press, 1958); R. W. Young, *Lines of Thought* (London: Oxford University Press, 1958).

suspend judgment as to when in the school program teaching should be organized around the individual disciplines, and when around the broad groupings of the disciplines. In all likelihood, different patterns of organization will be found to be appropriate for different levels of the school program. Dewey's notion of the "progressive organization of knowledge" might serve as a guiding conception in planning the sequence of the program through the elementary and secondary school years.

The significant point is that there is need for a broader context for curriculum planning than the separate disciplines, as is the case with most of the national projects now underway. Furthermore, the broad fields furnish a context within which we can consider fields of knowledge not now included in the programs of most schools, but which seem to have reasonable claims to a place in the curriculum. For example, in the social sciences, anthropology, political science, sociology, economics, and social psychology are given little or no attention at the present time. That these fields can make significant contributions in helping students understand the social and cultural changes now taking place around the world goes without saying.

In sum, scholars in the various disciplines must now be invited to join us in a search for new structures for teaching that avoid undue fragmentation of knowledge. The various fields must find their place in a pattern of studies that provides a substantial measure of coherence and relatedness for the program as a whole.

Let us not underestimate the difficulties that we face in these efforts, for the tendencies in the academic world are almost all in the opposite direction. This fall, for example, Columbia University suspended one of its courses in Contemporary Civilization that had been taught for over thirty years as a social science offering. This course, as it was reported in the *New York Times,* was a "casualty of the trend in social sciences, especially economics, anthropology and sociology, having become so technical as to defy the attempt of 'translating technical language into ordinary discourse.' "[12] At the same time, there is growing recognition that new approaches must be found. Recently, Professor Zacharias of the M.I.T. Physics Project urged that we reconsider the entire pattern of science education from the elementary years on and commented, "You can't carve up a discipline there (in the elementary schools) the way we do in graduate school. A youngster has to see problems whole."[13]

[12] *New York Times,* July 9, 1961.

[13] *Saturday Review,* October 21, 1961, p. 52.

RELATIONSHIPS OF KNOWLEDGE TO HUMAN AFFAIRS

That the schools ought to provide students with the means for intelligent action is not a new or controversial idea. When, however, it comes to deciding what to teach and how to teach to accomplish this goal, we find marked differences of opinion.

Is it sufficient in general education, for example, to have students learn how to behave like physicists, historians, or economists? I think not. For the economist *as* economist (to mention just one field) is in no position to prescribe courses of action regarding the host of public policy issues we face, and questions of public policy and decision loom large in general education. To be sure, economics does provide us with a body of theory that is essential in examining the probable consequences of alternative economic policies, and a good many of these analytical tools ought to become part of the intellectual equipment of all students. Economists are able to tell us what the probable consequences will be if the supply of money is increased, or if the interest rates are lowered; but they cannot *as* economists tell us whether or not we ought to take either of these two courses of action. Decision regarding these alternative courses of action involves weighing of values *and* technical economic analysis.

It is therefore clear that both values and economic theory come into play in deciding courses of action in economic affairs, and both must find their place in social studies teaching. Here the different modes of thought suggested by Peterson's approach come prominently into play. Technical economic analysis involves the empirical mode of thinking (i.e., it is concerned with matters of fact and theory), while considering alternative values involves the moral mode (i.e., it is concerned with criteria of what is desirable or undesirable). The teacher's job is to help students learn to make these necessary distinctions, so that they recognize when questions of fact and analysis are under consideration and when questions of value are at stake.[14] This would seem to hold as well for instruction in fields of study other than economics, which I have used here for purposes of illustration.

Thus far we have been talking about problems associated with a single field. But problems in the world of human affairs do not come neatly labeled "historical," "economic," or "political." They come as decisions to be made, and force us to call upon all we know and make us wish we

---

[14] See *Economic Education in the Schools,* Report of the National Task Force on Economic Education, 1961.

knew more. It was concern for broad cultural and moral questions that go beyond the boundaries of any one discipline that led the progressives to urge that students have the opportunity to deal with them in all their complexity. They proposed a new curriculum, one centered on the problems of youth and broad social issues, and drawing upon the academic disciplines as they become relevant to the problems under study. This idea became the hallmark of progressivism in curriculum building. It gained wide acceptance among educators and found expression in many influential statements of policy and opinion during the 1920's–40's. Attempted applications of this viewpoint were made in courses labeled "core," "common learnings," and the like.

Difficulties in this approach soon became apparent, not the least of which was the students' lack of first-hand acquaintance with the disciplines that were the source of the concepts and ideas essential to structuring problems under study. Without adequate understanding of the various fields of knowledge, students had no way of knowing which fields were relevant to problems of concern to them. As a matter of fact, without knowledge of the organized fields, it was difficult for them to ask the kinds of questions that the various disciplines could help them answer.

And yet, one feels that giving students an opportunity to grapple with broad social and cultural problems was basically a promising innovation. At the same time one is forced to recognize that problem solving on such a broad base cannot be pursued successfully without growing understanding of the fields of knowledge on which the problem solver must draw.

Recognizing then (1) the value in systematic study of the fields of knowledge and (2) the importance of developing competence in dealing with problems and issues that are broader than those of any one field, the question arises why opportunities for both types of activities should not be included in the program for all students. One might envision a general education program that would include basic instruction in the major fields defined earlier in this paper (the natural sciences, physical sciences, mathematics, and the humanities) together with a coordinating seminar in which students dealt with problems "in the round" and in which special effort is made to show the intimate relationships between the fields of study as concepts from these fields are brought to bear on these problems. Such a seminar would also furnish excellent opportunities to help students become aware of the different modes of thought or various types of language usage involved in dealing with problematic situations and the necessity for making clear distinctions among them.

REDUCING THE BEHAVIOR GAP

*Mario D. Fantini
and Gerald Weinstein*

The acuteness of our present "crisis" with so-called disadvantaged learners is forcing educators to examine closely virtually everything they know about learning and teaching in an effort to provide more effective education for such children. This offers educators unusual opportunities to consider anew basic educational questions and to introduce needed innovation and reform which may benefit *all* learners.

We suggest, as a start, that a close look be given to an important goal of education—the encouragement of certain kinds of social behavior. We must all concede that there is a wide discrepancy between much of the behavior of individuals in society and what they have been taught in school. This behavior gap is wide enough to stimulate us to examine the few established channels in education for changing or affecting behavior.

Traditionally, these channels have been the subject matter per se of the school—the courses offered, the curriculum taught. An examination of these channels, however, confronts us with a startling realization: The objectives of the subject matter itself have become the ultimate aims of the school. These aims can satisfy only the more obvious objective of education—to provide the child with necessary academic skills. They cannot meet the need every child has for positive self-definition, for positive relationships with others, and for some control over what happens to him. What we require, therefore, is another channel which will lead to more consonance between education and the way people ought to behave in society.

In seeking greater consonance, we consider again our crisis clientele, the disadvantaged. It is they who are most acutely symptomatic of the problems confronting all learners. One of the most glaring deficiencies of their education is its lack of contact with them: "School is phony—it has nothing to do with life like we know it."

The person caught in the bind of attempting to make a difference with such students is the teacher. Most teachers and administrators who work with the disadvantaged ask, "How can we make contact with our children,

From *NEA Journal,* LVII, No. 1 (January, 1968), 22-25. Used by permission of the author and publisher.

make education more meaningful to them?" Hungry for answers, they flock to the many workshops and institutes recently made available by federal legislation, where they learn a great deal about the nature of the "culturally deprived child"—primarily in terms of *description.*

As one teacher explained, "I understand my children better now, but I still don't know what to do with them. I learned, for example, that one-third of my children probably come from broken homes and that this poses severe problems for the growing child. Now that I know this fact, what do I do to teach them better?"

The task now is to develop *prescriptions* that are functionally linked to these descriptions. The few rudimentary prescriptions that currently exist have not touched the core of the problem; they lack intrinsic relevance for many children and for the disadvantaged in particular. And it is relevance, the linking of what he learns to what he feels and cares about, that makes schooling meaningful to the child. We suggest that there are at least four levels in education on which relevance may be achieved:

1. Teaching procedures and learning styles should be matched. If disadvantaged children learn best in kinesthetic, concrete, inductive, and relatively nonverbal situations, their teachers should use methodology suited to this learning style. Thus, there would be a degree of relevance in whatever is being taught because of *how* it is being taught.

2. The material presented should either be within the learner's knowledge of his physical realm of experience or it should be easily connected with it. Relevance is achieved by making *what* is being taught germane to the child's knowledge and experience.

3. *What* is being taught and *how* it is being taught must not ignore the learner's *feelings* about his experiences. A teacher may plan to use a unit on city policemen because the learner "knows" them. If the child's experience with policemen has led him to fear them, however, learning may in fact be inhibited unless the teacher gives him a chance to express his real feelings and to think them through.

4. Teaching must not ignore the *concerns* of learners. Concerns are the deep-felt feelings and emotions, the persistent, persuasive anxieties and underlying uneasiness children have about themselves and their relationship to the world. Education gains relevance on this level if the teacher attempts to deal with the questions people most consistently ask themselves: "Who am I?" "What can I do about things?" "Who am I really connected to or concerned about?"

The most effective teaching utilizes all four areas of relevance. At present, educators are beginning to use the first two, but they must give more attention to levels three and four. It is this area of emotion, feeling, concern that is undernourished by the school in terms of its content.

The school is not helping to answer the spoken and unspoken questions that trouble all children: "Why do I feel the way I do?" "What made me do that?" "Do they think I'm any good?" Instead, the school asks children: "What do we mean by the Common Market?" "How are animals and people different?" Ignored in the process is one of the child's primary enigmas: "What does it have to do with *me*?" By directing themselves to supplying acceptable answers to this pervasive query, educators can make the connection between the child's basic emotions and feelings (affect) and his processing of information and developing of concepts from that information (cognition).

The relationship between cognition and affect cannot be too strongly stressed. Cognition appears to be a natural way of equipping the individual with the capability to deal with the basic drives that direct and control behavior. It should link those drives to his environment and provide him with the means to cope with the demands the environment makes. In other words, cognition should not only be functionally linked to affect; it should *serve* affect.

Although educators have hinted at such a relationship between affect and cognition, the functional linkage is seldom made. Too often, the school severely limits the relationship between the two with its very definition of *affect*. It considers affect only in terms of play, interests, classroom climate, readiness, teacher-pupil interaction, motivation, and the like, all of which it can utilize to induce the child to accept prescribed academic content.

Feelings are made to serve as basic hooks for linking outside content (curriculum) to inside natural dispositions. They are the tools used to get to the institutionalized cognitive content—the subject matter. In the standard educational process, cognitive development is equated with a "knowing about" a variety of academic subjects, rather than with an understanding of how these subjects may serve the student's needs. Too many instructional roads seem to lead to cognition as the end product.

Yet it is obvious that knowing something cognitively does not always result in behavior that follows on that knowing. This is because knowledge alone cannot influence total behavior. Moreover, all kinds of knowledge are not equally influential. The missing ingredient in this equation seems to be knowledge that is related to the effective or emotional world of the learner.

What most often prompts action, or behavior, is a feeling or emotion about something rather than knowledge per se. It may be that "knowing about" can prompt feeling, but it is feeling that generates behavior. *Unless knowledge relates to feeling, it is unlikely to affect behavior appreciably.* When education begins to make better use of this basic concept, we will have taken a giant step toward reducing the behavior gap—the discrepancy between how people behave and how they have been taught to behave.

It appears to us that the child's concerns, wants, interests, fears, anxieties, joys, and other emotions and reactions to the world contain in them seeds of intrinsic motivation and are legitimate content in their own right. Moreover, when we deal with this inner content, we tell the child, in effect, that he *does* know something. This is perhaps the most important factor in linking relevant content with self-concept. For when the school tells the child that the experience he brings with him—that is part of him, that *is* him—has nothing to do with the "worthwhile" knowledge and experience that the school intends to set before him, it is telling the child that he is worthless.

Every teacher is familiar with the marked increase in attentiveness when the class has embarked on a discussion of the problems the students are facing. This is because the students are relating what they are learning cognitively to their own concerns. We conclude, then, that *relevance becomes a matter of functionally linking extrinsic curriculum to these basic intrinsic concerns and feelings.*

One of our fundamental premises is that achieving curriculum relevance is largely a matter of allowing the intrinsic (affective) dimensions of learning to direct more of the extrinsic (cognitive) dimensions. This line of movement is crucial, but it is usually reversed, with the cognitive dictating what areas of affect should be included.

An illustration of this may be helpful. A science teacher decides that Johnny must learn the substance of matter, which is a cognitive task. The teacher may then ask himself, "What do I have to know about Johnny's concerns or feelings to help him learn about matter?" He would be attempting, then, to make Johnny's feelings facilitate the acquisition of this bit of knowledge.

On the other hand, if he is aware of the important connection to be made, he may start with: "I want to work with Johnny on his concerns and feelings, on the things that bother him. What in science can help him to cope better with them?" By approaching the material in this fashion, he would be starting with the affective; he would have selected a piece of cognition that can serve the affective. This is the sort of spiraling direction that we are suggesting.

Our observations force us to conclude that the school has virtually ignored the insistent demands of the child's feelings and instead assumes that if enough pressure is placed upon them, students will be motivated to adjust to an extrinsic body of content, the curriculum. The learner is asked to give up his inner content in favor of an outer content which too often bears little connection to him. This adjustment, although made, appears at best an exercise to be tolerated or a system to beat.

We are not suggesting that all the skills and subject matter which make up school curriculum be replaced or discarded. We *do* suggest that linking academic content to the affective drives of the child represents a more natural process, one that can increase learning ability as well as influence social behavior.

This in no way minimizes the role of cognition. On the contrary, cognition gains greater potency because of its instrumental relationship to the affective. Content so linked is less irrelevant or phony, for it is connected with the learner's concerns, the very foundation of his motivation and actions. Affect thus becomes the basic reality and gives to cognition real meaning.

It will clarify the relationship of skills and concepts curriculum to the programing of the affective realm if one visualizes a school with three interlocking tiers of content.

One tier contains the basic skills, information, and concepts that are generally agreed upon as essential building blocks for the intellectual development of the child. These include reading, computation, and writing skills, among others, as well as the basic information provided by such disciplines as social studies, science, language.

The second tier involves development of the learner's idiosyncratic interests and talents. This personal-discovery tier allows for individual creativity and exploration of interests.

The third tier consists of a group-inquiry curriculum dealing with social issues and problems (such as civil rights) that are related to the personal, and with common personal concerns. (We are *not* suggesting that the classroom become a place for solving individual emotional problems. When we speak of "personal" concerns, we do so only in terms of the threads of *common interest* that run through these issues.)

Inherent in this tier is the development of the individual's interpersonal relationships: identifying, articulating, and evaluating his feelings, concerns, and opinions; comparing and contrasting them with those of others in a group. Although the affective may be used in *any* of the tiers in terms of process, it is chiefly in this third tier that we see the affective used as fully developed content.

We are very much aware that what we suggest here is far from simple. To shift content emphasis from cognition to affect means that school people will have to search for new points of departure for subject matter approaches that have been hallowed by time and custom. But our swiftly changing society requires great flexibility and dynamism of its educational system. It requires that new channels be found, new ways be opened, to reach the deep-down sources that motivate the student to learn and are the primary factors in influencing his social behavior. If educators can meet these requirements, if they can link the student's feelings with what they hope to teach him, they will be making a good start in reducing the unacceptable gap between the way people behave and the way they have been taught to behave.

STRUCTURE OF THE DISCIPLINES AS AN EDUCATIONAL SLOGAN

Herbert M. Kliebard

Almost half a century ago, William Heard Kilpatrick raised the question as to whether the new and exciting term *project method* ought to be admitted into educational discourse (5). He gave it an unqualified endorsement. Ever since the publication of Jerome Bruner's influential book (3), *structure of the disciplines* has generated the same kind of excitement, not only on the part of educationists, but among academicians as well. The proposal that the structure of the disciplines can provide a workable basis for curriculum organization seems to have struck a responsive chord among many who apparently see it as a desirable substitute for such other watchwords as *core* and *life adjustment,* which are falling or have fallen out of popular and professional favor. In just a few years, *structure of the disciplines* has become a kind of rallying cry occupying about the same position that the whole child and *education for democratic living* have held in other times. More than any other term, it seems to reflect the new intellectual rigor which is supposed to be characteristic of such recent

From *Teachers College Record,* LXVI, No. 7 (April 1, 1965), 598–603. Used by permission of the author and publisher.

educational phenomena as the modern mathematics programs and the National Science Foundation's science curricula.

As with other slogans, one of the difficulties with *structure of the disciplines* is that there is some confusion as to what it means. *The Process of Education* was basically a conference report of fewer than 100 pages, less than a third of which was devoted to this topic. It was admittedly not intended to provide definitive answers, merely to state hypotheses. As a result, the problem of defining the term and resolving its implications was left open to debate and interpretation. In time, *structure of the disciplines* has been imbued with almost mystical qualities, and its stature as an educational slogan has grown, but its usefulness as an educational concept may have become somewhat obscured.

WHAT DOES IT MEAN?

The question of what is a discipline, and the question of what constitutes structure, have been central to the discussion of the new term. Several articles have been written, attempting the job of definition, which have either directly or implicitly expressed approval of Bruner's point of view *vis-a-vis* the problem-centered or directly functional approach to curriculum organization. One description ascribed to disciplines the properties of analytic simplification, synthetic coordination, and dynamism (8); another the characteristics of a domain, a methodology, and a history or tradition (4); and a third sees disciplines as having conceptual and syntactical dimensions (9). These analyses were intended, at least in part, to demonstrate that the organized intellectual resources we call disciplines possess certain attributes which uniquely qualify them for teaching and learning. Unfortunately, it is easy to misinterpret these statements as implying a kind of caste system in which certain fields can be placed in a more exalted position in the academic hierarchy than others. Characteristics which have been ascribed to disciplines are taken to be criteria which in effect qualify certain fields as *bona fide* disciplines and which serve to exclude others. Certain prestigious disciplines, like mathematics and physics, become paragons which other fields of study are to emulate. As a matter of fact, a considerable amount of speculation in educational circles has taken the form of agonizing over whether education itself qualifies as a discipline or whether it has to be assigned to some kind of academic limbo. The tendency has been to use the term *field of study* for areas like education which presumably do not possess the proper set of credentials, and to reserve *discipline* for fields like mathematics and physics which are well established. One problem arising from such a distinction is that, by implication, disciplines are considered as entitled to a place in the curriculum, whereas fields of study are not.

Speculation about the term *structure* has sometimes involved the dissection of certain recognized disciplines with a view to exposing their elemental framework. This has occasionally taken the form of constructing models which are designed to illustrate graphically the complex inter-relationships within a discipline. The assumption has been that once the superficial characteristics have been stripped away and the bare bones revealed, the problem of organizing the field for teaching purposes will become markedly simplified.

THE SIMPLE ORIGINS

By contrast, the examples which Bruner himself used to illustrate what he means by structure are simple and undramatic. The structure of biology, he says, may be seen through the "basic relation between external stimulation and locomotor action" to which concepts like tropism and explanations of the swarming of locusts can be related (3). In algebra, structure is related to the fundamental concepts of commutation, distribution, and association. Emphasis on these "three fundamentals" presumably will provide the basis for understanding a wide variety of algebraic operations. The structure of English involves "the subtle structure of a sentence" and the way in which variety can be introduced into the form of language without changing the meaning. Not only do Bruner's illustrations fail to suggest a kind of magical inner core of interrelated principles to which everything in that field may be related, but they all represent quite different orders of things. At one point, Bruner even suggests that structure may take the form of a kind of feeling of empathy or an ability to see parallels. Thus, in history, "If a student could grasp in its most human sense the weariness of Europe at the close of the Hundred Years' War and how it created the conditions for a workable but not ideologically absolute Treaty of Westphalia [sic], he might be better able to think about the ideological struggle of East and West—though the parallel is anything but exact" (3). According to Bruner, then, the structure of a discipline may include, but is not limited to, basic concepts, explanatory principles, generalizations, and insights. Much seems to depend on what kind of discipline it is, and to some extent, on one's individual perception of what is fundamental to that discipline. No one would claim that historians, for example, are of one mind as to what *the* structure of history is or how history should be taught.[1]

None of Bruner's illustrations, therefore, implies that the disciplines are necessarily modeled around a skeleton of interrelated principles the general form of which is common to all disciplines and which must be relentlessly sought out and exposed before that subject can be properly taught. What does seem to be implied are two simple but important propositions: The first is that the curriculum ought to be organized around certain familiar subdivisions of knowledge, which Bruner chooses to call disciplines, and not around problems, social or personal. There is no suggestion, however, that any field of study must present an approved pedigree in order to be admitted to membership as a discipline. As a matter of fact, one important matter which Bruner leaves unresolved is the question of which subdivisions of knowledge are appropriate for study in the various stages of schooling and which should be excluded. The second proposition, implied by the word *structure,* is that the curriculum in these subjects ought to reflect what is central rather than what is peripheral to the fields. It is an attempt to avoid such obvious pitfalls in the teaching of subject matter as the mechanical manipulation of formulae in mathematics and the barren teaching of history as a congeries of unrelated dates and events. The problem of organizing a field for teaching and learning, then, is not one of searching for *the* structure and then transmitting it *in toto*, but one of determining which of the basic principles, theories, concepts, and the like can be adapted for this purpose.

IS IT USEFUL?

As an educational watchword, *structure of the disciplines* is certainly not without merit. The most obvious feature of the term is that it focuses the educational spotlight on knowledge in its various dimensions as the basic stock in trade of the schools. In the recent past, educationists have paid lip-service to the importance of knowledge as a fundamental factor in curriculum planning, but they have rarely given it the attention it deserves. The least that can be said is that *structure of the disciplines* may enliven

---

[1] Samuel Eliot Morison has recently criticized the approach to the teaching of history that was developed by Educational Services, Incorporated, an organization of academicians from Harvard and MIT. Recognizing that his views are outside the " 'Brunerian' frame of reference," Professor Morison nevertheless expressed a preference for the narrative tradition in history. Morison also confessed to some difficulty in understanding the aims of the group because their material was written "in 'pedagese' idiom." Apparently the scholars who worked on the probram developed fluency in that dialect as a byproduct of dealing with pedagogical problems (6).

the debate as to whether knowledge should be used instrumentally in the schools as a means of solving problems or whether it should be studied directly. Out of that debate a new consensus may eventually emerge, perhaps along the lines that Bellack has already suggested (1).

As has been noted, a second feature of the term is that it distinctly implies that in planning the curriculum around organized fields of knowledge, an effort must be made to emphasize what is fundamental to those fields and to minimize what is peripheral. This is not an unimportant consideration because there is reason to believe that a curriculum organized around subject-matter fields may lead to mechanistic teaching and learning unrelated to the kind of intellectual activity that characterizes the highest levels of scholarship. It is, however, not the first time that an effort has been made to plan a curriculum around what is basic to a field of study (2).

There are also some negative aspects to the way that *structure of the disciplines* has been interpreted and used, and if we are at all serious about the reevaluation of the curriculum which seems to be taking place, we ought at least to be aware of them. One of the obvious facts of life in curriculum planning is that not all of the subdivisions of knowledge can be incorporated into the curriculum. There simply is not enough time available, even assuming twelve years of schooling, to do this in any systematic kind of way. One is faced, then, with two basic alternatives: The first is to reorganize several subdivisions into broader units. This has been reasonably successful in certain instances and has met with undistinguished results in others. Botany, zoology, and physiology have been successfully combined and taught under the rubric of biology, but unresolved problems still plague the broad fields of social studies and English. The other alternative is simply to make choices from among the various disciplines, selecting those that seem more important than others.

SOME DANGERS

If we are to be guided by a narrow and limiting conception of *structure of the disciplines* in attempting to resolve this crucial problem, we would tend to exclude the first alternative out of hand because these broad fields have no stature as disciplines and would presumably lack well-defined structures. In considering the second alternative, our tendency would be to favor those fields of study that can readily exhibit a network of interrelated principles as their structure. While the existence of this kind of structure may make the curriculum in that subject in one sense easier to organize, its presence does not insure that that field of study is a more desirable component of a program of general education than one that does not. If structure is interpreted this way, then the social sciences and the humanities would be relegated to a permanent position of inferiority to the natural sciences and mathematics. The danger is that the question of *how* the curriculum shall be organized will become confused with the question of *what* shall be taught.

A second danger associated with the concept of *structure of the disciplines* is that so much attention will be directed to internal investigation of each of the fields of study that the curriculum as a whole will receive only superficial consideration. The curriculum generalist, the person who is concerned with the curriculum from a broad perspective, is rarely a participant in those commissions which have sought to develop programs in the individual subject areas and have been identified with the *structure of the disciplines* point of view. As a result, there has been little attention given to questions of balance and integration in the curriculum broadly conceived. A program of general education, after all, is not a collection of independent studies. It is (or at least prople try to make it) an approximation of what it is important to know.

There are signs already that this critical question may reduce itself to a power struggle among the various disciplines and will be decided on such factors as which discipline can gain enough federal and foundational support to secure a foothold in the curricula of American schools. The American Anthropological Association, for example, has succeeded in acquiring financial support from the National Science Foundation and is seeking a place for anthropology in the high-school curriculum. No major support has been forthcoming, however, for the claims of astronomy, psychology, social psychology, and philosophy. Few people would conceive of this as a desirable situation. It seems to be occurring, however, as a byproduct of an extraordinary emphasis on the curriculum in individual subject fields and a corresponding lack of attention to how all of the parts fit together.

The third danger implicit in some of the proposals associated with the *structure of the disciplines* is perhaps the most subtle. It is that schooling and the world of affairs will become even more sharply disjoined than is already the case as part of an unwholesome fission between theory and practice. This, of course, is a recurring and complex problem. It has become particularly acute, however, as a result of the tendency on the part of academicians who have been developing courses of study in the various disciplines in effect to interpret structure almost exclusively in terms of theory. An academician's bias is almost inevitably toward theoretical concerns because theory frequently represents the crowning accomplishment in his field. This does *not* mean that theory ought to dominate every stage of instruction. This criticism is not intended to resurrect the old cry of "subject-matter specialist" once again as a term of opprobrium. It does recognize that a scholar's commitment to his discipline and his expertise in that field are not the only qualifications that are appropriate to planning a curriculum. It is a little late in the day to argue that the academician has no place in the development of courses of study, but it is quite another thing to hold these scholars in such awe as to preclude a useful dialogue among educationists and academicians mutually concerned with school programs.

THE ISSUE OF RELEVANCE

Paradoxically, it was a professor of physics who, in a recent interview, made the overemphasis on theory a focal point of what is perhaps the sharpest attack on some of the new "structured" courses in the sciences and mathematics. Referring to these new curricula as a form of "educational carpet baggery" and to the superintendents and school boards who implement them as "scalawags," Professor Calandra directed much of his criticism at what he considers to be a decided overemphasis on theory in programs like the ones sponsored by PSSC and CBA and an "unfortunate divorce of pure mathematics from applied mathematics" in the new mathematics programs (7). Over-emphasis on theoretical abstractions and the creation of a dichotomy between theory and practice, in turn, may serve to obscure the relevance of schooling to the world of affairs. It is at least possible that intensive and continuous stress on theory will, in the mind of the student, remove that discipline from the arena of human activity out of which it arose. Structure, when equated with theory, can contribute to that unfortunate detachment.

It should be obvious that none of the dangers enumerated here is a *necessary* concomitant of *structure of the disciplines* as an educational slogan. As a matter of fact, several of the programs which are now identified with that term were under way before the publication of *The Process of Education.* Nevertheless, the phrase seems to capture the tenor of much of what has been done in the name of the new academic excellence and is presently very much in vogue. Its effect, however, is difficult to assess. On the one hand, the term has served to stimulate novel curriculum thinking and sharpen debate on certain issues; on the other, it has generated some complex problems. Each of these problems poses a potential obstacle to the development of a coherent and effective program for our schools. On balance, one must conclude that the recent emphasis on *structure of the disciplines* as the cornerstone of curriculum planning is a rather mixed blessing.

REFERENCES

1.   Bellack, A. A. Selection and organization of curriculum content: an analysis. In Bellack, A. A. (Ed.) *What shall the high schools teach?* Washington, DC: Yearb. Assn. Supervis. Curric. Dev., 1956.

2.   Billings, N. *A determination of generalizations basic to the social studies curriculum.* Baltimore: Warwick and York, 1929.

3.   Bruner, J. S. *The process of education.* Cambridge: Harvard Univer. Press, 1960.

4.   Foshay, A. W., Discipline-centered curriculum. In Passow, A. W. (Ed.) *Curriculum crossroads.* New York: Teach. Coll. Bur. Publ., 1962.

5.   Kilpatrick, W. H. The project method, *Teach. Coll. Rec.,* 1918, *19,* 319-335.

6.   Morison, S. E. The experiences and principles of an historian. In Morison S. E., *Vistas of history,* New York: Knopf, 1964.

7.   The new science curriculums: A sharp dissent. *School Mgmt.,* 1964, *8* 76-82.

8.   Phenix, P. H. The disciplines as curriculum content. In Passow, A. W. (Ed.), *Curriculum crossroads.* New York: 1962. Teach. Coll. Bur. Publ., 1962.

9.   Schwab, J. J. The concept of the structure of a discipline. *Educ. Rec.,* 1962, *43,* 197-205.

LOGIC, THINKING, AND TEACHING

B. Othanel Smith

My purpose is to explore the proposition that logic is relevant to thinking and teaching, and that preparation of the teacher should include the study of what I shall call educational logic. I shall discuss three points: First, that in the course of separating psychology from philosophy, the logical basis of education was lost in the shuffle and that in consequence pedagogical thought became psychologized; second, that the reduction of thinking to psychological processes left us without an adequate criterion of disciplined reasoning and that such a criterion is to be found in logic; third, in order to give rigor to the educative process the teacher must himself have command of logic, and that therefore, teaching depends as much upon logic as it does upon psychology.

LOGIC AND PSYCHOLOGY

At the outset I wish to say that by logic I mean inductive and deductive logic and along with it, semantics in its descriptive and philosophic sense. Logic is neither thinking nor thought. It has nothing to do with the creative processes. It does not tell us how we in fact do think, nor does it tell us how we ought to think. It is not a set of laws to be imposed upon thinking. It simply gives us the rules and techniques by which to assess the results of our mental efforts.

It is easy to see from what I have said that I hold logic and psychology to be different subjects. This view is out of step with that generally held in pragmatic educational theory wherein psychology and logic are meshed together to form a theory of problem solving. It conflicts also with the main line of the empiricist tradition stemming from Locke and Hume, which until about fifty years ago, held that logic and psychology were merely different ways of talking about the same thing. Logic supposedly described the processes of thinking; that is, the rules of logic were thought to be laws describing the way thinking actually occurred. Psychology as the

From *Educational Theory*, VII, No. 4 (October, 1967), 225-233. Used by permission of the author and publisher.

science of the mind purported also to describe thinking processes. The fact that both of these disciplines claimed to do the same thing was seen in their mutual concern with questions about ideas or mental images.

F. H. Bradley is usually given credit for entering the wedge between logic and psychology. In developing his own special brand of idealism, Bradley found it convenient to abandon ideas or mental images as the concern of philosophy. They did not provide the universality he required. In his view, images were mere mental events or psychic facts, having no independent existence or subsistence of their own. These were therefore in the domain of psychology. In Bradley's view philosophy was concerned with what was inferred from mental images. It dealt with their meanings and not with their occurrence. Now according to Bradley, that which is inferred from a mental image takes the form of a judgment. A judgment is not an idea or concept. The study of judgments and their relations is the task of logic. Hence the two subjects were entirely different—psychology dealing with mental events, and logic with inferences and judgments. Russell and Whitehead, in their mathematical logic, struck the final blow to separate logic from psychology.

In this country it was the psychologists who did the separating of logic from psychology—and this by radical surgery. At the very beginning of his epoch-making studies of learning, Thorndike formulated the laws of learning in terms of repetition. Ideas were replaced by the stimulus-response schema. A response became fixed to a stimulus by association through repeated contiguity of the two, in which the surviving response was selected by chance in the process of trial and error and reinforced by success. Thinking was thus reduced to a train of unitary stimulus-response reactions governed by the laws of readiness, exercise, and effect. Thorndike had apparently succeeded in demonstrating in miniature what Darwin claimed nature did on the grand scale. By variation, selection, and survival organic forms emerged. By trial, selection and survival of response the forms of behavior were determined. A hungry cat trying to get out of a box became the model of thinking and learning. Thus logic was completely undercut. To be correct was to be successful.

In Dewey's pragmatism events took a different turn. The Darwinian conception was Dewey's working model just as it was for Thorndike. But where Thorndike spoke of the stimulus Dewey talked instead of the perplexing situation. Yet both ways of talking had reference to observable circumstances of behavior. Instead of "learned behavior," Dewey spoke of the resolved situation, settled by appropriate modes of response. But at this point the parallel breaks down. To Thorndike there were no mental events between stimulus and response. There were only neurone connections. Dewey filled the gap with his Complete Act of Thought.

His formulation of the Complete Act of Thought included both logical and psychological elements. The first and third phase of the Complete Act, namely, the felt difficulty and the occurrence of suggested ways of overcoming it are psychological rather than logical. Phases four and five, that is, the examination of the grounds and the implications of the suggestions together with experimental testing of them are logical. The location and definition of the difficulty, constituting the second phase, appears to be a mixture of the two. While Dewey never abandoned this formulation, he did later modify his interpretation of it. In his major work on logic the Complete Act of Thought became the pattern of inquiry, and he there made it clear that he was concerned with the question of how situations were worked out rather than with thought. Indeed, Dewey was even doubtful that there was anything called thought as a physical existence.

To Dewey the rules of inquiry constituted logic. These rules were formulated from a study of what people do when they seek to settle situations. Once formulated, the rules of logic then become the criteria by which other inquiries are to be assessed. They set the conditions which investigations must meet if their results are to be acceptable. When put in this way, Dewey's conception of logic is no longer a psychological one. For the rules do not describe the supposed mental processes. Rather, they constitute the norms for assessing results of inquiry and for checking upon proposed steps.

LOGIC AND RIGOROUS THINKING

Had the normative significance of Dewey's theory of inquiry been understood in pedagogical circles, the course of educational development might have been different. For one thing, we might have had a logical basis for developing in students the capacity to direct and control their own thinking. As it was, the slogan that we teach "how to think" and not "what to think" was largely empty. For the pattern of inquiry which Dewey had earlier called the Complete Act of Thought was taken to be a description of how thinking and learning in fact occur, and not as a set of norms for judging inquiry. The stripped-down model of thinking presently found in educational psychology texts and other pedagogical literature consists of the following phases: feeling uncertain, locating barriers to action, getting hunches and trying them out in imagination, acting upon the promising one, and deciding whether the action ended with the desired result. Now these are psychological. They describe what we do when as hungry cats we try to escape from our box. They may be fairly good descriptions of what we do, but the crucial point is left out—the basis for appraising results. Blind imitation of past performance is one thing, judging and improving it, another.

There is another important point: from the standpoint of psychology, these five steps do not necessarily involve the use of language; for behavioristic theory assumes that observable actions and not talking are the true index of psychological events. What men say is one thing and what they do, quite another. The psychologist trusts in the doing and rules out language as significant behavior. This mistrust of language is due partly to the fact that experimental psychology developed largely from the study of lower animals and partly to the discredited status of language as a result of its use in introspection which was repudiated. In any event, the mistrust of language by psychologists infected educational thought in spite of the obvious fact that both teaching and human learning are practically impossible without it.

If we look in educational literature for criteria by which to evaluate the steps we take to get out of the box, we find that we are admonished to be alert, careful, open-minded, and whole-hearted. This is not very helpful. In the first place, these terms are elusive and hard to pin down. How can we tell when we are sufficiently alert, let alone when someone else is alert? If A says he is alert and B says no, A is not alert, by what criterion can we decide whose claim to accept? The same vagueness appears in the advice to be careful, open-minded, and whole-hearted. In the second place, these exhortations refer to ways of acting rather than to statements in which ideas can be formulated and tested. We can say that an individual is alert, careful, and so on. But it is a bit odd to say of a statement that it is alert, careful, whole-hearted, or open-minded.

Yet, since much of what we do—especially in matters of reasoning—is done with language, these vague psychological criteria are practically useless. They are useless in dealing with verbal formulations by which the logical soundness of thinking may be tested. Since they refer to ways of acting, these criteria are part and parcel of the psychological version of problem-solving, where results are tested in terms of success, and where success means to find a satisfying way out of a difficulty. But a mere state of psychological satisfaction offers no guarantee that we are not mistaken, nor that the way we solved the present problem might not lead to unsatisfactory consequences the next time we try it. Thus, the surrender of intellectual standards to psychology has all but robbed education of a theory of rigorous thinking.

By virtue of language and logic, thinking takes on a dimension in man different from that of the cat in the box. Man is a language-using creature;

this fact opens to him spheres of experience not given to other creatures. A point so obvious might go without saying were it not for the fact that the epithets "merely verbal" and "verbalism" have dulled the edge of understanding where language and logic are involved in teaching and learning. The plain fact is that without language, nothing can be taught or learned about the past, nor about things removed from immediate observation. The laws of science can be learned only through language and retained in symbolic form alone. Without language the scientific method could not progress beyond the scramblings of the cat in the box. An adequate theory of control over our thinking will acknowledge the central role of linguistic behavior.

But unless a theory of disciplined thinking is based on logic, it is apt to emphasize language in its literary and sociable uses, and to neglect it as an instrument for directing the exploration of the environment and as a vehicle of knowledge. When this happens, the existential and logical monitors of our judgments are by-passed. Instead, we are exhorted to control our emotions—to prevent ourselves from being swayed unduly by prejudice and from losing our heads in anger, fear, or envy. But how can one tell whether or not he is controlling his feelings and prejudices, or whether someone else is doing so? Unless we are to fall back upon such vague and shifting psychological criteria as satisfaction and success, we must appeal to the norms of inductive and deductive logic. We know that one's feelings and prejudices do not interfere unduly with his thinking if he takes such precautions as these: uses a fair sample, recognizes what is true by definition, avoids fallacious reasoning, reduces ideas to observation sentences when an empirical test is to be used, and controls relevant conditions. The point of this analysis is that logical and not psychological criteria are used to judge the efficiency of such operations as these. Therefore the individual is disciplined in his thinking only to the extent that he has taken on the logical and linguistic criteria by which the intellectual work of man is brought under control.

Now I want to explore the ways in which the thinking of an individual can be said to satisfy logical criteria. His thinking meets these criteria, we would say, when the results of his verbal behavior—statements, arguments, descriptions, and so forth—correspond to the rules. But the matter is not so simple, for there are different ways in which verbal behavior is found to abide by these rules. Consider the case of a child learning his mother tongue. As he does so, the child's sentence structure will conform to that of the adults. The child is not aware of such things as linguistic rules. In the same way, the child's reasoning may be said to conform to the rules of logic. His sentences may express valid arguments. This is rarely the case at an early age, but as the child progresses through the elementary school, he begins, though unconsciously and irregularly, to take on the forms of valid reasoning. In conforming to the rules, the child's reasoning is valid even though the idea never occurs to him that he should reason validly. He cannot verbalize the rules to which his reasoning corresponds. He has no words for talking about the rules of thinking or about mistakes in thinking. Hence his reasoning has not reached the threshold of conscious control. Now in cases of this sort we can say that the extent to which rules are satisfied at all, they are satisfied only by unconscious accommodation of behavior.

Let us now suppose that one who has learned to speak his native language goes to school and begins to study grammar. He is taught to classify words and to see relations among them in sentences. This gives him a set of words and rules for talking about language. He can then examine his own discourse and that of others to find and correct points where it fails to satisfy grammatical rules. But just as he can learn to use rules of grammar to guide his use of language, so can the individual learn to govern his own thinking and experimental investigations by using rules of reasoning and inquiry. He thereby acquires greater power over his own intellectual activities and clearer insight into those of others. For now he can rise above, survey, and assess them in the same sense that a referee rises above the game to judge the plays. This ability to perform at more than one level of the intellectual game, both to play it and to stand off and judge it, frees our thinking from unconscious habits conditioned by chance circumstances. Now when the individual examines his thought and brings it into line with criteria of effective thinking, we can say that this is a case of deliberate control, and is in direct contrast to unconscious accommodation.

Now I wish to make two qualifications. First, I do not wish to say that the individual is to make conscious use of logical rules every moment of his thinking. Constant mindfulness of these rules would be a serious impediment. It would have the same effect upon the thoughtful behavior of the individual as awareness of his feet was supposed to have had upon the march of the centipede. No one can act effectively if he is required at the same time both to perform and to think about whether or not he is performing correctly. But there are occasions when an activity can be improved by paying attention to its performance. Thus, one who is able to make deliberate use of rules when judgments about his own thinking or that of someone else are called for, is more apt to catch defects than one who has no command of logic. The disposition to use the rules when they count rather than the constant use of them distinguishes the discerning critic from the crass one.

The second qualification is about the rules themselves. It is usually thought that when one speaks of rules, he is talking about statements such as those in official rule books. But of course this need not be the case. Knowing rules does not mean knowing a particular set of words. The controversy over the teaching of formal grammar was not about the question of whether or not to teach grammatical rules. It was over the question of which rules to teach as well as the context in which the rules were to be taught, whether to teach them in relation to writing and speaking or as formally ordered elements in the official rule book.

When does one know the rules of a game, say, the game of checkers? Suppose he says, "No, you can't make that move" when someone moves a man backward, and he says this on any occasion when that move is made. Should we say that he knows one of the rules of the game, even though he cannot give a sophisticated statement of it? I think we should claim that he does know the rule. So it is with the rules of logic. To know that affirming the consequent is invalid is to recognize such affirmation when it occurs and to recognize thereby that the truth or falsity of the conclusion is still up in the air. The particular verbal form in which the rule is put is of no consequence in playing the game or in refereeing it.

The analogy between the game of checkers and thinking breaks down at least in one significant respect. A player in checkers is always called for infraction of the rules; learning to play the game entails learning the rules. But with thinking it is different. A player in this game, except among professionals, can take all sorts of liberties without anyone calling him for infraction of the rules and without the player himself even knowing that he is breaking them. In some cases, however, he will pick up certain logical rules in an *ad hoc* sense. Suppose a beginning high school student is given the following argument: If it rains, the streets are wet. The streets are wet. Therefore it rained. He will tell you quickly that the conclusion does not necessarily follow because the streets may be wet for some other reason. Perhaps the street sprinkler has come along. But when the content is unfamiliar and the argument complex, the student will seldom recognize the fallacy. He may fail to recognize the fallacy as such, if his reasoning is still at the level of concrete relations. Hence he could not go beyond cases of particular content. Nor could he recognize the fallacy in any general sense. Hence if the material relations in an argument go beyond his concrete knowledge, the student who has only an *ad hoc* command of the rules cannot detect logical mistakes.

To recognize fallacies in a generalized sense is to see them in abstraction from any particular content. The individual is able to lay his finger on any instance of a particular fallacy and to tell what is wrong, even though he is not familiar with the subject matter. He can thereby use logical rules to monitor his own thinking as well as that of others. It does not require a formal study of logic and scientific method to give the individual such generalized control over his thinking and judgment. To be good at the game of thinking, one does not need to be a professional. At the professional level we find logicians and critics of logical and scientific systems. Here the individual can examine relations among rules, study them as a system, and propose changes in them.

To sum up the levels at which rules may be known, the first is the level of accommodation. At this level, the individual knows how to play the game of thinking, though he does not explicitly know the rules. At the next, the *ad hoc* level, the individual knows the rules only in a special context. At the third, or general level, we now add the ability to deal with the rules in their general applicability. Finally, at the professional level, the individual goes beyond the general grasp of the rules to a command of them as a formal system.

I believe that at best the rules of the game of thinking are now being learned in an *ad hoc* sense. Both in school and out, the individual simply picks up rules of reasoning from the material relations in the content he studies. I suspect that many persons play the game of thinking without even knowing that there are rules. The teacher plays it too, and often on the same level, checking the students' thinking by the textbook, by what the teacher has himself been taught to be the correct answer, or by his own common sense notions of clear and accurate thinking.

LOGIC AND TEACHING

To continue a little longer in the metaphor, in the game of thinking the teacher is player, coach, and often referee. As a player, he engages students in thinking by asking questions and responding to their answers, by receiving questions and giving answers, and by many other devices and activities. In each of these there is a sort of give and take between teacher and students. But, having little knowledge of logic and being preoccupied with getting the student to understand facts and ideas, the teacher usually overlooks the logic of both his subject and of the class discussion. For instance, a history teacher discusses with his students the imperialism of a nation. He goes into the question of the extent and cause of the imperialism. But the concept of imperialism is not itself explicated, so that the students have varied notions of what is being talked about. The whole discussion is based on a vague and ambiguous term and thus thinking and learning are short-changed.

Now the teacher moves from the role of player to that of coach when he turns to the task of helping students work out a definition of imperialism. To handle this task, the teacher needs criteria by which to decide the adequacy of the definition worked out by himself and the students. As the teacher and students together analyze the concept of imperialism and give it the form of a definition, the teacher will help students from time to time to see what it means to define a term and to understand the kinds of rules by which the adequacy of a definition may be decided. He will show them, as appropriate occasions arise, that a definition lays down criteria for the use of a word, and that the definition we decide to give a word, or the usage we select, is related to the purpose we have in mind. He will show them that sometimes we define words by assigning whatever is named by the word to a class and then distinguishing it from other members of the class. On other occasions the teacher will show how to define words by pointing to instances, and in still other cases by reference to the operations we perform.

To reflect upon the work of the teacher is to see that there are many occasions when he could readily teach procedures of analysis and logical appraisal. He could teach how to distinguish between logical validity and empirical truth, how to tell when an argument is valid and when a proposition is true. Through his instruction students could learn how to identify assumptions, how to tell when conditions are logically necessary and sufficient, how to to identify hypotheses and to tell whether or not they are confirmed by particular instances, and many other procedures too numerous to mention. In order to teach for effective thinking at this higher level of operation, the teacher must possess a working knowledge of logic in an amount far in excess of that picked up through his own incidental learning. This claim that the teacher should be trained in logic rests upon two premises: first, it is important to develop the student's ability to think critically; second, in order to develop this ability the student must be given experience in controlling his own thinking under the guidance of the teacher.

Logic is not only necessary in teaching the student how to control his thinking but it is also an inherent part of teaching. Two lines of reasoning suggest this conclusion. In the first place, instruction in knowledge starts with an intent to arrive somewhere, to reach a conclusion. It is not a form of sociable conversation meandering wherever fancy leads. Rather it is studied discourse which aims not only at conclusions but also at showing the steps and reasons leading to the conclusions. This kind of discourse is logical. In trying to teach students to understand a conclusion and how it is reached, a teacher does not lead them down the blind alleys, detours, and mistaken paths which he himself may have taken, nor does he expose them to the false leads taken by the race. He strips off these mistaken moves, and starting at some take-off point, he tries to show by a chain of ideas that the conclusion is warranted.

In the second place, observation bears out the fact that instruction in knowledge involves logic. Even cursory observation of teaching will show that the teacher performs certain logical operations. He defines, interprets, explains, justifies, proves, evaluates. Now each of these activities is an operation done with words, sentences, and statements, and which we cannot perform without these linguistic instruments. Thus when we explain an event in science, we show it to be a special case of a law. In proving a proposition in mathematics, we show it to be a conclusion from a set of premises. When justifying our action, we give reasons to show that it is a wise step to take. In defining a word, we state the rules for using it. Now all of these operations fall in the domain of logic.

These operations are to be sharply distinguished from psychological processes. To talk about the operations of defining, proving, explaining, and so on, is not to talk about psychological events. Psychologists talk about certain processes: perceiving, emoting, conceiving, inferring, judging. Now it may well be that these processes occur when we prove a proposition or justify a course of action. But I do not think that teachers work with such processes even though they may be going on. Rather the teacher works with words and statements, their meanings and relations. He may decide that certain psychological events are taking place at a given moment, and so modify what he is doing. Still he is dealing with signs and symbols and performing the logical operations entailed by verbal instruction. So the changes he does make in his activities are largely changes in verbal behavior.

Some critics might object that my analysis presupposes an old-fashioned way of teaching and would then go on to make the point that nowadays no good teacher uses the methods of talking and telling. Instead of such verbal methods, these critics would say, the teacher engages students in problem-solving activities where they learn by planning and working out things together. It would then be said that the methods of involving and directing students in these activities require no special knowledge of logic on the part of the teacher. What he needs instead is suitable knowledge of human relations and skill in the techniques of group organization and control.

But it would be easy to show that the usual practice of teaching, especially in high school and college, is neither group work nor problem solving. Then, too, it can be shown that the assertion "a good teacher uses such and such methods" is logically circular because the meaning of "good teacher" may be interpreted to include "uses such and such methods." It is like saying all black cats are black. However, since these replies are not likely to convince the critics, I shall forego the pleasure of playing around with them.

Yet it should be noted that this objection to the claim that teachers need command of logic does not touch upon the point that the control of thinking involves deliberate use of logical rules. Such objection bears only on the claim that the acts of teaching are themselves logical operations. But, suppose it were the case that all teachers use problem-solving and group work. What would the teacher do in the classroom? If one insists that all learning is to result from problem-solving, or from instruction by one's peers through group work, what is the teacher's role? Is he no more than a mechanic who pushes psychological buttons to activate students and to keep them from getting out of hand? Of course not. The teacher who uses problem-solving and group work is inescapably involved in all the talking and telling that normally goes on in teaching. He must work with individuals and groups helping them to clarify meanings, to analyze and evaluate reasons and arguments, hypotheses and plans of action. The teacher helps students in testing the truth of statements about matters of fact, and in dealing with many other linguistic and logical operations. Even in problem-solving and group work the teacher cannot do these things without talking, and he will be intelligent about his talking only to the extent that he exercises deliberate control over it.

You have probably been wondering for several minutes whether or not I am advocating a return to the study of formal logic by teachers. If the expression "formal logic" means symbolic logic, that is not what I have in mind. Although for teachers of physical sciences and mathematics, acquaintance with it is not undesirable. If the expression means deductive logic, that is part of what I mean. I would certainly not want everything that is traditionally taught in deductive logic to be included in courses for teachers. Nor would I want the logical training of the teacher to be limited to deductive logic. In addition, I would surely include inductive logic, semantics, and some elements of the philosophy of science. Logicians have made progress in ways of teaching their subject as well as in pushing back the frontiers of the subject itself. I believe that in most schools philosophy departments could be persuaded to give appropriate courses in logic for teachers. But the work given by departments of philosophy, while necessary, is not sufficient. That would merely be preprofessional training. In addition, there is need for work in educational logic as a part of our professional program. This is not the place to outline such work, but I shall say that the course should deal with the logic of teaching—defining, explaining, interpreting, proving, justifying, verifying, applying, and the like. And such a course should use actual activities, events, and instructional materials found in the classrooms of elementary and high schools. Teaching has so many logical aspects that no one should fear that educational logic would be empty and formal, detached from the work of the classroom.

My efforts to justify the claim that teachers should have command of logic may be inadequate. As is often the case, I feel more certain of my conclusion than I do of the defense I have made for it. This confession is not entirely without merit, for we sometimes gain by holding on to an idea long enough to find out whether or not sufficient evidence for it can be accumulated. I hope that I have succeeded in raising some new questions about the role of logic in teacher education. If I have done this, I can trust that you will continue to turn these questions over in your mind until the answers you give them are grounded in fact and theory.

THE MEDIUM IS THE MESSAGE

Marshall McLuhan

In a culture like ours, long accustomed to splitting and dividing all things as a means of control, it is sometimes a bit of a shock to be reminded that, in operational and practical fact, the medium is the message. This is merely to say that the personal and social consequences of any medium—that is, of any extension of ourselves—result from the new scale that is introduced into our affairs by each extension of ourselves, or by any new technology. Thus, with automation, for example, the new patterns of human association tend to eliminate jobs, it is true. That is the negative result. Positively, automation creates roles for people, which is to say depth of involvement in their work and human association that our preceding mechanical technology had destroyed.

Many people would be disposed to say that it was not the machine, but what one did with the machine, that was its meaning or message. But in

From the *NEA Journal*, LVI, No. 7 (October, 1967), 24–27. Used by permission of the author and publisher.

terms of the ways in which the machine altered our relations to one another and to ourselves, it mattered not in the least whether it turned out cornflakes or Cadillacs. The restructuring of human work and association was shaped by the technique of fragmentation that is the essence of machine technology. The essence of automation technology is the opposite. It is integral and decentralist in depth, just as the machine was fragmentary, centralist, and superficial in its patterning of human relationships.

The instance of the electric light may prove illuminating in this connection. The electric light is pure information. It is a medium without a message, as it were, unless it is used to spell out some verbal ad or name. This fact, characteristic of all media, means that the "content" of any medium is always another medium. The content of writing is speech, just as the written word is the content of print, and print is the content of the telegraph. If it is asked, "What is the content of speech?" it is necessary to say, "It is an actual process of thought, which is in itself nonverbal."

An abstract painting represents direct manifestation of creative thought processes as they might appear in computer designs. What we are considering here, however, are the psychic and social consequences of the designs or patterns as they amplify or accelerate existing processes. For the "message" of any medium or technology is the change of scale or pace or pattern that it introduces into human affairs. The railway did not introduce movement or transportation or wheel or road into human society, but it accelerated and enlarged the scale of previous human functions, no matter what freight it carried.

Let us return to the electric light. Whether the light is being used for brain surgery or night baseball makes no difference to human society. It could be argued that these activities are in some way the "content" of the electric light, since they could not exist without the electric light. This argument merely underlines the point that the medium is the message because it is the medium that shapes and controls the scale and form of human association and action. The content or uses of media are as diverse as they are ineffectual in shaping the form of human association.

Indeed, it is typical that the "content" of any medium blinds us to the character of the medium. Only today have industries become aware of the various kinds of business in which they are engaged. When IBM discovered that it was not in the business of making office equipment or business machines, but that it was in the business of processing information, then it began to navigate with clear vision. The General Electric Company makes a considerable portion of its profits from electric light bulbs and lighting systems. It has not yet discovered that, quite as much as AT&T, it is in the business of moving information.

The electric light escapes attention as a communication medium just because it has no "content." And this makes it an invaluable instance of how people fail to study media at all. For it is not till the electric light is used to spell out some brand name that it is noticed as a medium. Then it is not the light but the "content" (or what is really another medium) that is noticed. The message of the electric light is like the message of electric power in industry, totally radical, pervasive, and decentralized. For electric light and power are separate from their uses, yet they eliminate time and space factors in human association exactly as do radio, telegraph, telephone, and TV, creating involvement in depth.

In accepting an honorary degree from a university a few years ago, the chairman of the board of one of the television networks made this statement: "We are too prone to make technological instruments the scapegoats for the sins of those who wield them. The products of modern science are not in themselves good or bad; it is the way they are used that determines their value." That is the voice of the current somnambulism. Suppose we were to say, "Apple pie is in itself neither good nor bad; it is the way it is used that determines its value." Or, "The smallpox virus is in itself neither good nor bad; it is the way it is used that determines its value." Again, "Firearms are in themselves neither good nor bad; it is the way they are used that determines their value."

I am not being perverse. There is simply nothing in the speaker's statement that will bear scrutiny, for it ignores the nature of the medium, of any and all media, in the true Narcissus style of one hyptonized by the amputation and extension of his own being in a new technical form.

The paradox of mechanization is that although it is itself the cause of maximal growth and change, the principle of mechanization excludes the very possibility of growth or the understanding of change. For mechanization is achieved by fragmentation of any process and by putting the fragmented parts in a series. Yet, as David Hume showed in the eighteenth century, there is no principle of causality in a mere sequence. That one thing follows another accounts for nothing.

The greatest of all reversals occurred with electricity, which ended sequence by making things instant. With instant speed, the causes of things began to emerge to awareness again as they had not done with things in sequence. Instead of asking, which came first, the chicken or the egg, it suddenly seemed that a chicken was an egg's idea for getting more eggs.

Mechanization was never so vividly fragmented or sequential as in the birth of the movies, the moment that translated us beyond mechanism into the world of growth and organic interrelation. The movie, by sheer speeding up of the mechanical, carried us from the world of sequence and connections into the world of creative configuration and structure. The message of the movie medium is that of transition from lineal connections to configurations.

To a highly literate and mechanized culture, the movie appeared as a world of triumphant illusions and dreams that money could buy. It was at this moment of the movie that cubism occurred. Cubism has been described by E. H. Gombrich (*Art and Illusion*) as "the most radical attempt to stamp out ambiguity and to enforce one reading of the picture—that of a man-made construction, a colored canvas." For cubism substitutes all facets of an object simultaneously for the "point of view" or facet of perspective illusion. Instead of the specialized illusion of the third dimension on canvas, cubism sets up an interplay of planes and contradiction or dramatic conflict of patterns, lights, textures that "drives home the message" by involvement.

In other words, cubism, by giving the inside and outside, the top, bottom, back, and front and the rest, in two dimensions, drops the illusion of perspective in favor of instant sensory awareness of the whole. Cubism, by seizing on instant total awareness, suddenly announced that the medium is the message. Is it not evident that the moment that sequence yields to the simultaneous, one is in the world of the structure and of configuration? Is that not what has happened in physics as in painting, poetry, and in communication? Specialized segments of attention have shifted to total field, and we can now say quite naturally, "The medium is the message."

Before electric speed and total field, it was not obvious that the medium is the message. The message, it seemed was the "content," as people used to ask what a painting was *about*. Yet they never thought to ask what a melody was about, nor what a house or a dress was about. In such matters, people retained some sense of the whole pattern, of form and function as a unity. But in the electric age this integral idea of structure and configuration has become so prevalent that educational theory has taken up the matter. Instead of working with specialized "problems" in arithmetic, the structural approach now follows the lines of force in the field of number and has small children meditating about number theory and "sets."

Detribalization by literacy and its traumatic effects on tribal man is the theme of a book by the psychiatrist, J. C. Carothers, *The African Mind in Health and Disease* (World Health Organization, Geneva, 1953). Much of this material reappeared in an article in *Psychiatry* magazine, November 1959, entitled "The Culture, Psychiatry, and the Written Word." Again, it is electric speed that has revealed the lines of force operating from Western technology in the remotest areas of bush, savannah, and desert. One example is the Bedouin with his battery radio on board the camel.

Submerging natives with floods of concepts for which nothing has prepared them is the normal action of all of our technology. But with electric media Western man himself experiences exactly the same inundation as the remote native. We are no more prepared to encounter radio and TV in our literate milieu than the native of Ghana is able to cope with the literacy that takes him out of his collective tribal world and beaches him in individual isolation. We are as numb in our new electric world as the native involved in our literate and mechanical culture.

Electric speed mingles the cultures of prehistory with the dregs of industrial marketeers, the nonliterate with the semiliterate and the post-literate. Mental breakdown of varying degrees is the very common result of uprooting and of inundation with new information and endless new patterns of information. In our own world as we become more aware of the effects of technology on psychic formation and manifestation, we are losing all confidence in our right to assign guilt. Ancient prehistoric societies regarded violent crime as pathetic. The killer was regarded as we do a cancer victim. "How terrible it must be to feel like that," they said.

Literate man is quite inclined to see others who cannot conform as somewhat pathetic. Especially the child, the cripple, the woman, and the colored person appear in a world of visual and typographic technology as victims of injustice. On the other hand, in a culture that assigns roles instead of jobs to people—the dwarf, the eccentric, the child create their own spaces. They are not expected to fit into some uniform and repeatable niche that is not their size anyway.

Consider the phrase, "It's a man's world." As a quantitative observation endlessly repeated from within a homogenized culture, this phrase refers to the men in such a culture who have to be homogenized Dagwoods in order to belong at all. In our IQ testing we have produced the greatest flood of misbegotten standards. Unaware of our typographic cultural bias, our testers assume that uniform and continuous habits are a sign of intelligence, thus eliminating the ear man and the tactile man.

The American stake in literacy as a technology or uniformity applied to every level of education, government, industry, and social life is totally threatened by the electric technology. The electric technology is within the gates, and we are numb, deaf, blind, and mute about its encounter with the Gutenberg technology, on and through which the American way of life was formed. It is, however, no time to suggest strategies when the threat has not even been acknowledged to exist. I am in the position of Louis Pasteur telling doctors that their greatest enemy was quite invisible, and quite unrecognized by them.

Our conventional response to all media, namely that it is how they are used that counts, is the numb stance of the technological idiot. For the "content" of a medium is like the juicy piece of meat carried by the burglar to distract the watchdog of the mind. The effect of the medium is made strong and intense just because it is given another medium as "content." The content of a movie is a novel or a play or an opera. The effect of the movie form is not related to its program content. The "content" of writing or print is speech, but the reader is almost entirely unaware either of print or of speech.

Arnold Toynbee apparently has not turned his attention to how media have shaped history. He seriously suggests that adult education is a useful counterforce to the popular press. He considers that, although all of the oriental societies have in our time accepted the industrial technology and its political consequences: "On the cultural plane . . . there is no uniform corresponding tendency." This is like the voice of the literate man, floundering in a milieu of ads, who boasts, "Personally, I pay no attention to ads."

The spiritual and cultural reservations that the oriental peoples may have about our technology will avail them not at all. The effects of technology do not occur at the level of opinions or concepts, but alter sense ratios or patterns of perception steadily and without any resistance. The serious artist is the only person able to encounter technology with impunity, just because he is an expert aware of the changes in sense perception.

The operation of the money medium in seventeenth-century Japan had effects not unlike the operation of typography in the West. The penetration of the money economy, wrote G. B. Sansom, "caused a slow but irresistible revolution, culminating in the breakdown of feudal government and the resumption of intercourse with foreign countries after more than two hundred years of seclusion." Money has reorganized the sense life of peoples just because it is an *extension* of our sense lives. This change does not depend upon approval or disapproval of those living in the society.

Arnold Toynbee made one approach to the transforming power of media in his concept of "etherialization," which he holds to be the principle of progressive simplification and efficiency in any organization or technology. Typically, he is ignoring the *effect* of the challenge of these forms upon the response of our senses. He imagines that it is the response of our opinions that is relevant to the effect of media and technology in society, a "point of view" that is plainly the result of the typographic spell. For the man in a literate and homogenized society ceases to be sensitive to the diverse and discontinuous life or forms. He acquires the illusion of the third dimension and the "private point of view" as part of his Narcissus fixation, and is quite shut off from the old truism that we become what we behold.

If the formative energies in the **media** are the media themselves, that raiscs an important consideration that can only be mentioned here, although it deserves volumes: Namely, that technological media are staples or natural resources, exactly as are coal and cotton and oil. Anybody will concede that a society whose economy is dependent upon one or two major staples like cotton or grain or lumber or fish or cattle is going to have some obvious social patterns of organization as a result.

Stress on a few major staples creates extreme instability in the economy but great endurance in the population. For a society configured by reliance on a few commodities accepts them as a social bond quite as much as the metropolis does the press. Cotton and oil, like radio and TV, become "fixed charges" on the entire psychic life of the community. And this pervasive fact creates the unique cultural flavor of any society. It pays through the nose and all its other senses for each staple that shapes its life.

That our human senses, of which all media are extensions, are also fixed charges on our personal energies and that they also configure the awareness and experience of each one of us may be perceived in another connection mentioned by the psychologist C. G. Jung:

> Every Roman was surrounded by slaves. The slave and his psychology flooded ancient Italy, and every Roman became inwardly, and of course unwittingly, a slave. Because living constantly in the atmosphere of slaves, he became infected through the unconscious with their psychology. No one can shield himself from such an influence.

THE DEMAND FOR CONTINUAL LEARNING
IN MODERN SOCIETY

Howard Y. McClusky

It is generally understood that the school reflects the society it serves. And if that society does not change too fast, the school may be able to educate youth for a lifetime. But modern conditions are forcing us to be a society

From *The University of Michigan School of Education Bulletin*, 34, No. 8 (May, 1963), 113–118. Used by permission of the author and publisher.

of constant learners just to keep abreast of the times. This accelerating development will undoubtedly produce drastic changes in the formal schooling of youth, as well as broader and more abundant provisions for adult education.

Our society of learners, our "learning society," becomes one in which learning is a central feature of its agencies, and where for the individual, learning is not an option but an indispensable condition of a meaningful existence. In such a society every one will need to learn and to keep on learning. The alternative will be estrangement from the main stream of life.

Recognition of this startling and pervasive fact is giving new urgency to the assessment of formal schooling. It is the generating force behind a national effort to bring the first twelve years of instruction up to the highest possible level of effectiveness for all young people. It has also gone far toward making two years beyond high school the preferred norm of educational achievement for the majority of American youth. But the striking outcome of this fact is increasing stress on the importance of the continuing education of adults. The logic of this emphasis is decisive.

For the first time in the history of civilization, the time of drastic cultural change has been telescoped into less than the lifetime of the individual. The current generation of mature adults now represents the first generation faced with managing a culture different *in kind* than the one originally transmitted to them. The consequences of this new fact of life is such that the well educated youth of today is an obsolete man tomorrow. The implication of this sudden turn in the tide of civilization is clear: a society that makes its educational investment almost entirely in children and youth is on the way to becoming obsolete and is reducing its chances for survival.[1]

That this last observation forecasts a major expansion in education for adults is obvious, but less obvious is the new perspective it gives on schooling for children and youth. Almost completely in the past and for a majority today, childhood and youth education is presumably a preparation for adult living. But in a learning society elementary, secondary, and higher education will be preparation for adult learning and living. Earlier (youth) and later (adult) education will not occupy separate domains, but will be part of a seamless garment of instruction covering the entire span of life. Every teacher of youth will, in an anticipatory sense, be regarded as a teacher of adults. It is our premise that a saturated application of this

---

[1] Gale Jensen, A. A. Liveright, and Collie Vernor (editors), *Adult Education: A New Imperative for Our Times,* p. 15. Chicago: Adult Education Association of the U.S.A., 1961.

viewpoint will ultimately produce basic changes in the entire apparatus of formal instruction.

Let us begin our forecast with the heart of the educational program, namely teaching. In this realm, "learning to learn" and "learning to want to learn" will become central goals of instruction. Reduced to essentials, "learning to learn" will require a dual emphasis: one on teaching the structure of subject matter and the other on the "why" of method. To illustrate, note Bruner's reference to one aspect of structure in biology:

> Take first a set of observations on an inchworm crossing a sheet of graph paper mounted on a board. The board is horizontal; the animal moves in a straight line. We tilt the board so that the inclined plane or upward grade is 30 degrees. We observe that the animal does not go straight up, but travels at an angle of 45 degrees from the line of maximum climb. We now tilt the board to 60 degrees. Now he travels along a line 75 degrees off the straight up line. From these two measures we may infer that inchworms 'prefer' to travel uphill along an incline of 15 degrees. We have discovered a geotropism. It is not an isolated fact . . . there is a preferred level of illumination toward which lower organisms orient, a preferred level of salinity, of temperature and so on. Once a student grasps this basic relation between external stimulation and locomotor action, he is well on his way toward being able to handle a good deal of seemingly new but in fact highly related information . . . Grasping the structure of a subject permits many other things to be related to it meaningfully. To learn structure, in short, is to learn how things are related.[2]

Similar examples can be readily found in the fields of language, mathematics, geography, physics and other disciplines.

The "why" of method may be illustrated by the whole-part-whole sequence of covering a unit of subject matter. This procedure means simply that one begins with a preliminary view of the whole, continues with a more detailed study of its parts, and concludes with a recapitulative view of the whole.

The "why" of this method may be found in Gestalt psychology which affirms that the "whole is more than the sum of the parts." But since, according to this theory, the parts derive their meaning from the whole, they should, as far as possible, be studied in the context of the whole of which they are a part. This reasoning explains the use of the pre- and post-overview as a means of providing context for the subdivisions of a unit of subject matter. This example also suggests a way by which the pupil

[2] Jerome S. Bruner, *The Process of Education*, p. 97. Cambridge: Harvard University Press, 1961.

may become explicitly aware of the "why" behind other methods and thus may greatly expand their range of transfer.

The discriminating reader could at this juncture argue that a solid grasp of the structure of subject matter and an understanding of the "why" of method has always been a valued goal of good teaching. This might be conceded, but the learning society will insist on bringing practice closer to intention much more rapidly than we are now doing. It will give relatively less attention to "covering the subject" and the mechanical feedback of discrete details, and place much greater stress on the derivation and generalization of relationships. But above all, the learning society will require schools to give major attention *to teaching for transfer from earlier to adult learning*. An unqualified acceptance of this emphasis would profoundly modify programs of most present day schools.

As indicated above, the objective of "learning to learn" would be one approach to teaching for transfer to future learning. Another, and a related approach is contained in Bruner's concept of the "spiral curriculum." As he says "the basic ideas that lie at the heart of science and mathematics and the basic themes that give form to life and literature are as simple as they are powerful." These elements could be introduced into the curriculum much earlier than they are now, and turning spirally back on themselves, be take-off points for transferring their application both to higher levels of complexity and to later stages in the life span. Thus by the introduction early of essential themes for re-use in later contexts, transfer from youth to adult learning would be greatly favored.

The learning society would produce another significant shift in the approach to education. At no time in the lives of youth would instruction be regarded as terminal. There would always be an open-end quality to teaching, and material beyond any unit of instruction would always be waiting to be discovered. Moreover, the student's career as a potential learner would never end. It could be interrupted, or intermittent, but never regarded as final. We would scrap the impossible notion that in 12, 14, or 16 years one can acquire enough knowledge to last a lifetime. The entire enterprise of schooling would be oriented to the idea that what we now know as elementary, secondary, and collegiate education is only preliminary to a lifetime of learning. The high school and college diploma, implying the completion of studies, would give way to a "Certificate of Transfer" from earlier to later instruction and the ultimate test of formal schooling for youth would be the extent to which it contributes to the continuing education of adults. Thus all the apparatus of admissions, achievement testing, marks, promotions, graduation, etc., would be reconceived in favor of procedures designed to sustain the individual in an ongoing life-span process of educative self-renewal and development. The learning society now being created by a growing technology allows us no alternative, for the continuing renewal of the society's members will be the price of its survival and an indispensable condition for the maintenance of its viability.

Consider the dropout. If in a learning society, learning must necessarily be forever, the dropout would constitute not only a tragic loss of resource, but also an intolerable incompatibility between individual status and societal purpose. A pupil might withdraw temporarily to work, with a built-in plan to return for later study, or he might drop out of one program in order to "drop in" to another. But in a learning society the act of dropping out could never be accepted as determining the final status of the pupil as a learner. He would be presented with multiple opportunities for instruction until he could find something that would enlist his talents and keep alive his ability and interest in learning.

There are two cogent reasons why the learning society invests the problem of the dropout with a new sense of urgency. One is that the competitive gap between the "drop-out" and the "stay-in" widens much more rapidly and leads to much more serious consequences for the individual in a learning society. And the other is that the hurt of dropping out, unless somehow constructively alleviated, will probably lead to a resistance to learning in the adult years when a return to learning is most needed to keep up with the pace of a rapidly changing community. This was not too serious in a pre-learning society, for a person with limited schooling could usually secure a respectable foothold in the economy. But those days are past. If dropping out of school means the end of organized learning, as it too often does today, it is in effect dropping out of the principal means for achieving most of the life chances provided by modern society. The growing irreversibility of the low social position to which the early dropout is usually condemned is one of the tragic consequences of the failure of our present educational system. The learning society would be compelled to remedy this breakdown in educational services by providing equal opportunity for everyone to learn throughout the entire span of life.

Another impact of the learning society would be the development of a network of linkages between the formal apparatus of schooling and the agencies in the community and elsewhere for the instruction of adults. The purpose here would be to surround the pupil with a knowledge of the connections between what he has started in school and the programs to which he can turn for continuing these inquiries in later years. He would be constantly reminded by the administration, guidance personnel, and his teachers that somewhere in the adult program of his own school system, university extension, correspondence study, the military services, business, industry, churches, labor unions, libraries, museums, etc., there is an attractive array of facilities waiting to be used for the renewal of a former skill or for the cultivation of a late-blooming interest.

The initiative for the creation of a linkage mechanism would be the responsibility of the school. Its formation would increase the relevance of regular formal instruction, but would also increase the possibility of transferring youth to adult learning by creating expectations with built-in facility for fulfillment. It is our premise that the inclusive character of education in the learning society would compel a much more thorough articulation of the formal schooling of youth with the agencies of adult education.

In brief we are saying that we are well on the road to developing a culture where learning in some form must become increasingly a way of life for the vast majority of all ages of the population. To a degree unknown in any other time in history, schooling for youth will become a relatively smaller part of a larger, more inclusive societal effort. As emphasis on the importance of education inevitably increases, adults will step up their demands for continuing education for themselves, as well as that kind of education for their children which they will more and more recognize as necessary for the viability of their future. The educative effort released by this massive involvement will re-orient systems of formal instruction to lifelong educational needs to an extent only partly fore-shadowed by current programs of schooling for youth.

QUESTIONS FOR DISCUSSION

THE NATURE OF KNOWLEDGE

1. What are the major elements of a discipline, as Foshay delineates them?
2. What is meant by the "structure of the disciplines"? Is this concept useful in curriculum building and teaching? What learning methods does Bruner recommend?
3. Do you agree with the statement in the introduction to this section that the only knowledge of worth to the individual consists of the structure of data which he himself has constructed from the facts discovered and organized by others? What might be the implications of this statement for curriculum planning and teaching?
4. Would broad groupings of the disciplines such as science, mathematics, social science, and the humanities help in resolving some of the problems of curriculum development?
5. Do Bellack's four "main modes of intellectual activity" offer a suitable way to organize knowledge for the school curriculum?
6. Do you agree with Fantini's and Weinstein's statement that "unless knowledge relates to feeling, it is unlikely to affect behavior appreciably"?
7. Is it possible that knowledge should be structured in all of the ways proposed in this section (the knower's structure; the structure of the disciplines: broad groupings) at different times for different purposes?
8. What is meant by the "discovery method of learning"? Should this method be used in dealing with knowledge at all grade levels— elementary, junior high, senior high, and community college?
9. How should a teacher decide which knowledge is of greatest worth for his own students?
10. What does McLuhan mean when he says, "The medium is the message"?
11. What does McClusky mean when he says that the "learning society" will force the school to give greater emphasis to "teaching for transfer from earlier to adult learning"?

5 Curriculum Criteria

A criterion is a standard on which a decision or judgment can be based; it is a basis for discrimination. Curriculum criteria are guidelines or standards on which instructional program decisions can be made.

If you have come this far consecutively in *Readings In Curriculum,* you should now have some understanding of the significance of social forces, human development, the nature of learning, and the nature of knowledge in planning a curriculum. It is necessary that all four of these bases be considered in any adequate curriculum planning. A major goal of this section is to emphasize that the curriculum-maker should consider *all* of the four bases presented in Sections 1 to 4 as curriculum criteria: they should be used together as guidelines for instructional decisions.

A knowledge of social forces and human development represent two ways of approaching the task of understanding the learner and his needs. Learning theories suggest that there are different ways of learning that may be superior in different circumstances, for different learning tasks, or for different learners. Knowledge theories indicate that learners have a personal organization of knowledge that may be different from the structure of the disciplines, and that both should be considered by the curriculum planner or teacher.

As you grow in knowledge and understanding of the bases of curriculum-decisions studied so far, it is hoped that you will try to use them together as a teacher or curriculum planner. Theories of human development, theories of learning, theories about the individual in society, and theories about the nature of knowledge each describe only a portion of the learner's setting, nature, and action. But used together they constitute multiple curriculum criteria to aid the teacher and curriculum maker in planning and evaluating.

One other consideration is also important: what objectives are to be

367

sought through the program of learning? Without having the objectives for learning clearly in view, teachers cannot make professional judgments on any sound basis. They cannot utilize their knowledge of the curriculum bases to make choices of content, materials, or procedures that will further student learning toward intended ends. To choose among curriculum alternatives or instructional strategies, the educator must know the goals he is seeking to attain, and the curriculum bases on which he may make these choices. Otherwise his selections will be little more than random; they cannot be termed professional in the light of today's knowledge of cultural and social forces, human development and learning, and knowledge and cognition.

A number of statements of objectives of American education have been issued by the Educational Policies Commission of the National Education Association. "The Central Purposes of American Education" presents several of the earlier statements of objectives and then asserts that today the development of the ability to think is the common thread in all of education and is the major goal of today's schools.

Brameld ("What Is The Central Purpose of American Education?") disagrees. He believes that the development of world citizenship should be considered as the major goal of education today.

Fox, in "Curriculum Development With A Purpose" describes the role of values in curriculum improvement. He believes that curriculum development will be facilitated if teachers and learners will specify their values and objectives as clearly as possible.

Haberman ("Behavioral Objectives: Bandwagon or Breakthrough") discusses the significance of the current emphasis on behavioral objectives and states that there are both benefits and limitations in conceiving the goals of school experiences in terms of behavioral objectives.

While the statements of objectives of the school program found in this section are helpful, every school faculty and each teacher should consider the goals that are pertinent for the learners with whom they work. Objectives in a particular setting are related to the social setting, values and needs of that community, the needs for individual development revealed by study of particular learners, and the significance of knowledge for interpretive use both in the local and the larger society.

In addition to objectives and the four bases of the curriculum, other curriculum criteria often mentioned as important are individual differences, balance, continuity, flexibility, and systematic planning.

Each of the curriculum bases—social forces, human development, learning, and knowledge—aids in developing understanding of individual differences and suggests ways of providing for them. "Labels and Fingerprints" discusses individual differences as a curriculum criterion, and examines nine school practices in the light of this criterion.

Balance as a curriculum criterion suggests the need to consider all four of the bases. Wiles ("Seeking Balance ' In The Curriculum") discusses problems in seeking balance in the curriculum and explains its relationship as a criterion to the four curriculum bases.

Continuity as a curriculum criterion is related to the four bases of the curriculum. Miel ("Let Us Develop Children Who Care About Themselves and Others") believes continuity is particularly meaningful when considering the learning of an individual and planning a curriculum for him.

If the curriculum is to provide for individual differences it must have flexibility and be systematically planned.

The process of curriculum planning should include many persons. Hass suggests how teachers, curriculum workers, scholars, parents, and students should work together in curriculum planning.

The editors of Readings In Curriculum placed "Curriculum Criteria" as Section 5 because they hope you will utilize the objectives, bases and criteria discussed here and in Sections 1–4 in thinking about and evaluating the curricula described, and proposals for change, in the subsequent sections on the elementary school, the junior high school, the high school, and the community college.

THE CENTRAL PURPOSE OF
AMERICAN EDUCATION

Educational Policies Commission

In any democracy, education is closely bound to the wishes of the people, but the strength of this bond in America has been unique. The American people have traditionally regarded education as a means for improving themselves and their society. Whenever an objective has been judged desirable for the individual or the society, it has tended to be accepted as a valid concern of the school. The American commitment to the free

From the *NEA Journal*, L, No. 6 (September, 1961), 13-16. Used by permission of the publisher.

society—to individual dignity, to personal liberty, to equality of opportunity—has set the frame in which the American school grew. The basic American value, respect for the individual, has led to one of the major charges which the American people have placed on their schools: to foster that development of individual capacities which will enable each human society—to individual dignity, to personal liberty, to equality of opportunity—has set the frame in which the American school grew. The basic being to become the best person he is capable of becoming.

The schools have been designed also to serve society's needs. The political order depends on responsible participation of individual citizens; hence the schools have been concerned with good citizenship. The economic order depends on ability and willingness to work; hence the schools have taught vocational skills. The general morality depends on choices made by individuals; hence the schools have cultivated moral habits and upright character.

Educational authorities have tended to share and support these broad concepts of educational purposes. Two of the best-known definitions of purposes were formulated by educators in 1918 and 1938. The first definition, by the Commission on the Reorganization of Secondary Education, proposed for the school a set of seven cardinal objectives: health, command of fundamental processes, worthy home membership, vocational competence, effective citizenship, worthy use of leisure, and ethical character. The second definition, by the Educational Policies Commission, developed a number of objectives under four headings: self-realization, human relationship, economic efficiency, and civic responsibility.

The American school must be concerned with all these objectives if it is to serve all of American life. That these are desirable objectives is clear. Yet they place before the school a problem of immense scope, for neither the schools nor the pupils have the time or energy to engage in all the activities which will fully achieve all these goals. Choices among possible activities are inevitable and are constantly being made in and for every school. But there is no consensus regarding a basis for making these choices. The need, therefore, is for a principle which will enable the school to identify its necessary and appropriate contributions to individual development and the needs of society.

Furthermore, education does not cease when the pupil leaves the school. No school fully achieves any pupil's goals in the relatively short time he spends in the classroom. The school seeks rather to equip the pupil to achieve them for himself. Thus the search for a definition of the school's necessary contribution entails an understanding of the ways individuals and societies choose and achieve their goals. Because the school must serve both individuals and the society at large in achieving their goals, and because the principal goal of the American society remains freedom, the requirements of freedom set the frame within which the school can discover the central focus of its own efforts.

FREEDOM OF THE MIND

The freedom which exalts the individual, and by which the worth of the society is judged, has many dimensions. It means freedom from undue governmental restraints; it means equality in political participation. It means the right to earn and own property and decide its disposition. It means equal access to just processes of law. It means the right to worship according to one's conscience.

Institutional safeguards are a necessary condition for freedom. They are not, however, sufficient to make men free. Freedom requires that citizens act responsibly in all ways. It cannot be preserved in a society whose citizens do not value freedom. Thus belief in freedom is essential to maintenance of freedom. The basis of this belief cannot be laid by mere indoctrination in principles of freedom. The ability to recite the values of a free society does not guarantee commitment to those values. Active belief in those values depends on awareness of them and of their role in life. The person who best supports these values is one who has examined them, who understands their function in his life and in the society at large, and who accepts them as worthy of his own support. For such a person these values are consciously held and consciously approved.

The conditions necessary for freedom include the social institutions which protect freedom and the personal commitment which gives it force. Both of these conditions rest.on one condition within the individuals who compose a free society. This is freedom of the mind.

Freedom of the mind is a condition which each individual must develop for himself. In this sense, no man is born free. A free society has the obligation to create circumstances in which all individuals may have opportunity and encouragement to attain freedom of the mind. If this goal is to be achieved, its requirements must be specified.

To be free, a man must be capable of basing his choices and actions on understandings which he himself achieves and on values which he examines for himself. He must be aware of the bases on which he accepts propositions as true. He must understand the values by which he lives, the assumptions on which they rest, and the consequences to which they lead. He must recognize that others may have different values. He must be capable of analyzing the situation in which he finds himself and of developing solutions to the problems before him. He must be able to perceive and understand the events of his life and time and the forces that influence and shape those events. He must recognize and accept the practical limitations which time and circumstance place on his choices. The free man, in short, has a rational grasp of himself, his surroundings, and the relation between them.

He has the freedom to think and choose, and that freedom must have its roots in conditions both within and around the individual. Society's dual role is to guarantee the necessary environment and to develop the necessary individual strength. That individual strength springs from a thinking, aware mind, a mind that possesses the capacity to achieve aesthetic sensitivity and moral responsibility, an enlightened mind. These qualities occur in wide diversity of patterns in different individuals. It is the contention of this essay that central to all of them, nurturing them and being nurtured by them, are man's rational powers.

THE CENTRAL ROLE OF THE RATIONAL POWERS

The cultivated powers of the free mind have always been basic in achieving freedom. The powers of the free mind are many. In addition to the rational powers, there are those which relate to the aesthetic, the moral, and the religious. There is a unique, central role for the rational powers of an individual, however, for upon them depends his ability to achieve his personal goals and to fulfill his obligations to society.

These powers involve the processes of recalling and imagining, classifying and generalizing, comparing and evaluating, analyzing and synthesizing, and deducing and inferring. These processes enable one to apply logic and the available evidence to his ideas, attitudes, and actions, and to pursue better whatever goals he may have.

This is not to say that the rational powers are all of life or all of the mind, but they are the essence of the ability to think. A thinking person is aware that all persons, himself included, are both rational and non-rational, that each person perceives events through the screen of his own personality, and that he must take account of his personality in evaluating his perceptions. The rational processes, moreover, make intelligent choices possible. Through them a person can become aware of the bases of choice in his values and of the circumstances of choice in his environment. Thus they are broadly applicable in life, and they provide a solid basis for competence in all the areas with which the school has traditionally been concerned.

The traditionally accepted obligation of the school to teach the *funda-*

mental processes—an obligation stressed in the 1918 and 1938 statements of educational purposes—is obviously directed toward the development of the ability to think. Each of the school's other traditional objectives can be better achieved as pupils develop this ability and learn to apply it to all the problems that face them.

Health, for example, depends upon a reasoned awareness of the value of mental and physical fitness and of the means by which it may be developed and maintained. Fitness is not merely a function of living and acting; it requires that the individual understand the connection among health, nutrition, activity, and environment, and that he take action to improve his mental and physical condition.

Worthy home membership in the modern age demands substantial knowledge of the role that the home and community play in human development. The person who understands the bases of his own judgments recognizes the home as the source from which most individuals develop most of the standards and values they apply in their lives. He is intelligently aware of the role of emotion in his own life and in the lives of others. His knowledge of the importance of the home environment in the formation of personality enables him to make reasoned judgments about his domestic behavior.

More than ever before, and for an ever-increasing proportion of the population, *vocational competence* requires developed rational capacities The march of technology and science in the modern society progressively eliminates the positions open to low-level talents. The man able to use only his hands is at a growing disadvantage as compared with the man who can also use his head. Today even the simplest use of hands is coming to require the simultaneous employment of the mind.

Effective citizenship is impossible without the ability to think. The good citizen, the one who contributes effectively and responsibly to the management of the public business in a free society, can fill his role only if he is aware of the values of his society. Moreover, the course of events in modern life is such that many of the factors which influence an individual's civic life are increasingly remote from him. His own first-hand experience is no longer an adequate basis for judgment. He must have in addition the intellectual means to study events, to relate his values to them, and to make wise decisions as to his own actions. He must also be skilled in the processes of communication and must understand both the potentialities and the limitations of communication among individuals and groups.

The *worthy use of leisure* is related to the individual's knowledge, understanding, and capacity to choose, from among all the activities to which his time can be devoted, those which contribute to the achievement of his purposes and to the satisfaction of his needs. On these bases, the individual can become aware of the external pressures which compete for his attention, moderate the influence of these pressures, and make wise choices for himself. His recreation, ranging from hobbies to sports to intellectual activity pursued for its own sake, can conform to his own concepts of constructive use of time.

The development of *ethical character* depends upon commitment to values; it depends also upon the ability to reason sensitively and responsibly with respect to those values in specific situations. Character is misunderstood if thought of as mere conformity to standards imposed by external authority. In a free society, ethics, morality, and character have meaning to the extent that they represent affirmative, thoughtful choices by individuals. The ability to make these choices depends on awareness of values and of their role in life. The home and the church begin to shape the child's values long before he goes to school. And a person who grows up in the American society inevitably acquires many values from his daily pattern of living. American children at the age of six, for example, usually have a firm commitment to the concept of fair play. This is a value which relates directly to such broad democratic concepts as justice and human worth and dignity. But the extension of this commitment to these broader democratic values will not occur unless the child becomes aware of its implications for his own behavior, and this awareness demands the ability to think.

A person who understands and appreciates his own values is most likely to act on them. He learns that his values are of great moment for himself, and he can look objectively and sympathetically at the values held by others. Thus, by critical thinking, he can deepen his respect for the importance of values and strengthen his sense of responsibility.

The man who seeks to understand himself understands also that other human beings have much in common with him. His understanding of the possibilities which exist within a human being strengthens his concept of the respect due every man. He recognizes the web which relates him to other men and perceives the necessity for responsible behavior. The person whose rational powers are not well developed can, at best, learn habitual responses and ways of conforming which may insure that he is not a detriment to his society. But, lacking the insight that he might have achieved, his capacity to contribute will inevitably be less than it might have become.

Development of the ability to reason can lead also to dedication to the values which inhere in rationality: commitment to honesty, accuracy, and personal reliability; respect for the intellect and for the intellectual life;

devotion to the expansion of knowledge. A man who thinks can understand the importance of this ability. He is likely to value the rational potentials of mankind as essential to a worthy life.

Thus the rational powers are central to all the other qualities of the human spirit. These powers flourish in a humane and morally responsible context and contribute to the entire personality. The rational powers are to the entire human spirit as the hub is to the wheel.

These powers are indispensable to a full and worthy life. The person in whom—for whatever reason—they are not well developed is increasingly handicapped in modern society. He may be able to satisfy minimal social standards, but he will inevitably lack his full measure of dignity because his incapacity limits his stature to less than he might otherwise attain. Only to the extent that an individual can realize his potentials, especially the development of his ability to think, can he fully achieve for himself the dignity that goes with freedom.

A person with developed rational powers has the means to be aware of all facets of his existence. In this sense he can live to the fullest. He can escape captivity to his emotions and irrational states. He can enrich his emotional life and direct it toward ever higher standards of taste and enjoyment. He can enjoy the political and economic freedoms of the democratic society. He can free himself from the bondage of ignorance and unawareness. He can make of himself a free man.

THE CHANGES IN MAN'S UNDERSTANDING AND POWER

The foregoing analysis of human freedom and review of the central role of the rational powers in enabling a person to achieve his own goals demonstrate the critical importance of developing those powers. Their importance is also demonstrated by an analysis of the great changes in the world.

Many profound changes are occurring in the world today, but there is a fundamental force contributing to all of them. That force is the expanding role accorded in modern life to the rational powers of man. By using these powers to increase his knowledge, man is attempting to solve the riddles of life, space, and time which have long intrigued him. By using these powers to develop sources of new energy and means of communication, he is moving into interplanetary space. By using these powers to make a smaller world and larger weapons, he is creating new needs for international organization and understanding. By using these powers to alleviate disease and poverty, he is lowering death rates and expanding populations. By using these powers to create and use a new technology, he is achieving undreamed affluence, so that in some societies distribution has become a greater problem than production.

While man is using the powers of his mind to solve old riddles, he is creating new ones. Basic assumptions upon which mankind has long operated are being challenged or demolished. The age-old resignation to poverty and inferior status for the masses of humanity is being replaced by a drive for a life of dignity for all. Yet, just as man achieves a higher hope for all mankind, he sees also the opening of a grim age in which expansion of the power to create is matched by a perhaps greater enlargement of the power to destroy.

As man sees his power expand, he is coming to realize that the common sense which he accumulates from his own experience is not a sufficient guide to the understanding of the events in his own life or of the nature of the physical world. And, with combined uneasiness and exultation, he senses that his whole way of looking at life may be challenged in a time when men are returning from space.

Through the ages, man has accepted many kinds of propositions as truth, or at least as bases sufficient for action. Some propositions have been accepted on grounds of superstition; some on grounds of decree, dogma, or custom; some on humanistic, aesthetic, or religious grounds; some on common sense. Today, the role of knowledge derived from rational inquiry is growing. For this there are several reasons.

In the first place, knowledge so derived has proved to be man's most efficient weapon for achieving power over his environment. It prevails because it works.

More than effectiveness, however, is involved. There is high credibility in a proposition which can be arrived at or tested by persons other than those who advance it. Modesty, too, is inherent in rational inquiry, for it is an attempt to free explanations of phenomena and events from subjective preference and human authority, and to subject such explanations to validation through experience. Einstein's concept of the curvature of space cannot be demonstrated to the naked eye and may offend common sense; but persons who cannot apply the mathematics necessary to comprehend the concept can still accept it. They do this, not on Einstein's authority, but on their awareness that he used rational methods to achieve it and that those who possess the ability and facilities have tested its rational consistency and empirical validity.

In recent decades, man has greatly accelerated his systematic efforts to gain insight through rational inquiry. In the physical and biological sciences and in mathematics, where he has most successfully applied these methods, he has in a short time accumulated a vast fund of knowledge so reliable as to give him power he has never before had to understand, to predict, and to act. That is why attempts are constantly being made to apply these methods to additional areas of learning and human behavior.

The rapid increase in man's ability to understand and change the world and himself has resulted from increased application of his powers of thought. These powers have proved to be his most potent resource, and, as such, the likely key to his future.

THE CENTRAL PURPOSE OF THE SCHOOL

The rational powers of the human mind have always been basic in establishing and preserving freedom. In furthering personal and social effectiveness they are becoming more important than ever. They are central to individual dignity, human progress, and national survival.

The individual with developed rational powers can share deeply in the freedoms his society offers and can contribute most to the preservation of those freedoms. At the same time he will have the best chance of understanding and contributing to the great events of his time. And the society which best develops the rational potentials of its people, along with their intuitive and aesthetic capabilities, will have the best chance of flourishing in the future. To help every person develop those powers is therefore a profoundly important objective and one which increases in importance with the passage of time. By pursuing this objective, the school can enhance spiritual and aesthetic values and the other cardinal purposes which it has traditionally served and must continue to serve.

The purpose which runs through and strenghthens all other educational purposes—the common thread of education—is the development of the ability to think. This is the central purpose to which the school must be oriented if it is to accomplish either its traditional tasks or those newly accentuated by recent changes in the world. To say that it is central is not to say that it is the sole purpose or in all circumstances the most important purpose, but that it must be a pervasive concern in the work of the school. Many agencies contribute to achieving educational objectives, but this particular objective will not be generally attained unless the school focuses on it. In this context, therefore, the development of every student's rational powers must be recognized as centrally important.

WHAT IS THE CENTRAL PURPOSE OF
AMERICAN EDUCATION?

Theodore Brameld

I

In its most recent pronouncement, the Educational Policies Commission of the National Education Association undertakes to answer the question posed by the title of this article. The title of its own twenty-one page document is, however, declarative and not interrogative. "The Central Purpose of American Education," we are informed, "is the development of the ability to think. This is the central purpose to which the school must be oriented if it is to accomplish either its traditional tasks or those newly accentuated by recent changes in the world. . . . In this context, therefore, the development of every student's rational powers must be recognized as centrally important."

Is the answer adequate? I do not think so. Despite elaborations and qualifications that reveal the commission's awareness of some of the complexities involved, despite fruitful proposals emanating from the central theme, the document performs a greater disservice than it does a service to American education. It is sometimes illogical. It begs at least one crucial question. It subordinates other questions equally crucial. At a period in our evolution when the role of the schools is being subjected to searching scrutiny, when teachers, administrators, and parents all require vigorous guidance and direction, the Educational Policies Commission issues a statement that, in my judgment, compounds present bewilderments and invites evasion of responsibility.

The question of the central purpose of American education is more imperative than at any moment since our public schools began. The document is to be commended for facing it. But it is not. to be commended for so unsatisfactorily delineating the scope and substance of that purpose.

Such an indictment requires, in all fairness, a more satisfactory delineation. I shall try to suggest that this lies in the crystallization of an overarching purpose that is definitive not only in its integral methods but

From *Phi Delta Kappan,* XLIII, (October, 1961), 9-14. Used by permission of the author and publisher.

in its character as a substantial goal—a purpose that views the obligations of contemporary education in terms, first of all, of our crisis-age, and that places upon us the supremely difficult and radical task of contributing powerfully to the creation of a world civilization.

II

Let us note, meanwhile, some typical elaborations of the document's major argument that education's central duty is to develop the ability to think.

This ability focuses in the individual's "rational powers"—a master term in the discussion. These powers include "the processes of recalling and imagining, classifying and generalizing, comparing and evaluating, analyzing and synthesizing, deducing and inferring. These processes enable one to apply logic and the available evidence to his ideas, attitudes, and actions, and to pursue better whatever goals he may have."

At the same time we are asked not to overlook the importance of other purposes. These are the spokes, as it were, of which rational powers are the hub of the wheel. Thus, time-worn objectives such as learning the fundamental processes of reading, writing, and computation are still necessary, as are health, worthy home membership, vocational competence, effective citizenship, worthy use of leisure, and the development of ethical character. All of these objectives, however, are made effective through rational powers.

Nor does the commission disregard the fact that the human being is not merely a rational animal but a many-faceted one. He possesses, for example, intuitive and esthetic powers, and these too should be enriched by education. But again they are not the central powers. Physical and mental health exemplify the principle that their own maximization is possible only through "reasoned awareness" of their value and of the means required to achieve them.

Properly, attention is likewise paid to the interdependence of rationality and freedom. A man cannot really be free unless he understands the conditions, social and personal, necessary to gain freedom. "The free man, in short, has a rational grasp of himself, his surroundings, and the relation between them."

III

To continue with citations from the general theme is tempting: there is always the likelihood that, in attempting to encapsulate, one has omitted some important emphasis. More practicable is my urgent suggestion that readers of this article obtain copies of the pamphlet from the NEA. Careful reading of the whole will, I hope, indicate that though I have neglected its ramifications I have sought for the policy's essence.

But is this essence clear to the commission itself?

For two reasons, at least, one may wonder. In the first place, just how central is the central purpose supposed to be? That the nourishment of rational powers is not the *exclusive* purpose of education is evident enough. What is not equally evident from the document is the comparative *importance* of others. I have already quoted the statement that the ability to think is "the central purpose to which the school must be oriented." Yet in the foreword we are told that this is "a central outcome of education."

The articles "the" and "a" make a great deal of difference. If I grasp one of the commonest rules of the very logic that we are enjoined to practice, "the" central purpose means that all other purposes are ancillary and secondary, while "a" central purpose means that there must be other purposes that share with rationality the central position. One cannot logically have it both ways at the same time. Yet, in the light of several passages besides the one quoted, we are asked to have it both ways. The commission can ask us, of course, but only at the cost of illogicality.

In the second place, and even more alarmingly, the proposed policy commits the fallacy of begging the pivotal question of what, precisely, is meant by rational powers. True, a plea for intensive research in such areas as the psychology of learning is one of the better features of the document. Yet one is hard put to discover what basic approach to the philosophy of rationality is, in fact, endorsed.

Indeed, at this significant point I find little if any improvement in the final version by comparison with an earlier, preparatory draft which the commission invited a number of us to comment upon. I take the liberty of quoting (with brief modification) from my own comment. It applies equally well here:

You are aware, of course, that any treatment of rational powers presupposes deep-seated assumptions of a philosophic nature. Everyone, or almost everyone, would agree that education should concern itself centrally with the development of rationality, but this agreement is deceptive and dangerous until it is subjected to rigorous analysis of what the term means. For example, Robert M. Hutchins would doubtless welcome many of your statements but he would interpret them according to his own neo-Aristotelian, perennialist conception of what rationality means. Equally, a follower of John Dewey would applaud much of your plea for the development of rational powers, but he would mean by this something radically different from what Hutchins means. For a Dewey progressivist, rational powers at their best are equated with intelligent action manifested in the processes of scientific inquiry. For a Hutchins perennialist, rational powers at their best are equated with the capacity to conceive and define self-evident principles. All of these terms presuppose, of course, a whole body of assumptions about the nature of human nature and thought. And though it is impossible in your brief document to delineate them in detail, I do not think you can avoid making perfectly clear that you are not using the term rational powers so ambiguously as to invite totally conflicting interpretations.

IV

Thus far we have been confined primarily to questions of logic. Turn now to two further questions, both of them stemming from a concern that the new pronouncement is overweighted with the methodological purpose of critical thinking and underweighted with more substantial purposes. That is to say, it is weakened by much more preoccupation with how to develop the rational processes essential to a sound education than it is with the graphic content of personal and cultural ends or goals—ends or goals for the achievement of which these processes are predominantly means.

To begin with, where in the entire statement are we challenged to cope thoroughly with such tremendous institutional and cultural alternatives as nationalism and internationalism, capitalism and communism, war and peace, ethnocentrism and cosmopolitanism? Where are we informed that the schools of America share a serious obligation to examine and compare with scrupulous care the precise institutional arrangements which these and other alternatives demand? One or two passages, to be sure, hint at their importance and even imply preferences. In largest part, however, the reader's attention is drawn to the exercise of rational processes which, it is alleged, lead inevitably to the study of such issues.

Yet, even assuming for the moment that rationality is clearly defined (which it actually is not), what guarantee do we have that the schools will then provide opportunity for searching, sustained analysis of the great political, economic, moral, and religious issues of our time? It is very well to hope that they will do so. But the range of opportunities to practice rationality is sufficiently vast (consider only the field of mathematics) to mitigate, if anything, against the possibility. We are told, and rightly so, that the schools cannot do everything. Thus, whether they will choose to provide time and resources for the *central* study of the moral and cultural dilemmas with which humanity is now beset depends, certainly in part, upon whether a policy-formulating body of the stature of the commission first chooses to press with candor, specificity, and vigor for such inclusion. It does not do so in this document.

The other question follows. Just as the commission's stress is much less upon concrete institutional issues than upon the instrumentalities of reason through which they might be raised, so too is its stress much less upon tangible choices among values—in other words, upon the qualitative character of normative commitments—than upon the requirement to practice rationality in approaching these choices. The point becomes clearer from another excerpt:

> The development of *ethical character* depends upon commitment to values; it depends also upon the ability to reason sensitively and responsibly with respect to those values in specific situations. . . . In a free society, ethics, morality, and character have meaning to the extent that they represent affirmative, thoughtful choices by individuals. The ability to make these choices depends on awareness of values and of their role in life.

As far as it goes, this is an admirable statement. It is also incomplete. To urge students and teachers to achieve rationally grounded commitment to values, yet not to demonstrate the act of such commitment by at least one or two bold and positive choices avoids the very ethical responsibility demanded of others. The commission, in brief, appears unwilling to dramatize an attempt to practice its own canons of rationality—to carry through the mandate handed to the rest of us.

To argue that the policy does carry through by its commitment to freedom is not a persuasive answer. For freedom, like rationality, is not necessarily, as such, a qualitative or substantial value. It becomes so, as Bronislaw Malinowski points out in his *Freedom and Civilization,* only when and if it is embodied in the cultural meanings of real people—above all, in their personal and public goals and then spelled out in institutional charters that select among alternatives in definite time and place.

Nor is it enough to be reminded, as the document does, of the two lists of qualitative purposes formulated by earlier educational commissions—lists which, when not innocuous, almost totally fail to anticipate the global transformations and unprecedented obligations resulting from them that have occurred in the quarter-century since the last cited list was published. Yet, nowhere does the current statement explicitly and unequivocally commit itself to a single new cultural goal beyond those of the 1918 and 1938 pronouncements. At most, under the heading, "The changes in man's understanding and power," it suggests that some new goals, thanks largely to rational powers, are already emerging. Nevertheless, the commission's own major commitment remains confined to the circular, safe, and often ambiguous equation of rationality-and-freedom.

V

The preceding questions raise, I readily admit, still others of an intricate nature about the legitimate role of education in a democracy. We have often heard that the prerogatives of the public-school classroom do not include the right to teach commitments about social institutions or even about values—that its function, rather, is limited to reflective inquiry into all of them. To allow more than this, it is sometimes argued, is to open the door to indoctrination and other iniquities which have weakened and even prostituted the educative process in authoritarian cultures.

As has also been pointed out, however, American education in fact continually commits itself to what it does and does not regard as the proper value orientation to be taught to our children. Numerous research studies, going back considerably farther than Howard K. Beale's *Are American Teachers Free?*, support his own largely negative answer and prove that a vast amount of indoctrination continually occurs in behalf of vested economic interests, political and patriotic pressure groups, religious sects, and other segments of community life which manifest very strong commitments.

Although it is curious that even in so brief a pamphlet almost no attention is paid to the invasions of academic freedom that such commitments often perpetrate, my point is not to suggest that the commission condones them. On the contrary, it surely does not. My point is more fundamental—that education conceived in an anthropological sense as the pivotal transmitter and innovator of cultural evolution, is forever involved in teaching and learning both the personal and institutional norms of the communities it serves. Aside from the question, at the moment, of which norms are desirable and which are not, education, it is safe to say, has never been and will never be clearly understood so long as its purpose is framed primarily in methodological terms. Rather, education has always been and will very likely always be, by the same token, saturated with implicit and explicit commitments to social institutions, to commensurate values, and to the substantial character that both of these acquire.

From this viewpoint, the key issue is not whether the central purpose of American education is to achieve normative commitments; in any case education invariably does so. Nor is that issue whether education shall concern itself profoundly with the enlargement of rational powers; how many citizens would care to reject such a purpose? The key issue, rather, is whether these powers shall be used to achieve values and institutions appropriate to an age undergoing, as ours is undergoing, lightning-like change—values and institutions that represent the widest, deepest aspirations of the greatest number of human beings everywhere on earth.

I have contended that, though the document pleads with us to effect "affirmative, thoughtful choices," it does not itself see fit to provide a model for them. I have not, however, thus far ventured to suggest any reasons for its hesitation. Here once more the problem is complex, and one cannot pretend to offer more than a hypothesis: I believe that the commission, as a sensitive educational barometer of the American cultural climate, has yielded, knowingly or not, to much the same mood of caution and complacency that for some years has been far more pervasive of this climate than any mood of moral audacity and social indignation. As the drama critic, Howard Taubman, recently observed in *The New York Times,* the American theater today suffers from a paucity of vital and controversial themes; its stages are cluttered with trivia. And just as the theater avoids such themes, so now and for perhaps culturally similar reasons does much of our education.

It was by no means always so. For example, in the 1930's and early 1940's, when Broadway (as Taubman also reminds us) was bursting with powerful dramas and prodigious themes, more than a little of the same kinds of cultural excitement reached into our schools. Some of it spread from the world's foremost center of professional education: Columbia's Teachers College. Some, in the form of grassroots experimentation, came directly out of local communities. And some was generated by publications of the Educational Policies Commission itself—for example, *Learning the Ways of Democracy* (1940) and *Education for All American Youth* (1944).

I suggest to some enterprising doctoral candidate in education that, for his thesis, he critically compare the range and content of the central commitments radiating from documents such as these with documents published by the commission in the past dozen or so years. He will find, I dare to predict, that a close correlation can be established between the swing toward conformity and conventionality in American life as a whole and the equivocal tone of several recent pronouncements. I point to only one of these published before the present statement: *Public Education and the Future of America* (1955).

And, as an interesting footnote, our candidate might also consider the relevance for his thesis of the *Harper's* article: "Teachers College: Extinct Volcano?"

VI

Yet, in one sense, the reasons that might help to explain such retreats from educational leadership are also reasons for hoping that the malaise I have so briefly diagnosed is temporary and curable. For, if and as the American culture begins to show less insecurity and greater readiness to pioneer again, we may be reasonably sure that such arts as the theater and such avenues of exploration as the school will react in comparable ways.

Are there signals that these shifts are already under way? In another publication I have tried to show that there are—the gradual decline of complacency among college students being but one instance. Far more significant is the groping yet ever-widening realization that either American civilization joins forces with other civilizations—including those of under-privileged peoples—or no civilization at all can very long survive.

These and other signals point, in turn, to the search in a number of countries for fresh and magnetic educational policies that could supersede our present vacillations. I venture to suggest three requirements as a minimum for such policies, all of them controversial, all obviously needing more thorough treatment than is possible here.

First, if marked improvement of rational powers is to be among the central purposes of education, as it certainly should be, we shall have to clarify the meaning of these powers, to take sides among various meanings, and thus to avoid further begging of the question. In this connection, since it still applies, I should like to quote further (again with slight amendment) from my comment submitted to the commission concerning an earlier draft:

> It is my view, and certainly that of the main stream of thinking in the Educational Policies Commission in past years, that the more fruitful and modern conception of rational powers has centered in the experimentalist orientation rather than in the neo-Aristotelian orientation reflected by Hutchins. If so, however, then it would be a cause of profound concern, if your forthcoming document were to reveal a shift, perhaps induced by partly unconscious pressures from outside, away from this main stream. In a sense, such a shift could mean a tragic setback, for the experimentalist orientation has far from succeeded in establishing itself as the dominant one. On the contrary, progress has been very slow and irregular. A vast amount of spadework and experimentation in our schools is yet to be done before we could claim that this orientation is commonly understood and practiced. For these reasons, I am disturbed that the overall impression left by your document, insofar as it fails to take a clearcut stand in its philosophy of rationality, is one of comfort to the anti-experimentalist orientation toward the meaning of rational powers.

Second, the dilemma mentioned above—namely, whether the advocacy of definite, qualitative purposes does not violate the tenets of reflective inquiry and non-indoctrination—should be reconsidered and resolved. The path to solution lies, on the one hand, in perceiving that substantial values and concrete social commitments are in any case inexplicable from education as a cultural institution. It lies, on the other hand, in the emergence of newly cooperative processes of teaching and learning that encourage students to reach group decisions and thus to choose deliberately and consciously from among the crucial normative options confronting our time.

These processes are completely antithetical to indoctrination. They require searching examination of the relevant evidence for and against every economic, political, moral, or other proposal. They require frank, un-inhibited communication about every aspect of all proposals. They require the right of minority dissent and respect for such dissent. They require patient consideration of the strategies needed to achieve any proposal and, wherever practicable, opportunity by students to engage in active imple-mentation. Finally, they require diligent effort to attain as wide a consensus about the desirability or undesirability of each proposal as evidence, communication, testing, and minority dissent can possibly provide.

The commission, in urging research into the theory and practice of rationality, could profitably support research in the multidimensional processes here suggested. They are, I believe, not only in accordance with hypotheses now influential in fields such as psychiatry, holding that man as a goal-seeking animal must, to be healthy, commit himself to goals that he believes in zealously enough to motivate his constant seeking of them; they are compatible also with the psychological bases of democratic decision-making in the wider community.

Third, the needed new policies should state as directly and clearly as language allows that, among the goals to be sought by education, one above all is paramount. This is the goal of a world civilization. Its full significance should be stated both in negative terms of the alternative—probable death to the human race—and in positive terms of the technologi-cal revolutions that have, for the first time, made a world civilization both workable and imperative.

Issues that arise in the course of examining the import of this central purpose are, of course, intricate. The structure and operation of enforce-able world government; anthropological questions of similarities and dif-ferences among the cooperating cultures; the crosscultural role of the arts, religions, sciences, and other creative achievements of highly diverse peoples; the gigantic obstacles that impede progress toward the goal—these are but exemplary issues. To a tragic extent they are also neglected by the schools of today. Yet they invite a plenitude of knowledge already available or fast developing—knowledge only waiting to be channelled into the curriculum at virtually every level and in virtually every subject.

If the objection is raised that the American people are not ready to accept such a purpose as this, one may ask whether they were ready, say in 1944, to accept the stirring proposals to educate all American youth. The Educational Policies Commission, as I understand its history, has not operated from the premise that its major task is to reinforce the school's transmissive cultural role. Rather, its task has been in much greater measure to lift the sights of the educational profession toward its innovative role.

The paramount innovation that is now required is not, however, chiefly intellectual in its derivation. It stems directly from the crisis that now threatens the survival of mankind. But equally it stems from a thrilling opportunity to share in the creation of a new epoch by and for mankind. In placing this central purpose before the schools of America, the commission need not and should not expect all of the profession to accept it. In accordance with the principles of consensus-building, any teacher or any student should feel wholly free to oppose the goal of a world civilization. At the same time he should be expected, as a partner in the enterprise of free education, to engage in full, open study of both pro's and con's, looking toward reconsideration of whatever judgments he may earlier have held.

The same rule applies equally, of course, to commitments of the commission itself. These commitments too, not being eternal or absolute, are subject to analysis, to improvement, even to repudiation by the same processes of cooperative study. Meanwhile, however, attainment of the goal of a world civilization should be enunciated as the first of all educational goals. And the highest powers of reason that education can possibly develop should be fostered and disciplined in behalf of its attainment.

CURRICULUM DEVELOPMENT WITH A PURPOSE

Robert S. Fox

Practical-minded educators are concerned that their investment of time and energy in the curriculum-improvement process be as rewarding as possible; that curriculum activities "pay off." Not only are they genuinely interested in seeing that the curriculum does, in fact, get "improved," but they seek evidence that the many precious hours during the school week and year devoted to committee work, discussions, creative thinking, writing, and trial of new procedures and materials essential to the curriculum-improvement enterprise. are productive hours. Such willingness to examine critically the traditional approaches to improvement of the school's instructional program is commendable and can lead to more purposeful and productive efforts.

In this context, the question is raised about the need to devote time to the clarification of values and the identification of purposes. Statements of objectives look nice on paper—they give respectability to a curriculum plan that is to be shared with others—but of what use are they? Don't teachers go ahead and do what they want to do, anyway? Is it not true that the realities of the situation take over when a proposed curriculum change is implemented at the classroom level? Is devoting time to the development of statements of purpose merely delaying attack on the more practical problems of curriculum change?

The thesis of this article is that values are the basic determiners of action—and purposes are statements of values in terms of the specifics of the problem being confronted. What the individual teacher does with the pupils in his classroom, what the superintendent does in supporting or resisting curriculum modifications, what the school-board member does in proposing new. emphases or a revival of the old—all are results of those values to which each is committed. These may be explicit, open to examination by others, or they may be implicit in the individual's actions.

From *Theory Into Practice*, I, No. 4 (October, 1962), 202–207. Used by permission of the author and publisher.

THE ROLE OF VALUES IN CURRICULUM IMPROVEMENT

Curriculum theorists identify sources of the curriculum. They point to the needs of the society, the nature of learning and of child development, and the disciplines of organized knowledge. Some see the basic problem of curriculum improvement as that of determining the amount of emphasis to be given to one or another of these sources; others would strive to integrate the three, finding them not incompatible, but essential, aspects of a total process—the warp and woof of the curriculum fabric.[1] However these three foundations for the curriculum may be related, they do provide guidelines for determining how the curriculum shall be organized, for deciding upon the appropriate content, for selecting teaching methods, and for obtaining instructional materials.

This all sounds very logical and scientific. It is, until we begin to examine the results of the process and discover the wide range of practice in the classroom. Something is amiss! Mackenzie suggests that we have addressed ourselves to the question, "What *should be* the sources of the curriculum?" rather than "What *are* the sources of the curriculum?" (italics added). The real sources, he says, are the individuals and groups that exercise influence over the curriculum—the teachers and educationists, students, boards of education and other legal agencies, and various individuals and organizations from the community at large. These, through their power to influence practices and to make decisions which affect what is done in the classroom, are the sources that make a difference.[2]

Neither of the foregoing analyses seems to describe the matter completely. Is it not possible the real difficulty is that the people who are in positions to have some influence on the curriculum are operating in terms of value systems that condition the use they make of the available resources? Principles of learning, analysis of the society and the community, the disciplines of subject areas—these are resources that can be used or discarded; or more frequently, used in part, to the extent that they support the values held. Figure 1 illustrates some of these relationships.

---

[1] *What Are the Sources of the Curriculum? A Symposium.* Washington, D.C.: Association for Supervision and Curriculum Development, National Education Association, 1962.

[2] Mackenzie, Gordon N. "Sources and Process in Curriculum Development," *ibid.,* p. 72.

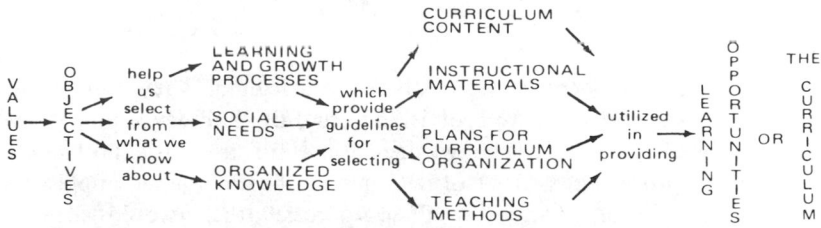

FIGURE 1. The Sources of Curriculum Development

Participants (they may be you or I) in the curriculum-improvement process may make use of what is known about effective motivation of the learner if it fits the values they are trying to implement. Otherwise they will select other, less effective ways to motivate. For example, it is known that if a child is engaged in solving a problem that is real to him, his motivation is high and his learning efficient. But if we deem it important for the child to learn something which does not make sense to him, we may "require" it, or grade him on it, or tell him that it's good for him. Similarly, the person interested in promoting "transference of the cultural heritage" may give close attention to research on the most efficient ways of committing a body of knowledge to memory, overlooking the research on rate of forgetting. The person who puts a high value on an intensely nationalistic kind of patriotism places considerable emphasis on knowing the rules for displaying the American flag, but overlooks the importance of young people being familiar with the functions and activities of the United Nations' Security Council.

Not only do one's values influence the choice of basic principles or guidelines, but they are involved at the level of implementation. Decisions regarding teaching methods, the design of learning experiences, or instructional materials can be and are circumvented by the classroom teacher who finds his own values and objectives inconsistent with these resources. Since "curriculum" ultimately consists of the actual learning experiences in which the pupils are engaged, the classroom teacher has the "last word," and his values may prove to be the most influential of all.

Describing this state of affairs is not to imply that it is wholly undesirable. However, the curriculum-development process will be facilitated if persons will *specify their values and objectives as clearly as possible,* making them genuinely visible. The large number and variety of persons concerned with and involved in curriculum improvement can then *work toward some mutually acceptable objectives.*

WHAT VALUES?

It is not the purpose of this article to propose an ideal system of values for use in curriculum-building. Nor is it feasible to compile a listing of all possible values which might be drawn upon. It may be helpful, however, to illustrate the complexity of the problem of clearly identifying values by examining a commonly accepted objective: An important function of the school is the intellectual development of the child.[3]

Few persons would quarrel with the general proposition. But just what values underlie this objective as it is understood by various people? Unquestionably for different people it carries grossly different implications. By way of illustration, I have suggested five general positions that might be taken toward the proposition that the job of the school is to promote the intellectual development of the child. These statements are not intended to represent the views of extremists, but of reasonably well-informed lay and professional people.

Position 1. The primary responsibility of the school is intellectual development. Intellectual development is conceived as mastery of subject-matter, and education should be concerned primarily with helping the learner develop a store of information, skills, and values which may be useful to him at some later time. An individual holding these values may select from the available resources on the learning process the point of view that the intellect is an independent and highly important "faculty" to be trained through exercise. He may emphasize the "inner logic" of the subject-matter within the various disciplines, and consequently propose a fairly rigid sequence of curriculum content.

Position 2. Again, the primary responsibility of the school is intellectual development, but here intellectual development is conceived as being directed toward creative problem-solving—the use of education as a tool, the fostering of curiosity, experimentation, and the reorganization of ideas. The person taking this position may have the psychological orientation of the behaviorist. He may, because of his view of the central needs of the society, advocate that the schools not waste valuable time on the practical

---

[3]Further amplification of this illustration may be found in the 1961 Yearbook of the Association for Supervision and Curriculum Development—Fox, Robert S. "Balance and the Problem of Purpose in Education," *Balance in the Curriculum.* Washington, D.C.: National Education Association, 1961, pp. 49–58.

arts, the development of social skills, or problems of personal adjustment. He may support a highly selective system of education, similar to that of some European countries, where those few pupils who possess superior academic aptitude are groomed for increasingly higher levels of intellectual achievement, while dropouts are channeled into the labor force.

Position 3. Intellectual development is the primary responsibility of the school; however, since the individual is an integrated organism, his intellectual development is but one part of his total growth. Emotional health, personal-social adjustment, group-process skills, and physical vitality all contribute to and are essential to intellectual effectiveness. The society requires that all of the talents of each of its citizens be fully developed. In working toward this objective, force field theory and Gestalt psychology are useful conceptual tools. A curriculum framework should be sufficiently flexible to provide for interrelationship of subject-matter and for participation of the learner in planning curriculum activities.

Position 4. All areas of development are important in and of themselves—schools should educate for life. Students need all-around development —social, emotional, intellectual, and physical. The person who implements this value position may draw heavily upon the principles of child growth and development. The public schools should work co-operatively with all agencies in the society which are concerned with the socialization of the child—the church, the family, and youth-serving organizations. Both teacher and students should have maximum opportunity for planning and implementing a curriculum designed to meet pertinent needs and concerns of the particular group. Instructional materials should be provided in great breadth and depth.

Position 5. The academic emphasis is appropriate to only a small portion of the student body. For many, general problems of life, particularly the immediate, practical, personal needs of the pupil are the appropriate subject-matter. Vocational skills are of primary importance; intelligence is developed and utilized in relation to these practical problems of living. There should be maximum utilization of community resources, including field projects, co-operative work assignments and internships. The curriculum structure should have enough flexibility to allow the program to be adapted to the particular needs of each pupil.

HOW ARE VALUES TO BE UTILIZED?

This complexity of value orientation in respect to an objective that seems to be commonly accepted points to a need for examining the process through which objectives in curriculum are identified and decided upon. Four suggestions follow:

1. Recognize the need for looking beyond the simple statements of purpose presented by those who propose curriculum modifications. The statements appearing in curriculum handbooks, in descriptions of new course plans, and in proposals for the use of programed learning materials, are undoubtedly sincere, but seldom reflect clearly the underlying values held by the proposer.

2. Give careful attention to specifying objectives and their underlying values as an essential part of the curriculum-improvement process. More is involved than merely getting statements down on paper. Group discussion, face-to-face interaction in a setting conducive to frank expression of ideas, may be essential.

3. Test your understanding of the proposed objectives by exploring some of the means-ends relationships. Work through the implications of the proposal in terms of learning principles, social philosophy, and relationships to the disciplines of organized fields of knowledge. Explore the meaning of the objectives when translated into curriculum content or instructional materials. What kinds of teaching methods are implied? Such an exploration may serve to clarify the true objectives.

4. Provide opportunities for interaction among the various individuals and groups concerned about the curriculum so that they may explore problems of values; achieve understanding of the various positions held; and, to the extent required by the nature of the program being considered, arrive at some consensus or decision.

This kind of interaction has been described as a political process.[4] Essentially, this is what it must be, for differences in values frequently may not be resolved by compromise or by seeking additional facts. Such differences reflect the basic postures of individuals or groups toward life and the world as they see it. Wiser curriculum decisions will be made if individuals are provided opportunity for intelligent examination of values and exploration of their implications for the classroom.

[4]See Mackenzie, "Sources and Process in Curriculum Development," *op. cit.,* pp. 76–78.

BEHAVIORAL OBJECTIVES:
BANDWAGON OR BREAKTHROUGH

Martin Haberman

Fads in curriculum development are not unlike those in the world of fashion: they emerge and are quickly in and out. Unlike clothes which can be given away, however, curriculum changes are often pushed into an already bulging school program. Revisions that are poorly conceived may be taught to youngsters long after the "mod" curriculum developers are back in longer skirts.

Before joining or pooh-poohing the behavioral objective approach, it is necessary to consider what it is and to lay open some of the common arguments raised for and against this process of curriculum development. Behavioral objectives are one means of conceiving the long-term goals of school experiences, as well as the purposes of the day-to-day instruction which lead to these ultimate goals. They are stated in a form that requires a specification of what the pupils are to do, under what conditions, and how such behavior will be evaluated. By learning specific behaviors, students are moved through a sequence of ever-increasing difficulty and abstraction that culminates in the achievement of the major generalizations within a particular established discipline. Obviously, behavioral objectives are a way of thinking and cannot be intrinsically good or bad. What makes them desirable or not is their applications. Following are some of the values and limitations of using this approach.

BENEFITS

Teachers and pupils have clear purposes. When people know what to do and what is expected of them, they do better. The teacher's planning is facilitated when he can specify his intentions in terms of pupil behavior, e.g., the child will add three columns correctly in three ways. Pupils are able to join in evaluation when criteria are open and demonstrable, e.g., Did I get the right answer? Did I do it a different way each time?

From *The Journal of Teacher Education*, XIX, No. 1 (Spring, 1968), 91-94. Used by permission of the author and publisher.

Broad content is broken down into manageable, meaningful pieces. Global, long-term goals are a source of guilt rather than direction for many teachers. Appreciating literature is a desirable objective, but of little value as a guide for planning what to do from 10:10 to 10:25 on Tuesdays. Assuming that one part of the grand goal of appreciation is voluntarily to choose to read when given several appealing alternatives, the teacher can now frame a specific objective for a given time period: the child will select a book and read; he will do this with increasing frequency for longer periods.

Organizing content into sequences and hierarchies is facilitated. As teachers use this approach, they will learn more about which abilities lead to others and about the relative difficulty of various learnings. At present there is little, if any, justification for the order in which youngsters are offered various kinds of content. What are the components of a particular piece of knowledge? What does the pupil have to know before he can do this? The major generalization, i.e., the basic processes as well as the key concepts, are broken down into their components. The most efficient, logical steps for learning these components are then traced back to the individual lesson. The exclusion of nonbehavioral objectives makes this approach plausible.

Evaluation is simplified. In most cases it becomes self-evident. Could he do it, or couldn't he? Grades and global subjective judgments are replaced by checklists next to specific behaviors. Can the pupil add two columns and exchange correctly? Can he skip? Can he identify the mammals? Can he reproduce a tone? Can he end the story in a different way from the author's?

Teacher training is facilitated. Teachers can practice and become expert in putting their subject matter into behavioral expectations for their pupils. In essence, their in-service training becomes planning to teach their own classes specific behavioral objectives. The search for "ideal" methods is abandoned, and teachers have the much simpler job of identifying particular strategies for moving particular pupils to demonstrate particular objectives.

Selection of materials is clarified. The result of knowing precisely what youngsters are to do leads to control in the selection of materials, equipment and the management of resources generally. Television, programed learning, language laboratories, or anything else is easily evaluated in terms of whether it will move pupils to a particular objective more effectively than some other instrumentality. Teachers and educators, armed by knowing specifically what they want to accomplish, play the machines rather than have the machines play them.

Research and planning become part of the mainstream of the educative process. Finding the best means of achieving clear goals is the way to make use of researchers. Currently, educators are asking experts in design and evaluation the wrong questions, e.g., What should be the school's purposes and direction? Using the behavioral approach, educators will more readily define their own goals and then ask researchers more fruitful questions, e.g., What are the most efficient means of achieving the goals we have already identified?

LIMITATIONS

The most powerful element in the process of schooling is social interaction, not content. Teachers are accused by technologists in the behavioral objective area of not being able to think in behavioral terms. This is not true! Teachers think in behavioral terms constantly as they face the problem of how to get Joey Franklin to sit down, not to disturb his neighbor, and to complete a particular assignment. Experts who limit their thinking to developing behavioral objectives in terms of content rather than dealing with the range of youngsters' classroom behavior are reserving the easiest job for themselves. Teachers believe that these experts don't have useful suggestions, let alone answers, for their already highly clarified and specific behavioral goals. Teachers express the belief that the forms of living behavior demonstrated by pupils take precedence and pervade the instructional and learning behaviors.

The interrelations of content are internal as well as external. Pupils organize content psychologically as well as logically. Though scope, sequence, and hierarchy seem to make sense, people don't learn that way. The three-year-old who learns that he must break candy into two equal parts before sharing with his friend has learned a basic concept of division long before he has learned to subtract. The best that can be said about the ordering of any content is that the curriculum developers have some rationale; it is naïve to believe that this is the best or only order for learning the material.

Skills become overemphasized—generalizations are undervalued. Critics of the behavioral objective approach point to the obvious predisposition to value those aspects of content that can most easily be put into behavioral terms. Skills of notation will take precedence over the difficult job of finding demonstrations of musical appreciation, techniques of computing will be emphasized at the expense of reaching for new or untried applications of a mathematical idea, remembering the names of characters will be easier to teach than offering personal interpretations and securing reactions to them. In essence, this criticism is that the sum equals more than its discrete parts—even when those parts are more easily cast into behavioral terms.

All content does not fit the behavioral approach. The danger of emphasizing the technical over the general aspects of a discipline has a curriculum counterpart: subjects that are more easily framed in behavioral terms can take precedence over those that are more difficult. Not only will the technicalities of a subject take precedence over the basic and real meanings but one discipline can take precedence over another. Consider the likelihood that art will be valued equally with math in a behaviorally oriented curriculum.

Experts become more critical than teachers and children in the decision-making process. Neither child development nor the development of instructional know-how can have more than an instrumental effect on curriculum. What is to be learned can be developed by experts with no personal experience in schools or with children. Such a process is inimical to the basic nature of the process of curriculum development; there are things which *should* be done in school that lie beyond the range of behavior capable of conception in a discipline of knowledge. These behaviors derive from the nature of children, the needs of teachers, and the interaction between these groups.

This limited discussion has touched on some of the common issues related to the behavioral objectives approach to curriculum development. They cannot be ignored and must be contended with, since this approach promises to be the major vehicle for revising curriculum in the future.

LABELS AND FINGERPRINTS

The individual is as unique as his fingerprints. Even a label cannot obscure his individuality. He may be a Kansan or a Californian, but these names do not describe him. They merely sort him. So it is with all labels. But the fingerprint is unmistakably individual—always symbolic of the uniqueness of every personality.

Used by permission of the American Association of School Administrators, National Education Association, Washington, D. C. (not dated). Joint statement issued by AASA, ASCD, NASSP, DESP, and DRE.

Basically, life is individual. A child is born, grows up, goes to school, makes a living, marries, finds a house or apartment, rears his children, gradually gets older, and, when the time comes, dies. All along, the erstwhile child thinks, talks, eats, sleeps; represents himself to the other people in the world, and struggles with his environment.

How does man or woman go through all these experiences of life? As an individual? By himself? Of course. The universe insists that a child, himself, be born, and a man, himself, die. No one can inhabit his body; no one can live and die for him.

Now what has all this to do with education? If values are kept straight, it has everything, it has everything to do with it. And that is what "Labels and Fingerprints" is about.

The signs today are ominous. The heritage that America has so well guarded, full personal development in ways most suited to each man's nature—this heritage now is threatened; and when the individual is threatened, our democratic society is in danger. The danger becomes more acute when the teaching profession is under pressure from many directions to bypass its obligations to the individual child, or when it deserts its own responsibility and high purpose.

Are we retreating from that ideal which has made American citizenship the envy of much of the world? Are we drifting away from making the dignity and inherent worth of the individual person pre-eminent among our values?

It is not in the might of the military, the productivity of industry, or the efficiency of transportation and communication that the true greatness of America lies. Rather, it is in the high esteem accorded the individual personality. Here, indeed, is our greatest contribution to men everywhere, and here is America's greatest secret weapon. Our philosophy of government from its very beginning, our deepest convictions, and our highest ideals have sought to clothe the individual with a sense of dignity, to recognize his potentialities, to unloose his creative powers, and to stimulate his initiative. It was on this platform that Jefferson, Adams, Lincoln, and Wilson rose to greatness.

And yet, despite these fundamental concepts and ideas, we seem to be drifting toward impersonality in almost every sphere of our culture. Individuality is tending to be submerged in gigantic organizations, in chain-belt production, in monolithic economic enterprise, and in the complex cultural interdependencies of our society.

Caught in this cultural drift, the schools too are veering toward impersonal solutions to vital educational problems. Mass grouping, standard curriculums, standard examinations, standard test scores, and standardized institutions are squeezing individuals into a common mold. Standard school products are demanded by short-sighted and frightened adults and frequently accepted by school boards and teachers. With an eye to masses rather than to individuals, the schools are departing from their unique historic character by manipulating pupils and teachers into organizational patterns and by leaning on administrative and mechanical devices that tend to destroy the very quality which has made them great. All this is becoming acceptable practice in spite of the commitment to the individual so clearly and forcibly avowed by the founders of this government.

Now let's look at the child when he first enters a schoolroom. The excitement and anticipation each child brings to the day he begins his formal education may well be the major common trait that he shares with the six-year-olds he finds in his first-grade class—an organized, formal learning group. Because he is in a group of six-year-olds, he acquires some labels that would make it seem he is like the others. He is tagged "a first-grader," "a pupil in Miss Smith's room"; described as a child who likes books, a child who does not like books, a wiggly, squirming six-year-old; a bright child, a slow child; a quiet, solemn child. He reads well, or he fails to read well; so he becomes a member of a blue-bird or red-bird or yellow-bird group. He plays well with other children, or he does not; he follows instructions, or he does not. He doesn't act like the others; he cannot do what some of them can do, just as some of them cannot do what he can do. So judgments are made and labels are given. As the child is labeled, so does he begin to think of himself; he begins to feel he must at least try to be like others in groups he is assigned to by his various labels—labels which describe what is expected of him.

Yet, he is as different as his fingerprints. And he has the American right to be different—the right to be individual—in spite of all labels, groupings, and attempts that have the effect of stamping him as being like all others of his age.

Each child or youth coming to school expects the education that will be best for him, the education that will enable him to continue to grow, develop, and learn in his own way. And it is true that learning for each child is a personal, individual experience. He comes to grips with subject matter in terms of his own physical, social, emotional characteristics. These characteristics are the ones that make him the person he is at grade one or grade twelve and at all the grades between.

Respect for all this, and more, is the cherished birthright of the American child. The right to be different; the right to be alone at certain times; not part of any group; and the right of an individual to pursue his own interests: these are evidences of respect for the worth of the individual.

How to accept and develop the differences among individuals is one of the great and persisting problems facing school people—teachers, administrators, and all who share a responsibility for teaching. It is easy to drift toward impersonal and mass solutions. Of all the mistakes we might make, the worst, in the long run, would be to alienate or ignore the individual. In most aspects of American life, the trend of the times is toward impersonality. Schools reflect this direction. Down this road toward impersonality are mass measures to care for the increasing number of learners. Also, down this road lies the challenge to an American's greatest right; his right to be an individual, to be himself.

When we talk of education for all the children of all the people, we have to keep in mind that unique individuals comprise the group. Sometimes we camouflage the issue by setting the individual need against the national need in our debates. If we fail to realize that this is a false antithesis, we tend to accept the massive solutions to educational problems, which are the most accessible ones. Problems of size and cost lend themselves to impersonal solutions which too often ignore the needs of the individual. This is what has been happening, and *it is not good enough* for the sixties. The drift must be halted.

The problem of numbers of students has been approached in many ways. We are convinced that the problem is not primarily one of techniques, but of philosophy. It is how to avoid losing the individual in the mass. We must prepare ourselves to find solutions that deal with students, not a million at a time, not hundreds in one class at a time, not even twenty or twenty-five in one class at one time, but *one at a time*. Every teacher knows well that learning takes place *one learner at a time*. The teacher plans lessons and learning experiences, provides materials to evoke learning; yet what ultimately counts most is what the individual learner makes of what is presented. The real quality of a learning experience, a single lesson, is not inherent in the material to be learned or in what the teacher expects will be learned. It inheres in the way the individual child or youth comes to grips with the material—selecting with the help of the teacher what is significant for him in terms of his own background, capacity, attitude, and interest. This is an individual problem, not a mass problem, and must have solutions in terms of each learner, not in terms of masses.

Who should learn *what* is a problem demanding new answers. Much more is involved than the grade placement of subjects, or some kind of ability grouping, or electives in the high schools. How can subject matter be organized and paced so that it will "come alive" for individuals of widely varying potentialities? To conceive of certain subject matter simply as appropriate for college-bound students, and less appropriate for all other students, is unimaginative and impractical. Decisions about who should learn what should be reached through the cooperation of teachers, administrators, curriculum specialists, and college professors in selecting the knowledge of most worth in specific fields of learning, and should be sought in the relationship between the teacher, the subject, and the individual student at a given moment.

How do goals set for the individual in school relate to the world scene? How do they relate to the need for skilled manpower? Skilled manpower is often defined in terms of proficiency in science, mathematics, and foreign languages, without regard for other areas of knowledge. Some people insist there is an urgent need for all learners to study these subjects if America is to maintain her freedom in the conflict of ideologies now prevalent in the world. They would subordinate the individual, his interests, his goals, his abilities and aptitudes; they would direct into these three fields all who have the capacity to master them.

If America chooses to combat the ideologies prevalent in today's world by means that conflict with American ideals, America cannot remain free. America is committed to freedom of the individual—freedom from tyranny, ignorance, fear, superstition. America is committed to the belief that each person can choose his own way of living and, at the same time, live within a framework of basic national commitments. In carrying out this ideal, America stands foremost in the world. The state and all its institutions—especially the schools—exist to serve this purpose. Even the problem of the national need for skilled manpower is solved by assuring the nation's children the opportunity to develop a galaxy of diverse interests and great range of specific individual capacities.

All kinds of youngsters come to school. They are Smith or Smythe; Jones, Jankowski, Izoma, or Brown; O'Leary, Ming, or Stalzanbach. Their fathers are lawyers, doctors, executives; store owners, truck drivers, day laborers. Their homes are fashionable mansions on exlusive streets, modest ranch-style houses; fancy apartments, one-room shacks, farm houses. They live in big cities, small towns, or villages. Their schools are grey, concrete monsters; colorful, glass delights; or one-room, tree-shaded retreats.

These youngsters are tomboys or dreamers; rambunctious or orderly. They are curious and wondering; excited about everything from jazz to guided missiles. Sometimes they are jubilantly happy and sometimes dismally depressed because they feel, as well as think, their thoughts. They are individualists. Homes, parents, cultures with their expectations, neighborhoods, friends, all have made their demands on each learner, demands to which he has responded in his own way. Teachers hear these youngsters, watch them, see them grow, and teach them as individual learners.

We have talked a lot in the past thirty years about individual differences and individualized instruction, but at this time when our knowledge and know-how are crystallizing into an education that nurtures all talents, education seems to be beating a retreat to formalized mass instruction with conformity, not diversity, as the goal. The old stereotypes of the "class" and the "grade" are now in ascendancy. The greater the stress of the times and the public demand for high standards of quality, the greater likelihood that we will seize upon the methods of mass production in the school. Although we know it is the individual who learns, it is the class, the group, that gets the attention. Teach the class and expect the individual to adapt himself to the pace set—this is the order of the day.

Within the schools of America can be found dozens of practices and procedures which obscure the individual and promote the group pattern. Although many of these practices were originally designed to make teaching of the individual easier, they seldom have achieved the goal. In fact, by eliminating the obvious deviate, they sometimes obscure the differences which still remain. Many present practices need reexamination; and the assumptions underlying them and their effects, both good and bad, on the individual pupil need careful scrutiny. Among these practices may be listed the following:

Graded organization. Although this plan of grouping children by the "ladder" concept—changing one whole rung once a year or remaining on the same rung for another whole year—is almost a universal practice, the need for reexamination of the plan is obvious when it is viewed in the light of individual differences.

Ability or homogeneity groupings within graded organization. The gains or losses for the individual child as a result of this plan should be examined and reexamined. The assumptions and methods of teachers in "ability" grouping schemes may be that little attention is given to any characteristic of a child other than the trait used as the basis for grouping. How valid are the assumptions, the beliefs, the philosophy, the psychology behind the drive toward making school learning difficulty, tough, or even frustrating? Emerson once said, "The great teacher is one who makes the difficult seem easy."

Emphasis on acquisition of facts. Stimulated by many forces, including TV quiz programs, information test programs, and demands for quality, the public is coming to think of education largely as the acquisition of facts, often by memorization; little attention is given to education through reasoning, questioning, and developing hypotheses. How is acquisition of information related to education of high quality?

Horizontal enrichment. What is the value of expanding learning opportunities for certain pupils beyond the content being mastered by the majority in the same grade? Does this plan enhance learning for *all* individuals in a group? Does it stimulate and help the abler pupil, the average pupil, the slower, the handicapped? In short, what does it do for the individual pupil?

Vertical enrichment—acceleration. Many plans now permit certain pupils to advance up the promotion ladder faster than standard practice dictates. Some plans permit early graduation from high school and early entrance into college or the work world. Other plans provide for study at the college level in high school and result in college entrance at normal age with advanced standing. Do these plans tend to freeze students who do not accelerate into fixed groupings? Do these plans have bad as well as good effects for the individuals they are intended to benefit?

The image of master teachers. Is the stereotype image of the master teacher becoming fixed? Is he one who deals with the individual? Is he one who assumes that telling or showing is masterful teaching? If this is the role of the master teacher, is not the concept of individual differences denied?

Standard time allotments. Time is used as a measure of learning (Carnegie Units, four years for high school, four years for an undergraduate college degree). Doesn't a uniform, rigid time schedule deny individual differences? If so, in what particular? What can be done to rescue the individual learner from the time-block lock-step?

Organizational structures. Many prevalent structural designs have been built on the belief that administrative procedures and special organizational structures will aid learning. Among those currently being promoted are (a) longer school day; (b) longer school year; (c) curriculum tracks; (d) X, Y, Z grouping; (e) team teaching; (f) schools within schools; (g) honors groups; (h) special schools for special talents; (i) teacher aides, and others. Will manipulation of the external aspects of a learning environment increase learning?

Using outside testing instruments. At no time in history have American schools placed so much faith in tests made by agencies outside the school system. What is the effect on the individual learner of the storm of examinations now imposed on him, often without regard for what the teacher has tried to teach? If the individual pupil counts, is good or evil to be found in a barrage of standardized tests, college board examinations, searches for talent, state-wide examinations, and national survey tests? Is conformity developed? Or is diversity developed by use of outside testing programs?

It is obvious that restrictive influences in school organization require regularity of pace and seldom permit an individual rate of progress. Whenever student pace is regularized, some are bored, while some are abused. Regardless of type of school organization, good teachers have always attempted to make learning a personal and important matter so that every child has a local habitation for learning—*his* habitation for *his* learning. Every good teacher makes sure every child is a person in his own right—a person identified by his own name and known and respected for himself. Effective teachers increase opportunities for individuals to assume responsibility for their own learning; for each learner must be allowed to proceed as quickly as he needs to and at other times to progress slowly. A significant achievement will be made when the amount of laboratory-like experiences is increased and attempts to see how many students can be put into a large room or an auditorium are decreased.

Each student deserves a program planned for him as an individual, planned in terms of a reliable estimate of his ability and his level of achievement. The individual program should be planned cooperatively by teacher, guidance personnel, the student, and his parents, and it should be revised from time to time to allow for changes in purpose and more accurate estimates of abilities. Such individual planning is possible only when a school has facilities, materials, and teachers to make it work. Each youth must have the individual freedom to select vocational and personal goals for himself and pursue a course that will help him reach his goals.

How school organization can facilitate the advancement of students more nearly at their own best pace raises some questions:

How can we preserve and promote the most effective and beneficial relationship in education—that between teacher and pupil?

If the teacher is the main element in the educational process, how can he be assisted with intraclass grouping?

What are the possibilities for individual study, apart from class work?

How essential is the concept of selective acceleration in encouraging each student to progress more nearly at his own best pace?

How can those students be identified who can proceed at a pace that does not conform to traditional regularity?

How can teachers be freed to do the professional job of assessing student strengths and weaknesses in order to plan programs which allow them to proceed at their optimum pace?

The school must recapture the program and the organization which will instill in the individual the desire to find himself in a group, not bury himself in it, and it must give him the means. If the individual citizen is not helped by the school to self-realization, to personal power, to self-assertion; then the whole concept of self-government will prove futile.

It must be remembered that individual teachers individualize instruction. Teachers constantly select and develop materials of instruction and methods of teaching that will help some learner to learn better. These teachers must be highly skilled in working with one child at a time.

Teachers are individuals, too. Teachers are different, too. They have the right to differ in their conceptions of teaching. If their individual competence is to be capitalized on, then each one must be free to use the diversified approaches which are his own unique power. Every teacher must be respected for his own individual powers and encouraged in his efforts to recognize individual differences among children. He must have the right to improvise and adjust teaching procedures on the basis of what is known about a learner, his abilities, and the learning process.

It is the individual teacher working with the individual learner who will continue to find solutions to the problem of individualizing instruction in the sixties.

"LET US DEVELOP CHILDREN WHO CARE ABOUT THEMSELVES AND OTHERS"

Alice Miel

Many changes are being made or are strongly urged today which really are not curriculum changes at all and which, in fact, make it more difficult to

From *Audiovisual Instruction*, VII, No. 6 (June, 1962), 355–357. Used by permission of the author and publisher.

achieve some of the curriculum changes we advocate. Some changes that I wish could gain ground were made years ago by a few people in education. Other changes that I will advocate would require work far out on an unmapped frontier. I prefer, then, to make some proposals on enhancing the quality of the curriculum at the elementary-school level.

CONCEPT OF SELF

The items I have put first in planning a better curriculum at the elementary level is fostering in each child a healthy concept of self. By this I mean that the child feels that he has the worth and dignity, the basic rights, of any human being. By this I mean, also, that he realizes the extent to which he depends on others and they on him for that very humanness—how inextricably interwoven are the self and the other.

A child who is maintaining a healthy view of himself as he changes with each year of living is a child who approaches most new situations with a feeling that "I can (or I can learn to) cope with this." The "I can'ts" for this child are based on realistic assessment of self and requirements and not on false teaching by others.

The elementary school can just as easily offer opportunities for girls to learn that they can run a projector, or use a hammer and saw, or do arithmetic or handle a snake, or perform an experiment in science as it can reinforce the belief possibly held by their mothers that certain learnings are too difficult for girls. The elementary school can just as easily offer opportunities for boys to feel successful in handling needle and thread, or running a sewing machine, or preparing a simple meal, as it can reinforce the helplessness about household matters they may be picking up from the males whom they admire.

Both boys and girls have a right to opportunities in the elementary school to find that they can read, that they can understand poetry and art and music and dance, and that they can take responsibility for managing their own conduct and learning. All children have a right to build a view that any kind of honest work they find themselves interested in and capable of performing in later life will be a worthy extension of themselves.

The concept of self which the school helps a child to develop is so basic to all of education that the 1962 yearbook of the Association for Supervision and Curriculum Development was devoted solely to this aspect of the curriculum. Those of you who have not read *Perceiving, Behaving, Becoming: A New Focus for Education* will find there many of the things which must be left unsaid today because of lack of time.

CREATIVITY

The second item we have selected for emphasis in our improved curriculum is *creativity*. It should not be necessary to make a case for creativity to an audience such as this. With the increasing mechanization of our society, the tendency toward depersonalization that comes from crowded living, and the increasing complexity of situations faced by human beings in this age, creative approaches to problem solving and to life in general are much needed by all members of the society.

Some do not agree that creativity can be developed in all persons, for they reserve the quality for a few truly original individuals. However, what harm can it do to treat every child as if he had the potentiality for creativity and to give him opportunity and encouragement for engaging in a creative *process*. The creativity of the product may range all the way from something new under the sun to something new to the individual making it, yet the process seems to be the same. The imagination produces a new way of seeing something, a new combination of familiar elements. The individual judges that the new idea is potentially useful and proceeds to work at it until he has expressed it in what is to him a satisfying finished form in some medium—materials of some kind, sounds, movements, or words. The product may be a new tune, a mobile, or a plan for improving flow of traffic.

Those interested in fostering creativity in children will want to consider carefully where some of the new applications of technology to education may be leading. Some of you may have heard or read Calvin Taylor's paper presented at the seminar on a theory of instructional materials sponsored by the ASCD in St. Louis in April 1960. The paper was entitled, "Possible Positive and Negative Effects of Instructional Media on Creativity." One possible negative effect Taylor pointed out was that "the largely ignored areas in education will continue to be ignored." Here he referred in particular to the development of creative talent. Another danger is that "of producing single views, single structures, single approaches in the minds and experiences of students." Creativity requires, of all things, that the individual play around with various approaches, gather data from many sources, and do his own ordering and structuring. Taylor suggests ways in which instructional materials can be made to stimulate diversity of response and also cautions that certain instructional media, such as teachers, should perhaps specialize in creativity, allowing other devices, such as machines "to specialize in those things for which they are so efficient in the total learning situation."

COMMITMENT

The third emphasis we wish to suggest in changing the curriculum is working for *commitment.* We realize that psychologists use this word to cover the case where an individual is so bound by one approach to a problem or one way of viewing a situation that he is blinded to other possibilities. This is just what must be avoided if the individual is to be creative. However, when we say that a person is *committed* to a democratic way of life, we have a useful meaning in mind. We think of a person pledged to uphold the basic values of our society, of someone who cares deeply about people, and who is willing to work hard and intelligently to help democracy to fulfill itself. In the 1962 yearbook of the ASCD referred to earlier, Maslow writes, ". . . character disorders and disturbances are now seen as far more important for the fate of the world than the classical neuroses or even the psychoses. From this point of view, new kinds of illness are most dangerous, e.g., the diminished or stunted person, i.e., the loss of any defining characteristics of humanness, or personhood, the failure to grow to one's potential; valuelessness." "The human being needs a framework of values . . . to live by and understand by," Maslow goes on to say, "in about the same sense that he needs sunlight, calcium, or love."

Maslow uses the expressive term "value-illnesses" for conditions like apathy, hopelessness, and cynicism.

We know that values cannot be taught to children in the way that facts are taught, we know also that adults in this period need help in clarifying their own values. Thus the task is doubly difficult. The responsibility of education for helping children develop a useful commitment to guiding values will not be fulfilled unless we work deliberately toward that end. Again, participants in this conference will want to think of the role of instructional materials. It will be equally important to do two things: (1) develop commitment that opens the way for more humane living; and (2) take precaution against developing commitment that narrows vision and closes doors.

CONTENT

The fourth curriculum emphasis we wish to propose is development of *content* that is comprehensive to help a modern child deal with his many-faceted environment and significant enough to mean all that is *contained* in opportunities for experience provided by the school. We must include within the term not subject matter alone, but also skills for searching out, organizing and using information and skills for handling various types of symbols, media, and tools. We must include also thought processes such as reasoning and criticizing and both analytical and intuitive approaches to data taken in by the senses.

The strengths and limitations of various media and instruction must be judged on the basis of their promise to develop some of this broad range of content. A special caution relates to what Taylor describes as using so many channels simultaneously for input of information that children have "too few channels free for scanning." A research study now in progress at Teachers College, Columbia University, has revealed the confusion of many of today's young children as a result of unexamined and unorganized information collected here and there in the process of growing. (Dorothy Mugge, *Social Studies Information of Seven-Year-Old Children.*) When the seven-year-old children in the study were asked what countries they had heard about, some of their replies were:

I just see countries but never heard of any. I saw when we went to New Jersey.
There's a country school in this book, I know.
You mean a country that's in a state?
We live in a country right now.
What's a country? Is Allentown a city or a country?

Asked about oceans they had heard about, the children said things like this:

Pocono Ocean. I think that's the ocean around here.
Mississippi Ocean, "Elantic" City Ocean, New Jersey Ocean, Delaware.
I only heard of a bay ocean at the seashore—bay and ocean together.

Confused time concepts were revealed in answering the question, "How often do you attend the movies?"

About twice some days.
Sometimes a week or five times a week.
Sometimes eleven days and then we go.
A whole bunch of times.
About a few months.
Two times a week or month.

Hearing such replies raised questions in the mind of the investigator about the great amount of information children supposedly have today and the desires of some scholars to introduce their disciplines to the very young. It caused her to wonder how these children could be helped most at school—by having a great deal more information fed in, or by assistance in getting order out of information already introduced?

COMMUNICATION

The fifth item in our list is *communication.* Under the heading of content, I have already included a broad range of skills, many of which are essential for communication. At this point, let us attend to the essence of the act of communication—having a real conversation with another human being. We say in elementary schools that we should give children "listening" experiences. Some of the activities we think of for this purpose are useful as far as they go, but how often do we help children really to listen to one another in ways that result in sharing and thus shifting their perceptions? The oneway communication of most media of instruction, including teachers at times, must be amply supplemented by provisions for genuine two-way communication. Much of this communication will be through language used as a means of clarifying one's own thoughts, quite as much as a means of conveying ideas to another. However, children will be cheated in school if they do not experience the many ways there are, in addition to words, for people to communicate.

COUNSELING

The sixth item for consideration is *counseling.* The elementary school, organized to provide one teacher as coordinator of all the experiences and as instructor for many of the experiences of one group of children, has a built-in opportunity for counseling by a familiar person as need arises. Not all teachers make good use of this counseling opportunity and not all problems of children can be handled by the classroom teacher. However, the direction of change that seems most promising is to make better use of the counseling advantage afforded by the so-called self-contained classroom and to build additional counseling services on that base.

CONTINUITY

The seventh and last point of emphasis, *continuity*, is like the rest, overlapping and pervasive. We hear a great deal nowadays about the proper sequence of learning tasks. Programing of subject matter so that one idea is established before the next was the concern of textbook and workbook writers for many years before the latest revival of interest in the teaching machine. In the world "continuity" there is quite a different idea from the straight line of progression conveyed by the word "sequence."

Continuity is a better term to use when thinking of the learning of an individual. We may say there is continuity in learning only when an individual must be achieving an integration of the different facts of his forward in life. Continuity is not just continuing in the same way. The individual must be achieving an integration of the different facts of his experience and distilling useful ideas and generalizations for testing in new situations. He must be transforming his ideas and his skills of relating to others as he grows up and moves into wider and different circles of people, each year of his life. Exposure to external sequences of subject matter may or may not hinder continuity within the individual. But in any case, the setting up of such sequences cannot be expected automatically to foster continuity. Some of the best opportunities for helping a child to maintain continuity in his learning occur in the in-between times in a school, the times unfortunately devoted in some schools largely to passing to another room or activity.

CONCLUSION

These seven suggested emphases in changing the curriculum have been reviewed all too briefly. Yet you must have noted that each of them suggested a slow, difficult way to improve rather than a panacea. In concluding, may I leave this statement in your mental notebook? Let us develop children who care about themselves and others around the world and who care also for the higher values of our society; children who are competent and therefore moving into the future with continuing confidence; children who (and here I run out of appropriate words beginning with the letter "c") are masters, not slaves of channels of communication, in school and out.

SEEKING BALANCE IN THE CURRICULUM

Kimball Wiles

In the controversy over education since Sputnik was placed in orbit, many persons have made a plea for balance. Some have asked for more math and science. Some have insisted that we continue to devote the same proportion of school time to the social studies and the humanities that we did before Sputnik. One professional association has designated the study of balance in the curriculum as a major emphasis in its national program.

Demands for balance are not new. Whenever people ask for a new emphasis in the curriculum or argue to maintain the present status, the plea for balance is a typical appeal to reason.

Some ask for even distribution of time among science, math, art, music, English and history.

Some ask that more attention be given to the cultures of the Far East, Africa and Latin America.

Some ask for more study which will enable pupils to develop ways of solving social problems.

Some ask for inclusion of more information about local community.

Some ask for more attention to problems of social adjustment.

Some ask that a variety in social points of view be represented in the curriculum and instructional materials.

Some ask for more time for TV teaching.

Some ask that pupils be made more anxious and concerned about failure.

Some ask that pupils be helped to be more secure so that they will be free to venture.

Some ask for a greater amount of creative activity.

Some ask for more teaching of common values.

Some ask for more stress of the fundamental skills.

What is the balance sought? How can it be attained?

From *Childhood Education,* XXXVI, No. 2 (October, 1959), 69–73. Reprinted by permission of the Association for Childhood Education International, 3615 Wisconsin Avenue, N.W., Washington, D. C.

ATTEMPTS TO ATTAIN BALANCE

Balance in the curriculum has been sought in various ways. Some school systems follow a curriculum pattern designed by scholars, in which all youngsters are brought into contact with the facts, concepts and generalizations it is assumed all students should know.

Some schools attempt to develop balance by assigning portions of days to designated subjects—fifteen minutes for spelling, twenty minutes for reading, twenty minutes for arithmetic, and so on. Certain assumptions are made about desirable balance in amounts of time provided for different activities.

Some schools try to obtain balance by having a classroom teacher plus some special teachers who come in to teach music, art, physical education and things the administrators think the classroom teacher cannot or does not teach well.

Other schools seek to achieve balance by maintaining self-contained classrooms in which the teacher knows all the activities in which youngsters engage. It is assumed the teacher has some criterion by which he can tell if there is a balance.

Some systems appoint supervisors to guide teachers toward more balance than they are providing. It is assumed the supervisors have a gauge by which they can determine proper balance.

PROBLEMS IN SECURING BALANCE

From the point of view of recent developments in research, seeking balance through division and allocation of content or administrative procedure has little chance for success. The research on perception (Kelley's report in *Education for What is Real* or the research of McClellan and others at the University of Chicago) indicates that *people perceive differently, in terms of their purposes, their needs, and their background.* Acceptance of this evidence leads to the proposition that a curriculum provided by a school is not the same for any two people going through it and that a balanced curriculum for the individual cannot be achieved by attempting to give everybody the same thing.

Difference in maturation rates makes it difficult to provide balance for the individual. American education is organized around homogeneous grouping by age. But the evidence being provided about maturation rates reveals that some nine-year-olds are as large as the average seventeen-year-old and some seventeen-year-olds are as small as the average nine-year-old. Willard Olson's studies show that *people grow at different rates and mature at different ages.* When teachers talk about developmental tasks as though they occur for all eleven-year-olds at the same time, they are not supported by research. When balance is sought by establishing a curriculum structure ahead of time, it is gained for one youngster and hindered for another.

Further, *learning rates differ.* If schools do a good job, the longer youngsters are in school, the greater the difference in range of achievement at a given grade level. It seems rather hopeless to look at balance as something that can be pre-structured by organizing concepts and activities into scope and sequence for given grades without consideration of a specific individual or class.

Add to differences in rates of maturation and learning variation in the purpose and the problems that children have, and the pre-structuring approach appears even less productive. Statements like Daniel Prescott's "Persistent emotional problems decrease the range of facts that are significant for the individual" illuminate the task of attempting to achieve balance by organizing content.

BALANCE FOR THE INDIVIDUAL

What alternative is left? How can balance be obtained? *Balance must be sought for the individual.* It is the assumption of the writer that each faculty must decide upon the types of growth it wants to develop and must use the program of activities to promote these growths in each child. Curriculum balance is determined by the extent to which a child's experiences promote *in a satisfactory manner* all of the growths the faculty deems important.

In arriving at the decision concerning desired growth, community groups, such as advisory groups or homeroom parent groups, should be brought in on the thinking. If not, lack of communication or lack of agreement may separate the school and homes, jeopardizing both support for the program and balance in the program.

Continuous evaluation and planning are necessary if balance is to be obtained. Evidence must be collected concerning the amount and kinds of growth being produced and the program for individuals revised in terms of the data secured.

The program that is balanced for one pupil may not be for another. The staff or the individual teacher must revise the schedule, method or activity when the evaluation reveals that classes or individuals are not making some of the growths sought. *Judgments must be made continuously by parents and teachers as to whether the present balance of pupil growth is satisfactory.* The basis for determining satisfactory balance should be the personal and social needs and purposes of the individual.

To maintain balance in the curriculum means that the teacher must be experimental to the extent that he will change his procedures when the evidence indicates he is ineffective. Each school needs a curriculum committee responsible for continuous evaluation of the program and recommendation of needed changes to the faculty.

THE METHOD IN OPERATION

How does this formula work in a school? Let's examine the operation of one school.

This school, faculty and parents, agreed on the types of growth desired. They said they wanted continuous growth of pupils in eight areas. Note the use of *continuous*. They do not expect all students to achieve given levels at any grade but want *uninterrupted progress* for all pupils in all of the types of growth desired.

First, they want continuous improvement in mental and physical health. A six-year-old observed students leaving the school at the end of the day. He looked at his mother and said, "This is a happy school, isn't it?" Even a six-year-old could see the youngsters as they came out of the school were happy. If the learning environment is to produce mental health, the people who go there must enjoy it and be happy.

In the kindergarten the five-year-olds go to the teacher when they are troubled, tug on her skirt and say, "lap." She sits down and holds them until they are ready to get down and face the world again. She gives them confidence of their worth. Evidence of her contribution is illustrated in the following incident. Joe, a five-year-old in Miss Jones' class, was being disciplined by his mother. She said, "If you don't behave, people won't like you." The little boy replied, "You know, Mother, no matter what Joe does, two people will like him. God and Miss Jones."

It is hoped all children will develop this sense of worth and acceptance.

Second, they want continuous growth in the fundamental skills. The official testing program is designed to sample growth in reading and arithmetic at the end of the second, fourth and sixth grades, and this is supplemented by each teacher's collecting evidence of progress.

At the beginning of the year the fifth-grade teacher asked each youngster to put into a Manila folder samples of all the work during the year of which he was proud. During January she asked each youngster to go through his folder and make a list of the ten most important things on which to work during the second semester. One boy, who read at the eighth-grade level and did arithmetic at the third-grade level, put as Number 1 on his list, "Work on my 8 tables." He did not have to be told to do it. He was using the evidence to make decisions about his status and desirable next steps. In a good intellectual climate, growth in fundamental skills is an individual matter in which pupils move ahead at their own best rate.

Third, they want continuous growth in the development of a set of values. The kindergarten teacher has the kind of relationship with children that enables them to discuss their problems with her. Even some youngsters in the first and second grades come back to talk with her. One little girl went to her and crawled upon her knee and said, "What happens if lightning strikes you?" The teacher said, "It may kill you." The little girl said, "What happens if you die?" The teacher said, "Different people believe different things." The little girl said, "Do you go to heaven?" The teacher knew that this little girl's parents did not believe in heaven or hell and she said, "Some people think so." The little girl said, "Is heaven near the sun?" The teacher said, "Some people think it is." The little girl said, "It is warm there?" The teacher said, "If it's near the sun, it would be." The little girl said, "Then I want to go there." Each person chooses his own counselor, and the essence of guidance is creating the kind of situation where people can analyze their values with people they trust. The school recognizes this phenomenon and seeks to keep the type of flexible organization which facilitates its operation.

Fourth, they want continuous growth in creative ability. Great emphasis is placed on seeking solutions to problems and on expression of feelings and perceptions. When the second-grade teacher asked her class to draw a picture of their family, one girl drew a picture of five fish. In the center was a great big fish and in the corners were four little fish. It would have been very easy to look at this picture and assume that the big fish in the center was the little girl. When the teacher asked her to explain the picture, the little girl said, "The big fish in the center is my big brother and all the rest of us are out on the edges." The picture was drawn at the height of the football season and her brother was the fullback.

When teachers give youngsters a chance to express themselves creatively, not only do they develop a skill that will be important the rest of their lives, they reveal to teachers the learnings that they are doing in such a way that teachers can know how to relate to them. Teachers in this school examine their methods and the activities they provide to see if they are encouraging creativity.

Fifth, they want continuous growth in skill in making independent and intelligent decisions. The fifth-grade teacher described previously asked each child as he went back through his folder to decide, "What are the ten most important things for you to do?" Each was asked to analyze himself to determine his strengths and his weaknesses and to say, "These are the important next steps to take." By this process, the staff hopes the school will develop mature, self-directing people.

Sixth, they want continuous growth in skill in democratic group participation. From kindergarten to the sixth year, teacher-pupil planning and teacher-pupil evaluation occur daily. Teachers try to foster this growth by the way they work. Group work and committee work are a part of every class. When John Lovell, of Auburn Polytechnic Institute, studied the way teachers develop group participation skill in this school, he found that at every level the way the teacher operated with his class was reflected in the way the committee chairmen behaved with student groups. People learn as much about group participation by the way the teacher operates as by anything they read or hear.

Seventh, they want continuous growth in individual interests and skill in following individual interests. When a boy from the north moved to Florida, the thing he became most interested in was poisonous snakes. He went to his third-grade teacher and said, "I want to read about moccasins, rattlers and coral snakes." She didn't say, "That's not in the third-grade curriculum; that's in tenth-grade biology—you'll get it there." She didn't say, "We don't have any instructional materials in the third grade which will permit you to read about poisonous snakes. We didn't buy any last year." She said, "Let's go to the school library and see if the librarian can help us find something." Because this teacher was willing to let this boy follow an individual interest for a portion of the day, his reading ability jumped from the third grade to the sixth grade in one year.

A fourth-grade boy was much interested in writing. He went on Saturday mornings to meet his fourth-grade teacher and began writing a book. It was never published, but the teacher took his time to work with a youngster on the pursuit of an individual interest.

Eighth, they want continuous growth in acquisition of an understanding of our cultural heritage. Experiences which acquaint pupils with social studies, language and literature are a part of the program; and administration of standardized tests at regular intervals throughout the elementary program determines whether or not classes and individual pupils are meeting expectations for pupils of their age and grade. The achievement of others assists in the interpretation of progress but is not a pattern or profile to seek.

Each teacher in this school believes these eight types of growth are important. He uses them as criteria to judge the curriculum of each pupil. He checks each youngster's progress and the things that he does by them. *He brings pupils and parents into decision-making situations at which it is decided if types and amounts of growth are in proper balance.* Teachers cannot make these judgments alone and be assured of validity. The purposes and concerns of those involved must enter the decision as to whether rates of growth in the areas are in balance.

Each teacher attempts to achieve balance by planning with the parents. Both share evidence that they have of growth or lack of growth in any of the eight areas and decide how they can supplement each other to bring a youngster up in an area where he may not be progressing as satisfactorily as they hope.

Not all faculties would establish the same types of growth as important. Differing values and community pressures might lead to the establishment of a different set of desirable outcomes. The formula that looks most promising is:

clear definition of the types of pupil growth sought

continuous collection of evidence concerning pupil growth in the specified areas

revision of the individual student's program when he is not making satisfactory progress in all areas

continuous study of the total program to discover ways of providing flexibility which permits greater adaptation of program to individual needs.

WHO SHOULD PLAN THE CURRICULUM?

Glen Hass

In this time of rapid change and increasing attention to education it is important that professional educators and others take a fresh look at the question, "Who Should Plan the Curriculum?" Recent developments suggest that some new answers to this central question are in order.

Today, the educated man is the central resource of society. The supply of such men and women available to each nation is the real measure of its economic, political and military potential. We are now undergoing the educational revolution because educated people are the capital of industrial society. Every chemist, every doctor, every engineer creates opportunity and need for more men who can apply knowledge and concepts.

In addition, change is so rapid in our innovating, industrial society, that today's education is unsuited for tomorrow's world and is as outmoded as the Model T for the world of 20 years from tomorrow—the world whose leaders are now in the classrooms of America.

THE CURRICULUM WE NEED

Today's curriculum planners should study conditions and trends in contemporary society and probable conditions and requirements for democratic living in the last half of this century. It may be we are planning to educate children for a society that does not now exist. Education for the immediate future in our rapidly changing society is almost useless unless it prepares learners to meet problems that are new and that neither they nor anyone else has ever encountered before.

The planners will almost certainly find that we need a curriculum which emphasizes the central concepts of the disciplines, concepts that explain phenomena in terms of their future state and direction. The increase in knowledge is becoming unteachable without emphasis on the rules for discovering the nature of the discipline.

The curriculum planners will learn that the school which faces toward the future world must teach innovation, problem solving, a love of learning;

From *Educational Leadership*, XIX, No. 1 (October, 1961), 2-4 and 39. Used by permission of the publisher.

its students must acquire the tools of analysis, expression and understanding. They will surely find that learners must be prepared for work that does not yet exist. They will see that our democracy will have numerous increasingly complex tasks as buyers, voters, legislators and cooperative planners.

It is apparent that the curriculum planning which will be needed involves an interrelationship of factors that go beyond the scope of any single discipline or profession.

In America, all interested citizens, parents, learners and scholars from all of the disciplines must work with teachers, principals and supervisors in the planning. This planning should go on throughout America on a local, state and national basis. A democratic society cannot permit uniformity and centralization. The onrushing future requires many different autonomous, competing efforts to cope with its problems.

In the past the columns of *Educational Leadership* have contained many statements that laymen should work with professional educators in planning the curriculum. We have, however, given inadequate attention to the particular role of each type of planner in the planning process. Lacking adequate role definition we may have often, as professionals, over-emphasized our mission to instruct the public, and may have been undersensitive to, or intolerant of suggestion and dissent. Let us try to define the particular role of each group in the planning.

ROLE OF THE SCHOLAR

In this period when the front line of our defense has moved from the trenches, to the factory, to the classroom, it is fortunate that professional educators are learning again how to communicate with the scholars and research workers in the various disciplines. It is doubly fortunate that scholars in other disciplines are showing renewed interest in the public school curriculum and are frequently now working with professional educators in curriculum planning.

What is the particular role in curriculum planning of the scholar from a discipline other than education? There are at least two ways in which he can help. He can often give crucial advice regarding *what* should be taught; and he can often suggest *means of implementing* curriculum decisions.

For instance, scholars in biology, mathematics, and physics are now working with teachers and other curriculum workers in determining what should be taught. These planners found that the textbooks in use contained almost none of the modern concepts, although greater change in knowledge has occurred in the past 50 years than in the preceding 500. They have also learned that much of the grade placement of the material seemed to be wrong and that greater emphasis was needed on unifying concepts so that the total number of basic ideas to be taught might be reduced.

The sociologist can give particular assistance in determining the means by which the goals of education may be achieved and in identifying the essential values and behavior patterns which must be taught as society changes. Of greatest importance, perhaps, is the fact that the sociologist can aid the educator in understanding the nature of the society in which his students will live in the future. Together they can devise an educational program to prepare for it.

The anthropologist can throw light on the reasons for the development of various aspects of the culture. He can help the school to plan to counterbalance current pressures for conformity and to attach greater emphasis to creativity and critical judgment. He can help in planning to develop in each student an understanding of his powers and limitations for creating and modifying society.

The scholars from all disciplines can aid in curriculum planning by identifying the central concepts and rules for discovering the nature of the discipline. In the terms in which they are now represented many of the disciplines are increasingly unteachable. We need a philosophical synthesis, appropriate to our world and to the learners, that can be taught—and only the scholar working alongside the educator can achieve this.

ROLE OF PARENTS AND OTHER CITIZENS

In the long run, we can only build the curriculum and use the teaching methods which the active school public will accept. We must work with the public and have orderly patterns for its participation. People need to be involved in the process of planning and curriculum in order to change their beliefs, attitudes and behavior regarding it.

It is a matter of crucial importance that many school systems invent structural devices to bring about a sharing of thinking about the curriculum by the lay citizens of the community and the professional staff members.

Staff members must learn to work with citizens; citizens must take part but not take over. This should begin at the level of the parent planning with the teacher about the needs of his child and should move from there to the citizens' advisory council and the curriculum committee. The profession, in each community, is responsible for establishing these channels.

ROLE OF THE STUDENT

The student is the major untapped resource in curriculum planning. Students are in the best position to explain many of the advantages and deficiencies of the present curriculum. Their ideas and reactions are of very great importance. Learning is significantly improved by putting greater responsibility on the student.

Too little use is made of teacher-pupil planning. The understanding and skills of planning are among the most important outcomes of education in our society. Perhaps more teachers would plan with their students if they realized that student-teacher planning has at least six aspects:

1. What is to be studied?
2. Why are we having this learning activity?
3. How shall we go about it?
4. Where do we do what needs to be done?
5. When do we do it?
6. Who will do each part of the job?

While student participation in the choice of topics may be possible only in certain subjects, there is no reason why extensive use of the other aspects of teacher-student planning should not be used in all subjects.

ROLE OF THE EDUCATOR

The role of the professional educator is one of growing stature and is one that will continue to grow as he works with the scholars and other members of the community.

It is the job of the professional educators to provide structure for planning with others, to inform, to offer recommendations, to bring together contributions from all sources, and to work out a recommended plan of action for curriculum change. In the analysis of the curriculum which is planned, the professional educator must be certain that it takes account of the nature of the learner and of the society of which he is a part. The part of the professional educator's role is not new but it will have increasing importance as he works and plans with others who are not so likely to give adequate attention to these bases for curriculum decisions.

The professional educator must be alerted to the necessity for relating schools to the surrounding political, economic and social forces so that the means and goals of education harmonize with the lives of men in particular circumstances. He should seek the unifying norms as he works with others in curriculum planning.

Frequently educators need to take a stand for what they believe, sharing what they know and feel. The public relies on the vision and courage of educators to present recommendations for curriculum improvement. Such recommendations should be related to a sense of purpose, the ability to think and analyze and a proper respect for the requirements of human response. The educator, in recommending, must carefully avoid the appearance that the curriculum is solely the professional's business. Experience over time in working together will help to solve this problem.

A most important part of the teacher's role is to communicate to students his own valuing of learning. Teachers motivate young people by their own motivations. Learners learn to like to learn from teachers who exhibit the intellectual accomplishment of regularly acquiring and acting on new knowledge.

Finally, the professional educator must evaluate and interrelate the contributions from other disciplines and evolve a curriculum plan for the approval of the curriculum committee or council and the school board.

MOVING AHEAD

If if is recognized that all public policy in education is the product of professional-lay interaction, then the main roadblocks to progress can be removed. The increasing communication between scholars in various disciplines and professional educators is a valuable step forward. A next step is to make greater use of that largely untapped resource—student contributions to curriculum planning. In each community professional educators should move to establish the structural devices needed so that scholars, citizens, students and professional educators may plan the curriculum needed for the 1970's. It will be particularly helpful if the persons are recognized and utilized. Because of the importance of education in today's world, each should be enabled to make his particular contribution to curriculum planning.

Who should plan the curriculum? Everyone interested in the future of America; everyone concerned for the quality of education being experienced by the leaders of the future who are now in our classrooms. . . .

QUESTIONS FOR DISCUSSION

CURRICULUM CRITERIA

1. How would *you* list the objectives of education today?
2. Do you agree that "Developing World Citizenship" is the major goal of education today? Why?
3. Do you agree that the clarification of values is a major activity in curriculum planning as stated by Fox? Why?
4. What is the meaning of the term "behavioral objectives"? Do you agree with Haberman that this way of stating objectives has both limitations and benefits? Why?
5. How should methods of instruction be selected by the teacher?
6. How unique should the program for each student be?
7. What content or experience should be required for all students?
8. What balance is needed in the curriculum? How should it be sought?
9. Who should participate in planning the curriculum? Why?
10. Who should participate in evaluating the curriculum? When?
11. Do you agree with Miel that healthy self-concept, creativity, commitment, content, communication, counseling, and continuity are important curriculum criteria?
12. Should the aims of the school be reflected in the curriculum? Is this an important curriculum criterion?
13. If you could do so, how would you change the process of curriculum planning in your school system? Why?

Part Two

The Curriculum

6 Preschool and Elementary

In the movement to change American education, many changes have been proposed for the elementary school level. In the last five years, virtually all aspects of the elementary program including teaching methods, organization for instruction, learning materials, as well as teacher education have undergone criticisms, and suggestions for changes have been made. Many innovations are now in use including modern mathematics, inquiry-approach science, non-graded organization, independent study, and team teaching.

During this same period there has been a remarkable growth of concern for early childhood education. In addition to Head Start programs, much support has developed and many new ideas have been tried in the schooling of two- three- and four-year olds. The 1964 national convention of the National Education Association advocated the addition of education for three- and four-year olds to the public school program.

Extensive research supports the view that the child's environment during the first five years of life is the significant one for intellectual and emotional development. Edwards ("Kindergarten Is Too Late") presents this research, as well as a summary of a number of the recent approaches to learning for young children. Norma Law ("Are the Public Schools Ready for Preschoolers") discusses the planning of programs for young children in terms of four basic "realities" that must be considered.

Harold Shane "Elementary Education: Objectives" traces the changes in the objectives of the elementary school curriculum from 1900 to the present. Today the elementary schools attempt to assume substantial responsibility for total human development.

What shall the elementary school teach is a recurring question. Dorris May Lee ("What Shall We Teach?"), and John U. Michaelis ("Educating Children for Change") each examine this basic question.

Probably the most common approach to curriculum content is that of attempting to revise the offering in a field. All agree that teaching reading is a function of the elementary school. But when to start reading is still an unresolved question. With a growing concern for the disadvantaged, the elementary school has taken on a new challenge in providing reading programs. Warren G. Cutts ("Reading Unreadiness in the Underprivileged") stresses the importance of special reading programs for the underprivileged.

Each field represented in the elementary school curriculum is undergoing changes and each has its problems. R. C. Bradley ("Improving the Social Studies Curriculum at the Elementary School Level") and Ivan Johnson ("Potential of the Arts in Elementary School") describe developments occurring in these two fields and suggest ways for improving each of them.

The American Association for the Advancement of Science has developed a new program in elementary science, which emphasizes skill in using the processes of science, and uses content selected from the various science disciplines. Arthur Livermore ("AAAS Elementary Science Program") describes this program, which begins in the kindergarten and continues through the sixth grade.

Controversy with regard to the curriculum of the elementary school is not restricted to content. With equal sincerity, questions have been raised about the organization that keeps age groups together and makes one teacher primarily responsible for the pupils' education for a year. The articles by Rodney Tillman ("Self-Contained Classroom: Where Do We Stand?"), Philip Lambert ("Team Teaching for the Elementary School"), and Robert H. Anderson ("The Nongraded School: An Overview") all deal with facets of the organization of the elementary school program.

What will the elementary school of the future be like? William D. Hedges ("Will We Recognize Tomorrow's Elementary School?") tells us that the large-scale entry of big business and technology into the schools will have profound implications for the elementary-school curriculum. Such terms as "hardware" and "software" have found their way into the vocabulary of educators. Massive federal support, especially in early elementary programs, evidences a positive national interest in our elementary schools. Will we be ready for the changes brought about by these developments and others in the future?

More important, do we know how to evaluate and make decisions about new developments and to judge their merit in comparison with present programs? The consideration of objectives of the program, the bases of the curriculum, and the criteria for a good curriculum, as presented in earlier sections of this book, provide criteria to guide the elementary school curriculum planner in making these decisions.

KINDERGARTEN IS TOO LATE

Esther P. Edwards

Education of the young child has come with a rush and a swirl out of the quiet backwater where it sat so long in its own reflection and has swept into the mainstream of American concern and controversy. At last we are hit hard with the fact that young children's experiences in their first years are of crucial creative importance for their total future lives. The heredity-environment dilemma having been laid to rest with the recognition that both are significant in continual interaction, we are ready to accept the thesis that intelligence is not fixed once and for all at birth but can be shaped by experience. We are just beginning to look seriously at the kinds of stimuli we provide for children. What should these be? When should they occur? How should they be presented? By whom? In what setting?

But what is the basis for this growing awareness that the early years are of incalculable significance? Any attempt to give a capsule explanation will be an oversimplification; yet the attempt must be made.

The word "cognition"—knowing—became respectable in American psychology in the Fifties. Piaget in Switzerland and Vygotsky in Russia had shown as long ago as the Twenties and Thirties that human intellectual functioning could not be sufficiently explained in any purely mechanical fashion. American psychology of the ruling behaviorist school came more reluctantly to recognize that thinking, learning, and behaving as we know them cannot be reduced wholly to a direct stimulus-response hookup.

What gives an intelligent adult the ability to focus his attention on *this* rather than on *that?* What allows him some degree of choice, of voluntary control? What gets him out from under the domination of his environment —not always, not entirely, but in part, and part of the time? Why can the absorbed reader fail even to hear the clock tick in the corner, the rain on the roof, the hiss of the fire, yet leap to instant attention when his child cries out softly in its sleep? Why, and how, have we human beings attained waking consciousness, that demanding burden and endless delight? What gives us alone of all life on this planet symbolic language—created, shared, used to build and sustain our cloud-palace cultures that float from generation to generation on the mind of man?

From *Saturday Review* LI, No. 24 (June 15, 1968), 68-70, 76-78. Used by permission of the author and publisher. Copyright Saturday Review, Inc., 1968.

D. O. Hebb of McGill University has shown that there is a relation between the level of complexity of a species, the slowness and difficulty of early learning in its members, and the ease and speed with which they can deal at maturity with complex ideas. Whatever an ant learns—if it learns anything at all, functioning as it does chiefly through instinct—may be learned in the first moments of its life, learned once and for all. Thereafter it functions well as an ant, but with no possibility of varying its set pattern. "Go to the ant, thou sluggard"—but not for help with calculus. A rat reared in darkness, Hebb tells us, is capable of a selective visual discrimination, definitely learned, after a total visual experience of less than fifteen minutes; within an hour or so it has learned to function as well as its peer reared normally. A rat is an ingenious and canny beast, but calculus is not its meat either.

The young human creature spends months and years completing the intellectual structures which at his birth are present only as possibilities. Slowly he develops, with little visible change from hour to hour or day to day. His early learning is more laborious than that of neurologically simpler creatures. It is not only that the baby's period of development is longer than the ant's or the rat's, but that the human child is involved in a more difficult task. So difficult, indeed, that his first learning is less efficient, less fluent than any other creature's. It has been said: "The longest journey in the world is the journey from the back of the head to the front of the head." The infant is building the pathways that will make this journey at first possible, then easy, then lightning swift and marvelously effective. What pathways these, through what trackless jungle? Connected and interconnected systems of neurons, branching and coiling back, going off in new directions and returning, making patterned avenues through the forest of nine billion nerve cells that lies between the incoming sensory areas of the brain and the outgoing motor centers. Without this development, conceptual thought is forever impossible.

So at maturity the intelligent adult, whose potential has thus been translated into reality, perceives with understanding, speaks and thinks symbolically, solves problems, categorizes, appreciates, and does all this with an instantaneous flash of insight that is alone of its kind in nature. He deals conceptually with the universe—a universe he first had to construct for himself. How does he do this? As each of us must, he has built it during his earliest years out of the myriad perceptual cues coming into the nervous system from "out there"—cues impinging continually on nerve endings, but meaningless until his system has built the structures that allow a reading of the signals and a response to them.

This is what the infant in his cradle is doing. We adults, rushing about harassed and busy, look at the baby and think: "How restful—to be fed, kept warm and clean, to have nothing to do but play with a toe, eat, cry a little, sleep. . . ." But the infant lying there is building his universe, and building himself. He must do both of these things, do them *then,* do them *at once* (for one is the converse of the other), or never do them at all. Never to do them is never to develop, to be cut off, to be a thing and not a man.

How construct a universe? The newborn baby possesses a nervous system which already receives and responds reflexively to signals from the outer world—to light, sound, temperature, pressure, and other stimuli. But though he responds through reflex action, the baby does not yet understand the signals: he cannot *read* them. He must learn to interconnect sets of cues—to see what he hears, for instance, and to learn that a light and a sound may describe one and the same object. So he begins to define reality. He must develop ability to deal with more and more signals at once. In time, perceptual cues gain meaning: the baby has begun to know what they signify. Memory, judgment, intention all stem from this moment in his intellectual life. First he acts as a purely physical being and learns how to solve problems by means of bodily acts. Then he learns to represent physical action by mental symbol, and thought has begun.

His first symbols are images, pictures which allow him to hang on to fleeting reality ("I remember my mother's face though she is out of the room"). Then the child learns a word, and another, and another, and begins to put words together. At eight months, or a year, he has begun to grasp the shorthand which allows him to hold in his head the whole of reality and to manipulate it, to solve the problems it sets him, through mental operations. Until he is five or six or older, the chief intellectual task of his life will be the creation of a symbolic vocabulary, or several of them (words, numbers, images, musical notes), which become the medium of his life as a human being.

How vital this is to human development is implied by the linguists' suggestion that the supremely difficult feat of building language recognition and response which takes place during the first years of life can occur because there is a built-in neurological mechanism for language learning present in every normal human organism. But like the image on the sensitized negative, this potential will not appear as reality unless the proper circumstances develop it. Experience—the right experience—is essential.

Heredity and environment interact. Hereditary possibilities are shaped by the influences that only human culture can provide; they are potentialities that must be developed while the young neurological organism is still rapidly growing, malleable, open to stimulus. If the "critical periods in learning" hypothesis applies to human beings (as we know it does to other creatures—dogs, for instance—and as evidence increasingly indicates it does to us), then the right experience must come at the right time, or the potential must remain forever unrealized.

Benjamin Bloom of the University of Chicago implies this when he says that the early environment, during the first five to seven years of life, is the significant one for intellectual development. This is why we are finally realizing that the young child's experience is of indelible importance, not only for his emotional life, but also in the formation of that aspect of man which is perhaps most crucially his own—his sapience.

If all this can be accepted as in some degree reflecting truth, where are we? We are at a point where we can see why education for the young child can matter enormously. It matters not as much as the family. The family is basic. But the good family is good precisely because it provides so much of the young child's education. Still, other appropriate experiences can add to what even the best family can do.

For the child born into a family which cannot give him what he needs in emotional security or intellectual stimulus, such experiences may act as a lifeline to essential development. What early education is offered to what children becomes, therefore, of first importance. Perhaps the right choices here can make a difference comparable to the release of nuclear energy—a release of human potential energizing our whole society.

This sense that the choices matter tremendously is why the present debate as to what constitutes good education for young children is more a battle than a scholarly discussion: Montessori—or not; "Teach your child to read at two"—or don't; imaginative play as the focus of the preschool experience vs. structured cognitive stimulation. Every aspect of the preschool is up for reconsideration, defended with zeal, attacked with fury. Partisanship is prevalent, the grounds for decision-making uncertain.

Part of this malaise stems from the attempt of psychologists and teachers to create activities appropriate for the thousands of urban—and rural—slum children who have come into preschool classes through such programs as Head Start. Once these children would never have seen the inside of a nursery school classroom. Now they are here. Teachers are responsible for them. And teachers have found that their tried and true techniques don't work with these children. How do you make contact with a nonverbal, uncooperative, frightened, dirty, doleful, thumb-sucking four-year-old dragged to school by a slightly older sister who can't tell you anything about him except that his name is Buzzer?

So it is perfectly true that many Head Start programs are not making a significant difference in the intellectual capacities or the academic readiness of children thrust into them for a brief six to eight weeks the summer before they go to "real" school. Head Start has been oversold in an effort to enlist citizen support: "It will bring the slum child up to the level of his middle-class age mates in one quick and easy exposure." That was a line that salved the taxpayer's conscience with a minimum of damage to his bank account. But it was a lie. No one with the faintest understanding of the realities of mental, social, and emotional growth ever thought it could do any such thing. Head Start may be better than nothing (in some cases even this is questionable), but it is vastly less good—and *less* than is needed.

The solution, however, is not to damn previous educational goals and means across the board. New circumstances and children with new needs do not prove that the established ways of going at the education of young children are valueless—only that we now are dealing with a wider range of children and must supplement the older ways with different aims, content, and techniques. We need a more varied repertoire. We need to know when to do what, and why. That's all. But that's a tall order.

The situation, then, calls for a plea to the embattled camps in preschool education to beat a few swords into plowshares, to leave their respective strongholds, to stop maintaining that each holds all the truth, and to begin to share questions and insights. A vast amount of hostility can be dissipated if we can accept two basic truths:

1. There is no one method of teaching young children which is ideal for all of them. Like the rest of us, they differ in temperament, in background, in needs, in readiness for this or that experience. As children vary, so must educational approaches.

2. Human beings are totalities: they have bodies, and they have minds; they exist in social contexts within which they act and feel. Small children are people, and their life in school needs to be a whole life in which physical, emotional, intellectual, and social aspects of the self are all given adequate nourishment. It is wrong to leave out any major segment, though emphasis can and should vary with the particular set of circumstances.

Perhaps the first step is acceptance of the individual differences among children. Some of these are genetic in origin; others are caused by environmental accidents. Within groups of children from similar cultural and social strata are wide ranges in health, energy, temperament, aptitudes, and innate potential. Even among children in the same family this is so. Dozens of factors can affect the quality of early experience. One child's mother was sick when he was at a vulnerable stage; another child had an .

illness that required hospitalization; for a third, everything went along smoothly and success bred success. The gap between one socioeconomic group and another magnifies the differences. The early life histories of children living within a few blocks of each other in an American city may be as remote from one another as is the Arabia Desert from Manhattan. How foolish then to think that any one approach can be the best, much less the only one for such diverse bits of mortality, so variously shaped by their three or four years of life.

Proponents of cognitive preschool experience have recently leveled severe criticism at the less-structured types of nursery school curricula. "Only play," they say, "only messing around with finger paints. . ." The Montessori schools point to their abundance of graded materials which can be used by the individual child to move step by step from growing mastery of sensory-motor skills to a knowledge of letters, of numbers, of ordering and labeling. The child's attention span increases. He learns to work independently, systematically, following a coherent pattern established by materials and setting. For children from the often chaotic homes of poverty this may mean a significant gain.

O. K. Moore, of the University of Pittsburgh, uses his "talking type-writer" (actually a total language environment, rather than a typewriter in an ordinary sense) as a tool whereby children as young as three years have learned to read and write in the natural way in which they learn to talk—inductively—with personal choice of activity and pace. Carl Bereiter and Siegfried Engelmann, formerly of the University of Illinois and now of the Ontario Institute for Studies in Education, have created what is perhaps at the moment the most controversial program in preschool education. It has been called a "pressure-cooker approach." In this setting, under direct academic force-feeding, groups of four- and five-year-olds from lower-class families are taught verbal and number patterns:

This is a ball.
This is a piece of clay.
Is this a ball?
Yes, this is a ball./No, this is not a ball.
This is a what? This is a ball. . . .

The aim of this exercise is to develop the ability not merely to label "ball" and "clay," but to know the use and significance of such essential carriers of meaning as the simple word "not." Verbal skills, numbers, and reading are taught. Drill is the medium. The adults unashamedly pressure children to learn. Hopefully their own desire to achieve competence will be fired by the sense that they are doing something tough and important, but praise, exhortation, and tangible rewards and punishment are freely used. The atmosphere is intense. These children have no time to lose. They must move into the world created by adult society. The whole thrust of the program is to make this possible for them.

These and other preschool programs focused on cognitive development add a dimension that was underplayed if not lacking in the older nursery schools, organized as these were around the child's social and emotional growth, his creative activity in the graphic arts and in music, and (with varying degrees of effectiveness) around introductory experiences in those areas recognized at a higher level as the basic disciplines (literature, mathematics, sciences, social sciences). Such a curriculum assumed that the young child entering preschool brought with him a fund of organized sensory and motor learnings. His language development was already well under way, chiefly through many months of interaction with an intelligent, loving, verbal, and attentive mother. Often what he needed most was to be a child among children in an environment which allowed him to explore and to play. He had already been molded and stimulated by the adult world, represented by his vitally concerned parents, and every day he went home to continue this part of his education.

But the Head Start children come from homes which have failed to nourish them in health, in emotional stability, in intellect. They need desperately to develop language, to learn to think. For these children such a program as Bereiter and Engelmann's can perhaps give the all-essential forward thrust without which nothing else can have meaning. They come to school late in the day to establish basic learnings. Their tendency is *not* to listen, *not* to focus. They know in their bones that no one is paying attention to them. They have to undo false beginnings. From a mile behind the starting line they have to start the race their more fortunate peers are already running. Under such circumstances, if pressured instruction will get them ready for school, blessings on it and let them have it.

But young children are being made ready for more than the first grade, and there is more to them than a brain, however vital that may be. William C. Rhodes of the National Institute of Mental Health writes in *Behavioral Science Frontiers in Education:*

> The imposition of culture upon the child, without relating the culture to his inner substance, is forcing a foreign body into his being. . . He will only mobilize defenses against the culture in an attempt to neutralize its harsh, abrasive denials of what he is.

This we must not make children do by being too demanding in our concern for cognitive growth. There are other values also of major importance.

Maya Pines, in her October 15, 1967, *New York Times Magazine* article "Slum Children Must Make Up for Lost Time," quotes disparagingly from the Head Start *Guide to a Daily Program,* which advocates that children:

. . . learn to work and play independently, at ease about being away from home, and able to accept help and direction from adults. . . . learn to live effectively with other children, and to value one's own rights and the rights of others. . . . develop self-identity and a view of themselves as having competence and worth.

This is not mere cant. It is not necessarily accomplished, but these are worthy goals. Anyone who has worked with young children, whether they be culturally deprived or not, knows it to be the most sober of cold facts that such children do need to develop independence, social competence, and a sense of self. Until they do, their growth toward other sorts of learning is enfeebled. The child who lacks adequate ego development neither cares nor dares to learn.

Hopefully children can learn both to use their minds and to become more fully human. Social and intellectual growth are not mutually exclusive. The valid criticism of the Bereiter and Engelmann program is not made on the ground that it gives drill in cognitive patterns, but that it gives little else except such drill, in a setting where teacher imposes and child conforms. This is too narrow a segment of experience. It ignores vital components of the totality that is a child. What the end result for these children after some years will be, no one knows. But one must wonder whether so intense a focus on the growth of knowledge and the means of its verification will not diminish other aspects of personality.

Preschool educators criticize the Bereiter and Engelmann program because of its frank admission of dependence on rewards (cookies, praise) and its use of punishment (physical coercion, isolation in unpleasant surroundings). These are gross inducements toward learning. If they are used only to prime the pump, as is recommended, then one may consider them symptomatic not of the program so much as of the damage already done to the child by his stultifying early experience, a damage demanding heroic measures to overcome. But if they must remain in the teacher's repertoire, if they are not left behind in favor of satisfaction from the achievement itself, then they form an indictment of the meaningfulness of this approach to children. A learning that takes place only when the teacher doles out candy or brandishes a switch (hypothetical or not) is a learning without intrinsic satisfaction. Performance can be evoked temporarily through pressure, but will not last. This is one touchstone of valid education. But why must we wait so long, and then resort to pressure? Already there are several experimental programs which are attempting significant intervention before the age of two in the lives of "high risk" children (the younger brothers and sisters of academically retarded children from deprived homes, or children from markedly nonverbal backgrounds). Appropriate education must be made available to every child as soon as he can benefit from it. We know that as early as eighteen months disadvantaged children start trailing their middle-class age mates in tests of general intelligence and language development. Already the subtle undermining brought about by inadequate experience has begun. It is simply not true that all lower-class children are lacking in potential compared with their middle-class peers. Some, no doubt, are. But for many, if not most, the deficit that so early becomes visible is more likely caused after conception by various environmental lacks (poor nutrition, the mother's ill health during the baby's intrauterine life, and inadequate sensory-motor stimulation after birth). Such lacks can be reversed, and they ought to be.

We are going to have to make educational stimulation available from babyhood on for the children whose families cannot provide it for them. Whether tutors should go into the homes, whether children should be brought into carefully planned, well staffed *educational* (as distinct from baby-sitting day-care) programs, we do not now know. Experiments going on in several places in the country should help us decide. But however we do it, intervention by the age of eighteen months should be the rule for the children of deprived inner-city or poor rural families. As it is now, few children reach Head Start before the age of four. We are not making use of the golden period when we can most easily and effectively work with children without using pressure, without having to force on them a culture already so foreign that it cannot be learned unless, as William Rhodes says, we make the child "give up completely the content of the self." We are not coming to children when there is still time to help them build effective roadways through the neurological labyrinth, to help them create a universe rich, diverse, satisfying. We can, if we will. And we must.

We must build programs designed to amplify the child's world as the middleclass child's parents do, when he is still an infant in the crib. We must do this not to cut the lower-class child off from his home and his family, but to assist his overburdened mother, to help make the family milieu better for the child. We must create kinds of stimulation that become a constant part of his life, involving him daily in meaningful interactions, just as the child from a more fortunate home interacts with his mother every day for years, until the time that the thousands of exchanges, each modifying and adding to his understanding, give him mastery of thought and speech. We know that this is the most deeply meaningful education for the one-, two-, or three-year-old child. We must try to approach it for every child.

Such special interventions are not yet widely available. Large numbers of deprived children remain, in a sense, accident victims in need of first aid. Perhaps the Bereiter and Engelmann type of program is that first aid. Perhaps it is the best solution to an unfortunate situation. Perhaps it can build in children who have missed out on the normal growth toward competence some of the abilities they would have developed more gradually had their backgrounds been more intellectually stimulating. Perhaps it cannot. We do not know, but surely it is worth trying, with the sobering thought that force-feeding programs, though they rescue the starving, do not make up for deficits already incurred.

But because people who have been hurt need first aid is no reason to prescribe first aid as the all-important component of everyone's experience. Because deprived children may benefit from intensive work in the cognitive areas where they lack development does not mean that a broader, more inclusive type of program which meets the equally real needs of the intellectually advanced child deserves ridicule. What we really want is to bring into our repertoire a much wider range of experience from which we may select intelligently those aspects which are most useful and appropriate for each group of children—indeed for each child.

Here we take issue with Miss Pines's description of the "established" nursery school, quoted from her *New York Times Magazine* article but similar in tone to what she writes in her new book, *Revolution in Learning: The Years from Birth to Six*. Miss Pines states:

Middle-class nursery schools operate on the theory that they can directly influence only the child's emotional and social development—not his mental growth. They assume that if they build up a shy child's confidence, or redirect an angry one's aggression, the child's intellectual development will take care of itself, following a sort of built-in timetable. Therefore they concentrate on teaching children to "get along with others" and "adjust to the group."

Undoubtedly this neglect of the cognitive dimension is true of many preschools, but it is not true of the good ones, and certainly it is false to the philosophy behind early education. It overlooks a range of experience which is very present when young children are well taught by intelligent teachers who are themselves cultivated and concerned people. Children do not get over being shy; they do not learn to redirect their anger or interact with others in a vacuum. They are able to develop as people, in the social and emotional sense, most effectively when their minds are occupied with challenging ideas. "Why does the ice cube melt? What is *melting?* Why does the wind blow, and what is air, and what are the words that let me talk about it? How can I draw a picture of what I felt like when I was in the hospital? What is a dream? Why am I afraid? How many nickels do we need to buy fresh food for our guppies if a box of fish food costs a quarter? What makes my baby brother cry at night and wake me up? How can a rocket go around the world so fast? When is tomorrow? How far is far?" These, and the millions of other questions small children ask every day, are *intellectual* challenges. The preschool exists to help children formulate them, examine them, and, in some degree, answer them. It can only do this by giving children some of the multiplicity of interlocking experiences through which they can move slowly toward mature answers. As nursery-school children they will not arrive, but they make progress.

Because in the past the intellectual component of the preschool has been implicit rather than explicit, this does not mean that it has been lacking. It means that the skilled preschool teacher has done a good job only when she has turned every experience to the benefit of intellectual growth as much as to social or emotional growth. It has given her the task of picking up the children's leads and building her program about these, on the presumption that children are readiest to learn in areas where they already show interest.

Let us not be so foolish as to say that the established nursery school curriculum—if it is taught well—lacks intellectual content, or that it ignores children's growth toward cognitive ability, for it does not. It has been subtle in its approach to these. Perhaps it has been too subtle to allow the critics to recognize the presence of these strands of experience, but not too subtle for children to learn from them—provided the children were ready to do so.

But let us also admit that children who have lacked the requisite preparatory growth are *not* ready for such a program and need something else, something with a more explicit structure, something which is geared specifically to their level of attainment and their deficits. If these children are not always to be accident victims, they need educational intervention years sooner than we are giving it to most of them now. But in trying to do this, we must also bear in mind that to teach is not to bulldoze. Nonverbal, immature, dirty Buzzer is still a person, not a thing to be obtusely shoved into any mold we choose. This is why we need teachers to create programs that as yet do not exist, programs which can combine structured cognitive stimulation with full respect for the inalienable right of each human being to be himself.

Let us admit, also, that when we create these new approaches to cognitive growth, they may also be able to add something vital to the multiple stimuli offered by the middle-class nursery school. To object to an exclusive focus on structured intellectual learning for the middle-class child is not to say that he cannot gain from some of it. No one is talking in terms of taking the bloom off frail butterfly wings. Children who have learned how to learn are eager and resilient, and gobble up new information, skills, and insights in every conceivable way. If they are given some leeway to choose those aspects of a program on which they will spend most of their time, they can only benefit from encountering a wider range of possibilities. Teachers should know all the materials—the fullest spectrum of approaches—and should not be afraid to use them.

We are wasting time and energy, good humor and understanding, in opposing each other. No school of thought has all the light. There is no one ideal approach to learning for all young children. Instead, there are many possible variations of emphasis which can make the preschool experience maximally valuable for a wide range of children from differing family backgrounds, social strata, and levels of development. Let's stop this fruitless squabbling and instead fight ignorance (our own as well as that of others) and the limitations to children's potential growth, however these may occur. Let's be grateful for every addition to the armament of techniques and tools which we can use to help children. Let us try to find out how best to employ each approach: when, with whom, for what reasons, under what circumstances. And for heaven's sake, let's get going.

ARE THE PUBLIC SCHOOLS READY FOR PRESCHOOLERS?

Norma R. Law

Achieving the Great Society depends not only upon the eradication of economic and educational deprivation from our culture. Of equal signifi-

From *Young Children,* XXI, No. 6 (September, 1966), 323-328. Used by permission of the author and publisher.

cance is a "poverty of spirit" that could invade all segments of our society unless its children see themselves as contributing, intelligent people with potentialities to be developed fully because the world needs them just as they need the strengths of other people.

PRESCHOOL EDUCATION IN THE NEWS

Americans have always turned to the schools when they were in trouble. To the school administrator, who already has too many children, too little space, too few teachers, and too uncertain funds, the move to have children start school at four and perhaps three years of age can be downright frightening. In addition to the administrative hazards involved, his own insufficient experience in planning for preschool children constitutes a serious threat to professional poise. Those of you who lived through the advent of kindergartens in your states recognize the feelings well. Those who are just now beginning to open school doors to five-year-olds find little comfort in knowing that there still are many more questions than answers, not only about preschoolers but about the whole range of early childhood education—nursery school, kindergarten, primary grades—in the public school system.

At the moment, society has discovered young children. One could wish it had discovered them for their own individuality and developmental strengths instead of for the federal subsidy and public goodwill they represent to many school people, or for the status-by-proxy they represent to many parents, or for the national jump-ahead they represent to many other citizens. What we deeply want, we are always in danger of getting. School administrators had better look at certain popular assumptions in our culture—"Bigger is better," "Force works," "Speed wins every time." Such assumptions could lose us our children if we don't watch out.

WHAT YOUNG CHILDREN BRING TO SCHOOL

Children start school on our side. They have worked tremendously hard as infants and toddlers, learning to walk and talk and cope with the world's affairs as they have met them. They come to school wanting to grow, not needing to be pushed or prodded into maturing, but needing good people to help them become richly human beings. They come different, not only in initial inborn characteristics but also in life's experiences. They come whole, with no way to slice them into parts. They come self-centered and active, often messy and demanding, invariably touching and testing and wanting to explore in ways that can be mighty inconvenient for adults. George soaking up brown paper towels in the bathroom may be exploring physical properties, but the school principal has other concerns, and perhaps such low tolerance of early growth that his school really can't adapt to young children.

WHAT THEY NEED TO FIND

Let's not fool ourselves that it is easy to teach or plan a program for young children. Young children have to have a balance between strenuous motor activity and quieter interests. They require individual and small-group situations, in contrast to total group activities. They thrive when the interrelatedness of development is respected—esthetic, social, emotional and physical, as well as intellectual development. They need adequate equipment, materials, and space indoors and outdoors. They depend upon important grown-ups—parents, teachers, doctors, neighbors—working together.

When it comes to planning experiences for young children, four realities, it seems to me, have to be considered:

1. The basic needs of all human beings for adequate health care and nutrition, for the giving and getting of love, for self-esteem, for mastery, and for freedom to be independent and dependent at the same time. For the school, these basic needs of all children overarch every decision it makes.
2. The function of play in developing motor skills, in learning about self and others, in translating knowledge into actions, and in using vital sensory endowments. Children play with as much concentration and dedication as deeply interested adults bring to their work.
3. Individual differences in life space, in tempo, in style of learning and in developmental spurts and regressions and plateaus. To assess these differences accurately, the school observes and systematically records the behavior of children in a variety of stress and non-stress situations. It consults with parents and with specialists of other disciplines. It recognizes small groups or subgroups for the opportunities they provide for many one-to-one relationships and for communication.
4. The content of knowledge and the development of understandings. This is where public pressure can blind school people to what they know about human wholeness and sequential development. As the various disciplines study the structure of knowledge, their intermittent reports to the public have certain dangers for children and parents but

tremendous challenge for school people. We have never had such responsibility for sifting research, assessing its implications for good learning experiences for children, and raising pertinent questions for further study. Responsible administrators listen to zealous claims of break-throughs and great innovation, then carefully check the evidence that changes *in fact* have taken place. They also want to know what happened to attitudes and basic human values. Knowing and respecting the individual push to grow, they want to know if the outcomes were in fact better than spontaneous growth changes. And recognizing the availability to them of many young children, they encourage and help teachers test the ideas out, never failing to provide the sensory, first-hand sources of information young children reach for.

Such concrete experiences with things and people are needed in enough abundance to promote perceptual and sensory discrimination and to extend the boundaries of the child's world. With a wide range of such experiences, the eventual abstractions of reading and writing and numbers make sense. Raw materials are needed, such as sand, water, sawdust, dirt, paint, clay; living things, such as worms, plants, insects and animals; people, such as older children, visitors, community workers, school principals and aides; and beautiful junk, such as dress-up clothes, broken radios, clocks, scraps of wood, and other materials.

For the young painter, process is infinitely absorbing. Shirley would just as soon finger paint on a table as on a paper and is delighted to wash it off with a sponge and then start over again, maybe this time deciding to use her whole fist or the very sponge she cleaned up with, which suddenly becomes part of the painting process. Pride in a product will come for her in another year or two.

THE SCHOOL ADAPTS TO CHILDREN

The pressure for children to fit the school has been with us for centuries. The mounting figures on dropouts, children on tranquilizers, and college suicides suggest that the costs are too high. Young children try desperately to adapt—step in to your kindergarten or primary grades some day and watch them—but the costs tend to be high there, too, as evidenced by remedial programs and actual dislike of self.

Young children are not inappropriate for schools. Public schools may be inappropriate for spontaneous learners. The fact that they are coming younger and younger simply demands that we get our houses in order.

Qualified, carefully selected teachers who have had supervised experience with young children are essential. To them is given the responsibility for welcoming children and their parents and for knowing how to give professional direction to the aides who assist them. In the school that is ready for young children, group size is not subject to the manipulations of supply and demand. Teacher-child ratio in large part determines the quality of teaching done, the experiences provided, the equipment used, the parent involvement encouraged, the specialists consulted, and the cooperative planning actually done with the school staff for improved learning and supporting experiences throughout the early years.

Some administrators have found that a separate wing of the school or a separate building provides the informal, unostentatious setting teachers of young children can use to good advantage. The teachers in that wing or building are as busy teaching language, health, socialization, critical thinking, independence, self-expression, information about the world and its affairs as is every other teacher in the school. The children are busy, too, playing with ideas and trying themselves out in a variety of self-initiated activities with materials and people of their own choosing. To the eyes of the school administrator accustomed to seated children, rows of desks or tables, and open books, such kaleidoscopic learning may seem to be without structure. Its transitions are so gradual that he or she can't find a beginning or an end. The concepts on which children are working are maddeningly fluid.

YOUNG CHILDREN AT WORK

Imagine the bewilderment of one school superintendent, come to check the lease on a recently acquired building, overhearing this conversation in the kindergarten.

Two children were in the corner of the room with wooden crates, large blocks, and other building equipment and were pretending that they were in rockets. Bruce was on a high pile of blocks and was counting from 10 to 1. He repeated his counting several times and each time left out seven in the proper sequence. (The teacher standing by noted this error, but made no issue of a mechanical slip, which was unimportant to Bruce in the act of blasting off. She would watch for actual understanding in a genuine quantity situation later, such as putting away the blocks, or giving out carrot sticks at snack.)

Zita was on the floor next to Bruce's pile of blocks and was 'sitting in what vaguely resembled an airplance. She kept pretending to steer it, at the same time saying, "Don't do this to me. Don't do this to me. I'm scared. Don't do this to me." (For a child who initially had avoided other children, Zita's participation in this situation spelled achievement for her and for her teacher. This friendship had not developed without support from her teacher, alert to a watching child and quick to suggest, "Bruce could likely use some more blocks. Zita, maybe you'd like to take them to him.")

George came over and started to join in the play but Zita said, "George you can't come in here, just Bruce and me." George stood by the table for a· while and watched without saying a word and then wandered over to the monkey bars. (No need to help George. He was surveying the possibilities and eventually would choose his own activity.)

Zita and Bruce both climbed inside one of the big crates, pretending to take a trip into space. Zita asked, "What are we going to do in space? There is nothing to eat; we are going to starve." About that time Bruce said, "Hey look, a food store. Hey look, some food—it's sweet potatoes." Bruce got out of the space ship and went to the windowsill, where some sweet potatoes were growing in water. Zita followed him and said, "No, we can't take those. They belong to the morning children." They both went back and got into the space ship again. Zita, repeated, "What are we going to do in space—we will starve."

Robin came in and stood by the table watching them for a while but soon left without saying anything to either one.

Zita said, "Let's go get Phyllis," but Bruce answered, "No, Phyllis is a dirty rat." Zita agreed by saying, "Yeah, a dirty dog." Bruce continued the conversation with, "She's like a real dog." (The teacher made no move to question this interchange. Phyllis had been taunting Zita for days. This could be healthy come-uppance. At any rate it gave her a clue that Phyllis needed her help, and maybe soon.)

Zita was still talking about food, "I'm going to die—no food. When are we going to get food?" Bruce answered, "I'll give you some of mine when we get home. My food has lots of energy and makes you grow and you will feel good just like me if you eat some of mine." Zita asked, "When are we going back to earth?"

THE TEACHER'S ROLE

Play-solving may not be immediately comprehensible but neither is it without content. To the diagnostic teacher it provides as many, and often more, clues to confusions, accuracies, and individual readiness as any pencil and paper test to the teacher of older children. For example, the children who persistently called the new shipment of white sand in the sandbox snow or sugar but never sand—as though all sand must be brown. Or the four-year-old who spotted dog tracks in the snow. Or the two little girls who had a long conversation about who was big and who was little in their families.

The teacher's responsibility is to prepare the learning environment, not only in light of what is known about child development, the community, and subject matter, but also about the creative power that lies in making personal choices. Equipment is rearranged. Materials to expand learnings are brought out. Fresh ideas are introduced. The teacher knows that educational purposes are better achieved when they are adapted to the child's purposes. Good teaching supports the child. It is a harder way to teach—and administer—a school, but who ever said growing creative, independent thinkers comes easy?

Mark and Sammy were furious. Mark had actually loosened his belt and roared, "I'll thrash you!" The teacher decided it was time to move in. Without anger or panic she announced, "We'll talk about it at the carpentry table. There's more room." A firm hand was placed on Mark's shoulder, and they made it out of the line of traffic. Accusations came in a torrent. Gradually as their bodies relaxed with adult acceptance of young feelings, the teacher remarked that she had put a few new things in the odds-and-ends box next to the wood. It was Sammy who spotted the wheel. "A bike, we could make a bike!"

The teacher's questions were few. She had some more wheels but what else would they need? Steve, who had joined them, was already rooting in the lumber box. Having found one piece the other two boys liked, he dashed back to the blocks, where he was building something big and high, but from time to time he kept check on the "bike" activities too. Sammy and Mark vigorously nailed four wheels into the sides of the thick board. The teacher helped when the hardness of the wood threatened to discourage the builders.

Mark, sitting down to test drivability announced, "We've got to have a handle." His gestures and Sammy's indicated that it must be a crossbar. With one sitting in place, the other decided where the handle should be. After this extra piece was attached and the nail sticking up on the seat was hammered over, the boys concentrated on different ways to ride what they still called a "bike," for all its four wheels.

The contraption was painted, with each boy painting from each end, and, by the time they reached the middle, wondering if they should have used the same color but agreeing that the wheels looked fine. "Except they'll have to stay on the sidewalk. The snow would take the paint off." Watching and listening, the teacher buttoned Judy's coat and asked an aide to record what was going on while the boys set about planning another bike. "Then there'd be two—One for each of us. Let's do that."

When you need a teacher for young children, look for a professional with vigor and imagination who can tolerate informality, enjoys children and parents, and has emotional satisfactions independent of them both. A teacher is no less scholarly whose techniques are as simple as a shoulder bag for the postman, a toy truck to challenge riding balance, a suggestion that the wet mitt be put on the radiator to see what happens, a request for ideas about how to make block-building safer for the children inside.

Spontaneous play needs to be capitalized on. Both children and animals deprived of play fail to learn. What they learn at play can be enriched by the ideas the teacher puts in, the structure that beckons children to think, alone or in small groups, of consequences or alternatives or likely guesses. With a diagnostic and providing teacher the youngest children find new possibilities in various materials, different playmates, and themselves. Much further investigation is needed about sequence in intellectual development, individual learning styles, and how they are related to creative thinking in the elementary school. Nevertheless, despite the lack of final answers, available theory and basic human values support the need for spontaneous play and direct experience for young learners. They also support continued reinforcement of rich experiences for all children if long-range benefits are to be maintained.

Nursery schools and kindergartens give the school its first opportunities to assess strengths to be nourished and occasions to be capitalized upon for genuine partnership with parents. If the public school is ready for preschoolers, their parents will be the first to know. They will sense it in the early recognition of and conversations about the child's likes and dislikes, his daily routines, and his family's hopes for him. They will feel it in the empathy school people have for the concerns vital to them and to their children. They will spot any reservations, however, that the school may have about them as parents. They will know immediately whether a school is open or closed.

School administrators who enroll preschoolers have embarked upon an extended adventure. Like Bruce and Zita in space you will have problems. Hopefully your navigational skills will be less erratic. Certainly your desire to succeed will match theirs. And no one will be traveling alone.

ELEMENTARY EDUCATION: OBJECTIVES

Harold G. Shane

Changes in American Life since 1900 have created a number of mutations in the objectives of elementary education. The schools attended by our grandparents or great-grandparents sixty-five to seventy-five years ago generally sought to provide a rudimentary classical education, to preserve and strengthen established moral-religious values, and to help children attain the level of literacy and skill needed for social and vocational competence in the nineteenth century.

By 1920, as our culture changed rapidly, an increasing number of elementary teachers were making what Lawrence A. Cremin has called "a many-sided effort to use the schools to improve the lives of individuals." As a result, elementary education became more concerned with children's total development, with family-community life, and with the application of scientific research that had a bearing on teaching and learning.

Greater attention also was given to the problems that stemmed from an increased awareness of human differences and individuality in the increasingly complicated social environment that we were creating.

As goals for the elementary school broadened in the 1920's and 1930's, it became apparent that there was a deepening split between the proponents of *traditional* and of *modern* practices. During this twenty-year period, William C. Bagley, an eloquent advocate of "fundamental education" and William H. Kilpatrick, a major spokesman for "progressive education," symbolized the schism that developed.

In the early 1950's, viewpoints on what the elementary school should seek to accomplish remained a mosaic of conflicting opinions, and a decade of great debate was well under way. Even now the arguments continue to be lively ones, and as Adler and Mayer phrased it, "The traditionalist accuses the modernist of assuming that the world began yesterday, and the modernist accuses the traditionalist of assuming that it ended a century or two ago."

After prolonged and heated discussion, just where are we *now*, with respect to objectives for elementary education?

Trends in educational practices suggest current directions. The true

From *NEA Journal*, LI, No. 6 (September, 1962), 41-43. Used by permission of the author and publisher.

expression of an individual's goals resides in what he *does* rather than what he *says.* If this maxim be applied to elementary school objectives, it would appear that many persons working in the first six or eight grades—perhaps because of changed thinking resulting from the debates in the 50's—have become convinced that some important aims associated with traditionalist or fundamentalist education had been neglected.

To phrase it more bluntly, in the last three to five years there has been a distinct trend toward an intellectual or cognitive emphasis in elementary, instruction and some withdrawal from the pronounced social emphasis associated in the public mind with the label "modernist" or "progressive."

A recent article by William Van Til makes the point that American education "is engrossed with the application of technology to education,, with competing new proposals for organization of the school program," and with "updating knowledge through efforts by specialists in the disciplines."

This new preoccupation with technology, structure, and content reflects a departure from the extreme modernist position of the 1930's, when the orphic statement, "We teach *children*, not *subjects,*" was familiar.

Van Til's list of three emphases suggests a current search for the means of achieving more learning in less time, a concern for organizational devices that provide superior *machinery* and *techniques* for recognizing human differences, and a quest for advice from specialists with respect to content in the sciences, in the humanities, and in other fields.

What does the freshened interest in and trend toward more intellectual, educationally oriented programs suggest with respect to elementary school objectives?

If it is true—as certainly seems to be the case—that the aims of elementary education have become more forthrightly academic, does this increased intellectual emphasis threaten sound practice? Several points seem relevant.

First, and obviously, there is nothing inherently wrong with a judicious increase in tempo of attempts, through education, to improve the intellectual powers and extend the information of children. Any argument to the contrary is fatuous.

Second, there is a real and present danger that elementary teachers may become so mesmerized by the magic of technology, the appeal of novel grouping plans, and the respectability of more challenging content that they overlook the fact that these elements are means rather than ends in education.

The use of technology, for instance, is not a goal. It is a procedure in attaining a goal. Even mastery of content per se is relevant to aims only as it motivates the child to continue his education and to use his knowledge. In Alfred North Whitehead's well-known phrases:

> Culture is activity of thought, and receptiveness to beauty and humane feeling. Scraps of information have nothing to do with it. A merely well-informed man is the most useless bore on God's earth. What we should aim at producing is men who possess both culture and expert knowledge in some special direction.

Third, increased interest in the goal of enhanced academic achievement should be characterized by teaching that is stimulating and challenging rather than merely harsh and onerous. Standards are not improved by requiring that pupils engage in increased *busywork.* There is little or no point in their doing busywork in the first place.

Fourth, it is incongruous for elementary education to seek to improve itself by an all-out effort to ape the programs and practices of the junior or senior high schools. Such mimicry is not only foolish but ironic as well during a time when secondary school teaching is being influenced by instructional policies and by research in learning which were initiated in the elementary school.

Certain established objectives of elementary education should be preserved. Changes in the educational climate of the United States, as already noted, have generally reaffirmed devotion to intellectual growth and indicated the vitality of the school's concern for basic skills, problem-solving ability, and rational thinking. These are standing goals that merely have been restated with vigor. Plainly, they are worth preserving.

Other outcomes that merit our best efforts include the following durable goals: improved physical health, mental and emotional well-being, the cultivation of individual talents and ability through equal opportunity, the development of social and economic literacy and of moral values, improvement of skills in the realm of human relations, the achievement of an understanding of the workings of practical democracy, and an awareness of and loyalty to the ideals of democracy at the child's level of ability to understand them.

The objectives listed above are not controversial ones, and teachers of both "traditionalist" and "modernist" persuasions doubtless would accept them—although there might be disagreement as to *how* to attain them. Our task in elementary education, with respect to goals, therefore, is related to how they best can be achieved.

How successfully goals for elementary children are pursued depends to a large extent on the individual teacher in his daily life with children.

Therefore, it is important for him to acquire a body of intellectually examined educational values as a foundation for his leadership activities in the classroom. This quality of mind, this power of professional judgment, is what gives meaning to classroom activities and, indeed, to the teacher's personal life as well.

Phrased in another way, sound educational values, and the worthy objectives toward which they direct us, reside neither in things nor in phrases but in people. In this sense, "good" goals for elementary education are found within the teacher, and their attainment depends on his skill in organizing learning experiences for children.

In summary, during a span of sixty years our objectives in guiding the, progress of children toward maturity have shifted from a narrow concept of formal instruction stressing the three R's to an era in which the schools attempted to assume greatly increased responsibility for total human development.

In some instances efforts to shape the school's programs so as to improve the total lives of children and to remake community life were overly ambitious, and as a result we now find educational leaders reaffirming more explicitly elementary education's obligation to cultivate intellectual ability as a major ingredient in the experiences of children in school.

Our success in the future, with respect to objectives, depends on a consummate display of professional skill on the part of individual teachers in blending their quest for increased excellence in academic performance with educational experience that is equally effective in influencing the social behavior and emotional maturation of children in desirable ways.

In the process of continuing change in elementary education, let us hope that individual human development continues to be deemed of prime importance and that the nature and quality of our programs motivate boys and girls to continue their education throughout their lives.

WHAT SHALL WE TEACH?

Dorris May Lee

A changing world requires a changing role and a changing educational pattern for our schools. What we shall teach cannot be decided merely on the basis of what we were taught to deem valuable. Increasingly, we are aware that we cannot predict the state of the world in the future or the specific needs of its citizens. In light of this, it seems imperative that we reconsider what we teach children.

It seems fairly obvious that we cannot give children many of the answers they will need. Therefore, we must give them command of the processes by which they can determine their own answers in light of the situation at the time. They will also need some fundamental concepts about the world in which they live. Thus, we might well plan our teaching under the dual headings of processes and content.

WHAT PROCESSES ARE IMPORTANT?

What are the processes which the school should teach? Some of the more important may be:

the process of communicating
the process of conceptualizing
the process of seeing relationships
the process of generalizing
the process of making applications
the process of problem solving
the process of self-direction
the process of creating
the process of appreciating
the process of memorizing.

From *The National Elementary Principal,* XL, No. 3 (December, 1960), 12-16. Used by permission of the author and publisher.

It is apparent that these processes all represent certain skills in thinking. Too often when we have thought of developing skills, it was the mechanical skills to which we referred. Skills, however, are at all levels of behavior—from skill in letter formation to skill in human relationships. They may be more art than mechanics.

The process of communicating: Each facet of communication—reading, writing, speaking, and listening—is primarily a thought process. This fact should continually be uppermost in the teacher's plans and procedures. Equally important, it must be uppermost in the awareness and activities of the learners.

Reading is the process of bringing meaning and feelings to the printed page. Many of the thought processes other than communicating are obviously involved, such as seeing relationships between what is being read and knowledge gained from previous experiences and enriching and developing concepts.

In order to develop this process of reading, a variety of skills need to be learned. Some of these are the mechanical skills of analyzing word and sentence structure. Others are of a different order having to do with understanding—for example, the use of context clues. When a child reads orally and miscalls words in such a way that the material is quite meaningless, it is a dead giveaway that reading is not a thinking process for him.

Writing is a process of expressing thoughts and feelings so they are meaningful to others. Obviously here, too, there are mechanical skills involved, mainly penmanship and spelling, with a certain amount of skill in word derivatives. Most so-called poor sentence structure stems from unclear thinking and can only be strengthened by improving the clarity and sureness of the child's thought processes. Other skills needed are the ability to consider and empathize with the intended audience and modify the writing so it will be most meaningful to them; the capacity to have clearly in mind the idea to be communicated and plan ways of expressing it most effectively; and the ability to select words and compose sentences and paragraphs in a way that will help one work through an unclear problem.

Speaking is the process of exchanging thoughts and feelings orally with others in order to improve understanding. Included here are the mechanical skills of sound production so that words are intelligible. However, many articulation problems are the result of lack of clarity and sureness in the thinking being expressed. Other skills needed are the ability to organize ideas into meaningful sequence and, as with writing, gauge the listening abilities and interests of the audience and adjust to them. Development of these skills in school needs to begin in kindergarten and continue there-after.

Listening is the process of interpreting others' statements, ideas, and feelings. Schools have done a minimum of teaching this very important process. We continue to hope for greater cooperation all the way from between classmates to between world powers. Yet the ability to listen and understand how the other person is thinking and feeling, an imperative basis for cooperation, has received very little attention. We tell children to listen quietly and courteously but seldom do we say, "Listen to find out how another is thinking or feeling about something." Neither do we often say, "Listen to see what you think and feel about what someone is saying."

The process of conceptualizing: This process involves increasing differentiation. Throughout life, every concept deepens and sharpens from the first inkling one has of its existence. The school needs to be keenly aware of the important concepts in all areas of living. Teachers need to know what stage each child has reached in developing these concepts so as to correct misconceptions and advance the depth and sharpness of thinking.

The process of seeing relationships: The school should so teach and organize learning that children are constantly being helped to recognize interrelationships. Teaching the fact that in some way and to some degree all things are related stimulates children to look for relationships. And seeing them increases effective learning many fold.

The process of generalizing: This might be called the process of integration, for it involves finding common elements among concepts. Research has long documented the fact that generalizations are far more effective learnings than specifics. When children are led to make their own generalizations, the effectiveness of the learning is increased. They also learn how to make generalizations for themselves and test their accuracy.

The process of making applications: Since generalizations are better remembered, then surely children must learn how to apply them to new situations and do it accurately. Since the only value of anything we learn in or out of school lies in the success with which we can apply it in various situations, the school must deliberately and consciously teach such a process of application.

The process of problem solving: Life is a series of different kinds of

problems to be solved in varying contexts. The greatest difficulties we have
stem from an inadequate solution of such problems. By using significant
problems, both valuable content and needed processes can be learned. Also
a procedure will be established which will help children recognize and deal
with the innumerable problems of living at which we now cannot even
guess but for which they must have answers in the future.

The process of self-direction: Almost everyone agrees that learning the
process of self-direction is important. Yet we have far to go in teaching it
adequately. On the development of this process depends the continuing
growth of each child in accordance with his potential, the habit of lifelong
learning which is essential, and the amount of freedom which teachers will
have to give guidance to individuals and small groups.

Self-direction includes the more negative aspect of self-control but puts
emphasis on the positive, constructive, forward-moving activity of the child
under his own steam. He has this self-direction to some degree on his first
day of school. It can be strengthened and developed in his subsequent
learning experiences, or it can be so inhibited that he becomes more
dependent on teacher direction.

The process of creating: Much confusion has resulted from the failure to
separate consideration of the creative process from that of the created
product. The former is a way of thinking, an approach to life and its
problems. It involves always being ready to take a new look, to search for
more adequate alternatives.

The creative process depends on a healthy self-concept, a confidence on
the part of each child that *his* thinking and ideas are valuable. This may be
one of the most important learnings in the elementary school. It is an
approach to living which is essential for the adequate development of each
individual and our national life. Skill in the process of creating can be
developed in some aspect of every content area, in every process to be
taught. It means seeking new ways of looking at situations, new relationships and their implications for action. Only as the child develops
confidence and trust in his own thinking and ability to solve problems in
ways that are new to him, will he develop these processes to the point
where they make larger contributions in later years.

The process of appreciating: Richness of life comes from the enjoyment
of the good, the true, and the beautiful wherever we may find them. This
is far broader than an appreciation of the Old Masters, Shakespeare, or
Beethoven. It is a way of life and can be a part of every hour of every
school day.

How does one learn appreciation? Perhaps through respect for others and the products they achieve. We can learn to appreciate certain aspects of nearly anything while at the same time recognizing their inadequacies. We also learn to appreciate in terms of the effectiveness with which a purpose is served. Most of all, we can learn to appreciate differences.

The process of memorizing: In the early schools, memorization was the main process that was taught. With greater understanding of how children learn and, even more important, how they learn to use what they know in life situations, memorization has taken quite a different role. We know that rote memory produces mechanical performance. And with certain skills this is important. We also know, however, that for intelligent application even these skills must be based on understanding. We know further that many of the learnings that require memorization are much more usable if experiences requiring understanding and application are provided.

WHAT CONTENT IS IMPORTANT?

Processes are fundamental. But none of them can be developed without content, for they have no content of their own. This content is derived from the society in which we live—both present and future as far as we can predict. It is indefensible to teach content which is inaccurate or superfluous. Even though a "good case" can be made for any particular learnings, it is always necessary to ask if they will be more important to children tomorrow than other things that might be put in their place. It is equally indefensible to omit learnings which it is almost certain children will need as they take their place in adult society.

What is this content? Or perhaps, how do we determine it? All content deals with the world in which we live—a world which can be divided into the physical-biological world and the world of people. Basic information about both and ways of dealing with them are essential.

For instance, certain content in science may be used to develop the processes of thinking, such as forming concepts, seeing relationships, making generalizations and applications, and communicating all these. All the facts about the physical world can never be taught to any one person. However, basic information can be learned when content is selected to develop overriding concepts and essential thought processes with material meaningful to the child. Understanding why something is so and what the consequences and implications may be for himself and others are fundamental learnings for the child.

All this is equally true in relation to the world of people. Since this science is newer and less fully developed than the science of things, it has been even less well organized for the curriculum. The older disciplines of history and geography have been included, but the newer ones of sociology, anthropology, psychology, and economics have only begun to be tapped for the elementary school. Yet these developing sciences perhaps involve more concepts and understandings necessary for effective living than do the older ones. We should look carefully at these disciplines— determine basic principles appropriate for elementary school children and weigh their potential contributions against the goals of the elementary school.

IMPLICATIONS FOR CURRICULUM

What does the foregoing mean as far as what the schools shall teach? It means that teachers would be far more conscious than they are today of the processes they are developing. They would realize that any of these processes can be developed through a wide range of content. Thus, content can be selected on its own merits.

It would mean that nothing needs to be retained in the curriculum just because it has "always been there." In no other area of life do we believe that what was good enough for us is good enough for our children. And certainly, this is not true in education. Our infinitely increased knowledge, including our understanding of how children learn to live effectively, must rule this out.

Certainly, it means we will teach the skills of communication—reading, writing, speaking, and listening—and of arithmetic, and teach them better than ever before. But we will realize that only an extremely small portion of these skills are mechanical. The art must be taught along with the mechanics since there is no value in and of the mechanics themselves. And we will remember that a child has not learned a skill until he has learned how to use it artfully and effectively for his own purposes in a "real" situation.

The social studies program needs most careful consideration as to content, for it breaks the most sharply of all with tradition, and goals are often not clear. As it fits into the total program, its purpose seems to be to help children live more successfully in the world of people. The child needs to understand himself and his associates, why they do what they do and how to deal with both himself and them more effectively. He needs to understand groups of peoples in both near and far places—how they live, how they have solved their problems, and why they do as they do—for they are all becoming his neighbors in this shrinking world.

He cannot possibly begin to know all of these things about any one group, nor much of consequence about all groups. A decision needs to be made as to whether studying a few representative groups in some depth or surveying many groups leads to greater understanding. A meaningful study of a group needs to include all the major activities of living: communication, transportation, food, clothing, shelter, education, creative efforts, values, and other cultural factors. It should consider the political, economic, geographic, and cultural factors. It should consider the political, economic, geographic, and cultural forces which have influenced their historical development; their place in the family of nations today; the likenesses and differences between their situation and ours; and the implications of their life and development for understanding our own.

Such study could only be undertaken for a limited number of groups. Hence, in making our selection, we should choose representative groups and those which have the greatest significance for understanding our own and world history. As time brings changes to the world scene, so may the choice of what should be studied change. A program of this nature may contribute extensively to the development of all the processes mentioned earlier as well as provide extremely important content.

Science will be a part of children's learning in school from kindergarten on. It will be a matter of continually developing concepts and understanding through observation, experimentation, and research which at the same time will be developing the processes of thinking. Children need to know mathematics as the language of science.

Scientists and educators working together need to help teachers by outlining basic concepts and providing illustrations of ways and materials through which they may be developed. The use of a structured science program depends on whether or not teachers use situations in other content areas and in daily living to provide continuity in developing the important concepts.

The foreign language program in the elementary school has made considerable headway in the last decade. It has met with much lay approval, partly because of the status factor. This needs to be recognized and taken into account in our evaluation.

The greatest weakness in our elementary school foreign language programs is probably the lack of a clear purpose. Is it for communication pruposes? Then selection of the language is important and should meet either local need or national need in the international field. Is it for appreciation of another culture? Then quite different content, procedures, and goals need to be established. While the study of any language may give the basis for understanding a culture different from our own, efficiency seems to demand that a culture which most needs understanding at this time should be selected.

Implications of answers to the above questions are significant. If communication is the aim, then continuity of language instruction is essential. What about mobility of students? of teachers? Would all children participate? If not, on what basis would they be selected? What does this mean for teacher education programs? For new skills for teachers in service? The new mechanical aids could help, but all studies show these to be simply aids, in no way ruling out teacher skill.

If appreciation is the aim, then a different procedure would be more adequate. Diversity rather than continuity might be the goal. Could some familiarity with the language become a part of the study of any people? How would mechanical aids fit into such a program? Would teachers need more information on the interrelationships of language and culture, the interrelationships and basic differences in the languages themselves, and the implications for the enrichment of our own language?

The most crucial question of all is this: Are the benefits which come to children from the study of a foreign language greater than those which might be attained in other ways? Are there better ways of spending the child's time and effort during these elementary school years?

The arts contribute to the processes of appreciation, and enjoyment, and creativity. How clearly does the school distinguish this in its content? There is considerable content and skill in the field of music, as well as in the other arts. To what extent are these areas taught also as bases for creativity?

Graphic art is probably the area in which greatest creativity is encouraged. Are children being helped to use it as a basis for appreciation and communication? The number of small storms kicked up today by those who are unable to appreciate art different from the traditional or to gain communication from it certainly indicates a lack in the development of these processes.

Now, what shall we teach in the elementary school? Will the *content* need to be continually re-evaluated in terms of the needs of a rapidly changing society and in light of continually expanding and altered knowledge? Will the *processes* become ever more important as skills to be used in discovering solutions to current problems of living together in this contracting world? We have had much experience in teaching content, but how well do we know how to teach processes? Or will the deliberate teaching of processes alter our methods of teaching content?

EDUCATING CHILDREN FOR CHANGE

John U. Michaelis

Four facets of education for change have been singled out for consideration in this statement. Certain points about the child's frame of reference for reacting to change are made first. This is followed by attention to selected aspects of two interrelated processes involved in dealing with change. Illustrative concepts related to change as found in basic sciences are summarized next. Finally, a few pitfalls and related challenges are noted. Because definitive research is not available, only tentative inferences and general suggestions can be made.

A fact that must not be overlooked is that children are actually living change in a day by day complex of experiences. They are a part of it and they interact with change via TV, radio, the press, experiences in school, community activities, and experiences in a variety of non-school educational agencies. What may seem like a dramatic change to an elderly person is really just life today for the child. For example, in the 1920's an expression of great speed was "going like forty" which later was changed to "going like sixty" and still later to "going over a hundred." Recently the writer heard children say as they engaged in dramatic play with jet planes, "Okay, let's try for three machs." This is indeed a change for the person accustomed to "going like forty." Yet for the child it is life today which will become his frame of reference for considering change tomorrow.

Thus an individual born in a world of jets, TV, nuclear fission and fusion, automation, social welfare programs, international agencies, and the like builds a background for thinking about change quite different from that of an individual born in an earlier generation. Both a great challenge and a difficulty arise because of this. The great challenge is to nurture the child's developing background in such a way that he becomes truly at home in the world today—finds a role to play, is aware of the effect of change upon one's role, learns to deal with change-producing forces, senses the emerging nature and direction of change, and is not frightened by change. The great difficulty is to develop a creative and inquiring sensitivity to changes needed in non-material phases of our culture to meet problems created by changing from "going like forty" to "let's try for three machs."

From *Educational Leadership*, XIV, No. 6 (March, 1957), 336-341. Used by permission of the author and publisher.

Changes within children themselves cannot be overlooked, since they condition the child's view of change and of others as they react to change. Expert guidance is needed as children move from dependence to independence, from a *me* to *we* to *me-we-other* concept of human relations, from gangs and cliques of one sex to heterosexual groups, and from self-centered to in-group-centered values to broader values and ideals vital in democratic living. Acceptance and understanding of changes within children should be coupled with experiences designed to enable children to understand and cope with changes within themselves and within their groups. The child's changing self-concept needs special attention so that a wholesome self-concept emerges as he moves from a *me* to *we* to *me-we-other* approach to others. Key outcomes are reasoned self-understanding and self-acceptance which are related to understanding and acceptance of others.

BASIC PROCESSES

Children need to become increasingly self-directive in dealing with change. A variety of competencies are needed, ranging from first level communication skills to a high level of critical-creative thinking. Two interrelated processes which combine a multitude of competencies are problem solving and the making of choices.

A dimension of these processes needing systematic attention is that composed of feelings and attitudes. This element is of crucial importance because of the emotional involvement created by change. In any given personal or social problem of real interest and concern, feelings and facts are intertwined and decision making typically is based on both. Preferences, interests, tastes, likes, dislikes very properly enter the thinking process. The problem is not to rule them out, or to ignore them, but to recognize them as a part of the process. It may well be that the feelings of the group, or of individuals within the group, will be of first importance in reaching a decision. Or it may be that once feelings and facts are both considered the decision will be based primarily on facts, and plans will be made to eliminate or control insecurities or threats to individuals because of the feelings involved. In either event, growing competence in handling both feelings and facts should be a primary outcome of problem-solving experiences that entail emotional involvement.

Related to this are the competencies needed to reap maximum benefits from mass media and non-school educational agencies which present current changes in an unsystematic way. Analysis, synthesis and some organized consideration of changes in light of values and current problems are necessary if effective understanding and action are to be achieved. High order skills are involved. For example, skills in critical and evaluative viewing and listening are needed to detect and share change-in-process and problems created by change as they are portrayed on TV and radio. Critical and selective reading abilities enable the child to note recent and long-term changes reported by the press and in resources found in libraries. Critical observation and research skills can be used on study trips to museums which offer concrete opportunities to develop insight into changes whether they are related to interventions, race relations, intercultural contributions, or to other human problems. Similarly, participation in youth groups and activities of civic and welfare agencies, and analysis of materials produced by various groups bring children face to face with new developments and proposals for meeting change. Competence in evaluating conflicts, sifting out critical elements, making choices and working with others to further common goals are brought into play.

Because change forces individuals and groups to make choices, the process of making choices in light of sound values becomes increasingly important. Involved are such elements as predicting the consequences of various choices, clarification of pertinent values, reconciling conflicts of values where possible or understanding and appreciating conflicting values where reconciliation is not possible, using mutually acceptable values as guides to choice making, balancing adherence and flexibility in applying values in new situations, and continuing evaluation and revision in light of acceptable values. While some choices will be primarily an individual matter, increasingly the trend is toward the making of choices in a group context. Here the individual needs to learn to work within a group-value frame of reference with sensitivity to individual variations. Fundamental attitudes of cooperation, concern for others, respect for the individual, and open-mindedness can be brought to bear directly upon specific choice options. Without such specific application these broad attitudes do not yield maximum returns to the improvement of choice making in a group setting.

BASIC CONCEPTS RELATED TO CHANGE

Concepts related to change as developed in the basic sciences and the humanities need to be considered systematically in planning and revising the curriculum. Such concepts are helpful to school workers in their own search for a better understanding of change and as a possible dimension of learning experiences for children if pertinent to a given problem. In order to keep ourselves up to date we need the continuing counsel of experts in the various disciplines. The following examples are illustrative of concepts related to change in different areas of human activity.

How people react to change is conditioned not only by physical factors in their environment but also by factors in their culture and subcultures. Likenesses and differences here and in other places need to be explored to points of understanding and appreciation in light of multifactor rather than single-factor causation.

Change is an imperative condition of human society, but may or may not be progress. As value systems change, cultures change and the desirability of change is appraised in light of values. Change has accelerated in the recent past in some areas of human activity and not in others with resultant dislocation and strain.

Use of the method of free inquiry is essential to the making of decisions in light of change and to the appraising of rightness and wrongness of action. Decisions and actions are right if they lead to a better way of life; they are wrong if detrimental to the individual or to society. Each individual needs to fashion a framework of values for such appraisal, and each individual is ultimately responsible for ethical matters in his own life. Through religion and philosophy man seeks and expresses values, and tries to relate his life to value-producing and personality-producing forces in the universe.

Increasing interdependence coupled with the struggle to achieve a better life in widely varying social-physical environments accentuate the need for teamwork in meeting human problems resultant from change. Needs, conflicts, tensions, hopes and aspirations need to be considered in light of varying human values and in light of varying means employed to deal with them.

Social groupings develop and change to meet individual and social needs. In varying degrees groups condition individual behavior, induce conformity, tap individual uniquenesses, and conserve individual and group integrity. Group values are strong motivating forces, they differ greatly in various cultures and subcultures, and frequently are obscured in conflicts and tensions. What may appear to be nonconformity to one group is really conformity in light of another's values. Effective communication between and within groups is essential to progress in coping with change.

Demands and problems created by change have forced individuals to resort to group action in an increasing number of situations. Loss of individual identity in groups not only has altered the roles that individuals play, but has created new concepts of group action essential to the achievement of both individual and group goals. New challenges and responsibilities face each individual as steps are taken to maintain personal integrity and individualism in certain spheres of activity while an all-out group effort is made in other activities.

Governments exist and change to serve the people and to regulate certain activities in the public interest so that security, justice, welfare and freedom may prevail. An increasing sense of brotherhood and concern for others is being expressed at home and in other places through changes in laws and institutions. Great civilizations have declined because of the failure to meet changing conditions through institutional adjustments. A belief in progress appears to be basic to the improvement of government.

Changes in a given culture are due to cultural inventions of other times and places as well as to inventions of the given culture. Invention, accumulation, diffusion and adjustment are processes in cultural evolution. Increasing cultural interaction has accelerated these processes, increased interdependence, and led to the development of new institutions.

Rate of change in both material and non-material aspects of culture varies greatly among cultures and subcultures. Isolated groups change slowly. Individuals in isolated cultures have little or no opportunity to move from a *me-we* to a *me-we-other* concept of human relations.

A dual stimulator-perpetuator role for schools and certain other institutions has emerged in connection with the rapidly changing material aspects of our culture and the slowly changing non-material aspects. On the one hand schools utilize and pass on material change to youngsters; on the other hand they conserve and pass on certain basic values of long term importance in our culture. Education is expected to stimulate technological and scientific change in line with material needs, yet must perpetuate and pass on many traditions, customs and norms in social areas, some of which may be out of line with emerging human relations needs. Material changes transmitted through schools by mandate of the people constitute a stimulating and changing influence in our culture. Social norms transmitted through schools by mandate of the people constitute a conservative, stabilizing influence. The great challenge here is to note needed changes in social norms and to use reasoned persuasion to bring about their inclusion in the instructional program.

TO BE AVOIDED

There are several pitfalls or dangers that should be avoided in our efforts to educate for change. One of the most serious is the tendency of some adults to become alarmed by change. If we do become alarmed and reveal anxieties we may create a real psychological problem for children as well as for ourselves. Inevitably children take on some of our worries and anxieties. They may even become frustrated, as are many adults, by rapid changes that are taking place.

On the other hand if we adults do not become alarmed by change, or do not reveal anxieties, if we can ride the changes as children do when they interact with secure persons, we can make a real and immediate contribution to the education of children for change. This calls for a high level of self-discipline because experiences in our past are vastly different from experiences in the present. If we exercise such self-discipline and endeavor to develop it within children, they will be better equipped to accept and to deal with change in the future when present-day experiences become their past and when changes crowd into their lives as adults. And in our teaching about change let us avoid the creation of fears about the future and attitudes toward change that are based on hopelessness, futility, and inevitable determinism.

A second pitfall is that of stopping short of helping children to generalize about change and to find a role to play as changes occur in home, school, community, or in the broader environment. It is one thing merely to perceive change; it is quite another to move on to develop generalizations and plans of action to meet change. Generalizations about change should be developed by children to enable them to meet and understand change in a variety of situations and to bring order to their thinking about change. Plans of action should be developed where appropriate to help them work out a role to play. The challenge is to help children move from a level of mere awareness of change, to understanding and generalizing about change, to finding a role to play in dealing with change.

A third pitfall is the belief held by some that non-material elements of a culture should change as rapidly as material elements. What psychological and social chaos we would have if certain basic values and ideals found in the home, church and other institutions were to change as rapidly as have certain technological elements of our culture! Stability, security and a steadying frame of reference are needed to deal with change. Frustration, anxiety, insecurity, poor choice making, and unintelligent problem solving can be expected in any situation in which there are no stabilizing factors, no operating values in which individuals have confidence, or no sound ground rules for action. The plea here is not for the maintenance of archaic institutions. Rather, let us make those modifications in non-material elements needed to deal with change and at the same time identify and utilize the steadying, security-giving elements needed to enhance individual and group welfare.

A fourth pitfall is the tendency of some to "chuck the old and grab the new" and to take on an attitude of unreasoned skepticism regarding a given cultural heritage. Change for change's sake emerges as their mode of operation. Let us recognize that any brand of authoritarianism is inimical to education for change whether it be based on either a status quo or on an anti-status quo approach. The tendency of some to desire pat answers derived through exclusive consideration of externals must be supplanted by a consideration of all the factors both internal and external that are related to a given problem created by change.

A fifth pitfall is the tendency of some to lose sight of the individual. The emergence of groups as power elements in all phases of our culture, and subgroups as power elements within large groups, quite properly has focused attention upon group processes. And group approaches will be used increasingly to meet problems and to deal with change. But what about the individual? Is maximum self-realization neglected? There need not be inconsistencies and neglect, provided consideration is given to both individual and group dynamics in a given situation.

A sixth pitfall is the introduction of conflicting values which children cannot handle without developing serious anxieties and frustrations. Home-school, majority-minority, and child-adult values are conflicting in a variety of individual and group situations. Many conflicts will arise even though we would wish otherwise. But let us not add to this burden by introducing conflicts of value resultant from change which are far beyond the child's ability to handle. The challenge here is not to avoid conflict, rather it is to avoid the introduction of conflicts which lead to hostility and threats to integrity. The second challenge is to help children develop competence in maintaining emotional balance and integrity in the face of what appear to be irreconcilable conflicts of value of a given moment. And thirdly, let us help children develop creative persistence in continuing to try to resolve some of the conflicts that appear at the present time to be irreconcilable.

READING UNREADINESS IN THE UNDERPRIVILEGED

Warren G. Cutts

Huh? . . . unh-hunh . . . nuttin . . . naw . . . wuh? . . . 'cuz . . . uhn-hnh . . . sho!

Is this a readiness-for-reading vocabulary? Definitely not! Yet, unfortunately, these "words," with variations for emphasis and inflection—plus a few other one-word sentences and a generous sprinkling of vulgarities—comprise the speaking vocabularies of many culturally disadvantaged first graders. These and other strange noises that take the place of standard American English reflect the impoverished language background of these children.

Although listening, speaking, reading, and writing skills are only a part of the needs characteristic of language-handicapped children, they are a vital part. Without mastering communication skills, culturally disadvantaged youngsters can never unlock the doors that lead to useful, productive citizenship; they can never become first-class citizens.

The above is not to say that culturally disadvantaged children cannot communicate with each other. Some of them have developed "scat" language to a rather high level of fluency. Nonetheless, this scat talk does not belong to the worlds of books or of business—worlds which are foreign to these children. Thus, teachers need to approach English language instruction for these children as if they were teaching a foreign language.

The foreign language approach might be coupled with one used successfully by some teachers. They have used the analogy of work clothes, play clothes, and Sunday clothes to convey the concept to their pupils of a different language for a different purpose. Different occasions call for different modes of dress, they explain, and the same thing is true of language.

As inconceivable as it seems, some teachers expect mastery of reading and writing skills by children who reveal gross deficiencies in listening and speaking.

Obviously, children who lack readiness for reading in terms of their oral language development and background of experience must have a prolonged

From *NEA Journal,* LII, No. 4 (April, 1963), 23-24. Used by permission of the author and publisher.

readiness program either in school or before they enter school. Six-year-olds who cannot talk coherently can scarcely be expected to begin reading as soon as they enter school.

Children whose language is limited to grunts and crudities need extensive experiences before they are ready for any formalized reading instruction.

If these children are to master the basic language skills of listening and speaking, they must have a wider range of experiences—both real and vicarious—than their more fortunate counterparts.

Such experiences should include listening to stories told or read by the teacher; taking field trips to parks, farms, zoos, airports, fire stations, and other points of interest; using and listening to tape recorders; hearing records; and seeing movies and film-strips. In all these activities, the main objective is to provide pupils with opportunities for language experience. They must, therefore, have plenty of time to react to and talk about the things they have seen and heard.

Teacher attitude is extremely important in helping disadvantaged children. The teacher needs to realize that vocabulary and language concepts develop slowly. He must learn to accept each child as he is and to respect him as an individual. He must take nothing for granted and carefully check all his assumptions concerning the child and the child's experiences.

For example, the teacher should not assume that children are familiar with points of interest in their own cities or, indeed, within their immediate neighborhoods. Many culturally deprived children have extremely limited horizons; many have never traveled more than two blocks from home before entering school.

That children learn largely through imitation suggests another important consideration for the schools: Culturally disadvantaged children cannot be kept out of the educational main stream without perpetuating the inadequacies that set them apart in the first place. Although culturally disadvantaged children generally cannot progress as rapidly as other children, they must have an opportunity to associate with them. (For the sake of over-all progress, however, probably no more than four or five disadvantaged children should be assigned to any one classroom.)

Whatever the school's approach, something must be done to overcome the handicaps resulting from cultural deprivation, particularly as it affects readiness for reading instruction. Otherwise, American teachers and administrators must be prepared to answer for the failure of an ever-increasing number of children to master the necessary skills of communication.

If the schools are to help the culturally deprived, I believe that a radical departure from typical educational procedures and instructional techniques is needed. One such innovation might be to reach down into the preschool years to provide these children with some of the experiences which other children typically have had before coming to school.

Such experiences might be arranged through special nursery schools and day camps. Adaptations might be made, for example, from the All Day Neighborhood Schools program of New York City.

Day camps and nursery schools can also provide an opportunity for teachers and others to work cooperatively with parents. This is important, for if parents are not brought into the program and shown how they can supplement the school's work, teachers and parents of culturally disadvantaged children may foster concepts that are diametrically opposed to one another.

Of course, all of this would call for a larger staff and for a greater expenditure of money than at present.

More and more educators are recognizing the importance of working with culturally disadvantaged children during the early formative years. School systems such as those of Dearborn, Michigan and Quincy, Illinois are now shifting emphasis from the junior high and high school to kindergarten and first grade. This shift is long overdue and should be extended downward until it reaches into the preschool years.

Culturally disadvantaged children must be helped to accept themselves and to realize, at the same time, that different kinds of language are appropriate as situations vary. They must come to understand that without better language mastery they cannot hope to bridge the gap which lies between themselves and profitable occupations—between second-class and first-class citizenship.

Culturally disadvantaged children have much to contribute to society. Many of them are talented in music, in art, in athletics, and in other fields, but few of them have had the opportunity to reveal these talents. Most of them depend primarily upon the school as the socializing force that can help them to find their places as contributing American citizens.

School and preschool enrichment programs may never be able to compensate fully for deficiencies in the experience and training provided by the home. Nevertheless, such programs can go a long way toward overcoming the handicap of a poor start, and without such enrichment, culturally disadvantaged children are certain to show irreparable gaps in their learning and to fall hopelessly behind the rest of society.

IMPROVING THE SOCIAL STUDIES CURRICULUM
AT THE ELEMENTARY-SCHOOL LEVEL

R. C. Bradley

The general direction being taken in the reorganization of the social studies curriculum is familiar to most educators. Obvious, too, is the fact that some tend to wait to see what their neighbors in education are going to do before they exercise more than opinion.

There is little need here, I believe, to argue whether content or method brings forth better achievement in youngsters. It is safe to assume that without a knowledge of the content, a method or methods would be of little value to the teacher, for she cannot impart that which she doesn't know. Hence, it should be stipulated at the outset an awareness of the need for a knowledgeable teacher. Moreover, personal observation suggests there is too much "telling" by the social-studies teacher, instead of motivating the child through a realistic problem situation in which he must think critically for himself.

This leaves one additional problem to be resolved. There is a need to consider the problem of *planned obsolescence.* That is, any questionable part of the social studies program should be studied by administrators and teachers alike, and procedures for deleting the superfluous content and the reduction of repetitive teaching of certain subject matter should be a matter of combined efforts and written policy. Succinctly, it is no longer only an assumption that children in primary grades know much of the social studies content prior to instruction.

Few persons would quarrel with the soundness of the general objectives of elementary-school social studies, which emphasize the need for developing in children a consciousness of the interdependence of people and nations, a realization of citizenship in action, an understanding and perpetuation of the American way of life, a critical awareness of the local, state, and national world about them, and an opportunity to extend into real life situations the basic objectives of education.

Possibly the main argument against modern school practices in social studies is that they are factless. If one is not careful, social studies can become a mass of vague generalities, falling to the point of erroneousness

From *The Social Studies,* LIX (February, 1968), 63-67. Used by permission of the author and publisher.

on the one hand and rising to pseudo-scientific pleasantries on the other. Teaching all too frequently has been by textbook assignment with emphasis on word or fact retention. And objective tests of the true-false category make it unnecessary for clever children to know much at all.

Then, too, youth evidences shocking unfamiliarity with some periods of history. One radio commentator reported a holiday survey at an East Coast beach, where he asked, "Why do we celebrate today?" Most replies ranged from "It's firecracker day" to "It's connected with some war." Believing that there is poor retention of historical knowledge and that its significance for current living has not been widely enough grasped, many educators express growing concern that those facts which contribute to reasoned thinking must become a part of the social studies curriculum.

CONSIDERATIONS

Among significant research findings which should be given consideration prior to revision of the local social studies program are these:

New insights regarding child growth and development as related to the teaching of certain subject matter.   Simply because a child *can* learn something at a given time should not be interpreted to mean that he *should* be taught it. However, there is evidence that children can learn some things in social studies not previously accepted wholeheartedly by educators. One study by Edward Beaubier involved the deliberate presentation of social studies material of greater complexity than is normally taught to children of grade 6. His findings were that these children can learn more than is typically expected of them.

Val Arnsdorf conducted a study with 536 sixth-graders dealing with activities stressing chronology, and concluded that pupils can profit from systematic instruction in the social studies which is undertaken to increase their understanding of and ability to use time relationships.

As repetition and duplication of subject matter is reduced to a minimum at all grade levels pupil boredom is also reduced in large measure. Hence, time might be used more wisely on those things of higher quality.

There are new developments in reading in the social studies. Training in the critical reading of the subject may begin as early as the primary grades if it is directed by the teacher. The judgments, inferences, and conclusions drawn by pupils may be compared and evaluated. Ethel Maw's study shows a strong indication of the effectiveness of the lessons in improving the thinking skills required by the test of critical thinking. Students in this study showed improvement in the thoughtful consideration of problems, the tendency to suspend judgment, and a desire to obtain evidence before forming conclusions.

New topics and units in social studies that merit attention. Although several areas merit consideration for inclusion in the curriculum, certain urgent ones should have priority. First, in recent months, public preoccupation with the status of the cold war between the United States and the USSR has been reflected in increased demands for school studies to help in understanding and combating communism. Recent studies support the statement that a majority of our schools have major inadequacies in the locally prepared topics and units for teaching about the evils of communism. Moreover, a few studies indicate expressions of hostility or indifference of students to excessively exhortatory or dogmatic programs of cold-war education. Although more research is needed, there is evidence that teachers will want to steer clear of dogmatic programs, and also of the extreme reflective approach which attempts to bring an intellectual discipline to bear on the study of controversy. Possibly the direct comparison of the democratic way of life to dialectic materialism would bear fruitful results. However, it should be recognized that communist rule is a continuous campaign against alleged hostile forces, and therefore not a normal system of government.

Secondly, the child's basic political orientation to regime and community undergoes little change during the high-school years, and there is little evidence that fundamental attitudes and values toward regime and political community are any different if one considers that point at which the child began and ended his high-school work. A new insight from research is that the ages of three to 13 seem to be the most formative years in political maturation.

Lastly, the teaching of economics in the elementary school is receiving increased attention. Among learning experiences reported as useful in building economic understanding are visits to places such as construction sites, freight yards, chain stores; use of current news; utilization of audiovisual materials, including graphs, charts, and scrapbooks; and visits of resource persons from banks, loan companies, and the like. Luther Hartwell Hodges has stated, "Americans can—and must—learn their economic ABCs, for at the bottom the case for economics is the case for democracy itself—government by the people. If a democracy is to cope effectively with economic issues, the people must understand."

PRIORITY

What should receive first priority in improving the social studies?

The quality of any program depends in large part on the willingness of the teacher to become better informed about her subject and her desire to improve basic ideas necessary for effective learning by the pupils. Social studies teachers need to think quite often in the way the historian thinks. Of first priority, then, is the need for the teacher to understand the structure of the discipline itself.

When the teacher recognizes that social studies is not a body of precise, memorizable facts, social studies will become, in a sense, constant controversy with her students. It will become alive when the students recognize that historical interpretations change as man examines events at different times and in different places. The scientist draws conclusions, formulates principles, and makes generalizations. Is this not also true of the historian? One of the chief duties of the teacher is to point out how history attempts to delineate, assess, interpret, and give relative place to the efforts of people, to important ideas, and to national achievements which may help the students deal with contemporary affairs. Textbook conclusions must be properly analyzed by the learner.

The teacher who points out these significant scenes behind the movements of various historical periods makes a contribution to the growth of our civilization. Hence, the teaching of social studies is more than reading and discussing a text. It involves a study of change and progress, human motives or drives, morals and ideals, material wants and needs, peaceful cooperation and warlike coexistence, conflict and hostility, communication and transportation, and the placing of historical events in appropriate perspective. The teacher of the social studies must relate history within the learner's grasp to time past, time present, and time future.

POTENTIAL OF THE ARTS IN ELEMENTARY SCHOOL

Ivan Johnson

In the elementary curriculum one may find grouped under the arts the visual arts, drama, music and dance. Occasionally industrial arts may be included. Generally music and art are the most common components of the arts area. Dramatics frequently is an outgrowth of creative writing or story telling in the elementary classroom, with little opportunity given for creative interpretation and forming illusions. Dance is perhaps the most neglected area; it is all too often a rainy day activity carried out in the name of physical exercise.

Whether the arts program is an expanded one (embracing the visual arts, music, drama and the dance), or one with two areas, the contribution to learning may be a rich and meaningful one. To make a significant contribution to the elementary school program, the arts need thoughtful study, strong support, and continuous evaluation.

Within the past decade the public has been deeply concerned about the curriculum of the schools, particularly with the programs for science and mathematics. Focusing on math and science education diverted temporarily the attention of educators from other areas in the curriculum. Public concerns, however, seem to swing like a pendulum. In recent months attention has been drawn to areas other than science and mathematics that need study. The public began to wonder if other areas of the curriculum did not also need re-evaluation, since mathematics and science had been in need of study. Questions were raised about the relative importance of this or that content in the curriculum. There were critics, in the pursuit of greater emphasis on the sciences and mathematics, who clamored loudly about "frills" consuming valuable learning time. The arts were among the areas to be labeled "frills."

Actually, this approach had a positive effect on arts education. It has brought about the rediscovery of the value of the arts to our culture in general and to learning in particular. Sterling McMurrin, U. S. Commissioner of Education has said:

We must guard against the tendency to suppose that our national well-being is served primarily by advances in technology, however

From *Educational Leadership*, XIX, No. 7 (April, 1962), 445-448. Used by permission of the author and publisher.

important and timely these may be. Knowledge is of value for its own sake as well as for its uses, and unless the sciences are supported in their own right the capital of knowledge on which our technology is nourished will surely diminish. And the social sciences and the humanities and fine arts are as important to the quality of our culture and eventually to the strength of our nation as are engineering and the physical sciences, upon which now so much obviously depends.[1]

In the process of reexamination, educators have begun to eliminate the superficial, produced-for-show activities and supplant these with arts learning experiences of a more meaningful kind. Interdisciplinary investigations, drawing upon findings in philosophy, psychology and sociology, have added new dimensions to the arts. Research, as well as experimental curricula, have more clearly defined new concepts.

CONTRIBUTION OF THE ARTS

The body of new material on the arts in education supports a more vital role in the growth and development of the child. The arts are not insular in their position in the curriculum. While strong as learning experience in themselves, the arts also gain strength from within the total curriculum of the school program.

The arts program is predicted on the assumption that the aesthetic principle is deeply imbedded in man and that its presence contributes to his well-being. The aesthetic needs of man are manifested in many ways. As they have throughout the history of civilization, the arts today reflect man's continual quest for life's meaning and his progress in solving the problems of his time. Man is frequently in contact with the arts through enjoying and reflecting on them as he finds them in his environment, or through creating the arts for his own purposes.

In the arts the individual, more than in almost any other human endeavor, must become personally involved, whether he is creating directly or is a listener or spectator. When the individual is participating in the arts by creating form directly, he is involved in the act of perceiving, judging, selecting and acting upon his judgments as he creates. As a spectator or listener, he becomes personally involved through his senses as he discovers new aspects, assimilates or establishes empathy in the visual or audile

[1] Sterling M. McMurrin. "A Crisis of Conscience." *The Education Supplement of Saturday Review*, September 16, 1961, p. 58-59, 77-78.

stimulus and gains new meanings in the art form he is perceiving. The arts, according to Manuel Barkan,[2] may be viewed as a means of both communion and communication. Viewed as communion, the arts are a way of perceiving and a means for rediscovering things one has taken for granted. As communication, the arts are a form of language and a medium of expression.

Understanding the arts cannot be accomplished by externalized or appreciational means alone. Research in the arts has shown that knowledges have greater depth and contribute more to our lives when we learn through direct experience or involvement in the creative art processes. Frequently citizens, and even teachers, seem to assume that the arts program in the school is one and the same as the program for the development of the professional artist. The nature of the learning in the arts for the professional must differ from that which seeks to deepen the knowledge of the arts for the child or youth. The arts learning for the child or young person must be designed to build on his particular values, interests and needs to the extent to which he may relate to them. Therefore the arts program in the public or community education must be conceived in terms of the broader, nonprofessional aspects of the arts-in-action in our society. The arts teacher or arts specialist, however, must be familiar with both the professional and nonprofessional approaches. The vitality of the arts in our society is derived from the ferment of change and a continuous search for creative solutions. Thus, the arts program in the elementary school grows and changes as it keeps pace with growing children in a changing world.

GOALS FOR THE ARTS

Although there are specific goals for each area, the arts have common aims which cause them to be so grouped. They also have interrelations that strengthen them as a group as well as individually.

In the elementary school, the teacher seeks the realization of certain goals in a good arts program. This program should help the pupil develop an understanding of his creative self and to appreciate the creative work of others. Through learning experiences in the arts, the pupil has an opportunity to form aesthetic judgments. He learns to value the creative, not the imitative, in the arts. The program should help the student to become

[2] Manuel Barkan. *A Foundation for Art Education* (New York: The Ronald Press, 1955), p. 6.

sensitive to aesthetic form, to sharpen his visual and audile perception. Integrated with and directly related to ongoing creative learning should be knowledge of our arts heritage—the art forms which have so greatly enriched civilization. Development of skills and knowledge of technical processes and media adapted to the developmental levels of the pupil and his needs is a part of the educational process in the arts.

In carrying forward the goals for arts education, the teacher is a catalyst for creative learning. When he becomes directive, imposes his own adult concepts on his pupils, the teacher operates in direct conflict with the aims of a good arts program. It is through the realization of these goals that the arts program contributes significantly to the education of the child.

It is assumed that since the elementary curriculum is already crowded with content that "must be taught," a program for arts education might be watered down or restricted in scope. If we can focus on the quality of experience more than the quantity, there is no reason why a rich program in the arts cannot be effectively provided in spite of limited time.

TEACHER ORIENTATION IN THE ARTS

Teachers, principals and supervisors have little opportunity to experience the arts in their professional preparation. Thus, when confronted with teaching the arts as part of the elementary curriculum, they may feel insecure. Generally they are aware of the importance of the arts per se in education but their lack of experience usually causes them to substitute how-to-do-it crutches for method and practice which at best provide little more than busywork for the child. In order to bring about more effective teaching in elementary school, we must help teachers, principals and supervisors, through professional and in-service education, personally to explore the arts in depth. Through personal experience, teachers may gain insights into the nature of the arts, creative behavior and the rich range of media (whether it be art, drama, dance or music).

In school systems where specialized personnel, such as art or music teachers and supervisors, are employed, there are usually workshops and laboratory sessions for helping teachers become more effective in the teaching of the arts. The help classroom teachers receive from these in-service activities is dependent upon the quality of leadership. A teacher, feeling insecure or unknowing, needs in-service activities which constitute orientation and are of a self-discovery kind. As he gains confidence through personal experience in the arts, he relates this to his teaching and the way in which children can be helped to develop creativity. The specialist must be able to see the teacher's problems through his (the teacher's) eyes. This requires inspirational leadership attuned to the teaching needs of those who seek help.

Yet what if there are no special teachers, no special supervisors? The writer has visited many elementary schools in which the faculty has organized an arts curriculum committee. The arts curriculum committee develops resources for teaching, organizes problem-solving study groups and workshops and stimulates self-evaluation. Some of the committees have brought specialists to their schools for workshops.

In one school the teachers had expressed interest in working with their pupils on a mural, but most of them were uncertain about how to get started. The general supervisor (elementary) discovered their problem and suggested that since she herself was not too familiar with mural making, it would be interesting to have a work session in which she and the teachers could develop one before teaching children about it. A film and several good books on the topic were obtained. In the work session an exciting mural was created and evaluated. This was only the beginning. Since the mural making session, workshops on such topics as papier-mache, picture making and ceramics have taken place. The supervisor's office, it might be added, is now resplendent with art (which she created) hung between the shelves of the state adopted readers and social studies books.

Ideally there should be a provision for equipment, facilities and materials needed for a good arts program. For example, a piano and a record player are important to a good music program. The need for the specialized resources for the teaching of the arts cannot be denied and should be recognized by school administrations. A long-range plan is needed in most instances to acquire gradually the resources for teaching the arts. There are, however, ingenious and imaginative ways that facilities and materials can be improvised and found, so that valuable learning experiences can be provided. The lack of facilities, equipment and materials can be studied by teachers, supervisor, principal and parents to find a way of developing an arts program. Sometimes it is surprising to find how many resources for teaching exist in the school community, especially when the faculty, administrators and parents explore the problem together.

SELF-EVALUATION IN THE ARTS

The quality of the arts program is dependent on self-evaluation. The arts continuously reflect new ideas in our culture. Thus, an arts program must be ever-changing, sensitive to new developments. Growth in the arts is stimulated by exploration of the unknown as well as the known.

In a meeting with the parents of an elementary school, a mother asked the writer if in a good art program her child should be making potholders each year as her parents' Christmas present. Apparently in grades 2, 3, 4 and 5 the children had made potholders every year. In this particular school no ongoing evaluation of the art program had taken place; a dull program was reflected in this instance. Through self-evaluation teachers ascertain the creative growth in their pupils, appraise their teaching effectiveness, identify problems needing study, and discover new potentials for the further development of the program.

In another school where parents were invited to participate in the evaluation of the arts program, it was a revelation for them. They became aware of the purposes of a good arts program and the means for implementing it. Prior to their participation, they, as members of the P.T.A., had regarded the arts as sources of supply for their programs—a musical or dramatic performance (usually precisely drilled) by pupils, or nut cups, posters and program covers for their social affairs (to which the children were not invited). As a result of the evaluation, the P.T.A. began to supplement the record collection in the school. New interest was taken in plays and music, which now became more creative and more closely related to the ongoing program of the school. The point here is that when we reflect on the true purposes of education, we focus on those learning experiences which are more significant to the intellectual and emotional growth of children. Stated goals for arts education are meaningless unless they are studied in all their dimensions.

Through personal experiences in the arts, the study of new ideas and practices and continuous evaluation, the arts program becomes increasingly dynamic. When teachers and parents discover the potential of the arts in the elementary school program the results are richly rewarding.

AAAS ELEMENTARY SCIENCE PROGRAM

Arthur H. Livermore

The American Association for the Advancement of Science Commission on Science Education was established by the board of directors of AAAS in the spring of 1962. The Commission has accepted the responsibility for stimulating improvement in science education at all academic levels. A major activity of the Commission since it was established has been the preparation and evaluation of science materials for the early grades. These materials are a series of exercises designed to improve the child's skills in using the processes of science. They are published in trial edition under the title *Science—A Process Approach.* Exercises for kindergarten through grade three develop the child's skills in these processes: observing, classifying, measuring, communicating, recognizing space/time relations, recognizing and using number relations, inferring, and predicting.

In each successive exercise in a sequence the child is expected to increase his skills in using that process. Observing, for example, starts with simple observations using various senses, and progresses to observations of animal motion, bacterial growth, and plant growth.

Recognizing space/time relations starts in kindergarten with simple activities designed to develop skill in recognizing two- and three-dimensional geometric shapes and in recognizing these shapes, or close approximations of them, in animate and inanimate objects. The sequence includes exercises on direction, time, straight and curved lines and surfaces, rate of change of position, and, finally, relative position and motion.

The titles of the exercises in the measuring sequence illustrate how a process is treated as a continuing thread.

Kindergarten.   Beginning Measurement—Comparing Lengths; Linear-Measurement.
First Grade.   Metric Measurement; Ordering Plane Figures by Area; Making Comparisons Using a Balance; Comparing Volumes; Measuring Forces with Springs.
Second Grade.   Are Pictures Always Life Size?; Measuring Volumes; Describing and Representing Forces; Estimations and Comparisons Using

From the *Journal of Chemical Education,* XLIII, No. 5 (May, 1966), 270-272. Used by permission of the author and publisher.

the Metric System; Separating Materials from Mixtures; Measuring Drop by Drop.

Third Grade.   Introduction to Temperature and Thermometers; Measuring Rate of Change—Evaporation of Water.

Fourth Grade.   Measurement of Volume by Displacement of Water; Units of Force; Measurement of Angles; Introduction to Probability.

In the first kindergarten exercise, Beginning Measurement—Comparing Lengths, the child arranges sticks of different lengths into sequences of increasing or decreasing lengths and learns to select objects of the same length by matching them to each other or to a third object. In the second exercise, Linear Measurement, the child uses sticks or blocks as units to measure the lengths of objects larger than the units.

Metric units of length are introduced in grade one. The children learn to use a simple equal-arm balance and to use metric units of mass. They also learn to use a spring scale to measure the force of earth-pull. The idea of area is introduced in first grade and area is measured by counting the number of similar objects—books, or squares on a transparent grid—that just cover the area being measured.

The participants at the summer writing conferences at Stanford University in 1963-64 agreed that we should include both the metric and the British-American systems since the latter *is* taught in schools. Several of our tryout teachers suggested that we stay with the metric system in our program. Both the teachers and the children like it. The writing group at Michigan State University in the summer of 1965 therefore decided to use only the metric system in the third experimental edition.

The second grade exercise on forces not only gives the child some experience using arrows to represent direction and magnitude of forces, but also introduces him to the idea that equal and opposing forces act on objects that are at rest.

In the exercises on measuring volume the child learns metric units and gets some idea of the volume of a drop of water.

Measurement of temperature and of rate of change in a physical system are the subjects of the third grade exercises.

In grade four the students measure volumes of solids by displacement of water. The idea that a solid can displace its own volume of water is not self evident to children of this age. This method of measuring volumes of solids is used later in grade six in an exercise on density in the operational definitions sequence. The newton as a unit of force is introduced at this grade level.

TRYOUT AND EVALUATION

The program has been prepared by a group of scientists, science educatois, and teachers who met for eight weeks each summer in 1963-65. During the summer writing conferences, the writers were asked to consider carefully the objectives of each exercise they prepared. It was suggested that they first ask themselves, "Just what is it that I would like a child to be able to *do* after he has finished this exercise that he could not do before?" The answers to this question are the statements of objectives that are listed at the beginning of each exercise. With objectives stated clearly, it should be possible to devise simple tests to determine whether the child has achieved the desired skills. Two such tests are provided.

First, at the end of each exercise thère is an "appraisal activity" that the teacher uses to find out how well the children in her class have achieved the abilities. Second, each teacher is provided with a competency measure which she administers to a random sample of children after each exercise has been taught. This competency measure is the backbone of our evaluation system. The tests are simple ones and the teacher checks "yes" or "no" for each child depending on whether he does or does not exhibit the appropriate behavior. ("Point to the blue triangle." Check *yes* if he does and *no* if he does not.)

The results of the testing with the competency measure are returned to AAAS where the results are tabulated by D. Henry Walbesser and his staff. The results of the first tryout year when we had about 120 teachers (K–3) in 12 centers teaching the program, were encouraging. On the average, 90% of the children tested with the checklists exhibited 90% of the desired behaviors. Control children were checked, and the best results showed 50% exhibiting 50% of the behaviors. During the second tryout year approximately 80% of the children tested with the checklists attained 80% of the desired skills. The decrease between the first and second year seems to be due mainly to the increased difficulty of the revised exercises.

In the summer of 1965, a writing group composed of more than 50 participants[1] revised the K-3 materials for the second time and the grade four and five exercises for the first time, and wrote new exercises for grade six. The processes for grades four through six are rooted in the elementary processes.

Exercises for grades four through six develop the child's skills in these processes: formulating hypotheses; making operational definitions; con-

---

[1] Two astronomers, eight biologists, seven chemists, two geologists, four mathematicians, six physicists, five psychologists, one sociologist, four education teachers (science), and 13 teachers and administrators.

trolling and manipulating variables; experimenting; formulating models; interpreting data.

THE QUESTION OF CONTENT

Science processes are the major themes or threads around which the AAAS program is constructed, but it is clear that process cannot be taught in the absence of content. The content has been selected from various science disciplines. In fact, one reason for selecting science writers from biology, chemistry, physics, geology, and psychology was to provide a balance of content topics for the process exercises. In a sense, process is the warp and content the woof of the fabric of the AAAS elementary science program.

In grades K–6 there are at least 28 (out of 184) exercises that are related to the field of chemistry. Some of these are quite simple, but they all lead to the more intensive study of chemistry in later years. The exercises that are concerned with the properties of matter are listed in Table 1 and the exercises in which changes in properties—chemical changes—take place are listed in Table 2.

In the exercises involving changes in properties, listed in Table 2, the children are not told that they are observing chemical changes taking place. In the kindergarten exercise, Observing 12, Observation of Color and Color Change in Plants, the emphasis is on careful and accurate observation. The children observe a colored plant, for example red cabbage, being boiled in water, notice the color changes, and the fact that some of the color goes into solution in the water. They then observe the changes in color that take place when vinegar or baking soda are added to the solution.

In the third grade exercise, Prediction 3, Case of the Suffocating Candle, the children observe the burning time of a candle under jars of different volumes. They measure the volumes of the jars and plot burning time against volume on a graph. Using this graph they then predict what the burning time would be under a jar of different volume from any that they tested. They then determine the burning time under that jar to test their prediction.

In the fourth grade exercise the students mix cornstarch, talcum powder, baking soda, or baking powder with water, a dilute iodine solution, or white vinegar. They observe the changes that take place when each pair is mixed. They are given an unknown solid, selected from the group of four with which they have been working, and are asked to carry out tests to identify it.

In a fifth grade exercise, the students learn something about the effect

Table 1. Exercises on the Properties of Matter

Grade	Process	Subject
K	Observing 1	Perception of color
	Observing 6	Perception of odor
	Observing 9	Observing solids changing to liquids
1	. . .	. . .
2	Classifying 6	The solid, liquid, and gaseous states of matter
	Inferring 2	Differentiating between similar things
3	Inferring 6	The displacement of water by air
	Communicating 10	Describing an experiment (Settling of sand and pebbles in water)
	Classifying 8	The color wheel–An order arrangement
4	Classifying 10	A punch card system for identifying minerals
	Classifying 11	Classifying and describing materials of the earth
	Formulating hypotheses 1	Evaporation and condensation
	Controlling variables 5	Thermal expansion
	Experimenting 1	Separating mixtures
5	Predicting 7	The pressure-volume relationship of air and water
	Formulating hypotheses 2	Air has mass and occupies space
	Formulating hypotheses 3	The atmosphere exerts pressure
6	Experimenting 3	Semipermeable membranes
	Formulating models 4	A mechanical model of a semipermeable membrane system
	Formulating hypotheses 6	Viscosity
	Formulating hypotheses 8	Small particles (An introduction to colloids)
	Experimenting 6	Chromatography
	Experimenting 8	Growing crystals

of temperature on reaction rate in an exercise in which they measure how long it takes Alka Seltzer tablets to dissolve in water at different temperatures.

An exercise on fermentation introduces them to a biochemical system. In that exercise they identify the gas produced by a mixture of yeast and sugar as carbon dioxide, measure rate of fermentation by counting bubbles, and investigate the effect of changing concentrations and temperature on fermentation rate.

Table 2. Exercises on Changes in Properties

Grade	Process	Subject
K	. . .	. . .
1	Observing 12	Observation of color and color change in plants
2	. . .	. . .
3	Predicting 5	Case of the suffocating candle
4	Interpreting data 2	Identifying unknowns
5	Interpreting data 11	Effect of temperature on rate of change
6	Controlling variables 13	Fermentation

CHILD PARTICIPATION

We consider the development and tryout of the AAAS program to be a major experiment in education. The emphasis on developing skills, the clear identification of objectives and the built-in evaluation program are significant aspects of the experiment. How the skills are developed—whether in group activities or in individual ones—is also a part of the experiment. Some of the exercises can only be done by the individual alone, for example the fifth grade exercises on The Effect of Practice on Memorization, and Why Do We Forget?, where the child determines the effect of practice on his ability to remember the Latin names of 20 familiar animals. Other exercises can be done by groups. In general we have tried to emphasize activities which are done by small groups, and we have provided some equipment and supplies to the tryout teachers to encourage child participation rather than teacher demonstration.

Representative of the exercises which are done by small groups is a fifth grade exercise, Interpreting Data 4, Magnetic Fields—The Nature of the Earth. Each child uses his small compass to trace the force field around a magnet which has been fastened to a large sheet of paper taped to the floor. The completed diagram is the work of a group of four or five children. Each group compares its diagram with the diagrams of other groups whose magnets were oriented in different directions and the class interpret their collective data.

The tryout of the program is continuing in 14 centers by about 250 teachers.

SELF-CONTAINED CLASSROOM: WHERE DO WE STAND?

Rodney Tillman

One-teacher-to-a-classroom is the predominant pattern of organization in elementary schools throughout the United States. "Self-contained classroom" is the term usually applied to this arrangement. In many school systems this organizational pattern was a direct outcome of study and research in the area of human growth and development. During the 1940's several studies of elementary school organization were made. Each study reported an increase in the number of school systems having the self-contained classroom as its basic organizational pattern.

Most educators who work in elementary schools define the self-contained classroom as one in which a pupil is under the guidance of one teacher for most of his school-sponsored activities. The teacher is expected to have much knowledge about each child in the class and to use this knowledge in providing guidance and assistance to the pupil and to his class. The self-contained classroom does not exclude the pupil from having contact with other teachers, other pupils, various specialists and school and community resources.

Within a school system, assignments of elementary school classroom teachers are generally made in one of two ways. Either a teacher works with one class and has responsibility in all subject matter areas or a teacher works with several classes and has responsibility in a limited number of subject matter areas. At the present time, various proposals and demonstrations which require a teacher to work with several classes during the school day are receiving nation-wide publicity.

There is at present a lack of carefully documented research evidence to show comparisons between patterns of organization and achievement in subject matter and growth in other areas of learning which are generally accepted as goals of the elementary school. It is important, therefore, to re-emphasize those values which come to children whose teachers know them well. Clara R. Chiara has written: "The teacher who knows the learner as an individual does not fragment the child, neither does he assess him solely on his ability or talent in one narrow field. Rather he views

From *Educational Leadership,* XVIII, No. 2 (November, 1960), 82-84. Used by permission of the author and publisher.

each student in his totality as a person of innate worth who has strengths and weaknesses in varying degrees in the many different life activities in which he engages. This climate of acceptance and respect encourages each student to move toward optimum realization of self." [1]

Perhaps the safest prediction one can make regarding today's elementary pupils and the years ahead is that the pupils will experience a continually accelerating rate of change in all areas of life. Basic to comprehending these changes will be an ability to understand the many interrelationships which exist in our society. This ability is best developed in the elementary school when pupils are given opportunities to work on problem areas which cut across subject matter lines. Emphasis given to these lines by teachers and parents is primarily responsible for their being recognized at all by pupils.

Separating the elementary school curriculum into specific areas and assigning a portion of the program to a certain teacher is an extremely complex matter. This becomes apparent as one studies the time allotments and the fusions of subject matter areas being made in some school systems where classroom teachers are assigned to teach specific subjects. Almost any subject can be found fused with practically every other subject taught in the elementary school. In studying time allotments for a specific subject one also finds great variation.

Alice Miel has discussed the possible contributions of the self-contained classroom to efficiency in learning with respect to mental health factors, use of time, and availability of resources and facilities. She states, "If a type or organization has more promise for accomplishing certain goals (better mental health, more integrated, more complete learning), then our best course is to work toward the realization of the potential that is there." [2]

PROMISING PRACTICES

It is also important to identify practices that are considered most promising in today's elementary schools. We can then determine how each practice will be promoted or hindered by a specific organizational pattern. Some promising practices promoted by the self-contained classroom include the following:

[1] Clara R. Chiara, "Effective Education in the Self-Contained Classroom," *The Self-Contained Classroom* (Washington, D.C.: Association for Supervision and Curriculum Development, NEA, 1960), p. 2.

[2] Alice Miel, "The Self-Contained Classroom: An Assessment," *Teachers College Record*, LIX, No. 5 (February, 1958), p. 286-87.

1. Parent-teacher conferences can be held. In these it is possible to discuss a pupil's intellectual, physical and social achievements and cooperatively plan next steps for working with the pupil.
2. Special resource teachers and classroom teachers can work as teams in teaching groups of pupils. A team approach enables the teacher specialists to be of maximum assistance to the group. Significant all-school activities such as sings, exhibits and special programs are possible when the resource teachers and classroom teachers work cooperatively on such undertakings.
3. Field trips can be conducted that extend over a longer period of time than normally allotted for one class.
4. Upper elementary school pupils can work in many ways with younger elementary school pupils. This practice should enrich the school program for both the older and younger pupils. Planning for such activities should involve all teachers and pupils who participate or who are affected by the program.
5. Activities that are under way simultaneously can be aimed at taking care of individual needs and interests. In each classroom, frequent periods of time should be provided for each pupil to work in those areas in which he is weak, or those in which he is strong or has special interest. The teacher who knows the pupils well will be able to guide each pupil into activities that will provide a balanced program for him.
6. Materials can be used in various ways that seem appropriate to the learning activity in progress. For example, the arithmetic book is very helpful, not only for mathematics but for the development of specific reading skills; and a map is often used in the teaching, not only of geography, but of arithmetic.
7. Problems can be studied that do not lend themselves to any one subject matter area. For example, a study of conservation or weather would draw upon areas such as reading, science and social studies.

It is true, of course, that one can identify situations in which the human relations and the promising practices possible in a self-contained classroom do not actually exist. One must realize, however, that no single pattern of organization can always assure a good school program. There is at present considerable public pressure for improving our schools. Many persons apparently believe that almost any change in organization will bring about the desired improvement. Educators, therefore, need to channel the public interest into constructive improvements, such as expanded in-service programs and longer periods of employment for professional personnel. Taking the easy, and often regressive, way of dealing with such pressures by drastically changing the existing pattern of organization may prove to be too costly to the pupils as well as—eventually—to the society.

A self-contained classroom offers the pupil opportunities for: (a) the development of strong human relationships, (b) a teacher who knows him well, (c) integration of subject matter areas, (d) individualized instruction, (e) growth in self-understanding and self-respect, and (f) choices in the use of his time. Since these opportunities are easier to provide in the self-contained classroom organization, this pattern should continue to be the predominant one in the schools of the United States.

Reaching the full potential of the self-contained classroom is an ever-continuing process. It is hoped that each reader will view his own situation not only in terms of "what it is" but also in terms of "what it might be."

TEAM TEACHING FOR THE ELEMENTARY SCHOOL

Philip Lambert

Among current developments in education, there is one which today is causing interest and excitement, as well as some negative reactions. This development is *team teaching*. Through many experiments with instructional teams have been made in junior high and high schools, the team teaching plan seems to have equal if not greater relevance to the needs and objectives of the elementary school.

The basic principle behind team teaching is not new, but older than formal education itself. The family unit, made up of many cooperating members—parents, grandparents, aunts and uncles, older brothers and sisters—was in the teaching business long before the first school was built. Today, children continue to learn basic skills from the members of their families most interested or best qualified to teach them. Team instruction, too, is based upon the idea that every teacher excels in some, but not all, of the abilities and techniques that are necessary for the education of a single child. Ideally, these special abilities should be used to the fullest extent, so that each child will get the best possible education his school can offer in every area.

From *Educational Leadership*, XVIII, No. 2 (November, 1960), 85-88 and 128. Used by permission of the author and publisher.

The present system of elementary school organization, however, attempts to give every teacher the same number of pupils, the same time schedule and curriculum, and the same responsibility, regardless of his or her special training, experience, skill, or capacity for taking responsibility. In addition, many elementary school teachers are overwhelmed with non-professional duties. Up to 40 percent of their time is spent in keeping attendance, collecting milk money, typing stencils, correcting routine tests, supervising playground and lunchroom activities, etc. Although most elementary teachers are sold on the educational importance of these tasks, actually how educational are they? This use of professional personnel for routine work that could be done at far lower cost by a secretary or a student aide is a waste of our limited teaching resources. It is as if qualified doctors were required by law to spend from two to three hours a day taking temperatures, filling in charts, and sending out bills.

In its simplest form, team teaching occurs whenever more than one teacher has responsibility for the same group of children at a given time—for example, whenever a certified teacher is assisted by a student teacher. In a more complex form the instructional team is a group of teachers of different experience and abilities aided by various non-professionals. The team may have from three to six or more members and be responsible for an elementary school class of as many as 150 or more children. The class may be all of the same grade level or of varying grade levels.

There is no typical instructional team. Let us look, however, at one team that might be assigned to a class of about 125 children ranging in age from five to eight years. At its head is the team chairman—an outstanding and experienced teacher who, let us say, is especially strong in the fields of language arts and social studies. He is assisted by two other fully licensed teachers: one has had several years of experience and some special preparation in the teaching of primary math and science, while the other, who has just received his credentials, is especially interested in arts and crafts. There are also two teaching interns who are completing their college or university preparation, and an instructional secretary, perhaps a mother, who serves as a part-time teachers' aide. The salaries of these last three staff members added together come to less than that of two fully qualified teachers. Since the team chairman receives an increased salary in recognition of his special responsibilities, the cost of the whole team is approximately the same as that of the teachers who would have been assigned to the same number of children under the present system.

Team teaching should not be confused with the departmentalized plan in which each teacher is responsible primarily for one subject area. The members of an instructional team, though they are all specially competent in certain areas, have their primary responsibility towards all the children in their large class. For example, if one teacher presents a science demonstration to the large class, the other teachers assist the demonstration teacher during the presentation. Therefore, when the groups break down into small work groups, each teacher has heard and participated in the demonstration from the beginning. This enables them to be effective small group leaders.

More than a dozen communities in the country have initiated team teaching in the elementary school. In most instances the experiments are in a developmental stage, and the staff members involved are not ready to evaluate their efforts completely at this time. However, both the Franklin school in Lexington, Massachusetts, in cooperation with Harvard University, and the Washington school in Madison, Wisconsin, in cooperation with the University of Wisconsin, are developing experimental designs to compare team teaching with present methods of teaching. This serious effort is taking place despite the fact that some researchers believe there are too many variables to make it possible to set up a completely valid experimental situation, in which only one aspect of team teaching would be tested at a time.

Preliminary results from the Franklin school have been inconclusive. However, the staff has reported that pupil achievement and adjustment remained the same notwithstanding the unsettled conditions of experimentation. The Washington school has begun a five-year project designed to answer such questions as these: What effect does team teaching have on pupil achievement in the various subject areas? What changes took place in children's perception of authority figures under team teaching conditions?

Informal evaluation seems to show that team teaching works in a variety of situations.

WHAT PROBLEMS ARE SOLVED?

Let us look now at some typical everyday problems of elementary education and see how team teaching might help to solve these:

1. Ricky has just had a fight in the play yard; he is now crying uncontrollably in the hall as class begins. What was the fight about? Who started it? What should be done? A few minutes' attention from someone who can learn the answers to these questions and who knows Ricky would probably clear up the matter. But Ricky's teacher cannot leave the rest of the class even for a few minutes. She will have to send

him to the principal's office, even though this may make him more disturbed. With an instructional team, someone who is familiar with both the child and the immediate situation is always available to help.

2. Mrs. McKay, a third grade teacher, has been ill off and on for several weeks. What effect will this have on the lives of the children in her class? Under the present system, each time she is absent a substitute will be sent in, and the chances are that each time it will be a different substitute who is completely unfamiliar with the children, the lesson plan, and perhaps even the school building and personnel. She will not know that David has trouble with division or that Susy will quiet down if she does not sit by Jane. She does not know whose turn it is to take attendance, what to do with the two turtles that have been brought to school, or where the nurse's office is. Probably she will be able to do little more than baby sit with the children until Mrs. McKay is well enough to continue their education.

The team system does away with this problem. In an emergency, any one of the other team members can pitch in and the instructional program can continue unimpeded. If a substitute is assigned to the class, there will always be someone available to answer her questions and tell her whatever she needs to know.

3. Sally just cannot get along with her teacher, Miss Grey. Sally has never been a disciplinary problem before, but she is lively and boisterous, and Miss Grey, though an excellent teacher, is a quiet, reserved kind of person. An experienced principal knows that all teachers cannot work effectively with all children. Should he move Sally to another room? Even if the child is not upset by this change, the principal may have to spend weeks reassuring Miss Grey that it was not her fault that she couldn't help Sally adjust and that she is not a failure as a teacher. If Miss Grey is part of an instructional team, however, this situation need not arise. An ideal teaching team will be made up of teachers with varying personality types, and it should contain someone who will find Sally easy to teach. Others may have special ability when it comes to dealing with the slow child, the shy child, etc.

4. Peter is an exceptionally bright boy who is considerably ahead of most of his classmates academically. However, he is rather small for his age and not unusually mature emotionally. Should he be moved ahead into a class with larger and older children, or should he stay where he is, with less and less interest in what is going on in class? Under the present system there is seldom any really satisfactory solution. But in the type of team teaching plan in which children of different ages are grouped together, Peter will be able to work at the level of his ability and still continue to play with friends of his own size and age. Even if the class

does not include older children, its large size means that it is more likely to contain enough other bright children so that special rapid-progress groups can be set up.

5. Mr. Johnson, one of four sixth grade teachers in a large elementary school, is an enthusiastic amateur scientist and has taken a course in elementary science teaching. Under the present system, only the 30 children who have the luck to be assigned to Mr. Johnson's class each year will be able to profit from his interest and preparation. Team teaching is still too new to have definitely established the best patterns of organization for all content areas. It has been shown, however, that subjects like science and social studies are particularly well suited to large-group teaching and the use of visual aids. In a team teaching setup, Mr. Johnson can make the introductory science presentations to a group of 120 children. He will also be available to help the other members of his team in planning follow-up work for smaller groups.

These are only a few examples of how team teaching might help a school to carry out some of the practical objectives of elementary education. A good team teaching program has other important advantages. It presents exceptional opportunities for the preservice education (and financial support) of undergraduate student teachers and also of students who already hold an A.B. degree but must take certain courses in order to earn a teaching certificate. For the qualified teacher, it provides an opportunity to move ahead in the profession without leaving the classroom where his ability and experience can be of most use. Team teaching also gives staff members a chance to work together on a common task, to share their ideas and their problems. They will be able to see good teaching practices in action and to learn new techniques. Some teachers today tend to look upon supervision as a threat to their autonomy. Perhaps the supervisor is seen as an investigator from outside from whom all problems must be concealed, rather than as someone who can give help in solving problems. In team teaching, the supervisor is regarded as a team member who shares both the work and responsibility.

Are there disadvantages in team teaching? In the beginning, the fears most often expressed were that the children would feel lonely or lost in such big groups, that they would be confused by the continual changing of rooms and teachers, and that they would miss having one person to relate to (or cling to). In practice, these fears have proved to be more or less unfounded.

The real problems of team teaching have centered around such matters as organization, curriculum planning, budgeting, and school architecture.

Team teaching is still in an experimental stage today, and setting up a good instructional team requires a great deal of skilled organizational work. Many observers have remarked on the vast amounts of time that are spent in discussion and planning. Though an established team teaching program should cost no more than the present system, getting one started is expensive in terms of money as well as time. New curriculum materials suitable for large-group instruction must be found or created, rooms rearranged and refurnished, audio-visual and clerical aids purchased, etc.

For these reasons, many school systems will move slowly in setting up instructional teams, in spite of all their apparent advantages. Nevertheless, it seems certain that team teaching is going to play a more and more important role in the future of American education. How can it lose, after all, when the children are behind it? Most of the children who have experienced team teaching have been enthusiastic. They seem to adjust quickly to the idea of having several teachers instead of one. They make more friends and join more activities. Most of all, they find school more interesting. With team teaching, the old-fashioned picture of the hopelessly bored child, forced to sit and squirm day after day in a certain seat in a certain room, listening to the droning voice of the same teacher, becomes a thing of the past.

THE NONGRADED SCHOOL: AN OVERVIEW

Robert H. Anderson

Few topics on the current scene are of greater interest to elementary school teachers and administrators than the nongraded school. The subject of a rapidly expanding literature, nongradedness has probably received more attention over the past decade in national, state, and regional meetings than any other aspect of school organization, and DESP's mailbox is constantly full of inquiries about it. Yet, for all the publicity it has received, nongradedness apparently remains a somewhat nebulous, even confusing, concept. It is therefore both timely and fortunate that DESP has

From *The National Elementary Principal,* XLVII, No. 2 (November, 1967), 4-10. Used by permission of the author and publisher.

reserved two issues of *The National Elementary Principal* for a thorough examination of the nongraded plan.

NONGRADEDNESS DEFINED

One reason for the uncertainty that surrounds the concept of nongradedness is that its vocabulary is both imprecise in meaning and negativistic in tone. "Nongradedness" is a clumsy and unsuitable term, since it refers primarily to what it is *not* rather than to what it *is*. Furthermore, the label "nongraded" has often been applied to programs which have made only very limited departures from conventional gradedness (for example, only the reading program has been rendered more flexible), or are merely a version of homogeneous grouping or even departmentalization. Often, too, visitors to so-called nongraded classes discover that terms such as "first grade" and "third grade" are still in common use and pupils may still be confronted by conventional A-B-C-D-F report cards, as well as the administrative machinery of promotion and nonpromotion. In the absence of agreement concerning its meaning, and because of the carelessness with which it is used, "nongradedness" is therefore a term for which the profession desperately needs alternatives. For the moment, however, we must struggle along with it as best we can.

Nongradedness refers to at least two dimensions of the school and its atmosphere: 1) the philosophy (or, if you will, the value system) that guides the behavior of the school staff toward the pupils, and 2) the administrative-organizational machinery and procedures whereby the life of the pupils and teachers is regulated and facilitated. It is, in short, both an operational mechanism and a theoretical proposition. It is not a new staffing pattern, as is team teaching. It is not a technological innovation, as is educational television. It is not, as such, a component of the curriculum reform movement, though it may very well be the chief inspiration behind curriculum reform. Rather, it is a concept of what is right and a plan for implementation of that concept.

Many definitions have been offered, and for the most part they differ in the elegance and the comprehensiveness with which their authors have stated them, rather than in conceptual meaning. Without exception, the emphasis is upon individualizing instruction and upon developing each individual up to his full potential for physical, social, intellectual, and civic accomplishment. Without exception, too, there is reference to the fact that provision should be made for both differentiated *rates* of pupil progress and variations in the *kinds of programs* offered to this child and that.

Many, though not all, refer to the need for more suitable forms of evaluating and reporting pupil progress, and most make some reference to the various *means* for individualizing instruction via pupil group, independent study, and other procedural arrangements. The titles of nongraded programs vary, many using phrases like "Continuous Progress Plan" or "Continuous Growth Plan," but others simply referring to the name of the school or city in a phrase such as "The Middletown Project."

Although most publications on nongradedness and an overwhelming number of pilot programs are at the early elementary level, the movement is in fact inclusive of all school levels from nursery schools through the university. The writings in this field are primarily in the form of magazine articles and pamphlets published by local school systems, although there are now a number of complete volumes dedicated to this topic. Several of those most recently published are in effect case histories of certain specific programs.

John I. Goodlad, in one of the three major volumes[1] produced by the NEA Project on Instruction, points out that there are several different models of school organization, or variants thereof, to be found in American schools today. One of these is the graded pattern which, we fervently hope, is rapidly disappearing from the American scene. Gradedness grows out of an assumption that schools are intended to cover and to inculcate in the pupils a specific body of subject matter which is carefully laid out in the successive grades and closely identified with those grades. In this model, the fact that children differ from each other is viewed primarily as an explanation for the differences in children's actual performances, and not as a basis for planning the program. Pupils who make slow progress are adjusted to the system by means chiefly of nonpromotion.

In the learner-centered, nongraded model which Goodlad then describes, the following assumptions are made:

School function: Schools are learner-centered—designed to develop the learner as an individual and as a member of society.
Means of fulfilling function: Focus should be on ways of knowing and thinking. Emphasis is on the individual.
Organizational structure: Graded structure is either ignored as meaningless or replaced with a nongraded plan. Grouping patterns are flexible. Individual differences tend to be accounted for through intraclass provisions rather than interclass provisions.

---

[1]Goodlad, John I. *Planning and Organizing for Teaching.* National Education Association, Project on the Instructional Program of the Public Schools. Washington, D.C.: the Association, 1963. pp. 54-57, 65-68.

Individual differences: Differences in many aspects of development are recognized and used in planning highly individualized programs.
Pupil progress: Provision is made for both differentiated rates of progress and variations in kinds of program, according to individual needs and abilities.

Nongradedness should not be confused with departmentalization, self-contained classrooms, or cooperative teaching plans. The latter three arrangements represent the major alternatives in horizontal school organization (i.e., the way the progress of children is regulated over a period of years). Every school must commit itself to both a vertical and a horizontal plan, and therefore if one believes in nongradedness he can, if he chooses, combine it with team teaching or with the self-contained classroom pattern, or (as in the Dual Progress Plan) with a form of departmentalization.

There is increasing reason to believe, as I do strongly, that nongradedness is both easier to develop and more effective in practice in schools that abandon the self-contained classroom arrangement in favor of its horizontal alternatives, especially cooperative teaching. It appears to be considerably more difficult for any one teacher by himself to carry on an appropriately flexible program for his class than it is for a group of teachers who share a larger number of pupils. However, having made this strategic suggestion let us return to our attempt at definition of a nongraded program.

In a full-fledged nongraded program, all of the following statements would be justified:

1. Suitable provision is being made, in all aspects of the curriculum, for each unique child.
   a. This implies flexible grouping and subgrouping of pupils.
   b. It implies an adaptable, flexible curriculum.
   c. It implies a great range of materials and instructional approaches.
2. The successive learning experiences of each boy and girl will be, to the greatest possible extent, pertinent and appropriate to his needs at that moment. Easier said than done, of course, but this—*not* teacher convenience or administrative convenience—is the creed that guides our professional decisions!
3. Each child is constantly under just the right amount of pressure—not too much, as in the graded school for slow learners, nor too little, as in the graded school for talented learners. Again, easier said than done—but we strive to do it!
4. Success, with appropriate rewards, is assured for all kinds of learners so long as they attend to their tasks with reasonable diligence and effort. Such success spurs the child to a conviction of his own worth, and to further achievement.

a. Failure and frustration occasionally? Yes, but not nearly as much as faces the below-average child in the graded school!

b. Over-confidence and complacence occasionally? If so, the system isn't working right.

5. Absent are grade labels (1st grade, 6th grade, etc.) and the related machinery of promotion-and-failure.

6. There is a reporting system consistent with the philosophy that says each child is a unique and precious individual. Teachers abolish the ridiculous and cynical system of A-B-C-D-F report cards.

7. There is more sophisticated curriculum planning, evaluation, and record-keeping on the part of teachers than one finds in schools still loyal to graded practices.

Admittedly an element of propaganda seems to color the foregoing statements, but it seems reasonable to link some of the hoped-for qualities of the school atmosphere with the mechanism itself so long as our intent is to define the idea at its best.

One further dimension of the nongraded concept requires explanation before we proceed to a discussion of nongradedness in practice. One of the characteristics of the graded school, especially in this century in urban schools, has been the separation of children into classes by age. Granted that there is nonetheless a spread of two or more years within each class because some children progress more rapidly (for example, via double-promotion) or more slowly (via nonpromotion), the typical graded class is composed mostly of children who are approximately the same age.

In a nongraded school, it is possible to continue this practice although there is increasing reason to believe that heterogeneous, multi-aged class groups may be preferable. It is argued that children require regular social and intellectual contacts, not only with other pupils of like mind, talent, and experience, but also with pupils of differing backgrounds and predispositions. This implies that a nongraded class (or, preferably, team) of children spanning several years would be preferable to a class or team of youngsters all about the same age. Deliberate heterogeneity, therefore, is recommended as the broad criterion for establishing pupil groups. Subgroups within the total pupil membership, for example a reading group, may of course be homogeneous.

NONGRADEDNESS: A RECENT HISTORY

Nongradedness is by no means a new idea in American education. Even before 1900 the rigidity and the psychological invalidity of the graded school were under attack from various educators here and abroad, and numerous efforts were made to introduce more humane and appropriate practices into the schools. It is possible to trace a steady, though distressingly slow, erosion of the literally graded school throughout the first half of the 20th century, with such devices as "social promotion" or equivalent practices blunting the worst features of gradedness even though some of its outward forms remained. More recently, the profession's protests against gradedness have increased to the point where Francis Keppel, in 1966, proclaimed nongradedness to be the fastest-moving innovation on the elementary school scene.

At the same time, Keppel and others took note of the somewhat sorry state of the research and literature, and the need to link nongradedness with other reforms such as curriculum revision, the reorganization and retraining of personnel, and the like.

At the present time, indications from the federal government and from NEA and other sources suggest that about one school system in every four is known to be engaged in a serious effort to develop nongraded practices in one or more schools. Probably an even larger number of schools have been moving without fanfare in the direction away from gradedness, and it is interesting to speculate upon the percentage of classrooms in America within which there is not yet any appreciable sign of rigid and unrelenting gradedness giving way. Let us hope that this percentage is small indeed!

We have, then, at least four arrangements in American elementary schools today: 1) uncompromising gradedness; 2) nominal but eroding gradedness (perhaps this is the prevailing arrangement); 3) nominal nongradedness, but within which one finds disappointing evidence of gradedness still in the atmosphere; and 4) nongradedness which is, in large measure, faithful to the definition offered in the preceding section. Though the latter group may at present be small, our hope is that this will soon constitute the majority.

RESEARCH ON NONGRADEDNESS

Partly because the concept itself is difficult to define and is subject to various interpretations, partly because the "educational research community" (to use Keppel's phrase) has not yet developed appropriate research technology, and partly because excellent examples of nongradedness are all too few, there is as yet very little research evidence on which the profession can base its decisions. Further difficulty results from the tendency of researchers to rely heavily upon inappropriate research designs. Goodlad[2] has discussed this problem in some detail, along with commentary on specific studies published up to 1962. Unfortunately, most of the studies published since that date are marred by the same design problems, and it may be some years before more appropriate research studies become available.

A common problem in research using the "control-group-vs.-experimental-group" design is that the researchers fail to indicate the specific, functional ways in which the two groups actually differ from each other. Presumably, the control (graded) group is being treated in ways that differ significantly from the definition of nongradedness as applied to the experimental group. Presumably, too, the experimental group *is* being treated according to the definition. However, one reads many research reports in vain for this type of information. Sometimes, in fact, one discovers information that tends to deny the project's validity.

A case in point is an article published in 1965 regarding a project in Los Angeles County.[3] In the article, there is no description of the ungraded primary organization reportedly being used in twenty schools. Within the text, however, there are comments from which the reader can deduce that the so-called ungraded plan was mostly a system of homogeneous grouping. Several other comments suggest that the ungraded plan was not given sufficient administrative support (for example, in instructional materials, or curriculum work). There is, further, no reference to differential procedures for inducting the primary pupils into 4th grade. The reader is therefore left to wonder whether there were any real differences, either operational or psychological.

Virtually the same question arises in connection with a study reported by Williams.[4] Although information is furnished to show certain administrative differences between the experimental and control groups (for example, use of grade labels and nonpromotion policy), there are statements which suggest that teachers in the so-called graded schools in fact made virtually the same adjustments to the individual differences in their classes as, supposedly (though no evidence is furnished), did the teachers of the so-called nongraded schools. A fascinating reference is made to the fact that the nongraded classes averaged 45 pupils per teacher, whereas the

[2] See Goodlad, John I., and Anderson, Robert H. *The Nongraded Elementary School.* Revised edition. New York: Harcourt, Brace and World, 1963. pp. 213-19.

[3] Hopkins, Kenneth D.; Oldridge, O.A.; and Williamson, Malcolm L. "An Empirical Comparison of Pupil Achievement and Other Variables in Graded and Ungraded Classes." *American Educational Research Journal* 2: 207-15; November 1965.

[4] Williams, Wilmajean. "Academic Achievement in a Graded School and in a Non-Graded School." *Elementary School Journal* 67: 135-39; December 1966.

graded classes averaged 27! It seems doubtful that a better understanding of nongradedness can be gained by studies of this sort, whatever their conclusions.

A different sort of problem arises in connection with a 1966 report from Naperville, Illinois.[5] The article describes the difficulties encountered when the parents of four boys, all capable of completing the primary unit in two years, preferred that they not be accelerated (as were 25 others), and therefore "withdrew" their sons from the program. Apparently, too, there is relatively rigid graded structure (as perhaps in the Los Angeles County program) from 4th through 12th grades, and no opportunity within the primary school program for the brighter youngsters to engage in 4th grade-level work. One suspects that the limitations under which the program operates are both self-imposed and artificial.

David Lewin[6] makes the altogether reasonable plea that educators should report the weaknesses as well as the strengths of nongradedness if and when they appear. He then proceeds to examine what he as a supervisor in New York City perceives as problems: better teachers, supported by assistants, are needed; available materials and techniques for individualizing instruction are inadequate; nongrading requires heavy reliance on programed material; costs (for example, in guidance services) are greater; teachers need more conference and planning time; new systems of reporting progress must be developed; testing programs must be revised; administrators must work harder. While his concluding statement that perhaps the goal of greater individualization may also be achievable in graded classes is not supported by argument, Lewin has contributed a great deal by revealing the tough problems that exist in many of our schools. Obviously, as he and many of the other authors are saying, excellent education is not just a question of overhauling our organizational machinery.

In fact, if research and experience tell us anything, it is that the basic problems in improving instruction can be resolved only by a "package approach" in which nongradedness is merely one major component. To quote Calvin Gross: "Nongradedness takes its place among the other promising components of what I like to call 'the innovative package'; team teaching, flexible space, and hierarchies of teaching personnel backed up by mechanical and electronic instructional systems and devices. This mosaic of mutually reinforcing concepts and arrangements has demonstrated greater

[5]Barnickle, Donald W., and Lindberg, Ruth T. "The Unwilling Accelerate—A Problem of the Nongraded School." *Elementary School Journal* 67: 84-87; November 1966.

[6]Lewin, David. "Go Slow on Non-Grading." *Elementary School Journal* 67:131-34; December 1966.

potential potency for individualizing instruction than any other design conceived so far."[7]

FURTHER COMMENTS AND REACTIONS*

Several writers have listed reasons why some observers do not consider the nongraded school as desirable. Alleged weaknesses are shown in the left hand column. In the right hand column, I offer my comment in response:

ALLEGATION	COMMENT
1. Nongradedness leads to soft pedagogy; it lacks fixed standards and requirements.	1. This is probably true in the early stages, but as we grow more skilled in curriculum development, appropriate standards for each type of child are likely to emerge. Nongradedness may, indeed, lead us away from soft pedagogy by enabling all youngsters to master what they study.
2. It places an impossible burden on the teacher.	2. Quite true, especially if we persist in having self-contained classrooms! The burden will lift as we find ways of sharing teaching responsibilities.
3. It replaces grade requirements by reading levels.	3. Only in the primitive stages and where nongradedness is not well understood.
4. It results in a lack of information on pupil progress to parents.	4. Only when the teachers are lazy, foolish, or incompetent in their reporting.
5. It is difficult to put into prac-	5. True. Therefore, let's start a

[7]Gross, Calvin, in the Foreword to *How to Organize a Non-Graded School,* by Howard, Eugene R., and Bardwell, Roger W. Englewood Cliffs, New Jersey: Prentice-Hall, 1966. p. 4.

*This section is adapted from pp. 61-63 of Robert H. Anderson, *Teaching in a World of Change.* (New York: Harcourt, Brace & World, Inc.) 1966.

tice, because teachers are in-adequately and insufficiently prepared.

revolution in teacher education!

6. It does not have minimal standards for all children.

6. It is better to have standards for *each child,* is it not?

7. Its curriculum sequence tends to lack specificity and order.

7. Again, if true it may be just as well! What we need, it must be admitted, is a far more adequate curriculum. The graded curriculum is scarcely the ideal.

8. It is only an improved means to an unimproved end.

8. This sounds like double-talk, but if the end is individual fulfillment then nongradedness is a better way to get there.

9. It does not guarantee that improved teaching will result.

9. No organization provides such a guarantee. To improve teaching is a very difficult task.

10. It suffers from widespread use and even abuse of the term "nongraded."

10. Amen!

11. There is some difficulty in aligning graded with non-graded schools (for example, a primary unit and a graded intermediate program).

11. This is true only if the graded unit continues to deal with youngsters in an inappropriate way. And even so, it is no problem for the children; the annoyance is only to the grade-minded teachers.

·12. Teachers and parents are so conditioned to the graded structure that they continue "grademindedness."

12. Yes, but over time this is a disease that can be cured.

13. Extensive records must be kept for each child.

13. Some teachers may regard this as a disadvantage but they are wrong!

14. Planning new methods of reporting to parents demands much time and work from the already heavily burdened faculty.	14. Very true. Administration must make better provision for supporting services (for example, substitute teacher help) and for retraining teachers in the technology of reporting.

As one considers the complaints that are raised against nongraded plans, he notes that often the critic displays an ingenuous faith in organizational structure as panacea. Would that it were so easy! If all it took to modernize and and improve school offerings was an edict to abolish the graded plan, we could all have been in Educational Heaven long ago!

But organizational reform is only a part of the job that must be done. Given the will, we could do it easily and quickly. Then at last we could turn our energies to the really crucial tasks of reform, namely the renovation and redevelopment of curriculum. Judging by their relative detachment from the school reorganization movement thus far, the curriculum people themselves seem not yet to have appreciated this fact; and it may be that nongradedness will ultimately be appreciated because of the curriculum work that it forced educators to do.

WHAT, THEN, SHOULD WE DO?

In this article I have tried to show that nongradedness is not merely an organizational gimmick but rather a framework within which educators try to express and accomplish what they consider essential to each child's development. I have acknowledged that the idea is as yet underdeveloped, and have endorsed the notion that it offers greatest promise when developed in conjunction with such arrangements as team teaching, multiage pupil grouping, and technological innovations. Note also that extensive curriculum work and teacher education activities must both precede and accompany nongradedness, along with such important work as the revision of evaluation and reporting procedures.[8] In short, if the idea of nongradedness is to flourish as it deserves, and if children are indeed to be served according to our profession's earnest intentions, our schools and teacher training institutions must literally overhaul themselves. Are we prepared to go this far?

---

[8] See the May 1966 issue of *The National Elementary Principal.*

WILL WE RECOGNIZE TOMORROW'S ELEMENTARY SCHOOL?

William D. Hedges

Though we will continue during the next 10 to 15 years to improve the quality of education *as we conceive it today,* there is now in the mill, I believe, a quantum jump in education that may completely remake the elementary school: the application of systems analysis and the entry of technology via big business into education. At the core of this quantum jump is the electronic computer.

The computer promises to help the teacher accomplish what he has always desired and dreamed of but has too rarely been able to bring about—virtually complete individualization of instruction according to the child's rate of learning, his interests, and his approach to learning (his style). We face the possibility that we can humanize the process of education for the many rather than the few.

This kind of individualization of instruction is almost certainly going to be accompanied by the large-scale entry of big business into education. Educational companies have already begun luring prominent educators into their employ, thus equipping themselves to more effectively develop new products and market them to the public schools. As Silberman has said, "Technology is knocking at the schoolhouse door."

Peering into the murky future, I can visualize something of a reversal, three or four decades from now, of the traditional roles of the school and the home. Historically the school has taught the three R's, and has left much of the process of socialization and the development of values—at least officially—to the home, church, and community. It is conceivable that we may someday see the home formally assuming the student's intellectual education, with the school becoming primarily a center for socialization. If this happens, how will it come about?

Technology will eventually enable each child to learn at his own optimum rate, will maintain careful records on him, including a complete and continuously updated growth profile, and will make suggestions for the teacher and the parents to consider about future steps in his development.

From *N.E.A. Journal,* LVI, No. 9 (December, 1967), 9-12. Used by permission of the author and publisher.

When this time comes, it will be as logical for students to have instructional terminals in their homes as it is today logical and commonplace for them to have TV sets and telephones. During an interim period on the way to this arrangement, the teaching terminals will be located in centers or "schools" allowing easy access for large numbers of pupils.

But any organized system of education that has faced up to and tried to answer the question, "Education for what?" will conclude that the process of growing up requires more than mere information; it requires interaction by each child with his fellows. Meeting this latter need will require seminars for the discussion of ideas, team sports, choral and band activities, dramatics, debate, and the like. Such group activities can only be accomplished at a site equipped to deal with numbers of persons working together—a school.

The school of the future will also provide diagnostic services for each child, including consideration of his emotional and physical, as well as his intellectual development. Teachers will cease to be primarily disseminators of information and will instead know each child thoroughly, work with children in seminars, tutor, evaluate new curriculum materials, alter commercial materials for specific needs, and simply cogitate on the nature and meaning of the educative process. As a result, educational programs will be tailored to the needs, interests, and abilities of the individual child and thus maximize diversity among people.

Important considerations remain: Much of the software, the curriculum materials needed for use by the computer, has yet to be developed. Also, we still have much to discover about how learning actually occurs. And most important, the preparation of our teachers needs to be revolutionized.

The hardware and the technology for doing the things I am projecting is essentially available now. It is so costly, however, that implementation must await the appearance of a mass market, the refinement of time sharing, and the development of huge quantities of software or curriculum materials.

Time sharing already permits real-time operations (using a computer to process more than one job at once) by mathematicians, physicists, and engineers. Tomorrow will see hundreds of thousands of children in school buildings and homes studying arithmetic via the computer at varying rates and by different approaches and in a way that maximizes success for each child. Gone will be the practice of predicating the failure of one child on the success of another (a characteristic of group-paced instruction).

Personally, I welcome the large-scale entry of big business and technology into the schools for developing curriculum materials as well as hardware. For those who feel that the outcome will be dehumanizing, I can only state my belief that the converse may well be true instead. For one thing, the teacher should be able to increase his personal contact with his students. He will be rid of much of the trivia characterizing his present job—grading papers, taking the roll, counting lunch money, running the duplicator, and so on. Machines will release him for doing those things only a human being can do—being creative and being human.

For those who fear that big business will determine the curriculum and, because of its emphasis on profit, promote its products to the detriment of both teachers and students, I have several responses. First, I acknowledge that the fears *may* be justified but submit that for years business interests have determined much of the curriculum through the writing and sale of textbooks, with very little protest on our part. Furthermore, business clearly wants to provide a product designed, developed, and approved by the profession.

In any event, as William Van Til has said: "Educational technology will not go away. It is here to stay. In the last half of the twentieth century an industrial revolution which was long overdue has finally reached education."

Since whether or not business is going to be in education is no longer open to debate, the question the education profession should be coping with right now is what kind of curriculum materials are to be used, and why, and how. I would add that during the next decade or so the educator will have to avoid the gimmickry and hard sell that characterized some facets of the recent boom in teaching machines and other kinds of programed instruction. Educators should look for and accept only materials that have been carefully field-proven.

For the future, we will increasingly see a systems approach brought to the process of education. We will see America's talents and resources brought to bear in a systematic and efficient fashion on our greatest resource—our children.

Even though many of us welcome the onset of these changes, we must note that while we were developing the automobile and the factory we were also creating major sources of fumes to poison the atmosphere. During the next two decades we will need our educational philosophers as never before to probe the implications of the changes we introduce into our schools. The line between mass education that releases and cultivates the potential diversity of the human race and mass education that enforces conformity can be quite thin. So can the line between what purports to be a humanizing of the process of education and what turns out to be a mechanization of education for a robot society.

QUESTIONS FOR DISCUSSION:

ELEMENTARY SCHOOL

1. What is the basis for the new concern for education of younger children? Should free public kindergartens be available to all five-year olds? Should there be expansion of schooling for three- and four-year olds and younger children?
2. What have been the major strengths of the elementary schools? What weaknesses do they still have?
3. What are the purposes of the elementary program? What order of priorities in purpose would you establish for the elementary school?
4. How should the content of the elementary curriculum be determined?
5. How individualized should the program of the elementary school be?
6. How should reading be taught in the elementary schools? Why are special reading programs in elementary schools for the disadvantaged so important?
7. What are some of the changes occurring in the social studies in the elementary school? In the arts? Science?
8. Describe a self-contained classroom. What are your reasons for opposing or defending it?
9. What place does team teaching have in the elementary school?
10. How does the nongraded elementary school function? Why do you advocate or condemn it?
11. What do you think will be the influence of big business and technology along with increasing federal support on the elementary school curriculum?
12. What can elementary schools do to encourage the learners to have a continued interest in learning?
13. What information or concepts in Sections 1–5 of this book have particular significance for curriculum planning in an elementary school?

7 Junior High School and the Middle School

Some students of education insist that the junior high school is the forgotten portion of the school program. They assert that its function has never been clearly defined, that its program is partly elementary and partly secondary, that teachers are not prepared to teach in the junior high schools, that little thinking has been done with regard to the design of the program that is needed.

On the other hand, other educators claim that the junior high school is the land of real opportunity. They hold that the people who work in the junior high schools are not shackled by tradition and are free to experiment and to develop the kind of learning activities appropriate to early adolescence, that students at this age are most receptive, and that major experimentation can be undertaken in the junior high school.

One of the issues that any junior high school faculty faces is what the school's role should be. William Van Til and John H. Lounsbury ("Meet Junior") describe the conditions out of which the junior high school emerged, the hopes of its proponents, the contribution it has made as a home of experimentation, and the present fluidity.

Mauritz Johnson, Jr. ("School in the Middle") proposes that "changes be in the direction of greater emphasis on significant ideas as opposed to inert facts; greater continuity of intellectual development; greater flexibility of programing, particularly in the 'arts' for pupils who differ so greatly; at least as much attention to independence in studying and thinking as in the social and emotional spheres."

Many people who have studied the junior high believe it should be an exploratory experience. The courses should be arranged so that students get an opportunity to sample many experiences and fields of knowledge. Exploration should be carried on, too, in the student activity program. Morrell J. Clute ("Student Activities for Early Adolescents") offers a desirable student activity program for the junior high school and some objectives that can be used as criteria in making judgments about a given student-activity program.

Although junior high schools are relatively free to change and to develop unique programs, the pattern has remained amazingly static. Foreign language programs have been offered in junior high schools for years, yet such programs still fail to reach large numbers of students (Joseph Vocolo, "Foreign Language Program in the Junior High School"). Core programs seemed to gain momentum in this portion of the secondary school, but appeared to die out in the sixties. Gordon Vars ("The Core Curriculum: Lively Corpse") tells us that the core curriculum idea in the junior high school is still very much with us.

Some junior high educators have questioned the grade arrangements found in junior high schools. William M. Alexander ("What Educational Plan for the In-Between-Ager?") indicates that there is a growing dissatisfaction with the present 7, 8, 9 junior high school organization. He raises many issues relating to the value of retaining the junior high school or replacing it with a new school called the Middle School.

What is a middle school? A number of educators have suggested that the junior high school has become a school more like the high school, better geared to the teenager than the early adolescent. At the same time, children in the upper-elementary grades are maturing earlier and knowledge is expanding. The traditional self-contained classroom organization of the elementary school seems inadequate to some for those learners moving toward adolescence. The middle school including grades 5 to 8 or 6 to 8 has been suggested as the arrangement best suited for these years.

Although the middle-school idea is gaining ground, there are many who question the necessity for the creation of a middle school. Articles by Richard Post ("Middle School: A Questionable Innovation") and Samuel Popper ("Institutional Integrity and Middle School Organization"), both deal with the merits of junior high organization versus middle-school organization.

Emmett Williams ("The Middle-School Movement") describes the experience of a number of schools with the middle school organization as well as innovative practices they are using. Some new problems arise as new organization is tried.

Some educators at the junior high school level believe that team teaching and flexible scheduling can be used to meet the individual needs of each student and to provide a wider range of exploration than is now possible. ("Brookhurst Junior High: An Innovative School"). Brookhurst is doing this within the present junior high school framework.

In making decisions regarding the curriculum and school organization at this level the important considerations are the following: What are the objectives of the school? What is the nature of the society and what are the major social forces in which the school exists? What learning principles and what knowledge about human development at this age level should be considered? What aspects of the nature of knowledge and cognition are particularly important? Professional decision-making requires that all of these questions be considered and that curriculum decisions and instructional strategies be based on multidimensional answers.

At least this will be necessary if the decisions made are to be adequate, or more than random.

MEET JUNIOR

William Van Til
and John H. Lounsbury

The junior high school in America grew out of the times. As the nineteenth century became the twentieth, America was at the "watershed of American history," as Henry Steele Commager put it. On one side of the watershed, in the past, lay a country which was predominantly rural and agricultural. On the other side, in the future that was emerging, lay a country which was predominantly urban and industrial.

In 1907 alone, well over a million immigrants entered the United States. By 1910, one-third of the American people were either foreign-born or of foreign-born parentage. Effective citizenship education for the immigrants and their children was desperately needed if they were to become Americans.

Some went West to farm. But the greater majority of the newcomers settled in the teeming cities of the Northeast and contributed their "cheap labor" to the building of an industrial nation.

In the prosperous times of the early twentieth century, many workers were needed. Children worked, in addition to men and women. In 1910,

From *NEA Journal,* XLVI, No. 9 (December, 1957), 594-596. Used by permission of the authors and publisher.

almost one out of every five children between the ages of 10 and 15 was employed.

In depressed times, armies of unemployed burdened urban society. City residents, including former farmers and often illiterate immigrants, were almost wholly dependent on factories and wages.

New social problems developed. In the new fast-growing cities, the individual family was less effective as the social, recreational, and educational center for family members' lives. More time was spent away from the family, both at gainful employment and in commercial recreation. People were faced with the problem of living and working together with those who were of different national, religious, and racial backgrounds.

Labor conflicted with capital. Both giant corporations and organizations of labor grew more powerful. Government expanded its activities, and America entered the ear of reform called the progressive ear. The United States began to acquire international responsibilities as an aftermath of the Spanish-American War at the turn of the century.

What was to be done with the growing number of young people who had acquired an elementary education but apparently were not going to college to become the future ministers, business executives, and other professionals? They lived primarily in urban environments. They were a very few years (or a few months) away from employment in industry. Many were of foreign birth and background, yet they were destined to be American citizens. In a democracy, they too were to have a voice in solution of social problems.

One answer was to create a school between elementary and secondary school that would be characterized by vocational education, citizenship education, and concern for social problems. There they might be helped as individuals thru new ways of grouping and organization, thru recognition of widely varying abilities and interests.

Proposals for the reorganization of education, including the creation of a junior high-school stepladder, did not frighten many people. The cultural context was one of change. The reorganization movement, which centered in the junior high school, grew out of the times. For some years, a number of national committees of educators, possessed initially with the economy-of-time idea, had been considering the downward extension of secondary education. Their influential reports also helped to pave the way for the organization of the junior high school.

Although the 8–4 plan had gained acceptance as the standard way to organize a school system, it came under fire in this age of re-examination and alteration. Organizing a junior high school was proposed as a means of alleviating many of the bad conditions that were apparent in the schools of the early 1900s.

Especially deplorable was the mass exodus of public-school pupils between the fifth and tenth grades. Too many youngsters were leaving school without adequate preparation for living or for making a living.

Educators believed that many drop-outs were caused by an inappropriate educational program marked by high rates of failures, as well as by economic necessity. Drop-outs, they argued, were caused in part by the great gap in content and methods that existed between elementary and secondary education.

The junior high school could help to bridge this gap, reasoned early proponents like Leonard V. Koos and Thomas H. Briggs. It would also be better able to equip those who continued to leave school early, for it would supply them with needed vocational education and guidance. With a departmentalized program, the junior high school would be able to reduce retardation thru promotion by subjects.

An intermediate institution might better take into account the findings of the new psychology of individual differences. The junior high school could permit students to take electives on the seventh- and eighth-grade levels and could group youngsters according to their abilities. Establishing a new school received added justification from G. Stanley Hall's then popular theories. To Hall, adolescence was a "psychological second birth"; he referred to the early adolescent as a "new kind of being which demands a new environment, new methods, and new matter."

As Thomas H. Briggs wrote, "The special functions of the junior high school have been stated as: first, to continue, insofar as it may seem wise and possible, and in a gradually diminishing degree, common, integrating education; second, to ascertain and reasonably to satisfy pupils' important immediate and assured future needs; third, to explore by means of material in itself worthwhile the interests, aptitudes, and capacities of pupils; fourth, to reveal to them, by material otherwise justifiable, the possibilities in the major fields of learning; and fifth, to start each pupil on the career which, as a result of the exploratory courses, he, his parents, and the school are convinced is most likely to be of profit to him and to society."

As the junior high school grew up, the cultural context in which it operated continued to undergo rapid alteration. Industrialization and urbanization which heralded the beginning of the junior high school marched remorselessly onward. So the junior high school had to change.

Take, for instance, the rate of vocational education as a major purpose of the junior high school. Child labor steadily decreased in the American economy. Industry no longer wanted, nor would new laws allow, the regular employment of early adolescents. Vocational education as a purpose of the junior high school became a dead issue. Vocational orientation and exploration took its place.

Compulsory-attendance laws also altered the junior high school's responsibility toward another early and related purpose, improving holding power. While by no means irrelevant to the junior high school, this problem has become more of a direct concern to the senior high school.

The junior high-school movement has made many contributions to American education. It has made available to early adolescents special facilities and instructional areas such as industrial arts, laboratory science, and, to an increasing degree, typing. It has made possible richer library and instructional materials for seventh- and eighth-graders.

The junior high-school movement has advanced materially efforts to take care of both the retarded and the gifted. It has furthered the development of a sound teacher-centered, counselor-supplemented guidance program. It has helped to narrow the gap between classroom work and student activities. It has brought more men teachers and administrators into the school program below the ninth grade. It has furthered the development of integrated, problem-centered teaching and the block-scheduling of time needed to facilitate such an approach in general education.

In the final analysis, however, the greatest contribution of the junior high-school movement is not a specific but a spirit, the spirit of experimentation which it brought to secondary education. Reorganization meant opportunity to try things out in a new school which was less handicapped by precedent and tradition. Despite the dominance of the senior high school, the junior high school has been a testing ground for such newer practices as the core curriculum.

Much remains to be done. The unfortunate tendency to mimic the senior high school is still a factor. The dearth of teachers specifically trained for work with young adolescents imposes a real obstacle to progress. The inadequate facilities often provided for junior high schools handicap programs.

The absence of adequate standards, regulations, and policies at the local and state levels hinders the proper development of junior high-school education. The lack of prestige accorded education at this level is damaging. The very name of this intermediate institution reflects its all-too-often subordinate position.

SCHOOL IN THE MIDDLE—
JUNIOR HIGH: EDUCATION'S PROBLEM CHILD

Mauritz Johnson, Jr.

Every so often some indignant or exasperated soul prescribes major surgery for the American educational enterprise, and more often than not the object of the incision and derision is the junior high school. In an atmosphere of such dire threats, fervent supporters of the junior high school brook no criticism of their beloved institution, however valid it may be. But, while detractors who advocate decapitation to cure a headache are of scant help to the patient, neither are his well-intentioned friends who call the headache an illusion or a normal condition.

The junior high school is an American invention which dates from the first decade of this century. In 1920 there were fewer than 400 of them; in 1940 there were over 2,000; and now the number is probably close to 5,000. In quantitative terms the movement has been a distinct success.

Actually, it was an integral part of a larger movement which involved the downward extension of secondary education through the annexation of grades seven and eight from the elementary school. In large school systems, physically separate three-year junior and senior high schools were established, but in small ones a single six-year secondary school became the mode. In the latter, the old four-year high school usually persisted as a unit, with the two appended grades occupying an indefinite status. Rarely has the junior high school idea been a guiding force in the six-year high school.

What is the junior high school idea? In a word, asylum. The junior high school is supposed to be a bridge between the elementary school and the upper secondary level and, indeed, a bridge between childhood and that attenuated near-adult stage we call adolescence. Within this "transition school for early adolescence," a very special environment is to be created in which pubescence can be experienced without trauma or trepidation. The forbearance of understanding teachers and the comfortable camouflage of the "peer group" (all of whom are in the same boat), facilitate the rapprochement of the sexes, the learning of new social skills, the exploration of bodily changes, and tolerant acceptance of ambivalent vacillation

From *Saturday Review*, XLV, No. 28 (July 21, 1962), 40-42, 56-57. Copyright Saturday Review, Inc., 1962. Used by permission of the author and publisher.

between childish dependence and brash assertiveness. At the same time, the right combination of wide "exploration" and wise guidance would assure that, when the metamorphosis was complete, the physically healthy, emotionally stable, socially adjusted, civic minded specimen which emerged from the cocoon would be well prepared to take advantage of whatever opportunities later adolescence might offer.

If this description appears to be a caricature, such is not the intent. Realistic or not, defensible or not, these are the goals that junior high schools have sought to achieve. It is easy to extend our overly sentimental view of childhood too far, but it cannot be gainsaid that in the contemporary American culture the phenomenon of adolescence is characterized by a quest for heterosexual social relationships and emancipation from adult control, and this phenomenon cannot be ignored. Apparently, the leap from childhood dependency to sophisticated individuality can rarely be accomplished in advanced Western societies without the intermediate use of the group of contemporaries as a transitory source of security. In a world in which adults expound one set of values and espouse another, in which schooling is prolonged and economic dependence is protracted, and in which social life is largely outside the family, the value of a haven the junior high school attempts to be is readily recognized by many parents of this in-between age group.

If this phase of development is often a difficult one for those passing through it, it is even more so for the adults around them. To establish and maintain a junior high school which fully exemplifies the idea underlying that institution is not easy, and many schools, it must be conceded, have been less than successful in this regard. And, as with the girl with the curl, a good junior high school can be very, very good, but a poor one can be horrid.

It is not difficult to find some teachers who view youngsters at this level as obnoxious nuisances, rather than as energetic, curious, fumbling individuals on the threshold of adulthood. Some junior high schools provide social activities as formal and sophisticated as those in which high school seniors engage. Some promote extensive interscholastic athletic programs which feature strenuous physical exertion, intense emotional involvement, and often late hours. In some, the break from grade six to seven is as abrupt as it ever was between grades eight and nine. But these are shortcomings in human performance and institutional arrangements, rather than inherent defects in the idea, which in many schools is faithfully and skilfully practiced.

But if the idea itself makes a certain amount of sense, it also gives disconcertingly little attention to the primary responsibility of any educational institution—intellectual development. Not that the intellectual aspect is completely ignored or that it is incompatible with the concern for transition, but simply that the emphasis on it is not explicit and its nature is not defined.

It was not ever thus. When the first junior high schools were established, there seems to have been greater concern about the downward extension of secondary education than about the separation of the secondary school into two components. The chief motive for extending downward stemmed from a dissatisfaction with the elementary school curriculum and methods in grades seven and eight. To a large extent these were "review" years, preparatory for eighth-grade graduation (or nongraduation). For many pupils this review was considered unnecessary, and it only delayed their beginning more advanced academic studies under teachers who were specialists in these subjects. For the many overage pupils who populated these grades, the steady diet of review of common branch subjects seemed, perhaps not entirely futile, but at least of less value for imminent entry into the world of work than one accompanied by some specific vocational training. It was through this combination of earlier academic instruction and terminal vocational training that the "needs" of the young (and not so young) adolescents were to be better met.

The separation of the junior high grades from the upper ones was not at that time so much for social and emotional reasons as to make the *academic* initiation at grade nine easier for pupils, since approximately half of all high school students were in the freshman classes of the conventional high schools, and that was as far as many of them ever got. It was *this* transition that was of greatest concern, not the one from grade six to seven or the one represented by pubescence. Indeed, if social and emotional considerations entered the picture at all, they revolved about protecting the younger children *from* the unwholesome influence of the young adolescents in the seventh and eighth grades within the elementary school, not providing a haven for the new junior high school group.

Again, this is not to deny the usefulness of a separate and special social setting for this transition period, but merely to emphasize that the early concern for more suitable intellectual fare has of late been obscured. We may grant that the earlier vocational emphasis is less appropriate today because of longer compulsory education, diminished overageness as a result of changed promotion policies, and increased importance of intellectual development in a technologically more complex economy. But precisely because more people do need to develop further than ever intellectually, it is all the more important that those who wish to improve the junior high schools again turn their attention to this central area of the school's responsibility.

It is in regard to intellectual training that those who are inclined toward abolition of the junior high school must also consider the consequences of such a step. To return grades seven and eight to an elementary school status is unthinkable. Pupils at this level must have the intellectual resources which a secondary school is better able to provide—teachers prepared in specific subject areas; laboratory, library, studio, and shop facilities; and a sufficient concentration of pupils for differentiation in the curriculum consistent with the extensive range of abilities among pupils at this level. The elementary school as we now know it cannot provide these conditions.

Some communities, because of building considerations or sheer tradition, retain grade nine with the upper three and maintain a two-year middle unit. There is a feeling in some quarters that ninth graders fare better academically under such an arrangement. This is highly questionable, unless there is a great disparity in the qualifications of teachers at the two levels. Actually, when teachers are equally qualified, ninth graders in a junior high school setting appear to achieve as well or better than they do as freshmen in a four-year high school. Furthermore, a two-grade school lacks stability in that pupils enter one year and leave the next. Although it is better than no middle school at all, it has not been found to be as satisfactory as a three-year unit.

A legitimate question, however, is which three grades? While the seven-nine unit predominates today, there is increasing interest in a six-seven-eight combination, because it appeals to the four-year high school advocates, to the proponents of a three-year middle unit, and to those who want pupils introduced even earlier to teachers who are specialists in their subjects. It would be resisted by those who for several decades have introduced an elementary school philosophy into the junior high school to counteract what they consider to be too early departmentalization, too great an academic emphasis, and too much imitation of high school social and athletic practices. The wisdom of such a unit should not, however, be determined by how large a coalition can be mustered in its favor.

Since the middle school as a separate organization can be justified on social grounds only if it embraces the period during which the majority of pupils reach adolescence, the six-seven-eight unit would be valid only if it could be shown that large numbers of sixth graders are pubescent. There is some evidence that youngsters do mature earlier today than they did a generation or two ago, and certainly they acquire greater amounts of general information and social sophistication earlier. In some communities, however, this is not true and it is senseless to argue for the same organizational pattern everywhere. But it does not follow that the matter of organization is, therefore, inconsequential. What is important is that we be clear as to *why* a middle school unit with identity of its own is desirable, and what it needs if it is to be a stable, viable unit.

Junior high schools can be eliminated or altered, but pupils of junior high school age will remain, and who will teach them and what they will be taught are the really significant questions. Their teachers need to be as well versed in their respective subject fields as possible, and in addition be cognizant and appreciative of the relative immaturity of these pupils, their transitional status, and their tremendous diversity. Junior high school teachers must be willing and able to help pupils become students, equipping them with the tools and procedures for a lifetime of study, rather than assuming that they are already so equipped or can acquire, on their own, the ability to study effectively and independently. If junior high schools would address themselves to this problem seriously, pupils, their parents, and all of their subsequent teachers would be grateful.

Good junior high school teachers are even harder to come by than good elementary or senior high school teachers. It would be an oversimplification to say that some teachers are attracted to the profession out of a desire to be with children and others from an urge to engage in the transmission of ideas, and that at the junior high school level the pupils aren't lovable enough for the one group and the ideas dealt with aren't complex enough for the other. Nevertheless, a recent study at Cornell showed that among some 600 teachers who were surveyed, those teaching grades seven and eight were markedly less satisfied with their level of assignment than were teachers in the grades below and above. When the reasons were analyzed, the nature of the curriculum (the ideas), rather than the nature of the pupils at this level, seemed to be predominant. Teachers who enjoy teaching many subject areas cannot do so in the junior high school, nor can those who enjoy teaching advanced content do that. Perhaps this is inevitable in an "in-between" school.

Yet, there is a clue here that the curriculum at this level needs some careful rethinking and perhaps a complete overhauling. Typically, all seventh and eighth graders are required to take some nine or ten subjects for the same length of time, despite considerable differences in their abilities, interests, and accomplishments. No matter that a pupil is tone deaf and has been taught music by a specialist throughout six elementary school years—he must still "explore" it, along with his friend who plays in both band and orchestra and practices an hour each evening. No matter that a pupil is weak in the fundamentals of arithmetic—his mathematics teacher, fresh from a course in partial differential equations, must teach him the types of life insurance and what enters into overhead in retailing, just as he must teach these topics to all the mathematically eager pupils awaiting the delights of algebra, geometry, and the infinity beyond.

In all fairness, it must be said that many program changes are currently being made in junior high schools—some eighth graders study algebra; foreign language, taught by the direct method, is offered in grade seven; set theory, Venn diagrams, and other modern mathematical topics have been introduced; and more science is being given. But these changes represent only creeping improvement, not the giant step that is needed. It is true that the quality of teaching makes or breaks any program, but a poor curriculum is a millstone around the neck of the best of teachers.

Take the bright young social studies teacher who did graduate work in comparative economics or American foreign policy. A complete stranger in the community, he must begin by teaching that one Silas Wright established the first local grist mill, and then recount for the nth time the story of the Indian tribes which inhabited the area and the great contribution they made to American culture, and spend the rest of the year in a provincial tribute to the greatness of the particular state. Or, consider the English teacher, a literature major, of course—primarily British literature, particularly poetry, especially the Lake poets—with no study of grammar since high school (the college English department didn't offer it) and only vaguely aware (from an education course) of the current controversy between proponents of structural linguistics and advocates of conventional grammar. What will be the major emphasis in her junior high school English classes? Grammar, of course, and what literature there is may consist of whatever novel is in the anthology, some short stories by Poe and O. Henry, and a long poem by Longfellow. The rest will be free reading of "adolescent literature" on romance and nursing for the girls, and war, sports, and atuomobiles for the boys.

Somewhere, at this very moment, an engineer, a doctor, and an AAUW member on a school board are doubtless fighting the good fight to employ a junior high school science teacher who has his master's degree in physics rather than education. The fact is, however, that most students who do graduate work in physics will be advised by their physics professors (and their common sense) to sell their valuable talents to some one other than a board of education. Those who actually become junior high school teachers may find that Ohm's law is the most advanced physics they teach, and that a large part of the time they must deal with such matters as testing food for starch with iodine, reading a weather map, and tracing the flow of blood through the heart.

Nevertheless, a curriculum must obviously be planned with the maturity and requirements of the learners in mind, not the strengths and desires of teachers. Yet, if the nature of the curriculum affects the availability and enthusiasm of teachers, so, too, the improvement of curriculum depends in the main upon the discontent and initiative of teachers. Administrators, laymen, and professors from both the scholarly disciplines and professional education can encourage and assist them, but in the final analysis, teachers, singly and in groups, must do the job. What deters them is not so much their own shortcomings as certain beliefs which are prevalent in many communities: that the problems in the junior high school are inevitable and unsolvable; that the junior high school must forever remain as it has been; that some outside authority really decides all the questions; that getting rid of the junior high school altogether will take care of the problems.

Many specific suggestions could be offered for the improvement of the curriculum at this level, but this is a matter on which those who are in a position to make the changes must work. It might be urged, though, that the changes be in the direction of greater emphasis on significant ideas as opposed to inert facts; greater continuity of intellectual development; greater flexibility of programming, particularly in the area of the "arts," for pupils who differ so greatly; and at least as much attention to independence in studying and thinking as in the social and emotional spheres. The fact that many junior high school pupils are so preoccupied with their adolescent developmental problems that they are distracted from learning may be, in part at least, of our own making. If we could provide a curriculum which would engross their attention more fully, they might then be distracted from many of their physical, social, and emotional problems.

One can insist that the curriculum of the middle school, and specifically its intellectual component, is in need of reexamination without implying that efforts to take into account the transition from childhood should be abandoned or neglected. Many problems, such as those relating to the grouping of pupils and the maintenance of standards, cannot be solved satisfactorily until the curriculum is reformed. For example, we currently form instructional groups, and then either fail to provide curricular differences or attempt to adapt the curriculum to each group. Instead, we should reverse the process by organizing the curriculum first and then forming the groups accordingly. We define junior high school courses in terms of grades, when we know there are greater differences among pupils *within* seventh grade than there are *between* an average seventh grader and an average senior. It is impossible to speak of standards without reference to relatively specific and stable curriculum elements, and the grade concept has lost its usefulness for this purpose.

To return to the opening metaphor, euthanasia is not the answer to the junior high school's malady, but a curricular lobotomy may be necessary. The present dosage of vitamins will not give us the kind of middle school we need.

STUDENT ACTIVITIES FOR EARLY ADOLESCENTS

Morrel J. Clute

The most remarkable characteristics of the human organism are its growth and development. The miracles of growth and the evolution of the human personality are the schools' greatest concern and responsibility. The time for being "grown-up" is long, indeed, when compared to the time for "growing-up." If we recognize that the experiences of the growing-up years have profound effect upon the grown-up years, then the responsibility of the school as a nurturer of growth is clear. Although growth and maturation are continuous processes that go on all through life, there are periods of time in the development of an individual where growth is more dramatic and the outward manifestations of rapid change are more obvious. The years of growth encompassed by the public school are without question most dramatic during the junior high grades. Grades seven, eight and nine, almost without exception are the grades in which boys and girls are doing the most important growing of their lives. The period of adolescence has too often been thought of as a transition from childhood to adulthood—a period in which little of importance happens. It may be, as many authorities on adolescence believe, that the junior high school period is the most important of all the school years. Growth in all areas of development, physical, social, emotional, and mental, is so rapid that unique problems arise. The values, attitudes, and beliefs that young people form during these years are likely to be life-long and will in a large measure determine the degree of success or satisfaction they give to or take from life. Therefore, the junior high school has unique functions because it must provide for boys and girls who have unique problems that arise from a unique period of growth.

If the school is to fulfill its unique functions, it must provide the kind

---

From *The Teachers College Record* XXXIV, No. 2 (November, 1962), 62-63, 72. Used by permission of the author and publisher.

of nurture that will satisfy the growth needs of boys and girls. Thus the curriculum must be defined in its broadest sense. It includes all the experiences that touch upon the student in his school life. It includes all the activities in which students participate both in class and out. As the line between what is curricular and what is extra-curricular has become more and more obscure, junior high schools have come closer to satisfying the growth needs of adolescent boys and girls. The student activities program, then, can be considered as part of the regular instructional program. Some activities will grow out of regular class processes; others will be organized outside of the classroom.

The student activities in the junior high take on unique characteristics because adolescents have special needs. Although it is not easy to describe or classify traits of adolescent growth, it is possible to generalize. There is a wide range of *differences in physical development.* Growth in height, weight, and maturity varies greatly with individuals and particularly between boys and girls. Girls' development is usually from one to two years ahead of boys in maturity during the junior high years.

Rapid growth of external and internal organs and the development of secondary sex characteristics *create problems because of rapid change.*

Adolescents are striving for independence from adults. The peer group, the club, the chum, the hero-figure play an important role in the struggle for freedom from adult direction and in *understanding the sex role*—what it means to be a boy or girl.

Adolescents have special fears about growing up, not being accepted, not being liked, about inadequacy, or about being different.

Intellectual growth results in expanding but often unstable interests.

Early adolescents tend to be idealists, with an eagerness for social service.

This remarkable growth which results in physical and sexual maturity has a tremendous impact on all aspects of adolescent life. With the development of secondary sex characteristics which follows soon after the advent of puberty, the adolescent in reality becomes a new person in a new world. He has a new body with new feelings and sensations. It is like starting life anew with a vastly different world to discover and explore, new relationships to understand with new and different expectations and patterns for behavior.

In this struggle to understand his new world, the people in it, and himself as a person of dignity and worth, the adolescent finds that the student activity program plays a vital role. . . .

These adolescent growth needs should be the basis for organizing the activities program in the junior high school.

PERSONAL SOCIAL ADJUSTMENT

Although all school experiences provide opportunities for furthering social adjustment, it is important to recognize it as an important objective. Every activity that brings students together provides opportunities for developing peer relationships and learning social skills of interaction. Students' participation in the planning, carrying-out and evaluation of special programs and activities means experience in decision making—an aid to becoming independent.

Widened corridors in newer buildings provide social living space. The lunch period often can be used for a rich program of activities. Quiet social experiences can be provided by use of the library and other rooms for reading, chess, checkers, cards, recording-listening, movies, arts and crafts and others. The list of games which provide opportunity for physical activity and social interaction is almost endless. Table tennis, volley ball, softball, shuffleboard, singing and dancing are but a few of the activities that some schools build into a noon program. With adult guidance these activities can be student planned and directed thus fulfilling the need for social interaction and for learning democratic skills of leadership and cooperation. *Student government* is probably the most important single activity of the school. A student faculty Council which truly represents the students not only provides opportunity for learning the democratic skills necessary for democratic citizenship, but gives both students and faculty a responsible role in all school activity. School camping is growing rapidly as an activity in those states fortunate enough to have the physical facilities. The school camp combines in one activity many of the virtues sought in more diversified activity programs.

DEVELOPMENT AND EXPANSION OF INTELLECTUAL INTERESTS

In many ways the conventional class program satisfies the need to explore the physical and social world, but many classroom procedures are not flexible enough to provide for the many and varied interests of adolescents. Forums, discussion groups, Pen Pal clubs and other activities of this type provide additional chances to explore the world and the people in it. The clubs which form around the academic subject areas are a reflection of the desire of students to explore and develop their special talents.

SPECIAL INTERESTS AND HOBBIES

A good club program can do much to enhance prevocational and avocational exploration. Again the list of clubs that may be organized in these two areas is almost limitless. Such clubs as Future Teachers, Future Nurses, Future Homemakers, Future Farmers, and 4-H are well known, nationally organized, and commonly found in most junior and senior-high schools. The nature of special interests in the junior high, however, calls for more flexibility than in the senior high. Schools should be ready to form and close out clubs as changing interests indicate the need. Adolescents are more interested in the "here and now" and are less motivated by the longrange adult goals. Clubs for modeling, airplane building, photography, rock collecting, radio, for example, may represent short-range interests and may need to be replaced by others during the school year. Student activities growing out of the regular class program are usually exciting opportunities for students to discover special interests. The English program can develop special activities in creative writing, school paper or magazine as well as in speech and dramatic activities. The music and art areas of the school offer many opportunities for the exploration of interests and the development of talent.

SOCIAL SERVICE

One of the very real needs of adolescents is the need to be of service to others. Their concern for justice and fair play is coupled with compassion for the less fortunate. Not only are they concerned with helping others, but they develop feelings of worth when performing a service that obviously contributes to the well-being of others. The safety patrol, service squad, ushers club, hall guides (as contrasted to hall guards), pep club, booster club, Junior Red Cross, all provide opportunities for service. Students welcome chances to be of service to their fellow students and as a rule participate enthusiastically in orientation activities at the beginning of a new school year. Older students can be of great help to incoming seventh graders. They are in the best position to communicate what school is like and they enjoy planning mixers, parties, picnics, or assembly programs to help students become acquainted with their new school.

IN SUMMARY

The objectives of a good student activities program for a junior high school can be summarized as follows:

1. It should further the personal social adjustment with peers and with adults.
2. It should promote learning the skills and concepts of democracy through actual practice.
3. It should offer an opportunity for students to pursue a wide variety of interests and adjust readily to changes in such interests.
4. It should provide for discovery and development of abilities.
5. It should provide an outlet for the altruism and idealism of junior high school youth.

In conclusion, it should be pointed out that the over-all goal of students activities is an opportunity for successful participation for all students. There should be an appropriate activity for every boy and girl, and every boy and girl should be in an activity. Whether the school provides a regular period for student activities (a common practice in junior high schools) or whether they are undistinguishable from the regularly organized learning experiences, there must be concern for all students. Students who need the experiences most are often denied them because of excessive cost or by the use of academic achievement as a criterion for admission into club membership or activity. A few students should not dominate the program nor should students be exploited for aggrandizement of the school. Students need to feel pride in their accomplishments, but winning teams and excellence of school productions must not be the only goals of such activities. Adult frustrations about the quality of finished products often denies the desired ends. Student activities provide rich nurture for adolescent growth.

FOREIGN LANGUAGE PROGRAM
IN THE JUNIOR HIGH SCHOOL

Joseph M. Vocolo

INTRODUCTION

A discussion of foreign languages at the junior high school level invariably gets around to the problem of scheduling difficulties. This is so because (1) the school day is already pretty well filled up with mandated subjects, and (2) foreign languages are strangers to the junior high school curriculum and particularly below grade nine.

As the discussion progresses it soon is abundantly obvious that the problem involves much more than a sitting down and making decisions about the number and variety of courses to be given and deciding the hourly schedule. Of course, this is the purely mechanical aspect of the procedure, but the implications of the schedule are reflected in outlook on the curriculum, function of the junior high school, concept of the learner, and a host of considerations which go to make up an entire orientation to education. The aim of this paper will be to show that foreign languages should be part of the core program (the constants in the curriculum) open to all pupils and that there is room in the schedule for this kind of program.

THE PROBLEM

John Dewey said once of the good community and the right attitude toward education: "What the best family wants for its children, the community should want for all children." Authors Faunce and Clute[1] have written concerning the objectives of education:

The fundamental purpose of education is to help the individual discover

---

From *The Clearing House,* XLII, No. 6 (February, 1968), 358-361. Used by permission of the author and publisher.

[1]Roland C. Faunce and Morrel J. Clute, *Teaching in the Junior High School* (Belmont, California: Wadsworth Publishing Company), 1961, p. 81.

himself and the world in which he lives so that he may live a happy and useful life. In other words, education has two basic purposes: to enable each individual to realize his full potential so that he may enjoy the greatest personal happiness; and to enable him to develop to his fullest capacity for citizenship so that his fellow men profit from his service.

Now both these citations make explicit that all children should have this opportunity for self-discovery. The question, then, is what experiences are all children to have and what experiences will be had by only some of the children? And if and when we deny certain experiences to some children for whatever reason, how do we reconcile this action with the above quoted statements? On what facts, experiences, research are such decisions based? What is the reaction of the child being denied entry to an area of the curriculum?

There appears to be little justification for maintaining old ideas (which were wrong to begin with) regarding foreign languages and their place in the junior high curriculum, especially in the light of the stated purposes of the junior high school, contemporary society, learning theory, and the nature and psychology of language learning. Shane[2] has said, writing of provisions for program enrichment:

Whether in elementary school music, junior high schools sports, or secondary school dramatics, opportunities should be available for all, since some children are not more worth educating than others—although the extent of their education quite properly may vary as dictated by talent, aspiration, and intelligence. Emphasis on skill or level of performance per se, therefore, should not determine who "belongs" in an activity.

It is ironic that often the very children denied access to certain curricular areas are the very ones who would profit the most from the experience. I'm speaking here of the culturally disadvantaged who has so much to gain precisely because of the fact of disadvantagement. That Shane's proposal should apply to foreign languages is clearly indicated by the joint statement of the National Education Association and the Modern Language Association,[3] "Preferably not later than the third grade, all children should have the opportunity to listen to and speak a second language." All students, according to recommendations of the National

[2]Harold G. Shane, "The School and Individual Differences" in *Individualizing Instruction*, 1962 yearbook—Part I, NSSE (Chicago: University of Chicago Press), 1962, p. 60.

[3]Ilo Remer, *A Handbook for Guiding Students in Modern Foreign Languages* (Washington: U.S. Government Printing Office), 1963, p. 3.

Association of Secondary School Principals in 1959,[4] should have the opportunity to elect foreign language study and to continue it as long as their interest and ability permit:

At a time when events anywhere in the world can produce immediate and profound repercussions on our everyday life, when decisions in this country involving other world areas are commonplace, and when an individual from any part of our country may find himself dealing with non-English-speaking peoples, some experience with another modern language and some understanding of another modern culture became extremely important.

Essentially the same recommendation is made by the United States Office of Education.[5] The New York State Education Department recommends foreign language programs beginning in grade seven. Thus the case for foreign languages as part of the core program and not solely for the edification of the exclusive few has gained some very powerful advocates. In matter of fact, no governmental body, no important organization would disagree with these views. The recent action of the state of California mandating the study of foreign languages for three years and for all pupils beginning no later than grade six may portend a future course of events. A little known fact is that similar bills have been introduced in the New York State legislature.

STATUS OF FOREIGN LANGUAGES IN THE JUNIOR HIGH SCHOOL

Yet, despite the weight of all this support, what is the state of foreign languages in the junior high school? In short, persons charged with responsibility for curriculum at this level don't appear to be listening. As one reads textbooks and other professional literature in the area of the junior high school, it is quickly and abundantly obvious that this area has been totally ignored. Even in the area of exploratory experiences curriculum writers choose not to pay much attention to this question. Foreign languages usually appear as a ninth grade elective presumably for the more able or academically inclined individual.

What is the present situation regarding enrollments in foreign languages

[4]NASSP, "Modern Foreign Languages in the Comprehensive High School," *Bulletin of the NASSP* (September, 1959), p. 4.

[5]Remer, p. 1.

at the junior high level? While no completely accurate count is available, it is safe to assume that less than 25 per cent of the grades seven to nine population is involved in such programs and the largest portion of these pupils would be found in the grade nine program. One notable exception is the program in three Buffalo junior high schools which enrolls approximately 70 per cent of all pupils in grades seven and eight. Incidentally, two of these schools can be labeled disadvantaged or core-area schools.

SCHEDULING FOREIGN LANGUAGES

The policy regarding foreign languages, where they are offered in junior high schools, is usually one of election. Most often it is a ninth grade elective. Generally speaking, guidance policy recommends the election of a foreign language to the college bound youngster and one can assume that the kinds of youngsters that are in these programs are the high I.Q. and college oriented groups. This applies to the grades seven and eight program as well as grade nine. Authors Faunce and Clute,[6] while they make no recommendations for foreign languages other than as electives in grade nine, frown on the idea of electives below grade nine.

In a lively, well-adapted program in which account is taken of pupils' choices and interests, the elective system contributes little in grades seven and eight. Grade nine may offer elective opportunity that makes some sense because elections are built up as continuations of the various exploratory programs of grades seven and eight. We repeat that specialization is not the function of this program, or of the junior high school (or of the foreign language program).

One might hasten to ask: On what exploratory experiences in foreign languages can an election be made in grade nine when such programs are not generally found below grade nine? Furthermore, is not the goal of exploration just as important in grade nine?

Why, then, have not foreign languages made the inroads in the junior high school that one might reasonably assume would follow on the advice of all the expert opinion? Answers usually heard are (1) there is no room in the already crowded schedule, and (2) persons charged with responsibility are not cognizant of or do not accept the new thinking concerning foreign languages. Perhaps the real answer is due to the usual time lag associated with acceptance of innovations which incidentally has attended all aspects of the development of the junior high school.

[6]Faunce and Clute, pp. 115-116.

RECOMMENDATIONS

Concerning the problem of the tight schedule, while it is true there is not an overabundance of unused time, it is clear there is room for foreign languages. The many schools all over the country—Buffalo and especially now California—testify to this possibility. One wonders how much room there would be for art, music, or industrial arts and homemaking were it not for the fact that these subjects are usually mandated, which leads to the speculation that the example of California may offer the solution.

Scheduling hints are offered by Faunce and Clute[7] with their "Alternate Day" and "Short Course" schedules. Foreign language can be scheduled in the former plan three days per week opposite homemaking or art. Incidentally, minimal exposure to foreign language is recommended as three days weekly. Since both homemaking and art are constants (required of all pupils) this plan has the added recommendation that all pupils may move in groups throughout the week. This assumes, of course, that all pupils will take foreign languages. In the "Short Course" plan foreign languages could be scheduled on alternate days with physical education.

In Buffalo junior high schools foreign languages in grades seven and eight are scheduled on the alternate-day plan three days per week opposite music or art. In grade nine foreign language is an elective and is scheduled the customary five days per week. However, because of exploratory experiences in grades seven and eight, which we would hope are both pleasurable and profitable, the pupils have some basis for making elections in foreign languages. In grade nine some pupils, with the help of guidance, may decide to continue with the same foreign language, others may switch languages, and still others may terminate their foreign language education. In any event larger numbers of pupils will have experiences with a foreign language.

In summation, there seems to be little justification for the lack of involvement of large numbers of pupils in junior high school foreign language programs. The recommendations of organizations and governmental bodies such as the NEA, MLA, NASSP, and USOE require curriculum makers at this level to take stock of the situation and evolve a fresh approach to the problem unbiased by previous expectations and experiences.

It should be mentioned here that research studies[8] have indicated that

---

[7] Faunce and Clute, pp. 107-108.

[8] Barbara Von Wittich, "Prediction of Success in Foreign Languages Study," *Modern Language Journal* (April, 1962), p. 211; and Elton Hocking, *Language Laboratory and Language Learning* (Washington: NEA), 1964, p. 72.

I.Q., achievement, reading level in English, success in other school subjects, results of prognostic tests are all poor predictors of success in a foreign language. The only reasonable way to determine if an individual will succeed is to give him an experience in the foreign language.

Thus, in terms of the stated purposes of the junior high school, the nature of the task as revealed by research and experience, and the needs of contemporary society and the learner, there is no basis in fact for continuing the program of foreign languages prevalent in the junior high school. Indeed, the junior high school may offer the last opportunity for the large masses of pupils to have an experience in a foreign language as part of their general education.

THE CORE CURRICULUM:
LIVELY CORPSE

Gordon F. Vars

Despite premature efforts to bury it, the core curriculum is not dead. Hasty diagnosis based on insufficient data characterizes Harvey Overton's untimely obituary, "The Rise and Fall of the Core Curriculum."[1] Russell Hamm, a more recent mourner, deals more with the patient's recent illness than with its present strength.[2] Although somewhat shaky from its recent bout with the "academic-itis" that swept American education in the early 1960's, core today shows a renewed vigor of body and spirit that should be heartening to its many admirers.

SIGNS OF HEALTH

If attendance at conventions is any measure of the health of core, the

---

From *The Clearing House,* XLII, No. 9 (May, 1968), 515-519. Used by permission of the author and publisher.

[1] Harvey Overton, "The Rise and Fall of the Core Curriculum." *The Clearing House,* Vol. 40, No. 9 (May, 1966), pp. 532-537.

[2] Russell L. Hamm, "Core Curriculum at the Crossroads," *Teachers College Journal,* Vol. 39, No. 2 (Nov. 1967), pp. 62-64.

crowd of more than 300 at the 1967 national core conference in Omaha, Nebraska, was a far cry from the "handful of the faithful" to which Overton refers. True, this may seem to be a small turnout when compared with national meetings of English, social studies, or science teachers, but few core conferences have topped this figure since the first gathering at Morgantown, West Virginia, in 1953. Any inclination of conferees to "lament the demise" of core was quickly dispelled by the enthusiasm of teachers and administrators in both Omaha and Westside, Nebraska, school systems. The atmosphere was more like a "revival" than a "wake," as Ernest Melby challenged educators to take all humanity to their hearts and Edythe Gaines reminded participants of the basic principles of core that continue to carry forward the central purposes of American society.

Overton also makes much of the fact that the number of articles on core listed in *Education Index* has declined in recent years and that current discussion of educational innovation seldom refers specifically to core. What he overlooks is the extent to which the core idea appears in contemporary discussion of team teaching, humanities programs, the middle school, special programs for the culturally disadvantaged, etc. Anyone who would use *Education Index* to assess the status of core must look under these headings, too, as will be elaborated later.

A realistic diagnosis of the health of a complex educational concept such as core must consider both its "body," the block-time class, and its "spirit," a set of ideas that includes problem-centered learning, student involvement in instruction, the teacher as guide as well as instructor, education as a humanizing experience, etc.

THE CORE CORPUS

The quickest way to identify the possible presence of core in a school program is to look for its administrative framework, the block-time class. This is a class that combines or replaces two or more subjects ordinarily taught separately. Whether taught by one teacher or by a team, it appears on the daily schedule as a block of time extending over two or more periods. Block-time has been especially well received at the junior high school level. It provides a transition between a self-contained elementary school program and a departmentalized high school, and it facilitates teacher advisement and guidance at a time when youngsters are going through the stresses and strains that accompany adolescence.

U.S. Office of Education surveys have shown a steady increase in the proportion of junior high schools utilizing block-time, from 15.8 per cent in 1949 to 31.4 per cent in 1957 to 40.0 per cent in 1960. In junior high schools of 300 or more pupils the 1960 figure was approximately 50 per cent.[3] Lounsbury found that 50 per cent of the junior high schools he surveyed had block-time classes in 1961, a drop from the figure of 59 per cent he had obtained from the same schools in 1954.[4] In his 1965 survey of schools enrolling 300 or more pupils in grades 7, 8, and 9, Gruhn found block-time in 46 per cent.[5] Although subject to the usual limitations of sampling surveys and further complicated by the perennial problem of terminology, these studies suggest that, while the incidence of block-time has declined somewhat in recent years, there has not been the wholesale abandonment of the idea that some alarmists would have us believe.

That many educators remain committed to the block-time approach was evident when school systems throughout the country were invited to submit descriptions of their programs for a book tentatively entitled *Current Concepts of Core Curriculum*. It may be scheduled for publication as part of the *Bold New Venture Series* of Indiana University Press.

Some current block-time programs included are: a General Education program that has been in operation at Oneida Junior High School, Schenectady, New York, since 1931; one of the many "block-of-time" programs in the junior high schools of Detroit, Michigan; the Basic Education program in Kinloch Park Junior High School, Miami, Florida; the district-wide core program in Jefferson County, Kentucky; and several programs in campus schools attached to colleges and universities.

Other large districts that might have been cited include the public schools of St. Paul, Minnesota, the Charlotte-Mecklenburg Schools of Charlotte, North Carolina, and the Shawnee-Mission district of suburban Kansas City, Kansas.

Perhaps the core bandwagon is not making as much noise as it did in the 1940's and 50's, but it is evident that many schools continue to utilize the block-time class as the framework within which teachers may work toward the core ideal.

---

[3]U.S. Office of Education, *The Junior High School: A Survey of Grades 7-8-9 in Junior and Junior-Senior High Schools, 1959-60*, by Grace S. Wright and Edith S. Greer, Bulletin 1963, No. 32 (Washington: Government Printing Office, 1963), p. 20.

[4]John H. Lounsbury and Harl R. Douglass, "Recent Trends in Junior High School Practices, 1954-1964," *Bulletin of the National Association of Secondary-School Principals*, Vol. 49, No. 302 (Sept. 1965), p. 92.

[5]William T. Gruhn and Harl R. Douglass, "A Survey of Practices in Junior High Schools: Block-Time and Core Programs," (unpublished studies; quoted with permission of the authors).

THE CORE SPIRIT

How many block-time classes embody a "true" problem-centered, guidance oriented, humanistic curriculum? Evidence on this question is conflicting. Lounsbury found a slight rise in the per cent of schools reporting problem-centered block-time classes, from 12 per cent in 1954 to 13 per cent in 1964.[6] On the other hand, Gruhn found that the proportion of junior high schools with programs in which "subjects are well integrated, losing their separate identities" was 10 per cent in his 1964 survey but only 4 per cent in 1965.[7] Observers have often noted the gap between core theory and classroom practice, and it is difficult to say whether the present situation is any worse now than it was several decades ago when the core movement was getting under way.

What about manifestations of the core "spirit" in other educational practices? The limitations of team teaching as a vehicle for achieving core objectives have been set forth elsewhere.[8] Nevertheless, many schools are utilizing interdisciplinary teams, often under such labels as "Humanities," "American Studies," or "World Studies," to achieve a more humane, integrated curriculum. Consider this rationale for an 11th grade program in Pueblo High School, Tucson, Arizona:

> One of the chief advantages of the humanities approach over conventional courses is the breaking down of artificial barriers between disciplines. Students study a particular topic from historical, literary, art, and musical viewpoints concurrently, thus receiving a much more balanced picture than would otherwise be presented.[9]

Many early core programs were taught by interdisciplinary teams. History suggests that the team approach may in time evolve into the problem-centered instruction characteristic of core, depending upon the teachers' educational philosophies and the kind of leadership provided. Time will tell whether the values obtained by pooling teacher talents will outweigh the difficulties in interpersonal relations that hamper many team efforts.

Team approaches to core that are illustrated in *Current Concepts of*

---

[6]Lounsbury, *op. cit.,* p. 92.

[7]Gruhn, *op. cit.*

[8]Gordon F. Vars, "Can Team Teaching Save the Core Curriculum?" *Phi Delta Kappan,* Vol. 47, No. 5 (January 1966), pp. 258-262.

[9]Marjorie Benson and Richard Rodgers *A Humanities Approach to English and American History* (Tucson, Arizona: The Public Schools, 1966), p. 3.

Core Curriculum include a team-taught core program in Northern Hills Junior High School, North Topeka, Kansas, and interdisciplinary team programs at Niskayuna, New York; Santa Barbara, California; Arvada, Colorado; Park Ridge, Illinois; and Dearborn, Michigan. It is interesting to note that interdisciplinary team programs, often under the rubric of humanities, are gaining increasing acceptance at the high school level, where the single-teacher core has never made many inroads.

Characteristics that have made core especially popular at the junior high school level would appear to make it even more appropriate for a middle school that includes somewhat younger children.[10] It is significant that of the 20 school systems identified by the National Education Association in 1965 as having middle schools, a vast majority had either self-contained or partially departmentalized programs in grades 5 and 6.[11] This may represent either a carryover of the self-contained classroom concept from the elementary school or the introduction of block-time or core ideas typical of the junior high school. In either case, some kind of home-base group is found in many middle schools and is recommended in much of the current discussion of the middle school. Moreover, the fact that middle schools may employ teachers with elementary training and certification may represent a real breakthrough in the problem of staffing block-time and core programs.

Space does not permit an examination of the core idea as it is reflected in some contemporary nongraded and independent study programs. Suffice it to say that certain types of nongraded programs, especially those that utilize interdisciplinary teams working within large blocks of time, and independent study programs in which the student's individual investigation is shared with a class or seminar, bear a number of the earmarks of the core idea. *Current Concepts of Core Curriculum* cites specific examples of nongraded core programs and independent study that grow out of block-time classes in Illinois, Pennsylvania, Florida, Kansas, Ohio, and Michigan.

One of the most exciting examples of the viability of the core idea is its success in special programs for the culturally disadvantaged. Young people who have rejected conventional schooling often respond with enthusiasm to the personalized instruction and guidance emphasis characterized by such projects as "Operation GO," "Project SAVE," "Upward Bound," or "Operation HELP." Some experts are predicting that such projects, backed with millions of dollars from government and foundation sources, will

[10]Gordon F. Vars, "Core Curriculum in the Middle School," *Ideas Educational,* Vol. 5, No. 1 (Winter, 1967), pp. 25-28.

[11]"Middle Schools," *Educational Research Service Circular,* No. 3 (Washington: National Education Association, May, 1965), p. 3.

spark a renaissance of core. The core curriculum arose out of the desire to make education more meaningful to students. This challenge continues to face our schools today, not only in the big cities but throughout the nation.

Current changes in the educational climate also support a hopeful prognosis for the future health of the core idea. Although difficult to document, it appears that preoccupation with the separate academic disciplines is waning. Witness the rise of the new prophet, Marshall McLuhan, who stresses interrelatedness of knowledge and human interaction in an era of new media. Major curriculum revision projects are searching for concepts and processes that span the disciplines, and a renewed concern for man's wholeness is illustrated by the appointment of a new Commission on Humanism in Education by the Association for Supervision and Curriculum Development. Hamm's gloomy analysis seems out of tune with these developments.

CONTINUING INFIRMITIES

Lest it would appear that the core curriculum is completely hale and hearty, it is necessary to examine some of its persistent weaknesses. Both Overton and Hamm comment on the problem of definition of terms. That this is not unique to core is evident by the bewildering variety of programs today that are labeled team teaching, nongrading, or independent study. Hope lies in the fact that curriculum specialists are approaching consensus on this issue, which is an essential first step toward consistency in school practice.

Overton's charge that the core idea has been insufficiently researched also can be applied to most school practices. However, a partial listing of research on the effectiveness of block-time and core programs includes 39 comparative studies, 15 normative studies, and six major summaries of research.[12] While it suffers all the inadequacies typical of research in the complex field of education, this body of knowledge compares very favorably with that cited in defense of other educational innovations.

Schools have had difficulty obtaining qualified core teachers from the very beginning. Since schools never have had and perhaps never will have an adequate supply of core teachers, some recommend "symbiotic teams" in which one teacher's strengths counteract another's weaknesses. The

---

[12]Gordon F. Vars, *Bibliography of Research on the Effectiveness of Block-Time Programs* (Kent, Ohio: Department of Secondary Education, Kent State University, 1967).

limitations of this approach have been mentioned earlier. The problem of preparing core teachers is aggravated by the vicious cycle in which colleges and universities find it difficult to justify a program that prepares teachers for positions that exist in a limited number of schools, and schools are reluctant to embark on programs for which teachers are scarce or non-existent. Similar difficulties confront schools wishing to embark on team teaching, nongraded programs, programmed instruction, or other innovations.

Primary responsibility for breaking this cycle probably lies with public school personnel, who must establish innovative programs with the best teachers available, while at the same time making their wants known to teacher-preparation institutions. Needed are more arrangements such as those in Omaha, Nebraska, where students obtain pre-service preparation for core teaching at the University of Omaha, and then do their practice teaching in local core classes under the guidance of their core methods professor.

In the long run, solution to this problem probably lies in the general upgrading of teacher preparation at all levels and in all fields. Promising developments include the use of interaction analysis and self-study via videotapes to develop teachers who see their job as something far more creative than dispensing information.

PROGNOSIS

Three kinds of evidence have been cited to demonstrate that the core curriculum idea is far from dead. First, a sizeable number of schools continue to utilize the block-time format in their efforts to approach the core ideal. Second, concepts long associated with the core curriculum are manifest in other contemporary programs such as interdisciplinary team teaching, humanities courses, certain independent study and nongraded programs, modified self-contained classes in middle schools, and special programs for the culturally disadvantaged. Third, there appears to be a perceptible swing away from extreme concern with subject matter mastery toward a more human, personal, problem-centered approach to education.

Whatever label it bears, or in whatever form it appears, the core curriculum idea will undoubtedly continue to have an important place in American education—as long as there are human problems that do not fall neatly within the boundaries of conventional subjects, as long as education is viewed as essentially a human and humanizing encounter between youth and adult, and as long as educators keep in mind that young people learn best when they are actively involved in wrestling with problems that have personal meaning to them. There is plenty of life in the old core curriculum yet!

WHAT EDUCATIONAL PLAN FOR THE
IN-BETWEEN-AGER?

William M. Alexander

The junior high school was created some fifty years ago—usually by taking grades 7 and 8 from the elementary school and combining them with grade 9 from the high school. Although its original purpose was to provide a bridge between childhood and adolescence, opinions differ as to whether it still does perform this function. Critics of the present junior high school organization point to research which shows that children reach adolescence much earlier than children did fifty years ago; girls may be pubescent before grade 7, and boys have generally reached full-blown adolescence by the time they have reached grade 9.

Another factor which bothers the critics is what the label "junior" implies. It has become all too descriptive of an activity program (including interscholastic athletics), a departmentalized schedule, and a social system that look very much like those in the senior high school.

Education Editor Paul Woodring wrote in a recent issue of the *Saturday Review:* "It now appears that the 6-3-3 plan, with its junior high school, is on its way out." Whatever the accuracy of Woodring's statement, it is doubtful that school boards and other responsible agencies will want to revert to the 8-4 plan. If anything replaces the junior high school, it will probably be a "middle school."

Several of these schools have been organized in recent years to serve the bridging function that the junior high school was set up to do. Although the number of these middle schools is too small to substantiate Woodring's prediction, their existence does indicate some dissatisfaction with the present junior high school organization.

From *NEA Journal,* LV, No. 3 (March, 1966), 30-32. Used by permission of the author and publisher.

Many of the middle school reorganizations include grades 6, 7, and 8, a practice of long standing in some districts. Grade 6 is simply moved from elementary to junior high and grade 9 is returned to the high school.

Such a grade reorganization does not necessarily involve any change in the instructional program or methods of instruction. The departmentalized schedule and the same program of activities may carrry over into the new school, or grade 6 may be left on a self-contained basis and instruction for grades 7 and 8 departmentalized.

A few districts are making a more radical shift by setting up a middle school to serve children usually enrolled in grades 5 to 8—roughly those about 10 to 14 years of age. Such a school will take boys and girls from the years of upper childhood and see some 85 percent of them through to early adolescence. Unlike the tendency of the junior high school to precipitate adolescent behavior, this kind of middle school will prepare children over a period of years to meet the crises of adolescence.

A few school districts have reorganized along these lines, usually in conjunction with new building programs. Such schools have also been proposed in large cities as a way of ending de facto segregation in some neighborhood elementary schools. Whether this 4-4-4 plan would do this on a permanent basis is a matter of opinion. Nevertheless, such a plan, with its complete middle division of the school program, promises to span the years between childhood and adolescence better than the predominant 6-3-3 setup.

Whatever the faults of the present junior high school, American communities cannot be expected to move overnight into some new pattern of school organization—nor should they. Our nation's 6,500 junior high schools represent a large investment in facilities and employ many persons whose careers are intertwined with the present organization.

Furthermore, the junior high school represents a significant improvement over the old eight-year elementary school. It has enriched the educational diet of the preadolescent youngster and has frequently encouraged useful educational experimentation. It might still serve as a point of departure for experimentation in new forms of school organization.

As school authorities and others debate the value of retaining the junior high school or replacing it with some other kind of middle school, they will have to resolve many though issues such as the following.

What grades should be included? As already indicated, the new middle schools usually include either grades 5 through 8, or, more frequently, 6 through 8. The middle school, however, may be ideally suited for a nongraded organization because of the wide differences in children in its age groups. Programs of diagnostic services, frequent teacher-student conferences, and much individualized instruction would help children achieve optimum progress without arbitrary grade level expectancies. Some pupils might move through the middle school in three years and others might need a fourth year.

Should the program differ for boys and girls? Since, on the average, girls reach adolescence earlier than boys, some of them may be encouraged to move· through the middle school at least a year ahead of the average boy. This might help take care of the typical discrepancy in the interests of boys and girls inthe 10- to 14-year-old age range.

How could the program be made intellectually stimulating? Both the self-contained classroom organization of the elementary school and the departmentalized junior high school have been criticized for their lack of intellectual stimulation. The weaknesses of these organizations should be avoided in the middle school, where new patterns of organization can be carefully tested.

For example, the middle school could try a team teaching arrangement in which four homeroom groups of about twenty-five pupils each share the same four teachers. Each teacher would serve as a homeroom teacher-counselor and each would have a different field of specialization (language arts, social studies, science, or mathematics).

Such a plan would facilitate planning for individual pupils and also utilize teachers in their area of greatest interest and competence. Rather than having a routine rotation of pupils through departmentalized schedules, such sharing of instruction and flexibility of learning groups would permit pupils and teachers to know each other well and would ensure that each curriculum area is taught in an intellectually stimulating manner. In addition, the flexibility of this plan would make possible extensive use of individualized instruction, including independent study.

How should learning skills be taught and emphasized? Emphasis should, of course, be given to learning skills in all studies. But the middle school might be the strategic point at which to provide extensive use of many library and other learning resources. Special learning centers could provide individualized instruction in reading, viewing, and listening, writing (including typing), interviewing, problem-solving, and other skills.

What common or general studies ought to be provided? The basic subjects of the elementary and junior high schools would undoubtedly be retained in the middle school: language arts, mathematics, science, and social studies. Some schools would include the fine arts and a second language as common subjects; others would make one or both an exploratory, individualized-choice area.

The content of the common areas would be planned with reference to the programs of the elementary and high schools so that there would be as much continuity as possible throughout the school program. A specific plan of scope and sequence in the general studies would assist teacher teamwork and also permit variations in pupil progress.

What exploratory experiences should be provided? The exploratory program of the junior high school has been one of its strengths; a major reason for moving children into a middle school earlier is to offer them increased opportunity for exploring many interests. In addition to exploratory experiences in such customary areas as foreign languages, the fine arts, industrial arts, and home economics, a range of interests might be served by other experiences such as in acting, photography, personal grooming, creative writing, and in assisting in library, laboratory, lunchroom, and office.

Many students could explore their leadership and vocational aptitudes by participating in various student-managed enterprises such as assembly programs, exhibits, school stores and banks, lost-and-found departments, school publications, and student government organizations.

What type of an activity program should be provided? A major criticism of the junior high school is its copying of the high school activity program. Many regard the need to eliminate this program as a justification for the middle school. The middle school could probably do without an organized activity program other than the student-managed enterprises already suggested. Perhaps each instructional unit (that is, a group of four homerooms involving approximately 100 pupils) could be left to develop its own activities, at least until and if enough common interests are discovered to justify schoolwide projects.

In larger middle schools, a "school within a school" organization might be desirable, grouping four instructional units to constitute a "little school" of 400 pupils encompassing the full age range of the school. These units could develop intramural activities for themselves and cooperate on some activities with other units within the middle school. Interscholastic athletic competition between middle schools would certainly not be permitted.

What would be the best way to promote sound personal development?

With the perils of adolescence looming just ahead for most pupils, the middle school can give continued and direct attention to the formation of personal values and standards of behavior. In addition to many curriculum opportunities, the homeroom organization could help greatly in individual development. The homeroom teacher-counselor would be continually alert to the potentialities and problems of each of his advisees.

The school would seek maximum interaction with interested parents, as well as opportunities to plan with representatives of other community institutions and agencies.

Many other issues will undoubtedly arise as existing faculty groups plan reorganizations of educational programs in order to do a better job of bridging childhood and adolescence.

Two criteria may help to ensure the success of these plans: (a) The reorganization should provide such varied and excellent learning opportunities that each pupil, whether 10 or 14 years old, boy or girl, advantaged or disadvantaged, can find some success and challenge that will stimulate further learning; and (b) the plan should include instruments for rigorous evaluation of results.

This second criterion will help educational researchers answer with more certainty troublesome questions which they can now answer only with guesses.

MIDDLE SCHOOL:
A QUESTIONABLE INNOVATION

Richard L. Post

Possibly my greatest misgivings concerning the current interest in the middle school stem from a feeling that educational gimmickry is being substituted for genuine innovation. The innovations which intrigue me are those offering an opportunity to stimulate the individualization of instruction. Independent study, continuous progress curricula, team teaching, and flexible scheduling seem to be the issues worthy of our serious considera-

From *The Clearing House,* XLII, No. 8 (April, 1968), 484-486. Used by permission of the author and publisher.

tion. I fail to see how the transfer of the ninth grade to the senior high and the fifth and sixth grades to the middle school can help us move in this direction. In fact, if the ninth grade students are moved into a more subject-centered school, and if the fifth and sixth grade students are subjected to increased departmentalization, we may set education back 50 years. Our energies may be directed toward an innovation which does not really merit serious consideration, and the important new ideas in education may be ignored.

The grade organization adopted by a district may be 6-3-3, 5-3-4, 4-4-4 or 6-6, with little real difference in the quality of the education offered. The program and staff within each institution determine its quality, and it is improvement in these areas that should occupy our interests.

It has been my experience that teachers whose interests are more subject-centered than child-centered gravitate to the senior high. As a result I have felt that senior high schools are more inclined to set arbitrary standards and utilize more impersonal teaching methods than junior high schools. It seems unwise to place ninth grade students in this environment until sufficient changes have been made in program and practice to insure that their needs will be met.

At age 14 decisions about continuing in school, about value systems, and about social attitudes are of prime importance to students, and a school whose primary concern is with needs of these individuals is necessary. In our junior high we utilize the block-of-time, attempt to give continuous instruction in reading, offer alternate courses for the gifted and the handicapped, and in other ways attempt to center our interest on the individual student. I'm not certain that the ninth grade student could get any better program than this if he were moved into a senior high school.

My feelings are even stronger when we discuss the social aspects of such a move. We have no night activities and our ninth grade students do not attend senior high social events. We do not permit students to drive cars to school. I do not see what useful purpose can be served by having 14-year-old girls going to the junior prom and riding home from school in cars with 18-year-old boys. Even if it were granted that ninth graders are more mature than they were 30 years ago, this maturity should be directed toward worthwhile junior high projects such as adopting a foster child, community beautification, or planning assemblies and programs. I feel that in the four year high school the few social opportunities available might encourage the wrong sort of development. The fact that students mature earlier should not lead one to the conclusion that we should encourage earlier sophistication of their social activities, since early marriage is still an economic mistake and dating activities should be deferred as long as possible.

There are many real challenges facing educational leaders today. Because of a growing recognition of the role education plays in improving the quality of life, there is a new commitment to educational improvement. A move to shift grades from one institution to another hardly seems worthy of consideration when we are on the verge of beginning to understand the teacher-learner relationship, and when fundamental changes in the nature of teaching could result. Another realignment of grades seems ridiculous when the graded school itself may be on its way out.

INSTITUTIONAL INTEGRITY AND MIDDLE SCHOOL ORGANIZATION

Samuel H. Popper

The burden of this essay is twofold: to register an imperative for institutional integrity in middle school organization and to spotlight a case of cultural deviance in the 5-8 middle school structure.

The early adolescent we know comes apart at the psychological seam. Organismic disorganization, following Fritz Redl, and ego diffusion, following Erik Erikson, are concomitants of the physiological revolution at the onset of adolescence. Norms of specificity and affective-neutrality, which are dominant in the relational network of both the elementary school and high school, compound for early adolescent pupils a host of integrative problems they must resolve at this stage of human development. These pupils are overwhelmed now with self-adjustment problems, with the problem of cultural meaning, with the problem of identification, with the problem of ego resynthesis. Ego is now the all-absorbing interest of the early adolescent pupil, and alter—whether alter is a teacher, team of teachers, or school organization—is "a significant other" for the pupil only insofar as a relation with alter helps reduce the terrible personal anxieties of an identity crisis.

From the point of view of an early adolescent, significant interaction with others in the school environment is measured now by the diffuse

From the *Journal of Secondary Education,* XLIII, No. 4 (April, 1968), 184-191. Used by permission of the author and publisher.

interest they have in him as a human being beset suddenly by natural and cultural problems beyond his control. If he is to find significance in interaction with teachers and curriculum—that is, with the structure and process of school organization—diffuseness and affectivity have to be dominant in their relations with him, for his immediate need now is for the particularistic values of identification. Otherwise his motivation in the learner's role will be difficult to attain. It is a period when he needs a temporary refuge from the pressures of culture, from the norms of specificity and affective-neutrality which are value complements of the evaluative performance standard; a psychosocial moratorium as it were. But diffuseness and affectivity in the structure and process of school organization are dissonant values. Therefore, a "special case" has to be made by the school for this turn of events.

And the special case which has been devised for this purpose is the middle school unit of our public school systems. Instrumental capacities are by no means neglected in this organization, learning continues, but the human condition at early adolescence is the dominant evaluative focus of this school and not how much has been learned of cognitive skills. Diffuseness and affectivity in relations between the middle school and pupils is normative because the value loading of its paramount cultural goal is inclined toward the particularistic. It is this paramount cultural goal which characterizes the institutional mission of the American middle school. From the point of view of society, the social value of this mission is the source of legitimation for middle school structure and process. My own definition of this paramount cultural goal is given in *The American Middle School* as follows: "to intervene protectively in the process of education which was begun in the elementary school, mediate between the human condition at the onset of adolescence and the pressures of culture, and continue the general education of early adolescents with a curriculum applied in a psychosocial environment which is functional for learning at this stage of socialization."

Call it a middle school, call it a junior high school, or call it by any other name—and there have been several—here is a unit of public school organization whose dominant focus was meant to be on early adolescent development. As one of its architects put it in 1909:

The boys are becoming men; the girls are becoming women; and a flood of new impulses, new ideas, new emotions are crowding up in them, making it a very critical and important period of their lives. In the organization of our schools, however, we do not take this into account.

. . . The seventh, eighth and ninth grades should be placed in schools separated from the primary grades.[1]

Nothing more consequential than an accident of history accounts for its traditional name of "junior high school." Its model was the "middle school" of other societies, but only in the American adaptation was it given a dominant psychosocial orientation.

THE QUESTION OF ACCELERATED MATURATION

Having defined sociologically the functional differentiation of the middle school in terms of the "special case" of early adolescent development, it is now imperative, of course, to ask: What period of time is encompassed by early adolescence? At the historical beginning of the American middle school, this period included the years from about 12 to 15. And so it has been since then. Most pupils enter public school organization in September if they will be 6 years old by December first of that year. Given regular attendance, no retardation, and age-grade placement, the average pupil is in a middle school from age 12 to 15. This period approximates the span of puberty—12.76 to 15.57—calculated by Stolz and Stolz.[2] They define adolescent development of boys by four distinct phases of change in the growth rate:

1. prepuberty, a slightly accelerated growth
2. puberty, a rapid acceleration of growth
3. postpuberty, a decline in growth
4. late adolescence, a stage of slow growth

Historically, the record is clear that from its inception the American middle school has been differentiated on the second stage of this classification by Stolz and Stolz—the age from about 12 to 15. Some now claim the onset of puberty has shifted downward because of climatic change, improved nutrition, changing class statuses, and a host of other influences. A modified physiology, in any event, is offered in justification for middle school programs as early as age 10, or the fifth grade. This is, of course, an empirical problem, one which cannot be settled by speculation or debate. However, what can be gleaned from the research literature is not supportive

[1] Superintendent W. A. Greeson of Grand Rapids, Michigan quoted in Popper, *The American Middle School,* p. 37.

[2] H. R. Stolz and L. M. Stolz, *Somatic Development of Adolescent Boys* (New York: The Macmillian Co., (1951), p. 424.

of middle school programs before age 12, not when the legitimation of such programs is anchored in cultural and psychological values of early adolescent education.

Throughout the literature one finds hypotheses which suggest that such diverse variables as race, climate, intelligence, the age of parents, myopia, and the number of siblings have a bearing on the onset of puberty. No conclusive empirical evidence has been found in support of any of these. Quite the contrary, Donovan and Bosch have found that white and Negro boys under identical conditions reach puberty at about the same age.[3] Guidry and Holman found no significant difference in the attainment of menarche by a population of white and Negro girls in New Orleans.[4] Insofar as there is empirical evidence at all, it supports Tanner's conclusion that racial difference is not a significant factor in maturation.[5] Tanner also inclines toward the position that no substantive evidence supports the idea that children in different climates mature at different rates.[6] However, Tanner does report there has been a striking tendency for the menarche to come earlier during the past hundred years.[7] But even around the variable of menarche, there is room for questioning the conclusiveness of empirical investigations.

Tanner, as one example, cites data which indicate changes in the onset of menarche as reported from recall by the subjects[8] There are two groupings in these data: those subjects before 1905 cluster around age 13.2. Such a sudden change leads one to speculate how accurate is a woman's memory of this event years following its occurrence?

Altogether, from what reliable data there are in the research literature at the present, it would seem that west Europeans and North Americans are growing taller, but no adequate evidence supports a secular acceleration of maturation. Television and other mass media of modern life have no doubt accelerated the cultural sophistication of early adolescents, which perhaps accounts for the illusion of an accelerated secular maturation. But as

---

[3] B. T. Donovan and J. J. Van der Worff ten Bosch, *Physiology of Puberty* (Baltimore, Md.: William and Wilkins Co., 1965), p. 25.

[4] M. A. Guidry and R. L. Holman, "Comparative Maturation of White and Negro Children in New Orleans," *Journal of Atheroslerotic Research,* Vol. 2, 1962.

[5] J. M. Tanner, *Growth at Adolescence,* 2nd ed. (Oxford, Eng.: Blackwell Scientific Publications, 1962), pp. 104-15.

[6] *Ibid.,* pp. 104-05.

[7] *Ibid.,* p. 143.

[8] *Ibid.,* pp. 152-54.

Wattenberg points out, modern-day early adolescents "are more dichoto-mized than any previous generation."[9]

As for girls, it would seem that, despite unsure empirical evidence, the attainment of menarche by most females in our society occurs at about age 13 plus. However, in our type of society, why take a thirteen-year old girl out of the protective environment of a middle school? The esteem of competition which so pervasively marks our culture extends to the pursuit of a marriage partner—all is fair in love and war. In the light of contemporary vital statistics which show between 1950 and 1959 a three-fold increase of births to girls under sixteen, is there not greater social value to have girls of thirteen and fourteen learn in a middle school the nascent art of running *from* a male until she catches him than in the more "hep" social environment of a high school?[10]

Following clues gleaned from physiological literature, it seems that those who contemplate a downward shift of middle school grades, and justify such an administrative action on grounds of an earlier onset of the pubertal period, risk the institutional integrity of early adolescent education against outrageously high odds.

Finally, the question is: Does it matter? Does it really matter whether a middle school is of grades 5-8, or any other combination of grades? It matters very much when the cultural legitimation of the unit is claimed through a social value in education whose dominant orientation is to the human condition at early adolescnece. At stake here is the institutional integrity of the American middle school. Is it the norm to admit perfectly healthy people as patients in the hospital organization? Do we admit any but handicapped pupils to programs of special education? Why, then, admit other than early adolescent pupils to a unit of school organization whose legitimation turns on the "special case" of early adolescent education?

The legitimation of the American middle school from the first has been as a school for early adolescents. Grades 7-9 were assigned to this school not out of accommodation or change, but because the years from twelve to fifteen were defined by the science of that age as the transitional period between late childhood and postpubescent adolescence. And society wastes its resources in unrewarding duplication when a middle school is diverted from the paramount goal of early adolescent education. Once the human condition at early adolescence ceases to be the dominant focus of middle

[9] William W. Wattenberg, "Today's Junior High School Students," *Educational Leadership,* Vol. 23, December, 1965, p. 190.

[10] A. D. Claman and H. M. Bell, "Pregnancy in the Very Young Teen-ager," *American Journal of Obstetrics and Gynecology,* Vol. 90, Sept.-Dec., 1964.

school education, then the old pattern of 8-4 school organization would have a *more valid* administrative rationale for existing than a 4-4-4 pattern. Positive intercultural and interracial attitudes, excellence in education, the cultivation of creativity, and the acquisition of cognitive skills are expected outputs of all school units, from first grade through the twelfth, and it does not matter whether the pattern of system organization is 8-4, 6-3-3, or 4-4-4.

Cultural pressures which brought the American middle school into existence as a differentiated school for early adolescent education have intensified and multiplied since the 1910 period. The new Department of Housing and Urban Development attests to that. Will the larger social welfare be served now by abandoning this institution for any other purpose? What other social value is capable of sustaining the legitimation of a middle school's *right* to exist once its differentiated function is no longer early adolescent education?

Institutional integrity was compromised in the American middle school during and after World War I when school districts used the middle school unit to get out from under a building-shortage problem. To this day, early adolescent education in the United States has not recovered from that tragic episode.[11] Now it is the problem of *de facto* racial segregation in American cities which threatens institutional integrity in the middle school. Again, the lure of an easy solution to an excruciatingly complex social problem threatens its legitimation.

---

[11] For an extended "bill of particulars," see chapter 11, "Dysfunctions and Instability," in Popper, *The American Middle School.*

THE MIDDLE-SCHOOL MOVEMENT

Emmett L. Williams

How can we best serve the educational needs of pupils who are no longer children and not quite adolescents? In trying to answer this question, some school systems are making modifications and improvements within the present organizational framework. Others, making basic changes in the age-grade range included in the school for middle adolescence, are establishing middle schools.

Everyone is familiar with the junior high—its genesis, its development, its many successes, and some of its problems—but the new middle school is less well-known. What is it? How widespread is the movement? Are there common characteristics of the program nationally? What are some of the emerging directions of the middle school?

My colleague, William M. Alexander, an early proponent of the middle school, defines it as "a school providing a program for a range of older children, preadolescents, and early adolescents that builds upon the school for earlier childhood and is linked to but different from the school for adolescence."

Very simply, the middle school consists of the organizational and program arrangements for pupils ranging in age from 9 through 14—ages 10 through 13 being most usual. Middle schools typically house grades 5 through 8, although several other age-grade patterns exist in practice. As with most innovations in institutions, the middle school is characterized by extreme variety. However, despite the fact that middle schools probably differ from one another more than they resemble one another, they do have some features in common.

One shared characteristic of the emerging middle schools is an attempt to combine the best features of the self-contained idea of the elementary school with the best features of the specialization of secondary schools. A large number of middle schools, especially in the East, have fifth and sixth grades that are largely self-contained and seventh and eighth grades that are essentially departmentalized.

Sometimes this plan breaks down and preserves just those features of the status quo—over-isolation and extreme departmentalization—that gave

---

From *Today's Education* 57, No. 9 (December, 1968), 41-42. Used by permission of the author and publisher.

impetus to the middle-school movement in the first place. One middle school, for instance, has fifth and sixth grades on the first floor and seventh and eighth on the second, and the two staffs never have occasion to speak to each other.

Some schools manage to effect a better transition than this. The Chippewa Middle School in Saginaw, Michigan, achieves planned gradualism by assigning fifth graders to a completely self-contained classroom with one teacher.

In the sixth grade, although the students are assigned to one classroom and spend most of their time with one teacher, the teachers work in informal teams, and students move about to a moderate degree in groups of different sizes and types arranged by the teacher teams in accordance with pupils' needs. A student becomes acquainted with several teachers and different groups of children while remaining essentially attached to one teacher and one room.

Still another pattern for combining the advantages of typical elementary and secondary practices is one that schedules pupils with a home-base teacher for a block of time and then moves them out to special teachers and laboratory centers. The home-base teacher is coordinator of the students' several program components. This arrangement provides every student with a teacher who knows him well and at the same time gives him contacts with teachers who can help him develop special competence in particular fields of interest.

The Community Middle School at Eagle Grove, Iowa, has instituted an adviser-advisee program to help develop a strong teacher-pupil relationship. Each member of the faculty acts as an adviser to no more than twenty students. This gives the student one adult to relate to for the four-year span of the middle school, while he may be studying with a dozen or more teachers in special areas.

Another characteristic of the emerging middle school is the emphasis on self-understanding. To this end, the instructional program frequently includes units on the special concerns of young adolescents. Increasing numbers of middle schools are using various modifications of what are coming to be known as *encounter groups*. These are discussion groups led by an adult with special training and focusing on topics and issues identified by the young people themselves.

Still another observable common characteristic of middle schools is the definite, planned emphasis on greater student self-direction and self-responsibility for learning. Nearly all of the new middle schools have some form of independent study plan.

For example, two middle schools in Centerville, Ohio—the Hithergreen

Middle School and Tower Heights Middle School—have developed a highly creative approach to student self-direction through the concept of student-structured time. At the beginning of an individual student's program, all his time is scheduled for him. After he has had experience in independent study skills and techniques, a portion of his weekly schedule is devoted to activities of his own choosing or design. The more he demonstrates the ability to manage his own time, the more time he is allowed to structure or schedule for himself. Independent study need not be individual study. Often, two or three pupils working together on projects can stimulate and teach each other.

Middle schools are finding the independent study phase of the program rewarding but difficult to develop. Independent study can become busy-work, or students may develop the unreal, superficial attitude that only those projects they have chosen have merit. Undoubtedly, too, there is a certain amount of inefficiency in such a program. Middle schools are finding that a successful independent study program requires in-service preparation for both teachers and pupils.

Among the reasons advanced for a reorganized middle school was the need to escape the unwholesome pressures of too-early senior high type activities and the interscholastic rat races that often plague many junior high schools. Middle schools across the nation have succeeded, for the most part, in rejecting inappropriate activities. Few, however, have come up with appropriate alternatives.

The elimination of interscholastic athletics, for example, has not yet been matched by the initiation of an appropriate preadolescent activity. This area calls for the investment of much more time and creative thought.

Several innovative features common to middle schools are a result of the timing of their birth. Since the middle-school idea developed rapidly in the 1960's, it was only natural for these schools to adopt the educational innovations of the 60's—team teaching, nongrading, flexible scheduling, programed instruction, laboratory facilities, and a host of newer media.

It is difficult to find a middle school that isn't using some form of team teaching. Although these schools seem to have solved some of the expected difficulties in team teaching—the mechanics, the scheduling of students, the added time requirements for planning, and the complexities of group evaluation—some of the unexpected problems haven't been dealt with so well.

A major problem of team teaching in many middle schools has been the failure to identify specifically and completely those things that team teaching can accomplish. Too often, teaming has been an end in itself. Furthermore, educators have underestimated the complexities of the group dynamics of team teaching.

Nongrading is another innovation found in middle schools and junior high schools, but, like team teaching, it does not yet live up to its full promise. Continuous progress plans are an important goal for the middle school if every child is to have the advantages of his own success-oriented program. However, although middle-school staffs are using independent study plans, progress through units, frequent rephasing of students, special skills development laboratories, and programed instructional materials, they report that continuous progress is still only in the developmental stages. It is difficult to avoid an overemphasis on rate of progress rather than on differentiated paths to different goals for individual students.

The middle school is an eager customer for the newest educational media. Middle schools are frequently housed in new buildings, and new buildings are more likely to be open-concept in design and to have video and audio learning facilities and, occasionally, even closed-circuit television. All of these media can result in greater individualization in the student's program. They *can* be stimulating. They help prepare students to live in a world in which they can control technology or be controlled by it.

On the other hand, the expanded use of technology may result in a greater impersonality in the school program. Machines can only act like machines. If we want human-type beings, we must personalize education. If a middle school uses a laboratory to *individualize,* it must use a small group to *socialize* and an individual conference to *personalize* the meaning of school.

The middle-school movement is an exciting development, and part of the excitement grows out of its newness—the excitement of creativity is felt in these schools. But middle-school staffs are the first to admit that present middle schools are moving toward, not demonstrating, the patterns of education they espouse. This in itself is praiseworthy.

BROOKHURST JUNIOR HIGH:
AN INNOVATIVE SCHOOL

American education is emerging as a new frontier. Staggering challenges brought about by the contemporary demand for quality education for a

From a brochure published by the Brookhurst Junior High School, Anaheim, California, 1968, 1-3. Used by permission of the principal, Don H. Nielson.

bulging and diverse student population must be met. Old solutions for new problems will not suffice.

With this philosophy in mind, Brookhurst inaugurated the Daily Demand Schedule in 1962. It came about through the efforts of the community, parents, staff, and administrators. The following basic assumptions served as guidelines:

1. All subjects do not require the same amount of time or method of instruction.

2. All students do not have equal abilities nor do they learn at the same rate.

3. The teacher is best qualified to determine the student's academic needs, the method of instruction, and the time required.

Currently functioning under this program are all 8th and 9th graders, some 800 students.

The school day has been divided into 16 modules of twenty minutes each. Each disciplinary team may group its students as it desires; i.e., English may have three or four ability groups, History only one, etc. Students within these groups may be changed at the teacher's request and new groups may be formed without disrupting a schedule.

Each teaching team submits five daily lesson job orders to the scheduling office on Monday for one week hence. On the daily form they indicate in Column I the total number of students in each group. For example: Pre-Algebra may consist of 200 students, so this number would be indicated. In the next column is requested the number of modules desired. The team may indicate one module for a large-group lecture or 14 for a field trip. A third column indicates the number of students wanted in each class, e.g., the ten or 200 mentioned before. They may request specific modules in the next column, but this is usually left to the discretion of the scheduling office unless a guest speaker is requested. Additional instructional help may be requested. Teachers are asked to indicate the type of instruction to be given to facilitate assigning rooms, e.g., large group instruction, small group discussion, etc. This may also be used as a record by which the team may evaluate units at their completion. The job orders are then sorted by the office into three categories:

1. Office Schedule. Classes scheduled from job orders of this category provide the student no choice in the selection of subject or time. The subject, room number, and modules will be printed on the schedule before he receives it. All office scheduled subjects are then transposed

onto the teacher's schedule, and each teacher given a copy. This verifies where he is to be and at what time. Across the top the subject is indicated; the left hand column shows the modules the class will meet, the numbers under the subject heading are rooms and the circles indicate the inclusive time for each class. Special bulletin notices are also placed on the teacher's schedule.

2. Must schedule. Classes scheduled from job orders of this category provide for the teacher to control the subject, but the student may select the time he wishes to attend the class. Physical Education serves as a good example. The student must attend each day according to State Law, but the teachers are not concerned with what time of the day he attends class.

3. May Schedule. Classes scheduled from job orders of this category allow the student to control both the time and the subject. These classes are generally from his elective program, but are not necessarily so. Any teacher may put his classes on the May Schedule and this is often done for students needing make-up or remedial work in the academic areas. These are schedules in addition to, not in lieu of, the regular academic commitment.

Electives.   Most of the electives operate on a contract or agreement basis. During the summer a course description of the electives offered is mailed home for the parents and students to use in selecting electives for the coming semester. Elective teachers are encouraged to work out curricular courses of study in which the student may spend varying amounts of time from day to day and from week to week.

Units of credit from one to ten may be earned as the student finds time to work with the elective. The amount of credit depends upon the number of projects that the student has completed at the end of the grading period. Teachers are encouraged to individualize the types of projects and the number required for a particular grade if at all possible.

Students may change their elective program as the year progresses providing the grade level counselor and parents agree to the alteration. Students are encouraged, however, to complete at least a minimal number of projects before dropping a course. There is no limit to the number of subjects a student may take. An extremely qualified student may take as many as ten electives during the course of a year.

Teachers add new subjects as the need arises and disband classes when their usefullness is fulfilled. The program coordinator is of course involved in all decisions affecting their daily schedule.

The "Must" and "May" schedule categories are transposed onto a Daily Master Schedule which is distributed to the student each morning by his counseling teacher along with his individual program. The counseling group composed of twenty to twenty-five students meets from 8:10 to 8:30 each morning and it is during this time that the student fills in his remaining open modules as he can accommodate them. The counseling teacher then checks to see that all "must" classes are met, that all 16 modules have been filled, that the student has elected a program which will be in his best interests (well balanced and suited to his needs) and that any information pertinent to this individual is passed on to him, e.g., special music or athletic instructions, etc.

The counseling teacher then separates the schedules. The top copy will be returned to the student for him to follow that day. The last copy is alphabetized and filed in the office so we may rapidly find a student any time.

Attendance.   Attendance is taken in the "Office Schedule" classes from a print-out list made in the office. "Must" and "May" schedule attendance is by a spot check process in the classes at regular intervals. Any suspected problem attendance students are checked regularly by our attendance counselor. There is continual hall checking for attendance irregularities.

Machine Operations: Litton Industries, in conjunction with the school staff, has developed a print out list of office scheduled classes giving the teacher positive attendance. Also the machines print those office scheduled classes on the students' schedule card each day. The machines include a Photo-reader, a teletype machine, and a small rotary printer. Further inquiries may be made to Litton-McBee Systems Division, 1931 South Manchester, Anaheim, California.

We feel that the Daily Demand Schedule described is a forward step in the advancement of education. It gives the teacher control over subject matter, time, and the method of instruction. It allows the teacher to meet the individual needs of each student through scheduling of numbers and groupings in labs or independent study. It allows the student a wider range of exploration and involvement through the broader choice of subjects available. More significantly, the Brookhurst Plan places the responsibility, to a great degree, for each youngster's educational program on his own shoulders, giving him choices each day which will significantly affect his life-long education. He learns to make decisions, the correctness or failure of which are highly meaningful and which go toward making him the responsible, interested, involved personality that our complex society demands.

QUESTIONS FOR DISCUSSION

Junior High School and The Middle School

1. Why is a junior high school needed? What are its major contributions?
2. What should be the relationship of the junior high school to the senior high school? To the elementary school?
3. How should the junior high school attempt to provide for individual differences?
4. In what ways can the junior high school really help a pupil engage in exploration?
5. What student activities are appropriate for the junior high school?
6. What grades should be included in the junior high school? How should the junior high be organized?
7. What is a middle school? What are some of the arguments for and against the middle school?
8. On the basis of the articles in this section, which arrangement is better, in your judgment—the junior high school or the middle school?
9. Can you use the bases and criteria presented in Sections 1-5 to aid you in arriving at an answer to question 8, above?

8 The High School

Sputnik in 1957 probably brought more changes to high school education than any other single event in the last hundred years. The launching of the first Russian satellite was a direct cause of a vastly accelerated curriculum revision in the high schools, especially in the areas of mathematics and the physical sciences. Other forces since the late 1950's have brought about much experimentation in content, organization, and teaching procedures. Public interest in experimentation has increased tremendously. Not since the supercharged era of progressive education in the 1930's has educational investigation brought more general notice. More recently, changes in the humanities, the social studies, language arts, and other areas are being considered by many national studies and organizations.

Most American educators believe in a comprehensive high school. they see it as a major unifying force in our society and want to preserve it. Because they recognize the importance of maintaining it, they propose needed modifications. Robert S. Gilchrist ("What Is A Comprehensive High School?") provides some criteria by which to judge a school's program and states that "we have a long way to go before we can say truthfully that most American boys and girls are attending comprehensive high schools." James B. Conant ("The Comprehensive High School: A Further Look") compares today's comprehensive high schools with those he visited in 1957-1958 and concludes that many changes have occured in the school program in those years. He believes the continuance of the comprehensive high school is important to the future of our society.

Present secondary schools vary in size from less than 60 to over 9,000 students. Many have cited the educational disadvantages of small high schools and have called for consolidation of those schools. Paul Ford ("Small High Schools: Myth, Reality, Potential") discusses small high schools in rural areas and calls for more imagination in strengthening them.

The organization of the high school has been the subject of experimentation in recent years. Burt Kaufman and Paul Bethune ("Nova High: Space Age School") provide insights into new types of organization used at Nova (Florida) High School.

Extracurricular activities in the high school have undergone severe criticism. Robert N. Bush ("The Proper Place of the Extracurriculum in High School") suggests that a balance should be sought between curricular and extracurricular activities.

Secondary school personnel are making new courses available to students in the high school in their concern for strengthening content. One such course is the humanities (Carolyn Glass and Richard I. Miller, "Humanities Courses in Secondary Schools").

Another area of recent attention in the high school has been independent study. Donald Empey ("What Is Independent Study All About?") discusses independent study and tells what the Arcadia (California) High School is doing to develop independent study.

The Vocational Act of 1963 brought new life to the high school programs designed for the non-college bound students. What should be the role of the high school in developing vocational programs? Louis Mason ("School-Work Programs – The Vocational Education Act in Action") discusses the ways the Oshkosh (Wisconsin) High School, a pilot school, has developed work-experience programs in many areas.

New programs have also been proposed for the academically talented high school student. One such program provides for early entrance into college for those students who participate in the College Entrance Examination Board's Advanced Placement Program. John Bergeson ("Advanced Placement – A Report on Former Participants and their Subsequent Academic Performance") offers convincing evidence to those who see merit in this way of providing for individual differences.

What are the results and implications of recent research in secondary education? John C. Flanagan ("The Implications of Recent Research For the Improvement of Secondary Education") reports on the first results of Project TALENT, which involves the testing of nearly one-half million students over a twenty-year period. Other studies cited by Flanagan have implications for the improvement of secondary education.

And what does the future hold for secondary education? Secondary school administrators and teachers have evidenced a desire to propose new models for more effective high schools. Two proposals are presented for comparison and analysis (Robert Havighurst, "High Schools for the Future," and Wiles, "Education of Adolescents: 1985"). The future is open. What the high school becomes depends upon the decisions made about whom it should serve and the role it should fulfill.

Wilhelms ("Which Way to a Curriculum for Adolescents") examines the major social forces today, as he sees them, and predicts more education for work, efforts to shape citizenship education that counts, and education for humanity.

The authors believe that the bases of the curriculum presented in the sections of this volume on social forces, human development, the nature of learning, and the nature of knowledge, along with the section on objectives and other curriculum criteria, suggest ways in which we should think about the problems and opportunities in planning for superior programs.

WHAT IS A COMPREHENSIVE HIGH SCHOOL?

Robert S. Gilchrist

Ask any twenty educators and citizens for a definition of a comprehensive high school and you may get twenty different replies, each of which tells part of the story. Study the implications of the comprehensive high school ideal, and the pieces begin to fit into the larger picture. The danger in a restricted definition of the comprehensive high school lies in stressing one part or another of its program apart from the total purpose.

Comprehensive means inclusive or including much. A truly comprehensive high school provides learning opportunities for all the normal adolescents within a range from barely educable to the gifted and talented. Its purpose is to enable each pupil (a) to develop to his greatest potential for his own success and happiness and (b) to make a maximum contribution to the American society of which he is a part.

To achieve this purpose, the comprehensive high school must affect positively the behavior of its pupils as adolescents and later as adults in all areas and aspects of living—not only as wage earners, citizens, and family members, but as unique human beings. This requires maximum intellectual development within a context of sound physical, emotional, and social growth.

From *NEA Journal,* LI, No. 8 (November, 1962), 32-33. Used by permission of the author and publisher.

Enough is known about human development, learning, the demands of living, and democratic values to describe the essentials of a comprehensive high school.

Balance in the curriculum is the first essential. Courses are offered at levels of difficulty to challenge all pupils in basic academic subject fields. Opportunities are also provided for each pupil to take elective subjects consistent with his interests, needs, abilities, and plans for the future. There are courses in the fine and practical arts as well as a strong health and physical fitness program.

Social learnings are recognized as important, because the surest guarantee of good adult citizenship is good adolescent citizenship. Student government, service clubs, social functions, publications, athletics, and other voluntary activities are a valuable supplement to curricular learnings.

Depth in the curriculum is another prime requisite. No course merely covers the facts in a textbook. The ability to think through problems, to sense relationships, to generalize, and to develop and clarify values are essential to democratic living. Every subject and every activity can and should contribute to the ideal of democratic living.

Individualized education is a characteristic of the comprehensive high school. The home background, out-of-school experiences, abilities, interests, and plans for the future of each student are considered. A strong guidance program assists the student in clarifying goals, in assessing strengths and weaknesses, and in selecting a sound program. The student has opportunities to learn at a pace consistent with his abilities.

Functional learning is essential in the comprehensive high school. Each experience must have meaning for the student. Classroom learning must be related to life outside the classroom if education is to be effective. For this reason, a comprehensive high school is an integral part of the community, and the faculty works in close cooperation with parents and all youth-serving institutions. The total school environment, whenever feasible, encourages practice of whatever is learned in any subject.

Finally, the administration and organization of the high school are means to serve effective learning, never ends in themselves. Programs and schedules for students are determined by their relation to individual needs and abilities rather than by rigid timetables or classic academic criteria.

How important is it that boys and girls throughout America have an opportunity to attend a comprehensive high school? Here is what one mother says:

My daughters loved their high school, and we would not want them to have missed the opportunities for both the academic and the social learning that they had there.

It was an excellent comprehensive high school. It was multiracial, and its student body contained an economic and social cross-section of the community; it had a fine academic tradition, an exceptionally good teaching staff, and an excellent library; it had good shop and vocational programs; and it offered outstanding opportunities in music, dramatics, and other arts. It had a continuation program of combined work and school. It was strong in athletics, had an enthusiastic student government, and a number of faculty-sponsored clubs.

In other words, it was strong both academically and socially. It trained for college or early job; gave opportunities for recognition and development of talent; and provided a framework in which young people from widely differing backgrounds could gain familiarity and some sense of communication with each other.

A student body that is limited to one classification gives limited preparation for living in a world where communication and understanding between people is of ever-increasing importance. By my definition, a comprehensive high school believes in a comprehending program for a wide range of students. It provides academic challenge for the brilliant and seeks to raise the sights and stretch the minds of the less obviously gifted. It is dedicated to the premise that intelligence and ability cannot be categorized.

To what extent do American youth have an opportunity to attend comprehensive high schools? Although we have a right to be proud of our system of free public high school education, I believe we have a long way to go before we can say truthfully that most American boys and girls are attending comprehensive high schools.

Dr. Conant performed an important service when he stated clearly that our high schools should be comprehensive. But there are forces and pressures which are working against this development.

For example, because college entrance is determined largely by test scores in academic subjects, enrollments in the arts, in home and family living, and in physical education are decreasing in many secondary schools. Further, when financial limitations require budget cuts, courses for the pupils not going on to college are too often the first to be eliminated. Perhaps most damaging is the implication that the pupils not academically inclined are less important than the college bound.

America desperately needs the developed abilities of all its youth. Citizens and educators have, in the comprehensive high school, an exciting and valuable tool to fulfill America's needs for the future.

THE COMPREHENSIVE HIGH SCHOOL:
A FURTHER LOOK

James B. Conant

I intend to comment on certain of our findings in the light of my experience in visiting a dozen or so schools in some 10 states in the last two years. It is not necessary to tell this audience of practitioners that there are many aspects of a high school which cannot be revealed by a questionnaire but which can be discovered by a visit. Yet, as you know from my brief report at the last annual meeting, your committee decided it had no choice but to proceed in its study by means of a questionnaire.

In my visits to high schools, I was especially interested in comparing the present situation with what I encountered in 1957 and 1958. In some cases, I revisited the same school and could thus refer to my notes of nearly 10 years ago.

CHANGE IN PRINCIPAL'S ROLE

One change I discovered which may be of special interest to this audience. In more than one community, the single high school I had known had been found inadequate from the point of view of space. The increase in population of the school district has required the building of a second high school. As a consequence, in several cases, many of the decisions previously made by the high school principal were being made in the superintendent's office. One or more coordinators were concerned with the instruction in both of the two high schools. The leadership, it seemed to me, had passed from the principal to the superintendent or to one or more persons on the superintendent's staff. I have in mind not only decisions about curricula but recruitment to the staff.

As an outsider, it seemed to me that it was a pity that the role of the principal had changed. In my earlier study, I had been impressed by the importance of a school board's finding not only a first-rate superintendent, but also an excellent high school principal; and I had come to relate the

---

From the *Bulletin of the National Association of Secondary-School Principals,* LI, No. 319 (May, 1967), 22-34. Used by permission of the author and publisher.

degree of success of the school to the qualities of the principal. I do not doubt that under the new circumstances I have just described, good principals are still important. But their authority and responsibility is certainly diminished.

Realizing that as a layman I am inquiring into delicate matters far beyond my competence even as an investigator or reporter, I venture to raise the following question: If there are two or more high schools in a district, is it necessary to have policy made in the superintendent's office to any greater degree than if there was only *one* high school? I should think there ought to be ways of building up the importance of the position of the high school principal even in a multi-high school district. At all events, I venture to raise the issue because I have seen so many flourishing schools whose welfare clearly reflected the drive and imagination of the principal who had been given a free hand by the superintendent.

To turn now to some of the findings in the report. You will discover that many of the questions we asked were tied in with the recommendations in my study of nine years ago. At least one critical question, however, was entirely new. We asked the principal to give us the ratio of total professional staff to students. Since I made my past study, I have come to believe that this one figure tells more about a medium-sized high school than any other single criterion.

My attention was first drawn to the significance of staff-student ratios in the course of preparation of the essay on "Quality in Public Education" written by the Educational Policies Commission of the NEA and AASA in 1959. I was at that time a member of the Commission and remember very well the discussion which led to the incorporation in the report of the following sentences: "If fewer than 50 professionals are available per thousand pupils, some of the elements of a program of high quality are likely to be slighted. It should be emphasized that this ratio is a minimum." (Expressed in terms of the number of students per individual staff member, the minimum was obviously 20.)

The ratios reported from the 2,000 schools we questioned varied from 11.3 to 37.3. Since this ratio reflects quite accurately the per-pupil cost of the instruction, it is clear that the support of the schools in question varied by at least threefold. As is repeatedly pointed out in our report, our much vaunted ideal of equality of opportunity is far from being realized the nation over or even within certain states.

As is implied by the sentence in the Educational Policies Commission essay I have just read, a cross-correlation study showed that the chances of finding that a given high school offers calculus is three times as great in a school from which 40 to 59 percent go on to college if the staff-student ratio is 17.4 or less as compared with the same type of school when the ratio is 23.5 or larger. (You will find this particular comparison in Table VIII of the appendix.) Similarly, taking all the 2,000 schools together, the chances of a school providing an adequate number of English teachers is nearly six times as great if the staff-student ratio is 17.4 or less as compared with a ratio of 20.5 or more.

PUPIL LOAD FOR ENGLISH TEACHERS

What constitutes an adequate number of English teachers? As a consequence of my first study, I suggested that no English teacher in a senior high school be responsible for more than 100 students. The returns showed that very few schools have as yet met this standard. Nearly 26 percent, however, reported a "teaching load" for the English teachers of 120 or less. As compared to a figure of 150 or more which was common in the schools I visited in 1957-58, a ratio of one teacher to 120 students represents real progress. But I have not retreated from my ideal of 100, let me make clear!

There is no need to tell you why the reduction in the number of students in English taught by a single teacher looms so large in the minds of some of us. What is really at issue is instruction in English composition. My premise was that adequate consideration of the themes could not be given by a teacher who had to handle anything like 150 themes.

On this point, I had an interesting conversation with a high school teacher of English in one school. She was fortunate enough to be teaching in a school which was sufficiently well supported to enable her to be responsible for only 110 students and, at times, only 100. She had taught, however, in a school in which the number was not 110, but 140. What she could accomplish under the two different circumstances was as different as day from night. She told me that whereas now the themes she corrected and discussed with the students (on an individual basis) averaged 500 to 1,000 words a week, previously individual conferences were rare and the themes per week had to be short (something like a quarter as long as is now the case).

I admit that the testimony of this particular teacher was reassuring; it indicated that the standard I had set for the teaching level of an English teacher had real significance. This testimony was not unusual. In general, I found a similar viewpoint in the schools I visited in the last two years.

RATIO OF COUNSELORS TO STUDENTS

Another figure which varied greatly from school to school was the ratio of counselors to students. In this case my recommendation in the *American High School Today* was far from the actuality in most of the 2,000 schools from which we obtained returns. I have had to lower my sights (but only temporarily) to a ratio of 1 to 349 or less and, even so, only 3.5 percent of the schools met this standard. But this matter is discussed at some length in the report and I have nothing to add as a result of my visitations, except to say my belief in the importance of good guidance officers remains unshaken and that I realize excellent counselors are in short supply.

ABILITY GROUPING

Both from my visits and from noting the returns from the questionnaires, I conclude that a remarkable change in attitude seems to have taken place as regards to ability grouping. A very large percentage of the schools returning the questionnaire—namely, 96.5 percent—reported that they were using ability grouping in one or more subjects. As I visited in the schools, I found the old-fashioned objection to ability grouping seemed to have largely disappeared. Now it is widely accepted that, for the good of the students and the school, there should be separate classes, depending on the rate of learning of the student in the subject.

Just how many levels there should be in the required courses, I am not prepared to say. I am prepared to emphasize once again, however, that I am opposed to a "track system" and that I would favor individualized programs according to which a boy or girl might be in the top group in English, we will say, but in the second or third group in social studies, or vice versa, and might be in either the top or bottom group, we will say, in eleventh-grade mathematics. I must admit that if this is done, it may result in some schools in an imbalance racially as between the different classes. This is because , unfortunately, in some cities those who have recently arrived from other parts of the country have come with a totally unsatisfactory elementary preparation. Therefore, these handicapped students are not able to keep pace with those who have grown up in an adequate system.

But if there be worry among parents about homogeneous grouping being undemocratic, the attitude of the administration can be made clear if it adopts my recommendation about the twelfth-grade course in American

Democracy. I believe strongly that the classes in such a course should be heterogeneously arranged so that all the youths will have an opportunity of discussing problems with those who have varying scholastic records and family backgrounds.

If a comprehensive high school is to fulfill its social and political functions, there must be one course required of all in which the assignment to a class is not in terms of ability or promise, but is on a random basis. The existence of such a course stands out as evidence of the school's commitment to equality. I am glad to report that in 62.5 percent of the schools, those in charge agreed with my point of view; though, I may add, I am well aware some social studies teachers and professors of history do not.

STUDY OF FIVE ACADEMIC SOLIDS YEARLY

One of the questions we asked was designed to bring out whether or not it was possible for an ambitious student to take five academic solids in one year and, at the same time, art or music as well as physical education. The response was amazing to me—74 percent of the schools answered in the affirmative. There may have been some misunderstanding of the question and, perhaps, this figure is a little high. But on the whole, as I traveled around I got the impression that, far more than 10 years ago, people were aware of the importance of a bright student's studying both mathematics and a modern foreign language.

I have recapitulated in my report my old arguments of why, for those who have the requisite ability, it is advisable to study mathematics through grade 12 and a modern foreign language to a point where something approaching mastery is attained before graduation. If this is not done, many doors to future careers are closed. For example, without adequate mathematical preparation, engineering and science cannot be studied. Let me call my point of view the "open door policy." Let me defend it here once again.

As I travel around, I am more and more impressed by the differences between the communities served by a medium-sized comprehensive high school. I know there are communities in which no one seems to care whether the able student studies four years of mathematics or masters a foreign language or not. There are others in which pressures from parents tend to force a student who has not the ability to enroll in mathematics through the eleventh and twelfth grades. Protective devices must be installed in such a school. I found this to be the case in more than one instance. It is covered in recommendation 13 in *The American High School Today,* which reads as follows:

Standards in advanced courses should be such that those who enroll in each successive course of a sequence have demonstrated the ability to handle that course. To this end, admission to eleventh-grade mathematics should depend upon the student's receiving at least a "C" in tenth-grade mathematics, and for admission to twelfth-grade mathematics at least a "C" should be required in the eleventh-grade course.

Similar standards should be applied to other elective academic courses. Such a regulation is important as a protection for student and teacher against undue parental pressure. Unfortunately, in one state I discovered that the chief state school officer did not believe in such a policy. He maintained that in every course a person should be entitled to the next course in the sequence unless he actually failed the preceding course. A ruling of this sort is based on a misunderstanding, I believe, of the nature of a sequential course of study and the proper role of grading in assisting the guidance officers.

ROLE OF VOCATIONAL COURSES

I should like to record another observation based on my visits as well as on the returns from our questionnaire, namely the changing role of the vocational courses. It is quite clear to me that, as compared to nearly 10 years ago, the new federal legislation has brought an improvement. The strict limits of the old Smith-Hughes Act seem to have been removed to good advantage.

I found in one school that I visited that vocational shop work had been put almost entirely on a cooperative study basis. This meant that even in such fields as tool and die work, auto mechanics, and building trades, it was possible for the boy concerned to spend the two or three or four hours of the day in the twelfth grade in a shop run by industry itself and yet receive academic credit for this work.

This is a pattern which I met in my first study only in connection with "distributive education." It seems to have spread in some cities to a wide range of nonacademic work. From what I saw, it seemed to me this was an excellent development, though it has within it dangers which were pointed out. In the first place, the arrangement depends on the employment situation and the attitude of the employers; secondly, there must be good supervision from the school or else what happens is that the employer simply exploits the cheap labor of the student.

I had an interesting experience which illustrates how impossible it is to generalize about vocational education. I visited two schools of the type I am considering in adjacent states in the Middle West on successive days.

Both provided good vocational studies, which were well attended. But in one school, the training of future tool and die workers had been given up. "There are no longer any openings for graduates who are trained in our machine shop," I was told. In the other school not 200 miles away, I found a considerable number of boys in the machine shop, and was told the demand for graduates trained under what used to be called the tool and die program was never greater! Incidentally, I found that neither the teachers nor the administrators in either of the two schools had ever heard of the other school. Yet, I am sure one could have learned from the other, for the characteristics of the schools were very similar and their problems were almost identical.

VOCATIONAL STUDY WHERE?

The question of area vocational schools, I know, is agitating many portions of the country. I venture to question the wisdom of sending those who desire vocational education to a vocational school for the entire day. Such a development endangers the whole concept of a comprehensive high school. On the other hand, I recognize that in a school district which cannot afford to provide good shops and does not have cooperative facilities, it may be necessary to bus the students who are concerned with certain kinds of vocational instruction to a central spot for the use of shops. But, under such arrangements, I would hope the boy or girl would remain a member of a comprehensive high school in which he or she would do the academic work.

I should like to use this occasion to explain an attitude I developed as a consequence of my first study and which my recent visits emphasize still further. The importance of good instruction in such fields as business education, home economics, drafting, auto mechanics, tool and die work, and building trades is not to be measured by the marketable skills thus developed. As many people have said, the same skills could be developed more effectively if the vocational courses were postponed to a junior college. But if this were done a highly important motivating force would vanish from the high school.

I am of the opinion that, under proper conditions, the vocational courses I have named (and others) interest a certain type of youth who is apathetic at best about English and social studies and finds mathematics, foreign languages, and physics at the eleventh- and twelfth-grade levels too difficult. A few of the schools I have visited were not widely comprehensive according to the criteria I have used. (There were no shops, for example, except for the industrial arts.) In talking with the counselors and teachers, I got the sharp impression that in such a school a certain type of boy was far more inclined to be either a dropout or a listless student than in a widely comprehensive high school. If I am right about this, the point is not without its significance.

MATH, SCIENCE, LANGUAGES

I hardly need to call to your attention the considerable change that has taken place in the instruction offered in mathematics, science, and foreign languages. The changes spelled out in some detail in the report are highly encouraging. Yet, on the other hand, their impact is uneven. I am glad that 40 percent of the schools reporting (remember their type) offer calculus. Yet, clearly, those who attend the other 60 percent of the same kind of school do not have an equal opportunity to do advanced work in mathematics.

Similarly, as regards instruction in a foreign language, there has been a vast improvement in the last ten years. Yet, in 35 percent of the schools reporting, it is impossible for a youth to study a modern foreign language for four years, according to our returns. In fact, I think the situation is somewhat worse than this figure indicates, since I have visited schools which offer a fourth year of French and Spanish but, to save money, require the few in the fourth-year class to sit with the third-year class. Adequate instruction under such conditions is impossible.

On the other hand, in a certain school from which less than half the graduates go on with further education, a third of the students are enrolled in a modern foreign language class and over 20 percent of the twelfth grade are completing the fourth year of either German, French, or Spanish. Contrast this situation with that in schools which only offer a fourth year on the compressed basis of combining the third- and fourth-year classes! Here is a striking example of the different traditions in different schools which, in turn, reflect different attitudes of the community. But I cannot help asking: Cannot the school authorities change the negative attitude of a community by offering challenges in instruction?

WHY STUDY A MODERN FOREIGN LANGUAGE?

Let me emphasize once again the significance of the study of a modern foreign language. Granted that not all students can benefit by such instruction, yet it seems quite clear to me that almost all those whom we call academically talented can. Indeed, it may well be that a good many others might study a modern foreign language to good advantage. In some of the schools which I visited, it would appear that quite a number of students elected a modern foreign language and carried it through for four years because they liked it. They had done well, although they did not have the kind of ability that would enable them to take mathematics much beyond the tenth grade. For such students, I believe, one should emphasize that studying a modern foreign language is an essential element in the development of a knowledge and understanding of the humanities.

To my mind, those who have talked so much about the neglect of the humanities in our schools and colleges have failed to realize that the essence of the humanities is language. There is no use talking vaguely about the culture of another country. What is needed first of all is knowledge of the language. Unless one has had the experience of speaking and reading and writing the language of at least one other culture, one has not made a start in understanding comparative literature. To my mind, we went off the track some years ago when, discarding Latin and Greek, we failed to realize the cultural importance of a knowledge—and I emphasize the word knowledge—of a modern foreign language.

The inability or the unwillingness of many high school students to tackle the hard work of studying a foreign language is equivalent to students of science refusing to study mathematics; this, we now know, makes no sense. I submit that the unwillingness of those who talk the most about the humanities to prescribe the study of a modern foreign language in high school can only be bewailed by those who wish the humanities well in the days ahead.

Those of you who recall the recommendations in the *American High School Today* will remember my urging each principal to prepare an academic inventory of each graduating class. Such an inventory shows what percentage of the academically talented youth (roughly 15 percent in a school with the normal range of intellectual ability) have elected academic subjects. Some principals have used the idea and found it helpful. For obvious reasons, we could not ask 2,000 schools to prepare such inventories. Therefore, we had to be content with reporting only what were the course offerings. We had no information as to what fraction of the student body elected advanced mathematics or a foreign language, for example. Therefore, comparisons between the present and the past are expressed in general terms.

RESULTS OF ACADEMIC INVENTORY

It so happens, however, that I can provide a personal supplement to the volume. In 1965, I started but never completed a restudy of the 22 high

schools on which I reported in some detail in 1959. I sent out question-
naries, and on the basis of the returns, I have been able to construct partial
academic inventories of 19 of these schools and compare them with what I
obtained in 1959. The changes are striking, particularly as regards the study
of foreign languages. In all 19 schools with one exception, the percentage
of academically talented boys electing three or more years of one foreign
language (including Latin) increased markedly. In many cases, the change
was manyfold. In several instances, it was from 0 to 40 percent or over.
The results are only a little less striking with the girls.

The great shift for both boys and girls was in the percentage electing 18
or more academic subjects. Parallel to the change in the election of a
foreign language (and, indeed, responsive to the change) in all but one or
two schools, the increase was spectacular. Obviously, increases in the study
of language had not generally been at the expense of other academic
subjects. Rather, the total number of academic subjects has been increased.
There can be little doubt that as far as the 19 widely comprehensive high
schools we studied in some detail in 1959 and for which we have 1965
data, the change from 1959 to 1965 was most encouraging.

The other items in which we compared 1959 with 1965 were the
following: four years of mathematics, three years or more of science, seven
years or more of mathematics together with science. In mathematics, the
changes are also in the direction of a larger percentage of able boys and
girls electing four years or more. In one school, for example, the increase
was from 15 to 90 percent for boys and 29 to 95 for girls; in still another,
the shift was from 55 to 80 for boys and 20 to 40 for girls. Of the 19
schools, eight showed a marked increase in the able boys electing four
years of mathematics, only two a decrease; the remainder were essentially
constant. In the case of girls, only one school had a decrease and many of
the increases were larger than in the case of the boys.

The returns in the case of science and mathematics and science
combined followed much the same pattern as those I have just reported. As
might be expected, the percentage of academically talented girls electing
three years or more of science was found to have increased significantly in
half the schools and only in three was it somewhat less.

In a word, our academic inventory has yielded specific information in
full accord with the picture of the change in offerings set forth in the new
book *The Comprehensive High School—A Second Report to Interested
Citizens.*

SMALL HIGH SCHOOLS:
MYTH, REALITY, POTENTIAL

Paul Ford

I. THE MYTH

Discussion among laymen and educators in rural communities often focuses on the alleged educational advantages offered students in small high schools—high schools with 200 students or less. The advantages involve small class size, much attention for individual students, frequent opportunities for students to pursue independent study, opportunities for students to participate in a variety of school-related activities, and close, beneficial personal relationships among students, teachers, and the community.

To investigate whether these and other advantages do accrue to students educated in small high schools, 13 small rural high schools throughout Washington State were studied. The largest high school enrolled 198 students in grades 9-12; the smallest school enrolled 32 students. To gain information, two interview instruments were designed. One was used with students from the small high schools; one was used with teachers of these students. Fifty percent of all students enrolled in grades 10-12 were selected randomly and interviewed; all teachers of grades 10-12 were interviewed. Interviews were conducted in the schools under study. Each interview took from 40 to 50 minutes. A similar procedure was used in three very large urban schools in which ten percent of the teachers and students were interviewed.

II. THE REALITY

On the basis of data gathered in interviews, it was found that students in small schools attend much smaller classes than do students in large high schools. Students in the small high schools sampled have considerably more time for independent study than do their peers in the large high schools sampled. At the same time, there is much more frequent in-school and out-of-school contact among teachers and students in small high schools than in large high schools. This is occasioned by large numbers of extracurricular activities for which small-school teachers are responsible. Teachers in large high schools have far fewer responsibilities for these

From the *Bulletin of the National Association of Secondary-School Principals,* LI, No. 317 (March, 1967), 89-95. Used by permission of the author and publisher.

activities. In addition, the smallness of rural communities facilitates contacts among teachers and students.

Despite these advantages, the great majority of students in small high schools rank their schools significantly lower than do students in large high schools. Why?

First, it is clear that while students in small schools have much time for independent study or individual learning experiences, this time is not used productively. Students in small high schools spend an average of 25 percent of their time in independent study. But both teacher direction for students and resource materials are lacking. More than 60 percent of the students sampled in small high schools say that they are bored.

Because of small class size, it would appear that great flexibility could be built into learning experiences for students in small high schools. To the contrary, neither teachers nor administrators, according to interviews with students and teachers, have taken advantage of this flexibility to introduce innovative methodology. At best, the small schools studied merely imitate the methodology used by large, traditional high schools of the past and present. Innovative curricular materials are used far less frequently in the small schools studied than in the large schools.

The limited use of innovative or stimulating curricula in small high schools is probably because of inadequately prepared teachers. Teachers in the small schools studied average between five and six preparations in different subject areas each day. It is unrealistic to suppose that a teacher could be adequately prepared in this number of subjects and, in addition, keep up with current curriculum development in all the subjects. It appears, then, that the teachers depend on traditional curricula, mostly textbooks, and contribute little that is innovative or stimulating in the numerous subject areas for which they are responsible.

Extracurricular Activities

It is true, generally speaking, that students in small high schools participate to a greater degree in school-related extracurricular activities than do students in large high schools. But students in small high schools do not see these activities as helping them to achieve educational or occupational aspirations. In addition, students in small high schools do not consider the courses they take as particularly useful in helping them achieve future aspirations.

In contrast, students in the large high schools studied regard the variety of extracurricular activities and curricula to which they are exposed as extremely important in helping them fulfill their aspirations. Further, students in the large high schools do not perceive activities or curriculum only as means to gain admission to college, but rather as leading to a wider variety of experiences in life.

Occupational horizons of youth in small high schools are extremely limited. Only one of the 13 small high schools studied employs an individual with any training in guidance and counseling. In the other schools guidance and counseling are left to teachers, principals, and superintendents. But it is not carried on in a sequential and logical fashion. It is, to the contrary, hit or miss. As a result, students do not have access to the basic occupational and educational information to which they are entitled. For instance, one question in the interview instrument asked students what kinds of work were involved in a number of different occupations. A junior in high school, when asked what a pharmacist does, replied, "Oh, he inspects farms." Another student, when asked what a draftsman does, said, "He comes around and gets people for the Army." While such answers are probably meant to be humorous, they are also tragic.

The tragedy is most eloquently expressed in terms of the aspirations of youth in the small high schools. More than 85 percent of the students interviewed expressed a desire to go on with their education beyond high school. But exactly why they would go on or what their aims in the immediate or distant future would be was, at best, vague. Not so with students in the large high schools studied. These students demonstrated much keener perceptions about their plans for the future and ways to pursue these plans.

Aesthetic and cultural experiences for students in small high schools are severely limited. They watch television a good deal, read some magazines and books, but their experience with the arts is not evident. Such is not true, according to interviews, for students in the large high schools.

Views on Ideal School

Students in the sample were asked to describe what they thought an ideal high school would be like. Responses from students in the small high schools were extremely consistent. What students want is a broad, deep curriculum, teachers who are prepared to teach it, and resource materials to support it. Students from the small schools studied want access to intellectual stimulation which they apparently feel is not now provided.

It can be generalized, on the basis of interview information, that while there are definite advantages to smallness, neither administrators nor teachers used these advantages to design appropriate curricula and methodology. Rather, there is an adherence to the old and the traditional schemes of high school education, which probably never were suited to education in very small high schools. The results of this situation are important.

Bored, frustrated rural high school youth drop out of school. For instance, during 1964-65 in counties where small high schools included in this study were located, the dropout rate was six percent. In the most densely populated counties of the state, which include the Seattle-Tacoma complex and Spokane, the rate ranged from 3.69 to 3.99 percent. The state average was 3.89 percent. According to statistics released by the Oregon State Department of Education, the same situation prevails in that state. Hard data support the idea that there is an inverse relationship between the size of schools and the percentage of high school dropouts in the two most populous states in the Northwest region.

In addition, carefully documented studies in Oregon indicate that graduates of high schools with enrollments of 100 students or less do significantly less well in freshman college studies than do their peers from large high schools. These are the realities.

III. THE POTENTIAL

Throughout Washington, the Northwest region, and other of the nation's rural areas, there are and will continue to be remote, necessary high schools which cannot be consolidated. Climate, topography, and distance are the main deterrents to effective consolidation. Each state must develop its own criteria for assigning a high school to the "remote and necessary" category. Schools which do not meet the criteria should be encouraged with all possible means to effect consolidation. Where necessary, state aid to such schools should be withdrawn. But in cases where schools are designated remote and necessary, states should provide funds to enable these schools to have educational programs and plants equal in quality to those in fine, large high school districts.

The history of remote small high schools indicates that in general they do not adopt or develop innovations without stimulation, support, and reinforcement from some outside source. Compare, for instance, small high schools included in educational projects supported by large grants from philanthropic foundations with the majority of remote small high schools in the Northwest, where such activities have been at a minimum. Qualitative differences are immediately obvious. This is not to say that all schools benefited by foundation support have developed or maintained excellent programs. But a substantial number have.

As a consequence of such projects, the hardware and software they have generated, other research, and the evolution of our technological capabilities, sufficient means are presently available to revolutionize education in remote high schools. The means include application to educational problems of computer-assisted instruction, systems theory, short and long-step programing, television, modular scheduling, ungraded classes, shared services, and a variety of other developments. Historically, there have been two major blocks to such a revolution: inadequate means to communicate innovations to remote areas and insufficient funds to implement the innovations. To some degree, at least, we are now able to overcome these blocks.

In the past, many state departments of education have been understaffed. Thus, they were unable to communicate with or supply adequate consultant help to many remote schools. Today, under provisions of Title V of the Elementary and Secondary Education Act of 1965 (Public Law 89-10), funds are available for the strengthening of state departments. Federally supported teacher fellowship programs and institutes make it possible for teachers from remote areas to broaden and deepen their knowledge and skills. Funds available under Title III of this law make it possible for remote schools, working together and with state departments of education, to develop innovative approaches to solving educational problems. In Oregon, for example, the State Department of Education provided the leadership that led to a Title III project in which 50 small high schools are working together to improve curriculum and instruction.

Provisions of Title IV of Public Law 89-10 established throughout the nation a network of regional laboratories. Broadly speaking, the tasks of the laboratories are to get excellent practices and innovations into the schools by cooperating with state departments of education, colleges, universities, and cultural, social, and business agencies. In some regions, remote high schools will benefit immensely from laboratory programs. For instance, in the region formed by Alaska, Idaho, Montana, Oregon, and Washington, the Northwest Regional Education Laboratory has established a variety of activities aimed at improving instruction in remote and necessary elementary and secondary schools.

Of late, much attention has been given to the educational and social problems found in big cities. Rightly so. But our concern for the masses should not outweigh our responsibilities for the millions of individuals in rural America. The intellectually and socially impoverished of an isolated New Hampshire community are not unlike those of urban Watts. No student, anywhere, should be penalized educationally because of the section of the country in which he lives.

The precedent for improving education in rural areas has been set. State activities such as those undertaken in New York, regional activities initiated by the regional education laboratories, national legislation encompassed in the Vocational Educational Act of 1963, and the Elementary and Secondary Act of 1965 demonstrate this. Potentials for rural youth are unlimited, provided that rural educators avail themselves of the advantages that accompany smallness and utilize appropriate innovations. Further, it is obvious that increased federal and state leadership and support are needed if youth in small, remote high schools are to fulfill their potentials.

Editor's note: Research described in this paper was supported with funds from the Washington State Department of Public Instruction, the Northwest Regional Education Laboratory, and funds allotted under Title III of Public Law 89-10.

NOVA HIGH
SPACE AGE SCHOOL

Burt Kaufman
and Paul Bethune

The Nova High School, which opened in September, 1963, is an initial unit of the South Florida Education Center, an educational complex imaginative in design and advanced in concept. Eventually this complex will house tax-supported schools encompassing kindergarten through junior college, plus a private university with a graduate school. This long-range program, when completed, will present a continuous integrated process of learning unparalleled in education history. Known as "The Nova Plan," this new approach may well develop a model educational system for the county, state, and nation.

What makes Nova High School different? It is not experimental in curriculum but in concept. Its construction features, equipment, teaching

From *Phi Delta Kappan*, XLVI, No. 1 (September, 1964), 9-11. Used by permission of the authors and publisher.

aids, and instructional methods have been tested and proved in other school systems. In fact, the director of Nova High School, Arthur B. Wolfe, spent three full years visiting outstanding schools of the United States in order to incorporate the best of modern educational methods in the Nova plan for instruction. The educational specifications were completed in their entirety before the first brick was laid.

Nova is a space age school. Its philosophy is based on a concept best described as scientific learning for a scientific age. Interestingly, to achieve the goals of such a philosophy, there has been a return to a "hard-core" curriculum. Each Nova student pursues a schedule of studies which includes mathematics, foreign language, English, science, social studies, technical science, special studies, and physical education. A student may choose a foreign language from among Latin, Spanish, French, Russian, and German. His choice of a technical science or special studies course comes from electronics, mechanical and scale drawing, music, home economics, art, personal typing, mechanical technology, safety and driver education, physiology, and home nursing. A student who chooses a foreign language in one school year may elect two courses from technical science; a student who does not may elect five for that school year.

Despite the seeming rigidity of this curriculum, there is flexibility within its framework. Nova is a nongraded school and this is the main feature of its program. It is possible for seventh-year students to be studying math with tenth-year students, science with eighth-year students, and English with seventh-year students. In other words, a nongraded program allows complete homogeneous grouping within each subject area without any regard to age or year in school. This educational program is truly tailored to individual needs and brings into practice the theory of "taking each student as far as he can go." For example, the mathematics department strongly believes in vertical acceleration for the gifted. The nongraded organization allows this to be done with ease. It is expected, therefore, that many students will study college mathematics courses such as abstract and linear algebra, calculus, and probability and statistics, beginning these in some cases as early as the ninth and tenth year in school. It is anticipated that, in the future, mathematically capable students will be able, prior to their graduation from high school, to complete what is now considered a very strong undergraduate math major in leading universities. At the same time, many of the less capable students will not get through the normal high school curriculum, even though all students will study mathematics as long as they are in school.

Each discipline has identified the approach its faculty thinks best suited to remove extraneous retardation in the case of the gifted and relaxation of time pressures for the less able. The idea here is predicated on the fact that each student should go as far as his capabilities will carry him without pressures to complete material for the sake of artificially set standards which do not take into consideration the individual differences among students.

Instead of being promoted a grade level each year, students progress through a series of achievement levels called "units" in each subject area. At the end of each unit a test is given which determines whether the student may continue to the next level. A student performing below minimum levels on the test must repeat that unit satisfactorily before being allowed to advance. Thus no student ever fails a whole year's work in any subject. At graduation time it is not expected that all students will have completed the same amount of the curriculum. However, a student who reports for a certain unit is expected to have a set of values, skills, and knowledge in common with others who are promoted to the same units. The identification of material within a unit allows for ladder-like steps upon which the student is constantly building and will use in later units.

When students enter Nova they undergo area examinations and all information coming from their former schools is considered. The student is then placed in the appropriate units *in each discipline.* The class to which he is assigned may have students at various levels within the unit. For example, some students in the group may be working to considerably more depth than others in the same group. This is not intended to retard the more able students but rather to meet individual needs and interests. Some students need depth in chemistry; some do not. Even though the student does not elect major studies, he does in practice exercise control over a portion of his education.

A student whose interest is in science may elect to go far beyond what is required, while in English he may pursue a less time-consuming pattern. On the other hand, he may devote extra effort to languages and do a minimum of science and math.

As the student progresses through the sequence, he is aware of his status within the sequence. The units require approximately one month of time for the average student, about six weeks for the less able. During a major reporting period of seven and a half weeks a typical student would have completed at least one and often two units. Each student receives a quality grade and a quantity grade. These are recorded on the report card and averaged for a final grade for a period.

Students are encouraged to do independent study and research in every discipline. The student is taught from the very beginning that he is the person primarily responsible for his education. Far more freedom is allowed students at Nova than at traditional schools, the goal being to help students develop mature study habits before they enter college. It is expected that Nova students will find the transition from Nova to college a smooth one.

The end of one trimester and the start of another means very little to the individual student or teacher. It calls for no major rearrangements. The one exception to this is the end of the third trimester, when the students embark on a one-month vacation. At this time we try to finish a unit so that the students will be mentally free for their vacation.

Nova is not attempting to become an educational racetrack. Students may apply for early graduation, but each case will be judged on its own merit. Ultimately, Nova will hold three graduations a year, to coincide with the student's entrance into the junior college or to one of the universities.

The newest and best of educational techniques and media are utilized at Nova. Among these are team teaching; closed-circuit television; overhead projectors in every room; reading laboratory; science and language laboratories; and large group, medium group, and small group instruction. There is also wall-to-wall carpeting throughout the school, resource centers equipped with a large number of reference books, micro-film readers, teaching machines, and tape recorders. At hand is also a complete data-processing center. The closed television system permits telecasting throughout the school as well as the making of video tapes of lessons and lectures for reshowing at a later date. Nova is also completely air-conditioned. These innovations were financed by the omission of facilities which have long been considered as standard equipment in conventional schools. Nova has no large auditorium and no expensive kitchen or cafeteria. Students either bring their lunches or buy food at snack bars which are supervised by a dietician. The students eat outside in a protected area.

Nova has already become an educational showcase in its own locale, Broward County, and is rapidly becoming a national mecca for educators hoping to see the newest ideas in practice. It is anticipated that many of the ideas and practices alive at Nova will be adopted elsewhere.

THE PROPER PLACE OF THE
EXTRACURRICULUM IN HIGH SCHOOL

Robert N. Bush

The symposium this month was planned because of concern expressed in the current critical discussion of high school education that the extra-curriculum had grown beyond bounds. What is the proper place of the extracurriculum in the high school? What reforms, if any, are needed to bring it to this place?

That extracurricular activities are valuable and have a place in high school few would deny. Their extensive growth over the past half century, while the American high school has been taking shape, testifies to their need-fulfilling character. Investigations verify the contribution of activities and disprove the claim that pupils who participate suffer academically *by comparison* with those who do not do so. Nonetheless, a significant number of laymen and educators, sympathetic to the values of the extracurriculum, appear troubled lest the sideshow overshadow the main event.

WHAT IS OF MOST IMPORTANCE?

Unlike the question of the chicken and the egg, we know that the curriculum came first, and that it is of fundamental, prior importance. The Citizens Advisory Commission of the California Legislative Joint Interim Committee on the Public Education System has stated in its first *Preliminary Progress Report* that "The Primary objective of the public schools should be the fullest development of every individual to think and act effectively and creatively through the mastery, by each student, to the extent of his ability, of the skills, knowledge, thought and appreciation which embody the major achievements of civilization. They are mainly language, literature, art, music, history, geography, government, mathematics, and natural science." The statement continues that the school "cannot perform its primary function adequately if its efforts are widely scattered." This document expresses the conviction that the school's aim

---

From the *California Journal of Secondary Education*, XXXIV, No. 5 (May, 1959), 257-262. Used by permission of the author and publisher.

needs to be sharply focused upon its central task, which may be found embedded in the basic curriculum. That this emphasis has become necessary warns that excesses on the extracurricular side may have crept in.

Proponents of the extracurriculum need not feel defensive that their program is under scrutiny. Calls for needed reform in all parts of the school program may be heard: note the emphasis in the symposiums in the *Journal* this year. Without questioning that the extracurriculum has its place, we need to specify the changes needed to bring into proper perspective. Three troublesome problems may be identified: The effect of the extracurriculum upon the load of the teacher, the load of the pupil, and the load of the school day. *The plain fact is that the extracurriculum has overloaded the whole high school.*

The rapidity with which scholars discover new knowledge, disprove old theories, and develop new fields of inquiry has made the curricular task of the high school steadily more difficult over the past half century. In addition, during this same time, we have added an extracurricular program. Quite limited in 1900, it has come to occupy a substantial amount of time in the regular school day. But to accommodate this sizable addition, the school day has not been lengthened, load and expectation for the pupil have not been increased, and adjustment in the variety and number of assignments of the teacher has not taken place. The consequent pressures caused by this chain of events have accumulated to a bursting point.

THE LOAD OF THE TEACHER

Studies of the loads of teachers reveal that as much as one-third of their total time may be absorbed in extracurricular activities. The curricular load of teachers has not, however, been reduced as the extracurriculum has been added. As a result, either the teacher has had added to his total load the amount of time devoted to the extracurriculum, or he spends a smaller proportion of his time in the central curricular duties of teaching— unfortunate occurrence in either event. Probably some of both of these undesirable alternatives have been followed. Foreign exchange teachers often comment upon the heavy extracurricular load carried by American teachers.

An excessive extracurricular load has led teachers to begin to pressure for two kinds of adjustment: extra pay for these so-called extra duties, or relief from curricular responsibilities. School districts may follow either or both practices. Compelling arguments both for and against may be heard on both sides. The volume and intensity of discussion attest that the issue has not been resolved. The bargaining of teachers for extra pay for extra duty, while understandable, has had the unfortunate result of placing teaching in the same category as labor in its negotiations with management. This works against the realization of full professional status for teaching.

The public needs to know that teachers are not, in these discussions of extra pay for extra duty, trying to discover how they can do less work for more money. They are responding to the powerful pressures that have accumulated over the years, especially as a result of the addition of the extracurriculum, which prohibit them from performing their main function, which is to teach pupils worthwhile basic subject matter in a manner that enables pupils to develop a mastery of the material by independent thought rather than by rote. The two main avenues for helping teachers who have assumed extracurricular duties have been extra pay and reduced academic load. Added avenues that ought to be further considered are (1) over-all reduction in the total amount of time and energy directed to extra-curricular activities in the school; (2) more student-directed activities; and (3) shift in supervision of the extracurriculum from the shoulders of teachers to nonteaching personnel, both paid and unpaid. Especially in a time of teacher shortage should the full energies of teachers be directed to teaching.

Both in hiring and advancing teachers in schools today, administrators place high premium on ability and willingness to participate in the extracurriculum. With the present program this is understandable. The issue becomes how so to change circumstances that priority may be given to teachers who wish to devote themselves to teaching. This is a question easier to raise than to answer. But a good answer will not be forthcoming until high school principals resolve to think even harder about how the problem may be resolved in their schools. Today the rewards to teachers of additional money, administrative approval, and professional advancement, push mainly in the extracurricular direction.

THE LOAD OF THE PUPIL

The second main point where the extracurriculum impinges is upon the pupil. Does the extracurriculum loom too large in the mind of the pupil; has it become too elaborate, expensive, time-consuming? Have pupils become so absorbed that they have lost perspective concerning the purpose of schooling? Cars, athletic games, social affairs, and all that is associated with these constantly must be kept in check, as school officials well know.

But they alone cannot stem the tide. Parents and citizens must rally to help. Strong demands for fostering these activities come from the community and parents. Efforts of school officials to curb them are not infrequently protested by the community. The extracurricular part of the school program grows like wildfire unless vigorously kept under control. Both school officials and parents and community leaders must combine in resolute action. While the immediate and lively interests of pupils push strongly in the direction of increased attention to the extracurriculum, long-run interest will be best served if the wishes of the day be not given full sway.

The extracurriculum has risen to prominence over the years allegedly because of the admission of all youth to high school and of the necessity of finding a wide variety of activities in which all could participate and succeed, especially those whose talents were other than academic. Furthermore, citizenship objectives, e.g., the development of leadership, are especially well served by the extracurricular program. The more liberal inclusion of the extracurriculum in the school is the result both of broadened objectives and enlarged enrollment as well as the play of the natural forces of pupil interest and initiative. In view of the persuasive logic of these supports for the extracurriculum, it is troublesome to note how unevenly students participate in activities. Those students participate most who are judged to be in least need of participation. Indeed, those colleges and universities who use activity participation as one criterion for admission unwittingly have given impetus to the extracurriculum rather than to the curricular aspects of high school education. The pressure upon the collegebound student to participate is often very great. The barriers to participation are also often very great. Students who are less academically talented and those who come from less favored segments of social and economic life, often do not participate in the extracurriculum. Some who should not participate do—and some who ought to and cannot are forced outside into extra-school activities of an anti-social nature.

Part of the difficulty which surrounds us may be the result over the years of an increased blurring of the lines between the curriculum and the extracurriculum. The advantages of bringing these two fields more closely together are often listed, while the problems may not have been so fully discussed. The proponents of the extracurriculum may protest, but a case may be made for the proposition that the curriculum tends to relate more closely to the idea of work and the extracurriculum to the idea of play. Even though Poor Richard many years ago observed that all work and no play would make Jack a dull boy, schools long continued to operate as though this were not true or that the purpose of schooling was to produce dull boys. One great advance of modern thought has been the recognition that educational achievement need not necessarily be painful, and that a pleasurable experience is not necessarily bad and non-educational. We have come to accept that schools and learning need not be harsh and completely devoid of play and that work interspersed with play may produce results better than an uninterrupted diet of work. From this it would be a mistake to proceed to argue that the two are not different and that work can be made wholly like play. As Ruskin pointed out, " 'Play' is an exertion of body or mind, made to please ourselves, and with no determined end; and work is a thing done because it ought to be done, and with a determined end. You play, as you call it, at cricket, for instance. That is as hard work as anything else; but it amuses you, and it has no result but the amusement. If it were done as an ordered form of exercise, for health's sake, it would become work directly. So, in like manner, whatever we do to please ourselves, and only for the sake of the pleasure, not for an ultimate object, is 'play,' the 'pleasing thing,' not the useful thing. Play may be useful, in a secondary sense; (nothing is indeed more useful or necessary); but the use of it depends on its being spontaneous."

Recognition of the value of extracurricular activities in promoting desirable educational outcomes has led to a tendency to curricularize them, to bring them into the school day, to require participation, to give points in the form of marks or demerits, to require them to be taught by certified personnel, and to grant credit which may appear on the official transcript and be applied toward graduation. A tendency may be noted on the other hand, perhaps not so marked, to extracurricularize the curricular. Classes have been made less formal; grades, marks, credits have been de-emphasized to make classes more pleasant. If there be a genuine difference between work and play, between the curricular and the extracurricular, and that each, valuable in its own right, enhances the other, it may be that the strongest values may be lost if each attempts to become like the other. If each retains its identity, contrasting values may be enhanced. Tendency to blur the distinctions may have become too great.

A proper balance between the two will not be struck without persuasive leadership from teachers, administrators, counselors, parents and citizens. Youth understandably need little encouragement to argue the case for the extracurriculum. Was not play ever more attractive than work, especially to the young? Lack of policy and leadership on the part of adults in the school and the community can result in undue attention to the extra-curriculum. Has the pendulum swung to the point where the curriculum needs to be de-extracurricularized?

THE LOAD OF THE SCHOOL DAY

In the not-too-distant past schools began as early as 8:00 a.m. and, with an hour for lunch, ran until 4:00 p.m. Over the years the school day has been shortened. During the same period we have been trying to fit more and more into it. Not only have subjects been added to the curriculum, but the extracurriculum, which was once largely conducted beyond the regular school hours, has increasingly been incorporated into the school day. The educational arguments for so doing are hard to deny. If activities are educationally important, if they are to be made available to all, and if they are to be supervised by regular staff, having them placed in the regular school day makes much sense. But in forcing more and more into the school day, both curricular and extracurricular, the point may have been reached where something must give way. Further, if the school day is not lengthened, and if activities remain in the regular day rather than moving outside, they may compete with and disrupt serious intellectual effort.

We are persuaded that a larger share of a pupil's day and year should be used in his serious intellectual development. This can and should be accomplished with all possible speed. Society will benefit, as well as the individual. Objection to the proposal to lengthen the school day and year, apart from the understandable but not deep-seated loud cry of anguish from the pupils, appears to come mainly from teachers, who understandably think of their present overloads. But what we suggest is not an increase in the load of the teachers, but rather giving pupils increased responsibility for their own education, not always necessarily under the supervision of a teacher. Much of the work of the extracurriculum need not occupy teachers but could be assumed by others in the school, both paid and unpaid assistants, as well as by volunteer persons from the community. This would help to keep clear the distinction between the curriculum and the extracurriculum, to make more manageable the load of the teacher, and to preserve the inherent strength in the extracurriculum.

As educators scrutinize the total high school program and prepare to make recommendations for constructive change, we should consider seriously the question that citizens have posed as to whether or not the extracurriculum needs to be seen in a new perspective, whether its demands have not become too excessive upon teachers, pupils, and the time of the school which should be devoted to serious intellectual work. If this is found to be true, we should begin to formulate constructive proposals for remedying the situation. Serious consideration needs to be directed to the adjustment of the load of the teacher so that he may devolte his full energies to teaching, to limiting and redirecting the energies of many pupils, especially those more academically talented, as well as to revising regulations which prohibit pupils who ought to participate from participating, and providing enough time to fit in both the curricular and the extracurricular.

The proper balance will not be easily achieved. The forces are strong in the ·extracurricular direction. Pupils are overzealous about activities. It is in activities, especially athletics, where the school is most visible to the community. When administrators, counselors, and those teachers who are activities enthusiasts join in the parade, the remaining teachers, devoted to the curriculum, where lies, remember, the basic and primary purpose of the school, are likely to find themselves overpowered. Strong, steady, and enlightened leadership from school officials, supported by boards of education, parents, citizens, will be required to achieve the balance that is so essential—and to see that the full values of both the curriculum and the extracurriculum are realized.

HUMANITIES COURSES IN SECONDARY SCHOOLS

*Carolyn A. Glass
and Richard I. Miller*

Is there an increased interest in teaching a course in the secondary schools that is generally called the humanities? Are more secondary schools incorporating this course into the instructional program? Where? How? What content comprises the course? How do the teachers like the course? How about the students? These questions and others have prompted this study. Very little evidence is available on what has been called "the humanities movement."

One can list many reasons why a secondary-school course on the humanities might be expected to develop. These include: a growing concern about the effects of mechanization and mass society, with accompanying tendencies of alienation both from oneself and from society; a view that man's rich intellectual and cultural heritage is not being explored by young

From *Educational Theory*, XVII, No. 3 (July, 1967), 227-235. Used by permission of the authors and publisher.

people; the Hegelian-like view that the humanities can help counterbalance the increasing emphasis on vocational education; and the belief that man, the full man, should be the goal of education—the thinking, believing, acting, and feeling man.

Given conditions that are favorable to the development of the humanities, has this development, in fact, taken place? To help constructive thinking about this question, this background paper will take two approaches: the results of two questionnaire surveys are outlined, and some conditions are discussed that favor development of humanities and some obstacles are mentioned. A personal note concludes the paper.

I. QUESTIONNAIRE SURVEYS

Two questionnaires were constructed. The first one was sent to every state department of education in the U.S.A. as well as to the equivalents in the territories. A 100 percent response was received on this questionnaire.

Following up information received on the initial questionnaire, another questionnaire was sent directly to each school that was listed by state departments as having good humanities programs. This questionnaire sought information about the nature of the program.

Description, analysis, interpretation, and evaluation of answers to these two questionnaires form the basis of this report.

1. Has the State Department published materials, articles, etc., relating to this area of interest?
2. Is philosophy or any course (Humanities, Great Books, etc.) taught in any secondary school system in your state?
3. As you see it, do you believe interest in this area has *decreased* or *increased* in the past five years, and how about the future?
(Increased – I; Decreased – D; About same – S)
    1960-1965; interest evident
    1965-70; interest expected

The Role of State Departments in the Humanities Area

The first question was designed to determine whether state departments of education were publishing materials, articles, etc., relating to this area of interest. Of the 54 replies received, five (9.3%) answered "yes," 47 (87%) said "no," and two (3.7%) did not reply. The five that have published articles or teachers' guides on humanities courses for high schools are: Florida, Missouri, Pennsylvania, Puerto Rico, and Virginia.

An analysis of the responses on the first question would lead one to conclude that state departments have not taken an active part—with the exception of Pennsylvania—in establishing humanities programs in their states.

Secondary Schools Offering a Humanities Course

The second question sought to learn (a) whether the state departments of education knew about humanities programs within their states, and (b) what schools they would list as having good humanities courses.

Of the 54 replies received on the question about whether philosophy or any course (Humanities, Great Books, etc.) is taught in schools of their state, 31 (57.4%) answered "yes," 20 (37%) replied "no," and 3 (5.6%) indicated that they had no knowledge of such a course being taught in their state.

The reliability of these replies may be open to question on the basis of discovering two schools offering humanities courses that were in states that answered "no."

The pattern of answers do indicate that the humanities programs are filtered throughout the United States and its territories, with such states indicating humanities programs in their school systems as Alaska, Arizona, California, Hawaii, Kansas, Mississippi, New Hampshire, North Carolina. The greater concentration of courses does seem to fall within the eastern half of the country and specifically the northeastern section. This is evidenced by affirmative replies from such states as: Connecticut, Massachusetts, Michigan, Minnesota, New Hampshire, New Jersey, New York, Ohio, Pennsylvania, Vermont, Wisconsin.

The third question probed into state departments' estimations of the direction in which interest in the humanities is moving. One part of the question asked for an indication of interest evidenced from 1960 to 1965. Of the 54 replies, 37 (68.5%) answered "increased," 13 (24.1%) "about the same," and 4 (7.4%) made no indication.

Another part of the question asked for interest expected from 1965 to 1970. Of the replies, 43 (79.6%) answered that an increase was expected, 5 (9.3%) about the same, and 6 (11.1%) gave no indication.

In listing factors that were instrumental in determining the state departments' estimation of state interest in the humanities program, the results were correlated in two ways. First, the relationship between those states giving a "no" answer in question two and the amount of interest indicated; and second, the comparison between the amount of interest indicated and reasons or factors given for the conclusion.

Of those 20 states replying that no humanities course was being taught in their state, all but three (Canal Zone, New Mexico, Virgin Islands) give an indication of interest in this area. And the Canal Zone gave as reason for its conclusion that humanities had not been discussed.

Such states as Idaho, Iowa, Maine, Oklahoma and Oregon indicated that interest in this area either was about the same from 1960-65, or they expected it to continue about the same in the future. One factor given in this conclusion was that their curriculum was being revised but in the direction of the vocational areas; while another said that they hoped to move in this direction with the addition of an English consultant to their state department of education.

The greatest number of states replying "no" to question two indicated on question three a present interest in this area or an expected interest. This category includes such states as Arkansas, Colorado, Illinois, West Virginia. An increasing stress on academic excellence and a concern for enrichment programs for the gifted were two reasons listed for the anticipated interest.

Of the 31 states replying "yes"—that a humanities course was being taught within their school systems—all states indicated an increase in interest either at present or in the future. Some factors listed as instrumental in their estimations were: more attention paid to the individual needs of the learner, national publicity and conferences reflecting new interest in this type of program, and a need to bring about a balance in the curriculum. While these reasons were dominant, others were given: Nebraska stated that such materials were being read and discussed in a larger degree in their state as a result of Project English; a new emphasis upon literature and history is evident with a tendency to identify the "educated man" with great books; requests made to the state departments from schools systems for information in this area have increased; and finally, one state department replied that "apparently this is another of those cycles that education and society must go through. Usually takes a decade to get it out of their system."

It would appear, in conclusion, that those states having a humanities program within their school systems are more aware of the scope of such a program and of its value for education. They also seem to be taking part in establishing such programs in many instances, particularly from an indication of requests made to the state departments by the school systems for information about this area.

As one would expect, the large secondary schools dominated the scene—schools between 1700-1800. Schools with an enrollment from 300-600 were generally special or college-preparatory schools.

The larger schools would be the logical ones pioneering this field with greater faculty specialization and more instructional flexibility.

Respondents were asked to check one of the following course titles: Humanities, Philosophy, or Great Books. In some cases other titles were written in, such as: Society and the Arts, American Civilization, Arts and Man, Essential Ideas, and History of Western Thought.

The vast majority of high schools with a humanities course indicated it was entitled "Humanities" in their curriculum. Several schools offered a philosophy course—usually an introductory course or one on ethics. Other schools listed a Great Books course, either in their school curriculum or as independent study.

The humanities offerings appear to be rather evenly distributed throughout the United States. A course dealing with the Great Books appeared most frequently in school systems in such states as Delaware, Minnesota, and Texas. And the philosophy course appeared in a few school systems in states such as Delaware, New York, and Washington.

Respondents were asked to indicate whether materials presented to the students were in the form of a concepts course (Freedom and Man, God and Man, etc.); Allied Arts (Music, Art, etc.); or Philosophy (original works or textbooks).

The types of materials most frequently listed came under the heading of the Allied Arts or a combination of concepts, allied arts, and philosophy. Those schools which offered a philosophy course included readings of original works and a type of concepts course.

For the majority of secondary schools, the humanities course is defined as a study of the allied arts or a combination of the allied arts, concepts, and philosophy.

A vast majority of the school systems reported that their courses in the general area of the humanities had been initiated since 1960. Some school systems in New York and Washington indicated that humanities programs were started in 1954 and 1955. Large school systems in Minnesota, New Hampshire, and New Jersey indicated that humanities courses were initiated in 1957, 1957, and 1955, respectively.

The respondent was asked to indicate whether the students enrolled in humanities courses were intellectually superior, junior or seniors, or if the course was open to all students.

In comprehensive high schools, the humanities course is limited to juniors and/or seniors, and in many cases to the superior student. The college preparatory high schools likewise offer the humanities course primarily for juniors and/or seniors with no emphasis placed upon the superior student.

The great books course, both in the comprehensive and college preparatory high schools, is usually open only to juniors and seniors. The philosophy course in these same types of schools, is open to juniors and/or seniors, with emphasis placed upon the superior student.

Respondents were asked to indicate the professional training of teachers for such a course. The following suggested specialties were given: English major or minor, philosophy major or minor, special certificate, or other.

The majority of the teachers employed in teaching the humanities courses were either English majors or minors. Those who taught a philosophy course were either history or philosophy majors or had some graduate or undergraduate training in philosophy. The great books teacher seemed most frequently to have an English major.

The major trend among those schools having a humanities course, and particularly one which used the Allied Arts as source material, was toward team teaching. The average course in the humanities was taught by four teachers, frequently with majors in English, art, music, and history or social studies. Team teaching is also being used in some school systems in New York State which offer a philosophy course. Team teaching seemed most prevalent in school systems in the states of New York, Pennsylvania, and Washington.

On the second questionnaire, the individual schools were asked whether they had "any means of evaluating the relationship between student interest in this course and his further study?"

The majority of school systems reported that they did not have means of evaluating student response at the present time, primarily because their humanities programs were relatively new. The main source of information used by schools indicating some evaluation was interviews with college students returning to visit their high schools. According to these reports, the students believed that further study in the arts and humanities came as the result of interest stimulated by the humanities course in secondary school.

A final question to individual schools asked for an evaluation of the humanities course. Of the 51 individual schools answering this question, a substantial majority took evaluation to mean whether the course was good or bad. With one or two exceptions, these evaluations were glowing. Typical comments include: "very valuable to students," "one of the most exciting courses ever offered," "received with considerable enthusiasm," "fills a great need," and "exceptionally stimulating to the students."

Some responses were analytical rather than evaluative, with such comments as: "broadens horizons in vocational thinking," "great need for a balance in the curriculum," "for about top 15 per cent of student body."

"sharpens critical thinking and reading scope," and "biggest problems are qualified teachers and enough time for planning."

In general, the greatest value from the humanities courses in the sampled secondary schools seemed to be in helping to broaden the curriculum and in widening the horizons of college-bound students. Also, several schools indicated that the course helped to develop critical thinking and to broaden the outlook toward the arts.

II. SOME OBSERVATIONS AND CONCLUSIONS

This section is based upon a selective survey of the literature, the two questionnaire surveys, and first-hand visitations of a small number of secondary-school humanities programs. More appropriately, this section should be entitled "Some Informal Observations and Tentative Conclusions." More research and study is needed in order to fortify or modify many points that will be raised subsequently.

Three Themes Supporting Humanities Programs in Secondary Schools

At the start of this paper, several reasons for the current development of humanities programs were listed. This section will be addressed to some additional factors that favor the humanities movement.

1. Increasing mechanization and complexity in living requires greater intellectual and cultural expansion. —Stephen Vincent Benet recognized that man might be dominated by his inventions when he wrote of the machine as—

> The great, metallic beast . . .
> The genie we have raised to rule the earth,
> Obsequious to our will
> But servant-master still,
> The tireless serf already half a god . . .

To counterbalance tendencies toward greater mechanization and complexity, the schools need to offer opportunities that will help youngsters think about aesthetic and cultural experiences—the humaneness of man. As Jacques Maritain has written:

The Humanities are those disciplines which make men more human, or nurture in man his nature as specifically human, because they convey to him the spiritual fruit and achievements of the labor of generations, and deal with things which are worth being known for their own sake, for the sake of truth or the sake of beauty.[1]

2. Awakening sense of values on part of today's youth requires opportunities for intellectual probing. —The abundant response of American youth to the Peace Corps and other service-type opportunities has deflated some pessimistic views of today's youth. Harold Taylor has pointed out that the "new generation" is often misunderstood by those of the "older generation, especially among educators, who have not themselves had the experience of direct involvement with the situation of the world. . . ."[2]

Where in the secondary school program does youth have an opportunity to examine values? Social studies could provide some opportunities in this area of study although one seldom finds this to be the case.

In an age where science and technology play a vital role, the vast scope and rapid production of knowledge tends to leave little time for discussing philosophical and moral aspects of many critical developments in modern life. Educators are asking the question, "What can the schools do to help the students develop a sense of values without being dogmatic?" The humanities course offers one answer to this question. Clifton Fadiman argues that in terms of equipping students to meet demands of the adult world, this direction is important:

A great work of art, properly taught, performs work on the teenager; and—this is what somehow he must be taught to feel—it performs it more efficiently, more economically and even more lastingly than most of his so-called "practical experience." The Humanities *force* him to grow up. They are not a nosegay to put in his buttonhole as a mark of culture. They are, or should be, as much a part of his life as his relations to his family or the career he will later choose for himself.[3]

3. Increasing interest in self-realization evident among youth requires opportunities for individual and group introspection. —In Hamlet one finds these lines:

. . . What a piece of work is a man! how noble in reason! how infinite

---

[1]Quoted in: Clifton Fadiman, "The Role of the Humanities in Secondary Schools." An address given in Miami, Florida, November 23, 1962, p. 7.

[2]Harold Taylor, "American Idealism, 1965," *Saturday Review,* 48:16 (June 26, 1965).

[3]Clifton Fadiman, *op. cit.,* p. 7.

in faculty! in form and moving how express and admirable! in action how like an angel! in apprehension how like a god!

Literature courses may brush over such well known passages, but how often does the already crowded course outline allow probing analysis of such thoughts? A humanities course allows one to see oneself by viewing others, and by relating oneself to great men and women and to great ideas. A primary role of the Humanities is to entice and stimulate young minds into exploring the human experience through what man has written or done. A great painting, for example, is an eloquent statement speaking across the ages about human feeling and insight. And about the music of Bach and Vivaldi, Secretary-General Hammarskjold once said, "They have a beautiful way of creating order and perspective in one's mind."[4]

Three Obstacles to Expansion of Secondary-School Humanities Programs

This section will touch upon three problems of conditions that will continue to inhibit growth of this area.

1. Inadequate teacher preparation. —If the humanities program is to enjoy continued growth and interest, some provisions for special teacher preparation will need to be considered. At the present time, someone with a special interest in the area is given the course to teach. Interest is a vital prerequisite, but so is content competency. Even a cursory study of the background of teachers who offer the humanities course and the content of the course will reveal a high correlation—as one would expect. Is there a core of subjects or knowledge that should be included in the humanities, or is any approach as good as any other?

Encyclopedia Britannica Films is in the process of making a series of films on the humanities, and the University of Georgia has developed an interesting and provocative series of films for the general public on the great issues of mankind. Films can be particularly useful in in-service programs that are pointed toward developing competencies for teaching humanities courses in secondary schools. The in-service area offers excellent opportunities for the humanities area.

2. Curriculum fullness. —In describing the "creeping curriculum," Ole Sand has said, "Never has so much about so little been taught to so

---

[4]Richard I. Miller, *Dag Hammarskjold and Crisis Diplomacy* (New York: Oceana Publications, Inc., 1961), p. 17.

many!" Where does a humanities course belong in the secondary school?

Thus far, the course is predominantly an elective course for bright junior and senior students. If it is good for this group, is it also good for average students? Are we selling short the below-average students by assuming they could not master the content or they would not be interested?

The newness of the humanities course has not allowed time for curriculum specialists to analyze the course with respect to total school program, and experimental programs in this content area have been very slow in getting under way. The expected future growth of the humanities will need to reckon with curricular fullness, and an intelligent reckoning will require more research and experimentation.

3. Misconceptions about the humanities. —Too often the secondary school humanities course is a series of loosely related anthologies, with little analysis and with little inductive learning. Reading and knowing Shakespeare is one thing; understanding him is another. With understanding can come increased insight into human motives and behavior, the poetry of language, the power of words, and the historical parade of human events.

One suspects that a great many of the teachers offering humanities courses are doing a good job, but not an outstanding one. A good teacher has half the battle won, but the other half is mastery of content.

Some excellent programs have been developed—programs that have carefully considered what should be included in a humanities course. Three such programs are mentioned:

A report on the work of the Pennsylvania Committee on the Humanities has been published and will not be repeated here.

The Lexington, Massachusetts, high school developed a project called "A Pilot Project in the Study of Mankind." The statement of purpose for the program is as follows:

. . . the over-all objective was the development of a greater awareness on the part of the student of his relationships to mankind as a whole. A second purpose was to enable the student to become more objective toward himself in the perspective of other people immediately about him. A third was to place the student in a position where he could view the ideas, values, and aspirations of his own culture against a wider circle of different cultures. Still another objective was to help the student seriously consider whether or not there are common concerns shared by men everywhere—concerns which, in turn, could provide the foundation for a world community.[5]

---

[5]Richard G. Lyons, "Philosophy and Anthropology in the Study of Mankind," *Social Education*, 28:405 (November, 1964).

The evaluation of the results of this project are interesting from the standpoint of a reasoned optimism about the future of such programs:

The project was subjected to various techniques of evaluation which, although imperfect demonstrated to our satisfaction that students of high school age will respond to a searching examination of the great issues of our time, and that their own values will often be broadened to include more regard for their common interest with people everywhere on earth.[6]

A third humanities program, started in 1964, was offered to two classes of sixth-grade students in the Shelmire Elementary School of Southampton, Pennsylvania. It included one semester of a study of man's relationship to nature and the arts. It was considered to be quite effective. The rationale for offering such a course is stated in the following goals:

1.   Help develop a concept of the meaning of the word 'humanities.'
2.   Arouse new dimensions of interest, which would be reflected in choice of TV, motion pictures, and reading.
3.   See themselves as human beings in a world of humans.
4.   Deepen insights in respect to other cultures.
5.   Provide a different orientation in the arts—expressions about and reactions to man himself.[7]

These two surveys leave many important questions unanswered. Obviously a great deal more study is needed before sufficient data is available for effective decision-making about curricular aspects of teaching about the humanities in secondary schools.

[6]*Ibid.,* p. 406.

[7]Henry W. Ray, "The Humanities in Elementary Education," *Social Education,* 27:459 (December, 1964).

WHAT IS INDEPENDENT
STUDY ALL ABOUT?

Donald W. Empey

In recent years considerable attention has been focused on student independent study by both elementary and secondary teachers.

Basically, independent study is the pursuit and acquisition of knowledge and skills by students with limited assistance from their classroom teachers. This is in contrast to the imparting of knowledge from teacher to student as is provided through lectures, demonstrations, and discussions. For some students independent study may be limited to acquiring understanding through seeking the answers to problems posed by teachers. For others, independent study may involve a self-directed learning activity completely divorced from any course requirements. It places emphasis on self-responsibility and self-regulation for learning. It can involve research in the library, construction in the shop, or investigations in the laboratory.

Much of the professional literature pertaining to independent study is found in descriptions of such organizational plans as team teaching and flexible scheduling. Independent study need not be limited, however, to such plans. Schools with traditional programs can provide opportunities for independent study. To take full advantage of the opportunities available in team teaching and flexible scheduling, however, both teachers and students must know what independent study is all about.

Self-direction is one of the most important objectives of education. By the time a student graduates from senior high school, he should have developed a high sense of self-direction and motivation. Unfortunately, much of the education in our schools today consists of teachers talking and (hopefully) students listening. If pupils are to have an opportunity to develop self-direction, they must have an opportunity to experience it through independent study.

We live in a world of change in which the amount of knowledge is accumulating very rapidly. Much of what students learn today will be obsolete in the near future. Much of what they will need to know as adults is not yet known by anyone. The Educational Policies Commission of the National Education Association states that the average high school graduate

From *Journal of Secondary Education,* XLIII, No. 3 (March, 1968), 104-108. Used by permission of the author and publisher.

today will have to be reeducated at least three times during his lifetime just to keep pace with the acceleration of knowledge. It is obvious that one of the primary functions of education is to help students "learn how to learn."

Independent study is psychologically sound. An individual learns best what he discovers for himself. Much of what is known about the learning process suggests that there may be altogether too much emphasis in schools placed on the teacher "transmitting knowledge." Valid research indicates that learning is better acquired when the teacher creates situations whereby the student can discover knowledge for himself.

At Arcadia (California) High School independent study has been divided into four phases. This distinction has been made as a convenience for teachers to help clarify the objectives of various types of independent study projects. It is realized, of course, that all aspects of independent study do not fit neatly into these compartments but the following classifications have proven to be helpful.

Phase One (the lesson for tomorrow)   This level of independent study is initiated by the teacher. It is the customary daily or weekly homework assignment. The assignment may be an open-end or a closed-end activity. Drill or practice experiences, routine in nature, are examples of closed-end activities. Homework assignments may be left open-ended, thus helping the student learn how to use information in an orderly and creative way. For example, the assignment may call for the student to compare two characters in a literature selection, or see how many different ways a problem in mathematics can be solved.

To be truly effective, homework should be individualized; that is, the assignments given to pupils should be based on the student's need to acquire certain information or develop certain skills. In some cases, however, it may be an assignment that all students in the class are to complete. While the scope of the daily or weekly homework assignment is limited, it has a definite place in the total plan of independent study when used properly by teachers.

Phase Two (the self-instruction package)   Phase two of independent study is also teacher initiated but wider in scope than phase one. Suppose the teacher is planning a unit on the Civil War. As part of this plan the teacher might prepare a package of materials to guide the student through various independent study experiences. Part of this package might be distributed to the student in the form of directions, guide questions, and statements of problems. Much of the package would be kept in the library or learning resource center to be used by students during time reserved for independent study. Part of the student's instructions might call for the use of reference books, periodicals, and pamphlets. The student might be asked to listen to recordings of music of the Civil War period. He might be asked to study maps, to view slides, video tape reocrdings, films, and filmstrips concerning various facets of the war.

This type of independent study calls for a much wider range of instructional materials than has been used in the past. Learning takes place better when various channels of communication can be used. Since some students learn best by reading, some by viewing, and some by listening, the multi-media approach to independent study can be effective.

Phase Three (the project)   This phase of independent study may be initiated by the teacher or by the student and is very open-ended in nature. The student, upon his own initiative or upon the request of a teacher, selects a project to develop in some depth. Next, the student will do the necessary reading, viewing, listening, computing, examining or building. He will subsequently report the results of his work in some type of presentation to the class or to the teacher. This phase of independent study provides an opportunity for the student to be creative and self-directing in completing the project.

Care must be taken by the teacher and the student in outlining what the project will involve so that it does not become "busy work." So many classroom projects are the "cut and paste" variety, which has very limited learning value. The objectives of a project need to be well defined in advance.

Phase Four (individualized research)   Phase four is the highest level of independent study. It is student-initiated and self-directed with limited assistance from the teacher. It begins with the student selecting a topic of interest and value to him. He then asks a teacher to be his advisor and together they outline the objectives of the project, the procedures to be followed, and the system for reporting and evaluating the project. Such an activity may extend over an entire semester or year with the student reporting his progress to the teacher periodically. The project need not be in conjunction with a course in which the student is currently enrolled.

This type of independent study activity might involve a student in science research utilizing the facilities of the science laboratory and the assistance of the science teaching staff. It may involve a research paper for a student of history. It may involve the construction of an engine or the making of clothing for students in the practical arts.

Often, the quest for knowledge will lead the student outside the confines of the school. With assistance from the student advisor, it may be possible for interviews to be arranged with experts in the field of interest. The pupil doing research in science, therefore, may receive advice and assistance from staff members from a nearby university or industrial establishment. The student studying the problems of urbanization may spend time assisting staff members in a Head Start project.

So often teacher planning focuses on classroom presentations and discussions. Actually, as the teacher plans, consideration should be given to at least four types of learning activities. First, the teacher should consider what types of experiences need to be provided through presentations by the teacher. Second, the teacher needs to plan experiences which provide an opportunity for interaction among students. Third, consideration should be given to activities involving laboratory experiences. Finally, the teacher needs to determine what kinds of activities can be pursued by the student on his own.

As teachers consider the placement of activities into the four categories presented above, many are surprised at the number of things that are now being done in the classroom for all which could be done independently. As students assume more responsibility for their own learning, the role of the teacher, of course, changes considerably. He becomes an expert in helping pupils discover knowledge for themselves. Most independent study thus becomes a very integral part of the total learning strategy developed by the teachers. Its planning involves attention equal to that which is given to preparing for lectures and discussions.

One of the most difficult tasks facing educators today is the selection of materials to assist teachers and students in independent study. During the past five years, considerable emphasis has been placed on the manufacturing and acquisition of equipment. Much of this equipment, such as the teaching machine, has great potential for utilization in independent study. However, the "software" to be used in these machines is lacking.

In the past, educators have placed most of the emphasis in independent study on the use of printed materials. There is, however, great potential in the proper utilization of a wide variety of media. Materials for independent study include not only books and periodicals but also such items as tape and disc recordings, filmstrips, slides, and videotaped programs. Recent developments in the use of 8mm film are particularly applicable to individual study. Programmed learning has, perhaps, its greatest potential in the area of independent study. If a student is having difficulty in a particular segment of a course, or if he wishes to engage in enrichment work within that course, programmed learning materials have been and can be written to be of assistance to him.

Independent study takes many forms. Facilities for such learning also vary. Independent study may take place at a student's desk, at a study center within a classroom, at a library or at a resource center.

School libraries must be more than book collections. Space and equipment should be made available for listening and viewing stations. The use of audio-visual materials cannot be limited to the classroom only. These materials must be made available to students in the school library or instructional materials center.

The study carrel, equipped with facilities for viewing and listening, has a place not only in the library or instructional materials center, but also in certain classrooms. Primary grade teachers have found that students can benefit from viewing and listening in independent study carrels.

As the concept of independent study grows in a school, the library may be inadequate. Learning resource centers and open laboratories located throughout the school will provide additional areas for individual study. Resource centers for social science, English, and mathematics, as well as laboratories for science and industrial arts, will provide opportunities for independent study to become an integral part of the total instructional program. Such centers will be supplied with the necessary apparatus, supplementary textbooks, periodicals and pamphlets. Resource centers may have library books and audio-visual materials pertaining to particular topics assigned on a temporary basis. The centers should be equipped with tables and chairs, bookcases, study carrels, and listening and viewing stations. Experimental programs are under way in some school districts which will provide an interlocking system of informational retrieval in the resource centers, the library, and classrooms, through dial access.

SCHOOL-WORK PROGRAMS
THE VOCATIONAL EDUCATION ACT IN ACTION

Louis D. Mason

The Vocational Education Act of 1963 (P.L. 88-210 Part A) was passed by Congress on December 13, 1963 and signed into public law on December

From *The Clearing House*, XLII, No. 5 (January, 1968), 294-296. Used by permission of the author and publisher.

18, 1963. When the funds from this measure were appropriated in 1964, it marked the start of a new epoch in education.

Following the first Sputnik, the emphasis in education was on the academics and, more specifically, the maths and sciences. The Vocational Act of 1963 has been predominantly responsible for the burgeoning and reawakening emphasis in vocational education. It was this legislative act that initiated the current trend of "education for employability." In the past, federal funds for vocational education were pretty well restricted to courses in agriculture and homemaking.

By this time the impact of the Act has already had a wide-range influence in the state of Wisconsin. As soon as federal funds were allocated to the states, the Wisconsin State Department of Public Instruction proceeded to select 34 pilot schools to participate in the implementation of work-experience programs in vocational education. The basic objective of a pilot school is to develop cooperative work-experience programs which would prepare students for entry jobs in the world of work. A cooperative work-experience program is the culminating part of a total vocational education sequence in which fundamental concepts and skills are taught in the classroom and related training is received in a local business or industry. Scheduled in the senior year, a cooperative program provides a student with a realistic and practical experience in well-selected training stations (supervised by both employer and a coordinating teacher) as well as monetary compensation and school credit.

Following are some examples of how one pilot school, Oshkosh Senior High, has taken advantage of the 1963 Vocational Education Act to institute cooperative work-experience programs in office occupations, food services, distributive and marketing occupations, vocational welding, and radio-television services.

SELECTION OF STUDENTS FOR A PROGRAM

In order for a cooperative program to operate successfully, the student trainees must possess certain qualifications, here indicated in the following listing:

1.   A student should be at least 16 years of age so that he may be employed in a gainful occupation.
2.   Each student should have an occupational interest. He should have made a preliminary decision on the best occupational area for him.
3.   He must possess pleasant personal characteristics and traits such

as: neat appearance, proper physical stature, acceptable speech, dependability, and initiativeness.

4.   He must be occupationally suited for certain types of work.

5.   He should be capable of earning advancement on the job.

6.   He should be a good school citizen; one who can represent the school as a product of the total instructional program.

Prior to the actual initiation of a program, surveys should be taken to indicate a need for a cooperative program in certain areas. They should show an acute interest on the part of local business and industry to participate in such a program.

The pupils who desire to enroll in the program are tested, interviewed, and finally selected by a coordinating teacher. The last step in the selection procedure is a final interview by a member of the business who has previously agreed to participate in the program. When all work-station arrangements have been made ready, schedules are arranged so that students can be released from school at 2:30 p.m. to report to their jobs. In addition to receiving ½ credit towards graduation while working, students are also compensated at a rate of pay that is compatible to the type of tasks they are performing.

In October of 1965, 21 seniors in the Distributive Education program began working 15 hours per week in some phase of distribution—retailing, wholesaling, or marketing. The following January, 20 senior girls began work in the office occupations area—stenography, clerical work and bookkeeping.

ADVISORY COMMITTEES

An "advisory-steering committee" is a general committee formed in the initial stages of planning to give direction to the total program. A steering committee should be as representative of the various community forces as possible. The committee, appointed by the superintendent, provides valuable assistance in public relations and promotional activities within the school and the community.

Membership in the "individual occupational advisory committees" is representative of the occupational areas concerned. Those selected to serve on these committees are close to the job performance of workers in the occupations. These persons are community leaders and should represent well-known business organizations. Committee members are recommended by the vocational administrator and are appointed by the superintendent.

The "advisory committee" is used as a sounding board and a resource unit for the planning and operating procedures of a specific program. The committee may be asked advice on public relations, curriculum content, equipment, student selection, evaluation of programs, and assist in various activities. It may suggest sources of training stations, types of instructional materials, assist with promotional affairs, provide resource personnel for classroom related instruction, recommend minimum standards for students, assist with the employer appreciation banquet, and help identify adult education needs.

Finally, the advisory committee is just that—a group of qualified, interested people selected by the school administration to provide counsel for the program. Advisory committee members should understand very clearly their responsibilities and the limits of the activity. Used well, they can be an invaluable part of the total program. The control of educational policy, however, remains with the local board of education.

BENEFITS DERIVED FROM THE PROGRAM

The vocational administrator at Oshkosh Senior High has outlined the following benefits derived from a cooperative work-experience program:

1. Economical and practical training opportunities
2. Increased practical educational contribution from the school to society
3. Application of school training to needs of the community
4. Opportunities provided for personal and professional development
5. A return of taxes in the form of direct service
6. Reduced personnel turnover through better selection and training
7. Expanded school offerings

Coordinating teachers, advisory committees, and training stations were set up for cooperative programs in the areas of food services, radio-TV repair, and welding and metal fabrication services. There are, in addition, five programs in the planning stages. They are drafting, data processing, agri-business, graphic arts, and woodworking.

There are exciting possibilities for vocational education in the era that lies ahead and I, for one, am hopeful that educators, administrators, and businessmen can meet this challenge "head on" in order to provide even greater accomplishments in vocational education in the future.

ADVANCED PLACEMENT
A REPORT ON FORMER PARTICIPANTS AND
THEIR SUBSEQUENT ACADEMIC PERFORMANCE

John B. Bergeson

The problem of maximizing the effectiveness of education for all students is a major concern in the United States. For various reasons, however, attention to the needs of academically talented students is receiving proportionately more consideration. One result was the formation in 1950 of the College Entrance Examination Board's Advanced Placement Program. This is a form of acceleration at the college level that depends upon the results of proficiency tests given toward the end of high school. As of 1964-1965, it had expanded to include 34,278 students from 2,369 high schools who took 45,110 examinations and applied for credit to 994 colleges (1).

The purpose of the investigation reported here was to examine the academic performance of college students in subject fields in which they were accelerated as a result of their participation in the Advanced Placement Program.

BACKGROUND

Even though many nationally known educators have recommended the Advanced Placement Program as a method of meeting the needs of academically gifted students, few research studies evaluating its effectiveness have been undertaken.

Breinan (2), Ducanis (3), Ralston (4), McGregor (5), and Woolcock (6) reported research which ascertained the opinions of former Advanced Placement Program participants about its effectiveness in preparing them for accelerated college work. A great majority of the students indicated that the program was effective.

Chamberlain (7) examined the academic records of 26 college students who had been given credit as a result of their participation in the program.

From *The Clearing House*, XLI, No. 6 (February, 1967), 365-367. Used by permission of the author and publisher.

He concluded that their academic performance was "good to superior" and that they had no difficulty in handling the higher-level courses.

Norton (8) reported a study undertaken in 1955 in which he noted the grades received in chemistry by college students who had been Advanced Placement Program participants and who had been accelerated in that subject field. Without offering conclusions, he found that the students received 22 "A's," 23 "B's," 10 "C's," and no "D's" or "F's."

Wilcox (9) examined the grades that 1,704 college students received in the first course they took as accelerated students. All had participated in the Advanced Placement Program while in high school. He found that 30.8 per cent received "A's," 41.6 per cent received "B's," 22.5 per cent received "C's," and 5.1 per cent received "D's" or "F's." He concluded that, for the most part, students who received credit as a result of their participation in the program were "doing well."

TABLE I
Significance of the Difference in the Grades
Received in the Comparison Course in English

Grade Received	Accelerants Who Had Participated in the Advanced Program	Matched Regular-Progress Students	Chi^2
A	8	10	.22
B	25	22	.19
C	17	19	.11
D	2	1	.33
F	0	0	.00
Total df=4	52	52	.85

A chi-square value of 9.488 is significant at the .05 level

These studies, undertaken principally to evaluate the academic performance of the former participants in the program, indicate that the accelerants seemed to perform at a comparatively high level. However, students who participate in the Advanced Placement Program and who later receive college credit could be presumed to do well simply because they are talented in the subject field in which they received the credit. Therefore a more valid study would match accelerated college students with regular progress students of similar academic ability. Then the grades received in the first course taken by accelerated students could be compared with the grades received in the same courses by their regular-progress counterparts.

For the regular-progress students, however,the comparison courses would be preceded by preliminary courses in the same subject field. Thus the grades of accelerated students would be compared with the grades of equally gifted students in order to determine if academic performance was impaired as a result of acceleration. The present study was conducted with this additional control.

PROCEDURE

One hundred and four pairs of students who had enrolled as freshmen in the College of Arts and Sciences of Northwestern University, Evanston, Illinois, in 1962, 1963, and 1964 were selected for the study. One student in each pair had been given credit as a result of participation in the Advanced Placement Program; the other student—matched with the accelerated student on the basis of sex, the appropriate SAT subscore, and participation in the course upon which the grade comparison was to be made—had not been accelerated.

The 104 pairs of students were distributed in the various subject fields as follows: English, 52 pairs; mathematics, 28 pairs; and science (biology, chemistry, and physics), 24 pairs.

FINDINGS

The data were examined by utilizing the chi-square test and are summarized in Tables I, II, and III.

No significant differences were found in the grades received in the comparison courses by accelerated students, and in the grades received by regular-progress counterparts in the subject fields of English, mathematics, and science.

CONCLUSION

It is apparent from the results of this study that participation in the Advanced Placement Program and subsequent acceleration need not result in lower college grades, and, presumably, less learning. Critics of the program, therefore, who base their objections on the assumption that skipping preliminary courses in a subject field will necessarily result in lower-than-expected academic performance in subsequent courses, would not be supported by these findings. The results of this study also would not support the apprehensions of many academically talented students who resist participation in the Advanced Placement Program for fear that acceleration would result in lower grades in the more advanced courses.

TABLE II
Significance of the Difference in the Grades
Received in the Comparison Course
in Mathematics

Grade Received	Accelerants Who Had Participated in the Advanced Placement Program	Matched Regular-Progress Students	Chi^2
A	10	5	1.67
B	12	9	.48
C	6	11	1.47
D	0	3	3.33
F	0	0	.00
Total df=4	28	28	6.95

A chi-square value of 9.488 is significant at the .05 level

TABLE III
Significance of the Difference in the Grades
Received in the Comparison Course in Science
(Biology, Chemistry, and Physics)

Grade Received	Accelerants Who Had Participated in the Advanced Placement Program	Matched Regular-Progress Students	Chi^2
A	0	4	4.00
B	13	9	.73
C	8	9	.06
D	2	1	.33
F	1	1	.00
Total df=4	24	24	5.12

A chi-square value of 9.488 is significant at the .05 level.

Recognizing the need for this study to be replicated in other institutions and in other subject fields included in the Advanced Placement Program, three recommendations can tentatively be made. First, colleges and universities that do not grant credit toward graduation to students who have performed satisfactorily on Advanced Placement Program high school proficiency examinations should do so. Second, high schools that do not offer the Advanced Placement Program-recommended courses as part of the high school curriculum should do so if personnel and facilities allow. Third, academically talented high school students should not only be encouraged to take these courses but also, in the case of successful participants, be encouraged to apply for credit at the college or university of their choice.

REFERENCES

(1)   College Entrance Examination Board, *A Guide to the Advanced Placement Program* (New York: College Entrance Examination Board, 1955), 7.

(2)   Breinan, Alexander, "The School and College Program of Admission with Advanced Standing," *High Points,* XXXVIII (December, 1956), 13-23.

(3)   Ducanis, Alex J., *Advanced Placement in New York State, A Follow-up Study* (New York: The University of the State of New York Press, 1963), 1-24.

(4)   Ralston, Nancy C., "The Advanced Placement Program in the Cincinnati Public Schools," *The Personnel and Guidance Journal,* XL (February, 1962), 557-560.

(5)   McGregor, Warren M., *The Significance of the Present Advanced Placement Program at Massapequa High School, Massapequa, New York— With Recommendations for its Further Development.* Unpublished doctoral dissertation, Columbia University, 1962.

(6)   Woolcock, Cyril W., "We're Not Doing Right by the Gifted," *NEA Journal,* LII (November, 1963), 31-32.

(7)   Dudley, David A. and Eugene R. Chamberlain, "The College Board Advanced Placement Program—A Progress Report," *California Journal of Secondary Education,* XXXIII (May, 1956), 183-185.

(8)   Norton, Bayes, "College Admissions with Advanded Standing," *Journal of Chemical Education,* XXXIII (March, 1958), 237-241.

(9)   Wilcox, Edward T., *A Report of the Faculty of Arts and Sciences on the Progress of Advanced Standing, 1955-1961* (Cambridge: Harvard University Press, 1962), 1-16.

THE IMPLICATIONS OF RECENT RESEARCH FOR THE IMPROVEMENT OF SECONDARY EDUCATION*

John C. Flanagan

Education at the secondary-school level has been one of our most stable institutions during the past fifty years. During this period the percentages of young Americans entering the ninth grade and graduating from high school have risen to 90 and 65, respectively. However, there has been little change in the program of studies to which these students have been exposed. There have been strong influences for change, especially in recent years; and there are many signs that radical changes can be expected in the next ten years. If such changes are to represent progress and improvements in secondary education and not mere change and innovation, they must be based on systematic research and evaluation.

There has been relatively little research in the field of secondary education. The studies of Edward L. Thorndike about fifty years ago did much to remove scientific support from the doctrine of mental discipline as a basis for many of the courses and methods being used in secondary education. As a result, modern languages were substituted for the study of Latin and Greek. At about the same time a different type of factor, federal support for vocational education at the secondary-school level, became a strong force in shaping the secondary-school program.

This discussion of recent research and its implications for secondary education will focus on current status, findings, and conclusions in each of three aspects of education:

1. objectives, curricula, and the content of the instructional program;
2. methods, technology, and the development of procedures for efficient learning;
3. measurement, evaluation, and guidance of the individual student so that he may set and work toward realistic educational and occupational goals.

From *American Educational Research Journal,* I, No. 1 (January, 1964), 1-9. Used by permission of the author and publisher.

*Invited Address for Division 15 (Educational Psychology) of the American Psychological Association, presented August 29, 1963, at the Sheraton Hotel, Philadelphia, Pennsylvania.

The objectives and content of programs of instruction undoubtedly comprise the most important of these three aspects of secondary education. Efficient instructional methods and precise measurement of results cannot compensate for inadequate attention to objectives and content. It is unfortunate that this is the area in which there has been the last research. Individual textbook authors, educational publishers, and numerous *ad hoc* committees of teachers and scholars have given serious thought to these matters. Rarely, however, have they engaged in the systematic collection and evaluation of data which might provide a sound basis for their decisions and choices.

College-preparatory courses continue to include the same subjects that were required fifty years ago, except, perhaps, for Latin and Greek. Recently, committees of university scholars in the fields of science and mathematics undertook the revision of secondary-school courses in their fields. They found that much of the information being taught in mathematics and science was out of date. They have attempted to bring into these courses an approach and an appreciation of methods more appropriate to present-day activities in these fields. However, these committees have not usually applied research methods to the study of objectives and content.

Vocational-education courses in many instances have changed little over the past decades in spite of the technological revolution in industry. Except for a few questionnaires and interviews collecting impressions from former students and their employers, the vocational-education program has not been studied objectively in terms of the needs of business and industry.

Since decisions regarding educational objectives and course content depend on value systems, it is unlikely that various local school authorities can be expected to agree on the relative importance of each of the goals and topics. It *is* true that more data can be expected to result in more intelligent decisions regarding objectives. If the specific nature of the student learning that can be expected from each of various defined educational experiences is known, choices of instructional materials for educational programs can be made in terms of the desired types of learning.

A number of findings from a recent survey of a representative sample of American students in the ninth, tenth, eleventh, and twelfth grades appear relevant to the problems of objectives and contents. This study, called Project TALENT, involved the testing of 440,000 students, using a comprehensive set of tests and questionnaires. One finding was that high-school girls in the twelfth grade knew very little more about mathematics and the physical sciences than girls in the ninth grade. This poses a real question for educational planners. Should the women in this country continue to grow up in relative ignorance of science, with little appreciation of the power and value of mathematical and scientific developments?

Another finding from Project TALENT is the lack of progress made by the students in vocational schools in the tool subjects of reading, writing, and mathematics. The students in the twelfth grade are only slightly more advanced in these fields than students in the ninth grade. It appears likely that these basic skills will be of increasing importance for skilled workers in industry because of the growing need for learning new methods of operation and new information to adapt to new equipment and procedures.

Project TALENT findings indicate that although the students from small rural schools did about as well as those from large city schools on subjects such as English, history, and the first two years of secondary-school mathematics, they were markedly inferior in advanced mathematics and sciences. It appears that unless this situation is remedied a significant segment of the population with potential talent will be seriously handicapped, if not eliminated, from further training in science and mathematics.

Project TALENT has provided a large amount of other information regarding the levels of achievement now reached by our high-school students with respect to a variety of educational objectives. Through follow-up studies planned for 1, 5, 10, and 20 years after high-school graduation, much additional data should be forthcoming. These follow-ups will be helpful in establishing the relative importance for civic and occupational activities of the various objectives in secondary education programs.

Data of many other types and from many other sources are needed to provide a sound basis for choosing educational objectives. For example, objectives for college-preparatory students should be based on a systematic study of the types of college programs that they are likely to enter. This study should include necessary knowledge, skills, habits, and attitudes.

Probably the two most effective ways to study college programs are by making a comprehensive task analysis of a sample of learning activities and by collecting a large representative sample of college situations that reveal especially effective or ineffective preparation at the secondary-school level.

The analysis of learning activities should include the study of sample paragraphs from textbooks, lectures, and reference materials. Similarly, typical assignments should be analyzed to study the prerequisites necessary for satisfactory and for superior completion. To obtain a large representative sample of college situations that reveal especially effective or ineffective preparation, the critical-incident technique may be used. Students and instructors should be asked for specific examples of situations in which a student performed unusually well or poorly because of a particular aspect of his secondary-school training. It would be necessary to collect such data for a number of courses in each of a variety of fields of study.

Similar systematic studies of the preparation of graduates of vocational schools for effective performance on the job should be carried out. One badly neglected area consists of the study of the effectiveness of the school's program to prepare students for adult life as revealed by the same type of analyses of adult activities and situations. It is proposed that the studies mentioned above be carried out initially to establish a reasonably sound basis for formulating educational objectives. Following these steps, more precise information could be obtained regarding objectives and content for the secondary-school program by devising new formulations of objectives and conducting controlled experiments to evaluate them against later performance. These experiments would make it possible to discover new and more effective types of preparation rather than relying entirely on information as to which of the present practices produced the best results.

In summarizing this discussion of the objectives and contents of secondary education, it can be said that recent efforts of scientists and scholars have made some progress in removing out-of-date content from courses in their fields. Each group has made a number of judgments as to appropriate objectives and content. These judgments have not been based on research evidence, nor have they been evaluated. It is clear that research data now available suggest some of the directions that revisions of objectives and content should take. A systematic research approach is essential if these decisions are to be based on more than hunches and educated guesses.

Let us look next at methods, technology, and the development of procedures for efficient learning. There has been much research on these problems. The findings suggest many improvements with respect to current methods of instruction. The psychological study of intellectual processes has given us some basic data regarding the learning process. Even in a simple problem like acquiring specific items of information, such as the English meaning of words in a foreign language, recent studies indicate that current methods are much less efficient than they could be. Substantial increases have been obtained in the number of foreign words "learned per minute" by using a simple linkage rule.

Another set of research findings refers to the importance of structure. Many specific items of information can be much more readily learned and remembered if they are related to concepts and principles of which they are examples. That is, if items are examples of a structured system they need not be memorized, because any item can be reproduced by anyone knowing the nature of the system.

A well-known but seriously neglected body of psychological knowledge relates to forgetting and retention. It has been well established that information that has been learned must be reviewed and integrated with new information if it is to be retained. The principles governing review for various types of information are not fully known, but much of what is known about effective methods of review is ignored in typical secondary-education programs. For example, foreign languages, mathematics, and science are given as isolated course units and then dropped without regard for much-needed, systematically scheduled reviews. There is no application of these subjects to later courses in other fields. Only at the college-preparatory schools in which the students are preparing for external examinations is any thought given to review and retention of courses that have been completed, and for which "Carnegie Units" are duly entered on the student's record card.

Another area in which there is a large amount of well-established knowledge is transfer and generalization. Educational psychologists have learned a great deal about the kinds of presentation which are most likely to be generalized or transferred to new situations. Many psychologists believe that the burden of establishing generalizations should be placed with the student, and that he should be encouraged and stimulated to develop his own set of principles as part of his experience in learning how to learn. Certainly these new approaches to improving the student's ability to generalize should be given a trial, and evaluated in the school situation.

A topic which has attracted recent attention is creativity. A large amount of evidence has been obtained indicating that teachers and school procedures are combining to frustrate and discourage any creative tendencies shown by students. Recent studies have shown that beginning in the intermediate grades of the elementary school, teachers and fellow students alike regard the original, imaginative, and curious student as a "smart alec" and a trouble-maker (Torrance, 1959). Certainly, substantial changes will need to be made in our present secondary-school programs if we are to nurture and develop originality, imagination, and ingenuity in our students.

Another topic of fundamental importance in secondary education is motivation to learn. Recent studies in the field of industrial psychology have shown that the basic motivating factors leading men to work long hours under unsatisfactory conditions are not factors related to the context of the job, such as good pay, job security, a good supervisor, or good working conditions. (Herzberg, Mausner, and Snyderman, 1959). The effective motivators are more closely related to the contents of the job. They are based on feelings of accomplishment, achievement, and growth or advancement with respect to valued objectives. The same factors are very likely to be the most effective motivators of students. To develop these feelings, the student must have well-defined educational objectives and must be provided with some means for measuring his personal development and progress toward these objectives.

In recent years the greatest impact on educational methods has been made by technological developments. The use of motion pictures, television, sound tapes, teaching machines, and programed texts has opened up many new possibilities for instructional programs. There have been many studies comparing the new media of instruction with more conventional procedures. These have been valuable in demonstrating the promise of the new technologies. There needs to be much more research on the problems of determining how these new media can contribute most effectively to the total educational program. One recent study found that programing, combined with standard teaching procedures, substantially and significantly increased the amount of learning compared to the standard teaching procedures (Goldbeck *and others,* 1962).

The development of procedures for efficient learning has lagged behind research on methods and technologies. The very large individual differences in students at the secondary-school level have been known for a long time. The Project TALENT survey indicated that 25 to 30 percent of ninth-grade students in the high schools of the United States already know more about many educational subjects than the average twelfth-grade student. Similarly, the top 5 percent of the students in a grade can learn the English meanings of twice as many foreign words as the average student can in the same period of time. These findings suggest the need for adapting the instructional program to the individual. Clearly, to provide the same educational activities and experiences for all of the students in a grade cannot but be wasteful. Procedures must be developed which will take each student from his present level of information and skill to the next higher level at his optimal rate of learning. Focusing learning activities on the individual rather than on the class has long been advocated by educators. New developments in methods and technology now make this possible.

The present structure of secondary education with its one- and two-year courses is not at all well suited to meet the educational needs of the individual student. Each individual's instructional program should be based on his broad educational and vocational objectives. It should provide for review of materials already learned, integration of ideas from one field to facilitate learning of another, and the continuous development of a better understanding and appreciation of all fields of knowledge. Another benefit that could be realized in an individualized program of instruction is the coordination of out-of-school learning through hobbies and recreational activities with the in-school program. The results of the Project TALENT Information Test suggest that for many students almost as much is learned out of school as in it.

The teacher can be a crucial factor in a student's educational program. However, at the secondary-school level, the teacher's role has frequently become merely that of a lecturer and clerk. By eliminating much, if not all, of this activity through new methods and media, the teacher should be freed to get better acquainted with each student, thereby providing opportunities for individual tutoring and special assistance.

To take full advantage of the recent findings regarding methods and media, a comprehensive new program should be developed for secondary-school students. In the development of this program each segment should be evaluated in terms of its effectiveness in preparing students to reach their objectives. By designing the instructional program in terms of established research findings and systematically testing all materials in terms of the performance of the students, effective instructional programs can be developed. The importance of testing the effectiveness of new procedures is illustrated by the study of a televised science demonstration. On the basis of tryout and testing of students, the filmed demonstration was revised. The study showed that a comparison with the original film indicated that students learned about 50 percent more from the revised film than they did from the original film (Gropper, Lumsdaine, and Shipman, 1961).

As indicated above, the measurement, evaluation, and guidance of each student is essential to an effective instructional program. At the present time, measures of the individual's talents, interests, and personal characteristics are not effectively used to assist students in educational and vocational planning. Studies such as Project TALENT have demonstrated that not only do students differ very greatly in general ability to learn verbal materials from books, but also with respect to their pattern of talents for many activities such as mathematical reasoning, mechanical comprehension, clerical ability, creativity, memory, and inspection of objects.

To assist the student in appropriately interpreting his scores on various tests of aptitude, interest, and other characteristics, it is necessary to have a comprehensive picture of his family background, hobbies, reading habits, activities, and plans. There is a considerable amount of data available indicating the aptitude and other personal requirements for various educational and occupational activities. However, most attention had been given to a relatively small number of the more popular courses and jobs. Several hundred others need further study. Project TALENT hopes to carry out follow-up studies necessary to identify the aptitude patterns required for effective work in a large number of additional activities.

About half of the twelfth-grade boys in the Project TALENT sample in 1960 did not go on to college. An indication of the aptitude patterns that are likely to characterize various jobs entered by students just out of high school is provided by the results of a follow-up of these students one year after they left high school. The test scores of boys engaged in electrical work, for example, are substantially above the average of the scores for all twelfth-grade boys, including those going on to college, on the tests of mechanical reasoning, visualization in two and three dimensions, and creativity. They are somewhat above the mean in reading comprehension, abstract reasoning, arithmetic reasoning, mathematics, and object inspection. They are below the average of twelfth-grade boys on the English test and on the clerical checking test.

By contrast, the boys who have gone into bookkeeping and other computational jobs are well above the average for twelfth-grade boys on the tests of English, reading comprehension, clerical checking, and arithmetic computation. They are below average on mechanical reasoning and visualization in two dimensions. The group of boys who went into sales activities tends to be close to average on most tests. They were a little above average on arithmetic computation. The boys who entered farming and agricultural activities immediately after high school are about average or a little above on mechanical reasoning and the two visualization tests, and generally below average on all other tests. They are especially low in English and reading comprehension.

One other group deserving special comment consists of the boys who, after leaving high school, went into unskilled labor jobs. This group is somewhat below average on all tests except the clerical checking and object inspection tests, on which they were about average. They are especially low on the tests of English and mathematics.

The groups entering these various jobs uniformly expressed preferences for these types of activites on the *Interest Inventory.* They indicated much participation in the types of activities closely related to the jobs they entered. On sections of the *General Information Test,* they show a greater amount of information about the topics relating to jobs they subsequently entered than to other kinds of jobs.

It appears that as additional follow-up data are obtained it should be possible to describe the special aptitude and interest patterns of each of a very large number of jobs. These data can provide a sound background for individual plans and choices.

On the basis of a relatively comprehensive picture of his talents and other assets, and the degree of correspondence of these with those of successful participants in various courses and fields of work, a secondary-school pupil should be given the opportunity to work out his educational and occupational plans with a panel of advisors. At least one of the panel members should have had counseling-and-guidance training; the responsibility for choices would be placed with the student, but the burden of interpreting and advising him of the evidence of his potential for such choices would rest on his panel of advisors.

It has been found that many students in high schools set unrealistic objectives for themselves. The Project TALENT survey showed that more than 62 percent of the twelfth-grade boys selected occupations that require a college degree. Since it is known that only a few more than a quarter of these students will graduate from college, there is an implication that many of them make unrealistic choices.

It is proposed that a plan of the objectives to be achieved during his four years of secondary-school training be worked out by each beginning ninth-grade student with the help of his panel of advisors. These objectives and the student's progress with respect to each of them should be reviewed every two months. On the basis of the progress made, and any new evidence available, the objectives should be revised as necessary.

If the student's objectives and the measures of progress with respect to his objectives are to be effective, they must be given in terms that have direct meaning to him. Recent work on Project TALENT has provided some meaningful scores for certain types of measures. For example, the scores on the reading-comprehension tests can be interpreted in terms of the magazines and authors that the student is able to read and understand. Slightly less than half of the twelfth-grade students, for example, understand the subtler points in typical paragraphs from the stories of Sinclair Lewis, Jules Verne, and Rudyard Kipling. They also fail to grasp many of the points in typical articles in such magazines as the *Saturday Evening Post, Reader's Digest, McCall's,* and *Time.* Similarly, vocabulary in English and foreign languages can be given in terms of the number of words for which the meanings are known. There is a need for developing this type of meaningful interpretation for the other measures of the various objectives of secondary education so that the student understands clearly the nature of his progress in various fields and the practical need for attaining higher levels of competency in them.

In conclusion, the field of secondary education today presents an opportunity for substantial and important improvement. Whether one looks at objectives and the content of instructional programs; methods and technology; or measurement, evaluation, and guidance, it is clear that a comprehensive development program based on present knowledge could improve greatly on present educational activities in our secondary schools. In all of these areas there are also critical research needs. The area of greatest need and of least current knowledge is that of educational objectives and the contents of the educational program. Research is required to develop a sound, factual basis for describing objectives. Each objective should be defined in terms of specific procedures to be used in evaluating the student's progress with respect to it. It is time that educational psychologists take an active part not only in the theoretical and laboratory aspects of secondary education but in practical applied work aimed directly at improving the total educational program in secondary schools.

REFERENCES

Flanagan, J. C. and others. *The Talents of American Youth. 1. Design for a Study of American Youth.* Boston: Houghton Mifflin, 1962.

Goldbeck, Robert A., and others. *Integrating Programmed Instruction With Conventional Classroom Teaching.* San Mateo, California: American Institute for Research, 1962.

Gropper, George L.; Lumsdaine, Arthur A.; and Shipman, Virginia I. C. *Studies in Televised Instruction: Report No. 1–Improvement of Televised Instruction Based on Student Responses to Achievement Tests.* Pittsburgh: American Institute for Research, March 1961.

Herzberg, Frederick I.; Mausner, Bernard; and Snyderman, Barbara B. *The Motivation to Work.* New York: John Wiley & Sons, Inc., 1959.

Torrance, E. Paul, and others. *Explorations in Creative Thinking in the Early School Years:* I-XII. Minneapolis: Bureau of Educational Research, University of Minnesota, 1959.

HIGH SCHOOLS FOR THE FUTURE

Robert J. Havighurst

In looking ahead at the future of secondary education in this country there are two possible positions which one may take. One is the position which stresses the *problems*—the schools in the slums of the big cities, and the small schools in the small villages. This is a familiar approach, but it is not the one I am going to take in this paper. The other is the position which stresses the *opportunities* of the high schools in a rapidly developing society. This latter is the approach I will follow.

This is an optimistic position. It assumes that we are solving our domestic problems of social integration and of metropolitan area cooperation between central city and suburbs. As we solve these problems, the future will present us more and more urgently the problem of the wise use of leisure, and the high schools will have the opportunity and the responsibility of contributing in a major way to resolving this problem.

There are two interrelated characteristics of our system of producing goods and services which result in an increase of free time and a growth in our ability to use free time wisely. The first is the remarkable increase in economic productivity due to automation and cybernation. The man-hour productivity in 1960 was three times that of 1900, in the United States. The American people elected to produce more goods and many new products with this increasing productivity. At the same time they elected to shorten the work week from about 60 to about 40 hours. Every American has more leisure (time free from work) than his grandfather had, if he wants leisure time. Nobody is forced by iron necessity to work as long as his grandfather did at the beginning of the century.

The second characteristic is the increasing ratio of white collar to manual workers. In the year 1956, the white collar workers first outnumbered the blue collar workers in the United States. Now white collar workers have a five to four preponderance over blue collar workers. With increased proportions of white collar workers goes more flexibility in the use of free time. For blue collar workers, as a general rule, free time is a time for rest and relaxation and the simplest forms of recreation. For white

From *Bulletin of the National Association of Secondary-School Principals,* LII, No. 328 (May, 1968), 117-125. Used by permission of the author and publisher.

collar workers there is a greater tendency to use free time in a variety of forms of action.

The various forms of action can be seen in three major categories:

Service—unpaid, freely chosen activities for the welfare of the family or the community
Study and Contemplation
Play—activities which are enjoyable in themselves.

THE GROWTH OF LEISURE

What people do with their free time is the major human concern of our society. How they use space is incidental to their use of time. Thus time is the arena or the stage on which the drama of human development unfolds in our society. Free time is a promontory of the future jutting into the present—a kind of concrete, present utopia. In Thomas More's Utopia, people worked only six hours a day. We have now reached that state.

The goal of a highly productive society is to set the stage for the wise consumption of the goods and services that the society produces. As the task of production is accomplished more and more fully, the task of consumption becomes more important and more complex. How shall we use our time and our resources in our highly productive society? This question dominates the situation.

With the present level of life expectancy, the present norm of retirement at about age 65, and the present length of the work year and the work week, the average American has something like *20 years of leisure* more than his grandfather had.

This leisure time may be used for a variety of kinds of *action,* some of which are more strenuous mentally or physically than most work is. We shall increasingly speak of higher and more liberal forms of work and action rather than of work and nonwork.

If the business of life is living, with work just one form of living, then the old ethic of work on which our society has rested since the Reformation must be replaced by a broader ethic of the use of time.

Any system of ethics must have standards of better or worse. Accordingly, we must develop standards of better or worse that apply to use of time. These standards will be more flexible, more varied than the ethical standards that have been developed to apply to work.

The new ethics of the use of time should include not only moral standards but also esthetic standards.

INSTRUMENTAL AND EXPRESSIVE EDUCATION

There are two basic aspects of education, both of which are essential for lifelong learning. They are the *instrumental* and the *expressive*. Instrumental education means education for a goal which lies outside and beyond the act of education. In this form, education is an instrument for changing the learner's situation. For example, the learner studies arithmetic so as to be able to exchange money and to buy and sell things and to become a competent scientist or teacher. Or the learner as a young adult studies in his vocational field so as to get a promotion, or studies cooking so as to become a better housewife. Instrumental education is thus a kind of investment of time and energy in the expectation of future gain.

Expressive education means education for a goal which lies within the act of learning or is so closely related to it that the act of learning appears to be the goal. For example, the learner studies arithmetic for the pleasure of learning about numbers and quantities. The learning of arithmetic is its own reward. Or the learner as a young adult studies the latest dances so as to enjoy the dances he and his friends go to. He learns to dance "for fun," and not to become a teacher of dancing or even to make new friends. Expressive education is a kind of consumption of time and energy for present gain.

In a changing society a competent person needs to make a combination of instrumental and expressive learning at every stage of his life.

He cannot confine learning to one or two stages of his life. Not long ago it was customary to divide the life cycle with a period of infancy and childhood for play, of childhood and adolescence for study, of adulthood for work, and old age for play again. Today nobody can live that way and be a competent member of contemporary society. Rather, the life cycle should be conceived of as a rope with parallel strands of play, study, and work each extending all the way through life, but with the work strand having greater thickness in adulthood, while the study and play strands have greater thickness in childhood and adolescence.

John Maynard Keynes, one of the great thinkers about the economics of a productive society during the present century, saw this coming when he wrote his essay on "Economic Possibilities for Our Grandchildren." Writing about the high school students of the next decade, he said, "It will be those people who can keep alive, and cultivate into fuller perfection, the art of life itself and do not sell themselves for the means of life who will be able to enjoy the abundance when it comes."

The high schools of the coming decade will be the principal instrument for these changes in the American way of life. This will result in major changes in the high school curriculum.

THE CURRICULUM AND EXPRESSIVE EDUCATION

We may expect a drastic shift in high school curricula which will tend to place the arts and humanities in balance with the sciences and mathematics. Just as the decade of the 1960's will go down in educational history as the decade when the instrumental aspects of the high school curriculum were reformed and strengtheded, the decade of the 1970's will come to stand for the strengthening of the expressive aspects of the high school curriculum.

As the curriculum develops, we will come to recognize a new type of successful student—the student with a high Expressive element. This person will be somewhat different from the highly Instrumental student who is the model of the successful student today. There will be four combinations of the Expressive and Instrumental factors, as shown in the following chart:

Expressive Values

		High	Low
	High	A	B
Instrumental *Values* }	Low	C	D

The C-type, high in Expressive and low in Instrumental values and attitudes, is one who will come into greater favor in the decade ahead.

"Innovations in the High Schools" was the topic of the April 1967 issue of *Nation's Schools*. This reported a national survey in 1966 of 7,237 accredited high schools by the North Central Association of Colleges and Secondary Schools, to find out what innovations had recently been made. A list of 27 innovations was used in checklist form. Of eight curriculum innovations, seven were in science or mathematics and one was titled "Humanities Course." There were seven technological innovations, all of instrumental character. There were twelve innovations in the category of organization. Only one of them was clearly expressive in character, namely "Cultural Enrichment Programs," but some others would lend themselves to expressive activity, including "flexible scheduling," "honor study halls," "optional class attendance," and "student exchange program." Thirty-one percent of the schools reported that they had introduced cultural enrichment programs, while 18 percent reported that they had a humanities course, combining instruction in art, music, literature, photography, and history.

The coming upsurge of interest in the arts and humanities is not yet visible in this kind of survey, but it is seen clearly in the current grants being made by the U.S. Office of Education under Title III of the

Elementary and Secondary Education Act. A strikingly high proportion of these grants are going for cultural enrichment programs.

ESTHETIC STANDARDS AND EXPRESSIVE EDUCATION

A controversy will no doubt develop among the leaders of expressive education over the extent to which the arts and humanities can be taught effectively to the mass of high school students. What is the place of esthetic standards in such a program? This writer's view is that esthetic standards can and should be taught, but also that esthetic standards will evolve through the experience of many people with a variety of ways of using their free time.

However, there will be people who contend that high school courses in the arts and humanities should be limited to a minority of students who demonstrate a high level of skill or appreciation in these courses. This was illustrated in a conference on *Humanities and the Schools* held in 1965 at the University of Kentucky, under the chairmanship of Harold Taylor. One group of speakers, including the chairman, argued that all kinds of students can and should participate in the arts and in creative activities. There were others who insisted on the importance of maintaining standards. For example, Stanley Kauffmann, the film critic, said:

In this matter it is important to start with a clear, unsentimentalized view, free of democratic fallacies. A very small proportion of any country's population has at any time had a strong interest in art. I think it is a dangerous mistake to assume, as a dynamics in the teaching of humanities, that that proportion must be increased. If it happened to be increased, that would be lovely. What is much more important is, first, that it be maintained and, second, be continually refined. . . .

I am much more concerned with the touching of the few who will respond to art than with dabbling every member of the class with a little art vaccine. Of course one cannot reliably know in advance who the responsive few will be, and therefore the approach must be to the whole class. What I am concerned with is the intent of the approach; so that when those few are reached, they are given help instead of—as often happens—hindrance that may take years to overcome. It is culturally more important that those few get some glimmer of the mysteries and un-certainties of art than that the majority be given a few facile certainties to make them feel they have a grip on the subject.

Edgar Friedenberg, a facile critic of public education, argues that all

youth could enjoy and participate in the arts, if only the educational
establishment would permit it. He says:

What I want to see happen is for youngsters to experience the private
vision that any one, to the degree that he is an artist, must start with; the
discipline, derived from the properties of his medium and from the nature
of the available symbols, to which the artist must submit; and the growth
and development of that vision under discipline. But a public school,
socializing young Americans to enjoy the Great Society, is not a very
promising *ambiance* in which to try to bring this confrontation about.

The American society offers major resources for the pleasurable use of
free time that are now in full course of development. These are: the
outdoors, television, the performing arts, and a fourth agency, the National
Foundation for the Arts and Humanities.

1. Use of the Outdoors

As the population increases and society becomes more urbanized, the
outdoors will become increasingly precious as a leisure-time resource; at the
same time, the outdoors will be increasingly threatened by the incursions
of urbanism and technology. Air and water polution threaten to make the
outdoors unsafe in many areas. Industrial exploitation of rivers, lakeshore,
seashore, and mineral deposits endanger the recreational use of the
outdoors.

There is need for a clear statement of the functions of leisure activity
and a policy of using the outdoors to serve these functions. Three
functions of leisure in a crowded urban society are:

● to give isolation, at times, amid the shoving and sprinting and raucous
activities of the city
● to reduce nervous tensions, through an effective combination of
physical with mental activity
● to provide a setting for the experience of awe and reverence for things
that are not man-made.

2. Television

Mr. Lee Loevinger, a member of the Federal Communications Commission,
told the twentieth convention of the New Jersey Broadcasters Association:

It seems to me that television is the literature of the illiterate, the
culture of the low-born, the wealth of the poor, the privilege of the

underprivileged, the exclusive club of the excluded masses. . . . Television is a golden goose that lays scrambled eggs. And it is futile and probably fatal to beat it for not laying caviar. Anyway, more people like scrambled eggs than caviar.

This view of TV as an element in the mass culture will be challenged as the federal government moves to establish "public television" which will be separate from the advertising business. The Carnegie Corporation comments:

What commercial television cannot do because of its need to reach mass audiences, noncommercial television cannot do because it lacks the money, facilities, and personnel. Hence in the technologically most advanced society in the history of man, the greatest technological device for informing, delighting, inspiring, amusing, provoking, and entertaining remains pitiably unexploited, and the American public is the loser.

With the Ford Foundation also interested in making noncommercial television a force for better use of free time, it is clear that there will be a public television network financed at a level of at least $100 million a year. This network will assist the 124 existing educational television stations and will provide programs that go beyond the bounds of what is ordinarily called educational television.

3. The Performing Arts

It is generally claimed that there has been a kind of "cultural explosion" in the United States since World War II. The number of symphony orchestras has doubled in 20 years, to a total of more than 1,400. The number of groups presenting opera doubled to 754 in the decade before 1964. Much of this growth was in the amateur sector. Of 1,401 symphony orchestras, only 54 were composed predominantly of professional musicians. Two economists looked at the phenomenon with a critical eye and concluded that much of the increase between 1946 and 1963 was because of growth in population and increase in prices as well as in real income, rather than because of increased interest in the arts compared with interest in other activities. It is concluded that substantial subsidy from the federal government is needed to give the performing arts the kind of development they deserve.

4. National Foundation for the Arts and Humanities

The bill that was signed into law on September 29, 1965, may go down in history as the most important piece of legislation for that year and perhaps for that decade. Thus the national government acknowledged responsibility for the state of the arts and for the functioning of the arts in the improvement of the mass culture. Before that time, a number of states had set up State Councils on the Arts with programs that included sponsoring touring groups in the performing arts, art exhibitions, conferences on music, and providing technical assistance to local community groups that supported museums, galleries, theater, and music groups. While the amounts of money provided for the State Councils have been modest and the budget of the Foundation for the Arts and Humanities is only $12 million in its second year, the money has already set in motion some promising programs.

The level of federal government support for the performing arts will certainly advance to at least $100 million a year within the next decade, and this will support work in major regional centers in addition to assisting the State Councils in their programs.

THE HIGH SCHOOLS AND THEIR RESOURCES

The high schools will be related to leisure-time resources in two ways. First, the schools will make increasing use of them. Especially in the area of the performing arts, we will find the high schools taking a big part in the spread of active participation in local musical and dramatic activities. Wherever there is an adult theater or chorus or orchestra, we will find the high school carrying on a youth theater or chorus or symphony, as a junior version and a preparation for adult participation.

Second, the schools will be studying the matter of social policies for use of leisure. Young people will be getting ready to act as citizens on behalf of conservation of recreational areas. They will be advising their Congressmen about government appropriations for public television and for the National Foundation for the Arts and Humanities. The wise and pleasurable use of leisure will become recognized as a major social goal in the United States, to be studied and discussed by high school students as part of their preparation for citizenship.

EDUCATION OF ADOLESCENTS: 1985

Kimball Wiles

Although it is possible that schools in 1985 will be used as instruments of thought control and social classification, the writer, nevertheless, is optimistic enough to believe there will continue to be a social commitment to freedom, creativity and equality of opportunity. With this basic assumption, an attempt is made in the following statement to project the changes that technological advances and social problems will produce.

PURPOSES AND PROGRAM—1985

Planners of the education for adolescents hope that each pupil will: (a) develop a set of values that will guide his behavior; (b) acquire the skills necessary to participate effectively in the culture; (c) gain understanding of the social, economic, political and scientific heritage; and (d) become able to make a specialized contribution to the society.

The program of the school is designed to promote these goals and is divided into four phases: (a) analysis of experiences and values; (b) acquisition of fundamental skills; (c) exploration of the cultural heritage; and (d) specialization and creativity.

ANALYSIS OF EXPERIENCES AND VALUES

In the school each pupil spends six hours a week in an Analysis Group. With ten other pupils of his own age and a skilled teacher-counselor he discusses any problem of ethics, social concern, out-of-school experience, or implication of knowledge encountered in another class he or any student brings to the group. No curriculum is established in advance. The exploration of questions, ideas or values advanced by group members constitutes the primary type of experience.

The purpose of the Analysis Group is to help each pupil discover

From the *Educational Leadership*, XVII, No. 8 (May, 1960), 480-483 and 489. Used by permission of the publisher.

meaning, to develop increased commitment to a set of values, to provide opportunity to examine the conflicts among the many sets of values and viewpoints held by members of the society.

The membership of an Analysis Group is carefully selected to provide persons of relatively equal intellectual ability but varied social and economic values. The group remains as a unit throughout its high school program. Changes are made only when deep emotional conflict develops between students or between a student and the teacher-counselor.

The teachers of Analysis Groups are emotionally mature people. They were selected early in their teacher education program because they displayed a high degree of empathy and were warm, outgoing personalities that other people liked. They were given special training in counseling, communication and value analysis. Each has been taught to see his role as helping others feel more secure, clarify their values, and communicate more effectively with their colleagues. If a teacher of an Analysis Group attempts to sell his viewpoint, he is considered unsuccessful and is replaced.

Each Analysis Group teacher meets three groups, or 33 students, during the week. His time beyond the 18 hours in the discussion groups is for individual counseling with the 33 pupils and their parents.

The Analysis Group is considered the basic element of the educational program. In the sixties it was recognized that unless citizens had values they accepted, understood and could apply, the social structure would begin to disintegrate unless authoritarian controls were applied. To counter the danger of collapse of a democratic way of life, the school was assigned the task of making as sure that each child develop a set of values as that he could read. The Analysis Group evolved as the best means of performing the values development function.

ACQUISITION OF FUNDAMENTAL SKILLS

Citizens in 1985 must have fundamental skills far superior to those necessary in the late fifties to be considered literate.

In the home and in the elementary school, children learn to read, spell and compute at their own rate of learning by the use of teaching machines. In the school for adolescents, mathematics, foreign languages and many scientific processes and formulas are taught by machines supervised by librarians and a staff of technicians.

It has been proven that the machines can teach basic skills as effectively and efficiently as a human. The work of Skinner and of persons working with foreign language laboratories in the late fifties paved the way for this development. All the activities needed for teaching all fundamental skills have been programmed.

Each student planning a high school program is told the skills he must master. He works through the needed program as rapidly as he can. When he wants to work on a skill, he goes to the librarian, schedules a machine and a program and goes to work.

Certain skills are needed by all citizens, and each adolescent's program includes the requirement that these skills be acquired. Other skills are considered vocational in nature and are added to a student's program if he indicates he has college entrance or a specific vocation as a goal.

Some students complete their basic skills work early in their high school program. Others work on them until they leave the high school.

Two librarians, one to issue programs and the other to help on request, and a staff of mechanical technicians supervise the work of 200 students. Disorder is at a minimum because each person works on his own level and on his purposes. Moreover, each student works in his own soundproofed cubicle.

The teaching machines laboratories for the various subject matter areas, mathematics, languages, grammar, are an integral part of the Materials Center of the School.

EXPLORATION OF THE CULTURAL HERITAGE

The explosion of available knowledge in the first three quarters of the twentieth century confronts educators with the need for selecting, synthesizing, interpreting and seeking better methods of transmitting it. The things that an effective citizen needs to know in 1985 are a multiple of the knowledge necessary in 1960. Textbooks with less than master teachers are not enough, and ways of bringing each student into a working relationship with the best teachers available have been sought. Basic knowledge from the essential fields is prepared in the most easily understood media and presented as dramatically and forcefully as possible. This knowledge from the humanities, the social sciences, and the physical and biological sciences is considered the Cultural Heritage.

Roughly a third of the program of each high school student is designed to help him acquire the basic knowledge of his culture. By exposure to the experiences, ideas, and discoveries of the past, it is hoped that the individual will become literate enough about the basic ideas of his culture to participate in discussions of them or to understand reference to them. It is further hoped that the experience in the Cultural Heritage portion of the program will develop a desire to futher enhance the values on which the society is based.

Classes in the Cultural Heritage program are large. Sometimes as many as 500 or 1000 are in a single section.

Teaching is by television, films or a highly skilled lecturer. No provision is made for discussion because ideas that produce a response can be discussed in the Analysis Groups.

Only one teacher and an assistant are needed in each subject matter field in each school. The teacher lectures or presents the material by an appropriate medium. The assistant prepares quizzes and examinations and records the marks made on the machine scored tests.

The high pupil-teacher ratio in the Cultural Heritage area, 1 teacher for each 500 to 1500 students, makes possible the low ratio, 1 to 33, for Analysis Groups and highly individual instruction for the exceptional student.

Teachers for the Cultural Heritage program are selected early in their teacher education program. They speak well, like to be before an audience, have a sense for the dramatic and are attractive persons. In addition to intensive work in their field. they are given work in speech, dramatics, logic, and mass media.

SPECIALIZATION AND CREATIVITY

The Analysis Groups, the Cultural Heritage Courses, and the Fundamental Skills work constitute the program required of all. But, in addition, each student is encouraged to develop a specialization. It is not required, but the opportunity is presented.

Shops, studios and working laboratories are available for specialized activities. All students who wish are encouraged to engage in some creative activities since the Cultural Heritage phase of the program is essentially a passive reception.

Writing laboratories are staffed to help students who want to develop creative writing ability. School newspapers, magazines and telecasts are writted in the laboratories.

Other students select work experience in various industries and businesses in the community. These students have decided they will not seek higher education and are using their specialized program to insure a smooth transition to regular employment.

Special opportunities are available for the persons who qualify in terms of ability and intensity of purpose.

Seminars in the various content fields, and some of an interdisciplinary nature, are available for those who can qualify. Students must have displayed unusual ability and show evidence of a desire for individual investigation in a field before they are permitted to enroll.

Seminars are limited to 15 students. They meet for two two-hour periods per week and the remainder of the time the students conduct independent research in the library or laboratories.

Small laboratories are kept open for full time use by the individual researchers from the seminars. In fact, students who are not expected to become scientists or technicians in an area do not use laboratory facilities. Laboratory experience was abandoned as a general education procedure in the mid-sixties.

In the specialized fields the pupil-teacher ratio is low, 1 to 40 or 50 pupils. Teachers give individualized supervision and plan with the Analysis Group teachers the experiences individuals should have.

No longer do the colleges blame the secondary schools for inadequate preparation. Graduation days have been eliminated. Students continue to work in the secondary school until they pass their college entrance examinations or move to a job. Most students enter the secondary school at 13, but some leave at 15 and others at 20. A student's decision to leave the program is conditioned by his completion of the Cultural Heritage experiences, his acquisition of fundamental skills, and his individual purposes.

THE SCHOOL PLANT

The school plant has many different sized rooms. Analysis groups, specialized education classrooms, studios and laboratories are small. Cultural Heritage courses are held in large halls equipped for lectures and mass media programs. Libraries and studios and shops are large. Areas where individuals work with teaching machines to perfect basic skills are divided into small work cubicles. Buildings with uniform size classrooms are obsolete.

BASIS OF SUPPORT

The program described above is paid for from federal funds. It was recognized in the late sixties that, with a population as mobile as ours, neither local communities nor the national government could afford to allow the great differences in educational opportunity to continue. No community was immune to poor education in another and the national government was thus neglecting a large percentage of its human resources.

EVOLUTION OF THE PROGRAM

The program was not achieved without some difficult struggles. Many voices arose in the late fifties and early sixties clamoring for a copying of a European educational system. Some wanted to use tests and allocate the pupil to a specialized curriculum as early as ten years of age and give him the required courses the experts deemed suitable for him. They proposed restricting the curriculum of the secondary school to the intellectual pursuit of information in certain areas of knowledge. Values and social development were to be left to the home and church.

However, increasing juvenile delinquency, more homes with both parents working, increasing mental and emotional disturbance could not be ignored. The secondary school program had to be made broad enough to deal with values, human relations, fundamental skills in communication, the cultural heritage, as well as work in a student's special field.

WHICH WAY TO A CURRICULUM FOR ADOLESCENTS?

Fred T. Wilhelms

Do you want to know which way the secondary schools are going to move? The best signs to look for are the forces abuilding in our society.

In the 1950's those forces created a drive for "excellence"—interpreted to mean rigorous intellectual achievement for the abler students (largely disregarding the rest). The definition narrowed still further when our political leaders chose to save face about Sputnik by charging that the schools had not produced enough scientists and engineers. Within a year NDEA pronounced its prescription: more science, mathematics, and foreign language, again chiefly for the elite.

From *NEA Journal,* LVI, No. 9 (December, 1967), 12-15. Used by permission of the author and publisher.

But the attempt to ignore the masses and to exclude everything but a few "pure" intellectual disciplines promptly failed. By 1962 the tide was beginning to turn. And today two sets of forces are rising to such power that the curriculum simply must respond to them.

1. The American people are intensely concerned about the dropout, the culturally deprived, and every kind of disadvantaged youngster. Large-scale unemployment of youth—with the prospect of more—looms grimly before the public eye. The stark tragedy of millions sinking into lives of ignorance, misery, and hatred has become unbearable. And there is a massive determination to use the schools to create a new break for this "society of losers."

2. A fundamental revolution is rocking the thought and value systems of the younger generation. A powerful force in itself, it is reinforced by adult fear. Although the rebellion may be easiest to see in the colleges (and not at Berkeley alone), it affects the secondary schools as well. It is easy to lampoon because of its fringe manifestations of long hair, hippie dress, and the like. Some may be tempted to rule that it affects only a small, visible minority; but any sensitive observer must see far more than this: a profoundly disturbed generation of idealistic youth in search of values to live by, many of them so alienated by the adult society that they can find almost nothing in it to commit themselves to. And the pressure from their uneasiness is accentuated because, at bottom, many adults feel the same way.

Of course, many other forces are operating—far too many to treat in a brief article. But I believe these two are about to reshape American secondary education. And I believe they will hit hardest upon vocational education, the social studies, and a new humanities program.

EDUCATION FOR WORK

When the public began worrying about youngsters who do badly at school, who drop out, whose out-of-school prospects are dim, it swung easily to the question, "What can the schools really do to help these youngsters get their toe in the economic door?"

And then came the quick answer: *more vocational education.* When Congress passed the radically new Vocational Education Act of 1963, it not only added hundreds of millions in funds but also "opened up" the whole structure to encourage a great diversity of offerings. It backed *area vocational technical schools,* which are being built by the hundreds. Enrollments have risen steadily and offerings are expanding.

Clearly, further great expansion of vocational education is one of the signal changes coming up. So far, only about 15 percent of our students have been directly involved; the future may see that percentage doubled or tripled. So far we have concentrated on a narrow part of the total spectrum of jobs and students—a "middle stripe" in each case. Now we have an almost entirely new task: to develop appropriate vocational preparation for the less able, less aspiring students—simple preparation for simple jobs. This is crucial, for without our help *they may never get any job at all.*

It will be easy enough—though expensive—to add skills-oriented courses in a new variety of fields. But as we do it, we must keep a weather eye on other demands that hit workers in a high technology. In more and more jobs success depends on intellectual problem solving, the ability to communicate, and the ability to work as part of a team. Besides, change comes so fast that the ability to swing with it is crucial.

Lack of skills, furthermore, is a long way from being the whole story. Particularly among the hardest-to-salvage group, many of whom are frustrated and angry, the most damaging deficits are often poor attitudes toward work and toward authority, and lack of grooming and manners.

Thus, I predict that while vocational education is going to have a far larger role than ever in both junior and senior high school, simple skill training will not prove to be enough for the disadvantaged, whose needs are going to push us into much broader curriculum reform on their behalf. Work experience programs will probably place increasing emphasis on communication skills, citizenship, and general personal development.

In working with these young people, I believe we shall find great use for group counseling and even something akin to group therapy. Consumer education will be a valuable ally, to help disadvantaged youngsters reconsider their whole life style. There will be tremendous creative ferment in this entire area. And what starts as simple occupational preparation will reach out in a determined effort to raise the standards of life of a group who have had to live too meagerly.

EDUCATION FOR CITIZENSHIP

Any sensitive reading of the problems now rising to crescendo in our society leads automatically to a call for citizenship education geared to those problems. Our great cities, dying at the core, face nothing less than a struggle for survival. Pollutions of many sorts rise like a stench. Two great races suffer the agonies of a tragic confrontation that need never have occurred. The problems go on and on. But we also have enormous, unprecedented resources. The times cry out for inspired, creative action by a citizenry competent enough and devoted ·enough to plunge boldly into intricate, realistic, lasting reform.

But the production of that citizenry is not proceeding very healthily. At least among the urban lower classes—and especially within the slum-bound minority peoples—hostility to the whole "system" smoulders ominously, bursting all too often into flames of violence. Among middle- and upper-class youth a different sort of questioning—sometimes even revulsion—grips the minds of many. Both youth and adults are often overwhelmed by the sheer bigness of our system, and few citizens feel that they can do much about it. A questioning attitude may not be all to the bad—and, even if it were, the schools should not accept more than their share of blame. But certainly a basic commitment to constructive action is essential, and that does not flourish in a mood of alienation, bitterness, or helplessness. We absolutely must build a revitalized social studies program that gets at the harsh realities as our youngsters see them.

We must, but will we? I do not know. We have been stuck for decades with a program of history which, despite all the fine words, is still mostly a chronology of political and military events; and of civics, which is mostly a description of the dry bones of government. The whole thing is largely out of touch with the real agenda of our times. It is powerfully entrenched and has great inertia. And the cold fact is that very few schools possess a good enough system of either needs analysis or decision making to do much more than tinker with a piece at a time.

At one level there is tremendous ferment for the sweeping social studies reorganization we have to have. More than 40 curriculum projects are at work.* They offer a great range of organizational schemes and instructional materials. But much as one hates to argue against the riches of diversity, the fact is that their efforts are badly scattered and fragmented. No one group, no one set of ideas, has yet emerged into the commanding position it would need in order to effect so fundamental a change. There is no concerted leadership. There is not even general agreement that citizenship *is* their goal. Some projects are working aggressively for a mobilized citizenship education, but more are interested only in the intellectual refinement of their fields.

Anyway, there is yet to emerge a compelling program with the smell of sweat and hot asphalt pavement. Given the inertia of the present system

---

*See "The 'New' Social Studies" in the November 1967 Journal for discussion of some of these projects.

and the pulling and hauling among the leadership, we may achieve little more than to polish the existing pieces.

Still, the harsh exigencies of our time will continue to push us; our students' powerful urge for relevance will continue to pull. Together they may show the present program up for the expensive futility it is. We just *might* swing a real analysis of the agenda of our day—and then launch a concerted, problem-solving attack on the needs it reveals.

The resources are at hand. For the first time in history we have at least the beginnings of genuine science in such areas as sociology, economics, political science, geography, social and cultural anthropology, and history itself. The crucial question is whether we decide that *the social studies are for citizenship.* If we do, then we can bring the sciences to bear on the lives of people.

Whether we win or lose, the *effort* to shape up a citizenship education that counts is going to be one of the major priorities of the decade—because it has to be.

EDUCATION FOR HUMANITY

If there is widespread discombobulation among our youth, viewed as prospective citizens, there is even deeper turmoil within many of them in terms of their private thoughts and feelings. They have grown up in an anxious, turbulent time, when values old in the history of mankind have suddenly come into question. The problem is not peculiar to them—it is shared by many adults—but with some special sensitivity and with the all-or-none quality characteristic of youthful idealism, they have opened it up most completely.

The surge of questioning and questing is too powerful to be ignored if the schools mean to be relevant. It goes to the very center of the person and the ultimate significance of life. On the negative side there is much rootlessness, anomie, rejection, and something like nihilism. There is a kind of desperation that makes the lonely bleakness of existentialism congenial. There is enough sheer disgust and anger to erupt into bizarre-seeming forms of rebellion. But on the positive side there is an idealistic search for something better, a brave and honest quest for values to live by. Sometimes it seems that youth feel that, all by themselves, they must start *de novo* to hammer out a new morality, a new way of living.

Sensitive curriculum makers simply must respond to this great surge, which represents a tremendous opportunity. Our main resource lies in the humanities. And I predict that for the next decade the fashioning of a meaningful humanities program will be one of the great preoccupations of the secondary schools.

The development is already under way. A few hundred high schools now speak of themselves as having a "humanities program." But what most of them refer to is one course in the senior year, and that often for only an elite. And many of them have fallen into the trap of merely "teaching more about" literature and the arts—a sort of great-books-cum-great-art course in "cultural" erudition.

We shall be driven far beyond that. I am convinced that we shall soon be viewing the humanities as a broad, integrated stream running through all the years. We shall have to reach beyond the aesthetics of art, music, and literature to incorporate behavioral sciences like psychology and social anthropology and perhaps much from history.

The job will not be easy. It will call for a new setting and a new way of teaching, for the humanities cannot be "learned," linear fashion, as science is learned. The goal is not to "know about" literature, for example, but to live with it, soak in it, build out of it richer perceptions of mankind and of life and of one's own personal purposes. What we are after here is the very best of the long tradition of *liberal education:* to help a young person shape himself with the best aids that the race possesses.

Frankly, there is little in the works so far to justify a prediction that all this will happen. Nevertheless, I so predict that it will be the greatest of all curricular surges in the years ahead for the simple reason that the pressures building up in our youth will force it to be.

What I have tried to convey in this all-too-compressed statement is that secondary program development is going to be dominated by rising needs and pressures among our adolescents. The children of the poor face so frightening a risk of not being able to earn a decent living that just helping them make an entry into the world of work has to be an overriding consideration. Vocational education is not all they need, but they do need it, in a form that fits. In this respect the children of the middle and upper classes are different, for no group in history has ever had so bright an economic future as they have.

But this is about the *only* way in which the fundamental needs of the groups differ. As future citizens, all of them are moving into a society which has to solve some crucial problems—and solve them fast—to survive. And all of them have grave doubts about the system we have—some to the point of revulsion and hostility; all need help to learn to attack the real agenda of our day.

Yet, even more fundamentally, all the youth of our day are growing into an age of uncertainty about themselves and about their significance.

Without quite knowing what has hit them, they are unsure about ethical values old in the history of man, about religion, about the relation of man to man. They are threshing about, often in crudely rebellious or even bizarre ways; but the important thing is that they are *searching*, impelled by a fine idealism and a relentless honesty. They deserve our help. And to give it to them we shall have to shuck off a lot of scholastic impedimenta and go to where a young person meets the realities of adulthood.

QUESTIONS FOR DISCUSSION
HIGH SCHOOL

1. What is a high school? What are its unique characteristics?
2. Why do authorities recommend a comprehensive high school? By what criteria would you determine whether a high school was comprehensive?
3. What changes are taking place in the program of the high school? What influences have produced the modifications?
4. What are the implications of recent research in secondary education? What is project TALENT?
5. What portion of the student's high school program should be elective? How much freedom of choice should he have?
6. What types of growth should the high school seek to promote? What priority should be established among them?
7. What non-class activities are appropriately a part of the high school curriculum? What is the function of a non-class activity?
8. How should work experience be included in the high school curriculum? For whom should it be provided? What outcomes should be sought?
9. How should the high school curriculum be changed to provide better education for disadvantaged youth? For the non-college bound high school student?
10. What is your evaluation of the non-graded high school?
11. Will independent study be important in efforts to improve high school programs?
12. Do you see any advantages in the program at Nova High School that might be utilized at other high schools?
13. What should the high school of the future be like? Which arrangements do you prefer: Those proposed by Havighurst, Wiles or Wilhelms?
14. Try using the bases and criteria presented in Sections 1-5 for evaluating the Nova High program.
15. What are the objectives, as you view them, of the programs proposed by Havighurst, Wiles and Wilhelms? Are there differences among them in this respect?

9 Community College

A new educational institution, the community college, has become a major element of the American system of free public education. It evolved from the junior college, but it has been designed to serve many more social purposes.

The community college serves the community with an adult education program in a variety of fields. It provides a college-parallel program for those who wish to transfer to four year colleges or universities after two years. It offers terminal education in many vocational, technical, and commercial subjects for those who will go no further in formal education programs. A number of states have developed master plans to provide community colleges within commuting distance of all high school graduates.

The community college has grown from one serving a limited number of students to the present vision of providing education for all youth not in four year colleges and for many adults and senior citizens. This development is described by Clyde E. Blocker ("Comprehensive Community College").

The terminal programs vary from community to community. Usually they are determined by the kinds of vocational and technical competencies needed by the area in which the college is located. Alfred W. Nall ("What About 'Terminal' General Education in the Junior Colleges?") raises the unresolved question of the amount and type of general education that should be provided in the terminal program.

N. H. Frank ("Changing Requirements for Technical Education") believes that technical education should prepare people to function in a group of operations rather than for specific technical competence. He believes that two years are not enough for preparation in many technical education fields.

The community college is rapidly beginning to assume its role as a dynamic force in the community it serves. Ervin Harlacher ("New Directions in Community Services") predicts seven directions which community services will take in the decade ahead. He cites examples in which community colleges are already meeting community needs by offering a variety of services to all age groups.

William Moore ("Opening The College Gates to the Low Achiever"), after identifying himself as a two-time high school dropout and as third from the last in his undergraduate college class, describes the general curriculum for the educationally disadvantaged at Forest Park Community College of St. Louis, where he is Associate Dean. Students assigned to this program are in the lower third of their high school classes at graduation and at the tenth percentile or below on the School and College Ability Tests. Each course is organized around five broad headings: orientation, self, self and society, human relations, and values.

In spite of the rapid growth and acceptance of the American community college there are still unresolved problems. The article by John Kuhlman ("The Dilemma of the Junior College") deals with various facets of problems facing these colleges.

Alvin C. Eurich ("Higher Education in the 21st Century") examines community colleges and all other types of higher education as if he were looking from the year 2000 and describes the development he anticipates.

What this institution will become is not yet known. But the social forces presented in Section One give some strong clues. More than any other portion of the public school curriculum, the community college curriculum is being shaped by the current planners. They have the opportunity to plan in the light of objectives sought, and all curriculum bases and criteria.

COMPREHENSIVE COMMUNITY COLLEGE

Clyde E. Blocker

The typical case studies reported below (actual cases with the names changed) demonstrate that the comprehensive community college is the

From *NEA Journal*, LI, No. 6 (September, 1962), 20-21. Used by permission of the author and publisher.

solution to the educational problems of these students and many others who cannot or will not enter four-year colleges after graduation from high school.

What is the comprehensive community college? It is a community centered, locally controlled and supported post-high school institution dedicated to serving the educational needs of all individuals in the community through comprehensive curriculum guidance programs and community services.

In most states, community colleges are supported by a combination of funds from state aid, local taxes, and student tuition. These colleges strive to keep student costs as low as possible so that expense will not be a barrier to attendance. Further, the community college is located near its students so that their living costs can be further minimized.

The community college makes a unique contribution to education beyond high school in a number of ways. First, the college has an open-door policy of admissions; it welcomes all students who can profit from its program. As the three cases cited here illustrate, the community college admits students who otherwise might never have had a chance for higher education. And it offers a broad curriculum from which both the academically talented and the nonacademic, vocationally oriented student can profit.

Second, the college not only utilizes the resources of the community for teaching and learning, as in the case of Jane, but it is also responsive to community needs for trained workers.

Third, the community college offers opportunities for individuals of all ages and degrees of educational and personal development to grow as people without traditional limitations on programs. There are 314,527 part-time and adult students in community colleges.

Community colleges serve a more heterogeneous population than is generally found in four-year institutions. A comprehensive three-year study by Leland Medsker published in 1960 shows that forty-seven percent of 13,300 community college students were twenty-three and over; sixteen percent were thirty years of age and over. In six community colleges, twenty-three percent of the students were married.

The student population in community colleges is also more heterogeneous with regard to academic ability than the four-year college population. Medsker's data showed a lower average cutoff score in 1952 on the American Council on Education Psychological Examination for students entering community college. However, approximately thirty percent of the students entering community colleges could have qualified for entrance at universities or four-year colleges.

Further, the socioeconomic background of community college students is more largely middle class and lower middle class than the background of students in four-year colleges. A study of male students in a large metropolitan community college showed that sixty-seven percent of the students' parents were foremen, craftsmen, operatives, household workers, service workers, and laborers, and that eighty-six percent of the students had already exceeded the educational level of their parents.

One of the striking facts consistently cited by such studies is the upward social and economic mobility of community college students from families in semi-skilled and unskilled occupational categories and from the lower middle class.

Community college students give a number of significant reasons for attending a local institution. A follow-up study of several thousand students over four years showed that the majority (seventy percent) thought it was cheaper than attending a residential college; forty-three percent said they could not go to college if the community college had not been located in the city; twenty percent wanted to continue working; sixteen percent wanted to see if they could do college work; and twelve percent wanted a two-year course.

Thus economic factors have a strong bearing upon the opportunity to attend college, and the community college, because of its low costs, encourages college attendance. The college is also a strong force in encouraging students who are not sure of themselves to attempt college work.

The comprehensive community college is truly an opportunity school. Though it is a relative newcomer to American public education, it is already contributing extensively to the advancement of our people. The community college is offering Americans a new kind of educational adventure, and they are utilizing this opportunity in rapidly increasing numbers.

CASE NUMBER ONE

Charles has three younger brothers and a younger sister. His father is a bookkeeper and his mother is a housewife. His high school grades were only average although his IQ was 121 and he had scored above average on standardized aptitude and achievement tests.

Charles' parents encouraged him to continue his studies in college even though they could not afford to send him to the state university. He enrolled at the local community college where he made a C average the first year and a B— average the third semester. Charles was active in student government during his sophomore year, and in the course of participating in this activity, he met Mr. McIntyre, the student government sponsor. The relationship between teacher and student tended to draw Charles out of his shell. His grades improved markedly, as did his ability to work co-operatively with others.

Charles has now been accepted at a state college, where he hopes to complete a program in accounting and management. He has been able to save some money from his part-time job; these earnings, combined with some help from his parents, will make it possible for him to pay most of his expenses during his junior year. He is not certain whether he will have sufficient funds to complete his senior year, but he is not concerned about this problem.

CASE NUMBER TWO

Jane graduated from high school with Charles. She had difficulty with mathematics, English, and history, but did work that was average or above in those subjects which required less abstract thought and more class participation and personal social skills. Her parents were willing to send her to the state university, but she did not want to go.

The summer after high school graduation, Jane took a part-time job at a local women's clothing shop and was quite successful at the work. Mrs. Wilson, the proprietress, became interested in her new employee and late in the summer suggested to Jane that she enroll in the cooperative retailing program at the community college. Jane was somewhat reluctant to do so but agreed when Mrs. Wilson said she could continue working in the store part-time.

Jane had difficulty with the required general education courses, especially English, but she has done above average work in retailing and related courses. She will graduate at the end of two semesters and one summer session and then she plans to work full-time in Mrs. Wilson's dress shop.

CASE NUMBER THREE

Mrs. Mary C was sixty-seven years old when she began her college work. She had graduated from high school forty-eight years before and for three years after graduation had worked as a secretary to earn money in order to take nurses' training. She finished this training in 1910. She married in 1916 and subsequently had three daughters. After her husband died in 1923, she supported her family by working as a nurse until all the children were educated and self-supporting.

Upon retirement, Mary found that she had too much time on her hands and, as a result, life was boring and meaningless. She decided to enter the community college to take some courses and keep busy. After the first semester, stimulated by the faculty and fellow students, she decided to continue her studies. At the end of two years she received an Associate in Arts degree with honors. She then was admitted to the state university, where she continued her studies and obtained an A.B. degree after three semesters and one summer session.

WHAT ABOUT "TERMINAL" GENERAL EDUCATION IN THE JUNIOR COLLEGES?

Alfred W. Nall

For purposes of this discussion and for lack of a better word, the word "terminal," as applied to junior college general education, is defined in the following manner. It is a type and quality of college education which is intrinsically immediate in its appeal, its usefulness, and benefit to the participant. If "terminal" can be interpreted to mean "end," then the only connotation of "end" which is applicable here is that which implies that the type of education under discussion is valid in and of itself, and thus is an "end" in itself without specific reference to its positional value in a sequence of prescribed education—formal or otherwise.

"Terminal" general education's distinctive quality derives from the fact that it is designed to fit the characteristics of a specific group of students; to include knowledge, skills, and practice for living in a democratic society; to provide a particularly pertinent course content; to utilize the most appropriate study materials; to apply the most effective methods of instruction; to place special emphasis upon artistry in teaching; to diversify evaluation of student growth and achievement. It is college education that deviates from the traditional, the classical, and the preparatory in the sense that lower division courses must prepare for upper division courses.

For any particular individual, this type of college education takes into account the fact that he may terminate his formal, in-school study at any given time; therefore, the educational experiences in each course should

From *Junior College Journal,* XXXIII, No. 1 (September, 1962), 20–24. Used by permission of the author and publisher.

emphasize the relatedness and significance of the subject matter to various aspects of the student's immediate environment—personal, social, civic, and economic. For a democratic society, it is college education which should contribute to the extension of the social, civic, and occupational maturity of the majority of its citizenry.

The specific group of college students for whom "terminal" education is designed includes an ever-increasing number of those who graduate from high school with aspiration for post-high school education of some type, but whose level of scholastic aptitude is such as to raise doubts, based upon statistical evidence, as to their likelihood of succeeding in graduating from a typical four-year college or university. It has been estimated at various times that a student should demonstrate a minimum IQ of 110 to 115 if he is to complete a four-year college curriculum successfully. On the basis of population estimates with reference to IQ, those measured with an IQ of 110 and higher constitute approximately 30 per cent of the population. However, it has also been estimated that 50 per cent or more of the college-age population could profit by education beyond the high school. Statistical studies have indicated that a downward extension of the 110 IQ level to include an additional 20 per cent of the college-age population would place the lower limit at approximately 100 IQ. If the IQ range be further extended to include the estimated percentage between 110–95, the potential "terminal" group would approximate 30 per cent of the college-age population. This formulation would suggest the feasibility of providing some type of post-high school education for a possible 60 per cent of the college-age population.

Educationally speaking, it would certainly seem desirable and important to the national welfare to provide programs of post-high school education for the 95 to 110 IQ group. Many of these persons for various reasons will not seek any type of higher education. Others will be well provided for in programs of business, technical, and apprenticeship education offered by junior colleges and other education agencies. The fact remains, however, as evidenced by the experience of many junior colleges, there will be a large number whose interests and abilities indicate that the solution to their educational requirements lies in the development of a type of "second-track" general education program.

General education courses and curriculums for the above-mentioned group of students need to be broad in conception to carry forward and enhance those learnings and skills already begun in the elementary and secondary schools but which in the present age require an increasingly intricate integration with the complex personal, social, and economic life. In a democratic society, a well-informed and politically active citizenry is imperative for deciding issues of significant social consequence. The individual vote of the "common man" is equivalent to that of any other, and when totaled with those of his peers, likely to be more influential.

The design of a "terminal" general education curriculum demands not only a careful selection and balance of courses, but each course needs to be carefully worked out so that emphasis is given to the immediacy and pertinence of the curriculum as a whole and to the objectives of each specific constituent course. These courses must not simply be "warmed-over" or "watered-down" versions of the traditional lower division university parallel courses. Effective "terminal" courses call for a vital reorganization of subject matter. Priority and emphasis must continually be given to the "here and now" so that maximum advantage may be taken of the psychological key to learning—motivation. Mathematics courses must help to identify and train the manipulative skills necessary to solve practical problems. English writing courses would need to stress the functional as primary to the analytical and the abstract. Social studies courses, including history, should attempt to utilize a current issue or situation as a point of departure for increased understanding rather than beginning with a detailed study of principles and/or chronological beginnings. All of the sciences would give first importance to problem solving, which is the underlying rationale of scientific method and procedure. Appreciation courses would really seek to create increased appreciation and would not become overlaid with such monumental accumulations of names, dates, and places that the primary objectives become obscured. Moral philosophy should be included in such a curriculum through the introduction of specially designed courses in ethics and aesthetics. Each course in this type of curriculum should contribute educationally as an end in itself.

Obviously, courses like those mentioned above will depart quite radically from the traditional presentation of subject matter to four-year college and university students. Thus, the teacher of such courses will be frequently confronted with a formidable problem of finding suitable teaching material. This lack of easily obtained resources is a major obstacle to the successful development of these courses. They will require more work on the part of the teacher. The most common difficulty is to find interesting materials dealing with the appropriate subject matter written at the level of comprehension of which these 95 to 110 IQ students are capable. Such resources are available, but their acquisition and adaptation are often an arduous task. In recent years, suitable texts have been developed for junior college use in some subject areas. In others, creative and enterprising faculty have had to write their own.

As with the choice of materials, the selection and use of teaching methods frequently must vary from the commonplace and the "traditional." To obtain maximum motivation and maintain interest, increased use must be made of such procedures as field trips, a wide variety of visual aids, and community resources—including outside speakers.

In many classes and in many subjects, the approach must be diagnostic and remedial. In certain subjects individualized instruction will be desirable. Development and use of self-teaching devices may enhance the feasibility of this method. The project method lends itself well to this kind of instruction. Problem solving as an approach is broadly applicable. Major emphasis upon student participation wherever possible is valuable in cultivating practice and skill in the use of knowledge as well as in the acquisition of it. Methodology of this type includes such procedures as laboratory work, panel discussions, buzz sessions, role-playing, etc. A total reliance upon the lecture, reading, and examination in courses for this type of student simply will not do.

It would appear obvious that the highest quality of teaching is required for the success of this type of educational program. The capable "terminal" course teacher must not only be thoroughly educated himself in the subject matter with which he deals, but it is of equal importance that professional training develop his teaching skill to the level of artistry. Furthering the general education of "terminal" college students requires a high degree of imagination and enthusiasm. The ability to motivate the student intrinsically ranks high on the list of the teacher's attributes. The effective teacher in this program must possess the personal qualities to achieve rapport with his students. His own motivation must be energized by a desire to stimulate and enhance student growth and maturity as well as to impart subject matter and his own knowledge. Because of the more limited capability of these students in abstraction, analysis, and ideation, the teacher must continually utilize his own powers of perception and integration to lead them to a better understanding of the relatedness of knowledge and its transferability from one aspect of living to another. This type of teaching is a challenge to the superior performers of the profession.

And the end is not yet! Creative thought must be given to the reorientation of perspective in the evaluation of student achievement. Grades, as symbols of success and accomplishment in these courses, must be interpreted solely in terms of the objectives. This will require a completely independent determination of educational values without reference to "transfer" or grade-point differentials. Greater weight can be given to the intangibles of evaluation—the subjective factors, such as personal growth toward maturity. Local norms can be developed as standards rather than relying exclusively upon other normative measures derived from the performance of four-year college and university students. In "terminal" general education courses, less use would be made of such scholastic "war horses" as the documented research paper, the scholarly critique, the extensive analytical essay examination, lengthy reading reports on collateral reading requiring a high degree of speed and comprehension, and similar measures of scholastic competence appropriate to the baccalaureate student.

If the junior college is to fulfill its promise and be truly comprehensive, it must compound an appropriate education prescription for all of the students who can profit from post-high school education. The need is succinctly stated by Damon D. Reach in a recent issue of *Overview*, "Great scientific and technological changes plus major shifts in social and cultural events over the past fifty years demand a greater degree of sophistication on the part of every member of society. Immaturity—in a worker, a manager, or a citizen—is an obstacle to mid-twentieth-century living. The facts point to one conclusion: a longer period of formal schooling must be available so that our youth can meet the demands of life in a modern democracy. Twelve years is proving to be inadequate preparation for accepting one's civic, economic, social and personal responsibilities. Communities have been extending educational opportunities horizontally, now they must extend them vertically as well.[1]

Are the junior colleges really willing to accept the challenge of the "terminal" function in general education?

CHANGING REQUIREMENTS FOR TECHNICAL EDUCATION

N. H. Frank

The problems of technical education are many and varied—as are indeed the problems of all education. Needless to say, it is hazardous to try to foresee things to come, but if we focus on general trends rather than

---

[1]Damon D. Reach, "Make Way for the Community College," *Overview*, April, 1961, p. 52.

From *American Vocational Journal*, XLII, No. 4 (April, 1967), 21-22. Used by permission of the author and publisher.

specifics, I believe it is possible to anticipate with some degree of assurance the general patterns and requirements that will characterize technical education in the future.

The future will bring with it growing demands for enhanced competence and versatility of technicians. Versatility, in particular, is a difficult attribute to acquire but we must question whether current practice is adequate to meet forthcoming needs in this area.

The serious shortage of competent technicians is so well-known and is such an evident matter of concern that I will not take your time to pursue this aspect of the problem. I would submit, however, that the need for technical ability in interdisciplinary operations will grow rapidly. In fact, some of these needs are already with us, for example, in electromechanical and in biomedical technology.

INSATIABLE DEMAND

First, it is striking how much the requirements of individual segments of American industry for electromechanical abilities reflect the special interest of different companies. And this points clearly to the fact that it is virtually impossible to satisfy in any detail the multiplicity of skills and understanding needed by all industry. In fact, the broad spectrum of the American industrial enterprise—and this spectrum gets broader with uncomfortable speed—makes it evident that *total* dependence on industrial needs in fashioning programs of study will lead only to frustration, not only for technical education but for vocational education in general.

Of course, industry's needs must play a significant role but should not and cannot alone dictate desirable learning experiences.

Second, the wide range of special needs makes it extraordinarily and increasingly difficult to create a curriculum that will satisfy them.

Faced with the specter of rapid multiplication of such complex educational programs, what should we do in our planning to cope with them? Some of us would be more comfortable if we could ignore them in the hope that they would go away, but the realities of the situation preclude this as a sensible course of action.

Let me be bold enough to propose a new format for technical education that might help solve this kind of problem. I must stress that this proposal is presented primarily for discussion, hopefully to stimulate thinking along these lines, and makes no claim to be the answer. First, I shall state my proposition in general terms, out of deference to my professorial rank, and then try to illustrate its implications by special examples.

GOALS BEFORE TOOLS

I propose that one should regroup the manifold components of technical education, using functional operations and processes to provide the guidelines for different curricula instead of organizing them as is presently done according to common techniques. In other words, we should prepare people to function in a group of operations all of which have a broad common theme, rather than train them for specific technical competence that finds application in almost every segment of industry.

Thus the emphasis would be primarily on the goals rather than on the tools.

For example, we might cast our educational programs in categories such as these:

1. Energy Conversion Systems and Operations
2. Communication Systems and Operations
3. Transportation Systems
4. Materials Processing and Fabricating Operations.
5. Operations and Processes Concerned with Living Organisms.

Such an organization of curricula would have some obvious advantages. The fact that the techniques acquired would all bear on a host of operations with a central theme would facilitate the development of what I consider a much needed pattern of laboratory-centered learning, with text materials and theory providing a supporting rather than leading role.

For example, broad energy principles would dominate the first category, whether electrical, mechanical, thermal, chemical, nuclear or combinations of these. In the communications area, we would find electronics, acoustics, language, visual aids, computers and so forth. In material processing would lie construction, chemical processes, metallurgy, synthetics, etc.; in transportation, everything from simple means of locomotion to mass transportation to space travel. Finally, the living systems would obviously encompass the whole range of health occupations, food and nutrition, and biological processes in general.

In all the categories, one finds common characteristics, for example, an overlap of techniques, instrumentation, problems of stability and control, systems operations and computer use. This commonality of technical assets would be significantly helpful in providing cross-over potential from one kind of employment to another, and this ease of transferability should be effective both laterally and vertically.

CRITICAL FACTOR

It is evident that the success of these proposed programs would depend critically on the character of the prior education of those who entered them. Thus, pre-technical education itself would need to partake of similar taste and style, and this relates intimately to the outcomes of the 1965 MIT Summer Study on Occupational, Vocational and Technical Education.

You may already surmise that the causes of action I am proposing here have their origin in that study, and this is indeed the fact. May I urge this Association to concern itself with and to help in the task of recasting the patterns of learning at elementary- and secondary-school levels along the lines recommended by the MIT Study.

If for no other reason than self-interest, this involvement would be a most rewarding investment of time and energy.

Similarly, the apprenticeship programs of this country need reshaping and, I suspect, should move largely to the post-high school level. Here, the need for cooperative interaction is clear.

Furthermore, I hope it will be possible for you, as technical educators, to enter into cooperative ventures with engineering educators, with the aim of establishing goal-oriented, project-type learning experiences in which teams of student engineers and student technicians can work together, much as they have to do in practice. The mutual benefits derivable from this sort of cooperation hardly need elaboration.

ARE TWO YEARS ENOUGH?

Finally, let me play the role of provocateur and pose the question: How long can technical education continue to operate effectively with two-year programs? Much of the foreseeable increase in the demands for future technicians with deeper insight, enhanced sophistication, and a larger proportion of the use of "head" to "hands," indicates the necessity for a longer period of post-high school learning than two years.

There is already an uncomfortable gap between engineering and technical education. As our better engineering schools concern themselves more and more with pushing back the frontiers of engineering activities, this gap will widen. Perhaps we already face the need for a new type of institution, a sort of junior institute of technology, aimed at turning out people to operate effectively in this "no-man's land." This level of attainment would require cognitive learning beyond that obtained in most of our technical institutes, but there would be no intention of aiming for the sort of abstract, sophisticated type of activities in which a growing number of engineers engage.

In summary, it seems to me that at this point in history, the challenge to technical education with respect to its future evolution is both immediate and great. I urge you to meet this challenge head on.

NEW DIRECTIONS IN COMMUNITY SERVICES

Ervin L. Harlacher

The community college is fast becoming a dynamic force which affects the thought processes, habits, economic status, and social interaction of people from every walk of life, in every part of the country. More and more, it is becoming the most important element of this nation's educational structure.

The community college in implementing its full community dimension is breaking, once and for all, the lock-step of tradition, i.e., college is four walls; college is semester-length courses; college is credit; college is culturally and educationally elite.

It seems inevitable that the community college will place even greater emphasis on its community dimension in the decade ahead. The community college will demonstrate, to an extent even greater than it has to date, that college is where the people are, and that community services are designed to take the college program out into the community as well as bring the community to the college.

In its most significant role, the program of community services constitutes what might be called "Operation Outreach." Peter S. Mousolite has suggested that, "We emulate the English minstrel, the French jongleur, the Spanish trovador, the Chautauqua enterprise so popular not so many years ago," and though the use of mobile units move out into the community and create the program there.[1]

From *Junior College Journal,* XXXVIII, No. 6 (March, 1968), 12-17. Used by permission of the author and the publisher.

[1] Mousolite, Peter S. *The Edge of the Chair,* remarks presented to National Conference on Vocational and Technical Education. Chicago: May 16, 1967.

THE NEXT GREAT THRUST

While the full potential of the program of community services has not yet been realized by all institutions, there is reason to believe that the next great thrust of the community college development will be in the direction of community services. The American Association of Junior Colleges therefore authorized the present study.

In conducting this study the author during the summer and fall of 1967 visited thirty-seven community college districts in thirteen states, representing the small and the large, the rich and the poor, and the urban and the rural community college. He also corresponded with administrators of twenty-eight additional college districts in twelve states, with trustees and presidents of newly organized community college districts, and with officials of state agencies concerned with the goverance of community colleges. The sixty-five community college districts participating in this study operate 104 college campuses in nineteen different states.

The community college is dedicated to the proposition that, important as are formalized curriculums offered for youth and adults within its classrooms, informal education provided on a continuous basis throughout the community for all of the rest of the people is of equal importance in building the character of the citizens who make up the state.

The program of the community college may be conceptualized in two dimensions—formal education and informal education. Through its formal dimension, sometimes characterized as schooling, the community college provides transfer, occupational, general education, and guidance and counseling programs for youth and adults enrolled in regularly scheduled day and evening classes on the campus.

But it is through its community dimension that the junior college truly becomes a community college. Chancellor Samuel B. Gould of the State University of New York, has underscored the importance of this dimension of informal education:

It is my conviction that a college, in addition to its more readily accepted intellectual dimension, should have the dimension of community that offers a place for the general life enrichment of all who live nearby: young and old, artisan and farmer and member of profession, college graduate and comparatively unskilled. Thus many of the gaps or weaknesses that the new pressures of numbers are bound to create in formal education can be filled or strengthened as a college opens its doors and its resources to all in a friendly and informal fashion, without thought of credits or degrees or anything more than to assist the burgeoning of understanding in the individual as a member of a personal, physical, political, economic, artistic and spiritual world.[2]

The philosophy that the community college campus encompasses the length and breadth of the college district, and that the total population of the district is its student body, makes it possible for the community college, in a massive and untraditional way, to broaden the base for higher education. This philosophy also makes it possible to ease the problems of access to higher education by taking the college to the people. Furthermore, it offers freedom from the traditional image of the American college and university which sees college primarily, if not entirely, as an institution concerned with educating youth.

While the addition of community services has revolutionized the role of the community college, actually the community services concept is as old as Socrates—possibly older. Socrates first exemplified it by taking his wisdom into the streets and the market place and there created a student community representative of the people and actively concerned with the social and moral issues of the time.

By the eighteenth century, however, the idea of providing higher education for all the people had been abandoned, and the universities became storehouses for factual knowledge and retreats for the idle rich or select few.

The first step toward providing community services in this country was taken in 1826 by Josiah Holbrook when he established the American Lyceum. In later years, after the lyceum died out, chautauqua, initiated in 1874, carried forward the lyceum "spirit" and became a symbol of education and culture until its peak year in 1924.[3]

MORRILL ACT

Another step in the development of community services was the establishment of agricultural extension as a function of American universities under the Morrill and Smith-Lever Acts. The philosophy of agricultural extension focused on "helping people to help themselves."

[2]Gould, Samuel B. "Whose Goals for Higher Education," remarks prepared for delivery before 50th Annual Meeting, American Council on Education, Washington, D.C., October 12, 1967.

[3]Jones, Bertis L. *The History of Community Development in American Universities With Particular Reference to Four Selected Institutions.* Unpublished Ed. D. dissertation, University of California, Los Angeles, 1961, p. 329-332.

The community services function as defined in this study, i.e., educational, cultural, and recreational services above and beyond regularly scheduled day and evening classes, is completely foreign to the traditional idea of college education but it is the manifestation of what the community college was created for. The community college recognizes that by definition it has an obligation to: (1) become a center of community life by encouraging the use of college facilities and services by community groups when such use does not interfere with the college's regularly scheduled day and evening programs; (2) provide educational services for all age groups which utilize the special skills and knowledge of the college staff and other experts and are designed to meet the needs of community groups and the college district at large; (3) provide the community with the leadership and coordination capabilities of the college, assist the community in long-range planning, and join with individuals and groups in attacking unsolved problems; and (4) contribute to and promote the cultural, intellectual, and social life of the college district community and the development of skills for the profitable use of leisure time.

A COMMUNITY SERVICE AGENCY

The original idea of the community college was one that involved a "grass roots" approach. In theory, at least, everyone connected with such an institution would look around, find educational gaps, and help fill the gaps. The community college faculty and staff—teachers and doers in the broadest possible sense—would undertake to solve human problems in the community around them or point out the needs to other educational groups in the community to care for.

Rooted in the soil of the district community it serves and drawing its students and strength from that community, the community college is particularly suited as a community service agency:

1. The community college is a community-centered institution with the primary purpose of providing service to the people of its community. Its offerings and programs are planned to meet the needs of the community and are developed with the active participation of citizens.

2. The community college claims community service as one of its major functions and, according to Thornton, ".... the scope and adequacy of these services determine whether or not the college merits the title of community junior college...."[4]

---

[4]Thornton, James W., *The Community Junior College.* New York: John Wiley and Sons, 1960, p. 66.

3. Since the community college is usually a creation of citizens of the local community or area, and since it is most frequently governed by a board of local citizens, the community college is readily capable of responding to changing community needs.

4. Most community colleges are operated by a local district which encompasses several separate and distinct communities. The ideal locale for a program of community services is one "in which there are numerous communities and subcommunities with natural and compelling interrelationship. . . ."[5] The program of community services welds these separate communities and groups together.

5. The community college is an institution of higher education, and as such can draw upon the advanced resources of its staff in assisting in the solution of the problems of an increasingly complex society.

6. The community college, as a relatively new segment of American education, is "unencrusted with tradition, not hidebound by a rigid history, and in many cases, new and eager for adventure." Thus, it is able, without duplicating existing services in the community, to tailor its program to meet local needs and conditions.

At least seven directions which this major emphasis on the community dimension will take, seem safe to predict at this point:

I. *The community college will develop aggressive multiservice outreach programs designed to truly extend its campus throughout the entire college district.*

Through the use of extension centers, empty stores, portable units located on vacant land, mobile units, churches, schools, libraries, museums, art gallaries, places of business and other community facilities, the community college will establish communications links with all segments of the college district community, encouraging a free exchange of ideas and resources. The community college, stable yet unfettered by the permanence of buildings, will move in physical location in response to shifting needs.

Extension centers: Pasadena City College in California offers short courses, lectures, and forums in sixty-five different sites in every part of the six unified districts which compose the college district, which includes a unique course for wives of prisoners. And 600 students are enrolled in

[5]Seay, Maurice F., and Crawford, Ferris N., *The Community School and Community Self-Improvement.* Lansing, Michigan: Clair L. Taylor, Superintendent to Public Instruction, 1954, p. 144.

college credit courses offered by Miami-Dade Junior College, Florida, in a variety of community locations, including public agencies, hotels, airlines, the Miami Beach Center, and a local Air Force base.

In-plant training: Perhaps the most extensive in-plant training program in the country is operated by New York City Community College, resulting in pretraining or in-service training for 180 newly appointed building inspectors, 300 building inspectors, 320 dietary aides from eighteen hospitals, 1,000 nurses' aides, and 700 municipal employees. Top management training courses conducted by El Centro College in Texas for a Dallas hospital, including basic management, work simplification, problem solving and goal setting, reportedly saved the hospital $750,000 operating costs during the first year. And the in-service training program developed for federal employees by Cuyahoga Community College in Cleveland, Ohio, is expected to attract some 500 initially, with the federal government paying tuition.

Mobile and portable units: Hudson Valley Community College in New York last summer utilized effectively an "Opportunity Van" in two disadvantaged Albany neighborhoods, recruiting students for its urban center. Another excellent example is the community science outreach program being developed by Oakland Community College in Michigan, in cooperation with a local institute of science, and featuring mobile exhibits and demonstrations, traveling museums and short courses.

II. *The community college will place increased emphasis on community education for all age levels and all age groups.*

Increasingly, community education services are not limited to youth just out of high school or to adults of the community, but are provided for citizens of all ages—including elementary and secondary school youngsters—with varying interests and points of view, and are provided at all social and economic levels. More and more these educational services embrace the whole gamut of community life with the objective of preparing citizens to cope with rapid and sweeping social, political, and technological change.

Short courses: The Center for Community Educational Services, established by the State University of New York Agricultural and Technical

College at Farmingdale, offered 720 workshops, seminars, institutes and conferences last year, accommodating 32,000 persons. Since 1940 Abraham Baldwin Agricultural College in Georgia has offered 743 short courses for 98,699 farmers, stressing the latest techniques in farming and related fields.

In-service training: Suffolk County Community College in New York has developed, in cooperation with Civil Training Council, twenty-two county-financed in-service training courses for county employees, offered during the working day at seven different locations.

Baltimore Junior College in Maryland, under its new careers program, trained some 300 disadvantaged persons, twenty-two and up, with job problems as psychology aides, home visitation aides, government service aides, data processing aides, etc. Some 1,100 disadvantaged adults and young adults are enrolled in the East Bay Skill Center, funded under MDTA and operated by Laney College in California. Big Bend Community College in Washington provides, on a contractual basis, training programs in licensed practical nursing, nurses aide, and mechanics, i.e., riveting, for a local Women's Job Corps Center. And Oakland Community College's project SERVE, funded under Title I of the Higher Education Act, stimulates active participation of senior citizens in community affairs through a three-part program: free counseling and placement service for those needing additional income; a volunteer placement bureau; and carefully tailored short courses.

Meeting community needs: "The Destroyers," a forum on the illegal drug traffic, sponsored by Ceritos College in California in cooperation with fourteen local school districts, resulted in a change in the curriculum for the fifth and sixth grades.

III. *The community college will utilize a greater diversification of media in meeting community needs and interests.*

No longer can it be said that the community college fulfills its community responsibility by merely offering a new course "anytime ten or more citizens want it, if teachers, space, funds, and equipment are available." Increasingly, the class is only one of a plethora of media utilized in the program of community service: telecommunications; seminars and symposiums; performing groups; self-instructional packages; educational and cultural tours; workshops and conferences; counseling and consultative services; research and planning, recreational activities; science experiments and exhibitions, facility usage; leadership, coordination, and advisory assistance; public lectures, and fine arts events.

Short courses: Even short courses offered under the program of community service take on a different format. Especially designed as in-service training for personnel of paleontology laboratories located in the area, the biostratigraphy seminar, sponsored by Bakersfield College in California, is now in its sixth year and continues to fill a need for the petroleum industry.

Telecommunications: Chicago City College's TV College, on the air approximately twenty-six hours per week, since 1956 has permitted 100,000 persons to take seventy different credit and noncredit courses in their homes, generating 170,000 enrollments. Using FM radio, Long Beach City College in California serves 100,000 kindergarten through twelfth grade students of the Long Beach Unified School District. In order to provide educational opportunities in five outlying areas of its 2,600 square mile district, Los Rios Junior College District in California is developing the concept of the Little Red Electronic Schoolhouse, equipping the one-room facilities with thirty carrels for audio-tutorial study.

Tours and field trips: During August of 1967, a week-long nature study field trip into the Minarets area of the Sierra Nevada was organized by Foothill College in California for thirty-six members of the community. And an imaginative program of field studies in Mexico and South America has been developed by the College of San Mateo in California including "pre-Columbian civilization" in Mexico City; and "Mayan civilization" centering on the Yucatan peninsula and Guatemala; and a people-to-people exploration of Central and South America.

Community performing groups: The Music Makers of the Foothill Junior College District in California encompass three community performing groups; a 140-voice community symphonic choir, the Schola Cantorum; a select chamber ensemble, the Master Symphonia; and a ninety-piece symphony, the Nova Vista Orchestra.

Consulting services: A program of technical assistance to industry, including bulletins, newsletters, and general consultative services, is being developed by New York City Community College in the areas of optics, data processing, and numerical control.

Community counseling: Cuyahoga Community College's project SEARCH for the culturally disadvantaged of the Hought section of Cleveland features a counseling center to help individuals identify realistic educational and vocational goals for themselves. North Florida Junior College provided the leadership for the development of an area guidance center, where twenty counselors serve elementary schools, high schools, and junior colleges in six rural counties by providing 115 hours of guidance time daily.

IV. *The community college will increasingly utilize its catalytic capabilities to assist its community in the solution of basic educational, economic, political, and social problems.*

In the process of becoming an educational resource center, the community college is dynamically relating its programs to the existing and emerging needs of its district community. Through action programs aimed at closing ravines now dividing the inner city from the outer community; baseline data from community studies; the leadership and advisory assistance of college personnel in the mobilization of community resources; long-range planning; workshops, institutes and conferences; and the organization of community coordinating councils and other needed groups, the community college is becoming an agency for social change.

Programs for the disadvantaged: During the past year, 192 disadvantaged students have participated in the Neighborhood Youth Corps program at Westark Junior College in Arkansas, spending approximately half of their time in remedial reading, writing and arithmetic, and the other half in automobile mechanics, automobile body and welding programs. Baltimore Junior College has developed two programs to motivate youngsters from culturally disadvantaged sections of Baltimore to stay in school and seek college goals: (1) an Upward Bound program for promising tenth and eleventh grade students; and (2) Operation: College Horizons for junior and senior high school students and their parents. The Peralta Colleges in California are developing an extensive program for the culturally disadvantaged who remain in the inner city, which features a student service corps, community development centers offering educational and counseling services, a cultural enrichment program, and a scholarship assistance program.

Community leadership: In order to give maximum service to its community, Abraham Baldwin College initiated project SURGE (Systematic Utilization of Resources for Growth and Efficiency) for Tifton and Tiff County in 1964, utilizing fourteen committees, representing every aspect of community life and an annual "town hall" type meeting.

Workshops, institutes, and conferences: An extensive program of community workshops and seminars to provide information and education about local government, planning renewal, community organization, etc., has been developed by Essex Community College in Maryland.

Organization of Community groups: New York City Community College has proposed the establishment of an economic training institute to be designed by a task force in response to problems identified by the South Brooklyn Community Progress Center's clientele as well as its professional staff.

V. *The community college will be increasingly concerned about the cultural growth of its community and state.*

That this trend is already taking shape has been evident in many communities for some time. A survey of development in California four years ago, for example, resulted in this conclusion: "California communities from the Sierra to the sea, and the Siskyous to the Mexican border are experiencing a cultural, social, and intellectual renaissance. And much of the credit for the community rebirth is due California's seventy-one public junior colleges and their programs of community services." [6]

Cultural centers: Flint Junior College in Michigan has developed a cultural center which includes an intimate theater, auditorium, an art center, planetarium, museum, and a public library. Del Mar College in Texas has become a cultural center for the entire college district through its extensive cultural program which includes community performing groups—a chamber orchestra, a chorale, choral ensemble, and a full symphony orchestra; and festivals and series presentations. Rockland Community College in New York has taken a number of steps to join forces with community groups in creating a cultural center for the community which would feature an on-campus museum, a theater and/or auditorium, and a planetarium. A most ambitious and extensive composite of performing arts activities was initiated in the spring of 1967 by Bucks County Community College, Pennsylvania, when it undertook a multifaceted program of experimental theater, children's theater, elementary and secondary school visitations, an art festival, and a college-sponsored professional repertory company.

Arts councils: Delta College in Michigan was instrumental in the formation of a forty-member arts council which is housed on the college campus and publishes an annual calendar, functions as a "clearinghouse" for the scheduling of events, operates a central arts activity over the college-owned educational television station.

[6] Harlacher, Ervin L. "California's Community Renaissance," *Junior College Journal,* XXXIV (May, 1966).

VI. *The community college will place greater emphasis on interaction with its community.*

Increasingly, it is being recognized that the effective program of community services is built upon (1) a solid foundation of citizen participation and college-community interactions and (2) a thorough understanding of the community. Citizens actually participate in the planning, maintenance, and evaluation of the program; and the college, recognizing that it must be of the community and not just in it, participates in community life. In such a way, mutual interaction is achieved.

Institutional synergism: This term has been defined as simultaneous action of separate agencies, which together have a greater total effect than the sum of their individual efforts. Illustrative of this term is the concept of the "Health and Education Campus" being developed by Essex Community College in Maryland, the Franklin Square Hospital, and the Baltimore County Health Department, and featuring the sharing of physical facilities and human resources, the joint development of paramedical curriculum, and development of continuing education programs for patients and the community through television. Rockland Community College is developing a college library as a strong community-serving central reference and research library to complement existing library services in the county, and a media center capable of sending programs to all schools in the county. Approximately one hundred paintings of Chautauqua County Society artists are constantly on display in hallways and offices throughout the campus of Jamestown Community College in New York, making the entire campus an art gallery. And thirty-three companies cooperate with Rock Valley College in Illinois in the promotion of and recruitment for its unique Career Advancement Program which is permitting 174 company-employed students to work half-time and spend half-time in class.

Advisory committees: Ceritos College in California is aided in the planning and implementation of its program of community services by a citizens' advisory council and nine advisory committees, including adult education, business, civic responsibilities, community research and development, community volunteer services, fine arts, professions, recreation and youth.

Community councils: Vincennes University Junior College in Indiana has organized a council of top managers of industry in the area which plans educational programs for the welfare of industry.

Community-college sponsorship: Joining forces with a community organization, North Florida Junior College has created the North Florida Junior College-Madison Artist Series Association for the purpose of planning and financing high-level artist series programs for the college and the community.

VII. *The community college will increasingly recognize the need for cooperation with other community and regional agencies.*

In order to avoid unnecessary duplication of services, a greater effort is being made by community college personnel to coordinate the community college program of community services with programs of other community and regional agencies, i.e., public schools, recreation districts, governmental agencies, museums, art galleries, libraries, and four-year colleges and universities.

Community college cooperation: The San Mateo and Foothill Junior College Districts in California have entered into a special training program, co-sponsored by the Junior League of Palo Alto, for the purpose of training unpaid volunteers for the public schools. And seventeen junior colleges of Los Angeles County, California, are cooperating in the offering of a two-unit health education course over a local commercial television channel.

Cooperation with four-year colleges: The College of the Redwoods and Humboldt State College in California are cooperating in the extension of concerts and lecture series programs to local communities in northern California. The Community College of Philadelphia and thirty-six other two and four-year colleges are participating in a consortium, the College Bound Corporation, to provide admission counseling for community high schools. Big Bend Community College is coordinating with four other colleges and a public school district in a nine-county area in the state of Washington, a unique program designed to upgrade Japanese migrants to a fifth grade reading level and offering prevocational and vocational programs.

Cooperation with public schools: Oakland Community College during the past year offered some eighty credit and noncredit courses in twenty-nine different centers in the college district, in cooperation with local public schools.

Regional cooperation: Approximately eighty colleges in California, including a few four-year colleges as well as community colleges, have organized the College Association for Public Events and Services for the purpose of block-booking lectures, artists, and exchanging package programs and experiences. CAPES organizations have also been organized in Arizona and Michigan.

CONCLUSION

Through imaginative programs of community services, community colleges are beginning to assume their natural role as a catalytic force—providing the leadership, coordination, and cooperation necessary to stimulate action programs by appropriate individuals and groups with the community. The reciprocal relationship between the community and the community college is such that the community college both reflects and effects changes in the structure of its community, and the life patterns of its residents.

More and more, the community college is inserting into the life stream of its people forces that can change, revise, unify, and stimulate the individual, the organization, and ultimately, the tone of mind of the entire community.

OPENING THE COLLEGE GATES
TO THE LOW ACHIEVER

William Moore, Jr.

Since I grew up in the ghetto, was a two-time high school dropout, was in the lower tenth percentile when I enrolled in college, and was graduated third from the last in my undergraduate class, I can justifiably describe myself as having been academically unsuccessful. Add to these credentials the fact that I am a Negro, and I believe you will agree that I can speak with authority and conviction on the subject of the educationally disadvantaged student.

Each year thousands of low achieving students enter adult society with "worthless" high school diplomas. Many of these students have been sold

From *Today's Education*, LVII, No. 9 (December, 1968), 38-40. Used by permission of the author and publisher.

on the purported value of the diploma, but they will not receive any reward for acquiring it. For a few good students, the diploma is a passport to college; for some others it leads to a union card and the world of work; but for far too many, particularly Negroes in the cities it is no more than an attendance prize. Its holder cannot get into college or into desirable areas of the work world. Such students, who are denied additional schooling, who cannot go to work, and who are vulnerable to the draft, are potential dynamite.

Though the academically unsuccessful come from all races and social classes, a disproportionately large number come from minority groups, especially from the Negro race. They often live in ugly cities. They come from broken homes, dilapidated housing, seething streets, and crippling schools. Only a few of them are motivated toward education. Most of them feel rejected, almost all of them have experienced some failure, a considerable number have been poor, and few of them have had a second chance at an education.

Many people say that our institutions of higher learning are shutting out or flunking out too many kids in a society in which the number of unskilled jobs remains about the same while the number of unskilled persons continues to increase. In addition to producing trained professionals, is higher education turning out enough other people with different marketable skills?

With all its resources and all its expertise, higher education has shown little concern for disadvantaged youth. College people have insisted that they are doing what they are supposed to do. They have rejected the awesome burden of trying to salvage students who are "unqualified" for higher education. Traditionally, they have recommended that some other "more appropriate" educational agency should try to reach students judged academically unsuccessful. Only a few have asked soul-searching questions—and found challenging answers.

In this decade, what constitutes a bona fide educational opportunity for the socially and economically disadvantaged that would be beneficial both to the student and to society? It certainly cannot arise from the traditional attitude of higher education that says to these young men and women, "This is what we have to offer—take it or leave it." Few of the inept can take it; too many of the unmotivated leave it. And educational experience for these students has to be significant.

The disadvantaged—by the sheer magnitude of their numbers and the insistence of their voices—have created a climate where higher education can no longer remain comfortable with its habitual position of scholarly detachment. Consequently, a social and academic revolution is beginning to affect higher education. In its vanguard are new theories and techniques for dealing with the marginal students. As a result of the increased emphasis on higher education for the masses, community colleges are springing up at the rate of 50 per year. And some are stressing an open-door policy—one that will admit students who were underachievers in high school, those with limited ability but high motivation, and those who are culturally· and economically disadvantaged. This is a dramatic change for higher education, although Negro colleges have long provided educational experiences for such students. Upward Bound and similar groups are also operating on many college campuses, but the fact that such programs are too few needs no documentation.

Believing they had a responsibility to serve the marginal student, Forest Park Community College's board of trustees, president, administrators, and faculty decided to accept the open-door policy and the challenges it presents. (Such a policy *must* have commitment from the top down.) Assisted by grant funds from the Danforth Foundation, they structured a truly imaginative program—the General Curriculum: A Program for the Educationally Disadvantaged—which attracts financial aid from public and private sources.

General Curriculum is an experimental program developed on the premise that the student who enters it will need simultaneous assistance in the basic academic skills (reading, mathematics, grammar, and composition), and personal enrichment and adjustment to self and society. The program provides this assistance through programed learning, general education classes, and guidance techniques—including careful and proper placement (into college curriculum, an existing training program, or directly on a job).

Located between the city and the suburbs, the college's General Curriculum Division attracts both Negro and Caucasian students from both directions. Poor and affluent students alike are assigned to this program on the basis of two criteria: high school rank at graduation and percentile rank on the School and College Ability Tests (SCAT). *These ranks must be in the lower third and the tenth percentile or below, respectively.* To be assigned to the General Curriculum, the student must meet both criteria. He is not, however, locked into the program. If he makes satisfactory progress (B−) after a semester or a year in the program, he may move into the transfer, technical, or career programs.

To solve the basic skills problem, the college offers a multimedia approach to programmed instruction. All instruction in our Programmed Materials Learning Laboratory is individualized. Each student proceeds at his own rate and works only on those skills in which he is deficient. His periodic examinations are spaced for maximum reinforcement; he always knows at what level he is working and where he must go to reach his objective. We place on him the burden of responsibility for assimilating the material. (The present Laboratory has auxiliary laboratories in writing, mathematics, and reading. And we have added a psychologist to the PMLL staff to diagnose learning problems and to prescribe remedial procedures appropriate to the student's learning style.)

Forest Park Community College readily observed that educationally disadvantaged students know little about events beyond their day, beyond their age group, beyond their neighborhood. Thus, they lack both an understanding of the total contemporary culture and a basic historical frame of reference. Therefore, for personal and cultural enrichment of these students, two teams of teachers developed (and continue to develop and evaluate) a one-year program of general education designed to provide their students with a stimulating and successful classroom experience. These teams have interest and experience in working with low achievers.

The marginal student is frequently antagonistic, hesitant, and indifferent to the educative process. These attitudes are compounded when the curriculum content fails to touch him in a direct way. For these reasons, material for the general education courses is chosen in terms of its relevance. (Students would be unmotivated either to understand when Ptolemy lived or to appreciate the influence of his cosmological theory. According to one General Curriculum student, "Ptolemy goofed with his theory of the universe, anyway—so why be bothered with him?")

We use no textbooks in these courses. Instructors choose their materials from current articles and other supplementary readings that are interesting, timely, and provocative. The content of one course is not isolated from the content of other general education courses. Rather, each course is structured around five broad headings: orientation, self, self and society, human relations, and values.

Each team has a weekly conference, which gives its members an opportunity to evaluate a student's progress with every other member of the team, including the counselor who works with the student. Every teacher also has a chance to determine whether his material correlates adequately with the content other team members are presenting. He also can discuss, compare, and exchange teaching techniques that have been effective in instructing General Curriculum students.

In guidance—one of the most cohesive factors in this program—a low student-counselor ratio ensures that students can be seen at least once a week or daily if necessary. Students attend guidance classes two class periods per week—to appraise their attitudes and their abilities. The counseling program is student- and community-centered rather than institution-centered. This implies that counselors are trained to know intimately all facets of the community so that its total resources are at the disposal of the educationally disadvantaged student. People from business, industry, the professions, labor, and management meet with our students, answer questions, and provide information about requirements for employment and opportunities for advancement.

Other features of the Forest Park General Curriculum program include:

- A deliberate plan to work with the deprived community
- Provisions for articulation between the high schools, community, and the college
- Remission of fees (tuition, books, and so forth) for needy students
- Employment of a full-time social worker
- Internships (with stipends) for prospective college-level teachers of the disadvantaged
- Continuing workshops for in-service personnel and workshops on a national basis for those interested in learning techniques of the program
- Access to expertise (in terms of consultation) and funds to experiment and develop a model program for the educationally disadvantaged across the nation.

The essence of our program cannot be captured in this short article. It is more than an educational program. It is people—creative people who have endured the frustrations, conflicts, dilemmas, and dynamics of human interaction. It is the long hours, coffee-stained tables, overflowing ashtrays, skipped lunches, and forgotten dinners; the endless meetings, conferences, memos, reports, and deadlines. It is the persistent challenge of *doing* what we didn't know could not be done.

And it is also the conversion of an English teacher into a programmed-learning expert by trial and error, the small successes, the blundering into a new technique or procedure that worked, and unsolicited letters from students who said they were helped. All these are the human ingredients.

At this point, we lack definitive research that will tell us exactly where each student has gone and how each has performed after involvement in the General Curriculum. But we do know that many students now view education and their individual abilities in a positive light, that they no longer perceive education as an experience of frustration and failure.

Even though the St. Louis humidity is unbelievable, grandmothers who have deferred their education for many years come to learn. Fathers, after the day's work, come to perform the computations in fractions that the fifth graders they leave at home have already mastered. Some come because they want to earn more money on their jobs. Others come because they are bored. Somehow, they will accept the inconvenience. Neither the blond kid who cannot master decimals nor the black one who consistently fails to make subject and verb agree complains. And this makes it all worthwhile.

THE DILEMMA OF THE JUNIOR COLLEGE

John M. Kuhlman

The typical junior college finds itself in a multiple-dimensional dilemma. It faces a number of consuming publics with differing demands for particular outputs. This situation arises, in part, because of the relative newness of the institution as well as its rate of growth. But a more fundamental cause is the number of roles it is expected to fulfill.

First, there is the conflict between the terminal and transfer programs. On the one hand, the junior college is an integral part of the nation's four-year college program. An increasing number of college students are receiving their initial college training in junior colleges. But the junior colleges also offer a number of terminal programs of importance to the local community. Some are commonly associated with vocational schools but others are of a pre-professional nature. A well-financed junior college may be able to offer both programs; however, there will be the tendency to merge some of the terminal and transfer students into a single class rather than offering two (small) sections of the same course. This is, in effect, a conflict between the higher academic standards of a transfer program and the lower standards of the terminal program.

Second, the junior college instructor faces a professional conflict not faced by his colleague in the four-year institution. In the latter, instruction is highly specialized with each instructor being part of a particular academic discipline. Some junior college instructors find themselves offering instruction in several unrelated or, at best, slightly related fields. For example, some who teach economics also teach such diverse topics as physical education, music, business education, marketing, history, political

From *Junior College Journal,* XXXVII, No. 6 (March, 1967), 68-70 . Used by permission of the author and publisher.

science, mathematics, and so on. Under such circumstances, it will be difficult, if not impossible, to generate a sense of professional belonging. As a result, in the case of economics, very few belong to the American Economic Association while a relatively large number belong to such organizations as the N.E.A. and state teachers' organizations. Also, there is little professional association between the junior college instructor in economics and the departments of economics in the four-year institutions and relatively more between junior college instructors and the college of education.

Third, the junior colleges, like secondary schools, often base pay raises and promotions on the number of graduate hours and degrees. The instructor may select a field from one of the several in which he teaches, or he may choose to do graduate work in the college of education. The latter is often an attractive alternative, but the result is that the instructor becomes relatively weaker in his professional fields of instruction and his already weak professional contacts in these fields become still weaker. Furthermore, to the extent that the junior college instructor has professional ties with neighboring four-year institutions, they are often with the college of education rather than the various academic disciplines in which his students will be doing upper level and graduate work.

The result, then, may be summed up as follows: The junior colleges are the center of a growing struggle between colleges of education, local school boards, and the high schools, on the one hand, and the four-year colleges (and graduate schools) and the academic disciplines, on the other. To the extent that the former dominate, then junior college education will take on more of the characteristics of the high school and become more of a high school continuation program and less of an introductory college program. There will be less emphasis on a liberal education and less college-level preparatory work for many students selecting various professional careers.

The burden of this dichotomic nature of the junior college will fall upon the junior college student who transfers to a four-year institution to continue his college education. If he is to do third-year work, then the work in the first two years must correspond to that at the four-year institution. Instructors in the elementary courses must keep abreast of the developments in their professional fields. To the extent that the quality of the first course was lowered to meet the needs of terminal students and to the extent that the instructor was doing graduate work in education rather than the academic discipline being taught, the junior college transfer student will suffer when he is put in with a group that received their initial college instruction from people teaching in their own discipline.

It should be pointed out that this is not a dire prediction of some future event but, rather, a description of an existing situation. Already there is a tendency to have some junior college courses repeated at the four-year institution. Some junior college students find themselves at a considerable handicap during their junior and senior years after they transfer to the terminal institution. The junior college transfer student generally takes longer to acquire the initial college degree than does his counterpart who enrolls at a four-year institution following his graduation from high school.[1] In part, the problems involved in transferring from junior college to the four-year institution concern the kind of instruction offered in the former and its relation to the upper-level instruction in the latter.

It is difficult, if not impossible, to say that the situation is better or worse in one or the other of the many academic disciplines. One can point out, however, that the situation in economics (as well as the other behavioral sciences) is of a different nature, as well as a different order of magnitude, than the problem in the physical sciences, for example.

It would seem to be neither false nor unfair to observe that most colleges of education are oriented toward the "social studies" rather than the social sciences. This is evidenced by the fact that there will generally be several courses devoted to the teaching of social studies or problems in social studies, however, such courses dealing with social sciences (as well as the physical and natural sciences) are, for the most part, lacking. To the extent that social studies is related to an academic discipline, that discipline is quite often the field of history. The concept of a social science or a behavioral science is quite often lacking in the typical college of education.

"SOCIAL STUDIES" AND "SOCIAL SCIENCE"

Based upon a rather cursory examination of a small number of texts, social studies seem to be those parts of the social sciences which can be understood by younger students. Edgar B. Wesley thought of social studies in the following terms. "The social studies are the social sciences simplified for pedagogical purposes."[2] Beyond this, many authors define the subject through a process of inclusion. J. C. McLendon includes cultural anthropology, archeology, education, jurisprudence, social psychology, and social

[1]Knoell, Dorothy M. "Focus on the Transfer Program." *Junior College Journal* 35: 5-9; May, 1956.

[2]*Teaching the Social Studies.* Boston: D. C. Heath, 1942

work as the semisocial sciences in addition to economics, history, geography, political science, and sociology as the social sciences.[3]

The teacher and writer in social studies seem to have little grasp of the concept of a social science. They tend to emphasize the word "social" and select courses on the basis of whether they deal with man in his social environment. The term "science" seems to have no particular meaning for them and certainly little, if any, implication as far as methodology is concerned. The social scientist, on the other hand, is primarily concerned with the scientific (i.e., methodological) aspect of a particular subject. To him the word "social" is coming to be quite unsatisfactory as a basis for classification. The significant difference is the difference between "studies" and "science."

To cite McLendon again, "Social studies are distinguishable from social sciences in four basic respects: scope, size, purpose, and level of difficulty."[4] In size and scope, social sciences are larger, i.e., cover a larger subject matter. The purpose of social science is to discover truths about human relationships while the purpose of social studies is to guide young people in their learning of particular portions of what social scientists have discovered. Social sciences are more abstract while social studies transform the more difficult parts of social science into more learnable material, for social science is often too abstract or complex for secondary school students.

McLendon does devote some space to the question of methodology in the social sciences; however, it appears that most of those writing texts on social studies have little or no awareness of the significance or nature of the scientific methodology in the social sciences. The need for and the use of mathematics in the social sciences is ignored. When statistics is mentioned it usually refers to the higher descriptive type of statistics found in the *Statistical Abstract* of the *World Almanac*. The construction of abstract models may be referred to but only to point out that such activity is too difficult for students in social studies. This type of reasoning is somewhat amazing in view of the fact that the "new mathematics" has demonstrated that young children are capable of engaging in a relatively high level of abstraction. Primary and secondary school students can use abstract models in the physical and natural sciences and mathematics. Yet we accept the conventional wisdom that one must be a college student before it is possible to undertake a comparable level of abstraction in the social sciences.

[3]McLendon, J. C. *Social Studies in Secondary Education.* New York: Macmillan Co., 1965.
[4]Ibid., p. 68.

To the extent that the college of education and its preponderant orientation toward social studies dominate the social science departments in junior colleges, the academic work in such departments will have less of a scientific orientation and more descriptive material dealing with contemporary society. There will be less emphasis on analytical reasoning and the use of abstract models. The junior college student will be told that there is relatively little need for mathematics in such fields, and the junior college social science courses may well become refuges for those avoiding mathematics and statistics. In short, the initial exposure to social sciences will be postponed until the last half of the student's undergraduate program.

Social studies, at all levels, have received a veritable fusilade of criticism—trivial, erroneous, propagandistic, etc. Possibly the most serious aspect of the problem is the effect of social scientists. If one accepts the argument that we had more success in solving social problems, then the future supply of social scientists becomes an extremely critical problem.

Social studies, rather than increasing the supply of social scientists, may actually cause fewer scholars to select the various social sciences as a college major and profession.

Suppose, to take a simple example, two entering high school students indicate an interest in science—one in the physical sciences and the other in the social sciences. The first will be advised to take the appropriate high school science courses as well as mathematics. And he will probably be ready to enroll in calculus when he enters college. The other student will be counseled to enroll in social studies courses and may be advised to ignore mathematics. When he enrolls in college, he will not have been exposed to any science course in his chosen field not will he have had the necessary mathematics. As far as his professional career is concerned, the second student has made little or no progress toward his ultimate goal.

A person planning to be a social scientist needs considerable training in mathematics and statistics but instead we observe high school students who are still selecting social studies because no mathematics is required. Future social scientists need to be exposed, at an early point in their careers, to statements of judgment and statements of fact (normative and positive statements) and be able to clearly distinguish between the two. Instead we observe their being taught by persons who may not even know the difference between the two. Students in the social sciences should be exposed to abstract and analytical reasoning as soon as they are intellectually capable of doing so but many social studies teachers have systematically avoided those college courses which required this type of endeavor.

In sum, the social studies program in primary and secondary schools makes little contribution to the education of the nation's future supply of social scientists; as a matter of fact, one might even make a stronger statement for there is a possibility that the trivial nature of the social studies actually causes some superior students to select other fields of study.

As it stands now, the student taking his first social science course in the four-year institution receives his initial exposure to this branch of science during his freshman and sophomore years. The student taking the same course in a junior college may not receive this initial exposure until his last two years of college work. Certainly, it takes little imagination to predict the reaction of the physicists or chemists if their students were in a similar position. If there is to be an adequate supply of social scientists it becomes imperative that the courses offered in the social science areas of the junior college be true social science courses. And the responsibility for this rests, in large part, upon the academic departments of the nation's colleges and universities.

CONCLUSION

Possibly the greatest gain from the summer institutes for junior college instructors of economics was the establishment of a high degree of rapport between the junior college instructor and his colleagues in the four-year institutions. Most of the participants, though not thinking of themselves as economists before the program, developed a feeling of professional affiliation. Many now subscribe to the *American Economic Review* and a relatively large number now attend professional meetings including the annual meeting of the American Economic Association.

Their attitude toward economics has also undergone a rather drastic transformation. A number of participants have reported that they now spend a great deal more of their time on the more analytical parts of the introductory course in economics and proportionately less on the purely descriptive parts. Insofar as advising is concerned, a number of participants report that they are now urging advisees to take additional courses in mathematics and statistics if they plan to major in one of the social sciences.

Overall, then, the institutes expose the participants to the concepts and discipline of a social science. They return to the junior college with the training which will enable them to advance their advisees and students toward a fruitful career in the social sciences.

Much of the factual material as well as the impressions of the author were gained from conversations with the participants in the two Summer Institutes for Junior College Instructors in Economics which were conducted by the Department of Economics of the University of Missouri (Columbia) and supported by the National Science Foundation. The author would also like to acknowledge the assistance of the Reaearch Center of the School of Business and Public Administration.

HIGHER EDUCATION IN THE 21ST CENTURY

Alvin C. Eurich

As we turn into the new century we find a world very different from what our parents knew in the 1960s. Travel time to Europe has shrunk to only an hour or so. Television and radio are on a world-wide basis; computors translate languages automatically and instantaneously; satellites give us very accurate weather predictions; and we are on the verge of controlling typhoons and hurricanes.

We continue to avoid a Third World War. In the 1960s, when Russia and the United States were the two major world powers, we twice came precariously close to a nuclear holocaust, once when that atomic bomb was accidentally detonated in the Sahara. Fortunately there were few casualties, and fateful retaliation was avoided. The crater still stands as a tourist attraction and a warning.

Our population has expanded far beyond the optimistic estimates of forty years ago, when we numbered only 186 million people. Today we are approaching 350 million. Our rapid population growth forced many changes. During the first half of the twentieth century we established universal elementary and secondary education. During the second half we made education compulsory through the age of twenty. We needed the additional skills, and we had to protect the labor market, which no longer had jobs for untrained young people. In the process we rebuilt the structure of our educational system. Many of our former liberal arts colleges—there were once sixty-two in the state of Pennsylvania alone—were unable to solve their financial problems. Since their facilities were urgently

From *Atlantic*, CCXI, No. t, (June, 1963), 51–55. Copyright © 1962, by the Atlantic Monthly Company, Boston, Mass. Reprinted with permission.

needed, local communities transformed them into junior colleges. The result is that a two-year college within commuting distance from home is now available for every young man and woman.

These colleges prepare some students for more advanced college and university work; they also train most of the technicians essential to the professions. Half a century ago the Rochester Institute of Technology, under Mark Ellingson's presidency, set the pace. In the late 1960s the institute moved to a new $53 million campus. Now, after several periods of expansion, it enrolls more than 50,000 students. Its graduates have played important roles in developing the photographic computer systems which translate written messages. The institute's cooperative work-study program was, with Antioch's, among the first in the nation.

During the quarter century following World War II, teachers colleges disappeared completely from the American scene. Their place has been taken by multipurpose institutions which, together with the strong liberal arts colleges and the universities, have discontinued the first two years of higher education, since these now come almost wholly within the province of the junior colleges. The transition was accomplished with surprising smoothness. California and Florida took the lead, and, in the East, one remembers the pioneering of the University of Pittsburgh under Chancellor Litchfield.

The new multipurpose institutions, following the pattern set by Florida Atlantic University under its first president, Kenneth R. Williams, now admit qualified graduates from the junior colleges and offer three-year programs, culminating in the master's degree. During the last quarter of the century, there were heated debates at meetings of the Association of American Colleges on the question of whether the baccalaureate degree should be granted at the end of junior college work. The traditionalists won; the junior colleges continued to award the Associate of Arts or Associate of Science degree while the baccalaureate of arts or science fell into disuse because students going beyond junior college pursued a program leading directly to the master's degree or a professional degree.

The largest universities, with their clusters of professional and graduate schools and research institutions, have now become virtually self-contained cities. Some, like New York University, enroll more than 200,000 students. We continue to wonder whether these institutions are getting too big.

During the past half century, the content of education at all levels was profoundly strengthened in two ways: we became much clearer about the objectives of education; and leading university scholars from various disciplines became so alarmed about our soft education that they produced, in cooperation with schoolteachers and administrators, new curricula extending from the kindergarten through the graduate and professional schools.

Our economy of abundance and a better system of distribution have made us less concerned with the strictly professional or vocational aims of education. Even in the sixties students were ceasing to value a college degree by the additional earning power it conferred. We now minimize the time spent on acquiring practical skills and factual knowledge. Instead, we place more emphasis on developing wisdom about major ideas, as in the course on great issues which President Dickey inaugurated in his first years at Dartmouth. Our employment of knowledge, as of leisure, is more satisfying than it was in the early days of the affluent society, when men were consumed, to the point of boredom, with strictly materialistic pleasures. We recognize the truth expressed by Mark Van Doren fifty years ago: "Freedom to use the mind is the greatest happiness."

The revival of philosophy and of the humanities emerged gradually. By the late sixties it had become clear that a spiritual malaise afflicted American life. Studies of the national character seemed to indicate that America had "run out of gas"; individuals felt dominated by the vastness of their own social institutions and by a national style of conformity also referred to as "other-directedness." Conservatism gripped the nation, and the question arose whether America had "any more great business to conduct." People of all ages had difficulty adjusting themselves to the twenty-four-hour work week, and they began to question if the zealous accumulation of creature comforts had not reached a point of diminishing returns.

College students became impatient with vocational preparation and a general smattering of culture. Through such organizations as the "Challenge" symposia and the various groups concerned with civil rights, the movement gathered strength for the redesign of higher education. Graduate students rebelled against the sterile but exhausting competition for degrees; it was they who forced a revival of humanistic thought, so that even our great technical institutions, led by the Massachusetts Institute of Technology, sought a better balance in their curriculum through a renewed emphasis on the humanities.

Scientists, furthermore, had succeeded in creating life, so that human evolution need no longer be left to chance. This discovery intensified the philosophical search for better answers to the age-old question about the ultimate destiny of man.

We are just now beginning to take seriously Ortega y Gasset's insight set down years ago in his *Mission of the University:* "The need to create sound syntheses and systematization of knowledge, to be taught in the 'Faculty of Culture,' will call out a kind of scientific genius which hitherto has existed only as an aberration, the genius for integration." At Brown University, President Barnaby Keeney was one of the first to initiate an Institute for the Synthesis of Knowledge.

The most radical difference between today's colleges and those of fifty years ago, however, is not in the curriculum but in the use of learning resources. The use of television as an educational medium in colleges developed swiftly after it was introduced in the 1950s. Educators resisted, but demonstration after demonstration, such as those carried on at Pennsylvania State University, established the truth that televised instruction was educationally effective and economically feasible. In 1962 some 30,000 courses were given over television in the United States. But more years were to elapse before colleges recognized that television had made the standard lecture obsolete and the conventional laboratory demonstration inadequate and costly.

The objections to the use of television were essentially the same as those raised at Oxford and Cambridge in the latter part of the nineteenth century when the "university lectures" were proposed. At that time the Oxbridge dons predicted that the innovation would reduce the separate colleges to mere appendages. What actually happened was that the colleges became far more vital when professors were relieved of the responsibility for lecturing and could devote themselves to probing the minds of the students, individually or in small groups. The students, of course, were enabled to hear only the very best lecturers in each field.

So, too, with television. The first glimmer of this came in 1958–1959 when a basic college physics course was offered over a national network under the direction of Professor Harvey E. White of the University of California, one of the nation's best physics teachers. During the year, seven Nobel Prize winners—Brattain, Kusch, Rabi, Block, Seaborg, Anderson, and McMillan—and other distinguished scientists helped to teach the course. They represented an array of talent that no single university could possibly have afforded. The following year, a chemistry course was similarly offered, by Professor John Baxter of the University of Florida, an outstanding teacher. He, too, was aided by eminent chemists from academic, industrial, and governmental laboratories. Other courses in biology, government, economics, and the humanities followed in rapid succession, first on national networks and then, with the success of Telstar, across national boundaries.

Now, fortunately, lectures by some of the greatest scholars are available on electronic tapes. Because it was not until the middle of the 1960s that we began systematically to record the leading scholars of the world, we missed many great men who lived in the twentieth century, such as Enrico

Fermi, Henri Bergson, and Sigmund Freud. Under our present system, the senior faculty members, having been spared the drudgery of repeating over and over the basic substance of their fields, are in fresher mind to work with students on advanced topics. Moreover, the students themselves have a firmer grasp of the subject matter, because they have studied the taped lectures at their own rate of comprehension, reviewing them on kinescopes as often as necessary. Television has, in short, provided us with the technology we needed to build a genuine system of mass education, one in which each student has an equal opportunity to learn, no matter where his college is located or what its resources are.

We have also made enormous strides in the teaching of the individual student. Here the most exciting developments have been in independent study, honors work, programmed learning, and language laboratories. Programmed learning, so common today, was hardly known fifty years ago. True, Professor Sidney Pressey at Ohio State University invented the first teaching machine in the 1920s—a device which is now permanently on exhibit at the Smithsonian Institution. But it was not until the 1950s, when Professor Skinner developed another machine and carried on his experiments at Harvard, that programmed learning began to attract attention. After various experiments in the sixties at Harvard, Hamilton College, and numerous secondary schools had clearly demonstrated that students learned faster with programmed materials than with conventional texts and lectures, this scheme of instruction developed into one of the most effective resources for adjusting instruction to the individual student's rate of learning.

The resistance to programming was different from that which had confronted television. Educators knew what television was, but, perhaps because the commercial programming was so vulgar, they refused to grasp its pedagogical implications. In the case of programmed learning, though, most college teachers and administrators did not even know what the new technique was; they only knew that, because of its unfortunate linkage with teaching machines, they did not like it.

As we can now see so clearly, television and programmed learning, both introduced into education in the 1950s, defined the limits of a spectrum of instructional resources. Television provided the medium for mass instruction; programmed learning provided the ultimate in individualized instruction. Within this range, including other devices and procedures, such as motion pictures, filmstrips, language laboratories, and increased scope for independent study, a new diversity was added to the educator's repertoire. These resources enabled us to break the ancient framework that for so long had held college education in a rigid pattern. No longer do we have to divide the school day into fixed fifty-minute periods; no longer do we measure a student's progress by the number of credit hours he has banked; no longer do we march all students through the same series of lectures and classes.

Today, flexibility and adjustment to individual differences are axiomatic. Each student progresses at his own rate. Much of the time he studies on his own, or with fellow students, but always with instant access to the complete range of learning resources: taped lectures, programmed course materials, language audio-tapes, bibliographies, and original documents on microfilm.

Cooperative arrangements among colleges and universities provided another means of bringing the most competent faculty members and learning resources to more students. This, too, developed slowly at first. In the 1930s President Lotus D. Coffman of the University of Minnesota urged the Midwestern universities to share their library resources, but it took a full half century before institutions of higher learning saw the folly of competing with each other by trying to build up *all* academic disciplines. Dr. Coffman urged uniqueness and strength rather than standardization and mediocrity. The University of Minnesota, he rightly observed, was distinguished in Scandinavian literature. Why should other universities try to be equally strong in this area? Within its W. L. Clements Library, the University of Michigan possessed a rare collection of books and documents in American history. Why not send advanced students to Michigan rather than try to duplicate this resource? Some years after Coffman's death, his dream was partly realized with the construction in Chicago of the Midwest Inter-Library Center.

Seeing the major advantages of pooling library resources, the Midwestern universities moved forward quickly and cooperatively in other areas. Their Committee on Institutional Cooperation gave graduate students the opportunity to move freely from one institution to another on a short-term basis to take advantage of special opportunities—Purdue's bio-nucleonic laboratory, or star scholars, such as those in Egyptology at Chicago. Under the leadership of presidents Herman Wells of Indiana and Frederick Hovde of Purdue, a cooperative instructional program was further extended over a closed-circuit television system tying together the campuses at Lafayette and Bloomington and including the centers in Indianapolis, Fort Wayne, and Evansville. With the success of the Midwest Airborne television instruction of over five million school-children and the invention of multichannel electronic tapes for broadcasting, basic courses in the sciences and humanities were offered to students in all the major universities in Ohio, Indiana, Kentucky, Illinois, Michigan, Wisconsin, and Ontario. These courses supplemented the instructional program offered over Telstar on an international basis.

The universities also recognized the economy of combining their purchasing power. An Inter-University Authority now purchases and distributes supplies and equipment required on the various campuses. The need for such an operation was obvious in the 1970s, when very expensive computer systems for all types of activities became essential on every campus.

The smaller colleges were profoundly affected by all these cooperative arrangements. Their own initial efforts included groupings such as the Claremont Colleges, the Richmond (Virginia) Center, and the Connecticut Valley Colleges, involving Amherst, Mt. Holyoke, Smith, and the University of Massachusetts. For a long time, such simple matters as not having a common academic calendar prevented students from crossing campus lines in their programs of courses. But during the latter part of the twentieth century the colleges found that they were still competing too much and duplicating their instruction. Renewed efforts were made until there was hardly a college left that was not a member of a cluster of institutions sharing facilities and programs. Each group is affiliated with one or more universities, an arrangement which first became dramatically visible in 1963, when seven faculty members from the University of Chicago personally offered a course on Civilizations from South Asia to a hundred students from Swarthmore, Bryn Mawr, and Haverford colleges, with one of these faculty members flying to Philadelphia each week. This is another way by which students gained access to the educational resources of a widespread academic community instead of being limited to the offerings of a small institution. In the process, too, the advantages of a smaller group have been preserved.

Even more drastic are the changes in our libraries. As a result of research carried on not only in the United States but also in Japan, India, Belgium, Holland, France, and England, we have revolutionized the techniques of storing and transmitting information. Most of our documents are now reduced to pinpoint size and stored on film. We have established the National Research Library, which, as John Kemeny of the Dartmouth mathematics department predicted some years ago, has reached more than 300 million volumes in miniaturized form. Through a multichannel cable, we can instantly transmit information from these volumes to reading units on campuses throughout the country. The space previously used for storing books has been freed for faculty study, reading rooms, and independent work.

Even the architecture of our campuses reflects the innovations in teaching techniques. Iowa State University, the University of Miami in

Florida, with its visual communication building, and Stephens College, with its comprehensive learning center, pioneered in constructing academic facilities that make the maximum use of diverse learning aids. For the lectures over television, students now quite generally listen to portable television sets in their own rooms. These lectures are followed by small group discussions in dormitories, patterned after the "House Plan" first tried out some years ago by Stephens College. The programmed learning laboratories are open twenty-four hours every day, and students may study whenever they desire to do so.

Along with the clarification of objectives, the upgrading and updating of the curriculum, the use of a variety of devices and procedures for learning, and the new library system, we have also vastly improved the process by which students are admitted to the colleges and universities, and the way in which they progress through the course of study. Questions like these inspired reforms:

If students learn at different rates of speed, couldn't some of them achieve the goal in three years, or two, while others worked at it for five or six? Would it not be wise to tell the student what is expected of him, what the end result of his liberal education should be, and then let the student decide, with such guidance as John Finley used to give his students at Eliot House, Harvard, how he can best make use of the university's resources?

To answer these questions, the colleges had to define more precisely the goals they were striving for in the liberal education of students. Whereas under the old system the administration could lean heavily on the accumulation of credit hours as evidence that the student was acquiring an education, the new system required the colleges to devise adequate measures of achievement.

The important point was that students began to progress with complete flexibility. The principles or early admission and admission with advanced standing, which did so much to facilitate the transition from high school to college fifty years ago, were applied as well to the transition from college to graduate work. Standard measures of achievement in each basic subject were devised. But students could meet these standards at their own rate of learning and in a variety of ways.

The system which emerged was pioneered in California under a plan initially worked out by a commission headed by President Arthur Coons of Occidental and strongly supported by President Clark Kerr of the University of California. Virtually all California students progressed at their own rate from high school to a junior college. The top third of these students, plus some who entered advanced vocational programs, went on to college.

From college, approximately the top 12 percent advanced to the university. During the latter half of the century we also made great strides in the use of the educational plant and facilities. With the crowding of students on the campuses there was neither time nor money enough to build the necessary classrooms, laboratories, and dormitories. In the 1960s the idea of using the campus on a year-round basis caught on, and administrators discovered that existing facilities could accommodate at least 25 percent more students. Now it would be unthinkable to permit buildings to remain idle for three summer months.

Nor do we any longer tolerate such luxurious use of academic facilities as we did during the academic years of the first half of the twentieth century. Then, except for a very few metropolitan universities, we occupied our classrooms primarily in the morning and our laboratories in the afternoon. With the large federal student-aid program for veterans following World War II, some universities changed their practices. Stanford University, for example, was among the first to do so. Dr. Donald B. Tresidder, who was then president. appointed a director of planning—the first position of this kind to be created in any university. An analysis of plant use during the last pre-war year showed that with better use of available space the enrollment could be doubled.

To make maximum use of land, President Tresidder planned an industrial park. And to attract to the area industries whose research interests related to a university, he created the Stanford Research Institute. During the last half of the century, this compound of a first-rate university, the Research Institute, industries with broad research interests, and government projects such as the two-mile-long linear accelerator has set a pattern followed in most university centers of the country.

As we look back over the progress of higher education in recent decades, we may wonder when the major changes began to develop. It is difficult to fix an exact date, but I believe a turning point occurred in the mid-1950s and 1960s. First we were spurred by Sputnik; then, in the years 1964, 1965, and 1966, the colleges felt most keenly the increase in the demand for higher education. The college population nearly trebled during the sixties and seventies, with the most acute increases taking place in the mid-sixties.

It was this tremendous increase, I think, which galvanized the leading colleges and universities into action. Through such relatively simple reforms as year-round operation, control over proliferating courses, and better use of independent study, many colleges found they could enroll up to one-third more students without any significant increase in costs.

Now, here we stand in the year 2000, at the dawn of another century.

During the past forty years colleges and universities, like society itself, have moved farther than in all previous history. But as Oliver Wendell Holmes once said, "The great thing in the world is not so much where we stand as in what direction we are moving." We are a long way from a system of higher education that cultivates the full potentialities of man, regardless of race, color, creed, or economic status. But an orderly world of rationally free men can settle for no less.

QUESTIONS FOR DISCUSSION

COMMUNITY COLLEGE

1. What is the difference between a community college and a junior college?
2. How should the transfer program be determined?
3. How should the technical and vocational offerings of a community college be determined? How should they differ from the vocational programs of the high school? How should they differ from the vocational and technical offerings in the adult education program available in a community?
4. What should be included in the community service program of a community college? What type of courses would you exclude? What criteria should be used in making a decision?
5. What should be the relationship of the community college to the high school? What relationship should exist between the community college and surrounding universities?
6. Who should determine what the offering of the community college should be?
7. To what extent should students be able to transfer from one program to another in a community college?
8. What general education should be provided in the community college? What is general education at the community college level?
9. What should be the admission requirements of a community college?
10. What should be the graduation requirements of a community college?
11. Who should attend a community college? Should "low achievers" be admitted?
12. What information or concepts in Section 1–4 of this book have particular significance for curriculum planning in a community college?

10 Curriculum Issues

In a plural culture there will always be many issues. They represent the cutting edge on which new social knowledge is being formed.

Issues should not be seen as threats. They should be seen as opportunities for gaining new insights. As people clarify the issues that divide them, they become surer of the alternative positions that can be taken. If they are wise, they seek evidence as to which of the positions is most appropriate, and in the process, their decision becomes more mature and new issues are identified.

Dale Doak asks how the "practiced" and the "professed" can be brought into closer harmony in schools. Is the basic role of education intellectual development? Is it to develop a "healthy self concept" in every learner?

Van Til asks whether the question of freedom is not basic when one tries to produce positive reinforcement with teaching machines. He asks whether team teaching actually will improve learning and provide sufficiently personalized contacts and firsthand experiences so that learners can deal with significant problems. He asks, "Is Progressive Education Obsolete?"

Theral T. Herrick ("Curriculum Problems: Some Basic Issues") has stated ten of the major issues that have been inherent in most of the sections of this collection of readings. His article provides a good summary of the problems confronting educators in the curriculum decisions they are called upon to make.

MYTHS IN EDUCATION

E. Dale Doak

This presentation of myths is not intended as an indictment against a whole people—the teachers of our public schools. It is intended as a stimulus for reflective, divergent thinking. Do you consistently behave in congruence with your ideals and values? If not, why not? How can each of us become self-actualizing persons whose behaviors accurately reflect our beliefs?

Through the years many professional educators have come to believe in certain basic ideals, ideas, and values about teaching and learning, the teacher and the learner, that are often repeated and perhaps even more often violated. These are now presented as a study in mythology in public education.

The basic myth surrounding public education is that the emphasis for improvement of education should lie with the development of physical hardware and software and organizational changes rather than in the development of the human potential of teachers.

It is pure mythology to suggest that every class must meet for every day, that each student must spend one year per grade, that the magic number is 25 pupils per class, that all pupils should start to school at age 6, that there must be 1 guidance counselor for every 250 pupils, or that the number of library books per pupil, the A.D.A. expenditure, or the type of curriculum a child follows (academic, general, vocational) really has much impact on the quality of education received by any student.

The prime consideration is not what physical conditions exist, but how the human element, the teacher, makes use of the tools of the trade. Too many for too long have neglected this simple but basic fact of life. The emphasis must shift from the development of gadgetry to a major reemphasis and investment in the development of the human potential of teachers.

A crucial myth is the idea that schools really foster a healthy self-concept in every child. It is increasingly imperative that the schools' program recognize the basic need for dignity and worth inherent in the

From *The Clearing House,* XVIII, No. 5 (January, 1969), 288–290. Used by permission of the author and publisher.

socio-psychological make-up of every human being. While most of us have a basic philosophy which recognizes these needs of children, many of our schools' practices deny these needs and understandings.

What, for example, is the effect on a student of consistent, daily failure in his school work? Does failure make him feel that he is a worthy individual or does it deny him that opportunity? When we punish youngsters, by whatever means, because they have "different" cultural values than the majority, what is the effect? What is the effect of severe criticism of a youngster in the presence of his peers, self-worth or denial?

These and many more practices are practices which are incongruent with philosophy—our values and ideas. How can the "practiced" and the "professed" be brought into closer harmony?

One of the most interesting studies in mythology is the idea that we really know what is the basic role of the school. And even where statements of educational philosophy, goals, and objectives are written, is the curriculum of the school planned, designed, and implemented in accord with the statements? But every school writes such a statement. For what purpose? In the mind of the typical public school practitioner goal statements are abstractions of little or no value. How, then, can we give structure, consistency, and direction to curriculum planning?

Is the basic role of public education one of intellectual development? Presently many schools' practices limit the educational program essentially to this goal. Learning in most schools is practiced as the absorbing and storing of facts rather than the development of learners as persons who know how and are eager to learn.

Admittedly, knowledge is important, but to what end? What about the goals in the affective domain as contrasted with those of the cognitive realm? What about the development of effective citizens? Training for worthy use of leisure time? Vocational competence? Worthy home membership?

Learned men and societies have for centuries debated the issue of "What knowledge is of the most worth?" And this basic question has been complicated many times over in the highly complex, pluralistic society in which we live.

Should we educate only for intellectual competence? Do we? What are the alternatives? Can education be a panacea for all of society's ills?

Now is the time for facing up to and reaching decisions about this giant dilemma.

Another important myth is the belief that most teacher behavior is planned, deliberate behavior rather than random reaction to stimuli. When a teacher involves students in discussion, what is his purpose? Is he attempting to help students diverge in their thinking concerning a given topic? Or is he probing for convergency? Or evaluative thinking? Or perhaps he has no idea as to the level of thinking he is attempting to foster.

It is documented fact that the majority of verbal behavior in the typical classroom is at the knowledge level, the level of factual information. It would appear to be myth, then, that public schools generally encourage and attempt to develop the prime objective of critical thinking—an objective which most schools place high on the priority list.

Little classroom activity centers around analysis, synthesis, application or evaluative levels of thinking. How can high order thinking be stimulated in most classroom situations? Or, is thinking beyond factual acquisition desirable? Which type of thinking will have the highest educational residue?

That "teaching is telling" is indeed another myth. "Telling" is an occupational hazard for most teachers. What do students remember that is told to them? Very little! Perhaps if one viewed teaching and learning as problem solving, more meaningful learning experiences could be designed and made a substantial, integral part of each child's curriculum.

What are the alternatives to "telling"? Bruner, among others, suggests that the prime task of the teacher is activation and maintainance of problem solving behavior on the part of the learner. Implicit in this statement is the idea that teachers also become problem solvers directing a major portion of their attention to the how of "activating" and "maintaining" good oriented student behavior.

Still another important myth in public school education is that most school curricula are justified by criteria other than history and tradition. What is really different in today's curriculum from that of the 1930's? Much has been written about change in education, but how significant are the changes which are being made? Do we know?

The fact is that, in far too many schools, the emphasis is still on the subject and its acquisition as an end product rather than on the learner as a fully functioning, contributing member of society.

The myths examined here present only a partial picture, one taken without a wide-angle lens. The camera shows only a partial image of the panorama of public education and, if viewed out of context, presents a distorted view of an institution held in high esteem worldwide.

But each of you has your own camera. Focus it carefully on the problems of public education. What do you see? How can the combined talents of professional educators be directed not toward self-satisfaction but toward problem solution.

The answer lies somewhere in the realm of development of human potential!

IS PROGRESSIVE EDUCATION OBSOLETE?

William Van Til

Is progressive education outmoded? One's first impulse is to say "yes." Who today, among the voices being heard on education, is talking about the concerns which characterized many leaders of education during the first half of the twentieth century? Specifically, who today is talking about the ideas which occupied John Dewey, George Counts, Boyd H. Bode, and William Heard Kilpatrick, those symbols of the intellectual leadership of the "new education," symbols of the varied versions of the progressive movement in education? Practically nobody, at least nobody who is being heard widely.

Instead, American education in the early 1960s is engrossed with the application of technology to education, with competing new proposals for organization of the school program, and with stress on reconstruction of academic disciplines. The mass media foster the interest in technology, organization, and disciplines. If an educator tries to be heard on more fundamental aspects, he often encounters the silent treatment.

The Industrial Revolution has finally reached education. As a result, matters of technology have virtually become table talk in education today. In professional discussions and in the mass media reporting we hear constantly about educational television, language laboratories, courses on film, and programmed learning through teaching machines.

A second stress in today's education emphasizes organization of the school program. Proposals are varied and often conflicting. They include such organizational proposals as team teaching, the dual progress plan, the nongraded school, and increasing the course requirements within the existing Carnegie unit structure.

Currently, a third stress is the new interest in the academic disciplines.

From *Saturday Review*, XLV, No. 7 (February 17, 1962), 56–57. Copyright 1962, by Saturday Review, Inc. Used by permission of the author and publisher.

In part, the emphasis is upon updating knowledge through efforts by specialists in the disciplines. The work of such groups as the Physical Science Study Committee and the varied mathematics programs at Yale, Maryland, and Illinois are watched intently. Science, mathematics, and foreign languages ride high as the favored fields of the national government, which has become a significant curriculum maker on the elementary and high school levels. The fields of English and physical education make frantic and failing attempts to latch onto the benefits of the National Defense Education Act; leadership in reconstruction of the curriculum in these fields has been assumed by the College Entrance Examination Board and by a football coach, respectively. There are indications that Commissioner McMurrin intends to attempt to do for the arts as well as for English what post-Sputnik apprehension did for the sciences. Rumors, alarms, and confusions surround the status of the social studies. The phrase "structures of the disciplines" is being bandied about, with none too clear a definition emerging as yet.

Technology, organization, and the disciplines seem a far cry from the philosophical, social, and psychological ideas that engaged the leaders of the progressive movement in education in the first half of the twentieth century. There appears to have been a change in "fashions in ideas," to use the chilling and accurate phrase Irwin Edman coined for a phenomenon of our times. Consequently, progressive education seems outmoded. Lawrence A. Cremin even consigned it to history in his *The Transformation of the School: Progressivism in American Education, 1876–1957.* He began his preface as follows: "The death of the Progressive Education Association in 1955 and the passing of its journal, *Progressive Education,* two years later marked the end of an era in American pedagogy. Yet one would scarcely have known it from the pitifully small group of mourners at both funerals." Martin Meyer recapitulated the Cremin position in his widely read book, *The Schools.*

One might readily conclude that progressive education is outmoded save for a stubborn fact. The fact is that the questions raised by the progressive movement in education are not obsolete. They will not die. They cannot be killed. They cannot be exorcised by any voodooism yet known to technology, organization, or the reconstruction of disciplines which remains aloof from these questions.

The basic questions which men like John Dewey, William Heard Kilpatrick, George Counts, and Boyd H. Bode raised are inescapable questions: What are the aims of education? Upon what foundations should the school program be built? Given such aims and foundations, what should the schools teach? To these probing and fundamental questions, matters of organization and technique, while important, are necessarily subordinate.

The progressive education movement of the first half of the twentieth century, symbolized by Dewey, Kilpatrick, Counts, and Bode, was essentially a quest for workable answers for our times to questions such as these. No one claims that the Holy Grail was found; no one claims that the questioners came up with final, definitive, eternal answers. The "new educators" did not completely agree among themselves on workable answers for our times. But at least the "new educators" asked the right questions.

One wing of the progressive movement sought the answers primarily in the potential of the individual learner. A pioneer in this respect was the man whose ninetieth birthday was celebrated on November 20, 1961— William Heard Kilpatrick. Many of today's schoolmen will remember Kilpatrick's classes in the Horace Mann Auditorium of Teachers College, Columbia University. Hundreds attended each session, yet the quiet man with the mane of white hair used committees and reports so skillfully that each student found opportunities to speak out and battle over ideas.

The heart of Kilpatrick's first major contribution to education, "The Project Method," was founded on his faith in the potential of the individual learner. In back of the recurrent Kilpatrickian phrases which valued "purposeful activity," "intrinsic motivation," "planning," in back of his opposition to "extrinsic subject matter" which disregarded individuals, in back of his opposition to meaningless rote learning, lay Kilpatrick's belief that clues to significant content can be found within the learner and can be developed fully in collaboration with a mature adult who fosters self-direction and independent thought. The later Kilpatrick increased his stress on the importance of social orientation and the urgency of meeting social problems. But the mark Kilpatrick lastingly left on the progressive movement still derives largely from his faith in the potentiality of the learner when that potentiality is cultivated by skillful and sensitive teachers. To many educators, probably to most, insight into the relationship between the individual and his education was the major contribution of the progressive education which Kilpatrick espoused, though he was concerned for philosophical and social, as well as psychological, foundations. And—mistake it not—the insight derived from Kilpatrick made a massive contribution to education in an era that had lost sight of the importance of the learner and his purposes and potential.

A second wing of the progressive movement set forth answers to the perennial questions of aims, foundations, and content largely in terms of the society which surrounded the schools. George Counts, a battler for socially oriented schools in a democracy, serves as a symbol of this emphasis. To George Counts, for instence, the times cried out for an education realistically geared to the new social order which was emerging. He threw his eloquent challenge to the Progressive Education Association assembled in convention in 1932. He amplified his ideas in the pamphlet "Dare the Schools Build a New Social Order?" and for years educators found themselves forced to face the issues Counts raised. Whether one condemned aspects of his viewpoint as indoctrination and a potential abuse of the method of intelligence, thus classifying it as a new liberal's version of authoritarianism, or whether one hailed it as a realistic recognition of the overpowering importance of social problems, as an indication that the social sciences had come of age, an educator who heard Counts had to take into account stress on society. The role of education with respect to social change and to reform was an imperative and recurrent theme with Counts and his fellow social reconstructionists. The pivotal place of social realities in education could not be forgotten after Counts was heard, even though indoctrination might be repudiated.

George Counts lived his faith. He helped turn back Communist infiltration of teachers' unions. He was a tower of strength in the Liberal Party; he was a candidate for public office and in the vanguard of social movements of his time. He is still active in his retirement.

To others equally immersed in the progressive movement, democratic values were central to all considerations. For instance, to Boyd H. Bode, the Lincoln-like man from Illinois who made his major contribution through Ohio State University, the crucial need was for the clarification of differences between the democratic way of life and the way of its authoritarian competitors. As he saw it, the road out of value confusion led through a remorseless and unremitting use of the method of intelligence in human affairs. To Bode, progressive education was at the crossroads and a child-centered view would never suffice. Nor was indoctrination the road to a better world. He conducted his classes in philosophy of education through the Socratic method and he fostered thought with every heckling, humorous, or trenchant exchange of ideas into day-by-day learning experiences.

I venture for your consideration the bold hypothesis that each of these men touched on part of the whole, that each perceived and particularly stressed an aspect of education which we neglect at our peril, that each succeeded nobly, and, where he failed, failed gallantly in building the "new education." Each asked the right questions; each responded with relevant contributions toward workable answers for our times.

The thinker who came closest to the reconciliation of the individual, society, and philosophical foundations—was the extraordinary John Dewey, whose centennial was celebrated by the John Dewey Society in 1959 through meetings in scores of universities across the nation. The word "extraordinary" is used advisedly. During his long lifetime, this incredible man lived a full life as a person, participated in social and civic action, conducted the most famous laboratory school in history, became the father figure of the progressive education movement (and, to shift the analogy, sometimes served as mother hen by reconciling conflicts and even smoothing ruffled feathers in the flock), became a towering figure in philosophy, and, in the process, managed to leave for posterity a legacy of 5,000 pages of articles and 18,000 pages in book form.

Yet even Dewey, prodigious though his endeavors were, never achieved extensive translation of his ideas into a new curriculum. Underbrush in philosophy needed to be cleared. After his Laboratory School experimentation, and after setting forth his pedagogical creed in such books as *The School and Society* and *Democracy and Education,* Dewey gave himself to this Herculean labor as he built his philosophy of experimentalism. He constantly reacted to trends and tendencies in progressive education, as he did in his critique "Experience and Education." He made only occasional critical forays into program building. He would be the first to admit, were he alive, that much remained to be done to implement his ideas on what he preferred to term simply "education," rather than "progressive education."

So we turn back to the thinking of representative intellectual leaders of the progressive movement in education, not in any spirit of ancestor worship, but for the inescapable questions they raised and for the insights they contributed toward workable solutions for our times. Cremin says it well in his final paragraphs: "There remained a timelessness about many of the problems the progressives raised and the solutions they proposed. . . . And for all the talk about pedagogical breakthroughs and crash programs, the authentic progressive vision remained strangely pertinent to the problems of mid-century America. Perhaps it only awaited the reformulation and resuscitation that would ultimately derive from a larger research and reform in American life and thought." With these words Cremin partially redeems the strange inconsistency of pointing out brilliantly in early chapters that social currents created progressive education well before the official establishment of a Progressive Education Association, yet conveying the impression in his final chapter that the demise of an organization and a magazine meant the death of progressive education. The fact that ideas live beyond organizations apparently escaped the overanxious gravediggers who gleefully greeted Cremin's book as the definitive obituary for progressive education as a force in American ideas.

The questions raised and many of the tentative answers ventured by the early leaders of progressive education are not dead nor will they die. In time, the sponsors of new educational technology, the advocates of varied forms of educational organization, the proponents of study of the structure of separate disciplines, must face the inescapable questions and consider the possible solutions proposed.

The problem for sponsors and users of programmed learning through teaching machines does not lie in the capacity of the machine to produce positive reinforcement, whether it takes the form of a kind word, a pat on the head, or, indeed, a bottle of Coca-Cola. Given technical ingenuity, a reinforcing reward will be forthcoming. The harder problem for sponsors and users of the teaching machine is whether positive reinforcement will be used to bring nearer George Orwell's "1984" and Aldous Huxley's "Brave New World," or whether programmed learning, using positive reinforcement selectively and with discrimination will reduce the skill-drudgery of education and free teachers and students for more humane aspects of learning and human development, such as creativity, the use of reflective thought, and experiences in freedom. Consider, for instance, this quotation from *Walden Two,* a Utopia envisioned by the pioneer of teaching machines, B. F. Skinner of Harvard, a Utopia which appears to some of us an authoritarian nightmare world of behavioristic conditioning. T. E. Frazier, spokesman for *Walden Two,* says approvingly, "Now that we *know* how positive reinforcement works and why negative doesn't . . . we can be more deliberate, and hence more successful, in our cultural design. We can achieve a sort of control under which the controlled, even though they are following a code much more scrupulously than was ever the case under the old system, nevertheless *feel free.* They are doing what they want to do, not what they are forced to do. That's the source of the tremendous power of positive reinforcement—there's no restraint and no revolt. By a careful cultural design, we control not the final behavior, but the *inclination* to behave—the motives, the desires, the wishes.

"The curious thing is that in that case *the question of freedom never arises."*

In the light of this quotation we can understand why Aldous Huxley recently reminded us in *Brave New World Revisited* that it may be later than we think. He wrote as his conclusion, "The older dictators fell because they never could supply their subjects with enough bread, enough circuses, enough miracles and mysteries. Nor did they possess a really effective system of mind-manipulation. . . . Under a scientific dictator, education will really work—with the result that most men and women will grow up to love their servitude and will never dream of revolution. There seems to be no good reason why a thoroughly scientific dictatorship should ever be overthrown."

The problem before the sponsors of educational television is not how wide a circle over six states, or indeed a nation, can be reached by a plane flying for Midwest Airborne Television. Nor is it bouncing beams off satellites for global television. Technology will solve those problems. The real problem is whether the device will realize the gloomy prophecy of an old Vanderbilt University professor who once said at a meeting of the American Association of University Professors, "Gentlemen, the time is coming when one Harvard University professor will determine through his history course on television what history is taught in the United States—and even if it's Arthur Schlesinger, Jr., I say the hell with it!"—or whether imaginative educational TV will provide learners with a magic carpet to a wider world of experience made at once more expansive and more closely detailed.

The problem before the sponsors and users of team teaching is not precisely how many students to instruct at any given time in any given space. It is not whether a new magical number combination, proposed for better staff utilization, or some flexible magic of numbers out of Lexington, Massachusetts, will take the place of the former magic number—25 or 30 in each classroom. Experience and, we hope, genuine controlled experimentation, will supply the answer here. The real problem is whether team teaching actually will improve learning, whether it will evolve toward emphasis on the *interrelationships* of subject matter, whether it can provide sufficient personalized contacts with teachers and sufficient firsthand experiences by students to enable young people to deal with significant problems.

The problem before the sponsors and users of the dual progress plan is not the technical difficulty of introducing specialized science, mathematics, and arts teachers into elementary school organization through the demonstrations at Ossining and Long Beach in New York. The real problem for the sponsors and users of the dual progress plan is recognized by the originator of the plan as whether the dual progress plan will or will not better answer some of Dewey's persistent queries; George Stoddard poses the issue in his new book, *The Dual Progress Plan,* which should be read along with the Association for Supervision and Curriculum Development pamphlet, "The Self-Contained Classroom," for differing organizational approaches to possibly compatible goals.

The problem before the liberal arts professors currently reconstructing and updating knowledge in such disciplines as physics, biology, and mathematics is not whether they can cram all of man's new knowledge into separate water-tight compartments, which will then be siphoned off during the elementary and high school years. They can't. Even if they could, they would endlessly face true obsolescence, for knowledge swiftly dates and, like fish, won't keep. The real problem, of which some of the reconstructors of disciplines are aware and of which others appear quite unaware, is whether the scholars can identify concepts in their new knowledge which can be made meaningful to children and youth, appropriate to both the general and specialized education needed for living in today's society, crucial in the process of critical thinking and problem solving—or whether their reconstructed and amplified knowledge, however new, will prove to be inert subject matter in Alfred North Whitehead's sense.

The problem for those who are studying the structures of the disciplines may be first to make clear what they mean. Granted that they can and do, the question will face them as to whether their studies of structures of disciplines are to be achieved as culminations built upon the experience of learners, as Dewey recommended. Or will their studies of structures of disciplines be evasions of problems central to general education; formal orientations to content which bear little relationship to how young people live and learn?

One can derive little encouragement for the future of study of the structure of the disciplines from the views of Charles R. Keller, director of the John Hay Fellows Program, who believes "too many social studies teachers have emphasized the creation of good citizens rather than the content and discipline of their subjects." He says, "Attitudes cannot be taught in formal classroom situations. We weaken education—and schools—when we try to do so. What students should do in school is to study subjects and become acquainted with facts and ideas. Subjects as such have disciplines that will help to develop students' minds." Is this the conception of educational aims and psychology of learning which is to characterize the new advocacy of studying the structure of disciplines? Surely this was not the conception of Arthur W. Foshay when, in his presidential address to the Association for Supervision and Curriculum Development in 1961, he advised "that we educators take directly into account the nature of the organized bodies of knowledge, in addition to the nature of the growing child and the nature of our society, as we try to make curriculum decisions."

If their work is to have meaning, rather than to be innovation for unclear purposes, the sponsors and users of the new technology, organization, and approaches to disciplines must come to terms with the questions that engaged the intellectual leadership of the progressive movement in education. Questions of "why" and "what" have necessary precedence over question of "how" and "when." The inescapable questions relate to the aims of education, the foundations of the program, and what the schools should teach as appropriate content based on such aims and foundations.

Is, then, the progressive movement in education obsolete? I think not. The questions raised by the "new education" are remorseless, inevitable, demanding. The answers provided by the intellectual leaders of the progressive movement were promising beginnings, useful leads, valid foreshadowings.

When considerations of "why" are dodged, we get prescriptions which simply cannot be appraised. One cannot truly evaluate the proposals made in widely read books which are characterized by indifference to aims and purposes in the early chapters and which then constantly smuggle in unanalyzed value assumptions through the remainder of the pages. Two knights entered in the educational jousting show this tendency: both the great and good James B. Conant and the provocative and prancing Martin Mayer.

Conant, for instance, does not set forth aims for education in *The American High School Today*. Yet he steadily makes assumptions as to what knowledge is of most worth.

In "Slums and Suburbs," Conant says, "It is after visits to schools like these that I grow impatient with both critics and defenders of public education who ignore the realities of school situations to engage in fruitless debate about educational philosophy, purposes, and the like. These situations call for action, not hair-splitting arguments." Yet "Slums and Suburbs" is permeated with proposals for action which must be based on philosophic assumptions.

In *The Schools*, Martin Mayer colorfully rejects all possible formulations of aims. He says, "It is well to rid oneself immediately of this business of 'the aims of education.' Discussions on this subject are among the dullest and most fruitless of human pursuits. Whatever the ideal general 'aims of education' may be, they certainly cannot be accomplished in schools." He then proceeds to lace through his book individualistic approbations and denunciations based on his acceptance of undefined aims.

One of the myths of our times is that the several tendencies which characterized what is broadly termed progressive education prevailed, were fully achieved, and are now being repudiated. This sedulously cultivated myth is incomprehensible. The reality is that progressive education has never been tried on any significant scale.

As the inescapable queries reassert themselves and the tentative proposals of the varied interpretations of progressive education are reconsidered, educators will find it necessary to utilize the insights of Dewey, Bode, Counts, and Kilpatrick. An education which takes into account the individual, his society, and his values—an education which builds upon the soundest possible scholarship derivative from psychological, social, and philosophical foundations—is imperative in developing a curriculum appropriate for twentieth-century man.

The central questions posed and the relevant contributions toward workable answers for our times made by such interpreters of the progressive movement in education are not obsolete. They must and will persist. In time, they will be embodied in the form of new proposals for modern education, new syntheses which build upon our predecessors, as is common in the world of ideas. The overanxious gravediggers, and those who currently give them comfort, will discover as this twentieth century moves along that what they have mistaken for a corpse is indeed very much alive.

CURRICULUM PROBLEMS: SOME BASIC ISSUES

Theral T. Herrick

During the early days of our American public school system, the problem of what to teach was relatively easy to solve, since only a small portion of young people were in school, the emphasis was on preparation for college, vocational opportunities were limited, and the demands of society at large were few and far removed from the schools. Today, however, the problem of what to teach in our schools is complex and difficult. We have a far greater number of children from all strata of society, vocational choices are multitudinous, technical needs have been added to academic preparation, and the ever-increasing demands of society are now brought to bear upon the schools. If the public schools are to play an effective part in maintaining our democracy and our economic system, the problem of what

From *Teacher's College Record*, LX, No. 5 (February, 1959), 242–244. Used by permission of the author and publisher.

to teach must be given much closer attention by all concerned. A few of the basic issues are discussed below.

1. Who shall determine what is to be taught? As we work on the problem of what to teach in our schools, we might logically start with the question of who is going to determine the curriculum. Should it be the expert, the public at large, teachers, children, governments, or a combination of these groups?

2. How shall we organize and work to decide what is to be taught? If the decision as to what is to be taught is a cooperative process, then we have to decide how to organize and proceed with our work. Such questions arise as: Who shall assume leadership? How shall people become involved? How shall decisions be made and implemented? How shall the process be kept orderly, comprehensive, continuous, and cooperative?

3. What sources shall be used in determining what is to be taught? Today there seem to be as many opinions as there are people regarding what shall be taught in the curriculum. Unfortunately, too few people have spent the time and effort necessary to arrive at well-founded conclusions based upon thought and study. In many cases judgments lack substantiation, whereas Tyler suggests that determination of the curriculum might come from such defensible sources as the study of the learner, contemporary life, subject-matter specialists, philosophy, and the psychology of learning.[1]

4. Shall we provide a comprehensive curriculum for all children and youth? With more and more students in our schools, with more students remaining in school longer, with a greater diversity of student interests and needs, and with ever-expanding demands by our society, the question of how comprehensive the curriculum shall become must be settled before we can decide what to teach. Furthermore, a comprehensive curriculum leads to questions concerning means of meeting the individual differences of students, such as courses for slow students, courses for gifted students, ability grouping and multiple curriculums within each school.

5. What shall we regard as general and as specialized education? In deciding what is to be taught it makes quite a difference whether the course or subject is to be required of every student because of its general

---

[1]Ralph W. Tyler, *Basic Principles of Curriculum and Instruction,* Syllabus for Education 360, pp. 4–28 (Chicago, The University of Chicago Press, 1950).

value in everyday living, or is to be elective because of its unique value to the individual, owing to his special interests and needs. Some would argue that general education should always come first and specialized education second, if the budget permits. However, this is a difficult problem because it is often hard to determine what everyone needs and whether or not specialized subjects are as important to the individual as the general ones. The old question, What is a frill? enters into this argument because art or music might be frills for some students, whereas Latin and algebra might be frills for others.

6. How shall we maintain a balance in what is taught? The most thoughtful scientists and engineers are not arguing for a narrow science and mathematics curriculum, because they realize the need for other subjects such as English, social studies, foreign languages, physical education, and the cultural arts. The argument seems to be over the amount of emphasis scientific subjects in our curriculum should receive with a fair share of students entering science and engineering. However, there are people in our society who always ride tidal waves, whether these waves are citizenship, physical fitness, mental health, safety, science, or engineering. Perhaps educators need only to keep their heads and work calmly for a balance in the curriculum, with new emphases from time to time, while avoiding an avalanche of emotionalized, hasty decisions.

7. What subject areas deserve immediate consideration? If we believe in a well-balanced curriculum for all of the children of all of the people, and if we believe that improving the curriculum is a continuous process, then we should be ready and willing to give serious attention to some of the most controversial areas of the curriculum. This is not because these areas necessarily need to be added to or deleted from the curriculum, but because they may need to be improved, or to be more clearly interpreted to the public, or because new research and experience may be available to help in the study of these areas. In the elementary schools, some of these controversial subjects are: science, arts and crafts, music, physical education, health and safety, foreign language, geography, and in some cases civics. In the secondary schools, subjects for consideration include: reading courses, separate "tracks" and "speed-up" courses in mathematics, required science, driver education, home and family living, agriculture, conservation, art, music, physical education, health and safety, the Russian language, vocations, core, and advanced courses in the humanities. Furthermore, economic education and citizenship education in both elementary and secondary schools are becoming the concern of more and more people. The high school, with its elective system, may solve many of these problems more easily than the junior high school, where electives have been on the decline and where many people seem to want more and more high school subjects taught. Obviously the schools cannot teach everything that is requested, so choices will have to be made or differentiation within courses and blocks of time will have to be utilized

8. *How shall we teach what is to be taught?* In the process of deciding what is to be taught, we should always keep in mind *how* the curriculum will be taught. There is little or no value in placing a subject in the curriculum unless it can be taught effectively. In fact, some of the criticism now being directed at some areas of the curriculum may be due to ineffective teaching. Serious consideration should be given to the amount of teaching that still exists based upon the pure association theories of learning, using the low level rote-memorization, sit-still, pouring-in type of learning. The basic question may be, How can we encourage teachers to teach for insight through analysis, relationship, and generalization based upon the field theories of learning? The approach now used by many people in meeting social, economic, political, and educational problems might lead us to believe that much is yet to be done by the schools in teaching critical thinking through problem solving.

9. *How shall we finance what is to be taught?* Right now and for the next several years we are facing, and will face, a severe financial crisis in American education. Too many people use the sole criterion, Can we afford it? in determining the curriculum, whereas the criterion should be, Is this desirable and, if so, how do we pay for it? It is of little avail to talk about adding or improving courses in the curriculum unless the tax structure is such that we can raise the funds necessary for a desirable educational program for children and youth. Undoubtedly, every educator should assume some responsibility for improving our tax structure as he works on what is to be taught.

10. *How shall we evaluate the subjects that are taught?* Obviously some subjects are more important than others and some are taught better than others, but we have always been prone to add to the curriculum without removing anything. Perhaps it is time for us to establish some rather firm criteria based upon sources similar to those suggested by Tyler, so that we may exercise calmer and better judgment than has been used in the past in deciding what is to be taught.

American education is unique in that there is no national curriculum, and few state curriculum programs are superimposed upon local schools. However, this uniqueness places the burden upon all of us to consider carefully and intelligently what we should teach in our schools.

QUESTIONS FOR DISCUSSION

CURRICULUM ISSUES

1. Is the basic goal of the school program intellectual development? Why?
2. Should education be a positive social force? In what ways?
3. Toward what knowledge, understanding, and skills should learning experiences be directed?
4. How can curriculum planners provide for the freedom of the learners? Can programmed instruction threaten this freedom?
5. Is progressive education obsolete?
6. Are there additions that you would make to Herrick's list of 10 "Basic Curriculum Issues"?

Index